NEPALI IN

A Topical Approach to Learning Nepali

DANIEL P. WATTERS
NARENDRA B. RAJBHANDARY

EKTA BOOKS
KATHMANDU, NEPAL

NEPALI IN CONTEXT

A Topical Approach to Learning Nepali

Ekta Books Distributors Pvt. Ltd.
Prashutigriha Marga, Thapathali
GPO Box No. 6445, Kathmandu, Nepal
E-mail: ektabooks.nepal@gmail.com
<http://www.ektabooks.com>

1st Edition : 2000
2nd Edition : 2006
3rd Edition : 2010
4th Edition : 2018 (Updated)

ISBN 978-9937-1-0608-5

Printed In Nepal At Monaj Offset Press, Kathmandu, Nepal

Contents

UNIT THREE

The Physical World

UNIT FOUR

Nepali Attire and Society

UNIT FIVE

Nepali Life

UNIT SIX

Religion and Government

UNIT SEVEN

Additional Vocabulary

UNIT EIGHT

Appendices

Acknowledgments

The authors would like to express their appreciation to TEAM, without which this book would have been impossible. Because of their solid commitment to language learning, TEAM poured precious time and energy into this project from 1996-1998 in order to improve their language program, often when that time and energy was sorely needed elsewhere. In a very real sense, this is TEAM's book. Special thanks goes to Dr. Mahadev Awasthi for detailed proofreading and editing of Nepali text.

About the Fourth Edition

We consider it a privilege to have been able to work on the book once again. Even after the third edition of the book we found that much more could be added and several unnecessary inclusions had to be omitted. In this edition, the reader will find that the book is finer and important sections more conspicuous than it was before. This of course, does not mean that it is done. We will keep editing and re-editing the book to give you, our readers, the best and updated.

From this edition onwards, we have included an audio DVD along with the book. The following lessons have been incorporated in the Audio DVD the Devanagari Script, Devanagari Script Vowels, Lesson 1-4, Chapters 1-23, Appendix 2, Nepali Numerals, Vocabulary: Domestic, Medical, Administrative, Religions and Construction. Ms. Marcy Noble has done a wonderful work of handpicking the narrators and recording matter for the Audio DVD. We are grateful to Ms. Noble for her effort in preparing this product.

As far as the readers, students and teachers are concerned, we are certain that you will find this book user-friendly. We urge you to put the DVD to optimum use since listening will further enhance the learning of the Nepali language.

Any further suggestions from teachers and guardians for the improvement of the book will be gratefully accepted.

• Authors

Introduction

Philosophy

Learning *about* Nepali is not the same as learning *how* to use Nepali. Speaking is a social activity that requires participation in a social context. If you study this book only within the confines of four walls and never become actively involved in your community, then we will consider this book to have failed. It is the authors' goal that in the process of using this textbook you will build many meaningful relationships with Nepalis and that upon completion of this book you will be able to communicate in a wide range of situations. It is our conviction that the degree to which you learn Nepali will be the degree to which you cope, build relationships and work effectively in Nepal.

Balanced Methodology

Balance is the key to language learning. For you introverts that prefer a structured approach, if you don't go out into the community you'll only hear a small set of the spoken forms that are encountered and the Nepali you learn will have no social context. The goal is to communicate, not to finish the textbook. For you extroverts that thrive on the communicative approach, if you talk the day away drinking tea and never study, you will rarely be corrected and likely form bad habits. Your range of vocabulary and grammar will also suffer. If you commit to completing each chapter thoroughly, including the *In the Community* section, you will have achieved that balance.

Using this Textbook to its Full Potential

- Find a tutor that can fully work through the textbook with you, *one-on-one*, several hours at a time. This book was written with this assumption, particularly the *Practice* and *Let's Talk* sections of each chapter. It is only in this controlled environment that you will get needed correction and feedback.
- Be prepared for your sessions with your tutor. Tape record the vocabulary and know it well before class so that you can use your time productively.
- Resolve to shut this textbook and get into the community after each chapter. The *In the Community* section of each chapter suggests an activity that will help you do so, but this will require personal commitment.
- Build in a system of accountability so that you don't get stuck at a language learning plateau. Find someone who can encourage and push you on. Build in frequent testing and set thresholds for moving on. For an example of an accountability tool, see Appendix 1.
- The devanagri writing system should be learned in conjunction with chapters one and two (unit two). Following that, only devanagri is used.

Features of Each Chapter

- **Particular topic or domain**: Each chapter features a topic that is either very useful or commonly encountered. In the early chapters, these are topics useful for functioning; later they focus on a particular cultural aspect.

- **Common vocabulary**: Based on the chapter's topic, the most common 50-75 vocabulary words are given. Formal, archaic or rare words are avoided.
- ***Useful Phrases***: 5-10 phrases that are useful to know are given. Often these are helpful questions or phrases that illustrate a common vocabulary usage.
- ***Text***: Each chapter features a text (topic specific) in which all of the vocabulary words are found. Different types of texts are used throughout the textbook: dialogue, essay, narrative, folk-tale, etc.
- ***Grammar***: Any new structures or grammar points found in the text are explained with examples. Frequent overview charts are also given.
- ***Practice***: This section focuses on pattern and structure. This is done through the use of frame drills, translation, stem sentences, etc.
- ***Let's Talk***: This section focuses on conversation and production. This is done through the use of role playing, hypothetical situations, topics to discuss, games, interviews, etc.
- ***In the Community***: Designed specifically for an integrated language learning program, community assignments are given that take Nepali beyond the classroom and into the real world. The focus is cultural communicative competence.
- ***Did You Know?***: At the end of each chapter, topic specific cultural tidbits, taboos, national facts, etc. are given.

Integrating *Nepali in Context* into a Language Program

To serve as an example of how this textbook can be integrated into a language program, a program is here briefly summarized. In this program, each chapter is completed over a two week period using the following cycle:

Thursday and Friday: **preparation on own**, reading and memorizing.
following Monday through Friday: **with tutor**, 3 hours per day
following Monday and Tuesday: completion of **community assignment**
Wednesday: 3 hours of **professional material** with tutor

In addition to the above, this program features the following:

- Feedback sheets are given to a language coordinator after each chapter.
- Tape recordings of each chapter's vocab and text are listened to.
- Exams are given after ch. 8, 15, 20 and 23 (70% required before moving on).
- Cultural readings accompany each chapter.
- Regularly scheduled cultural outings are planned.
- Village living options are included.
- Planned trips outside the valley encouraged.

Going at this pace, *Nepali in Context* takes roughly one year to complete.

It is our sincere hope that *Nepali in Context* will make a real difference in the time you spend in Nepal. Enjoy.

Daniel P. Watters

For the Tutor
शिक्षक (ट्युटर) को निम्ति

हुन त प्रभावकारी भाषाशिक्षणका अनेकौं सिद्धान्त र तरिकाहरूको विकास भइसकेको छ । कति त अझै विकसित हुँदै छन् । सबै कुरा यहीं प्रयोग गरेर साध्य पनि हुँदैन । त्यस्तै विदेशीहरूलाई नेपाली भाषा सिकाउनको लागि धेरै पुस्तकहरू पाइन्छन् । सबै पुस्तकका आ-आफ्नो विशेषताहरू छन् । सबैमा एउटा-एउटा अपूर्णता अथवा अवगुण छ भनेमा अत्युक्ति नहोला । त्यस्तै यो पुस्तक पनि, चाहे जतिसुकै मिहिनेत र अनुभव सँगालेर तयार पारिएको होस्, पूर्ण र अवगुणरहित छ भनेर कदापि दाबी गर्न सक्तैनौं । तर यस पुस्तकलाई आकर्षक, उपयोगी, प्रभावशाली र प्रयोग गर्न सजिलो बनाउनको लागि यथाशक्य प्रयत्न गरेका छौं । नेपाली भाषाशिक्षणमा नरेन्द्रबहादुर राजभण्डारीको अनुभव र भाषाविज्ञानसम्बन्धी डेनियल वाटर्सको उत्कृष्ट ज्ञानको प्रतिफलको रूपमा हामीले यसलाई लिएका छौं । यसको मूल्याङ्कन शिक्षक/प्रशिक्षार्थीहरू आफैले गर्नुहुनेछ ।

अब यस पुस्तकको प्रयोग गर्नेबारे केही भन्न चाहन्छौं । यस पुस्तकको प्रयोग गर्नुअघि देवनागरी लिपिको साथै अलिअलि प्रारम्भिक अथवा आधारभूत भाषिक ज्ञान सिकाउन प्रतिदिन दुई/अढाई घण्टाको दरले २/३ हप्ता जति लाग्ला । हरेक पाठको सुरुमा नेपाली शब्दहरूको अङ्ग्रेजी रूपान्तर दिइएको छ । शब्दार्थ दिँदा सकेसम्म पाठ्य विषयमा प्रयोग गरिएको अर्थ र अरू वैकल्पिक अर्थहरू पनि दिइएको छ । उचित उच्चारणको अभ्यास जरुरी छ । यसका लागि यसै पुस्तकको सहायकको रूपमा श्रव्य टेप पनि उपलब्ध छ । ती शब्दावली र अर्थ पहिले कण्ठ गराउनुपर्छ । यस क्रममा विभिन्न रोचक, आकर्षक र प्रभावकारी तरिकाहरूको पनि प्रयोग गर्न सकिन्छ । यसो गरेमा छिटो (पछिसम्मको लागि) कण्ठ हुन्छ र पट्यार पनि लाग्दैन । यसको लागि चार्ट, कार्ड, सेतो पाटी प्रयोग गर्न, विभिन्न हाउभाउ गर्न, वास्तविक चीजबीजहरू देखाउन र अन्य विविध क्रियाकलाप गर्न सकिन्छ । नभए सिधै शब्दहरू कण्ठ गराउनुपर्ने हुन्छ । त्यसपछि व्यवहारमा प्रयोग हुने केही वाक्य/वाक्यांशहरू र अङ्ग्रेजी रूपान्तर दिइएको छ । रूपान्तर गर्दा पर्यायभन्दा भावार्थमा जोड दिइएको छ । यस्ता वाक्यांशहरू उपयोगी हुने हुँदा विद्यार्थीहरू यसलाई कण्ठ गर्न अभिप्रेरित हुने आशा गर्न सकिन्छ ।

पाठ सुरु गर्नुभन्दा अघि यसमा प्रयोग गरिएका व्याकरणगत बुँदाहरूको छलफल गर्नु जरुरी छ । कहिलेकाहीं पाठसँगसँगै व्याकरणको पनि छलफल र अभ्यास गर्न सकिन्छ । यहाँ पनि छिटोछरितो र स्पष्टसँग बुझाउने विभिन्न उपायहरूको अवलम्बन गर्नुपर्ने हुन सक्छ । अझ कहिलेकाहीं यस पुस्तकमा उल्लेख गर्न छुटेका बुँदाहरूका बारेमा र हाम्रो चलन/संस्कृतिको बारेमा पनि छलफल गर्नुपर्ने हुन सक्छ । यसरी सम्पूर्ण पाठ पढ्न र बुझ्न सक्ने भएपछि शिक्षकले अङ्ग्रेजीमा अनुवाद नगरीकनै नेपालीमै पाठको बारेमा प्रश्नोत्तर गर्न सकिने आशा गर्न सकिन्छ । तब पाठको रोचकता बढ्नेछ ।

पाठको अन्त्यमा व्याकरणमा आधारित अभ्यासहरू दिइएका छन् । अतिरिक्त गृहकार्य पनि दिन सकिन्छ । यो पूरा गरेपछि "अब हामी कुरा गरौं" भनेर स्वतन्त्र रूपमा कुराकानी गर्नको लागि निर्देशनहरू

दिइएका छन् । त्यसपछि विद्यार्थीले कक्षाकोठाको वातावरणभित्र सिकेको कुरा बाहिर वास्तविक समुदायमा वा स्थितिमा प्रयोग गर्नका लागि निर्देशन र पथ-प्रदर्शन गरिएको छ ।

यस पुस्तकको मूल उद्देश्य विद्यार्थी आफैलाई यो काम गर्न सक्षम बनाउनु हो । तर कहिलेकाहीं विद्यार्थीले चाहेको अवस्थामा शिक्षकको मद्दतको आवश्यकता पर्न सक्छ । अन्त्यमा केही नेपाली चलन र संस्कृतिको बारेमा जानकारी दिइएको छ । यहाँ पनि विद्यार्थीले नबुझेको कुरा सोध्न सक्छन् र शिक्षकले जाने बुझेसम्म यथार्थ उत्तर दिनुपर्छ ।

सुरुका प्रत्येक पाठ १०/१२ घण्टामा पूरा गर्न सकिन्छ भने पछिका पाठहरूको लागि १५ घण्टासम्म चाहिएला । तर छोटो समयमा काम चल्ने भाषा सिक्न देवनागरी प्रयोग गर्नुपर्दैन । आवश्यकता र उपलब्ध समयअनुसार केही आधारभूत पाठहरू रोमनमा लेखेर सिकाउन सकिन्छ । यसरी यस पुस्तकको उपयोगिता प्रयोगकर्ताकै हातमा सुम्पन्छौं ।

भाषाशिक्षणको अनुभव नगरेकाहरूको विचारमा नेपाली भाषा सिकाउनु त्यति गाह्रो नहोला । त्यसो भन्दैमा यो काम असाध्य गाह्रो पनि होइन । तर केही तालिम, केही अध्ययन र केही अनुभवले भाषाशिक्षणलाई रोचक र प्रभावकारी अवश्य बनाउँछ । कसैले पनि मैले सबै कुरा जानेको छु अर्थात् मलाई सबै कुरा थाहा छ भन्न सक्तैन । त्यसो भनेमा त्यो जस्तो झूटो अरू केही हुँदैन । घर्तीको त अर्ति मान्नुपर्छ भने अरूको के कुरा ? हामी पनि पूर्णज्ञ होइनौं । हामीले पनि अर्ती त सुन्नै पर्छ । तसर्थ यस पुस्तकलाई परिष्कृत र अझ प्रभावकारी बनाउनका लागि तपाईंहरूको अमूल्य सुझाव र सल्लाह पाएमा आभारी हुनेथियौं ।

दानिएल पी. वाटर्स
नरेन्द्रबहादुर राजभण्डारी

Contents: Grammar

Contents: Complex Verbs

UNIT ONE

Elementary Courses

- The Devanagari Script
- Nasalization
- Half Letters
- Common Consonant Clusters
- Irregular Half Letters
- Consonant Clusters with (र)
- Other Irregular Consonant Clusters

THE DEVANAGARI SCRIPT

	VOICELESS		VOICED		
	-ASPIRATED	+ASPIRATED	-ASPIRATED	+ASPIRATED	NASAL
Velar (Plosives)	क k	ख k^h	ग g	घ g^h	ङ ŋ
Alveolar (Affricates)	च ts	छ ts^h	ज dz	झ झ dz^h	ञ ɲ **(also** n**)**
Retroflex (Plosives)	ट ʈ	ठ $ʈ^h$	ड ɖ **(also** ɽ**)**	ढ $ɖ^h$ **(also** $ɽ^h$**)**	ण ɳ **(also** n**)**
Dental (Plosives)	त t	थ t^h	द d	ध d^h	न n
Bilabial (Plosives)	प p	फ p^h **(also** Φ**)**	ब b	भ b^h	म m
(Approx., flap, trill)	य j	र r/ɾ	ल l	व w **(also** b **and** β**)**	
Fricative	श ʃ **(also** s**)**	ष ʂ **(also** s**)**	स s	ह h	

INTERNATIONAL PHONETIC ALPHABET

ŋ	velar nasal--*song*	Φ, β	bilabial fricatives	ɾ	flap
ɲ	palatal nasal--*nya*	j	pronounce *y--yam*	ʃ	pronounced *sh*
ʈ ɖ ɽ	retroflex	r	trill	ʂ	retroflexed *s*

Lesson 1

Vowels:	Word initial and following vowels:	अ	आ
	Following consonants:		ा
	Common transcription:	**a**	**aa**

Pronunciation:

अ: ago, the, cup

आ: father, mom, not

*Consonants:

क्	ल्	म्	य्	ह्
k	**l**	**m**	**y**	**h**

Pronunciation: क: Voiceless unaspirated velar plosive. All Nepali plosives (stops) are either aspirated or unaspirated, *including* voiced plosives. Pay careful attention to aspiration.

Syllables:

क	ल	म	य	ह
ka	la	ma	ya	ha
का	ला	मा	या	हा
kaa	laa	maa	yaa	haa

Words:

आमा	aamaa	मा	maa
कम	**kam	मामा	maamaa
कलम	**kalam	माला	maalaa
काका	kaakaa	हक	**hak
काम	**kaam	हमला	hamalaa
मल	**mal	हाल	**haal

* The consonants here are marked with halanta ् . See also lesson 7. A halanta is marked on independent half consonants (without a final 'a' sound, e.g., आउनुस्, आउँछन्, छन्, हुन्, भन्, बस्, लेख् and some Sanskrit words like श्रीमान्, अर्थात् and so on. But, if a letter does not have a bar (like ङ, ट, ठ, ड, ढ, छ, ह) then a halanta is a must when it needs to be halved e.g., पढ्नु, उठ्छ, बस्छ्यौ, सट्टा (also सट्टा) and so on.

*If a consonant is word final, it is usually pronounced without the inherent *a* sound, particularly if it is a noun. Thus, कलम is *kalam*, not *kalama*.

Lesson 2

Vowels:			
	Word initial and following vowels:	ए	ओ
	Following consonants:	े	ो
	Common transcription:	**e**	**o**

Pronunciation: ए: pet, red, kept.

ओ: go, flow, hoe. Don't pronounce this as a glide (*ow*)

Consonants:

त्	द्	प्	र्	स्
t	**d**	**p**	**r**	**s**

Syllables:

त ta	द da	प pa	र ra	स sa
ता taa	दा daa	पा paa	रा raa	सा saa
ते te	दे de	पे pe	रे re	से se
तो to	दो do	पो po	रो ro	सो so

Words:

असार	asaar	पद	pad
आकार	aakaar	पसल	pasal
आराम	aaraam	पाका	paakaa
एकता	ekataa	पात	paat
ओरालो	oraalo	पातलो	paatalo
ओहो	oho	पालो	paalo
कपास	kapaas	पोका	pokaa
के	ke	पोते	pote
केरा	keraa	मसला	masalaa
कोदो	kodo	रात	raat
तर	tara	रातो	raato
तल	tala	समेत	samet
तातो	taato	साल	saal
ताल	taal	सेतो	seto
तास	taas	हरेक	harek
तेल	tel	दोहोरो	dohoro

Lesson 3

Vowels:					
	Word initial and following vowels:	इ	ई	उ	ऊ
	Following consonants:	ि	ी		
	Common transcription:	**i**	**i**	**ु u**	**ू u**

Pronunciation: इ / ई : **<u>ea</u>**t, s**<u>ee</u>**m, b**<u>ea</u>**n. In speech, the same. Not the glide *iy*.

उ / ऊ : c**<u>oo</u>**l, b**<u>oo</u>**t, st**<u>ew</u>**. In speech, the same. Not the glide *uw*.

Consonants:

ग्	छ्	ड्	न्	ब्
g	**chh**	**D**	**n**	**b**

Pronunciation:

ड: Medially, ड is pronounced as retroflexed flap (*ɽa*).

छ: As with plosives, affricates are also + or - aspiration. छ is pronounced *t* plus *s*, and then aspirating (ts^ha)

Syllables:

ग	छ	ड	न	ब
ga	chha	Da	na	ba
गा	छा	डा	ना	बा
gaa	chhaa	Daa	naa	baa
गि	छि	डि	नि	बि
गी	छी	डी	नी	बी
gi	chhi	Di	ni	bi
गु	छु	डु	नु	बु
गू	छू	डू	नू	बू
gu	chhu	Du	nu	bu

गे	छे	डे	ने	बे
ge	chhe	De	ne	be
गो	छो	डो	नो	बो
go	chho	Do	no	bo

Words:

उमारिनु	umaarinu	तिनी	tini
कुराकानी	kuraakaani	दिनु	dinu
गरिब	garib	नातिनी	naatini
गाडी	gaaDi	पिउनु	piunu
गुदी	gudi	बहिनी	bahini
छिनिनु	chhininu	बिदा	bidaa
छुनु	chhunu	बिरामी	biraami
छुरा	chhuraa	बुहारी	buhaari
छोरी	chhori	मुनि	muni
डराउनु	Daraaunu	रहिरहनु	rahirahanu
डाडु	DaaDu	सिउनु	siunu

Lesson 4

Vowels:			
	Word initial and following vowels:	ऐ	औ
	Following consonants:	ै	ौ
	Common transcription:	**ai**	**au**

Pronunciation: These are true glides (a combination of vowel sounds) For ऐ, first say *a* and glide into *i*. For औ, first say *a* and glide into *u*

Consonants:

ख्	घ्	च्	ज्	झ्
kh	**gh**	**ch**	**j**	**jh**

Syllables:

ख kha	घ gha	च cha	ज ja	झ jha
खा khaa	घा ghaa	चा chaa	जा jaa	झा jhaa
खि खी khi	घि घी ghi	चि ची chi	जि जी ji	झि झी jhi
खु खू khu	घु घू ghu	चु चू chu	जु जू ju	झु झू jhu
खे khe	घे ghe	चे che	जे je	झे jhe
खै khai	घै ghai	चै chai	जै jai	झै jhai

खो	घो	चो	जो	झो
kho	gho	cho	jo	jho
खौ	घौ	चौ	जौ	झौ
khau	ghau	chau	jau	jhau

Words:

ऐना	ainaa	चीन	chin
खबर	khabar	चैत	chait
खरायो	kharaayo	चोक	chok
खसी	khasi	चोरी	chori
खाजा	khaajaa	चौर	chaur
खुला	khulaa	जगत	jagat
खुब	khub	जतातत‍ै	jataatatai
खेती	kheti	जनता	janataa
खेल	khel	जमिन	jamin
खैरो	khairo	जागिरे	jaagire
खोपी	khopi	जाति	jaati
घडियाल	ghaDiyaal	जादू	jaadu
चरा	charaa	जुलुस	julus
चलन	chalan	जोगी	jogi
चामल	chaamal	झन्	jhan
चाहनु	chaahanu	झरना	jharanaa
चिया	chiyaa	झाडा	jhaaDaa

Lesson 5

Consonants:

ट्	ठ्	फ्	श्	ङ्	ञ्	ण्
T	**Th**	**ph**	**sh**	**ng**	**ny**	**N**

Pronunciation:

ङ: A velar nasal, this is like the *ng* in *sing*. It never occurs word initially.

फ: This can be pronounced as an aspirated bilabial (p^h) or as a voiceless bilabial fricative. The later is like *fa,* but with the lips only (like blowing out a candle).

ञ and ण: These are often used in formal or archaic words. Some dialects pronounce ञ palatalized and ण retroflexed, but more often they are pronounced the same as न. They do not occur with every vowel.

Consonants:

ढ्	थ्	ध्	भ्	व्	ष्
Dh	**th**	**dh**	**bh**	**w**	**sh**

Pronunciation:

ढ: Medially and finally, this is usually pronounced as an aspirated retroflexed flap (*ṭ*^{h}*a*).

व: Depending on the word, this can be pronounced several ways: *wa, ba* and as a voiced bilabial fricative. The later is like *va*, but with the lips only.

स श and ष: In speech, these are all pronounced the same - *sa*. They are written differently for historical reasons. Purists will say श is pronounced *sha,* and that ष is retroflexed.

Syllables:

ट	ठ	फ	श	ढ	थ	ध	भ	व	ष
Ta	Tha	pha	sha	Dha	tha	dha	bha	wa	sha
टा	ठा	फा	शा	ढा	था	धा	भा	वा	षा
Taa	Thaa	phaa	shaa	Dhaa	thaa	dhaa	bhaa	waa	shaa
टि	ठि	फि	शि	ढि	थि	धि	भि	वि	षि
टी	ठी	फी	शी	ढी	थी	धी	भी	वी	षी
Ti	Thi	phi	shi	Dhi	thi	dhi	bhi	wi	shi
टु	ठु	फु	शु	ढु	थु	धु	भु	वु	षु
टू	ठू	फू	शू	ढू	थू	धू	भू	वू	षू
Tu	Thu	phu	shu	Dhu	thu	dhu	bhu	wu	shu
टे	ठे	फे	शे	ढे	थे	धे	भे	वे	षे
Te	The	phe	she	Dhe	the	dhe	bhe	we	she
टै	ठै	फै	शै	ढै	थै	धै	भै	वै	षै
Tai	Thai	phai	shai	Dhai	thai	dhai	bhai	wai	shai
टो	ठो	फो	शो	ढो	थो	धो	भो	वो	षो
To	Tho	pho	sho	Dho	tho	dho	bho	wo	sho
टौ	ठौ	फौ	शौ	ढौ	थौ	धौ	भौ	वौ	षौ
Tau	Thau	phau	shau	Dhau	thau	dhau	bhau	wau	shau

Words:

टाढा	TaaDhaa
टारी	Taari
टालो	Taalo
टीका	Tikaa
टुसा	Tusaa
टोपी	Topi
ठमेल	Thamel
ठाडो	ThaaDo
ठूलो	Thulo
ढीलो	Dhilo
ढुकुटी	DhukuTi
ढोका	Dhokaa
थकाइ	thakaai
थाल	thaal
थाहा	thaahaa
थोक	thok
थोरै	thorai
फैलिनु	phailinu
फोहर	phohar
भएर	bhaera
भजन	bhajan
भदौ	bhadau
भरिया	bhariyaa
भलो	bhalo
भवन	bhawan
भाइ	bhaai
भाडा	bhaaRaa
भारत	bhaarat
भाषा	bhaashaa
भिड	bhiR
भिर	bhir
भेग	bheg
भेषभूषा	bheshbhushaa
भोटे	bhoTe

धनी	dhani	वन	ban
धागो	dhaago	वरिपरि	waripari
धुनु	dhunu	वा	waa
धेरै	dherai	वाक	waak
धोती	dhoti	विकास	bikaas
फँडानी	phaRaani	विनाश	binaash
फरक	pharak	विशेष	bishesh
फरिया	phariyaa	विष	bish
फल	phal	वैशाख	baishaakh
फाइदा	phaaidaa	शरीर	sharir
फागुन	phaagun	शहर	shahar
फुली	phuli	शिखर	shikhar
फेदी	phedi		

Lesson 6

NASALIZATION

Vowels are nasalized by placing either (ं) or (ँ) over the vowel. The (ं) is usually used when the vowel protrudes over the horizontal bar, though some insist that the other should always be used to nasalize a vowel.

कँ काँ किँ कीँ कुँ कूँ केँ कैँ कौँ

Words:

आँगन	aañgan	पहेँलो	paheñlo
काँटा	kaañTaa	गैँडा	gaiñRa
कहाँ	kahaañ	गलैँचा	galaiñchaa
चाहिँ	chaahiñ	औँठी	auñThi
छिँडी	chhiñRi	दसौँ	dashauñ
पिँढी	piñRhi	घुइँचो	ghuiñcho
दिनहुँ	dinahuñ	भुइँ	bhuiñ
सुँगुर	suñgur	दिउँसो	diuñso
हुँदैन	huñdaina	तपाइँ	tapaaiñ

The (ं) is sometimes used before य्, र्, ल्, व्, श् and ह्:
for example, संयोग, संरचना, संलग्न, संवाद, संशय, संसद्, संहार।

Special Characters:

रु	(र+ ु)	रू	(र+ ू)
ru		**ru**	

Words:

हरू	haru	बरु	baru
कुरूप	kurup	मारुनी	maaruni
अरू	aru	रुख	rukh
गोरु	goru	रुचाउनु	ruchaaunu
जरुरी	jaruri	रुनु	runu

Lesson 7

HALF LETTERS

All consonants that have a vertical bar have "half" letters that are used when writing consonant clusters. The "half" letter is written first, then the "full" consonant it joins with.

FULL	HALF	अर्को अक्षरमा जोडिँदा हुने रूप	EG.		FULL	HALF	अर्को अक्षरमा जोडिँदा हुने रूप	EG.	
क	क्	क्‍	क्ल	kla	न	न्	न्‍	न्त	nta
ख	ख्	ख्‍	ख्ल	khla	प	प्	प्‍	प्त	pta
ग	ग्	ग्‍	ग्ल	gla	फ	फ्	फ्‍	फ्न	phna
घ	घ्	घ्‍	घ्व	ghwa	ब	ब्	ब्‍	ब्न	bna
च	च्	च्‍	च्न	chna	भ	भ्	भ्‍	भ्य	bhya
ज	ज्	ज्‍	ज्न	jna	म	म्	म्‍	म्न	mna
झ	झ्	झ्‍	झ्न	jhna	ल	ल्	ल्‍	ल्न	lna
ञ	ञ्	ञ्‍	ञ्च	ncha	व	व्	व्‍	व्य	wya
ण	ण्	ण्‍	ण्ड	NRa	श	श्	श्‍	श्न	shna
त	त्	त्‍	त्म	tma	ष	ष्	ष्‍	ष्ट	shTa
थ	थ्	थ्‍	थ्य	thya	स	स्	स्‍	स्न	sna
ध	ध्	ध्‍	ध्न	dhna					

Lesson 8

COMMON CONSONANT CLUSTERS

Almost all consonants cluster with छ, थ्य, द, न, य and ल. For example:

क् + छ = क्छ	रोक्छ	rokchha
क् + थ् + य = क्थ्य	रोक्थ्यो	rokthyo
क् + द = क्द	रोक्दै	rokdai
क् + न = क्न	रोक्नु	roknu
क् + य = क्य	रोक्यो	rokyo
क् + ल = क्ल	रोक्ला	roklaa

ख् + छ = ख्छ	राख्छ	raakhchha
ख् + थ् + य = ख्थ्य	राख्थ्यो	raakhthyo
ख् + द = ख्द	राख्दै	raakhdai
ख् + न = ख्न	राख्नु	raakhnu
ख् + य = ख्य	राख्यो	raakhyo
ख् + ल = ख्ल	राख्ला	raakhlaa

Lesson 9

IRREGULAR HALF LETTERS

ङ् + क = ङ्क	शङ्का	shangkaa
ङ् + ग = ङ्ग	चङ्गा	changgaa
छ् + य = छ्य	ओछ्यान	ochhyaan
ट् + ट = ट्ट	छुट्टी	chhuTTi
ट्ट् + य = ट्ट्य	छुट्ट्याउनु	chhuTyaunu
ठ् + ठ = ठ्ठ	चिठ्ठा	chiThThaa
ड् + क = ड्क	अड्कनु	aRkanu
द् + द = द्द	उद्देश्य	uddeshya
द् + व = द्व	द्वारा	dwaaraa
द् + य = द्य	उद्याउनु	udyaunu
द् + ध = द्ध	पद्धति	padhdati

Lesson 10

CONSONANTS CLUSTERS WITH (र)

If र is the first consonant of a consonant cluster, र becomes (ʿ) and is placed over the vowel that follows the cluster. For example:

र् + छ = र्छ	पर्छ	parchha
र् + क = र्क	अर्को	arko
र् + म = र्म	गर्मी	garmi
र् + द = र्द	पर्दैन	pardaina
र् + ल = र्ल	पर्ला	parlaa

EXCEPTION:

र + य = र्‍य	भर्‍याङ	bharyaang

If र is the second consonant of a consonant cluster, र becomes (्र) and is joined to the first consonant. For example:

ग् + र = ग्र	पाङ्ग्रा	paangraa
ह् + र = ह्र	गाह्रो	gaahro
ख् + र = ख्र	बाख्रा	baakhraa

EXCEPTION:

क् + र = क्र/क्र	टुक्रा	Tukra
त् + र = त्र	भित्र	bhitra
ट् + र = ट्र	राष्ट्रिय	raashTriya
ड् + र = ड्र	ड्राइभर	Draaibhar
द् + र = द्र	समुद्र	samudra

3) In some Sanskrit words, *ri* (as in *river*) is written with a (ृ) underneath:

दृश्य drishya   संस्कृति sañskriti

Lesson 11

OTHER IRREGULAR CONSONANT CLUSTERS

क् + ष = क्ष	अध्यक्ष	adhyaksha
क् + त = क्त	मुक्ति	mukti
त् + त = त्त	हात्ती	haatti
ज् + ञ = ज्ञ	ज्ञान	gyaan

Sample Words (excluding clusters with र, छ, थ, द, न, य and ल):

चक्की	chakki	पाइन्ट	paainT
डाक्टर	DaakTar	चिन्ता	chintaa
भक्तपुर	bhaktapur	पन्ध्र	pandhra
ट्याक्सी	Tyaaksi	हप्ता	haptaa
सुख्खा	sukhkhaa	लाप्पा	laappaa
जग्गा	jaggaa	उब्जनी	ubjani
घ्वाइँ	ghwaaiñ	नब्बे	nabbe
पच्चीस	pachchis	सम्भिनु	samjhinu
मज्जा	majjaa	सम्धी	samdhi

अञ्चल	anchal	जम्मा	jammaa
ज्वाइँ	jwaaiñ	सम्पन्न	sampanna
अड्‌कनु	aDkanu	सम्बन्ध	sambandha
चिट्ठी	chiThThi	पुल्चोक	pulcok
घण्टा	ghaNTaa	पल्ट	palTa
डन्डी	DanDi	डँडेल्धुरा	DaDeldhura
वैकुण्ठ	baikuNTha	पश्चिम	pashcim
चित्त	chitta	ईष्ट	isT
आत्मा	aatmaa	प्रतिष्ठा	pratishThaa
उत्पादन	utpaadan	विष्णु	vishNu
महत्त्व	mahattwa	विश्वास	bishwaas
उत्सव	utsaw	स्कूल	skul
पद्धति	padhdati	स्टोभ	stobh
उद्देश्य	uddeshya	त्यस्तो	tyasto
द्वारा	dwaaraa	वनस्पति	banaspati
अन्जीर	anjir	स्वास्थ्य	swaasthya
सन्चै	sancai	हिस्स	hissa

UNIT TWO

Getting Around

1. To Be or Not To Be छ/छैन, हो/होइन
2. Introducing Yourself आफ्नो परिचय
3. Shopping किनमेल
4. Taxi ट्याक्सी
5. Househelper काम गर्ने दिदी
6. Telephone Conversation फोनमा कुराकानी
7. The Trip to Rukum रुकुमसम्मको यात्रा
8. My Organization मेरो संस्था

CHAPTER 1

"TO BE OR NOT TO BE..."
छ छैन/हुनु नहुनु/हो होइन

VOCABULARY

✎ **As you learn Devanagari, write in the words below. See the Nep-Eng glossary for help.**

____	yo	this
____	tyo	that
____	yi	these
____	ti	those
____	kalam	pen
____	sisaa kalam	pencil
____	kaagaj	Paper
____	kitaab	book
____	kaapi	notebook
____	jholaa	bag
____	kaalo	black
____	nilo	blue
____	khairo	brown
____	hariyo	green
____	raato	red
____	seto	white
____	paheñlo	yellow
____	raamro	good
____	parkhaal	wall (compound)
____	jhyaal	window
____	ghar	house
____	baar	fence, hedge
____	Dhokaa	door
____	koThaa	room
____	mech	chair
____	Tebul	"table"
____	ek	one
____	dui	two
____	tin	three
____	chaar	four
____	paañch	five
____	chha	six
____	saat	seven
____	aaTh	eight
____	nau	nine
____	das	ten

	-maa	in, at, on		ke	what
	naraamro	bad		kahaañ	where
	saano	small		katiwaTaa	how many
	Thulo	big		kasto	of what sort
	baliyo	strong		dherai	very / many
	kachchaa	weak; crude		ma	I
	pardaa	curtain		tapaaiñ	you (polite)
	bhuiñ	floor		kasko	whose
	bhittaa	wall (inside)		rang	color

USEFUL PHRASES

- tyo ke ho? — *What is that?*
- kahaañ cha? — *Where is (it)?*
- katiwaTaa chha? — *How many are there?*
- tyo kasto chha? — *How is that?*
- tyo kasko ho? — *Whose is that?*

TEXT

Note: The devanagari writing system should be learned from your tutor in conjunction with this and the next chapter. This can easily be done in two or three weeks. Starting with chapter 3, only devanagri will be used.

tapaaiñko kitaap mechmaa chha.

tapaaiñko kitaap bhuiñmaa chhaina.

✎

tyo tapaaiñko kitaap ho.

✎

tapaaiñko kitaap bhuiñmaa chhaina.

✎

tapaaiñko kitaap nilo chha.

✎

tapaaiñko kitaap raamro chha.

✎

mero kitaap kasto chha?

✎

tyo kitaap kasko ho?

✎

mero kalam Tebulmaa chha.

✎

yo mero kalam ho.

✎

mero kalam raato chha.

✎

mero kalam Thulo chha.

✎

tapaaiñko kalam chha?

✎

tapaaiñko kalam kasto chha?

✎

tapaaiñko kalam kahaañ chha?

✎

bhuiñmaa duiwaTaa jholaa chhan.

✎

euTaa mero jholaa ho, euTaa tapaaiñko jholaa ho.

✎

jholaaharu raamraa chhan.

✎

ti jholaaharu khairaa chhan.

✎

jholaaharu ThulThulaa chhan.

✎

ti jholaaharu raamraa jholaa hun.

✎

jholaaharu kahaañ chhan?

✎

GRAMMAR

➤ 1.1 *CHHA* VERSUS *HO.*

If you think about it, the English *is* has several different functions. *Is* can be:

- equative — *This **is** a pen (this = a pen).*
- existential — *There **is** a pen (a pen exists).*
- locative — *The pen **is** on the table.*
- descriptive — *The pen **is** nice,*

While English uses only *is* for all of the above, Nepali uses two forms of the verb *to be* (*hunu*). *Ho* is used for the equative while *cha* is used for the others:

• equative	*This **is** a pen*	yo kalam **ho.**
• existential	*There **is** a pen -- a pen exists.*	kalam **chha.**
• locative	*The pen **is** on the table.*	kalam Tebulmaa **chha.**
• descriptive	*The pen **is** nice,*	kalam raamro **chha.**

Sometimes either *ho* or *chha* may be used, but not without change in meaning:

raamro kalam **chha**?	(existential) *Is there a nice pen? Do (you) have a nice pen?*
raamro kalam **ho**?	(equative) *Is that a nice pen? Does that = a nice pen?*
yo kalam raamro **chha**?	(descriptive) *Is this pen nice?*
yo kalam raamro **ho**?	(equative) *Is this pen a nice pen?*

If the above explanation is confusing, just remember:

> USE *CHHA* TO TALK ABOUT:
> 1) WHETHER OR NOT SOMETHING **EXISTS,**
> 2) **WHERE** SOMETHING IS
> 3) AFTER AN **ADJECTIVE**.
>
> USE *HO* AFTER **NOUNS**.

One notable exception is an idiomatic expression for *Where are you from?* You will hear *ghar kahaañ ho?* (literally *Where is your house*). If you want to ask the literal question "Where is your house?" then you would use *ghar kahaañ chha.*

➤ 1.2 DETERMINERS *THIS, THESE, THAT, THOSE.*

SINGULAR		PLURAL	
this pen	**yo** kalam	**these** pens	**yi** kalamharu
this paper	**yo** kaagaj	**these** papers	**yi** kaagajharu
that book	**tyo** kitaap	**those** books	**ti** kitaapharu
that notebook	**tyo** kaapi	**those** notebooks	**ti** kaapiharu

*In Nepali, there are no definite or indefinite articles (in English, *a* and *the*)

➤ 1.3 PLURAL MARKER *-HARU.*

A plural noun is indicated by adding *-haru* to the noun.

Where *-haru* is **optional**:

- With the addition of *dherai 'very'*: *Tebulmaa dherai kitaap**haru** chhan* or *Tebulmaa dherai kitaap chhan.*
- When the plural noun is referred to twice *-haru* is optional on the second noun: *ti jholaaharu raamraa jholaa hun.*
- When a plural noun is modified by a number, the *-haru* is often omitted: *Tebulmaa tinwaTaa kitaap chhan.*

➤ 1.4 VERBAL AGREEMENT WITH PLURAL NOUNS.

The plural forms of *chha* and *ho* are *chhan* and *hun,* respectively. These are commonly ignored in everyday speech, but are often used in formal speech and writing.

Tebulmaa kitaapharu chhan and *yi kitaapharu meraa hun*

➤ 1.5 ADJECTIVE AGREEMENT WITH PLURAL NOUNS.

Adjectives ending in "*o*" change to "*aa*" before a plural noun. This is commonly ignored in everyday speech, but is often used in formal speech and writing.

Tebulmaa Thulaa kitaapharu chhan and
Tebulmaa saanaa kitaapharu chhan

Also, before plural nouns many adjectives will often display reduplication:

Tebulmaa ThulThulaa kitaapharu chhan and
Tebulmaa saansaanaa kitaapharu chhan

➤ 1.6 MEASURE WORD -*WATAA*.

In Nepali, every quantified noun requires a measure word (like with some English words: *one loaf of bread, two bars of soap, three sheets of paper*). For animals, inanimate objects and young children -*waTaa* is used:

tinwataa kitaap	*charwataa kaapi*	*paañchwataa kalam*
three books	four notebooks	five pens

*'One' is irregular: *euTaa. 'Two'* and *'three'* have the short forms *duiTaa* and *tinTaa.*

➤ 1.7 WRITTEN VS SPOKEN NEPALI.

There are endless debates as to what "correct" Nepali is. This is largely due to the fact that there is a great disparity between written and spoken Nepali; that and the fact that Nepali is a second language for almost half of the Nepalese. The Nepali of a newspaper and the Nepali of a villager are very different indeed. Plurality, as was discussed in 1.4 and 1.5, is one area where the spoken and written forms can be very different. The spoken forms given below will no doubt be regarded as "incorrect" by many in Kathmandu valley (your tutor included?); nevertheless, they are what you will hear.

- "Correct" Nepali: Plural nouns require the plural determiners *yi* and *ti*
  But, you will hear: *yo kalamharu* and *tyo kitaapharu* .
- "Correct" Nepali: *chhan* and *hun* should be used with plural nouns.
  But, you will hear: *Tebulmaa kitaapharu chha* and *yo kitaapharu mero ho*.
- "Correct" Nepali: An adj ending in *o* changes to *aa* before a plural noun.
  But, you will hear: *Tebulmaa Thulo kitaapharu chha*

➤ 1.8 POSSESSIVE -*KO*.

The possesive is formed by adding the possessive marker -*ko*.

**mero*	*my*	*jholaako*	*the bag's*
tapaaiñko	*yours*	*kitaapko*	*the book's*

*Note that *ma+ko* becomes *mero*.

➤ 1.9 *CHHAINA(N)* AND *HOINA(N)*.

Positive	Negative	Positive	Negative
CHHA	CHHAINA	HO	HOINA
CHHAN	CHHAINAN	HUN	HOINAN

PRACTICE

1. Supply the positive verb *to be* (see the key for answers):
   1. yi kitaabharu meraa ____________
   2. ti baarharu baliyaa ____________
   3. tyo kalam nilo kalam ____________
   4. raamro kalam ____________?
   5. tyo koThaa saano koThaa ____________
   6. koThaa Thulo ____________
   7. ti kaapiharu tapaaiñkaa ____________
   8. tyo Thulo jholaa raato ____________
   9. tapaaiñko kalam raamro kalam ____________
   10. jholaa Tebulmaa ____________
   11. tyo Dhokaa khairo Dhokaa ____________
   12. tapaaiñko raato kalam ____________?
   13. yo Thulo ghar ____________
   14. Tebulmaa kitaab ____________
   15. paheñlo jholaa ____________?
   16. koThaamaa mec ____________
   17. tapaaiñko ghar ____________?
   18. pardaa jhyaalmaa ____________
   19. yo kalam ____________
   20. tapaaiñko kaapi ____________?
   21. mecmaa nilo kitaab ____________
   22. yi kalamharu naraamraa ____________
   23. jholaamaa sisaa kalam ____________

24. tyo kitaap saano ____________
25. kaagajmaa kalam ____________
26. yo kalam nilo ____________
27. bhuiñmaa jhola ____________
28. yi gharharu Thulaa ____________
29. kaagaj Tebulmaa ____________
30. mero ghar nilo ____________
31. bhittaa seto ____________
32. jhyaalmaa pardaa ____________

2. Repeat #1, but supply the correct **negative** verb.

3. yo raamro kalam ho.

yo tyo yi ti	raamro	kalam	haru	ho hoina hun hoinan

4. Tebulmaa raamro kitaap chha.

Tebul jhola bhuiñ parkhaal	-maa	raamro	kitaap	-haru	chha chhaina chhan chhainan

5. Tebulmaa euTaa kalam chha.

Tebul jhola bhuiñ mec parkhaal	-maa	ek dui tin car kati	waTaa	kalam	haru	chha chhan

LET'S TALK

Bring for this section: Colored pens/pencils, paper, colored books, notebook, bag/backpack, game of UNO (if you have it).

1. With as many things as you can, complete the following dialogues. After going through each one once, repeat by reversing roles A and B:

A: yo/tyo ke ho?
B: yo/tyo _____ ho.

A: yo/tyo kasto chha?
B: yo/tyo ADJ chha.

A: NOUN kahaañ chha?
B: NOUN PLACE-maa chha.

A: NOUN kasko ho?
B: NOUN PERSON'S ho.

A: katiwaTaa NOUN chha?
B: NUMBER-waTaa NOUN chha.

2. Using the above dialogues loosely, elicit negative responses.

3. Take turns being Person A and Person B in the following settings. Greet each other and take leave from each other accordingly *with one or two words.*

Setting	Person A	Person B
1. At home ministry	Office Director	Home Minister
2. At the park	very good friend	very good friend
3. Visiting with landlord	tenant	landlord
4. Coming home from school	young child	parent
5. Greeting househelp at door	househelp	foreigner
6. Meeting someone new	whoever	whoever
7. Shopping	shopper	shopkeeper
8. Taking a taxi	taxi driver	traveler

4. If you have a game of "UNO", play a couple games with your tutor. When you lay down the card, state the number and color of the card. If you can't or are wrong, draw two!

DID YOU KNOW?

If you've been tempted to point at things with your finger, try pointing with your lips: that's what Nepali's do.

If you really want to emphasize the question "tyo ke ho?" (and lips aren't enough) flick your head upwards and spin your hand so that it ends up looking like this:

CHAPTER 2

INTRODUCING YOURSELF
आफ्नो परिचय

VOCABULARY

	parichaya	introduction		añgreji	English
	naam	name		baa, bubaa	father
	desh	country		nepaal	Nepal
	amerikaa	America		didi	older sister
	swayamsewak	volunteer		bhaashaa	language
	kaam	work		sikaaunu	teach
	garnu	to do		skul	school
	paaTan	Patan		daal bhaat	lentil and rice
	Thamel	Thamel		khaanu	eat
	basnu	sit, stay, live at		**Not in text, but required vocabulary**	
	ali	a little		bis	twenty
	nepaali	Nepali		tis	thirty
	bolnu	speak		chaalis	forty
	hindi	Hindi		pachaas	fifty
	uhaañ	he/she (polite)		saaThi	sixty
	aamaa	mother		sattari	seventy
	hunu	to be		assi	eighty
	kaaThmaaDauñ	Kathmandu		nabbe	ninety
				saya	hundred

USEFUL PHRASES

- tapaaiñko naam ke ho? *What is your name?*

- ma ali ali nepaali bolchhu. *I speak a little Nepali.*

- pheri bheTauñlaa. *See you later (lit. we'll meet again).*

TEXT

mero naam DewiD ho.

mero deshko naam amerikaa ho.

ma swayamsewakko kaam garchhu.

ma paaTanmaa kaam garchhu.

✎

ma Thamelmaa baschhu.

✎

ma ali ali nepaali bolchhu.

✎

ma hindi boldinã.

✎

wahaañ mero aamaa hunuhunchha.

✎

wahaañko naam kerin ho.

✎

wahaañ kaaThmaaDauñ gest haausmaa basnuhunchha.

✎

wahaañ kaam garnuhunna.

✎

wahaañ nepaali bolnuhunna.

✎

wahaañ añgreji bolnuhunchha.

✎

tapaaiñko naam ke ho?

✎

tapaaiñko deshko naam ke ho?

✎

tapaaiñ ke kaam garnuhunchha?

✎

tapaaiñ kahaañ basnuhunchha?

✎

tapaaiñko aamaa ke kaam garnuhunchha?

✎

tapaaiñko baa nepaalmaa hunuhunchha?

✎

mero didi amerikaamaa hunuhunchha.

✎

wahaañ añgreji bhaashaa sikaaunuhunchha.

✎

wahaañ skulmaa kaam garnuhunchha.

✎

wahaañ daal bhaat khaanuhunna.

✎

GRAMMAR

➤ 2.1 PRONOUNS.

For second and third person pronouns, the choice of pronoun is determined by factors such as age, sex, rank, familiarity, relative nearness to the speaker, etc. These factors all interplay to determine the level of politeness or respect required. (For first person pronouns, the only choice is singular or plural).

SECOND PERSON PRONOUNS *(YOU)*

	You should use:	**You might hear others use:**
hajur	To a high ranking gov't official.	To a person of high rank or a flattering shopkeeper to yourself.
tapaaiñ	*As a foreigner, almost always.* To your husband.	To an elder relative or person of equal status that's unfamiliar.
timi	To your child or wife.	To a younger relative, close friend or child.
tañ	To an animal or affectionately to your child.	To a *very* close friend, animal, or to someone they're *very* mad at.

If for reasons of equality you choose to use *tapaiñ* for your wife, know that it will be amusing to your listeners. It will also have the effect of saying that your relationship is extremely formal and distant. Pronouns are not chosen solely on the basis of rank; familiarity, is equally important.

THIRD PERSON PRONOUNS *(HE, SHE, IT)*

	You should use:
hajur	When referring to a high ranking official that is present.
uhaañ	*As a foreigner, almost always,* when the person being referred to is present. For your husband and older relatives.
far away close **uni, tini** **yini**	For historical persons and feminine forms. Fairly respectful -- may be used for your wife. Fairly literary.
uniharu, **tiniharu** **yiniharu**	Plural, for people unknown to the listener that don't require special respect. When referring to several people that aren't present.
far away close **u, tyo** **yo**	For 'it', your wife, children and people unknown to the listener that don't require special respect.

➤ 2.2 *HO* CONJUGATED FOR RESPECT.

The first sentence of our text, *mero naam DewiD ho*, is an example of an equative sentence (*my name = David*): thus *ho* is used. However, in our text we also find the sentence *wahaañ mero aamaa hunuhunchha*. This is also an equative sentence (*she = my mother*). But instead of *ho* , we find *hunuhunchha*. This is because in Nepali the verb displays subject agreement, changing depending on the level of respect required by the subject. The subject *my name* naturally doesn't require respect, while *my mother* does.

<table>
<tr>
<td>subject doesn't require respect
⇓
mero naam DewiD ho
⇑
respectless equative is</td>
<td>subject requires respect
⇓
wahaañ mero aamaa hunuhunchha
⇑ ⇑
respectful pronoun respectful equative is</td>
</tr>
</table>

➤ 2.3 THE SIMPLE INDEFINITE.

As we have found above, verbs agree with their subjects. That means, the verb changes depending on the subject. It also changes depending on the tense. In this chapter we encounter the simple indefinite, and it is inflected as follows:

SUBJECT	POSITIVE	NEGATIVE
ma	Verb root + chhu	Verb root + dinā
wahaañ	VERB + hunchha	VERB + hunna
tapaaiñ	VERB + hunchha	VERB + hunna

The simple indefinite can be used in several contexts. It is used for:

- Action that is being done in the present: *I am eating daal bhat.*
- General facts or things that are done habitually: *I eat daal bhat.*
- Reference to the future: *I will eat daal bhat/I am going to eat daal bhat.*

All of the above examples could be said, *ma daal bhaat khaanchhu*. Meaning is derived from the context.

➤ 2.4 VERBAL SUFFIXATION.

We have just looked at the simple indefinite tense; whenever *ma* is the subject -*chhu* (positive) and -*dinā* (negative) are suffixed to the verb. To add a suffix, we apply the following suffixation rule:

Find the first of the final consonant(s), and delete everything that follows. Then directly add the suffix to what's left.

Before we're done, two spelling rules need to be considered.

- **#1 [n] is deleted after [àu], nasalizing the preceding vowel**
- **#2 [n] is deleted before [d], nasalizing the preceding vowel.**

Applying our rules step by step, we get:

SUFFIXATION RULE		**SPELLING RULES**	
1. Find 1st of the last C's...	**...remove whatever follows and add the suffix**	**1. Delete [n] after [aau] and nasalize preceding V. 2. Delete [n] before [d] and nasalize preceding V.**	
garnu	gar-chhu		
sikaaunu	sikaaun-chhu	sikaauñ-chhu	sikaauñchhu
sikaaunu	sikaaun-dinã	sikaauñ-dinã	sikaauñdinã
khaanu	khaan-dinã	khaan-dinã	khaañdinã

You'll be happy to know that in order to conjugate for *tapaaiñ* and *wahaañ*, all you have to do is add *hunchha* and *hunna* to the infinitive verb (indefinite):

INFINITIVE	POSITIVE	NEGATIVE
garnu (to do)	garnu -hunchha	garnu -hunna
basnu (to sit)	basnu -hunchha	basnu -hunna
bolnu (to speak)	bolnu -hunchha	bolnu -hunna
khaanu (to eat)	khaanu -hunchha	khaanu -hunna
sikaaunu (to teach)	sikaaunu -hunchha	sikaaunu -hunna
hunu (to be)	hunu -hunchha	hunu -hunna

PRACTICE

1. mero naam DewiD ho.

ma	-ko naam	DewiD	ho
wahaañ			
tapaaiñ		ke	

2. ma nepaali bolchhu.

ma	añgreji	bolchhu
wahaañ	nepaali	**POS/NEG**
tapaaiñ	hindi	

3. ma swayamsewakko kaam garchhu.

ma		-ko kaam garnu
wahaañ		**POS/NEG**
tapaaiñ	*-ke	

*Note that *-ko* is not used with *-ke*.

4. mero aamaako naam keren ho.

ma	-ko	aamaa	-ko naam	keren	ho
wahaañ		baa			
tapaaiñ		didi		ke	

5. ma Thamelmaa baschu.

ma	amerikaa	-maa basnu
wahaañ	paaTan	**POS/NEG**
tapaaiñ	Thamel	
	*kahaañ	

*Note that -maa is not used with kahaañ.

6. wahaañ mero aamaa hunuhunchha.

ma	ma	-ko	aamaa	hunu
wahaañ	wahaañ		baa	**POS/NEG**
tapaaiñ	tapaaiñ		didi	

LET'S TALK

Bring for this section: Pictures of your family.

1. Listen to your tutors introduction, then introduce yourself to your tutor.
2. Have your tutor ask you the following questions. Then answers them based on your own experience (pay attention to intonation):

   tapaaiñko naam ke ho?
   tapaaiñko baako naam ke ho?
   tapaaiñko aamaako naam ke ho?
   tapaaiñko didiko naam ke ho?
   tapaaiñko deshko naam ke ho?

tapaaiñ ke kaam garnuhunchha?
tapaaiñko baa ke kaam garnuhunchha?
tapaaiñko aamaa ke kaam garnuhunchha?
tapaaiñko didi ke kaam garnuhunchha?

tapaaiñ kahaañ basnuhunchha?
tapaaiñko baa kahaañ basnuhunchha?
tapaaiñko aamaa kahaañ basnuhunchha?
tapaaiñko didi kahaañ basnuhunchha?

tapaaiñ nepaali bolnuhunchha?
tapaaiñ añgreji bolnuhunchha?
tapaaiñ hindi bolnuhunchha?
tapaaiñko baa nepaali bolnuhunchha?
tapaaiñko aamaa añgreji bolnuhunchha?

3. Without looking at the above questions, ask your tutor as many of the above questions as you can.

4. Using the pictures you brought to class, talk about your family, including the following information:
   - names
   - What they do (you can use the English word for your occupation).
   - Where they live.
   - What languages they speak.

5. Your tutor gives you an *answer* to a question. Come up with an appropriate *question* to the answer. For example, if your tutor says "*kitaap*", you may supply the question, "*Tebulmaa ke chha?*". Here's a few answers to start with:

   euTaa cha
   hoina, raato cha
   boldinã, nepaali bolchu
   amerikaamaa hunuhuncha
   nepaal ho

   Now reverse roles.

IN THE COMMUNITY

Until now you have been in a structured classroom setting; now it's time to apply what you know in the community. The only way to get into the community is to jump in!

Male language learners have it easy because there are men hanging out everywhere with free time. The challenge for a female language learner in Nepal is to find women to talk to (besides at a few shops and vegetable stalls). So, if you are a female language learner, it is absolutely essential that you break into the woman's world. Don't rely on being able to walk out into the street for many of the community assignments; you will need to get into their homes. Start your networking now, so that you have women you can meet with for future assignments. Target one or two women that you would like to befriend. As you grow in your relationship with them, ask them to introduce you to their friends. Then they can introduce you to their friends and so on.

So, now for the assignment. Male language learners: using the following text, initiate conversations that exchange the following information:

namaste. ma nepaali sikchhu. nepaali sikeko ek haptaa maatrai bhayo. mero parichaya ekchhin sunnus hai? .....[leaving] la, ma jaanchhu, namaste.

Hello. I am learning Nepali. I have learned Nepali for only one week. Please listen for a moment to my introduction...... Okay, I'm leaving. Bye.

Note: This sounds formal in English, but it is actually said in Nepali.

- Names.
- What you do (you can use the English word for your occupation)
- Where you live.
- What languages you speak.
- Your parents and elder siblings (if any) names.
- What your parents and elder siblings do.
- Where your parents and elder siblings live.
- What languages your parents and elder siblings speak.

This assignment is considered complete after exchanging all the above information with 4 individuals.

Female language learners: target one or two women to befriend and introduce yourselves to them (same info as above). If you can converse with more women, then go for it, but your strategy should be to get beyond the market or street and into the home. Your goal in the coming months should be to discover and be a part of several womens' social circles.

DID YOU KNOW?

Never ask, "Is she your wife?" or "Is he your husband?" If the answer is "yes", you're safe, but if the answer is "no", you will have no doubt caused a lot of embarrassment. If you need to, you can ask politely, "Who is she?" or "She is......?"

While it's okay to ask someone's name, Nepalis do not use first names to refer to each other, especially outside of Kathmandu valley. The best alternate is to use some appropriate kinship term, or use *-ji* after a name. You will even hear someone call their spouse by saying, "Hey, mother of my boy" or "Father of my child." You may on occasion hear someone trying to get your attention by saying, "Uncle/Aunt of my child."

CHAPTER 3

SHOPPING

किनमेल

VOCABULARY					
किनमेल	shopping	रूपैयाँ	rupee (written in bank note)	साबुन	soap
आज	today	सस्तो	inexpensive	चाहिँ	*particle*
साहुजी / साहुनी	shopkeeper (m/f)	किलो	kilo	पूजा	"Puja"
हामी	we	कति	how much	न	*particle*
बजार	market	पर्छ	costs	जम्मा	in total
जानु	go	दिनु	give	पैसा	money
तरकारी	vegetable	रुपियाँ	rupee (colloquial)	धन्यवाद	thanks
किन्नु	buy	लिनु	take	कुरा	thing, matter
फलफूल	fruits	महँगो	expensive	सिमी	bean
पसल	shop, store, stall	पच्चीस	twenty-five	बन्दाकोबी	cabbage
पाटन	Patan	कम	below, less	आलु	potato
ठमेल	Thamel	हुँदैन	not allowed	काँक्रो	cucumber
यहाँ	here	ल	alright, okay	गोलभेँडा	tomato
पाइनु	to be available	अर्को	another, the next	साग	spinach
चाहिनु	to be needed	पाउरोटी	loaf bread	गाजर	carrot
स्याउ	apple	पन्ध्र	fifteen	हस् / हवस्	okay
सुन्तला	orange	होला	probably	आधा	half
र	and	अरू	other, else, more	प्याज	onion
केरा	banana	कुन	which		
आँप	mango	धुनु	wash	**Learn numbers 11-19**	

USEFUL PHRASES

- तपाईँलाई के चाहिन्छ ? — *What do you need?*
- एक किलोको कति पर्छ ? — *How much does a kilo cost?*
- एक किलो आँप कतिमा दिने ? — *How much is a kilo of mangoes?*
- एक किलो आँपको कति (हो) ? — *How much is a kilo of mangoes?*
- एक किलो आँप कसरी दिने ? — *How much is a kilo of mangoes?*

TEXT

आज हामी बजार जान्छौँ। आज हामी पाटन जान्छौँ। आज हामी ठमेल जाँदैनौँ। म तरकारी किन्छु। उहाँ फलफूल किन्नुहुन्छ।

फलफूल पसलमा

क: साहुनी ! यहाँ के-के पाइन्छ?
ख: तपाईँलाई के-के चाहिन्छ?

क: स्याउ, सुन्तला र केरा। आँप छैन होला?
ख: छ ! सस्तो छ।

क: एक किलोको कति पर्छ? कतिमा दिने?
ख: तपाईँलाई तीस रुपियाँमा दिन्छु।

क: तीसमा लिन्नँ। त्यो त महँगो भयो।
ख: कति दिनुहुन्छ त?

क: बीसमा दिने?
ख: पच्चीसमा कम हुँदैन।
क: ल, दुई किलो दिनुस्।

अर्को पसलमा

क: साहुजी ! पाउरोटी छ?

ख: छ।

क: एउटाको कति?

ख: पन्ध्र रुपियाँ।

क: दुईवटा दिनुस्।

ख: हस्, लिनुस्। अरू के चाहिन्छ?

क: लुगा धुने साबुन छ?

ख: छ। कुनचाहिँ?

क: पूजा साबुन दुईवटा दिनुस् न !

ख: लिनुस्।

क: जम्मा कति भयो?

ख: ४६ रुपियाँ भयो।

क: पैसा लिनुस्। धन्यवाद !

GRAMMAR

➤ 3.1 INDEFINITE TENSE FOR हामी.

To conjugate the verbs of this chapter for the plural first person pronoun हामी, suffix -छौं for the positive and -दैनौं for the negative by applying our suffixation and spelling rules introduced last chapter. Since none of the verbs in this chapter end in [au], we only need to apply rule #2. We need to add one important exception to the above spelling rules: **Do not apply spelling rules to verbs that end in *-nnu*, as in किन्नु.**

SUFFIXATION RULE		SPELLING RULE(S)	
1. Find 1st of the last C's...	**...remove everything that follows and add the suffix**	**#1. Delete [n] before [d] and nasalize the preceding vowel.** **Exception: doesn't apply to verbs ending in *-nnu***	
jaanu	jaan-dainauñ	jaañ-dainauñ	जाँदैनौं
kinnu	kin-dainauñ	**does not apply** (*-nnu*)	किन्दैनौं
dinu	din-dainauñ	diñ-dainauñ	दिँदैनौं
linu	lin-dainauñ	liñ-dainauñ	लिँदैनौं
dhunu	dhun-dainauñ	dhuñ-dainauñ	धुँदैनौं

➤ 3.2 PASSIVES MARKER –इनु.

In active sentences, the subject is typically the actor, e.g. *I saw the orange*. In passive sentences, the subject is the recipient of the action, e.g. *The orange was seen [by me]*. The passive is created by attaching -इनु to the verb base (and then conjugating for tense). The passives given in the chart below cover the most common passives. It should also be noted that in colloquial speech, the active form is often used when the passive should. For example, *Are oranges available?* should be said सुन्तला पाइन्छ? but सुन्तला पाउँछ? is often heard.

ACTIVE		PASSIVE	
to get, receive, find	पाउनु	पाइनु	*be available*
to want, desire, intend	चाहनु	चाहिनु	*be needed*
to see	देख्नु	देखिनु	*to be seen, to be visible*
to do	गर्नु	गरिनु	*to be done*
to say, tell, ask to ..	भन्नु	भनिनु	*to be said, to be called*
to hear, listen	सुन्नु	सुनिनु	*to be heard, to be audible*
to reach, to be enough, to arrive	पुग्नु	पुगिनु	*be reached*
be able to do, can	सक्नु	सकिनु	*be do-able, to be possible, to be finished*

➤ 3.3 –लाई IN PASSIVES AND WITH INDIRECT OBJECTS.

- -लाई marks indirect objects:

म तपाईंलाई पैसा दिन्छु। — *I give money to you.*
उहाँ मलाई पैसा दिनुहुन्छ। — *He gives money to me.*

- -लाई is used in certian passive constructions:

  मलाई पैसा चाहिन्छ। — *Money is needed by me (I need money).*

  मलाई पनि पाइन्छ? — *Is some available to me as well?*

In a sentence like, हामी र तपाईंलाई के के चाहिन्छ only the second constituent of the noun phrase needs लाई.

➤ 3.4 REDUPLICATION FOR PLURALITY.

Reduplication is used with question words to indicate plurality:

के-के *what all* कहाँ-कहाँ *where all.* को-को *who all*

➤ 3.5 DISCOURSE PARTICLES.

Particles are those funny little things in a language that never really translate, but they give a sentence a different sense of meaning. In the short dialogue of this chapter we encounter six common discourse particles:

होला	Expresses uncertainty	आँप छैन होला।	*There **probably** aren't any mangoes.*
त	Emphasizes preceding word	त्यो त महँगो भयो।	***As for** that, it's expensive.*
चाहिँ	Emphasizes preceding word	मचाहिँ किन्छु।	***As for** me, I'll buy it. As for [Noun].*
चाहिँ	*The [Adj] one*	सस्तोचाहिँ दिनुस्।	*Give me the cheap **one**.*
ल	Signals acceptance	ल, दुई किलो दिनुस्।	***Okay**, give me two kilos.*
हस्	Equal to **ल**, but more polite	हस्, लिनुस्।	***Okay**, take it.*
न	Makes a request more polite	दुईवटा दिनुस् न !	*Give me two, **please**.*

➤ 3.6 -को कति पर्छ *HOW MUCH DOES X COST.*

There are two options for *How much does one kilo of mangoes cost:*

[आँप ↔ एक किलो] **को कति पर्छ**
[एक किलो ↔ आँप] **को कति पर्छ**

Several other common ways for asking how much something is:

एक किलो आँप कतिमा दिने? — *For how much will you give me a kilo of mangoes?*

एक किलो आँपको कति (हो)? — *How much is one kilo of mangoes.*

*एक किलो आँप कसरी दिने? — *For what will you give me a kilo of mangoes?*

*The later expression is very colloquial, very common in Kathmandu.

➤ 3.7 -ने FOR INFORMAL FUTURE.

Rather than fully conjugating a verb, -ने is used very commonly in informal, colloquial speech for reference to the future:

कतिमा दिने (instead of दिनुहुन्छ)	*How much will you give it for?*
बीसमा दिने?	*Will you give it for 20?*
त्यतिमा नदिने	*(I) won't give it for that much.*

➤ 3.8 -ने FOR DERIVATION.

Derivation is a process whereby a word changes part of speech. -ने is added to a verb to make it function as an adjective. In English the same is done with -*ing*: *drinking water, writing book, singing person, falling tree,* etc.

धुने साबुन	*washing soap*
चाहिने तरकारी	*vegetables that are needed*
गर्ने आमा	*the mother that does*

When adding suffixes that begin with an [n], as with the above -ने, always remove the entire -*nu* from the infinitive and add the suffix to whatever is left.

Spelling rules are not applied.

ADDING A SUFFIX THAT BEGINS WITH -*N*		
Remove all of and only ***-nu***	**... and add the suffix (eg. ने)**	**Don't apply any spelling rules**
sikaau.....**nu**	sikaau**ne**	सिकाउने
jaa.....**nu**	jaa**ne**	जाने
kin.....**nu**	kin**ne**	किन्ने
di.....**nu**	di**ne**	दिने
dhu.....**nu**	dhu**ne**	धुने

➤ 3.9 ALTERNATIVE SIMPLE INDEFINITE NEGATIVE.

For those verbs that end in -*(vowel)nu*, there is an alternative negative:

म	हामी
SIKAAU-NNÃ	SIKAAU-NNAUÑ
DHU-NNÃ	DHU-NNAUÑ
BIRSA-NNÃ	BIRSA-NNAUÑ
KHAA-NNÃ	KHAA-NNAUÑ
*DI-NNÃ	*DI-NNAUÑ
GAR- nonexistent; verb ends in consonant	

*The verbs that have [i] as the last vowel (after taking off *-nu*) more commonly take the *-nna* ending rather than *-dinã*. लिन्नँ is more common than लिँदिनँ, and दिन्नँ is more common than दिँदिनँ.

➤ 3.10 PAST TENSE OF हुनु.

The past tense of the verb हुनु is भयो. We will deal with this in detail later; you only need to note here that Nepali uses the past tense, त्यो त महँगो भयो, *That was expensive* when English would use *That is expensive*. Think of it as, the point in time at which the shopkeeper gave the price is now in the past tense.

➤ 3.11 THE POLITE IMPERATIVE -नुस्.

The polite imperative (command) is made by adding -नुस् to the verb base. You would use this, for example, when asking an elder to do something (but not for a child).

दिनुस्	*(please) give*	नदिनुस्	*(please) don't give*
बस्नुस्	*(please) sit*	नबस्नुस्	*(please) don't sit*

Remember, when adding suffixes that begin with an [n], always remove the entire **-nu** from the infinitive and add the suffix to whatever is left. **Spelling rules are not applied**. Thus we arrive at: सिकाउनुस्, जानुस्, किन्नुस्, दिनुस्, लिनुस्, धुनुस्.

➤ 3.12 अर्को VERSUS अरू.

अर्को - *One other, another, next, one more.* Used to modify a singular object.

अरू - *Other, more, else.* Used to modify a plural object, or to mean *more*. For example, if you want more daal bhat, you would say अरू दालभात दिनुस्।

अरू + Question word = Wh- else? e.g. अरू के चाहिन्छ? What else you need?
More politely अरू केही चाहिन्छ? Do you need anything else?

PRACTICE

1. Conjugate the following for the indefinite tense हामी, म, तपाईं, and वहाँ (+/–):
   जानु, किन्नु, दिनु, लिनु, धुनु, गर्नु, बस्नु, बोल्नु, सिकाउनु, खानु

2. Conjugate for the indefinite tense म and हामी using the two alternative negatives (-न and -दिन). Note for which ones you can't use -न, and for which ones -न is more common:
   जानु, किन्नु, दिनु, लिनु, धुनु, गर्नु, बस्नु, बोल्नु, सिकाउनु, खानु

3. Supply each sentence with the correct active or passive form (+ / –):

a) तपाईँ त्यो पसलमा पाउरोटी (**पाउनु**)
b) त्यो पसलमा साबुन (**पाउनु**)
c) तपाईँ के-के (**चाहनु**)
d) बजारमा के-के (**पाउनु**)?
e) म त्यो (**गर्नु**)।
f) नेपालमा त्यो (**गर्नु**)।

4. If the sentence is incorrect, correct it by adding -लाई :

a) म तपाईँ पैसा दिन्छु।
b) तपाईँ म आलु दिनुहुन्छ।
c) तपाईँ म त्यो दिनुस्।
d) हामी के-के चाहिन्छ?
e) हामी र तपाईँ के-के चाहिन्छ?
f) तपाईं म स्याउ दिनुस्।
g) म पनि अलि तरकारी चाहिन्छ?

5. Using a particle, add to each sentence the given meaning:

a) त्यो महँगो भयो। *Emphasize "that"*
b) आँप छैन। *Express uncertainty*
c) म किन्छु। *Emphasize "me"*
d) सस्तो *Emphasize "inexpensive"*
e) लिनुस् । *Express polite acceptance*
f) दुईवटा केरा दिनुस्। *Express acceptance*
g) आलु सस्तो भयो। *Emphasize "potatoes"*
h) स्याउ छ। *Express uncertainty*
i) दुईवटा दिनुस्। *Make request more polite*
j) मेचमा बस्छु। *Express polite acceptance*
k) मेचमा बस्नुस्। *Make request more polite*
l) म बस्दिनँ। *Emphasize "me"*
m) दुई किलो दिनुस्। *Express acceptance and make request more polite.*

6. आँप एक किलोको कति पर्छ?

आँप	एक किलो	-को कति पर्छ?
आलु	दुई किलो	
सिमी	चार किलो	
स्याउ		
केरा		

एक किलो	आँप	-को कति पर्छ?
	आलु	कतिमा दिने?
	सिमी	-को कति हो?
	स्याउ	कसरी दिने?
	केरा	

7. Translate the following using -ने.
   a) the washing soap
   b) the vegetables that are needed
   c) the mother that does
   d) the father that sits
   e) the shopkeeper that speaks

8. Conjugate the following verbs using -नुस् (+/–):
   जानु, किन्नु, दिनु, लिनु, धुनु, गर्नु, बस्नु, बोल्नु, सिकाउनु, खानु

9. Translate the following sentences using -ने.
   a) Are you going to the market?
   b) Are you going to buy vegetables?
   c) How much will you give me?
   d) Are you going to wash those vegetables?
   e) We will eat the fruit.

10. Translate the following sentences using अर्को or अरू:
   a) Give me some more vegetables.
   b) Take two more apples.
   c) Buy another kg of potatoes.
   d) Eat another apple.
   e) Eat some more dhal baat.

LET'S TALK

Bring for this section: Market vegetables and fruit that are in season and money to "go shopping".

1. Your tutor is a shopkeeper. Here is a shopping list of things for you to buy from your tutor:

bread - two loaves
soap - two bars

beans - 1/2 kg
cabbage
potatoes - 2 kg
cucumber
tomatoes - 1/2 kg
spinach
carrots
onions

2. Your tutor is now the shopper and you are the shopkeeper. Your tutor is to buy from you the above list of market items.

3. Your tutor is an Indian fruit vendor. Here's a shopping list of fruit to buy:

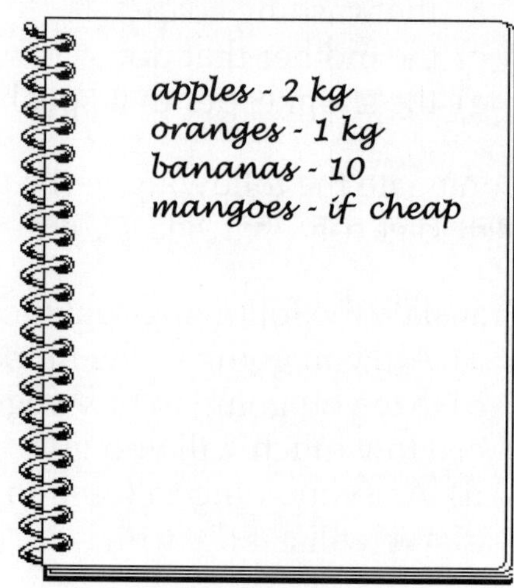

apples - 2 kg
oranges - 1 kg
bananas - 10
mangoes - if cheap

4. You are now the Indian fruit vendor. Your tutor is to buy the above fruit from you.

5. **Step 1.** Your tutor states a false price for the following items.
   Step 2. You then state whether the price given is expensive or cheap.
   Step 3. Your tutor then gives the normal, reasonable price for you to write in:

apple ___	bean ___	tomato ___
orange ___	cabbage ___	spinach ___
banana ___	potato ___	carrot ___
mango ___	cucumber ___	

IN THE COMMUNITY

1. Go to one or two large vegetable markets and note the following:
   a. Roughly the ratio of male vs. female vendors.
   b. Roughly the ratio of male vs. female shoppers.
   c. How much bargaining is going on.

2. At the same market(s), compare prices by asking different vendors the prices of different vegetables (it is acceptable to ask for the English equivalent for numbers you don't know). Tip: at each vendor buy a little bit of something. For example, if you need 2 kg. of potatoes, buy 1/2 kg. from four different vendors. The assignment is complete when you have spent a total of 3 hours at the market(s) or asked 50 different prices, whichever comes first.

DID YOU KNOW?

Vegetables are usually not vigorously bargained for. While you will hear it to a certain degree, it is certainly not to the extent that you hear bargaining for fruits. Bargaining should also not be done in the common little grocery stores, either. Bargaining *should* be vigorous with vendors of any kind (including fruit vendors), in tourist shops, appliance stores (though you won't get far), wages for a one time job, clothing stores, etc.

Money should always be given and received with the right hand.

It is very common for the men to do the shopping for vegetables and meat.

At the end of our text we find the shopper saying "thank you", but it really isn't that common. You will hear foreigners using it all the time, but listen to how often a Nepali says to another Nepali "धन्यवाद." Probably not very often. In fact, if you give someone a gift, you may never even hear a "धन्यवाद". It is not that they are not grateful; it just isn't said with words. "Thank you" is more commonly communicated through body language. The recipient may raise the gift to his/her forehead and something like food will be received with the right hand while the left hand is placed on the forearm of the right arm. An expression like "You need not have done it" may convey a sense of gratefulness.

CHAPTER 4

TAXI
ट्याक्सी

VOCABULARY					
ट्याक्सी	"taxi"	होइन	isn't; no	दायाँ	right
आजभोलि	nowadays	पनि	also, even	-तिर	towards
दिउँसो	(in the) afternoon	कि	or	पुग्नु	reach, arrive
मिटर	"meter"	अहिले	now	अब	now
चलाउनु	drive, operate, run	इमिग्रेसन	immigration	कता (तिर)	to which direction, whither?
तर	but, however	अफिस	"office"	सिधा	straight
साँझ	evening, dusk, twilight	डेरा	rented flat	गाडी	car, truck, vehicle
पछि	after, behind, later	-न चाहनु	to want, intend to desire to	पछाडि	behind
मोलतोल	bargaining	देख्नु	to see	रोक्नु	stop; obstruct
टाढा	far (distance)	पुल्चोक	Pulchok	हेर्नु	to look, watch
दक्षिणकाली	Dakshinkali	छिन	moment	पुल	bridge
ऊ	he, she, it	होटेल	"hotel"	देखाउनु	to show, demonstrate, exhibit
खाली	empty, vacant	नारायणी	Narayani	ठाउँ	place
ड्राइभर	"driver"	अगाडि	in front, before	साँघुरो	narrow, tight
बाटो	road, way, trail	हगि?	right?	फराकिलो	wide
सडक	street	चोक	courtyard, intersection, square	पीपल बोट	Peepal tree
भन्नु	say, tell	बायाँ	left	घुम्ती	bend (in a road)
आउनु	come	त्यहाँ	there	मोड्नु	to turn
-निर	near, beside, next to				

USEFUL PHRASES

- ट्याक्सी खाली हो? — *Is the taxi empty (available)?*
- कति भयो? — *How much (price)?*
- यहाँ रोक्नुस्। — *Stop here.*
- पहिले बायाँतिर मोड्नुस्। — *At first, turn left.*
- दायाँतिर मोड्नुस्। — *Turn right.*
- पीपल बोटमा पुगेपछि... — *After reaching the peepul tree...*
- मलाई थाहा छैन। — *I don't know. I've no knowledge.*
- म जान चाहन्छु। — *I want to go.*

TEXT

आजभोलि काठमाडौंमा धेरै ट्याक्सी पाइन्छन् । दिउँसो ड्राइभरहरूले ट्याक्सी मिटरमा चलाउँछन् । तर तिनीहरूले साँझ परेपछि मोलतोल गर्छन् र मिटरमा चलाउँदैनन् । तिनीहरूले धेरै टाढा जान पनि मोलतोल गर्छन् ।

जेम्स ट्याक्सीमा दक्षिणकाली जान्छ । ऊ ट्याक्सीमा पाटन जाँदैन । ऊ एउटा ट्याक्सीनिर जान्छ ।

जेम्स : ट्याक्सी खाली हो?

ट्याक्सी ड्राइभर : हो । कहाँ जाने?

जेम्स : दक्षिणकाली जाने ।

ट्या. ड्रा. : कति दिनुहुन्छ? धेरै टाढा छ । बाटो राम्रो छैन ।

जेम्स : कति लिनुहुन्छ ? तपाईं नै भन्नुस् ।

ट्या. ड्रा. : जान र आउन पच्चिस सय रुपियाँ दिनुस् ।

जेम्स : पच्चिस सय होइन । अठार सय लिनुस् ।

ट्या. ड्रा. : ल, पच्चिस सय पनि होइन, अठार सय पनि होइन । एक्काइस सयमा जाने कि नजाने?

जेम्स : ल ल, जाऔं ।

एलेक्स अहिले इमिग्रेसन अफिसमा छ । ऊ अहिले डेरामा जान चाहन्छ । उसले एउटा ट्याक्सी देख्छ ।

एलेक्स : ट्याक्सी खाली छ?

ट्याक्सी ड्रा. : छ । कहाँ जाने?

एलेक्स : पुल्चोक ।

ट्या. ड्रा. : ल, बस्नुस् । (एकछिनपछि)

ट्या. ड्रा. : पुल्चोकमा कहाँ?

एलेक्स : होटेल नारायणीको अगाडि एउटा बाटो छ, हगि?

ट्या. ड्रा. : हो । त्यो चोकबाट बायाँ जाने?

एलेक्स : होइन होइन, त्यहाँबाट दायाँतिर जाने ।

(पुल्चोक पुगेपछि ट्याक्सी नारायणी होटेलको अगाडिको बाटोमा जान्छ ।)

ट्या. ड्रा. : अब कता?

एलेक्स : सिधा जानुस्, ऊ...त्यो निलो गाडीको पछाडि रोक्नुस् । त्यो गाडीनिर ।

ट्या. ड्रा. : हुन्छ, ल ।

एलेक्स : कति भयो? मिटर हेर्नुस् ।

ट्या. ड्रा. : दुई सय पचास रुपियाँ भयो ।

एलेक्स : पैसा लिनुस्, धन्यवाद !

GRAMMAR

➤ 4.1 EMPHATIC -नै.

We have already encountered two emphatic particles: त and चाहिँ (3.5). The other emphatic particle that is very prolific is नै. In our text we have the sentence तपाईं नै भन्नुस्. It has the sense, *You (not me) say it.* As a short form of नै, only ऐ (ै) is added. It is added directly to words that end in a consonant. For words that end in a vowel, ऐ replaces the last vowel. For words that already end in ऐ thc full long form नै is used. नै is sometimes bound to a word or occurs more commonly than the ordinary form.

FREE FORM	EMPH.	SHORT
घर	घर **नै**	घरै
घरमा	घरमा **नै**	घरमै
तपाईं	तपाईं **नै**	--
म	म **नै**	मै
मात्र	--	मात्रै
--	--	धेरै

➤ 4.2 INDEFINITE TENSE FOR ऊ AND उनीहरू.

ऊ (यो/त्यो)		उनी/उनीहरू (यिनी/तिनीहरू)	
POSITIVE	NEGATIVE	POSITIVE	NEGATIVE
–छ	**–दैन**	**–छन्**	**–दैनन्**
भन्छ	भन्दैन	भन्छन्	भन्दैनन्
आउँछ	आउँदैन	आउँछन्	आउँदैनन्
चाहन्छ	चाहँदैन	चाहन्छन्	चाहँदैनन्
देख्छ	देख्दैन	देख्छन्	देख्दैनन्
हेर्छ	हेर्दैन	हेर्छन्	हेर्दैनन्
रोक्छ	रोक्दैन	रोक्छन्	रोक्दैनन्
पुग्छ	पुग्दैन	पुग्छन्	पुग्दैनन्

➤ 4.3 SUFFIXING A SUFFIX THAT BEGINS WITH A VOWEL.

In suffixing -एपछि, this is the first time we have added **a suffix that begins with a vowel**, so a few more spelling rules need to be added:

- **#3 Delete [n] between vowels, but if that results in a vowel cluster of three, delete the vowel before [n] as well.**
- **#4 [u] followed by a vowel becomes [o]**

You will only need to apply rules #1 and #2 **or** #3 and #4. So, adding the suffix -एपछि *after*, we apply rules #3 and #4:

SUFFIXATION RULE		**SPELLING RULES 3 AND 4**	
1. Find first of final C's...	**2. Add suffix to what follows**	**3. Apply spelling rules (unless ends in -nnu)**	**Devanagri Spelling**
bhannu	bhanepachhi	(ends in *-nnu*)	भनेपछि
aaunu	aaunepachhi	aaepachhi (# 3)	आएपछि
pakaunu	pakaaunepachhi	pakaepachhi (# 3)	पकाएपछि
*caahanu	caahanepachhi	*caahepachhi (# 3)	चाहेपछि
**jaanu	jaanepachhi	**gaepachhi (# 3)	गएपछि
dhunu (wash)	dhunepachhi	***dhoepachhi (# 3, 4)	धोएपछि
dek^hnu	dek^hepachhi	--	देखेपछि
hernu	herepachhi	--	हेरेपछि
roknu	rokepachhi	--	रोकेपछि
pugnu	pugepachhi	--	पुगेपछि
khaanu	khaanepachhi	--	खाएपछि

* Analyzing [h]'s as voiceless vowels, [hae] is a vowel cluster of three.

** When adding suffixes that begin with a vowel, [jaa] becomes [ga], except in the injunctive mood

*** Notice that rules 3 and 4 should be applied in that order.

Putting all of our suffixation and spelling rules together (and in case you're worried there's more, that's about it) we get:

SUFFIXATION AND SPELLING RULES

- **SUFFIXATION (unless suffix begins with *-n*):**
  Find the first of the final consonant(s), and delete everything that follows. Then directly add the suffix to what's left.

- **SUFFIXATION (with suffix that begins with *-n*):**
  Remove *-nu* (and only *-nu*) and add the suffix to what's left.

- **SPELLING (when adding a suffix that begins with a consonant)**
  #1 [n] is deleted after [aau], nasalizing the preceding vowel.
  #2 [n] is deleted before [d], nasalizing the preceding vowel.

- **SPELLING (when adding a suffix that begins with a vowel)**
  #3 Delete [n] between vowels, but if that results in a vowel cluster of three, delete the vowel before [n] as well.
  #4 [u] followed by a vowel becomes [o]

- **DON'T APPLY the above Spelling rules if:**
  A verb ends in *-nnu* or when adding a suffix that begins with *-n*.

➤ 4.4 DERIVATIONAL -न.

Among various other uses, -न is used to derive nouns out of verbs (nominalization). English does this by adding *ing* or using *to do X*. In our text we find the sentence जान र आउन छ शय रुपैयाँ दिनुस्. The English sense is, ***For coming** and going, give me 600 Rs.*

VERB	NOUN	VERB	NOUN
speak	speak**ing**	बोल्नु	बोल्**न**
teach	teach**ing**	सिकाउनु	सिकाउ**न**
eat	eat**ing**	खानु	खा**न**
go	go**ing**	जानु	जा**न**
come	com**ing**	आउनु	आउ**न**

➤ 4.5 ...पनि होइन, ...पनि होइन NEITHER..., NOR....

छ सय पनि होइन, चार सय पनि होइन। *Neither 600 nor 400 hundred.*
रातो पनि होइन, सेतो पनि होइन। *Neither red nor white.*
राम्रो पनि होइन, नराम्रो पनि होइन। *Neither good nor bad.*

➤ 4.6 INJUNCTIVE MOOD.

The injunctive mood is used to express a wish or desire. In questions, *shall* or *may*; in statements, *let's*.

verb	question	statement	verb	question	statement
गरौं	shall/may we do?	Let's do.	हेरौं	shall/may we see?	Let's see.
बसौं	shall/may we sit?	Let's sit.	भनौं	shall/may we say?	Let's say.
खाऔं	shall/may we eat?	Let's eat.	सिकाऔं	shall/may we teach?	Let's teach.
किनौं	shall/may we buy?	Let's buy.	धोऔं	shall/may we wash?	Let's wash.

verb	question	statement	verb	question	statement
गरूँ	shall/may I do?	Let me do.	हेरूँ	shall/may I see?	Let me see.
बसूँ	shall/may I sit?	Let me sit.	भनूँ	shall/may I say?	Let me say.
खाऊँ	shall/may I eat?	Let me eat.	सिकाऊँ	shall/may I teach?	Let me teach.
किनूँ	shall/may I buy?	Let me buy.	धोऊँ	shall/may I wash?	Let me wash.

* Some dialects use जाम instead of जाऔं for shall we go? or Let's go.
** 'न-' is added to make them negative e.g.
नगरौं - Let's not do. Shall we not do?
नगरूँ - Let me not do. Shall I not do?

➤ 4.7 WHEN -वटा IS NOT USED.

When a number qualifies a word that measures an amount or time period, -वटा is not used. For example, *one moment* is एकछिन, <u>not</u> * एउटा छिन. None of the following phrases would use -वटा: *one cup, two kilos, three hours, nine miles.*

➤ 4.8 -ले IN A STORY.

There are many different situations where ले is used. The particular usage of our text is: **in telling a story** or giving a narrative, the **third person subject** of a **transitive verb** takes the suffix ले. In our text we have the sentence उसले एउटा

ट्याक्सी देख्छ . In this sentence, ऊ is a third person subject, देख्नु is a transitive verb, and our text is telling a story. Most Nepalis will tell you that the sentence is okay with or without the ले but purists will insist upon it. While other uses of ले are obligatory , it's fairly safe to say that this particular use is optional.

➤ 4.9 अब VERSUS अहिले.

अहिले can be used to mean *at present*; अब cannot:

अहिले म खान्छु।	*I'm eating (at present).*
अब म खान्छु।	*I will eat (now).*

COMPLEX VERBS

• -एपछि — ***after...***

पीपल बोटमा पुगेपछि...	***After*** *reaching the peepul tree...*
साँझ परेपछि ट्याक्सीहरूले मोलतोल गर्छन्।	***After*** *turning dusk, taxi (drivers) bargain.*
पुल्चोक पुगेपछि	***After*** *reaching Pulchok.*

• -न चाहनु — ***to want to...***

ऊ अहिले डेरामा जान चाहन्छ।	*He* ***wants to*** *go to his apartment now.*
म जान चाहन्छु।	*I* ***want to*** *go.*
ट्याक्सीहरू मोलतोल गर्न चाहन्छन्।	*Taxi (drivers)* ***want to*** *bargain.*

PRACTICE

1. i. Emphasize the bolded words using the emphatic particle **-नै**.
   ii. Emphasize the bolded words using the short form, where possible.
   a) **टेबुलमा** किताप छ।
   b) मेरी **आमा** घरमा हुनुहुन्छ।
   c) मेरी आमा **घरमा** हुनुहुन्छ।
   d) यो घर **मेरो** हो।
   e) मेरी **आमा** नेपाली हुनुहुन्छ।
   f) मेरी आमा **नेपाली** हुनुहुन्छ।
   g) हामी **तरकारी** किन्छौँ।
   h) **गाजर** मलाई दिनुस्।
   i) गाजर **मलाई** दिनुस्।

2. Conjugate the following verbs for the indefinite tense ऊ , pos. and neg.:
   जानु, किन्नु, धुनु, गर्नु, बस्नु, सिकाउनु, भन्नु, आउनु, चाहनु, देख्नु, हेर्नु, रोक्नु, पुग्नु

3. Conjugate the following for उनी(हरू), positive and negative:
   जानु, किन्नु, धुनु, गर्नु, बस्नु, सिकाउनु, भन्नु, आउनु, चाहनु, देख्नु, हेर्नु, रोक्नु, पुग्नु

4. Link the pairs of sentences using -एपछि and conjugate the final verb.
   a) किनमेल गर्छु। — तरकारी खानु।
   b) तपाईं बोल्नुहुन्छ। — मेचमा बस्नु।
   c) हामी कितापबाट सिकाउँछौं। — हामी बोल्नु।
   d) म टेबुलमा बस्छु। — तपाईं मलाई सिकाउनु।
   e) म घर जान्छु। — म तपाईंलाई यो दिनु।
   f) तपाईं स्याउ किन्नुस्। — स्याउ धुनु।
   g) स्याउ धुनुस्। — स्याउ खानु।
   h) म तपाईंको घर आउँछु। — मलाई भन्नु।

5. Translate the following sentences using -न:
   a) buying vegetables
   b) giving money
   c) doing work
   d) teaching Hindi
   e) It is good to sit in a chair.
   f) It is good to speak Nepali.

6. Using the structure [X पनि होइन/छैन, Y पनि होइन/छैन], translate the following:
   a) That pen is neither blue nor red.
   b) That taxi is neither good nor bad.
   c) Not for 5 rupees or for 7 rupees
   d) Oranges are not expensive. Nor are they cheap.
   e) Neither left nor right; stop right here.

7. Using the injunctive mood, translate the following (+/–):
   a) Shall we go to buy vegetables? — Shall I go to buy vegetables.
   b) Let's go. — Let me go.
   c) Let's speak Nepali. — Let me speak Nepali.
   d) May we eat apples? — May I eat apples?
   e) Shall we teach him Nepali? — May I teach him Nepali?
   f) Let's sit for a moment. — Let me sit for a moment.
   g) Let's see. — Let me see.
   h) May we say it in Nepali? — May I say it in Nepali?

   Now do the above for negative also.

8. म घरबाट आउँछु।

म	घर	-बाट	आउँछु
ऊ		-निर	जान्‌
उनीहरू		-तिर	बस्‌नु
		-मा	रोक्‌नु
			खान्छु

LET'S TALK

Bring for this section: A map of Kathmandu city

1. Your tutor describes how to get from point A to point B. Then, taking the same two points, you describe how to get from point B to point A.

Point A	**Point B**
a. the zoo	the airport
b. the stadium	Pashupati
c. Royal Palace	Tribhuvan University
d. Pulchok	your house
e. Swayambhu	Bimsen tower
f. Boudha	Everest Hotel
g. Yak and Yeti Hotel	Summit Hotel

Some useful phrases that you should already know: to this direction.

After/before reaching X	*After/before the bridge*	*stop here*
From the intersection	*turn left*	*Turn at the first left.*
In front of/behind X	*turn right*	*Turn at the second right.*
After a little while	*go straight*	*After reaching ...*
At/from the hotel	*go towards...*	*In this direction*

2. **Step One** : Without letting your tutor see, write down the name of a place in Kathmandu on a slip of paper.

   Step Two : Your tutor points at a random place on the map.

   Step Three : Give directions to get from the random place your tutor pointed at to the place you wrote down. As you give directions, your tutor should trace with his finger the route described. For example, if you say, "आउने चोकबाट, दायाँ जानुस्" your tutor will move his/her finger from where it was to the next intersection and trace left.

Step Four : After you successfully have your tutor trace to the place you wrote down, show the paper to your tutor.

Repeat several times, and reverse roles several times.

3. Describe to each other what is:
   a) on your left
   b) on your right
   c) in front of you
   d) behind you

4. Use the picture below to talk about who is in front of/behind who:

IN THE COMMUNITY

1. Plan a travel route that takes you throughout the city. It should include five destination points. For example, your route might include the five destination points: German Embassy, CIWEC clinic, KTM Guest House, Blue Bird Hotel and home. Upon reaching each destination point, you are to change taxis. In other words, you will go on five different taxi rides. There are three rules:

   Rule One : You cannot give the name of the destination point or the name of the area. You must give directions *as you go*. (Plan your route well!).

Rule Two : You cannot point (to avoid "go this way...go that way").

Rule Three : NO ENGLISH

If you have a grouchy taxi driver, he might not like these rules, so start with the following excuse:

मलाई ठाउँको नाम थाहा छैन। ठाउँ टाढा छ। म तपाईँलाई बाटो देखाउँछु।

I don't know the name of the place. The place is far. I'll show you the way.

If the taxi driver can't agree to that, find another taxi. Only if you get *completely* lost can you use place names.

2. As you complete #1, ask *each* of the taxi drivers:
   a) his name
   b) where he lives
   c) if he has brothers and sisters
   d) what his family members do
   e) what languages he speaks.
   f) if he uses the meter at night
   g) and anything else that you can say!

DID YOU KNOW?

When you cross a river you may notice your taxi driver touch his forehead with his right hand several times. He may also do this when passing an important temple. In so doing, he is paying homage to that particular deity.

On the ninth day of Dassai sacrifices are made to the goddess Durga for protection of vehicles (taxis included) and their passengers. Blood from a sacrificed animal is sprinkled over the vehicle while flowers, rice and red powder are also offered. Durga is said to be the moving force of vehicles. All the tools of a car are also strewn out and flowers, incense, wicks, etc. are offered to Vishwa Karma, the producer of all tools.

When driving a vehicle, it is a worse offense to hit a cow than to hit a human.

CHAPTER 5

HOUSEHELP

काम गर्ने दिदी

VOCABULARY

तिनी	he, she (MH)	मीठो	tasty, delicious	आइतबार	Sunday
मद्दत	help	पकाउनु	cook	नजिक	near (distance)
बिहान	(in the) morning	खाना	food, meal	त्यसकारण	therefore
बजे	(at)...o'clock	उमाल्नु	boil (liquids, tr.)	शहर	city
सधैँ	always	पानी	water	चीजबीज	goods
हप्ता	week	श्रीमान्	husband	हिजो	yesterday
कुचो	broom	एकदम	very, quite (with negative पटक्कै)	सोमबार	Monday
लाउनु	apply	मन	mind/heart	मङ्गलबार	Tuesday
पुछ्नु	wipe, clean off	मात्र	only, merely	बुधबार	Wednesday
सफा गर्नु	clean (up), tidy	अनि	and (then)	बिहीबार	Thursday
सफा हुनु	be clean(ed)	रोटी	bread	शुक्रबार	Friday
छोरा	son	भाँडा	utensil, container, pot	भऱ्याङ/भरेङ	stairs, ladder
छोरी	daughter	माझ्नु	brush, scrub	थाल	plate, platter
हेरबिचार	supervision	सुक्नु	get dry (intran.)	चम्चा	spoon
हात	hand; arm	इस्त्री	iron (clothes)	काँटा	fork
मुख	mouth; face	कहिलेकाहीँ	occasionally, sometimes	चक्कु	knife (small)
-सँग	with, together	ऐना	glass; mirror	श्रीमती	wife
चामल	rice (uncooked)	शनिबार	Saturday	उसिन्नु	boil (solids)
केलाउनु	cull, clean (rice)			लुगा	clothe, dress

USEFUL PHRASES

- मलाई दालभात एकदम मनपर्छ। *I really like daal bhat.*
- मलाई दालभात खान मनपर्छ। *I like to eat daal bhat.*
- मलाई हिन्दी बोल्न आउँदैन। *I don't speak Hindi.*
- मलाई नेपाली अलिअलि आउँछ। *I speak a little Nepali.*
- म सवा एक बजे जान्छु। *I'm going at 1:15.*
- म साढे एक बजे जान्छु। *I'm going at 1:30.*
- म पौने दुई बजे जान्छु। *I'm going at 1:45.*
- कति बज्यो? *What time is it?*
- तीन बज्यो। *It's three o'clock.*
- मेरो बिचारमा... *I think.../It is my opinion that...*

TEXT

तिनको नाम माइम हो । हामी तिनलाई दिदी भन्छौं । तिनी हामीलाई घरको काममा मद्दत गर्छिन् । तिनी बिहान नौ बजे हाम्रो घरमा आउँछिन् । तिनी सधैं आउँदिनन् । तिनी हप्तामा पाँच दिन आउँछिन् । हाम्रो घरमा आएपछि तिनी कोठामा कुचो लगाउँछिन् ।

तिनी घरको भुइँ पुछेर सफा गर्छिन् । तिनी लुगा धुन्छिन् । तिनी छोराछोरीको हेरविचार पनि गर्छिन् । त्यसपछि तिनी हातमुख राम्रोसँग धोएर तरकारी धुन्छिन् । तिनी चामल केलाउँछिन् । तिनी मीठो दालभात पकाउँछिन् । हामी दिउँसो एक बजे खाना खान्छौं । हामी दालभातसँग उमालेको पानी खान्छौं । मेरो श्रीमान्लाई दालभात एकदम मनपर्छ । उहाँलाई मात्र होइन मलाई पनि दालभात मनपर्छ । हामी दालभात मात्र होइन, रोटीतरकारी पनि

खान्छौं । दिदी खाना खाएपछि भाँडा माझ्छिन् । तिनी कोठा सफा गर्छिन् र सुकेको लुगामा इस्त्री गर्छिन् । तिनी कहिलेकाहीं झ्यालका ऐनाहरू पुछ्छिन् ।

शनिबार र आइतबार दिदी आउँदिनन् । ती दिनहरूमा हामी धेरै काम गर्छौं । अलिअलि काम मेरा श्रीमान् गर्नुहुन्छ र अलिअलि काम म गर्छु । शनिबार र आइतबार हामी किनमेल गर्न जान्छौं । हाम्रो डेरा नजिक सानासाना पसलहरू मात्र छन् । त्यसकारण हामी शहरमा गएर फलफूल र अरू धेरै चिजबिज किन्छौं । शहरमा राम्रा-राम्रा सस्ता-महँगा चिजबिजहरू पाइन्छन् ।

हिजो दिदी आइनन् । त्यसकारण हामीले घरको काम गर्‍यौं । हामीले विदेशी खाना पकायौं । हामीले दालभात पकाएनौं । मेरो श्रीमान् नेपाली सिक्न जानुभयो । तर म सिक्न गइनँ । मैले छोराछोरीको हेरबिचार गरें । स्कूलबाट आएर श्रीमान्ले मलाई खाना पकाउन मद्दत गर्नुभयो ।

GRAMMAR

➤ 5.1 3RD PERSON PRONOUNS AND *SHE*.

With pronouns, there is no distinction between gender. You have already learned उहाँ and ऊ, both of which can be used for *he* or *she*. Another third person pronoun, तिनी, lies somewhere between उहाँ and ऊ on the honorific scale. However, when ऊ and तिनी are used as *she*, they require feminine verbs. That is, the verb is conjugated differently than for when the pronouns are used as *he*.

L	ऊ *he/she*	ambiguous
O	त्यो *he/she/it*	**far** from speaker
W	यो *he/she/it*	**near** to speaker
M	उनी *he/she*	ambiguous
I	तिनी *he/she*	**far** from speaker
D	यिनी *he/she*	**near** to speaker

The low and mid-honorific ऊ and तिनी belong to a set of pronouns that maintain a distinction of nearness to the speaker as well. In 1.2 you have already learned this distinction with यो and त्यो, *this* and *that*.

Now to compare the different uses of third person pronouns:

PRONOUN	**HE/IT**		**SHE**		**Simple past**
	conjugates:	**USE:**	**conjugates:**	**USE:**	
ऊ/त्यो/यो	-छ/दैन	low/familiar	-छे/दिन	low/familiar	-ई/-इन
उनी/तिनी/यिनी	-छन्/दैनन्	formal, historical figures	-छिन्/दिनन्	polite/honorific	v भयो/भएन
उहाँ/तपाईं	-हुन्छ/-हुन्न	polite/honorific	-हुन्छ/-हुन्न	middle	-इन्/-इनन्

Adding to our list the plural third person pronouns, they are simply उनी, तिनी, यिनी plus -हरू. Thus, उनीहरू *they* , तिनीहरू *they (far)* and यिनीहरू *they (near)*. These are always used with third person plural subjects and conjugate the same as उनी *he* .

To conjugate for तिनी *she* -छिन् is suffixed to the verb in the positive and -दिनन् in the negative. Remember to apply the spelling rules #1 and #2. It should be noted that though feminine conjugations are considered "proper" Nepali, they are often not spoken. In some dialects, feminine forms are the norm, however.

➤ 5.2 –लाई WITH मन पर्नु AND *FOR*.

You have already learned that -लाई is used to mark indirect objects and that it is used in some passive sentences (3.3): In this chapter we find two more uses:

- *For*. हामी तिन**लाई** दिदी भन्छौं। ***For** her, we say "sister"*
- With the idiom मन पर्नु the subject *always* takes **–लाई**.
  म**लाई** दालभात मन पर्छ। *I like daal bhat*. Lit. *daal bhaat heart-falls* ***to** me.*

➤ 5.3 THE SIMPLE PAST.

PRONOUN	POSITIVE	NEGATIVE
म	verb root + एँ	verb root + इनँ
हामी	verb root + यौँ	verb root + एनौँ
F	verb root + यो/ई	verb root + एन/इन
उनीहरू	verb root + ए	verb root + एनन्
उहाँ/तपाईँ	verb + भयो	verb + भएन

Only ऊ and उनीहरू are shown. ऊ/यो/त्यो and उनी/यिनी/तिनी conjugate the same verb ending.

Suffixes that begin with [y] are treated as suffixes that begin with a vowel.

➤ 5.4 -ले WITH A PAST TRANSITIVE VERB.

-ले is always used with **subjects of transitive verbs in the past tense**. This use is **obligatory**. A transitive verb is a verb that can (but doesn't have to) take a direct object: *John kicked* ***the ball,*** *Mary hit* ***the man.*** The following verbs are some of the transitive verbs you've learned. Whenever these are used in a past tense sentence, the subject **must** take -ले:

गर्नु, बोल्नु, सिकाउनु, खानु, किन्नु, दिनु, लिनु, धुनु, भन्नु, थाल्नु, देख्नु, हेर्नु, रोक्नु.

The following are intransitive verbs and therefore their subjects **never** take -ले:

हुनु, बस्नु, जानु, आउनु, पुग्नु, हिँड्नु, सुत्नु

➤ 5.5 -एर *IN X-ING, HAVING X-ED.*

-एर serves to connect two phrases. If the two phrases occur at the same time, it can mean *in x-ing, y; in an x-manner;* or *while X-ing*. If the two phrases occur one after the other, then it roughly means, *having X-ed, Y*; or X, *then Y:*

1. In/by X-ing, Y — तिनी भुइँ पुछेर सफा गर्छिन्। — *In/by wiping the floor, she cleans.*
2. In an X-ing manner, Y — हामी बसेर खान्छौँ। — *In a sitting manner, we eat.*
3. While X-ing, Y — घरमा बसेर ऊ पढ्छ। — *While sitting at home, he reads.*
4. Having X-ed, Y — म दाल भात खाएर सुत्छु। — *Having eaten daal bhat, I (will) sleep.*

	Clause One	Clause Two
The subject can be included in both clauses:	[**श्रीमान्** स्कूलबाट आएर]	[**उहाँले** मलाई मद्दत गर्नुभयो]
The subject can be included in 1 of the clauses:	[स्कूलबाट आएर]	[**श्रीमान्ले** मलाई मद्दत गर्नुभयो]
	[**श्रीमान्** स्कूलबाट आएर]	[मलाई मद्दत गर्नुभयो]
The subject can be omitted from both:	[स्कूलबाट आएर]	[मलाई मद्दत गर्नुभयो]

However, this raises an interesting point over which pure Nepali speakers don't agree. You will remember from 5.4 that the subject of a transitive verb must take -ले. In the previous example, the first clause has an intransitive verb and the second clause has a transitive verb: [स्कूलबाट **आएर**] [मलाई मद्दत **गर्नुभयो**]. Some speakers will insist that even if the subject is in the first clause (with the intransitive verb) it requires -ले: **श्रीमान्ले** स्कूलबाट आएर मलाई मद्दत गर्नुभयो while others insist that it doesn't: **श्रीमान्** स्कूलबाट आएर मलाई मद्दत गर्नुभयो. However, you can be sure that all speakers would use -ले if the subject was in the clause with a transitive verb, so that is your safest bet: स्कूलबाट आएर **श्रीमान्ले** मलाई मद्दत गर्नुभयो.

➤ 5.6 DERIVATIONAL -सँग.

As a regular postposition, -सँग can mean *with*. However, it can also derive adverbs from adjectives. In our text, for example, -सँग is attached to the adjective राम्रो, changing it into an adverb.

➤ 5.7 DERIVATIONAL -एको.

-एको is used similarly to the derivational -ने (3.8) in that it derives an adjective from a verb. Though very similar, however, -एको has reference to a *particular point in time* while -ने has no reference to time:

-एको	particular point in time	-ने	generally/habitually (timeless)
उमालेको पानी	the boil**ed** water	उमाल्ने पानी	water **used for** boiling (generally)
हिजो आएको दिदी	the didi who came yesterday	काम गर्ने दिदी	the didi who works **(habitual)**
बसेकी आमा	the sitt**ing** mother	बस्ने आमा	the mother who sits **(habitual)**
खाएको स्याउ	the eat**en** apple	खाने स्याउ	apple **used for** eating (generally)
कुचो लगाएको कोठा	the room that is cleaned	कुचो लगाउने दिदी	the didi who sweeps **(habitual)**
धोएको लुगा	washed clothes	धुने साबुन	soap **used for** washing (generally)

➤ **5.8 -मा** *AMONG.* In this chapter -मा is also used as *among*: ती दिनहरूमा among those days.

➤ **5.9 त्यसकारण** *THEREFORE, FOR THAT REASON.*

कलम छैन; त्यसकारण लेख्न सक्दिनँ।	*I don't have a pen, therefore I can't write.*
मेच कच्चा छ; त्यसकारण म त्यहाँ बस्दिनँ।	*The chair is weak, therefore I won't sit there.*

COMPLEX VERBS

- **-न मनपर्नु** — ***to like to...***

मलाई दालभात खान मनपर्छ।	*I **like to** eat daal bhat.*
मलाई तरकारी किन्न मनपर्छ।	*I **like to** buy vegetables.*

- **-न मद्दत गर्नु** — ***to help...***

तिनी हामीलाई घरको काम गर्न मद्दत गर्छिन्।	*She **helps** us do the housework.*
उहाँले खाना पकाउन मद्दत गर्नुभयो।	*He **helped** cook the food.*

- **-न आउनु** — ***to know how to...***

मलाई हिन्दी बोल्न आउँदैन।	*I don't **know how to** speak Hindi.*
मलाई नेपाली बोल्न आउँछ।	*I **know how to** speak Nepali.*

- **-न जानु** — ***to go (in order) to...***

मेरा श्रीमान् नेपाली सिक्न जानुभयो।	*My husband went to learn Nepali.*
उहाँ खाना पकाउन जानुभयो।	*He went to cook the food.*

- **-न जान्नु** — ***to know how to...***

म हिन्दी बोल्न जान्दछु।	*I **know how to** speak Hindi.*
म नेपाली बोल्न जान्दछु।	*I **know how to** speak Nepali.*

PRACTICE

1. Conjugate for the indefinite tense ऊ/त्यो/यो and उनी/तिनी/यिनी using masculine, negative and positive:

   लगाउनु, पुछ्नु, केलाउनु, पकाउनु, उमाल्नु, माझ्नु

2. Conjugate for the indefinite tense ऊ/त्यो/यो and उनी/तिनी/यिनी using feminine, negative and positive:

   लगाउनु, पुछ्नु, केलाउनु, पकाउनु, उमाल्नु, माझ्नु

3. Conjugate for the indefinite tense उनीहरू/तिनीहरू/यिनीहरू using negative and positive:

   लगाउनु, पुछ्नु, केलाउनु, पकाउनु, उमाल्नु, माझ्नु

4. Supply the correct indefinite tense conjugation for the given pronoun, using negative and positive:

   1. [she] त्यो बजारमा जानु।
   2. [he] यो पैसा लिनु।
   3. [she] यो धेरै दालभात खानु।
   4. उनीहरू बजार जानु।
   5. [he] ऊ मलाई कागज दिनु।
   6. [she] ऊ अलिअलि नेपाली बोल्नु।
   7. [he] त्यो बजारमा तरकारी धुनु।
   8. तिनीहरू मलाई पैसा दिनु।
   9. [she] यिनी भुईंमा कुचो लगाउनु।
   10. *[he] यिनी ट्याक्सी रोक्नु।
   11. [she] तिनी दालभात पकाउनु।
   12. *[he] उनी मेरो घर आउनु।
   13. [she] उनी पानी उमाल्नु।
   14. यिनीहरू नेपाली राम्रोसँग बोल्नु।

   *As *he* these pronouns are very literary.

5. Repeat #1-4, but conjugate for the simple past tense.

6. Using the verbs supplied, build a sentence using -एर:

बस्नु	-एर	सिकाउँछु
धुनु	-एर	खानु
जानु	-एर	किन्नु
दिनु	-एर	लिनु
पुग्नु	-एर	रोक्नु
लगाउनु	-एर	पुछ्नु
केलाउनु	-एर	पकाउनु
उमाल्नु	-एर	खानु

7. Using the negative of -एर (as न- इकन in 9.8), translate the following:
   a) I will teach without sitting.
   b) We will go wash the clothes without eating.
   c) We left (went) without buying vegetables.
   d) He stopped without (before) reaching the hotel.
   e) She cooked rice without culling it.
   f) They drink the water without boiling it.

8. Translate the following using either -एको or -ने, whichever is appropriate:
   a) The shopkeeper that works.
   b) My sister that is staying at home.
   c) The driver that spoke Nepali.
   d) My sister that stays at home.
   e) The shopkeeper that worked.
   f) The dried bread.
   g) The sister that sweeps.
   h) The road that goes to Patan.
   i) The water that is used for boiling.
   j) The driver that speaks Nepali.
   k) The taxi that stops.
   l) The stopped taxi.
   m) The water that has been boiled.
   n) The sister that is sweeping.

9. Complete the following sentences:
   a) दालभात मात्र होइन रोटी पनि ....
   b) आमा मात्र होइन बा पनि ....
   c) सोमबार मात्र होइन बुधबार पनि ....
   d) पानी मात्र होइन खाना पनि ....
   e) हात मात्र होइन मुख पनि ....
   f) हामीलाई मात्र होइन तपाईंलाई पनि ....
   g) छोरा मात्र होइन छोरी पनि ....
   h) बिहान मात्र होइन साँझ पनि ....

10. Using त्यसकारण give at least two results for *each* of the following:
   a) कलम छैन; त्यसकारण ....
   b) त्यो मेच कच्चा छ; त्यसकारण ....
   c) मलाई हिन्दी आउँदैन; त्यसकारण ....
   d) बजार धेरै टाढा छ; त्यसकारण ....
   e) त्यो पसलमा स्याउ महँगो छ; त्यसकारण ....

11. Translate the following using -न जानु:
   a) I'm going (in order) to buy vegetables.
   b) He's going (in order) to learn Nepali.
   c) They are going (in order) to get a taxi.
   d) She is going (in order) to sweep the floor.
   e) You are going (in order) to boil the water.

LET'S TALK

1. Listing as many things as you can, what do and don't you like? Here's a list of things that might help with ideas:

green bananas	living in Thamel	your classroom
yellow bananas	speaking Hindi	certain fruits / vegies
big houses	your older sister	Nepali taxis
orange curtains	school	sweeping the floor
America	daal bhat	lots of money
volunteer work	eating	
Patan	teaching	

2. On what days of the week do you go shopping? have class? eat daal bhat? watch the kids? cook? eat at a hotel? take a taxi? other?

3. तपाईं कुन कुन काम कहिलेकाहीं मात्र गर्नुहुन्छ? What things do you do only occasionally? go shopping? have class? eat daal bhat? watch the kids? cook? eat at a hotel? take a taxi? other?

4. Using each of the following verbs, describe to your tutor what you did yesterday. After each sentence, your tutor repeats what you did. For example, you say for the first verb: "हिजो मैले पाटनमा किनमेल गरें". Then your tutor says, "हिजो तपाईंले पाटनमा किनमेल गर्नुभयो".

   Verbs: गर्नु, बस्नु, जानु, आउनु, बोल्नु, खानु, किन्नु, दिनु, लिनु, भन्नु, देख्नु, लगाउनु,

   Reverse roles.

5. तपाईंको विचारमा पुरुषहरुले महिलाहरुलाई के के गर्न मद्दत गर्नुपर्छ? What do you think men should help women do? What do you think women should help men do?

6. What do you know how to do? Housework? Shopping? Bargaining? etc. Use both -न आउँछ and -न जान्दछु. What do you not know how to do?

7. What languages do and don't you know how to speak? Use both -न आउँछ and -न जान्दछु.

8. At what time of the day do you go shopping? have class? eat daal bhat? watch the kids? cook? eat at a hotel? take a taxi? other?

9. What time is it (round off to the nearest quarter hour):
    a) now
    b) one hour from now
    c) 15 minutes from now
    d) 15 minutes ago
    e) 30 minutes from now
    f) 30 minutes ago
    g) 1 hour 15 minutes from now
    h) 1 hour 15 minutes ago
    i) 1 hour 30 minutes from now
    j) 1 hour 30 minutes ago

10. Tell your tutor all the things that your househelp needs to do today.

11. You are your tutor's househelp. Your tutor is to explain the following to-do list to you.

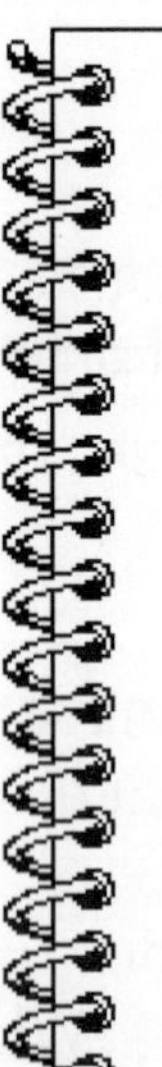

My to-do list for didi:
1. sweep the floor
2. wipe the table
3. boil water
4. Wash the fruit.
5. Give the kids some fruit.
6. After eating, wash the kids hands and face.
7. Cull the rice and start cooking by 11:00.
8. Put the plates and silverware on the table.
9. After lunch, wash the dishes.
10. Iron the dried clothes.
11. Wash the windows.
12. Buy some veggies at the market.
13. Watch the kids.
14. At 4:00, go home.

12. Your tutor is now the househelp. You are to explain the to-do list to your tutor.

IN THE COMMUNITY

As with every community assignment, if you ask someone a question about themselves, offer the same information about yourself as well.

1. Talk to different people about what they do on the different days of the week. Female language learners, continue to work on strengthening your friendships with women in their homes. Have a friend introduce you to a friend. What days do they work? don't they work? How many days per week do they work? What about yourself?

2. Of the same people you talk to above, ask the following:
   a) Do they have househelp (often a young girl or boy)?
   b) If so, does the househelp work every day? On what days?
   c) Who in the family does the following:
      sweeps the floor
      cooks the food
      washes the dishes
      buys the vegetables
   d) If the answer to (c) is mostly someone else, do they ever do any of the above?
   e) What chores do/don't they like to do?

In preparation for next chapter, if any of the people you talk to have a phone ask them if you can call them later (म पछि तपाईंलाई फोन गर्न सक्छु? तपाईंको नम्बर कति हो?). And don't worry, पछि can mean an indefinite amount of time later.

This assignment is considered complete when your conversation time totals 3 hours, or you have covered as much of the above as possible with 4 people (whichever is shortest).

DID YOU KNOW?

Westerners are used to casual relationships, even with those of the opposite sex. In Nepal, however, people are very gender conscious. It is probably a good idea that males keep their relationship with their househelp quite formal. This would also be in keeping with their deep seated concepts of rank.

If you have kids and your househelp is watching them, you may have very different ideas of discipline. Nepalis are usually very permissive with their children, especially someone else's. They will probably have a very difficult time telling your kids "no", so you will need to keep your kids accountable to your househelp yourself.

It is customary to give a full month's bonus to any hired help before the month of Dassai.

If you have a problem with your househelp, direct confrontation is not a good solution. It is extremely important they do not lose face. Be creative but don't confront. Never criticize your househelp in front of others; it won't get you very far.

CHAPTER 6

TELEPHONE CONVERSATION
फोनमा कुराकानी

VOCABULARY

फोन	"phone"	खाजा	snack	पैंतालीस	forty-five
कुराकानी	talk, chat	नि	"what about"	पचपन्न	fifty-five
भोलि	tomorrow	ठिक	right, correct, ok	पैंसट्ठी	sixty-five
पिकनिक	"picnic"	थर्मस	"thermos", vacuum flask	पचहत्तर	seventy-five
थानकोट	Thankot	चिया	tea	पचासी	eighty-five
पार्क	"park"	राख्नु	put down, place	पन्चानब्बे	ninety-five
मासु	meat	है	okay?	हजार	thousand
ल्याउनु	bring	बाहिर	out(side)	सुन्नु	listen, hear
पुलाउ	fried rice	केही	some (emph. of के)	छिटो	quickly, early, fast
सबै	all	खबर	news, message	बिस्तारै	slowly, gradually, carefully, safely
सबैजना	everyone	कि	yes or no?	दाइ	older brother
थोक	thing	बैठक	meeting-room	भाइ	younger brother
थाहा	knowledge	हजूर	Sir, lord (hon)	बहिनी	younger sister
ओहो	wow!, hey!	फुर्सद	leisure time	भित्र	inside, in, into
सन्चै	health; well	दालमोठ	crunchy snacks	टिप्नु	write down, pick up, pluck, note down
गोपाल	Gopal	-जी / ज्यू	Mr. (polite)	माथि	up, over, above
क्यारे	uncertainty, I guess	पढ्नु	to study, read	तल	below, down
हेलो	"hello"	पैंतीस	thirty-five		

USEFUL PHRASES

- को बोल्नुभएको? — *Who's speaking?*
- म मेथ्यु बोल्दै छु। — *This is Matthew speaking.*
- तपाईँलाई कस्तो छ? — *How are you?*
- फोन राख्छु, है? — *I'm hanging up, okay?*
- उहाँ बाहिर जानुभएको छ। — *He/she's out now.*
- केही खबर छ कि? — *Can I take a message?*
- माथि एकचोटि पाऊँ। — *May I speak to upstairs please?*
- यहाँ बस्नु ठिक छ? — *Is it okay to sit here?*
- नबिर्सनुस्। — *Don't forget.*
- मैले तपाईँलाई फोन गर्न बिर्सें। — *I forgot to call you.*
- म उहाँलाई बोलाइदिन्छु। — *I'll get him for you. (Lit. I'll call him out for you)*

TEXT

भोलि हामी पिकनिक जान्छौँ । हामी थानकोटको पार्कमा पिकनिक जान्छौँ । डी. बी. पकाएको मासु लिएर जान्छन् । माइकजी पुलाउ लिएर जानुहुन्छ । सबैजना एकएक थोक लिएर जान्छन् । म के लिएर जाऊँ मलाई थाहा छैन । म रेमीलाई फोन गर्छु ।

हरिकुमार : हेलो ! को बोल्नुभएको?

मेथ्यु : म मेथ्यु बोल्दै छु । तपाईँ को हुनुहुन्छ?

हरिकुमार : म हरिकुमार । त्यहाँ रेमीजी हुनुहुन्छ?

मेथ्यु : हुनुहुन्छ, म बोलाइदिन्छु ।

रेमी फोनमा --

हरिकुमार : हेलो, रेमीजी हो?

रेमी : हो, ओहो हरिकुमारजी ! तपाईँलाई कस्तो छ?

हरिकुमार : सन्चै छ । भोलि हामी पिकनिक जाने होइन? गोपालजी त आउनुहुन्न क्यारे !

रेमी : हो ! तपाईँ पनि आउनुहुन्न?

हरिकुमार : म त आउँछु, तपाईँ के लिएर आउनुहुन्छ?

रेमी : म खाजा लिएर आउँछु । अनि तपाईँ नि?

हरिकुमार : म के लिएर आऊँ मलाई थाहा छैन । के ल्याउनु ठिक हो भन्नुस् न!

रेमी : तपाईँ थर्मसमा चिया र राम्रो दालमोठ लिएर आउनुस् न, हुँदैन र?

हरिकुमार : हुन्छ । ल फोन राख्छु है?

रेमी : हुन्छ, धन्यवाद !

❀ ❀ ❀

हरिकुमार : हेलो, यो कहाँ पर्‍यो?

सेरी : यो बानेश्वरमा पर्‍यो ।

हरिकुमार : टीम नेपाल हो?

सेरी : हो ।

हरिकुमार : तपाईँ को बोल्नुभएको?

सेरी : म सेरी बोल्दै छु । तपाईँलाई को चाहियो?

हरिकुमार : त्यहाँ केशवजीलाई पाऊँ न !

सेरी : उहाँ अहिले यहाँ हुनुहुन्न । बाहिर जानुभएको छ । केही खबर छ कि?

हरिकुमार : उहाँलाई भोलि अफिसमा बैठक छ भनिदिनुस् ।

❀ ❀ ❀

हरिकुमार : हेलो, केशवजी हो?

केशव : हजुर, म बोल्दैछु, के छ?

हरिकुमार : ठिकै छ । भोलि तपाईँको फुर्सद छ?

केशव : भोलि शनिबार होइन?

हरिकुमार : हो ।

केशव : भोलि दिउँसो एक बजेपछि फुर्सद छ ।

हरिकुमार : भोलि अफिसमा एउटा बैठक छ । तपाईँ पनि आउनुस् है !

केशव : हुन्छ, कति बजे?

हरिकुमार : दिउँसो दुई बजेतिर आउनुस् न ! हुन्न र?

केशव : हुन्छ ।

हरिकुमार : ल, अहिले फोन राख्छु है ! धन्यवाद !

GRAMMAR

➤ 6.1 WHEN -मा IS OPTIONAL.

Often, the use of the postposition -मा is optional, as with हामी पिकनिक(मा) जान्छौँ. In certain cases it is more common to leave it off. These are often associated with the verb जानु:

म स्कूल- जान्छु   म बजार- जान्छु   म घर- जान्छु

In fact, in the above examples, using -मा would imply going about *in* school, *in* the bazaar, *in* the house -- not, *to* school, *to* the bazaar, *to* the house.

➤ 6.2 HUMAN CLASSIFIER -जना.

We have already encountered the object/child classifier -वटा (1.6). Whenever a human is quantified, the classifier -जना is used:

मेरा तीनजना भाइ My three younger brothers.
मेरा चारजना छोरा My four sons. (Children can take either -जना or -वटा).

In combination with सबै *all*, सबैजना means *everyone* or *everybody*.

➤ 6.3 PASSIVES AND -लाई.

In 3.2, the verbal passive marker -इनु was discussed. However, not all passive sentences display this marker. The passive subject however, is always marked with -लाई. Though the below sentences are passive, translations are given in both active and passive forms, since English prefers the active:

मलाई थाहा छ।	*Passive*: (It) is known by me.	*Active*: I know.
तपाईँलाई कस्तो छ?	*Passive*: How is it by you?	*Active*: How are you?
तपाईँलाई सन्चै छ?	*Passive*: Is health to you?	*Active*: Are you healthy?
मलाई पैसा चाहिन्छ।	*Passive*: Money is needed by me.	*Active*: I need money.
मलाई दालभात मनपर्छ।	*Passive*: Daal bhat is liked by me.	*Active*: I like daal bhaat

Remember that in active sentences, the subject is typically the actor, e.g. *I saw the orange.* In passive sentences, the subject is the recipient of the action, e.g. *The orange was seen [**by** me].* And again, remember that even though a sentence may be active in English, Nepali may prefer the passive. However, the Nepali passive may have an active counterpart, as can be seen below.

PASSIVE		ACTIVE	
तपाईँलाई कस्तो छ?	How is it by you?	तपाईँ कस्तो हुनुहुन्छ?	How are you?
तपाईँलाई सन्चै छ?	Is health to you?	तपाईँ सन्चै हुनुहुन्छ?	Are you healthy?
मलाई दालभात मन पर्छ।	Daal bhat is liked by me.	म दालभात मन पराउँछु।	I like daal bhat.

Important: in the active, there is no -लाई and the verb is inflected for the subject.

➤ 6.4 PRESENT CONTINUOUS AND –दै. (see also appendix 4/5)

-दै (imperfect aspect marker) is used to form the present continuous tense. This tense is used to describe something that is in the process of being done, at the present moment. The action has not been completed. The following are some of the verbs you've learned inflected for the present continuous tense, first person singular:

बोल्दै छु	*I am speaking.*	धुँदै छु	*I am washing.*
खाँदै छु	*I am eating.*	सुन्दै छु	*I am listening.*
पकाउँदै छु	*I am cooking.*	बस्दै छु	*I am sitting.*
जाँदै छु	*I am going.*		

See conjugation table also in the appendix.

Note:

1) This tense does not have a negative. A second present continuous tense will be learned that is used to express the negative.
2) बस्दै छु means ***in the process of*** *sitting,* ***but not yet*** *seated.* The action is not completed. The second present continuous tense is used to express, *I'm sitting here (stationary).*
3) The verbs जाँदै छु and आउँदै छु can mean both *about to* and *in the process of.*

➤ 6.5 MORE DISCOURSE PARTICLES.

As in 3.5, we encounter several more discourse particles in this chapter:

ओहो	ओहो! तपाईँलाई कस्तो छ?	*Wow/Hey! How are you doing!* **Exclamatory**.
क्यारे	ऊ आउँदैन क्यारे !	*He isn't coming, right? I think.* Expresses **uncertainty**.
नि	अनि तपाईँ नि?	***And what about** you?*
है	फोन राख्छु है !	*I'll hang up, okay? alright?* Seeks **approval**.
हजुर	हजुर, म बोलाइदिन्छु।	*Yes , I'll call (him).* **Polite affirmative**.
र	हुँदैन **र**?	*Is it unacceptable? (It is acceptable)* Implies **opposite response**. Rhetorical question.

COMPLEX VERBS

- **-इदिनु** — ***to do for..***

हुनुहुन्छ, म बोलाइदिन्छु।	*He's here. I'll get him (**for you**).*
ऊ मेरो काम गरिदिन्छ।	*He does my work (**for me**).*
ट्याक्सी होटेलनिर रोकिदिनुस्।	*Stop the taxi near the hotel **for me**.*
अफिसमा बैठक छ, भनिदिनुस्।	*Tell (him) for me--there's a meeting in the office.*

- **-नु ठिक छ/हो** — ***okay to..***

के ल्याउनु ठीक हो भन्नुस् न !	*Tell me what's **okay** to bring.*
यहाँ बस्नु ठीक छ?	*Is it **okay** to sit here?*

- **-न बिर्सनु** — ***to forget to..***

मैले तपाईँलाई फोन गर्न बिर्सें।	*I **forgot to** call you.*
मैले पैसा ल्याउन बिर्सें।	*I **forgot to** bring money.*
तपाईँले टिप्न बिर्सनुभयो।	*You **forgot to** write it down.*

- **-न पाउनु** — ***get a chance to*** (active), ***be allowed to*** (passive)...

उसले कुरा गर्न पाएन।	*He didn't get chance to talk. (He wasn't allowed to talk)*
म/मैले घर जान पाएँ।	*I was allowed to go home. (I got a chance to go home.)*
मैले किताप पढ्न पाएँ।	*I got a chance to read the book. (I was allowed to read).*
भोलि म तपाईँलाई भेट्न पाउँदिनँ।	*I won't be available to see you tomorrow.* *(I will not get a chance to see you tomorrow).*

PRACTICE

1. Translate the following sentences using the present continuous. Note: If you haven't already left, but you *will* be going, the simple indefinite is better (-छु). Remember, the simple indefinite can have reference to the future.
   a) I'm going home (in the process of).
   b) I'm going into the house (in the process of).
   c) I'm going to the market (in the process of).
   d) I'm going around (inside of) the market (in the process of).
   e) The two of us are going home (in the process of).
   f) The three of us are going to the market (in the process of).

2. For म, तपाईँ, and हामी, conjugate the following verbs for the present continuous tense, using -दै: जानु, गर्नु, किन्नु, धुनु, आउनु, माझ्नु, ल्याउनु, राख्नु, सुन्नु

3. Using -दै, can you guess what the conjugations for the other pronouns would be? Try conjugating the following:

   जानु, गर्नु, किन्नु, धुनु, आउनु, माझ्नु, ल्याउनु, राख्नु, सुन्नु

4. If incorrect, correct the following sentences:
   a) तपाईँ कस्तो छ? ....
   b) म नेपाली बोल्न मन पराउँछु? ....
   c) तपाईँलाई कस्तो छ? ....
   d) तपाईँलाई सन्चै छ? ....
   e) मलाई नेपाली बोल्न मन पर्छ। ....
   f) तपाईँ कस्तो हुनुहुन्छ? ....
   g) मलाई नेपाली बोल्न मन पराउँछु? ....
   h) तपाईँ सन्चै छ? ....
   i) म नेपाली बोल्न मन पर्छ? ....
   j) तपाईँलाई सन्चै हुनुहुन्छ? ....
   k) तपाईँलाई कस्तो हुनुहुन्छ? ....
   l) तपाईँ सन्चै हुनुहुन्छ? ....
   m) मलाई थाहा छ। ....
   n) म थाहा छ। ....
   o) मलाई पैसा चाहिन्छ। ....

5. Use -इदिनु to translate the following sentences:
    a) I'll eat the carrot for you.
    b) My little brother completely ate the orange.
    c) I'll speak Nepali slowly for you.
    d) Please sit down for me.
    e) Please speak a little Nepali for me.
    f) You teach us some Nepali; we'll teach you some English.
    g) He'll buy you some apples at the market.
    h) I'll wash the vegetables for you.
    i) I'll tell him for you.
    j) Please stop the taxi.
    k) Don't sweep the floor. I'll sweep it for you.
    l) We'll bring it for you.
    m) Put my bag in the room for me.

6. Supply the appropriate particle for each sentence:
    a) म नेपाली बोल्छु। अनि तपाईं *What about you*?
    b) तपाईं मेरो घर आउनुहुन्छ *Uncertain*?
    c) तपाईं मासु ल्याउनुस्, हुँदैन *Opposite response*?
    d) *Wow* त्यो झोला एकदम राम्रो छ।
    e) *Polite yes* म भोलि तपाईंसँग जान्छु।
    f) सुन्तला झोलामा राख्छु *Okay*?।

7. Translate the following using -नु ठीक छ or -नु ठिक हो/होइन Then supply an appropriate response.
    a) Is it okay to sit here?
    b) Is it okay to phone you tomorrow?
    c) Is it okay to talk in class?
    d) Is it okay to eat in class?
    e) Is it okay to talk quickly?
    f) Is it okay to put it here?

8. Translate the following using -न बिर्सनु.
    a) You forgot to phone yesterday.
    b) I forgot to tell you my name.
    c) We forgot to buy vegetables.
    d) I forgot how to say "thousand".
    e) She forgot to buy meat at the store.

9. Translate the following using -न पाउनु:
   a) I got a chance to see him.
   b) Sorry. I didn't get a chance to phone you.
   c) He was allowed to go home.
   d) He got a chance to go home.
   e) They weren't allowed to sit there.

LET'S TALK

1. Using various props in the room, your tutor directs you to place things using बाहिर, भित्र, माथि, तल.

2. With your tutor, mimic a phone conversation for the following situations:
   - Call your tutor to ask directions to your tutor's house.
   - Your tutor calls you to ask directions to your house.
   - You don't know the going price of apples and don't want to be cheated. You call your tutor to find out the price.
   - Your tutor is your househelp, and you need her to come tomorrow at 8:00. Call her and explain that she needs to come at 8:00 in order to cook a large meal for six people.
   - You call your tutor, but your tutor isn't home. Leave the following message for your tutor (your tutor will have to pretend to be someone else): The message is, your tutor is to call you at 9:00 at the following number - 472139. Your househelp hasn't come, so you will come to class at 11:00.
   - Your tutor calls you with the message that he/she won't be able to teach you today. But you aren't home. Pretending to be someone else, tell your tutor that he/she (you) has gone to the market and will be back at 6:00. Take a message.
   - Any other ideas for a phone conversation? Make up **two** more!

3. Last chapter you listed as many things as you could that you did and didn't like. Repeat that exercise, but this time use **active** sentences:

green bananas	school
big houses	daal bhat
orange curtains	eating certain fruits / veggies
America	Nepali taxis
volunteer work	sweeping the floor
living in Thamel	lots of money
speaking Hindi	
your older sister	

IN THE COMMUNITY

It's time to call some of your new acquaintances and try out your new phone skills. After learning the useful phrases till they roll off your tongue, make a total of six phone calls and maintain as long a conversation with them as you can. If the person you call wants to use English, at this point you can say something like तपाईं नेपालीमा बोल्नुस्। म नेपाली सिक्छु। म अलिअलि नेपाली बोल्छु। If the person you're trying to call isn't home, try calling back later. At this point, you can ask questions like:

> Are you eating? What do you eat? What times do you eat? What are you doing? Are you going shopping today? What are you going to buy? What fruits are available now? Are they expensive? Do you wash your vegetables? Do you like [x] ? Do you have househelp?

Your conversations don't have to be long, but they should exhaust what you know how to say. This exercise may feel awkward and contrived, but keep this in mind: in the future Nepali friends will call you for no reason other than to say "hi". Often, you don't have to have a reason to call. Also, the question तपाईंले भात खानुभयो *Have you eaten?* is very common. It's equivalent to the English question *How's the weather?* In other words, when you don't know what else to say and there's a lull, you can ask भात खानुभयो. It's a conversation filler and doesn't really mean you are interested to know whether they've eaten or not. Closing the conversation is as simple as saying ल, अहिले फोन राख्छु है.

As an option to the above assignment, you may make only 5 phone calls if (and only if) you do the following: go to a local phone exchange and sit and listen to how other people talk on the phone. By local phone exchange, I don't mean regular stores that you can call from but an actual store that has that as its main service. Sit and listen for 1 hour or to 10 conversations (whichever is shortest). You may want to make a few phone calls from there yourself to make the storekeeper happy, but then ask if you can just sit and talk. You may find yourself in several other conversations while there.

DID YOU KNOW?

Phone etiquette in Nepal may not be what you are used to. A common question that you will hear when you answer the phone is यो कहाँ पऱ्यो *Where have I reached?* The answer is always a place name. This is more of a convention these days, but it is probably because in the past, one could never be sure whether one was connected to the number they dialed.

Another common practice that may seem strange is, even when it is obvious to the caller that you are not who they want to talk to, they will want to know who is speaking.

Also, rather than the person who called asking to speak to so-and-so, the person who answers asks the caller who they would like to speak to. Otherwise you may get a volley of "*hello hellos*".

When a conversation is over and it's time to hang up, callers often hang up without so much as a good-bye. You just hang up. In our text, they say "*I'll hang-up, okay?*" but often you won't even hear that. Actually, in face-to-face meetings as well, when it's time to leave all you may notice is a slight nod of the head. No *good-byes, namastes* or *see-you-laters*.

CHAPTER 7

THE TRIP TO RUKUM
रूकुमसम्मको यात्रा

VOCABULARY					
रुकुम	Rukum	ज्याला	daily wages	उनी	he, she (MH)
-सम्म	up to, until	ज्यान	life	अछूत	untouchable
यात्रा	journey	मान्नु	agree	लाम्खुट्टे	mosquito
चौरजहारी	Chaurjahari	पहिलो	first	गर्मी	hot (weather)
सजिलो	easy	सक्नु	be able to	सुत्नु	sleep, lie down
बाटो	path, way, road, street, trail	उकालो	uphill, rise	भोलिपल्ट	the next day
नेपालगन्ज	Nepalgunj	ओरालो	downhill	सबेरै	early morning
हवाइजहाज	airplane	गाह्रो	difficult, hard	उठ्नु	get up, rise, stand up, arise
सामान	supplies	डर	fear	नास्ता	morning snack
सकिनु	be possible, can be, be finished	लाग्नु	feel (emotion)	बिदा लिनु	take leave
यसरी	thus, in this way	तेर्सो	level, flat	डाँडा	ridge, hill
मोटर	"motor"	तर्नु	to cross a river, ford	मनोहर	attractive, beautiful
पैदल	on foot, by foot, by peddle	अघि	before; in front, ago	दृश्य	view, sight
तुलसीपुर	Tulsipur	बास	lodging, stay	हिमाल	snow-peak
सल्यान	Salyan	खोज्नु	search for, seek	अत्यन्त	extremely
बस	"bus"	थाल्नु	to begin	खुसी	happiness, pleasure
हिँड्नु	walk	बल्ल	finally, at last	थकाइ	fatigue, tiredness
वर्ष	year	गाउँ	village	आराम	rest, ease
सुरु	beginning, inception, onset	पिरो	spicy hot	बेलुका/ बेलुकि	late afternoon, evening
विदेशी	foreign(er)	* छिँडी	ground floor	रमाइलो	pleasant, interesting
भारी	load, burden, heavy	पिँढी	porch	मिलनसार	sociable, friendly
भरिया	porter	किनभने	because	फेरि	also, furthermore, again
कहिले	when; sometimes	भएर	via (having been at)	मान्छे/मानिस	a person, man
खोला	small river, stream	घरबेटी	landlord	-बाट	from

* This term mainly applies to tall urban buildings and is not commonly used in rural areas.

USEFUL PHRASES

- (तपाईंले) बुझ्नुभयो ? — *Did you understand?*
- (मैले) बुझिनँ / बुझेँ । — *I didn't understand/yes, I did.*
- मैले बिर्सें । — *I forgot.*
- "..." भनेको के हो ? — *What does "..." mean ?*
- ऊ नआएसम्म बस्नुस् । — *Wait until he comes (as long as he hasn't come).*

TEXT

रुकुमको चौरजहारी (चौरझारी) जाने दुईवटा बाटा छन् । एउटा बाटो हो- हवाइजहाजको बाटो । हवाइजहाज नेपालगन्जबाट चौरजहारीसम्म नै जान्छ । तर धेरै सामान लिएर हवाइजहाजमा जान सकिँदैन । यसरी जान धेरै महँगो पर्छ । फेरि हवाइजहाज सधैं पाइँदैन । चौरजहारीसम्म जाने मोटर बाटो छैन । त्यहाँ जाने अर्को बाटो पैदल बाटो हो । नेपालगन्जबाट र काठमाडौंबाट पनि तुलसीपुर भएर सल्यानसम्म बस जान्छ । त्यहाँबाट दुई दिन हिँडेर चौरजहारी पुग्न सकिन्छ ।

गएको वर्ष अक्टोबरमा हामी त्यहाँ गयौं । हामीले सल्यानबाट पैदल यात्रा सुरु गऱ्यौं । हामी दुईजना नेपाली र दुईजना विदेशी थियौं । हाम्रो सामान चार भारी थियो । भरियाहरू सजिलैसँग पाइए । तर ज्याला अलि महँगो थियो । खाना खाएर दिनको दुई सय रुपियाँमा एकजनाले पनि कम गरेन । एक सय पचास दिने भनेको त ज्यान गए मानेन ।

पहिलो दिन हामी धेरै हिँड्न सकेनौं । हामी कहिले उकालो, कहिले ओरालो बाटो हिँडचौं । उकालो बाटो हिँड्न गाह्रो छ । ओरालो बाटोमा हिँड्न डर लाग्छ । अनि मलाई तेर्सो बाटो एकदम मन पर्छ । हामीले धेरै खोलाहरू पनि तऱ्यौं ।

साँझ पर्नुअघि हामीले बास खोज्न थाल्यौं । बल्लबल्ल एउटा सानो गाउँमा दुईवटा घरमा बास पायौं । त्यहाँ हामीले दालभात खायौं । दालभात र तरकारी मीठो थियो तर अलिअलि पिरो थियो । हामी भित्र छिँडीमा बस्यौं; तर भरियाहरू बाहिर पिँढीमा बसे । उनीहरू छिँडीमा बसेनन्; किनभने उनीहरू अछूत थिए । त्यहाँ लाम्खुट्टे धेरै थिए र धेरै गर्मी थियो । सुत्न एकदम गाह्रो थियो ।

हामी भोलिपल्ट बिहान सबेरै उठ्यौं । हातमुख धोएर हामीले चिया खायौं र अलिअलि नास्ता खायौं । त्यसपछि घरबेटीहरूसँग बिदा लिएर हामी हिँडचौं । त्यो दिन हामी धेरै हिँडचौं । हामीले डाँडाहरूबाट मनोहर दृश्यहरू हेऱ्यौं । हिमालको दृश्य हेरेर हामीलाई अत्यन्त खुसी लाग्यो । अलिअलि थकाइ लागेकोले हामीले एउटा घरको पिँढीमा आराम गऱ्यौं । बल्लबल्ल यसरी बेलुकासम्ममा हामी चौरजहारी पुग्यौं । त्यहाँ एकदम रमाइलो थियो र त्यस गाउँका मान्छेहरू एकदम मिलनसार थिए ।

GRAMMAR

➤ 7.1 यसरी/त्यसरी/उसरी.

You will remember that यो and त्यो are *near* and *far* from the speaker, respectively, and that ऊ isn't marked for nearness to the speaker. From these are derived यसरी/त्यसरी/उसरी:

यसरी	in this way, in this manner (action done near speaker)
त्यसरी	in that way, in that manner (action done away from speaker)
उसरी	in this/that way, in this/that manner (ambiguous--both near/far)

➤ 7.2 OBLIQUE PRONOUNS.

When ऊ/उनी, त्यो/तिनी, यो/यिनी and को? take को, लाई or ले, they become:

उसको	उसलाई	उसले
त्यसको	त्यसलाई	त्यसले
यसको	यसलाई	यसले
उनको	उनलाई	उनले
तिनको	तिनलाई	तिनले
यिनको	यिनलाई	यिनले
कसको	कसलाई	कसले

However, in colloquial Nepali you will still hear उल्लाई/उल्ले त्यल्लाई/त्यल्ले, यल्लाई/यल्ले

➤ 7.3 पनि + NEG VERB *NOT EVEN.*

When पनि is used with a negative verb, it means *(not) even*.

एकजनाले पनि सय रुपियाँमा कम गरेन ।	*Not even one of them would lower it from Rs. 100*
हामीले घरहरू पनि देख्न सकेनौं ।	*We couldn't even see houses.*

➤ 7.4 CONDITIONAL *IF* CLAUSE –ए

One way to express *if x, then y* is to suffix the main verb with -ए:

ज्यान जानु + –ए + मानेन	ज्यान गए (पनि) मानेन
*For life to go + **if** + he didn't agree.*	*Even **if** (his) life left, he didn't agree.* ("Over my dead body")
ट्याक्सी पाए म जान्छु ।	*If (I) find a taxi, I'll go.*
तरकारी किने पैसा पुग्दैन ।	*If (I) buy vegies, I won't have enough money.* *If vegetables were bought there wouldn't be enough money.*

➤ 7.5 कहिले..., कहिले... *SOMETIMES..., SOMETIMES...*

कहिले उकालो कहिले ओरालो	*sometimes uphill, sometimes downhill*
कहिले राम्रो कहिले नराम्रो	*sometimes nice, sometimes bad*
कहिले सानो कहिले ठूलो	*sometimes small, sometimes big*

➤ 7.6 IDIOMATIC लाग्नु AND –लाई.

लाग्नु can have the sense of *to capture* or *take possession of.* Together with *fear* it means something like *to be captured or possessed by fear;* or simply *to be afraid.*

Many physical ailments also use this verb. As they would say using the verb लाग्नु, *a cold possessed/captured me.*

Sentences which use the verb लाग्नु are often passive and therefore the recipient is marked with -लाई. For example, you would say मलाई डर लाग्यो, not *म डर लाग्यो. As a passive, it would translate, *Fear was possessed by me.*

➤ 7.7 TENSE WITH लाग्नु AND पर्नु.

Whereas the present tense is used in English for *I am afraid,* the past tense is used in Nepali: 'मलाई डर लाग्यो'. The indefinite tense is used to state habitual or general fact. (You will learn the Present Perfect later (-एको छैन), but it is given here to fill the paradigm):

POSITIVE		NEGATIVE	
मलाई डर **लाग्यो** ।	I **was** afraid.	मलाई डर **लागेन** ।	I **wasn't** afraid.
मलाई खाना मन **पर्‍यो**।	I **liked** the food.	मलाई खाना मन **परेन** ।	I **didn't like** the food.
मलाई डर **लाग्यो** ।	I **am** afraid.	मलाई डर **लागेको छैन** ।	I **am not** afraid (yet).
मलाई खाना मन **पर्‍यो**।	I **like** the food.	मलाई खाना मन **परेको छैन**।	I **don't like** the food (yet).
मलाई डर **लाग्छ**।	I **fear** (general).	मलाई डर **लाग्दैन**।	I **don't fear** (general).
मलाई खाना **मनपर्छ** ।	I **like** food (general).	मलाई खाना **मनपर्दैन**।	I **don't like** food (general).

➤ 7.8 किनभने *BECAUSE.*

उनीहरु पिँढीमा बसे, किनभने उनीहरू अछूत थिए । *(They) stayed on the porch because, they were untouchables.*

म लेख्न सक्दिनँ, किनभने मसँग कलम छैन । *I can't write because, I don't have a pen.*

म त्यहाँ बस्दिनँ, किनभने त्यो मेच कच्चा छ । *I won't sit there, because the chair is weak.*

➤ 7.9 हुनु IN THE INDEFINITE AND PAST.

The following chart is to fill in all the conjugations of *to be* in the indefinite and past tenses.

			POSITIVE		NEGATIVE	
म	Indefinite	Equative	हुँ	म डाक्टर हुँ । I am a doctor	होइन	म डाक्टर होइन । I am not a doctor
	Indefinite	Des, Loc, Exist	छु	म बलियो छु । I am strong	छैनँ	म बलियो छैनँ । I am not strong
	Simple Past	All	थिएँ	म बलियो थिएँ । I was strong	थिइनँ	म बलियो थिइनँ । I wasn't strong
हामी	Indefinite	Equative	हौं	हामी डाक्टर हौं । We are doctors	होइनौं	हामी डाक्टर होइनौं । We are not doctors
	Indefinite	Des, Loc, Exist	छौं	हामी बलिया छौं । We are strong	छैनौं	हामी बलिया छैनौं । We are not strong
	Simple Past	All	थियौं	हामी बलिया थियौं । We were strong	थिएनौं	हामी बलिया थिएनौं । We weren't strong
	Indefinite	Equative	हो	ऊ डाक्टर हो । He/she is a doctor	होइन	ऊ डाक्टर होइन । He/she is not a doctor
	Indefinite	Des, Loc, Exist	छ	ऊ बलियो छ । He/she is strong	छैन	ऊ बलियो छैन । He/she is not strong
	Simple Past	All	थियो	ऊ बलियो थियो । He/she was strong	थिएन	ऊ बलियो थिएन । He/she wasn't strong
उनी	Indefinite	Equative	हुन्	उनी डाक्टर हुन् । He/she is a doctor	होइनन्	उनी डाक्टर होइनन् । He/she is not a doctor
	Indefinite	Des, Loc, Exist	छन्	उनी बलिया छन् । He/she is strong	छैनन्	उनी बलिया छैनन् । He/she is not strong
	Simple Past	All	थिए	उनी बलिया थिए । He/she was strong	थिएनन्	उनी बलिया थिएनन् । He/she wasn't strong
तपाई	Indefinite	Equative	हुनुहुन्छ	तपाईं डाक्टर हुनुहुन्छ। You are a doctor	हुनुहुन्न	तपाईं डाक्टर हुनुहुन्न । You are not a doctor
र	Indefinite	Des, Loc, Exist	हुनुहुन्छ	तपाईं बलियो हुनुहुन्छ। You are strong	हुनुहुन्न	तपाईं बलियो हुनुहुन्न । You are not strong
उहाँ	Simple Past	All	हुनुहुन्थ्यो	उहाँ बलियो हुनुहुन्थ्यो । He was strong	हुनुहुन्नथ्यो	उहाँ बलियो हुनुहुन्नथ्यो । She wasn't strong

COMPLEX VERBS

• **-एकोले**	***because.., because of ... ing***
थकाइ लागेकोले हामीले आराम गऱ्यौं ।	***Because*** *we were tired, we rested.*
	Because of *being tired.*
ऊ आएकोले हामीले खाएनौं ।	***Because*** *he came, we didn't eat.*
साँझ परेकोले हामी पुग्न सकेनौं ।	***Because*** *it fell dusk, we couldn't reach (it).*
• **-न सक्नु**	***to be able to..***
म हिँड्न सक्छु ।	*I'm* ***able to*** *walk.*
पहिलो दिन हामी धेरै हिँड्न सकेनौं ।	*The first day, we weren't* ***able to*** *walk much.*
हामीले धेरै खोलाहरू तर्न सक्यौं ।	*We were* ***able to*** *cross many rivers.*
• **-न सकिनु**	***to be possible to...***
साँझ पर्नुअगाडि पुग्न सकिन्छ ।	*It's* ***possible to*** *arrive before dusk.*
पहिलो दिन धेरै हिँड्न सकिँदैन ।	*It's not* ***possible to*** *walk much on the first day.*
२ दिन हिँडेर चौरजहारी पुग्न सकिन्छ ।	*It's* ***possible to*** *reach C. by walking 2 days.*
• **-नु(भन्दा) अघि/अगाडि**	***before... ing***
हिँड्नु(भन्दा) अघि/अगाडि हामीले खायौं ।	***Before*** *we walked, we ate.*
	Before *walking, we at.*
साँझ पर्नु(भन्दा) अघि/अगाडि पुग्न सकिन्छ ।	*It's possible to arrive* ***before*** *dusk.*
बास खोज्नु(भन्दा) अघि/अगाडि साँझ पऱ्यो ।	*It turned dusk* ***before*** *we looked for shelter.*
• **-न थाल्नु**	***to begin to...***
उसले बोल्न थाल्यो ।	*He* ***began to*** *speak.*
साँझ पर्नुअघि हामीले बास खोज्न थाल्यौं ।	*We* ***began to*** *look for shelter before dusk.*
हामीले खोला तर्न थाल्यौं ।	*We* ***began to*** *cross the river.*
• **-न सुरु गर्नु**	***to begin to...***
उसले बोल्न सुरु गऱ्यो ।	*He* ***began to*** *speak.*
साँझ पर्नुअघि हामीले बास खोज्न सुरु गऱ्यौं ।	*We* ***began to*** *look for shelter before dusk.*
हामीले खोला तर्न सुरु गऱ्यौं ।	*We* ***began to*** *cross the river.*

- **न–एसम्म** — ***until...***

  ऊ नआएसम्म बस्नोस् । — *Wait **until** he comes (as long as he hasn't come...)*

  नखाएसम्म नहिँड्नुस् । — *Don't walk **until** you've eaten.*

  नसुतेसम्म कुरा गरें । — *I talked **until** I slept.*

- **–न गाह्रो हुनु** — ***is difficult to...***

  सुत्न एकदम गाह्रो थियो । — *It was very **difficult to** sleep.*

  उकालो बाटो हिँड्न गाह्रो छ । — *It is **difficult to** walk on uphill trails.*

PRACTICE

Bring for this section: two die (dice).

1. हामी नेपालगन्जबाट चौरजहारीसम्म जान्छौं ।

नेपालगन्ज	बाट	चौरजहारी	सम्म	जान्छौं
बेलायत		अमेरिका		
धरहरा		ठमेल		

2. तुलसीपुर भएर सल्यानसम्म बस जान्छ ।

तुलसीपुर	भएर	सल्यान	सम्म	बस	जान्छ
धनुकट्टा		बसन्तपुर			
भक्तपुर		नगरकोट			

3. भरियाहरू सजिलोसँग पाइए ।

भरियाहरू	सजिलो	सँग	पाइए
	राम्रो		
	खुसी		
	मिलनसार	---	

4. हामी कहिले उकालो कहिले ओरालो बाटो हिँडचौं ।

कहिले	उकालो	कहिले	ओरालो	बाटो	हिँडचौं
	राम्रो		नराम्रो		
	बलियो		कच्चा		
	साँघुरो		फराकिलो		

5. Complete the sentences with सकिन्छ or सकिँदैन.

   नेपालमा स्वयंसेवकको काम गर्न ....

   नेपालमा हिन्दी बोल्न ....

   नेपालमा अङ्ग्रेजी सजिलोसँग बोल्न ....

   नेपालमा सबै कुरा खान ....

   नेपालमा होटेलमा बस्न ....

   ठूलो गाडी सानो बाटोमा चलाउन ....

   यहाँबाट हिमाल राम्रोसँग हेर्न ....

   भात सजिलोसँग पकाउन ....

6. Repeat #5, expressing the sentences in the active (by choosing a subject).

7. Translate (Nepali and English) and complete each of the sentences **twice**.
   a) रुकुम जाने बस एउटा मात्र छ; त्यसकारण...
   b) हवाइजहाज चौरजहारीसम्म नै जान्छ; त्यसकारण...
   c) हवाइजहाजमा जान महँगो पर्छ (हुन्छ); त्यसकारण...
   d) स्याउ धेरै महँगो छ; त्यसकारण...
   e) मान्छेहरू धेरै मिलनसार छन्; त्यसकारण...
   f) Because there is only one bus to Rukum...
   g) Because the plane goes all the way to Chaurjahari...
   h) Because it's expensive to go by plane...
   i) Because we got up very early...
   j) We went on Tuesday because...
   k) We aren't going to walk, because...
   l) Are you going to walk because...?
   m) We went there last year because...
   n) We like the place because...
   o) We ate quickly because...

8. Translate (Nepali and English) and complete each of the sentences **twice**.
   a) तपाईंले मलाई फोन गरे...
   b) स्याउ सस्तो भए...
   c) लुगा धोए...
   d) मैले खाना पकाए...
   e) If he stops at the hotel...
   f) If the plane comes tomorrow...
   g) If you turn left at the intersection...

9. Translate (Nepali and English) and complete each of the sentences **twice**.
   a) पानी खानुअघि...
   b) साँझ पर्नुअघि...
   c) बजार जानुअघि...
   d) मेचमा बस्नुअघि...
   e) Before she washed the dishes...
   f) Before the bus came...
   g) Before phoning his mother...

10. Roll the two die (dice) brought to class and use the following corresponding words to construct a sentence with the correct "is" in the *indefinite tense.* Continue till correct sentences can be produced immediately after rolling.

1st dice	2nd dice
① म	① उसको दाइ
② हामी	② विदेशी
③ ऊ	③ बलियो
④ उनी	④ छिटो
⑤ तपाईं	⑤ पाटनमा
⑥ उहाँ	⑥ घरमा

11. Same as #10, but use the *simple past tense.* Continue till correct sentences can be produced immediately after rolling.

1st dice	2nd dice
① म	① भरिया
② हामी	② उहाँकी छोरी
③ ऊ	③ अछूत
④ उनी	④ रमाइलो
⑤ तपाईं	⑤ बाहिर
⑥ उहाँ	⑥ पिँढीमा

12. Repeat #10 and #11 using negatives.

13. Translate each of the following.
    a) It's possible to drink the water. (The water is drinkable.)
    b) It's possible to reach the market in 10 minutes.
    c) It's possible to cross that river.
    d) It's not possible to cross big rivers.
    e) It's not possible to go there.

14. Translate each of the following using both -न थाल्नु and -न सुरु गर्नु.
    a) He began to drink the water.
    b) I began to go to the market.
    c) We began to cross that river.
    d) You begin to speak first.
    e) They began to go there.

15. Translate and complete each of the following twice:
    a) उसले पानी नखाएसम्म...
    b) म बजार नगएसम्म...
    c) Until we cross that river...
    d) Until I begin to speak...
    e) Until they go there...

16. Translate and complete each of the following twice:
    a) तरकारी महँगो भएकोले...
    b) मेच धेरै कच्चा/कमजोर भएकोले...
    c) बाटो साँघुरो भएकोले...
    d) Because the taxi driver drove fast...
    e) Because he called me...
    f) Because we walked uphill...
    g) Because he drank unboiled water...

LET'S TALK

1. Tell your tutor what things you **are** and **aren't** able to do. Here are some ideas:

   I'm (not) able to speak...
   I'm (not) able to go to the bazaar (X time).
   I'm (not) able to walk uphill/downhill/on the level.
   I'm (not) able to teach...
   I'm (not) able to eat...
   I'm (not) able to go to...
   I'm (not) able to buy...

2. Take turns talking about what you are afraid of. Here are some ideas:

   eating green apples
   drinking unboiled water
   speaking Nepali
   teaching English
   riding expensive taxis
   walking downhill quickly

3. Take turns talking about whether or not you find the following difficult:

   walking uphill
   sleeping at night
   speaking Nepali
   teaching English
   cooking Nepali food
   walking downhill quickly

4. Take turns describing...
    a) what you did yesterday.
    b) what you plan to do today.
    c) what you plan to do tomorrow.

5. Describe to each other an overnight trip you've taken. If you can describe a trip taken in Nepal, describe that trip. In your conversations, include the following points:
    a) mode of travel
    b) route
    c) length of time required
    d) where you overnighted
    e) cost of travel
    f) food eaten

6. Pretend you are a trekker and your tutor is a trekking agent. Ask your tutor for advice on a trek.
    What route should you take?
    Is there a lot of uphill?
    Where can you sleep?
    Do you have to cross rivers?
    Are porters available? For how much?
    What modes of transportation will you have to take?
    What kind of food is available?
    Are there mosquitoes?
    What are the views like?
    Will you have to cross rivers or are there bridges?
    etc., etc., etc.

    Now reverse roles.

IN THE COMMUNITY

Have a conversation with at least 4 individual people *or* until your conversation time totals three hours, whichever is shortest. (Conversation time means time **talking**; this does not include time for travel, or lull time and you should be contributing to the conversation). Your conversation should minimally include the description of an **overnight trip** you've taken. If you can describe a trip taken in Nepal, describe that trip. In your conversations, try to include the following points:

a) mode of travel
b) route
c) length of time required
d) where you overnighted
e) cost of travel
f) food eaten

As an alternative to the above:
Plan an overnight trip somewhere on the Kathmandu valley rim. Plan your trip so that you can easily reach your destination in a day. As in our text, you will need to ask around for a place to spend the night. In most villages there is a "hotel" where you can get a *daal bhaat* meal, a sleeping mat and a room to spend the night. Otherwise, you can almost always find a family that is willing to put you up for the night (the best option for this assignment). Women should not attempt this assignment alone. Husbands and wives can plan the trip together and have it count for both of you, even though you may be on different chapters. *Resorts like Nagarkot, Dhulikhel and Hati Ban do not count!*

DID YOU KNOW?

Some Nepali superstitions regarding travel:

- If someone sneezes when leaving the house, it's best to wait a few minutes before leaving.
- When sleeping at an inn, sleep with the ceiling beams parallel to your body.
- When sleeping at an inn, never point your feet at the water containers.
- A married woman shouldn't visit her parents on a Tuesday or on the last day of the month.
- When traveling one should take some rice, one betel-nut and one coin in a piece of cloth for good luck.
- If you stumble while walking, a family member is thinking about you.
- One shouldn't return home on the ninth day of an absence. If one has to return on that day, spend the night at a friends.
- If you're going on a several day trip and as you leave a cat crosses your path, it's best to postpone the trip for a day.
- If you encounter a tree that has fallen over the path, don't go under the tree. If there's no other way and you must go under, place a rock on the tree where you go under.

Etc., etc., etc.! There are many variations to the above, and each ethnic group has their own set of superstitions regarding travel.

CHAPTER 8

MY ORGANIZATION
मेरो संस्था

VOCABULARY

संस्था	an organization	छुट्टी	holiday, leave, vacation	योजना	plan, arrangement
मुख्य	main, chief	घण्टा	hour	भेरी	Bheri (river), Bheri zone
सिक्नु	learn	अनुभवी	experienced	नदी	river
धेरैजसो	most, mostly, often, frequently	अस्पताल	"hospital"	किनार	edge, side
डाक्टर	"doctor"	महाकाली	Mahakali (zone)	भीर	precipice, cliff
इन्जिनियर	"engineer"	अञ्चल	Zone/Region	त्यसैले	because of that, that is why
विदेश	foreign country	जिल्ला	District	डेढ	one and a half
पहिले	at first, firstly, before, previously	पोखरा	Pokhara	उपकरण	equipment
संस्कृति	culture	कर्मचारी	employee, staff	पठाउनु	send
डँडेल्धुरा	Dandeldhura	धनगढी	Dhangadhi	ट्रक	"truck"
शिक्षक	teacher	-जति	about, approx	लग्नु	take away
नियुक्ति	appointment to a post	दिनहुँ	daily	भिसा	"visa"
भवन	building (large)	बिरामी	sick (person)	मिलाउनु	arrange, fix (see also 16.1)
भाडा	rent, hire, fare	औषधि	medicine	महिना	month
तिर्नु	pay, repay (bill, debt, tax etc.)	-को लागि	for the sake of, in order to, for	सरकार	government (adj. सरकारी)
तलब	pay, salary	हिजोआज	nowadays	अनुसन्धान	research, investigation
नर्स	"nurse"	क्लिनिक	"clinic"	अन्य	other
उपचार	treatment	बनाउनु	make, build, fix prepare, repair		

USEFUL PHRASES

- म "…" भन्ने संस्थामा काम गर्छु । — *I work in an organization called "…".*
- म नेपालमा आएको … भयो । — *I've been in Nepal for … time.*
- म दिनको दुईतीन घण्टा नेपाली सिक्छु । — *I study Nepali for 2 to 3 hours/day.*
- … जति लाग्छ । — *It takes/costs around ….*
- म त्यहाँ दुई हप्ताजति बसें । — *I stayed there for around two weeks.*
- म एक महिनाको लागि रुकुम जान्छु । — *I'm going to Rukum for one month.*

TEXT

म टीम नेपाल भन्ने संस्थामा काम गर्छु । यसको मुख्य अफिस काठमाडौँको बानेश्वरमा छ । यसले नेपालमा काम गरेको २८ वर्ष भइसक्यो । म टीमको स्कूलमा नेपाली सिक्छु ।

काठमाडौँमा टीमको स्कूल छ । धेरैजसो टीमका डाक्टर र इन्जिनियरहरू त्यहाँ नेपाली भाषा सिक्छन् । डाक्टर, इन्जिनियरहरू विदेशबाट आउँछन् । उनीहरू पहिले काठमाडौँमा नेपाली भाषा र संस्कृति सिक्छन् । त्यसपछि उनीहरू डँडेल्धुरा, रुकुम र अरू ठाउँमा काम गर्न जान्छन् ।

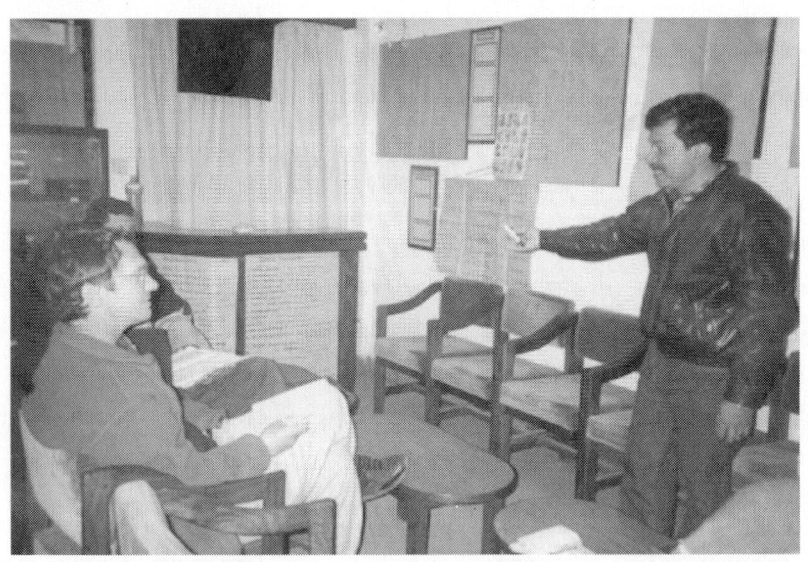

टीम अफिसले भाषा सिकाउने शिक्षकहरूको नियुक्ति गर्छ, स्कूल-भवनको भाडा तिर्छ र शिक्षकहरूको तलब दिन्छ। टीम स्कूलमा (विदेशी) डाक्टर, नर्स, इन्जिनियरहरू हप्तामा पाँच दिन भाषा सिक्छन् । शनिबार र आइतबार त्यहाँ छुट्टी हुन्छ । धेरैजसोले स्कूलमा दिनको दुईतीन घण्टा सिक्छन् । उनीहरू धेरैजसो बिहान सिक्छन् । शिक्षकहरू अनुभवी छन् । स्कूलमा भाषा सिकेपछि उनीहरू घर जान्छन् ।

अहिले टीम नेपालले दुईवटा अस्पताल चलाइरहेको छ । ती अस्पतालहरू महाकाली अञ्चलको डँडेल्धुरा जिल्लामा छन् । एउटा अस्पताल डँडेल्धुरामा र अर्को

सानो अस्पताल त्यहींको सानो पोखरामा छ । अहिले टीम अस्पतालमा तीनजना विदेशी डाक्टरहरू काम गर्नुहुन्छ । डँडेल्धुरामा दुईजना विदेशी नर्स र पन्ध्रजना नेपाली नर्सहरू छन् । अरू दश-बाह्रजना नेपाली कर्मचारीहरू पनि त्यहाँ काम गर्छन् ।

काठमाडौंबाट डँडेल्धुरा धेरै टाढा छ । यहाँबाट नेपालगन्ज भएर धनगढीसम्म बसमा जानुपर्छ । त्यहाँसम्म बसमा १८ घण्टाजति लाग्छ । नेपालगन्जपछि बाटो नराम्रो छ । काठमाडौंबाट धनगढीसम्म बसमा पाँच सय रुपियाँजति लाग्छ । धनगढीबाट डडेल्धुरासम्म पुग्न पाँच घण्टाजति लाग्छ । त्यहाँ पुगेपछि एकदम रमाइलो हुन्छ । त्यहाँ दिनहुँ धेरै बिरामीहरू उपचार गराउन आउँछन् । त्यहाँ औषधि किन्नको लागि बाहिर जानु पर्दैन । त्यहाँ अस्पतालभित्रै औषधि किन्न पाइन्छ ।

हिजोआज टीम नेपालले रुकुम जिल्लाको चौरजहारीमा एउटा सानो क्लिनिक चलाइरहेको छ । त्यहाँ एउटा अस्पताल बनाउने योजना छ । चौरजहारी भेरी नदीको किनारमा छ । तर त्यहाँबाट नदीसम्म पुग्न गाह्रो छ । किनभने त्यहाँ नजिक ठूलो भीर छ । त्यसैले एक-डेढ घण्टा टाढाबाट हिंड्नु पर्छ ।

काठमाडौंको अफिसले यी अस्पताल र क्लिनिकको लागि डाक्टर, नर्स, इन्जिनियर, औषधि र उपकरणहरू पठाउनु पर्छ । औषधि र उपकरणहरू ट्रकमा र भरियाले बोकेर लग्नु पर्छ । टीम अफिसको अर्को काम यहाँ काम गर्ने विदेशीहरूको भिसा मिलाउनु हो । भिसा मिलाउनको लागि नेपाली कर्मचारीले मद्दत गर्नुहुन्छ ।

गएको अक्टोबरमा म डँडेल्धुरा गएँ । म त्यहाँ दुई हप्ताजति बसेँ । आउने सेप्टेम्बरमा म एक महिनाको लागि रुकुम जान्छु । मैले त्यहाँ धेरै सामान लिएर जानुपर्छ ।

GRAMMAR

➤ 8.1 ...**भन्ने**... *..CALLED...*

टीम भन्ने संस्था	*the organization called TEAM*
राम भन्ने मान्छे	*the man named Ram*
पूजा भन्ने साबुन	*the soap named Puja*

This should be distinguished from the verb भने: तिनीहरूले भने *they said*

➤ 8.2 हुन्छ FOR GENERAL FACTS.

हुन्छ is used with general statements of fact or things that are always true:

शनिबार र आइतबार छुट्टी हुन्छ ।	*Saturday and Sunday are holidays (general fact)*
स्याउ महँगो हुन्छ ।	*Apples are expensive (general fact)*
एक दिनमा २४ घण्टा हुन्छ ।	*There are 24 hours in a day (general fact)*

➤ 8.3 -ले WITH GENERAL FACTS.

-ले is also used with a subject when the sentence expresses a universal or established fact, given the verb is transitive:

अफिसले भाषा सिकाउने शिक्षकहरूको नियुक्ति गर्छ।	*The office appoints teachers for language.*
धेरैजसोले दिनको दुई घण्टा सिक्छन् ।	*Most learn two hours per day.*
पुरुषहरूले सुरुवाल लगाउँछन् ।	*Men wear pants.*
महिलाहरूले साडी लगाउँछन् ।	*Women wear saris.*
दिदीले भात पकाउनुहुन्छ ।	*My sister cooks the meal (regularly)*

➤ 8.4 THE 2ND PRESENT CONTINUOUS.

In 6.4 you learned the first present continuous tense (बोल्दै छु *I am speaking*). The second present continuous is essentially the same. In our text we have चलाइरहेको छ, *is operating*:

① चलाउनु + ② इरहनु + ③ एको + ④ छ

- ① चलाउनु: *to manage, operate* or *run*. (Also *move, drive, stir, tease* and *use*!)
- ② इरहनु: *to last* or *remain*. When suffixed it means *to remain* or *keep on*. This verb is commonly suffixed to form several continuous tenses.
- ③ -एको: *had* or *have*.
- ④ It is the छ that makes this the **present** continuous tense. If थियो had been final, our verb would have been in the **past** continuous tense.

Putting it all together, we get:

① चलाउनु + ② इरहनु + ③ एको + ④ छ = चलाइरहेको छ

to run	to keep on	have	present	= to have been keeping on running

To have been keeping on running! What a mouthful! But if you think about it, that essentially means, *is running*.

This present continuous tense is equally as common as the first you learned in 6.4 and they are basically synonymous. However, there are some subtle differences:

- Unlike the first, this second continuous tense has a negative.
- Where the first continuous tense was restricted to something in *process*, the second can be used to express the continuation of an event:

बस्दै छु	*in the process of sitting*
बसिरहेको छु	*already seated and sitting*
सुत्दै छु	*in the process of going to sleep (head nodding)*
सुतिरहेको छु	*sleeping (asleep)*

The second continuous tense is conjugated as follows:

SUBJECT	POSITIVE	NEGATIVE
म	-इरहेको छु	-इरहेको छैन
हामी	-इरहेका छौं	-इरहेका छैनौं
तपाईं	-इरहनु भएको छ	-इरहनु भएको छैन
ऊ	-इरहेको छ	-इरहेको छैन
उनी	-इरहेका छन्	-इरहेका छैनन्
उहाँ	-इरहनु भएको छ	-इरहनु भएको छैन

➤ 8.5 त्यसैले *BECAUSE OF THAT.*

(Synonymous with त्यसकारण)

हाम्रो नजिक पसलहरू छैनन् । त्यसैले हामी शहर जान्छौं ।	*There are no shops near us, therefore we go to the city.*
उनीहरू अछूत थिए, त्यसैले पिँढीमा बसे ।	*They were untouchables, so they stayed on the porch.*
थकाइ लाग्यो, त्यसैले हामीले पिँढीमा आराम गऱ्यौं ।	*We were tired, so rested on the porch.*

➤ 8.6 CAUSATIVES.

Many of the verbs you've learned can be made into causatives by adding to the verb the ending -आउनु. To get an idea of what a causative is and how they work in Nepali, consider the following (some of them you already know!):

गर्नु	*to do*	➡	गराउनु	*to cause to do (get done)*
बस्नु	*to sit*	➡	बसाउनु/बसाल्नु	*to cause to sit (to set)*
खानु	*to eat*	➡	खुवाउनु/ख्वाउनु	*to cause to eat (to feed)*
सिक्नु	*to learn*	➡	सिकाउनु	*to cause to learn (to teach)*
चल्नु	*to move*	➡	चलाउनु	*to cause to move (to operate)*
देख्नु	*to see*	➡	देखाउनु	*to cause to see (to show)*
सुन्नु	*to hear*	➡	सुनाउनु	*to cause to hear (to tell)*

Although many verbs fit into this pattern, the relationship between the normal and causative are not always clear . Some verbs display only the causative.

COMPLEX VERBS

● **-इसक्नु** — ***finish...; have already...; have had...***

मैले भात खाइसकेँ। — *I **have already** eaten/I've **finished** eating.*

दुई महिना भइसक्यो । — *It's **already** been two months.*

हामीले त्यहाँ अस्पताल बनाइसक्यौँ । — *We've **already** /**finished** building a hospital there.*

● **-नु पर्छ** — ***should, must, have to...*** (note: tran requires -ले)

मैले भात खानु पर्छ । — *I **have to** eat rice.*

तपाईंले नेपाली सिक्नु पर्छ । — *You **must** learn Nepali.*

हामीले त्यहाँ अस्पताल बनाउनु पर्छ । — *We are **required to** build a hospital there.*

● **-नु पर्दैन** — ***don't have to, not necessary to...***(note: -ले)

मैले भात खानु पर्दैन । — *I **don't need to** eat rice (not necessary).*

तपाईंले नेपाली सिक्नु पर्दैन । — *It's **not necessary** for you to learn Nepali.*

त्यहाँ अस्पताल बनाउनु पर्दैन । — *It's **not necessary** to build a hospital there.*

● **-नु/न हुन्छ** — ***permissible, can, okay to...***

भात खानु/खान हुन्छ । — *It's **okay to** eat rice.*

नेपाली सिक्नु/सिक्न हुन्छ । — *You **can** learn Nepali; it's okay.*

त्यहाँ अस्पताल बनाउनु/बनाउन हुन्छ । — *It's **okay to** build a hospital there.*

- **-नु हुँदैन** — ***must not, should not ...***

मैले भात खानु हुँदैन ।	*I **must not** eat rice.*
तपाईंले नेपाली सिक्नु हुँदैन ।	*You are **not allowed to** learn Nepali.*
त्यहाँ अस्पताल बनाउनु हुँदैन ।	*It's **not okay to** build a hospital there.*

- **-एको TIME भयो** — ***...ago , since***

तपाईं नेपालमा आएको कति भयो ?	***How long ago did** you come to Nepal (here now)?*
म नेपालमा आएको १ वर्ष भयो ।	*I came to Nepal a year **ago** (been here a year).*
म नेपालमा **न**आएको १ वर्ष भयो ।	*It's been a year since I (last) come to Nepal.*
मैले खाना पकाएको १ घण्टा भयो । (tr)	***It's been** 1hr. **since** I cooked food (finished an hour ago).*
	*I **have been cooking** food for an hour (started an hour ago)*
मलाई डर लागेको १ घण्टा भयो ।	*I **have been** afraid for an hour.*
	*An hour ago, I **was** afraid (but not now).*

- **-न (को लागि / लाई)** — ***in order to...***

(also pronounced **(का लागि)**) ***for, for the sake of ... ing (purpose or intention)***

कोहि पनि औषधि किन्नको लागि बाहिर जानु पर्दैन ।	*No one has to go outside **in order to** buy meds.*
कोहि पनि औषधि किन्नलाई बाहिर जानु पर्दैन ।	*No one has to go outside **in order to** buy meds.*
कोहि पनि औषधि किन्न बाहिर जानु पर्दैन ।	*No one has to go outside **in order to** buy meds.*
भिसा मिलाउनको लागि ऊ मद्दत गर्छ ।	***In order to** arrange visas, he helps.*
भिसा मिलाउनलाई ऊ मद्दत गर्छ ।	***In order to** arrange visas, he helps.*
भिसा मिलाउन ऊ मद्दत गर्छ ।	***In order to** arrange visas, he helps.*
म तरकारी किन्नको लागि बजार जान्छु ।	*I'm going to the market **to** buy vegetables.*
म तरकारी किन्नलाई बजार जान्छु ।	*I'm going to the market **to** buy vegetables.*
म तरकारी किन्न बजार जान्छु ।	*I'm going to the market **to** buy vegetables.*

- **-न (को लागि / लाई) MEASURE लाग्नु** — **MEASURE *required to...***

(also spoken as **का लागि**)

नेपाली सिक्न(को लागि) एक वर्ष लाग्छ ।	*It takes **one year to** learn Nepali.*
त्यो किन्न(लाई) दुई रुपियाँ लाग्छ ।	*That **requires two rupees** to buy.*
त्यहाँ पुग्न दुई हप्ता लाग्छ ।	*It takes **two weeks to** reach there.*

PRACTICE

1. म टीम भन्ने संस्थामा काम गर्छु ।

टीम	भन्ने	_____	काम गर्नु
राम			
नारायणी			
होन्डा			

2. मैले काम गरेको २८ वर्ष भइसक्यो ।

मैले काम गरेको	२८ वर्ष	भइसक्यो
नेपाल आएको	५ हप्ता	
म स्कूल पुगेको	२ घण्टा	
मैले काम खोजेको	धेरै	
म सुतेको		

3. म औषधि किन्नको लागि बाहिर जान्छु ।

	औषधि किन्न	-को लागि	बाहिर जानु
Supply a subject	नेपाली बोल्न		घर जानु
	भुइँ पुछ्न		नजिक आउनु
	सुन्न		अगाडि बस्नु
	हेर्न		

4. Warm up by repeating -इरहेको, -इरहेको, -इरहेको... over and over. Tutor: correct pronunciation! Then repeat -इरहनुभएको over and over. Now that your tongue is loose, conjugate the following verbs for the second present continuous tense *positive* (for each pronoun): सिक्नु, तिर्नु, बनाउनु, पठाउनु, लग्नु

5. Repeat #4 (including warm-up!) but conjugate for the *negative*.

6. Translate and complete using त्यसैले each of the following sentences.
   a) रुकुम जाने बस एउटा मात्र छ; त्यसैले...
   b) हवाइजहाज चौरजहारीसम्म नै जान्छ; त्यसैले...
   c) हवाइजहाजमा जान महँगो पर्छ (हुन्छ); त्यसैले...
   d) स्याउ धेरै महँगो छ; त्यसैले...
   e) मान्छेहरू धेरै मिलनसार छन्; त्यसैले...

7. Rephrase each of the sentences in #6 using a) त्यसकारण b) किनभने and c) -एकोले.

8. Translate each of the following:

a) I've already eaten. *Give two results using* त्यसैले.

b) A hospital has already been built there. *Give two results using* त्यसकारण.

c) Because it's already been two hours. *Give two results using* -एकोले.

d) I've finished learning that.

e) He has already paid you.

f) The plane has already arrived.

9. Translate and complete the following:

a) काम गर्न जानुअघि मैले...पर्छ ।

b) काममा जानुअघि मैले...पर्दैन ।

c) काममा जानुअघि...हुन्छ ।

d) काममा जानुअघि...हुँदैन ।

e) घर जानुअघि काम गर्ने बहिनीले...पर्छ ।

f) It's not necessary for my housegirl to ... before going home.

g) It's okay if my housegirl ... before going home.

h) My housegirl must not ... before going home.

i) In order to ... we must...

j) In order to ... it's not necessary to...

k) In order to ... it's okay to...

l) In order to ... we must not...

10. Translate the following using -एको TIME भयो:

a) I came to Nepal one year ago.

b) He came to Nepal two years ago.

c) How long ago did you come to class?

d) I came to class an hour ago.

e) It has been two hours since I came to class.

f) I have been cooking food for an hour now.

g) It's been two days since I (last) cooked.

h) He has been afraid for 10 minutes.

i) It's been many days since I was afraid.

11. Translate and complete the following using -नको लागि:
    a) I have come (in order) to learn Nepali.
    b) I am going (in order) to buy vegetables.
    c) She comes on Mondays (in order) to clean our house.
    d) He has come (in order) to give us a message.
    e) Call me (in order) to talk Nepali.
    f) It takes one year (in order) to learn Nepali.
    g) It takes three days (in order) to reach my village.
    h) In order to reach my village, one has to walk.
    i) It takes eight hours to reach Pokhara by bus.
    j) It takes one hour to reach Pokhara by plane.

12. Repeat #11 using -न or -नलाई and *past tense.*

13. Convert each of the following sentences as illustrated:

    म एउटा संस्थामा काम गर्छु । त्यो संस्थाको नाम टीम नेपाल हो ।
    ➠ म टीम नेपाल भन्ने संस्थामा काम गर्छु ।

    a) हिजो एकजना साथी आउनुभयो । उहाँको नाम रवीन हो ।
    b) भोलि हामी घुम्न जान्छौँ । हामी घुम्न जाने ठाउँको नाम धुलिखेल हो ।
    c) त्यस पसलमा नेपाली टोपी पाइन्छ । त्यस पसलका साहुजीको नाम राम्चा हो ।
    d) म शिक्षकसँग नेपाली सिक्छु । शिक्षकको नाम शमा हो ।
    e) पोप जोन पाल भेटीकन सिटीमा बस्नुहुन्छ । त्यो संसारको सानो देश हो ।

LET'S TALK

1. Make as many statements of general fact as you can. Eg., *tomatoes are red.*

2. Tell each other what you've already done today. Using तपाईं(ले) repeat each other and then reverse roles.

3. Act out the following verbs. For each action your tutor describes what you are doing. When possible, use both the first and the second continuous tenses (-दै हुनुहुन्छ and -इरहनुभएको छ). When finished, reverse roles.

sitting (seated)	sitting down (moving)	falling asleep
listening	putting a book on the table	sleeping (asleep)

4. Your tutor is to tell you about an organization he/she belonged to (or used to belong to). Reverse roles.

5. Using मेरो x-ने योजना छ, your tutor is to tell you about his/her plans. Reverse roles.

6. Take turns providing three answers for each of the following:
   a) things you must do (-नु पर्छ)
   b) things that are allowed to do (-नु हुन्छ)
   c) things you can't (must not) do (-नु हुँदैन)
   d) things that aren't necessary for you to do (-नु पर्दैन)

7. How long does it take to...
   a) learn Nepali
   b) finish this book
   c) go to Pokhara by bus
   d) go to Europe by plane
   e) eat daal bhat

   How much money does it take to...
   f) buy a kilo of apples
   g) go to Pokhara by bus
   h) fly to Seattle
   i) cook daal bhaat
   j) wash your clothes

8. Finish and discuss the following sentences:
   a) In order to be happy...
   b) In order to clean a house...
   c) In order to learn a language...
   d) In order to sleep well...
   e) In order to be beautiful...

IN THE COMMUNITY

Have a conversation with at least 4 individual people *or* until your conversation time totals three hours (whichever is shortest). Minimally cover the following information:

1. Exchange information about organizations that you belong to.
2. Find out for each individual:
   a) Three things they're *not allowed to* do (तपाईंले के-के गर्नु हुँदैन ?)
   b) Three things they *have to* do (तपाईंले के-के गर्नु पर्छ ?)

As an alternative to the above assignment, find a Nepali who...

- ❑ has flown on an airplane
- ❑ has two daughters
- ❑ lives in Patan
- ❑ speaks Tamang (dominates the hills surrounding KTM valley)
- ❑ bought vegetables yesterday
- ❑ boils their drinking water
- ❑ doesn't like spicy food
- ❑ is from the Terrai
- ❑ has househelp

To complete this assignment, you have to have found and talked to each of the above individuals *or* spent at least four hours trying.

DID YOU KNOW?

If you represent an organization and are signing an official paper, the organization's stamp carries as much weight as your signature.

For any kind of business meeting in Kathmandu, it is considered good practice to exchange business cards. In some situations, a business card is almost equal to an identity card.

UNIT THREE

The Physical World

CHAPTER 9

CONCERNING HEALTH

स्वास्थ्यसम्बन्धी

VOCABULARY					
स्वास्थ्य	health	तिमी	you (med.)	औलो ज्वरो	malarial fever
सम्बन्धी	concerning, relating	कारण	reason, cause	कमलपित्त	Hepatitis A, jaundice
राति	night (at)	हुन सक्नु	to be possible	मस्तिष्क ज्वर	meningitis
अचानक	suddenly	निको	well, healthy	यौन रोग	venereal disease (STD)
ज्वर आउनु	get fever	झोल	liquid; soup	इत्यादि	etc.
जाडो लाग्नु	feel cold	जीवनजल	oral rehydration brand	रुघा ज्वरो	cold flu
जिउ	body	शरीर	body	दु:ख दिनु	bother, trouble
दुख्नु	be hurt, have pain	नुन	salt	कुनै-कुनै	some (emph)
बेर	time (short period)	अचम्म लाग्नु	feel amazed, surprised,	महामारी	plague, epidemic
पेट	stomach	घुम्नु	turn around (*intr.*) wander, stroll (*intr.*)	सर्नु (*intr.*)	shift, move, communicate/ transmit (a disease)
पखाला लाग्नु	get diarrhea	-को बारेमा	about X	फैलिनु	to be spread
वाकवाक	nausea	होसियार	careful	त्यति	that much
यस्तो/यसो	such as this, like this	खास गरी	actually, in fact, particularly	खोप	vaccination, vaccine
किसिमको	kind of, sort of	पिउनु	drink	-भन्दा	than, as compared to
गडबडी	upset, disorder	सतर्क	alert	पहिल्यै	before(hand), already before
विचार गर्नु	think, consider	धारा	water tap, faucet		
ओछ्यान	bed(ing)	त्यस्तै/त्यसो	just like that, in that manner	ज्ञान	wisdom, knowledge
ओछ्यान पर्नु	be bed-ridden	समय लाग्नु	to require time	महत्त्वपूर्ण	important
आफू	(one's) self	समस्या	problem	कसरी	how, in what way, in what manner?
फर्कनु	return; turn	साधारणतया	generally, ordinarily, normally, commonly	पटक	time (1 of a #)
ढिलो	late; slow, delay	रोग	sickness, disease	चक्की	tablet, pill
अझै	still, yet	झाडापखाला	loose stool, diarrhea	बेला	time (point of)
जस्तो	like, as if, as	विष	poison	सोध्नु	ask

पातलो	thin	-बाहेक	besides X, except X	साधारण	ordinary, general
पुरानो	old	गलत	wrong; error	कार्यकर्ता	worker (of org)
साथी	friend	तराई	Terai	सल्लाह	advice
अथवा	or (syn. कि)	मौसम	weather, season	बिमारी	alt of बिरामी, sickness
लक्षण	symptom	टोक्नु	bite	अर्थात्	that-is-to-say, that means, i.e., in other words
अध्ययन	study			खेर गइसक्यो	already wasted

USEFUL PHRASES

- कहाँ दुख्छ ? — *Where does it hurt?*
- अरू केही हुन्छ ? — *What else is wrong?* (Lit. Does anything else happen?)
- पक्का हो ? पक्का हो । — *Really, is it true? It's certain, you bet!* (Are you sure? I'm sure)
- साँचै हो ? साँचै हो । — *Really, is it true? It's certain, you bet!*
- एक दिन बिराएर खानुस् । — *Take it every other day (lit. miss a day)*
- तपाईंको सल्लाह के छ ? — *What is your advice?*
- यो गलत हो । — *This is wrong.*

TEXT

हिजो बेलुका मीठो खाना खाएर सुतेको माइक राति दुई बजे अचानक उठ्यो । उसलाई अलिअलि ज्वर आयो र जाडो लाग्यो । उसको जिउ पनि अलिअलि दुख्यो । केही बेरपछि उसको पेट पनि अलिअलि दुख्यो । उसलाई दिसा लाग्यो अनि वाकवाक पनि लाग्यो । यस्तो किसिमको पेटको गडबडी भएको कुरो पहिले उसलाई थाहा थिएन । उसले विचार गऱ्यो- "म त ओछ्यानमै पर्छु कि ? अब नेपालमा अरू कुरा देख्न सकिँदैन कि ? आफ्नै देशमा फर्कनुपर्ला कि ?"

भोलिपल्ट ऊ बिहान धेरै ढिलो उठ्यो । दिसा अझै पानीजस्तो पातलो थियो । ऊ डाक्टरकहाँ गयो । डाक्टर उसको पुरानो साथी थियो । डाक्टरले उसको रोगको लक्षणहरूको अध्ययन गरेर भन्यो- "तिमीलाई पखाला लागेको छ । यो मौसममा धेरैजसो विदेशीहरूलाई पखाला लाग्छ । बेक्टेरियाको कारणले हुनसक्छ । आफै पनि निको हुन सक्छ । छिटो निको हुनको लागि एक किसिमको एन्टिबायोटिक लिनु राम्रो हुन्छ । तिमीले धेरै झोल खाना खानुपर्छ । तिमीले जीवनजल मिलाएको पानी पनि खानु पर्छ । किनभने तिम्रो शरीरबाट धेरै पानी र नुन खेरगइसक्यो।" उसलाई डाक्टरको कुरा सुनेर अचम्म लाग्यो । दुई दिनपछि ऊ निको भयो र घुम्न जान थाल्यो ।

विदेशीहरू नेपालमा बस्दाखेरि आफ्नो स्वास्थ्यको बारेमा धेरै होसियार हुनु पर्छ। खास गरी खानेपिउने सबै कुरामा सतर्क हुनु पर्छ । नेपालीहरूले मीठो मानेर खाएको कुरा आफूलाई पनि खान मन लाग्छ होला । अरूले धाराको पानी सिधै खाएको देखेर आफूलाई पनि त्यस्तै गर्न मन लाग्छ होला, होइन त ? तपाईं त्यसो गर्न सक्ने हुन धेरै समय लाग्ला । बिर्सेर पनि अहिले नै यसो नगर्नुस् । खानेपिउने कुराबाट पेटको समस्या विदेशीहरूलाई मात्र होइन नेपालीहरूलाई पनि हुन्छ । नेपालमा साधारणतया पाइने रोग झाडापखाला अथवा ग्यास्ट्रोइन्ट्राइटिस हो । थाहा पाएर अथवा थाहा नपाई खाएको गलत खाना विषजस्तै भइदिन्छ ।

यसबाहेक नेपालमा अरू पनि रोगहरू पाइन्छन् । जस्तै: तराईमा लाम्खुट्टेले टोकेपछि लाग्ने औलो ज्वरो, कमलपित्त, मस्तिष्क ज्वर (मेनेन्जाइटीस), इन्सेफलाइटिस, टी.बी., यौन रोगहरू इत्यादि । कहिलेकाहीं रुघा ज्वरोले पनि अलिअलि दु:ख दिन्छ। कुनैकुनै रोग महामारी जस्तै सर्छ र फैलिन्छ । कुनै रोग त्यति सजिलोसँग सर्दैन । कुनै रोगको लागि खोप पाइन्छ अनि कुनै रोगको लागि पाइँदैन । कुनै खोप महँगो हुन्छ, कुनै खोप सस्तो हुन्छ । यी सबै कुराको लागि नेपालमा आउनुभन्दा पहिल्यै अलिअलि ज्ञान चाहिन्छ । रोगको उपचार गर्नुभन्दा रोग लाग्न नै नदिनु राम्रो हो ।

रोगको लागि आफै औषधि किनेर खानु राम्रो हुँदैन । डाक्टरको सल्लाह महत्त्वपूर्ण हुन्छ । कुन औषधि कसरी खाने, दिनको कतिपटक कति चक्की खाने, कुन बेला खाने इत्यादि सबै डाक्टरसँग सोधेर गर्नु पर्छ । शहरमा डाक्टर र डाक्टरका क्लिनिक धेरै पाइन्छन्; तर गाउँमा पाइँदैन । साधारण बिमारीको लागि स्वास्थ्य कार्यकर्ताले नै मद्दत गर्न सक्छ; तर ठूलो बिमारीको लागि शहरमै आउनु पर्छ । कुनैकुनै रोगको उपचार नेपालमा नहुन सक्छ अर्थात् त्यस्तो रोगको लागि विदेशमै जानुपर्ने हुन सक्छ ।

GRAMMAR

➤ 9.1 तिमी.

	Positive	Negative
Simple Indef:	-छौ	-दैनौ
Present Cont:	-दै छौ	-
Simple Past:	-यौ	-एनौ
2 Pres Cont:	-इरहेका छौ	-इरहेका छैनौ
Imperative	-ऊ eg. जाऊ/बस	न- -ऊ eg. नजाऊ/नबस
you are/aren't	छौ/हौ	छैनौ/होइनौ

In this chapter, the doctor uses तिमी for the patient because they are old friends. They are very familiar with each other. As a foreigner, however, you should be cautious using it with even good friends as it may be interpreted as ranking yourself higher. You should use it, however, when speaking to your children and other young children. Husbands would also use it when speaking to their wives. Using तपाईं for your wife would be highly amusing. See the table for how to conjugate. Its possessive is तिम्रो.

➤ 9.2 THE REFLEXIVE आफू

आफू can stand alone as *any* of the pronouns, but it has a reflexive sense (*own self*). It's meaning is then derived by the conjugation of the agreeing verb:

आफू कहिले आउनुभयो ? — *When did you (yourself) come?*

भोलि आफू जान्छु । — *Tomorrow I (myself) will go.*

It is commonly used in conjunction with a pronoun (often आफै):

भोलि म आफै जान्छु ।	*Tomorrow I myself will go (so you don't have to).*
म त गर्दिनँ, तपाईं आफै गर्नुस् ।	*I won't do it; do it yourself.*
मेरो आफ्नो देश	*my own country*
तिमी तिम्रो आफ्नो घर जाऊ ।	*Go to your own house.*
हामी आफैले यो गर्नुपर्छ ।	*We have to do it ourselves.*

Emphatic for आफु, आफुले, आफ्नो, आफुलाई, आफुसँग, आफुमा = आफै, आफैले, आफ्नै, आफैलाई, आफैसँग, आफैमा

➤ 9.3 INDEFINITE FUTURE (–ला).

	INDEF FUTURE	SIMPLE INDEF
म	खा-उँला	खान्छु होला
तपाईं	खानु -होला	खानुहुन्छ होला
हामी	खा -औंला	खान्छौं होला
तिमी	खा -औला	खान्छौ होला
उनी	खा -लान्	खान्छन् होला
ऊ	खा -ला	खान्छ होला

In our text we have धेरै समय लाग्ला. In the simple indefinite tense, this would have been conjugated धेरै समय लाग्छ, meaning *It takes/will take a long time.* In the indefinite future, it means *It will probably take a long time.*

It is possible to use the word होला after a simple indefinite sentence for the same effect. For example, धेरै समय लाग्छ होला has the same meaning as धेरै समय लाग्ला. The former is certainly easier to use, because otherwise you will need to learn how to conjugate the indefinite future for each pronoun.

➤ 9.4 –कहाँ *(often shortened as* काँ) *TO THE PLACE OF X.*

म साथीकहाँ जाँदै छु ।	*I'm going to my friends place.*

➤ 9.5 PRESENT PERFECT.

This tense expresses a present state resulting from a past action, or a past situation that has present relevance. It roughly corresponds to the English *have X-ed* and this covers the majority of the uses.

म पोखरा गएको छु ।	*I **have** gone to Pokhara.*
हामीले तरकारी किनेका छौं ।	*We **have** bought vegetables.*
मैले विचार गरेको छु ।	*I **have** thought about it.*

There are, however, a few uses that don't correspond to the English *have*. The first is in combination with the verbs लाग्नु and पर्नु.

मलाई डर लागेको छैन ।	*I am not afraid.*
मलाई खाना मनपरेको छैन ।	*I don't like the food.*
मलाई धेरै किन्नुपरेको छ ।	*I need to buy lots of things (this moment).*
मलाई त्यहाँ जान मनलागेको छ ।	*I want to go there.*

The literal meaning of these sentences is a little more consistent with *have*:

मलाई डर लागेको छैन ।	*Fear* ***hasn't*** *captured me.*
मलाई खाना मनपरेको छैन ।	*The food* ***hasn't*** *fallen into my heart.*
मलाई धेरै किन्नुपरेको छ ।	*It* ***has*** *fallen that I need to buy a lot.*
मलाई त्यहाँ जान मनलागेको छैन ।	*It* ***has not*** *grabbed my heart to go there.*

The second use that doesn't correspond to the English *have* is in connection with the verbs जान्नु *to know (a fact)* and चिन्नु *to know (a person).*

मैले नेपाली बोल्न जानेको छु ।	*I know how to speak Nepali.*
मैले उहाँलाई चिनेको छु ।	*I know him.*

The present perfect is conjugated as follows:

म	-एको छु	-एको छैन
हामी	-एका छौं	-एका छैनौं
तिमी	-एका छौ	-एको छैनौ
तपाईं/उहाँ	-नु भएको छ	-नु भएको छैन
ऊ	-एको छ	-एको छैन

➤ 9.6 -ले IN THE PRESENT PERFECT.

The primary use of -ले that you've learned so far is adding it to the subject if the verb of that sentence is transitive (5.4). This is also true for present (and past) perfect, which you've just learned.

हामीले तरकारी किनेका छौं ।	*We have bought vegetables.*

➤ 9.7 -(को कारण)ले (गर्दा) *BECAUSE, BY REASON OF.*

When suffixing -ले and -को कारणले to a noun, they are suffixed directly:

यो बेक्टेरियाको कारणले हुन सक्छ ।	*It could be by reason of bacteria.*
यो बेक्टेरियाले हुन सक्छ ।	*It could be because of bacteria.*
नउमालेको पानीले म बिरामी भएँ ।	*I am sick because of (drinking) unboiled water.*

त्यसैले म जाँदिनँ । *Because of that, I won't go.*

ज्वर आएकोले म सुत्छु । *Because of getting a fever, I'm going to bed.*

They cannot be directly suffixed to an adjective; only to the verb that the adjective modifies.

ढिलो आएको कारणले... *By reason of being late...*

ढिलो आएकोले... *Because of being late...*

For more on suffixing to a verb, see the *Complex Verb* section of this chapter.

➤ 9.8 –एर'S ALTERNATE –ई / इकन (Negative न–इ(कन)

-एर's exact alternative is -ई (sometimes written -इ):

थाहा पाएर अथवा थाहा नपाई... *With or without knowing.*

म खाना खाएर/खाई बजार जान्छु। *Having eaten, I will go to the bazaar.*

➤ 9.9 भन्दा *THAN, MORE THAN.*

उपचार गर्नुभन्दा रोग लाग्न नदिनु राम्रो हो। *It's better to prevent disease **than** to treat it.*

पोखराभन्दा काठमाडौं ठूलो छ । *KTM is bigger **than** Pokhara.*

काठमाडौं पोखराभन्दा ठूलो छ । *KTM is bigger **than** Pokhara.*

➤9.10 USES OF जस्तो. Emphatic: जस्तै Synonym: झैं

- ***LIKE, AS:***

मेरो घडी तपाईंको जस्तो छैन । *My watch is not like yours.*

योजस्तो घडी महँगो हुन्छ । *Watches like this are expensive.*

तपाईंको जस्तो कलम मेरो छैन । *I don't have a pen like yours.*

रोगजस्तो डरलाग्दो *dangerous like a disease*

जस्तो बाबु उस्तै छोरा । *Like father like son.*

म तपाईंजस्तो छिटो हिँड्न सक्दिनँ । *I can't walk fast like you.*

मजस्तो बिस्तारै हिँड्नुस् । *Walk slowly like me.*

- ***SEEMS LIKE, LOOKS LIKE:***

तपाईं बिरामीजस्तो देखिनुहुन्छ । *You look sick.*

आज पानी पर्लाजस्तो छ । *It looks like it's going to rain today.*

मलाई यो ठिक होइनजस्तो लाग्यो । *I felt like this wasn't right.*

- ***SUCH AS:***

धेरै पाइन्छ । जस्तै: साबुन, रोटी... — *A lot is available. Such as: soap, bread...*

COMPLEX VERBS

- **-एको कारणले (गर्दा) / एकोले** — ***because, by reason of...***(past events)

ढिलो आएको (कारण)ले (गर्दा)...	*By reason of being late...*
पानी परेको (कारण)ले (गर्दा), म गइनँ ।	*Because of it raining, I didn't go.*
ऊ आएको (कारण)ले (गर्दा)...	*Because he came...*

- **-ना(को कारण)ले (गर्दा)** — ***because, by reason of...***(past and present)

ढिलो आउना(को कारण)ले (गर्दा)	*By reason of being late...*
पानी पर्ना(को कारण)ले (गर्दा), म गइनँ ।	*Because of it raining, I didn't go.*
ऊ आउना(को कारण)ले (गर्दा)...	*Because he came...*

- **-दा(खेरि)** — ***while ... ing, when***

नेपालमा बस्दा(खेरि) खाने पानी उमाल्नु पर्छ।	***While*** *living in Nepal, drinking water needs to be boiled.*
नेपाली सिक्दा(खेरि) सुत्नु हुँदैन ।	***While*** *studying Nepali, sleeping is not allowed.*
पानी पर्दा(खेरि) म गइनँ ।	***While*** *it was raining, I didn't go.*

- **-नुभन्दा पहिल्यै / पहिले नै** — ***before..., already before***

हिँड्नुभन्दा पहिल्यै हामीले खायौं ।	***Before*** *we walked, we ate.*
साँझ पर्नुभन्दा पहिल्यै पुग्न सकिन्छ ।	*It's possible to arrive* ***before*** *dusk.*
बास खोज्नुभन्दा पहिल्यै साँझ पर्‍यो ।	*It turned dusk* ***before*** *we looked for shelter.*

- **-एको देखेर** — ***seeing, having seen...***

खाली ट्याक्सी आएको देखेर मैले त्यसलाई रोकेँ ।	***Seeing*** *an empty taxi come, I stopped it.*
अरूले धाराको पानी सिधै खाएको देखेर...	***Seeing*** *others directly drinking tap water...*
पानी परेको देखेर म गइनँ ।	***Seeing*** *it was raining, I didn't go.*

- **-ए(को) जस्तो / ए(को) जस्तै** — ***do as... / as, exactly as...***

म तपाईंले भनेजस्तै गर्छु ।	*I'll do* ***exactly as*** *you say.*
मैले पकाएजस्तो खाना पकाउनुस् ।	*Cook* ***as*** *I cook.*
मैले नेपाली बोलेजस्तो बोल्नुस् ।	*Speak Nepali* ***as*** *I speak (it).*

- **-ए(को) जस्तो गर्नु** — ***do as if, pretend...***

  उसले सुतेजस्तो गऱ्यो । — *He **pretended** to sleep.*

  उसले रोग लागेकोजस्तो गऱ्यो । — *He **pretended** he was sick.*

- **-न मन लाग्नु** — ***feel like, want to...***(takes -लाई)

  मलाई गाउँमा घुम्न मनलाग्यो । — *I **feel like** strolling in the village.*

  (तपाईंलाई) खान मनलाग्छ होला । — *(You) will probably **feel like** eating.*

  मलाई त्यहाँ जान मनलागेको छ । — *I **want to** go there.*

PRACTICE

1. For each of the sentences, translate (English and Nepali) and complete.

   a) तरकारी महँगो भएको कारणले (गर्दा)...

   b) मेच धेरै कमजोर भएको कारणले (गर्दा)...

   c) बाटो साँघुरो भएको कारणले (गर्दा)...

   d) Because the taxi driver drove fast...

   e) Because he called me...

   f) Because we walked uphill...

   g) Because he drank unboiled water...

   h) Because they were good friends...

2. Repeat each sentence of #1 using -एकोले and -ना(को कारण)ले. Give a new result for each sentence.

3. Translate (English and Nepali) and complete each sentence with *two* phrases.

   a) साहुजीसँग बोल्दा(खेरि)...

   b) मेरो लुगा धुँदा(खेरि)...

   c) ट्याक्सी चलाउँदा(खेरि)...

   d) भुइँमा कुचो लगाउँदा(खेरि)...

   e) ओरालो बाटोमा हिँड्दा(खेरि)...

   f) While studying Nepali...

   g) While working in the office...

   h) While searching for porters...

   i) While having a fever...

   j) While strolling around Kathmandu...

   k) While having a headache...

   l) While I am hungry

4. Translate (English and Nepali) and complete each of the sentences:
   a) पानी खानुभन्दा पहिल्यै...
   b) साँझ पर्नुभन्दा पहिल्यै...
   c) बिरामी हुनुभन्दा पहिल्यै...
   d) Before he sat in the chair...
   e) Before she got a fever...
   f) Before the bus came...
   g) Before phoning his mother...

5. Translate (English and Nepali) and complete each of the sentences:
   a) त्यस मान्छेले पानी खाएको देखेर...
   b) डाक्टर आएको देखेर...
   c) मेरी बहिनी सुतेको देखेर...
   d) Seeing the man bargain at the store...
   e) Seeing my wife studying ...

6. Using -इ, build a sentence with the verbs supplied:

वाकवाक लाग्नु	-ई	सुत्नु
सोध्नु	-ई	बस्नु
पुग्नु	-ई	रोक्नु
खानु	-ई	जानु
-न नसक्नु	-ई	-न थाल्नु

7. Repeat #6, but use negatives to give the meaning *without... ing.*

8. Using भन्दा make *two* comparisons using each of the following adjectives: राम्रो, ठूलो, टाढा, मीठो, छिटो, गाह्रो, अनुभवी, ढिलो, पुरानो, महत्त्वपूर्ण

9. Conjugate the following verbs in the present perfect, positive and negative (use -ले whenever necessary) for म, हामी, तिमी, तपाईं/उहाँ, ऊ, उनी: फर्कनु, पिउनु, टोक्नु

10. Translate the following using the appropriate tense:
    a) I had a fever.
    b) I didn't have a fever.
    c) I have a fever.
    d) I don't have a fever.

11. Using the word जस्तो , translate the following sentences:
    a) The shopkeeper looked just like my dad.
    b) My sister is just like my mother.
    c) This is tasty like a mango.
    d) That organization is just like TEAM.
    e) That house is just like mine.
    f) My house is not like your house.
    g) I don't have a house like yours.
    h) "like father like son"

12. Translate the following sentences using -ए(को) जस्तै/जस्तो:
    a) He can't do as I do.
    b) Shopping in Nepal is not like shopping in my country.
    c) Cook the food just as a Nepali cooks.
    d) Stop the taxi just like that car stopped.
    e) Speak Nepali just like that foreigner spoke.

13. Translate the following sentences using -ए(को) जस्तै/जस्तो गर्नु:
    a) Pretend you have a fever.
    b) Pretend your body hurts.
    c) I pretended I was thinking.
    d) He always pretends that he is sick.

14. Translate the following sentences using -बाहेक:
    a) besides this
    b) Besides Malaria, Nepal has other diseases.
    c) Besides me, no one went.
    d) Besides salt, we don't need anything.
    e) Besides him, we all speak Nepali.

LET'S TALK

1. Using the structure -भन्दा पहिल्यै your tutor describes his/her morning in reverse. For example, "Before I sat down, I opened the door. Before I opened the door, I walked to class. Before I walked to class, I cooked breakfast...". **Reverse roles.**

2. Each of you tell the other about what the immediate future holds. For example, do you have any travels planned? Are you going shopping, etc. However, things being uncertain as they are, use *only* the indefinite future.

3. Each of you name all the countries you *have* been to (present perfect).

4. Now, name all the countries the other person has been to (present perfect).

5. Make up and tell your tutor a story. In this story, *all* of the following words must be used (in any order--check them off as you go). You will have to be very creative.

कालो पर्दा	सानो कोठा	हिन्दी	आँप
साबुन	आलु	गाडी	पुल
कुचो	शनिबार	फुर्सद	भरिया
दिनहुँ	नदी	वाकवाक लाग्नु	खोप

6. Using the phrase म तपाईंजस्तो छु; किनभने... each of you describe at least ten things that you have in common. Using the phrase म तपाईंजस्तो छैन; किनभने... each of you describe at least five things that you don't have in common.

7. Using the phrase नेपाली सिकाउनाको कारणले... your tutor tells you five things that result. Using the phrase नेपाली सिक्नाको कारणले... tell your tutor five things that result.

8. Ask about the last time (पछिल्लो पटक) your tutor was sick. **Reverse roles**.

9. Using भन्दा take turns with your tutor ranking each of the following list according to your likes. If you can, give reasons why:

कालो	पाटन	स्याउ	बिहान	शनिबार
निलो	ठमेल	सुन्तला	दिउँसो	आइतबार
हरियो	पोखरा	केरा	साँझ	सोमबार
रातो	काठमाडौं	आँप	राति	बुधबार

10. Difficult as it may be, take turns giving each other different commands that can be acted out in the classroom *using the तिमी form*. Remember, you are role playing!

11. Use the present perfect tense to describe things that you *have* done. Take turns. Each of you should be able to produce some twenty or thirty sentences. For some ideas:

    foods you have eaten
    languages you have studied
    schools you have gone to
    work you have done
    place you have gone shopping
    illnesses you have had
    etc.

12. Recalling as much as you can of the other person from #11, retell what the other person did using the तिमी form. In other words, your tutor will tell you, "You have..., you have..., you have..." each time using तिमी. Then reverse roles. It may be awkward, but it requires practice.

13. Discuss what you do and don't feel like doing (using मन लाग्नु) when:
    a) you have lots of work
    b) you have a fever
    c) a friend comes to visit
    d) you make a mistake
    e) can't find a taxi

IN THE COMMUNITY

Remember, the goal of each chapter is to equip you for the community assignment. In other words, the chapter itself is secondary to what you accomplish in the community. Place the highest importance on that time. It's the difference between playing a flight simulator and actually flying the plane.

1. In the community, ask the following questions of at least 3 people, or until you've spent 2 hrs. in conversation.
    a) Do you boil your water?
    b) How important (महत्त्वपूर्ण) is it to boil drinking water?
    c) If you get a fever, what do you do?
       (Hint: since you only touched on if-clauses in 7.4, say "After you get a fever...")
    d) When do you go to the hospital? (तपाईं अस्पताल कहिले जानुहुन्छ ?)

e) When do you take medicine? (तपाईँ कहिले औषधि खानुहुन्छ ?)
f) Have you ever had malaria? (तपाईँलाई कहिल्यै औलो लागेको छ ?)
g) Do they know what causes malaria? (औलो ज्वरोको कारण के होला ?)
(Hint: using के होला ? is less demanding than के हो ?)
h) How are diseases spread? (रोगहरू कसरी सर्छन् होला ?)
i) What vaccinations have you had? (तपाईँले कुन-कुन खोप लिनुभएको छ ?)
j) You're free to ask other questions as well!

The following text may be helpful to you in starting out:

म तपाईँलाई केही सोध्न सक्छु ? म अहिले नेपाली पढ्छु । पढेको पाँच महिना मात्र भयो, त्यसकारण म अलिअलि मात्र नेपाली बोल्छु । अहिले म स्वास्थ्यको बारेमा पढ्छु । स्वास्थ्यको बारेमा केही सोध्न सक्छु ?

2. Ask the following questions of at least 4 young children below their teens (or until your conversation time totals 1 hour) and practice the तिमी forms:
   a) What is your name?
   b) How old are you (तिमी कति वर्ष भयौ?)
   c) Where do you go to school? (तिमी कुन स्कूल जान्छौ)
   d) Do you like school?
   e) Where do you live?
   f) Do you have brothers or sisters?
   g) Anything else you want to ask.

3. This is mostly an observational assignment. **Time required**: 1 hr. Find a local pharmacy (the bigger the better) to simply sit in. Watch and observe who comes for medicine. What ailments do they have? How much diagnosing does the pharmacist do? How many come with hospital prescriptions? As with any assignment in a store/market, you can always begin by buying *one* thing. A couple aspirins and a throat lozenge won't cost much but will eliminate suspicion. After you buy a little, ask if you can ask a few questions. Explain that you're studying Nepali. Then ask if you can sit down, and you're set to go. (Hint: if you are a medical professional, you might not want to let them know or they may feel like they're under scrutiny). When there are no customers, take the time to ask the pharmacist some questions. How long did he/she study medicine (उहाँले औषधिको बारेमा कति महिना पढ्नुभयो ?)? Where? Was it difficult? etc.

DID YOU KNOW?

There are literally thousands of home remedies and cures for every ailment imaginable. These may or may not have religious connotations. Nepalis seem to be willing to try anything for a cure, from home remedies to Aruvedic medicine to modern medicine. In the hills, consulting a shaman is very common. Other times, the sacrifice of an animal may be required. Physical sickness is often viewed as having a non-physical cause and is closely associated with ritual purity. It may be caused by the planets, eating something that is ritually impure, black magic, etc.

The jutho concept:
This is a very strong concept among Hindus and should not be underestimated. Any food that comes into contact with anything that has been in contact with the mouth is considered *ritually* impure, that is, *jutho*. For example, if I serve myself some food with a spoon I've been eating with, all the food in that container is considered impure. When drinking, if I touch my lips to the container, it becomes ritually impure and undrinkable for anyone else. While still eating, if I touch any food with my left hand, all the food in that container becomes *jutho*.

The evil eye concept:
You may have noticed onions and peppers hanging from the ceilings of tea shops and other stores. This is to ward off the evil eye. If someone looks at something (usually applies to children and food) with evil intent, jealousy or great desire, that object becomes contaminated. For example, complementing the appearance of someone's baby may signal underlying jealousy or desire to have such a baby. If so, the evil eye has struck and the baby may become sick and die. Therefore, some parents may not want people to compliment them about their baby. Or if you carry food in public that is not covered, someone who is really hungry may want it. As a result, whoever eats that food will get sick.

There are also numerous superstitions associated with health and physical well being. For example (all but the last taken from *Nepalese Customs and Manners*),

- If you touch your throat, blow on your fingers or you will grow a goiter.
- Wednesday is a good day to visit the doctor.

- After a trip to the Terai, some people drink a glass of water in which an "anti-malarial" herb has been soaked.
- Some foods should not be consumed in combination with other foods. For example, ginger and pumpkin is believed to cause leprosy.
- On the evening after a baby has been vaccinated for smallpox, no relative should place a red pepper over hot coals.
- During her menstrual period, a women is ritually impure. Any person or food she comes into contact with is considered impure. During that time, she is not even to enter the kitchen (one blessing!).

- For an earache, just across the Bagmati bridge going into Patan there is a shrine especially for that. Offer a coin there to the earache god.
- For a toothache, drive a nail into the block of wood found at Bangemuda, the toothache god.
- You shouldn't turn the head of your bed north because the magnetic attraction of the North Pole is harmful.

CHAPTER 10

NEPAL'S CLIMATE AND WEATHER
नेपालको हावापानी र मौसम

VOCABULARY					
हावापानी	climate	प्राकृतिक	natural	असार	June-July
नक्सा	map, drawing	समुद्र	sea	साउन	July-Aug
पूर्व	East	सतह	surface; level	भदौ	Aug-Sept
पश्चिम	West	उचाइ	height, altitude	असोज	Sept-Oct
उस्तै	same as, similar	लाग्नु	to begin, set off	कात्तिक	Oct-Nov
अनुसार	according to	बढ्दै जानु	continue increasing	मंसिर	Nov-Dec
फरक	different	बढी	a lot, so much, more, excess	पुस	Dec-Jan
पूर्वी	eastern	उत्तर	North	माघ	Jan-Feb
सबभन्दा	(the) most of all, compared to all	जमिन	land	फागुन	Feb-Mar
थोरै	a little	तथा	and (literary)	चैत	Mar-Apr
पहाड	hill, mountain	हुने हुनाले	because (it) is	मुसलधारे	torrential (rain)
पहाडी	mountainous, hilly	पसिना	sweat	भिज्नु	get wet, soaked
भेग	locality, area, region	जीवन	life; lifetime	आँधीबेहरी	big storm, hurricane, typhoon, cyclone
हिउँद	winter	कठिन	difficult	हिउँ पर्नु	to snow
वर्षा	rain; rainy season	हुस्सु लाग्नु	to fog, be foggy	घाम लाग्नु	shine, be sunny
-को बीचमा	in between/middle	कुहिरो लाग्नु	to mist, be misty	आकाश	sky
हुरी	gale, storm	शीत पर्नु	to dew	न्यानो	warm
बतास	wind	तुसारो पर्नु	to frost	तापक्रम	temperature
चल्नु	move (intr)	बाक्लो	thick	जम्नु	to freeze
मेघ गर्जनु	thunder (cloud roar)	सिरक	quilt	बादल लाग्नु	to become cloudy
-सहित	with, including	-को आवश्यकता	necessity of	तुवाँलो लाग्नु	to be hazy
असिना पर्नु	to hail	दक्षिण	South	छाता	umbrella
धूलो	dust	सुख्खा	dry		
देखि	from, since	बैसाख	Apr-May		
उड्नु	fly (intr)	जेठ	May-June	**Note: All these words are connected to table 10.2**	

USEFUL PHRASES

- पानी पर्लाजस्तो छ । *It looks like it's going to rain.*
- एकछिन पर्खनुस् । *Please wait a while.*
- कस्तो गर्मी, हगि ? *It's really hot, isn't it?*
- खाने बेला भयो *It's time to eat.*
- मलाई आज हतार छ । *I'm in a hurry today.*
- पानी पर्न लाग्यो । *It's about to rain.*
- जसरी भए पनि । *By all means. Whatever it takes. Anyhow, In whatever manner possible*
- मैले भने(को) अनुसार... *According to what I said...,*

TEXT

तपाईँ नेपालको नक्सा हेर्नुस् । नेपाल पूर्व मेचीदेखि पश्चिम महाकालीसम्म फैलिएको छ । तर नेपालका सबै ठाउँको हावापानी उस्तै छैन । ठाउँअनुसार यहाँको हावापानी फरक छ । नेपालको पूर्वी तराईमा सबभन्दा धेरै पानी पर्छ । हामी जतिजति नेपालको पश्चिमतिर जान्छौँ उतिउति थोरै पानी पर्छ । पश्चिम नेपालमा सबभन्दा थोरै पानी पर्छ । फेरि यहाँ तराईमा भन्दा पहाडमा कम पानी पर्छ । पश्चिम नेपालको पहाडी भेगमा एकदम थोरै पानी पर्छ ।

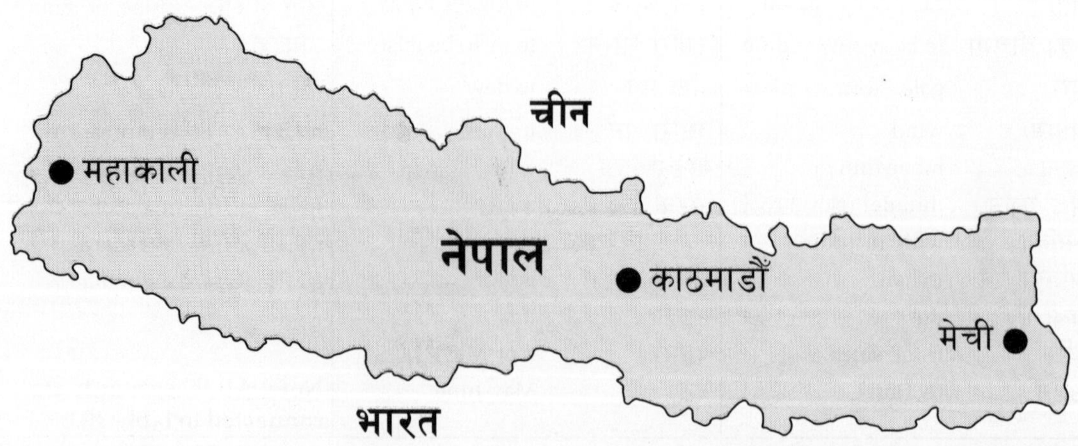

त्यसै गरी असार र साउनमा सबभन्दा धेरै पानी पर्छ अनि यहाँ हिउँदमा सुख्खा हुन्छ । हिउँद र वर्षा महिनाको बीचमा कहिलेकाहीँ हुरीबतास चल्छ र मेघगर्जनसहितको पानी पर्छ । यहाँ कहिलेकाहीँ असिना पनि पर्छ । त्यसबेला धेरैजसो सुख्खा हुन्छ र धूलो उड्छ । तर वर्षा र हिउँद महिनाको बीचमा मौसम एकदम रमाइलो हुन्छ । पानी उस्तो पर्दैन तर प्राकृतिक दृश्य पनि हरियो अनि सफा देखिन्छ ।

समुद्र सतहभन्दा थोरै उचाइमा भएकोले तराईमा गर्मी हुन्छ । हामी जतिजति पश्चिमतिर लाग्छौं त्यतित्यति गर्मी बढ्दै जान्छ । पश्चिम नेपालको तराईमा सबभन्दा बढी गर्मी हुन्छ । यहाँ तराईमा भन्दा पहाडमा कम गर्मी हुन्छ अनि हिमालमा सबभन्दा जाडो हुन्छ । हामी तराईबाट जतिजति उत्तरतिर जान्छौं त्यतित्यति जमिनको उचाइ बढ्छ । त्यसकारण जाडो पनि बढ्दै जान्छ ।

त्यसरी नै चैत-वैशाखमा सबभन्दा गर्मी हुन्छ र पुस-माघमा सबभन्दा जाडो हुन्छ । चैत-वैशाखमा गर्मी तथा सुख्खा हुने हुनाले पानीको दुःख हुन्छ । यतिबेला पसिना आउँछ, रोग लाग्छ, जीवन कठिन हुन्छ । पुसमाघमा अर्थात् हिउँदमा जाडो मात्र होइन सुख्खा पनि हुन्छ । त्यसबेला हुस्सु र कुहिरो लाग्छ । कहिलेकाहीँ बिहान शीत र तुसारो पनि पर्छ । बाक्लो लुगा, सिरक, ज्याकेट, स्वेटर, धेरै खाना यस समयका आवश्यकताहरू हुन् ।

GRAMMAR

➤ 10.1 –देखि VERSUS –बाट.

In ch. 7, you used -बाट to mean *from*. -देखि also means *from*, but it is a little broader in its use. -देखि can be used for both place and time (*from Pokhara* or *from 12 o'clock*), whereas -बाट is only supposed to be used with places. I say supposed to because it is also often used for time as well, particularly in West Nepal.

मेची**देखि** महाकालीसम्म	***from*** *Mechi to Mahakali*
मेची**बाट** महाकालीसम्म	***from*** *Mechi to Mahakali*
एक बजे**देखि**	***from/since*** *one o'clock*
एक बजे**बाट**	***from*** *one o'clock (considered wrong, but spoken)*
एक बजे**पछि**	***after*** *one o'clock*

➤ 10.2 DEMONSTRATIVES AND QUESTION WORDS.

Nepali has a myriad of demonstratives and corresponding words. The following chart is given so that you can see them all together in one place.

Question W	Emph	Demonstrative	Emph	Demonstrative	Emph	Demonstr.	Emph
के *what*	केही	त्यो *that (thing)*	त्यही	ऊ *far away thing*	उही	यो *this (thing)*	यही
को *who*	कोही	त्यो *he, she, it*	त्यही	ऊ *he, she, it*	उही	यो *he, she, it*	यही
कसले *who (tr.)*	कसैले	त्यसले *he, she, it*	त्यसैले	उसले *he, she, it*	उसैले	यसले *he, she, it*	यसैले
कसलाई *to whom*	कसैलाई	त्यसलाई *to him/her*	त्यसैलाई	उसलाई *to him/her*	उसैलाई	यसलाई *to him/her*	यसैलाई
कसको *whose*	कसैको	त्यसको *his/her/its*	त्यसैको	उसको *his/her*	उसैको	यसको *his/her/its*	यसैको
कहाँ *where*	कहीँ	त्यहाँ *there*	त्यहीँ	उहाँ *there*	उहीँ	यहाँ *here*	यहीँ
कता *whither*	कतै	त्यता *thither*	त्यतै त्यता नै	उता *thither*	उतै उता नै	यता *hither*	यतै यता नै
कसरी *how*	कसै गरी	त्यसरी *that way*	त्यसै गरी त्यसरी नै	उसरी *that way*	उसै गरी उसरी नै	यसरी *this way*	यसै गरी यसरी नै
कहिले *when*	कहिल्यै	तहिले *at that time*	त्यसै बेला	उहिले *at that time*	उहिल्यै	अहिले *now*	अहिल्यै
कति *how much*	कत्ति	त्यति *that much*	त्यत्ति त्यति नै	उति *(only relative)*	उत्ति उति नै	यति *this much*	यत्ति यति नै
कस्तो *what kind*	कस्तै	त्यस्तो *that kind*	त्यस्तै	उस्तो *the same*	उस्तै	यस्तो *this kind*	यस्तै
कुन *which*	कुनै	-	-	-	-	-	-

You will notice that the first and second set of demonstratives (त्यो, ऊ; त्यहाँ, उहाँ; त्यता, उता etc.) are fairly synonymous. Where they are synonymous, the first set is more common.

➤ 10.3 QUESTION WORDS AND RELITIVIZATION.

In our text, we have the sequence of words जति...त्यति and जति...उति. These are examples of relitivization. That is, the use of a relative pronoun (*who, which, whom, whose* and *that*) or relative adverb (*when, the more, however much,* etc.) to introduce a post-modifying clause: *the man* ***who****..., the bird* ***that****...,* ***when*** *I came*....They are formed from their corresponding question words. For example, the question word कहाँ becomes जहाँ to mean *wher**ever.*** कसरी becomes जसरी to mean *how**ever.*** The Tuborg beer signs you see everywhere say, तपाईं जहाँ भएपनि *wherever you are*. Study the table below to get an idea of how it works. Note that in complete sentences, the relative pronoun/adverb is always found first in a sequence that includes the corresponding demonstrative: *who...that, wherever...there, whenever...then*, etc.

QW	Relative Pronoun/Adverb		
के *what*	जे…त्यो / त्यही	जे छ त्यो दिनुस् ।	**Whatever** there is, give me that.
को *who*	जो…त्यो / त्यही	जो आयो त्यो मेरो भाइ हो ।	**The one who** came is my brother.
कसले *who (tr.)*	जसले…त्यसले / त्यसैले	जसले मह काढ्छ त्यसले हात चाट्छ।	**The one who** collects honey licks his hands.
कसको *whose*	जसको…त्यसको	जसको सिङ छैन त्यसैको नाम तिखे।	**The one** who dosen't have horns …
कसलाई *to whom*	जसलाई… त्यसलाई / त्यसैलाई	जसलाई म चिन्दिनँ त्यसको कुरा नगरौं।	**Let's not** talk about the one whom I don't know.
कहाँ *where*	जहाँ…त्यहाँ / त्यहीं	जहाँ हिउँ पर्छ त्यहाँ जाडो हुन्छ ।	**Wherever** snow falls, there it's cold.
कता *whither*	जता…उतै	जता हेर्‍यो*, उतै पानी ।	**Wherever** you look, there's water.
कसरी *how*	जसरी…उसरी / उसरी नै	जसरी सिकाएँ उसरी गर्नुस् ।	**However** I taught you, do it the same way.
कहिले *when*	जहिले…तहिले	म जहिले आएँ तहिले तिमी थिएनौ ।	**When** I came, you weren't there.
	जब…तब	जब म आएँ, तब तिमी थिएनौ	**When** I came, you weren't there.
कति *how much*	जति…त्यति	जति घाम लाग्छ त्यति गर्मी हुन्छ ।	**The more** the sun shines the hotter it gets.
कस्तो *what kind*	जस्तो … त्यस्तै	जस्तो मनपर्छ त्यस्तै किन्नुस्।	Buy **whatever** kind you like.
कुन *which*	जुन …. (त्यो)	जुन ठाउँमा बस्यो* त्यहीँ ठाउँ राम्रो।	**Whichever** place you live at you like.

* **gramatically it is** हेरियो, बसियो **instead of** हेर्‍यो, बस्यो

➤ 10.4 QUESTION WORDS USED AS ADJECTIVES.

You have already had two question words used as adjectives:

Ch 6- केही खबर छ कि ? *Is there **any** message?*
Ch 7- कहिले उकालो, कहिले ओरालो ***sometimes** uphill, **sometimes** downhill*

When a question word is used as an adjective or adverb, the emphatic form is almost always used. In a positive sentence, question words can be used to mean *some* or *any* : that is, *someone, anywhere, sometimes*, etc. It's meaning is derived from context. In a negative sentence, they mean *none*: that is, *never, nowhere, no one*, etc. Note the use of पनि in connection with these words.

WITH POS VERB - *SOME/ANY*		WITH NEG VERB - *NONE*	
केही काम छ ?	Do you have **any** work?	छैन । **केही पनि** छैन ।	No, there's **none**.
त्यो कोठामा **कोही** छ ?	Is there **anyone** in the room?	**कोही** आएन	**No one** came.
कोही पनि जान सक्छन् ।	**Anyone** can go.	छैन । **कोही पनि** छैन ।	No, **no one is there**.
कहीं पानी पऱ्यो ।	It rained **somewhere**.	पानी **कहीं (पनि)** परेन ।	It rained **nowhere**.
कलम **कतै** होला ।	The pen may be **somewhere**.	कलम **कतै (पनि)** छैन ।	The pen is **nowhere**.
कहिलेकाहीं त्यस्तो हुन्छ ।	**Sometimes** that happens.	म **कहिल्यै** त्यो खान्नँ ।	I **never** eat that.
कुनै ठाउँमा (कहीं)	In **some** place.	**कहिल्यै (पनि)** हुँदैन ।	That **never** happens.
कुनै पनि ठाउँमा	In **any** place.	**कुनै पनि** पैसा पाइएन ।	**No** money was found.

As you can see from the previous table, the use of पनि is not consistent. But since पनि is optionally or never used **in positive sentences, it is always safe to not use पनि**. And likewise, since पनि is optionally or always used **in negative sentences, it is always safe to use पनि.**

➤ 10.5 पनि WITH क-WORDS AND ज-WORDS.

In section 10.3 you learned how to use a ज-word in a relative clause. However, they can be used independently, similar to the क-words in 10.4. For example you can say, राम केही पनि खाँदैन *Ram eats nothing* (lit. *doesn't eat anything*) and राम जे पनि खान्छ *Ram eats anything*. You can say कोही पनि आउन हुँदैन *no one can came* or जो आए पनि हुन्छ *anyone can come.* Note that in this sentence कोही and पनि are immediately juxtaposed, whereas जो and पनि are separated by आए.

क...पनि (WITH NEG VERB)		ज...पनि (WITH POS VERB)	
केही पनि	nothing	जे पनि	whatever (anything)
कोही पनि	no one	जो पनि	whoever (anyone)
कसैले पनि *(tr.)*	no one	जसले पनि	whoever (anyone)
कसैलाई पनि	to no one	जसलाई पनि	whomever (to anyone)
कसैको पनि	no one's	जसको पनि	whoever's (anyone's)
कहीं पनि	no where	जहाँ पनि	wherever (anywhere)
कसै गरी पनि	in no way	जसरी पनि	however (in any way)
कहिले पनि	never	जहिले पनि	whenever (always)
कत्ति पनि	not at all	जत्ति पनि	however much
कुनै पनि	nothing	जुनै पनि	whatever (anything)

➤ 10.6 FORMING ADJECTIVES WITH –ई.

One way (among others) to make an adjective from a noun is to suffix -ई:

पूर्व	➡ पूर्वी *eastern*	दक्षिण	➡ दक्षिणी *southern*
पश्चिम	➡ पश्चिमी *western*	पहाड	➡ पहाडी *mountainous*
उत्तर	➡ उत्तरी *northern*	हिमाल	➡ हिमाली *Himalayan*
नेपाल	➡ नेपाली *Nepalese*	विदेश	➡ विदेशी *foreign(er)*

➤ 10.7 पर्नु, लाग्नु and हुनु FOR DIFFERENT WEATHER.

Things that are a liquid or solid (and therefore fall) collocate with पर्नु. Things that are gas or ethereal collocate with लाग्नु. Things that are conditions/states collocate with हुनु.

पर्नु : पानी पर्नु, असिना पर्नु, शीत पर्नु, तुसारो पर्नु, हिउँ पर्नु
लाग्नु : घाम लाग्नु, बादल लाग्नु, हुस्सू लाग्नु, कुहिरो लाग्नु, तुवाँलो लाग्नु
हुनु : गर्मी हुनु, जाडो हुनु, सुख्खा हुनु, हिलो हुनु,
चल्नु : हावा, हुरी, बतास, आँधि, आँधिबेहरी
जानु : भुइँचालो, भूकम्प (earthquake), पहिरो
आउनु : बाढी

➤ 10.8 WEATHER AND TENSE.

The tenses that are used for weather do not correlate neatly with English and can therefore be very confusing. For example, Nepali uses the past tense पानी पर्‍यो to mean *it is raining*. See the following chart:

SIMPLE INDEFINITE (for general or immediate future)			
पानी पर्छ ।	it rains (general)/it will rain	पानी पर्दैन ।	it doesn't rain (gen)/it won't rain
घाम लाग्छ ।	it's sunny (gen.)/it will be sunny	घाम लाग्दैन ।	it isn't sunny (gen.)/it won't be sunny
गर्मी छ ।	it's hot (now)	गर्मी छैन ।	it isn't hot (now)
गर्मी हुन्छ ।	it's hot (general)/it will be hot	गर्मी हुँदैन ।	it's not hot (general)/it won't be hot
SIMPLE PAST (positive also used for present)			
पानी पर्‍यो ।	it rained/is raining	पानी परेन ।	it didn't rain
घाम लाग्यो ।	it was/is sunny	घाम लागेन ।	it wasn't sunny
गर्मी थियो ।	it was hot	गर्मी थिएन ।	it wasn't hot
गर्मी भयो ।	it became/is hot	गर्मी भएन ।	it did not become hot

PRESENT PERFECT (positive also used for continuous)			
पानी परेको छ ।	it has rained (in the past); it is (and has been) raining (now)	पानी परेको छैन।	it hasn't rained/isn't raining (yet)
घाम लागेको छ ।	it has been sunny (in the past); it is (and has been) sunny (now)	घाम लागेको छैन।	it hasn't been sunny/isn't sunny (yet)
गर्मी भएको छ ।	it has been/has become hot	गर्मी भएको छैन।	it hasn't been/hasn't become hot (yet)
CONTINUOUS			
पानी पर्दै छ ।	it is raining now; it rains (these days)	(Negative rare, even for 2nd continuos)	
घाम लाग्दै छ ।	it is sunny now;		
गर्मी हुँदै छ ।	it is about to be hot		

Based on the above, this is how you would say...

1. It is raining: पानी पर्‍यो । It is hot: गर्मी छ, गर्मी भयो ।
   पानी पर्दैछ । It isn't hot: गर्मी छैन ।
   पानी परेको छ ।
   पानी परिरहेको छ । It was hot: गर्मी थियो ।
   It isn't raining: पानी परेको छैन । It wasn't hot: गर्मी थिएन ।
2. It rained: पानी पर्‍यो ।
   It didn't rain: पानी परेन । It will be hot: गर्मी हुन्छ ।
3. It will rain: पानी पर्छ, पानी पर्ला । It won't be hot: गर्मी हुँदैन ।
   It won't rain: पानी पर्दैन ।
4. It has rained: पानी परेको छ । It has been hot: गर्मी भएको छ ।
   It hasn't rained: पानी परेको छैन । It hasn't been hot: गर्मी भएको छैन ।
5. It rains (generally): पानी पर्छ ।
   It doesn't rain (generally): पानी पर्दैन । It is hot (generally): गर्मी हुन्छ ।
6. It has been raining: पानी परेको छ । It isn't hot (generally): गर्मी हुँदैन ।
   It hasn't been raining: पानी परेको छैन ।
7. There'll be rain tomorrow (a forecast): भोलि पानी पर्नेछ ।

COMPLEX VERBS

- **–दै जानु** — ***continue on, keep on...***

  गर्मी बढ्दै जान्छ । — *It continues to get hotter.*
  जाडो पनि बढ्दै जान्छ । — *It also continues to get colder.*
  तपाईं भन्दै जानुस्, म सुन्दै जान्छु । — *You keep on talking, I'll keep on listening.*

- **–एको (हुना)ले (गर्दा)** — ***because, by reason of...*(past events)**

  ढिलो आएको (हुना)ले (गर्दा)... — *Because of being late...*
  पानी परेको (हुना)ले (गर्दा), म गइनँ । — *Because of it raining, I didn't go.*
  थोरै उचाइमा भएकोले यहाँ गर्मी हुन्छ । — *Because of its low elevation, it's hot here.*

- **–ने हुनाले / –ने भएकोले** — ***because...*(general reasons)**

  सुख्खा हुने हुनाले... — *Because it is dry (generally)...*
  पानी आउने हुनाले... — *Because water comes (generally)...*
  हिउँ पर्ने हुनाले... — *Because it snows (generally)...*

- **–ए(को) अनुसार** — ***according to...***

  मैले भने(को) अनुसार गर्नुस् । — *Do **according to** what I said.*
  मैले मेरो बाले भने(को) अनुसार गर्नुपर्छ । — *I have to do **according to** what my father says.*
  उहाँले सुने(को) अनुसार... — ***According to** what he heard...*

- **–ने बेलामा** — ***when, at the time of...***

  पानी पर्ने बेलामा मान्छे भित्र जान्छन् । — ***When** it rains, people go inside.*
  बतास चल्ने बेलामा धूलो उड्छ । — ***When** it blows, dust rises.*
  लाग्ने बेलामा हुरी आयो ।/चल्यो । — ***At the time of** setting off, a storm came.*

- **–ने बेला भयो** — ***time to...***

  खाने बेला भयो — *It's **time to** eat.*
  जाने बेला भयो — *It's **time to** go.*

- **–न लाग्नु** — ***about to...; started...***

  पानी पर्न लाग्यो । — *It's **about to** rain.*
  गर्मी हुन लाग्यो । — *It's **about to** become hot.*
  मैले काम गर्न लागेँ । — *I started **working**. I'm about to work.*

- **-ए पनि** *_ever...*

जति खाए पनि	*however much you eat*
जहिले आए पनि	*whenever you come*
जहाँ बसे पनि	*wherever you sit/stay*
जे भए पनि	*whatever it is (however)*
जे गरे पनि	*whatever you do*

PRACTICE

As boring or difficult as the following three exercises may be, don't cheat yourself by going over them quickly. *Learn them well.* This is an area that foreigners continue to make mistakes in after living in Nepal many years, though it is very basic.

1. Make a set of flash cards with all the question words and their corresponding demonstratives, including emphatics (10.2). Using these, have your tutor drill you on each word. After going through them once, set aside those cards that you know well, and focus on the difficult ones. *Continue going through the cards until you know* ***each one*** *(including emphatics).*

2. Using all the cards in your flash card set, have your tutor begin by showing you the Nepali word. Then your task is to give the equivalent relative pronoun/adverb and use it in a sentence. The first time through, your tutor should first give an example sentence that you repeat. Thereafter, you should produce a unique sentence by yourself. For example, if your tutor shows you the card कहाँ, you need to produce a sentence using जहाँ. *Continue going through the cards until you feel confident using* ***each one*** *in a sentence.*

3. The same as #2, except use the Nepali word as an adverb in a positive sentence, then again in a negative sentence. For example, if your tutor shows you the card कहाँ, you need to use it in a sentence where it means *somewhere* and in another sentence where it means *nowhere*. Remember to use the emphatic.

4. Complete the following sentences, giving two endings for each one:

a) मेरो बाको अनुसार ……………………………………………………

b) त्यहाँको बाटोअनुसार ……………………………………………………

c) सुनेको खबरअनुसार ……………………………………………………

d) हावापानीअनुसार ……………………………………………………

e) भेगअनुसार ……………………………………………………

5. Translate and complete each of the following sentences twice:

a) मेरी आमाले भनेअनुसार ……………………………………………………

b) मैले सुने(को)अनुसार ……………………………………………………

c) Do according to ……………………………………………………

d) According to what my doctor said ……………………………………………………

e) According to what I saw ……………………………………………………

6. Translate and complete each of the following sentences twice:

a) म जति कुरा गर्छु, उति (त्यति) ……………………………………………………

b) जति हिउँ पर्छ, त्यति ……………………………………………………

c) जति बादल लाग्छ ……………………………………………………

d) The more my work continues increasing ……………………………………………………

e) The more unboiled water I drink ……………………………………………………

7. Translate and complete each of the following sentences twice:

a) तरकारी महँगो भएको (हुना)ले ……………………………………………………

b) मेच धेरै कमजोर भएको (हुना)ले ……………………………………………………

c) बाटो साँघुरो भएको (हुना)ले ……………………………………………………

d) Because the phone is bad ……………………………………………………

e) Because the road is uphill ……………………………………………………

f) Because he drank unboiled water ……………………………………………………

g) Because they were good friends ……………………………………………………

8. Translate and complete each of the following sentences:

a) तरकारी महँगो हुने हुनाले ……………………………………………………

b) मेच धेरै कमजोर हुने हुनाले ……………………………………………………

c) हिमालमा जाडो हुने हुनाले ……………………………………………………

d) बाटो साँघुरो हुने हुनाले ……………………………………………………

e) Because the phones are bad ……………………………………………………

f) Because the roads are uphill ……………………………………………………

g) Because they drink unboiled water ……………………………………………………

h) Because they are good friends ……………………………………………………

9. Translate and complete each of the following sentences twice:

a) जहाँ जाडो हुन्छ त्यहाँ...

b) बजारमा जे पाउनुहुन्छ त्यो...

c) जता हेर्‍यो उतै...

d) However I told you to come...

e) When you gave me a vaccination...

f) The more the wind blows...

g) Whatever you do...

10. Translate and complete each of the following sentences:

a) It's 6:00; time to... (morning)

b) It's 10:15; time to.. (morning)

c) It's 12:30; time to...

d) It's 2:25; time to... (afternoon)

e) It's 6:45; time to... (evening)

f) It's 10:00; time to... (night)

11. Translate the following using -न लाग्नु:

a) It's about to rain.

b) It's about to be the cold season.

c) We're about to go home.

d) The wind started to blow.

e) We started to walk uphill.

f) It has started to snow.

g) I started to get a fever.

12. Translate and complete each of the following sentences twice:

a) मैले जत्ति खाए पनि...

b) तपाईं जहिले आए पनि...

c) Wherever we sit...

d) Whatever you do...

e) However much I learn...

13. Study the following sentences:

i. पानी नपर्ने बेला	i. पानी नभएको ठाउँ	i. खाना पकाउने मान्छे
ii. ***जुन*** बेला पानी पर्दैन	ii. ***जुन*** ठाउँमा पानी छैन	ii. ***जुन*** मान्छेले खाना पकाउँछ
iii. ***जहिले*** पानी पर्दैन	iii. ***जहाँ*** पानी छैन	iii. ***जसले*** खाना पकाउँछ

Now for each of the following sentences, state the two counterparts:

a) जसले देख्न सक्दैन
b) जसको दृष्टि छैन त्यसलाई अन्धो भनिन्छ ।
c) जसको सन्तान *(descendents)* छैन
d) मेरो घरमा काम गर्ने मान्छे
e) जहाँ बास पाइन्छ त्यहाँ हामी बस्छौं ।
f) जस्तो तपाईंलाई मनपर्छ त्यस्तो किन्नुस् ।
g) जुनबेला धेरै जाडो हुन्छ त्यसबेला जीवन कठिन हुन्छ ।
h) जति चाहिन्छ त्यति लिनुस् ।
i) जहिले साथी आउँछ
j) जो ढिलो आयो त्यो मेरो भाइ होइन ।

LET'S TALK

1. Using फरक and उस्तै, talk about your differences and similarities. Taking turns, give as many examples as you can.

2. Taking turns for each sentence and using सबभन्दा, what is the.../when is the...

   a) sickest you've ever been
   b) coldest you've ever been
   c) hottest place you've been to
   d) the most important thing you've done
   e) the farthest you've ever walked
   f) the northern most point you've traveled to
   g) the southern most point you've traveled to

3. Taking turns for each sentence, what is...

   a) to the north of your house
   b) to the north of your home country
   c) to the south of your home country
   d) to the west of your favorite city
   e) to the east of where you are now

4. Taking turns for each sentence, what is...
   a) between your house and where you are now
   b) between the nearest market and your house
   c) between your home country and India
   d) between the palace and the Bagmati bridge
   e) between your house and your tutor's house

5. Using -दै जानु, what continues or increases after...
   a) going to sleep late
   b) not eating breakfast
   c) walking all day
   d) starting class
   e) meeting an old friend

6. Tell your tutor what the weather's like for each season where you come from.

7. Take turns describing what you think the weather will be like tomorrow.

8. Taking turns for each sentence, talk about...
   a) why there is *no* electricity in the mountains
   b) where there is *some* snow this time of year
   c) why *no one* lives on the top of Mt. Everest
   d) why *some* people drink water straight out of the tap
   e) why there is *no* malaria *at all* in cold places
   f) why you *always* need an umbrella when traveling

9. Using the following time words, your tutor asks you a question about the weather. Answer, in both the positive and negative. Reverse roles.
   अहिले, भोलि, आजभोलि, हिजो

10. Take turns talking about in what season or weather...
    a) खाना धेरै मनपर्छ..........मनपर्दैन
    b) गर्मी हुन्छ..........हुँदैन
    c) पानी पर्छ..........पर्दैन

d) कुहिरो लाग्छ..........लाग्दैन

e) रमाइलो हुन्छ.........हुँदैन

f) दिन लामो हुन्छ..........हुँदैन

g) रात लामो हुन्छ..........हुँदैन

h) कुनकुन तरकारी/फलफूल पाइन्छ..........पाईदैन

i) केके सस्तो/महँगो हुन्छ.........हुँदैन

11. Using -ने बेलामा, when do you...

a) visit your friends?
b) think very hard?
c) stay inside?
d) go to bed at 5:00 pm?
e) wake up at 5:00 am?

IN THE COMMUNITY

Remember, exchange information. Offer the same information about yourself.

1. Ask each of the following questions of at least 5 people, or until your conversation time totals 30 minutes. You are to conduct an opinion poll in order to practice भन्दा and सबभन्दा. You will also be using the phrase तपाईंको विचारमा...

   a) Compared to bananas, do you like oranges? Why?
   तपाईंलाई केराभन्दा सुन्तला मनपर्छ ? किन होला ?

   b) What is your favorite fruit? Why?
   तपाईंलाई सबभन्दा मनपर्ने फलफूल के हो ? किन होला?

   c) Compared to West Nepal, do you like East Nepal? Why?
   तपाईंलाई पश्चिमी नेपालभन्दा पूर्वी नेपाल मनपर्छ ? किन होला ?

   d) What is your favorite place in Nepal? Why?
   तपाईंलाई नेपालको सबभन्दा मनपर्ने ठाउँ कुन हो ? किन होला?

2. Talk about the weather, covering the following points with at least 4 people, or until your conversation time totals 3 hours.
   a) The current weather--what is it like?
   b) What do they think the weather will be like tomorrow? in a month?
   c) In what months is it hot? cold? windy? foggy? rainy? dusty? etc.
   d) Tell them about the climate and weather where you come from.
   e) Find out as much as you can about the weather and climate of Chitawan (Terrai district) and Solu Khumbu (Everest's district)

   If they have lived outside the Kathmandu valley:
   f) How does the weather and climate where they live(d) compare to Kathmandu? What are the differences?
   g) Where they live(d), does it ever snow? hail? frost? mist? get foggy?
   h) On the coldest day, what is the temperature? On the hottest day?

DID YOU KNOW?

- Staring at the clouds will make you lose your memory.
- If it rains on Tuesday or Saturday, it may continue for a week.
- There are three types of lightening: 1) fire--burns up anything it hits, 2) ax--splits whatever it hits and 3) cock--just makes a loud noise.

Indra is considered to be the giver of rain and grain and is celebrated at the end of monsoon with the big festival Indra Jatra. After monsoon, kite flying is very popular. Kite flying is equivalent to sending Indra a letter asking the rain to stop. Therefore, superstitious people don't fly kites before or during monsoon.

Rato Machhendra is also worshipped as the Rain god by the Newari Buddhists. Before the beginning of monsoon, a giant chariot carrying Rato Machhendra is pulled through the city in April/May while its devotees pray for rain.

On the day of Shivaratri, huge fires are built to warm Shiva and chase the cold season away.

The Buddhist symbol of the thunderbolt is the Vajra and is a requirement for every Buddhist ceremony. It is a symbol of the changeless absolute.

CHAPTER 11

NEPAL: A BEAUTIFUL COUNTRY
सुन्दर देश: नेपाल

Vocabulary					
चीन	China	बसोबास	inhabitation	खन्नु	to dig
भारत	India	छेउ-छाउ	vicinity	सिँचाइ	irrigation
निकै	very	बस्ती	village, settlement	सुविधा	convenience, facility
सुन्दर *adj*	beautiful	प्रमुख	main, chief	अन्न	food grain
सुन्दरता *n*	beauty	-को रूप	form of	भण्डार	warehouse, storeroom
झरना	waterfall	भोटे	Tibetan	औद्योगिक	industrial
ताल	lake	सेर्पा	Sherpa	जनसङ्ख्या	population (human)
वन	forest, woods	स्रोत	source	जङ्गल	jungle
भाग	part	क्षेत्र	area, region; field	फँडानी	deforestation
अग्लो	tall	मध्य	middle	बसाउनु	to settle, to set on, to establish
हिमालय-पर्वतमाला	Himal. Range	सुदूर	far, remote, distant	प्रवृत्ति	tendency (people's)
कहीं-कहीं	in some places	उजाड	desolate; wilderness	मध्ये	among, between
-पारि	across, other side	विभिन्न	various	विकास	development
भूभाग	region, territory	प्रकार	kind, sort, type	बाँकी	remaining, leftover
सिमाना	border, frontier, boundary	व्यापारिक	business, commercial	हावा	air, wind
छुट्टयाउनु	divide, separate	उपत्यका	valley	गुफा	cave
पग्लनु	melt (intr)	नाला	stream, ditch	मरुभूमि	desert
बग्नु	flow	डाँडाकाँडा	mountains hills	पृथ्वी	the earth (planet)
संसार	world	रमणीय	pleasant	हिलो	mud
सगरमाथा	Mt. Everest	धरातल	terrain	पोखरी	pond

शिखर	summit	यातायात	transportation	घाटी	mountain pass
-भरि	throughout; full	बिजुली	electricity	पैरो / पहिरो	landslide
प्रसिद्ध	renown, famous	मधेस	the Terai	भीरपाखा	terraced land, slope land
वनस्पति	vegetation	फाँट	cultivated plain (plot of)		
फेदी	foot, bottom of a hill	कृषि	agriculture		
काँडे	thorny	मैदान	the plains, plain, ground, field	***know all the PP's in 11.4**	

USEFUL PHRASES

- "..." लाई नेपालीमा के भनिन्छ ? — *What is "..." called in Nepali?*
- मलाई माफ गर्नुस् । — *I'm sorry. (Forgive me, excuse me, I beg pardon.)*
- हतार नगर्नुस् । — *Don't hurry.*
- बस समाउन हतार गर्नुस् । — *Hurry to catch the bus.*
- म विश्वास गर्दिनँ । — *I don't believe (it).*
- ढिलो नगर्नुस् है ! — *Don't be late, OK ? (Don't delay, OK?)*
- फरक पर्दैन । — *It doesn't matter.* Also, *I'm sure. (It doesn't make any difference)*
- काम गर्न बाँकी छ । — *There's work left to do.*

TEXT

चीन र भारतको बीचमा नेपाल देश छ । यो देश सानो भए पनि निकै सुन्दर छ। यहाँ किसिमकिसिमको प्राकृतिक सुन्दरता पाइन्छ । धेरै ठूला र साना नदी, खोला, झरना, ताल, हरियो वन, सेता हिमाल इत्यादि यहाँका प्राकृतिक सुन्दरता हुन् ।

नेपालको उत्तरी भागमा धेरै अग्लो हिमालय-पर्वतमाला छ । कहीं-कहीं हिमालपारि पनि नेपालको भूभाग पर्छ । हिमालय-पर्वतले नेपाल र तिब्बतको

सिमाना छुट्ट्याउँछ । नेपालको उत्तरी भागलाई हिमाली भेग भनिन्छ । हिमालको हिउँ पग्लेर ठूलाठूला नदीहरू बगेका छन् । धेरै हिउँ पग्ल्यो भने नदीहरू एकदम ठूला हुन्छन् । नेपालमा संसारको सबभन्दा अग्लो हिमाल सगरमाथा छ । यही शिखरको कारणले नेपाल संसारभरि प्रसिद्ध छ ।

हिमालमा बाह्रै महिना हिउँ नै हिउँ हुने हुनाले कुनै किसिमको वनस्पति हुँदैन । हिमालको फेदीतिर अलिअलि काँडे वनस्पति देखिन्छन् । त्यसैको छेउछाउतिर अलि तल मान्छेको निकै पातलो बस्ती देखिन थाल्छ । त्यहाँ प्रमुख रूपमा भोटे र सेर्पाहरूको बस्ती पाइन्छ । त्यहाँ जाडो महिनामा त बाक्लो हिउँ नै पर्छ । हिमाल प्रमुख ठूला नदीहरूको स्रोत भएकोले त्यहाँ पानीचाहिँ सफा पाइन्छ ।

हिमाली भेगपछि हामी पहाडी क्षेत्रको कुरा गरौं । पूर्वी पहाडदेखि मध्य पश्चिमी पहाडसम्म मानिसहरुको बस्ती राम्रै देखिन्छ । सुदूर पश्चिमी पहाडमा अलि उजाड र गर्मी बढी हुन्छ । पहाडी क्षेत्रमा सबै किसिमका मान्छेहरूको बसोबास छ । यहाँको पहाडी भेगमा विभिन्न प्रकारका वनस्पति पाइन्छन् । यस क्षेत्रमा धेरै गाउँ र शहरहरू छन् । यहाँ व्यापारिक क्षेत्र पनि छन् । उपत्यका, नदीनाला, डाँडाकाँडा आदि यहाँका रमणीय धरातल हुन् । यहाँ यातायातको समस्या अझै कम भएको छैन । धेरै ठाउँमा मोटरबाटो र बिजुली पुग्न सकेको छैन ।

तराई (मधेस) समथर फाँट हो । समुद्रको सतहबाट थोरै उचाइमा भएकोले यहाँ गर्मी हुन्छ । कृषिको लागि सबभन्दा राम्रो मैदान तराई नै हो । फेरि धेरैजसो ठाउँमा थोरै खने पनि पानी आउने हुनाले तराईमा सिँचाइको पनि सुविधा छ । तराईलाई नेपालको अन्न भण्डार भने पनि हुन्छ । औद्योगिक शहरहरू पनि यही क्षेत्रमा पाइन्छन् । सबभन्दा धेरै जनसङ्ख्या भएको क्षेत्र यही हो । जङ्गल फँडानी गरेर बस्ती बसाउने प्रवृत्ति यहाँको समस्याहरूमध्ये एक हो । पूर्वी तराईभन्दा पश्चिमी तराईमा विकासको काम धेरै गर्न बाँकी छ । पश्चिमी तराई अझ विकसित भयो भने त्यहाँ पनि जनसङ्ख्या बढ्दै जान्छ होला ।

GRAMMAR

➤ 11.1 *IF*-CLAUSE WITH भने AND –ए.

An if-clause is formed by joining two clauses with भने and conjugating the first verb (almost always) in the past tense. Thus (because of the past tense) the subject of first clause requires -ले if the verb is transitive.

पानी पर्‍यो भने म जान्नँ ।	*If it rains, I won't go.*
ऊ गयो भने म पनि जान्छु ।	*If he goes, I'll go as well.*
तपाईंले मलाई सिकाउनुभयो भने म सिक्छु ।	*If you teach me, I'll learn.*
तपाईंले मलाई सिकाउनुभएन भने म सिक्दिनँ ।	*If you don't teach me, I won't learn.*

Notice that even though the events are in the future, the first verb is still conjugated in the past tense. Very rarely, the first verb may be conjugated in the present tense, but only when both actions are expected to happen in the very immediate future.

There is also an abbreviated if-clause. In this structure, भने is left out and -ए is suffixed diffectly to the first verb. Using the same example sentences as above, note carefully how the negative is formed in the last sentence (using न-).

पानी परे म जाँदिनँ ।	*If it rains, I won't go.*
ऊ गए म पनि जान्छु ।	*If he goes, I'll go as well.*
तपाईंले सिकाए म सिक्छु ।	*If you teach me, I'll learn.*
तपाईंले नसिकाए म सिक्दिनँ ।	*If you don't teach me, I won't learn.*

➤ 11.2 तैपनि (emphatic of तापनि) *NEVERTHELESS, even in that case, even then*

पानी पर्‍यो । तैपनि म जान्छु ।	*It's raining. Nevertheless, I'm going.*
पानी पर्दैन । तैपनि वन राम्रो छ ।	*It doesn't rain. Nevertheless, the forest is nice.*

➤ 11.3 POSTPOSITIONS भरि, मध्य AND पारि.

- **-भरि**

a) *full of X;*	कपभरि पानी	*cup full of water*
b) *all over, X-wide*	संसारभरि प्रसिद्ध छ ।	*famous world-wide*
c) *all X long (time)*	दिनभरि	*all day long*

- **-मध्ये, मध्य** **बजारको मध्यमा** in the middle / centre of market.

d) *between X and Y*	घर र बजारको मध्यमा	*between the house and market*
b) *mid X, center* (मध्य)	मध्यपश्चिमी	*mid-western*
c) *among, between*	समस्याहरूमध्ये	*among the problems*

- **-पारि** *across, other side of* हिमालपारि *on the other side of the Himalayas*

opp. **-वारि**

नदीपारि	*on the other side of the river*
पुलपारि	*on the other side of the bridge*
बाटोपारि	*on the other side of the street*

➤ 11.4 POSTPOSITION REVIEW.

You have learned all of the following postpositions, but for some you have learned their meaning in reference to place only or in reference to time only. You will see that for some, both can be used. When writting, postpositions are almost always joined and spelled as one word.

PP	PLACE		TIME	
निर	घरनिर	**near** the house		
तिर	घरतिर	**towards** the house	एक बजेतिर aroun(one o'clock	
माथि	घरमाथि	**above/on top of** house		
भन्दा माथि	त्यहाँभन्दा माथि	**beyond** there		
तल	घरतल	**below** the house		
बाहिर	घरबाहिर	**outside** the house		
पारि	हिमालपारि	on **the other side of...**		
मध्ये	समस्यामध्ये	**among** the problems		
-को मध्यमा	X र Y-को मध्यमा	**between X and Y**		
-को पछाडि	घरको पछाडि	**behind** the house		
मा	कोठामा	**in** the room	तीन दिनमा	**in** three days
अघि	घरअघि	**facing** the house	तीन दिनअघि	three days **ago**
-को अगाडि	घरको अगाडि	**in front of** the house	तीन दिनअगाडि	three days **ago**
भित्र	घरभित्र	**inside** the house	तीन दिनभित्र	**within** three days

-को बीचमा	बजारको बीचमा	in **the middle of** the b..	कामको बीचमा	**during** work
भरि	संसारभरि	world **wide/all over**	दिनभरि	**all** day **long**
सम्म	घरसम्म	**to/as far as** home	पाँच बजेसम्ममा	**by** five o'clock
बाट	घरबाट	**from** home	*तीन बजेबाट	**from** 3 o'clock
बाट...सम्म	X बाट Y सम्म	**from X to Y**	**३ बजेबाट..सम्म	**from** 3 o'clock **until..**
देखि	घरदेखि	**from** house	पाँच महिनादेखि	**since** (for) 5 months
देखि...सम्म	X देखि Y सम्म	**from X to Y**	X देखि Y सम्म	**from X until Y**
देखि...भित्र			Xदेखि Y भित्र	**between X and Y**
पछि			तीन दिनपछि	**after** three days
भन्दा अघि			जानुभन्दा अघि	**before** going
भन्दा अगाडि			जानुभन्दा अगाडि	**before** going

* तीन बजेपछि is preferred **३ बजेदेखि...सम्म is preferred

➤11.5 NOUN–नै NOUN *N UPON N, LOTS OF N*

हिउँ नै हिउँ — *lots of snow, snow upon snow*

पानी नै पानी — *lots of water, water upon water*

जङ्गल नै जङ्गल/जङ्गलैजङ्गल — *lots of jungle, jungle upon jungle*

COMPLEX VERBS

• –ए(ता)पनि *even though, even if...*

देश सानो भए(ता)पनि... — ***Even though** the country is small...*

पानी परे(ता)पनि म जान्छु। — ***Even if** it rains, I will go* **or** ***Even though** it rains, I go (generally)*

पानी नपरे(ता)पनि वन राम्रो छ। — ***Even though** it doesn't rain, the forest is nice.*

ऊ नगए(ता)पनि म जान्छु । — ***Even if** he isn't going, I'll go* **or** ***Even though** he doesn't go, I go.*

- **-ए(पनि) हुन्छ** — ***okay if, doesn't matter if...*** (cf. नु/न हुन्छ)

भात खाए(पनि) हुन्छ ।	*It's **okay if** you eat rice.*
नेपाली सिके(पनि) हुन्छ ।	*It's **okay if** you learn Nepali.*
त्यहाँ अस्पताल बनाए(पनि) हुन्छ ।	*It's **okay if** you build a hospital there.*
...भने पनि हुन्छ ।	***It can be said that... /We can say ....***

- **-न बाँकी छ, थियो, हुन्छ, भयो** — ***...remaining to do***

विकासको काम गर्न धेरै बाँकी छ ।	*There's a lot of development work **left to do**.*
मैले/मेरो काम गर्न बाँकी छ ।	*I have work **left to do**.*

- **-न हतार गर्नु** — ***hurry to...***

बस समाउन हतार गर्नुस् ।	***Hurry to** catch the bus.*
बस समाउनको लागि हिँड्न हतार गर्नुस् ।	*In order to catch the bus, walk hurriedly.*
पिउन हतार गर्नुस् । जानै पर्‍यो ।	***Hurry up** and drink. (We) have to go.*

- **-एदेखि** — ***since, from when...***

म पोखराबाट फर्केदेखि पानी परेको छ ।	*Since I returned from Pokhara it has been raining.*
अन्जीर टिप्न गएदेखिको कथा	*The story from when (she) went to pick figs.*

PRACTICE

1. Translate and complete each sentence with *two results*; the first using भने and the second using -ए:

a) पानी पर्‍यो भने...
   पानी परे...
b) पानी परेन भने...
   पानी नपरे...
c) घाम लाग्यो भने...
   घाम लागे...
d) घाम लागेन भने...
   घाम नलागे...
e) हिउँ पग्लेन भने...
   हिउँ नपग्ले...
f) If you drink unboiled water...
g) If he speaks Hindi...
h) If she comes tomorrow...
i) If the store is close to home...
j) If I am careful...
k) If I buy only expensive vegetables...
l) If you don't get vaccinated...
m) If the weather is nice tomorrow...
n) If you don't live in the Terai...
o) If I walk uphill all day...
p) If we don't take a taxi at night...
*q) If I haven't called you by 3 o'clock...
*r) If she hasn't eaten all her food...
*s) If I haven't studied the book...
*t) If they've asked you a difficult question...
*u) If I have said something wrong...

*In the present perfect, -ए is the only option.

2. Rephrase each sentence in #1 using -ए(पनि) हुन्छ (eg. *It's okay if it rains*).

3. Translate and connect each pair of sentences using तैपनि, then express the sentence using -ए(ता)पनि.

a)	पानी पऱ्यो ।	म पिकनिक जान्छु ।
b)	गाडी ढिलो भयो ।	म रिसाएको छैन ।
c)	त्यो क्षेत्र सुदूर छ ।	मान्छेहरू त्यहाँ बस्छन् ।
d)	पानी नपरेको एक हप्ता भयो ।	बिरुवाहरू अझै हरिया छन् ।
e)	धेरै हिउँ पग्लेको छ ।	नदी सानो छ ।
f)	There are no clouds in the sky.	I think it is going to rain.
g)	The waterfall is beautiful.	Don't drink the water.
h)	There is a border.	It's as though there isn't a border.
i)	Nepal is a small country.	It is famous worldwide.
j)	There is lots of development.	There is lots of development remaining (to be done).
k)	He has taken medicine.	He still has a fever.
l)	He has no symptoms.	He can still spread the disease.
m)	I was vaccinated for Hepatitis.	I got Hepatitis.
n)	It is very important.	People aren't careful.
o)	He doesn't have any money.	He came home with a new umbrella.
p)	He didn't have an appointment.	He came into my office.
q)	He had a long holiday.	He was very tired.
r)	The road was level.	The car drove very slowly.
s)	It was very cold.	I slept on the porch.
t)	I knew he was home.	No one answered the phone.

4. Two phrases for each postposition given in 11.4 are given below (scrambled). Translate each one.

near the mountain	outside the school	from my house to the office (2)
towards the border	among the problems	in the room
beyond the sea	outside the clinic	to/as far as the river
towards the stream	beyond the forest	facing him
in front of the hotel	on the other side of the forest	among the diseases
below the house	below the hospital	behind the school
on top of the summit	behind the house	all over the village
near the car	between the village and the lake	in the bag
between Pokhara and KTM	on the other side of the ridge	in front of the gate

in three hours
inside the house
all evening long
facing the road
inside the book
from 2 until 2:30
after three weeks
in the middle of the forest
all over the world
to/as far as the lake
on top of the mountain
from India (2)
after 2:15
from far (2)
from night until day
between 3:30 and 4:15
in three days
three months ago
since (for) 5 months
five years ago
in the middle of the road
within three days
during work
during the afternoon
all week long
by 3:30
before going (2)
from India to China (2)
by 4:45
after 3:15
from 1:15 until 1:45
since (for) 5 years
from morning until evening
within three hours
between 2 and 3 o'clock
after three days
before eating (2)

5. Translate and complete the following twice:
   a) नेपाली सिकेदेखि...
   b) घरबाट फर्केदेखि...
   c) Since opening the door...
   d) Since drinking that unboiled water...
   e) Since crossing the river...

6. Translate the following using -न बाँकी छ:
   a) I have lots of work left to do.
   b) There is lots of development left to do.
   c) I have a little tea left to drink.
   d) He has a few things left to say.

7. Translate the following using -न हतार गर्नु:
   a) Hurry up and finish this.
   b) Hurry up and finish eating.
   c) I'm hurrying to get a taxi.
   d) We hurried to get home.
   e) They hurried to drink their tea.

8. Make complete sentences from the following table:

तपाईं(ले)	चढेको	सबभन्दा	अग्लो पहाड...
म(ले)	गएको		सुन्दर ठाउँ...
हामी(ले)	खाएको		मिठो खाना...
(ले)	लेखेको		लामो चिठी...
...(ले)	देखेको		राम्रो मान्छे...

LET'S TALK

1. Describe to your tutor the geography of your home area. What are its distinctive features? What does it have in common with Nepal? Are their lakes, rivers, waterfalls, mountains, etc? Is the population high?

2. Directed Interview. Take turns answering each of the following questions:
   a) In your opinion, what is the most beautiful place you have been to? **Why**?
   b) What is the highest mountain you have climbed?
   c) What is your favorite form of transportation?
   d) Because of the terrain, where is the place you would least like to live? **Why**?
   e) Have you ever been in a cave? If so, where and how did you like it?

3. Reverse Interview. Below are 12 answers given in an interview. You don't know what the questions were, but your task is to think of creative questions that fit these answers. **Step 1**: Together with your tutor translate the phrases and write the translations following each phrase. **Step 2**: Think of an appropriate question to fit each answer. **Step 3**: Your tutor answers the question with the given phrases. **Reverse Roles** on steps 2 and 3.
   a) Yes, I have.
   b) I forget.
   c) In my opinion, it's well known.
   d) I stayed there for around two years.
   e) Not only is it hot, it also rains a lot.
   f) Only in the woods.
   g) Mainly on the plains.
   h) There is a lot remaining.
   i) I will never go there again.
   j) That place is very beautiful.
   k) Only across the river.
   l) No problem.

4. Write down the name of a country, without letting your tutor see. Your tutor then has to ask questions until he/she has figured out the name of the country. *You can only answer "yes" or "no"*. **Reverse roles.**

5. Take turns describing the differences between northern and southern Nepal.

6. You are stranded by yourself in the middle of a desert. Take turns ranking in order of importance the following items. Give reasons why:

कागज	एउटा स्याउ
ऐना	औषधि
साबुन	एक कप पानी
छाता	कुचो

7. Take turns giving your opinion for the following. Why do you think...
    a) ...the price of vegetables changes from season to season?
    b) ...Nepalis usually work six days per week?
    c) ...electricity hasn't reached many places in Nepal?
    d) ...TEAM has an office in Kathmandu?
    e) ...it's important to learn the language of the country you're living in?
    f) ...many Nepalis don't boil their drinking water?

8. Take turns talking about what you do if...
    a) ...you have a fever?
    b) ...you have no tea and a good friend comes to your house?
    c) ...you are very tired?
    d) ...you run out of gas to cook with and there's none at the stores?
    e) ...someone calls but it's the wrong number?
    f) ...you eat very spicy food but there's no drinking water?
    g) ...you are late for an appointment?
    h) ...it is snowing but you don't have a coat?
    i) ...it is very hot and you can't sleep?

IN THE COMMUNITY

Field trip. Take a trip to Chobar gorge and the Adinath Lokeshwar temple. They are located 6 km past the Ring Road on the way to Daksinkali (lit. South Kali), just before the large cement factory. If you don't have your own transportation, you can take the public bus or a taxi. For a taxi you'll have to negotiate a day rate before you leave, but it's around Rs. 600/half day. It also makes a pleasant (but steep) bike trip.

If you do choose to taxi out, use the time to talk to the taxi driver about:

a) The geography of your own country.
b) The geographical differences and similarities between your country and Nepal.
c) The most beautiful places you've been to.
d) The least favorite place you've been to.

Once you get to the gorge, don't just look. You are required to *talk* to the locals for a minimum of 2 hrs. about the area. Since the area is becoming more known to tourists, you will have to make it explicit that you only want to speak in Nepali. When at the gorge, include in your questions:

a) How did the gorge come to be?
b) What was there before the gorge?
c) Who put the bridge there and when?
d) How do they feel about the river? What did it used to be like?
e) Find out as much as you can about the caves.

Visit the temple Adinath Lokeshwar. Visit the temple and find out (by talking!):

a) What is the significance of the kitchen utensils?
b) Was there lots of rain last year? Why (not)?
c) Will there be lots of rain this year? Why (not)?
d) How do they feel about the river? What did it used to be like?
e) How do they like the view from their village?
f) What is it like living on a ridge?
g) How long has the village had electricity?
h) Ask them to teach you a Newari phrase and see them light up!

This assignment is considered complete when your conversation time totals a minimum of 2 hrs. If you took a taxi, this does not include conversation with the driver.

If you are adventurous enough *and have the time,* explore the caves (remember to pack a flashlight)! As a kid, that was one of my favorite things to do. They are some of the longest caves in S. Asia and yet surprisingly unknown. A word of warning--the passages are narrow, honeycombed and wet. People have gotten lost in them. If you want a guide, many of the local boys will jump at the chance to make a few rupees and show you around. I also suggest taking an umbrella for rain *and* shade.

DID YOU KNOW?

- Westerners are prohibited from entering almost all temples. Remove your shoes when others are removing theirs. You may have to remove leather items as well, such as leather belts. Circle a temple in a clockwise direction.

- Nepal not only contains the highest mountain in the world, but also the deepest river gorge (the Seti Gandaki River).

- There are 14 peaks over 8,000m in the world. Of the 10 highest of those, 8 are in Nepal. Yet in Nepal's short width, the elevation goes from 100m above sea level to the highest mountain in the world.

- The Himalayan mountains continue to grow as a result of the Eurasian and Indo-Australian plates colliding.

- Landslides during monsoon are a common occurance, wiping out roads, trails and water supply pipes. They have even been known to cover entire villages.

- Nepal has an estimated 83,000 megawatts of hydroelectic potential, enough to light the Indian subcontinent!

- People are migrating to the Terai and cities at an alarming rate, in search of better land and work.

CHAPTER 12
NEPAL'S WILDERNESS
नेपालको वन

VOCABULARY

महत्त्व	importance, significance	वाहन	vehicle	घडियाल	slender nose alligator
विनाश	destruction	उम्रनु	sprout, germinate	गोही	crocodile
चोरी	theft	तामा	bamboo shoot	जात	species; caste
कटानी	cutting, deforestation	टुसा	bamboo shoot (thin)	दाँत	tooth
व्यवहार	behavior, practice, treatment	जङ्गली	wild	पङ्क्ति	line, row
रुख	tree	खेती	cultivation	माछा	fish
बिरुवा	seedling, sapling	सिसौ	tree - Dalbergia Sissu	आहार	diet, food
वन्यजन्तु	wild animal	स्तरीय	quality, standard	जीव	life, living being
साल	tree - Shorea Robustas	सिङे	horned	शाखा	branch, division, section
काठ	wood, timber	गैंडा	rhinosaurus	वासस्थान	habitat, dwelling
प्रयोग	use	छाला	skin, hide, leather	चितुवा	leopard
संरक्षण	protection, conservation	दृष्टि	sight (sense); eye	ओगट्नु	to cover (area), occupy
स्याउला	branch (leafy)	कमजोर	weak, tender, impotent	ढुङ्गे	stoned, rocky
पात	leaf	सुन्ने	hearing (sense)	छोटो	short
व्यावसायिक	vocational	सुँघ्ने	smell (sense)	थुतुनो	snout
उचित	proper, reasonable, appropriate	शक्ति	power, strength, might, potency	निधार	forehead
व्यवस्था	management, arrangement	एकान्त	loneliness	ठाडो	very steep, erect
जरुरी	important, urgent	हमला	attack, invasion	चिउँडो	chin
सल्ला	pine tree	हात्ती	elephant	हल्का	light (color, weight...)
लेक	highlands	चढ्नु	to mount; ascend, climb, ride	फाइदा	profit, benefit, merit, advantage
नरम	soft	चर्नु	to graze (intr)	बाँदर	monkey

वृक्षारोपण	tree planting	पाटे	striped (black)	रौं	fur, hair
बाँस	bamboo	बाघ	tiger	किरा	insect, bug
निगाला	bamboo (thin)	राजा	king	चरा / पंक्षि	bird
छाउनु	to thatch (roof)	चिन्नु	know, recognize	फूल	flower
छाप्रो	hut	लामो	long	लालीगुराँस	red rhododendron
आदि	etc.	पाटा	stripe	डाँफे	pheasant
भर्खर	just, just now	रहनु	to remain	पुच्छर	tail

USEFUL PHRASES

- म भर्खर चिया खाएर आएँ । — *I just had tea and came (so no thanks).*
- म तपाईंको कुरा मान्छु । — *I agree with you.*
- यो कुरो धेरै जरुरी छ । — *It's very important/urgent.*
- यो कुरो धेरै महत्त्वपूर्ण छ । — *It's very important.*
- मलाई जान दिनुस् । — *Allow me to go.*
- यो धेरै फाइदाजनक छ । — *It's very advantageous/profitable.*
- (तपाईं) उहाँलाई चिन्नुहुन्छ ? — *Do you know him?*
- उहाँलाई देखेको मात्रै हो । — *(I) only know him by sight.*

TEXT

वनजङ्गलको महत्त्व धेरैलाई थाहा छ । कसैकसैलाई यसको महत्त्व थाहा छैन होला । तर वनजङ्गलको विनाश धेरै भइसक्यो । त्यसबाट धेरै बेफाइदा भइरहेको छ । वनजङ्गलको चोरी-कटानी रोकिएको छैन । जनसङ्ख्या बढेर र मान्छेहरूको नराम्रो व्यवहार भएर वनविनाश हुँदै छ । अब नेपालको वनजङ्गलका केही रुखबिरुवा र वन्यजन्तुका बारेमा कुरा गरौं:

सालः यस रुखको काठ घर बनाउनको लागि प्रयोग गरिन्छ। तराईको जङ्गलमा साल धेरै पाइन्छ । सबभन्दा धेरै विनाश भएको रुख पनि यही हो । तर कटानी गरिएको ठाउँमा संरक्षण गरियो भने यो आफै आउँछ र बढ्छ । यस रुखका स्याउला र पातको पनि धेरै प्रयोग गरिन्छ । सालको पात व्यावसायिक रूपमा प्रयोग गरिन्छ । यसको उचित व्यवस्था हुनु जरुरी छ ।

साल *सल्ला*

सल्लाः नेपालमा धेरै पाइने अर्को रुख सल्ला हो । सल्ला धेरै किसिमका हुन्छन् । पहाडदेखि लेकसम्म विभिन्न किसिमका सल्ला पाइन्छन् । यसको काठ अलि नरम हुन्छ । पहाडी भेगमा वृक्षारोपणको लागि यसको धेरै प्रयोग गरिन्छ ।

बाँस र निगालोः बाँस र निगालो धेरैधेरै कामका लागि प्रयोग गरिन्छन् । घर छाउन, घर बनाउन, छाप्रो बनाउन आदि धेरै काममा यिनको प्रयोग हुन्छ । बाँसको भर्खर उम्रेको तामा र टुसा खानको लागि पनि निकै प्रयोग गरिन्छ । बाँस र निगालो जङ्गली पनि हुन्छन् र यिनको खेती गरिएको पनि पाइन्छ ।

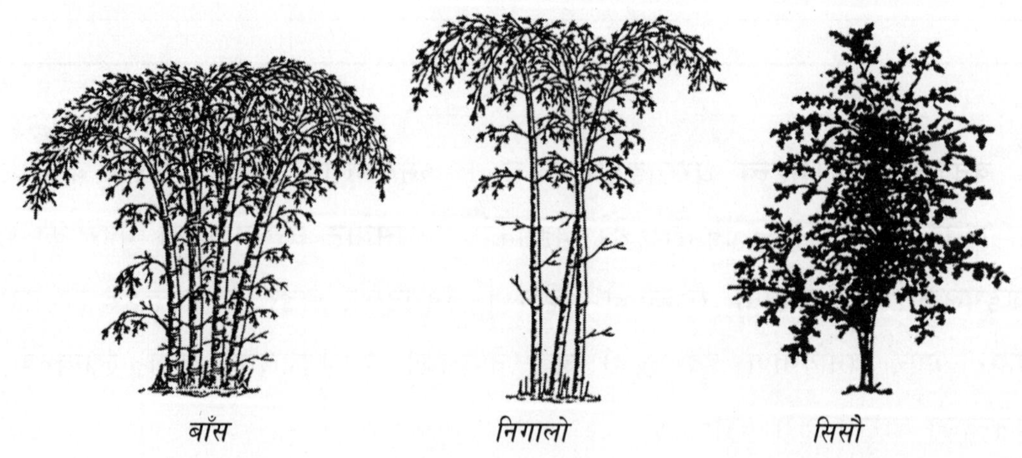
बाँस *निगालो* *सिसौ*

सिसौः राम्रो फर्निचर बनाउनको लागि सिसौ स्तरीय काठ हो । पहिले जङ्गली सिसौको धेरै प्रयोग गरिन्थ्यो । तर आजभोलि यसको खेती गरिन्छ । यसको खेतीबाट निकै फाइदा हुन्छ रे !

केही जङ्गली जनावर

एक सिङे गैँडाः यो नेपाल, भारत, बर्मा र अफ्रिकाका केही ठाउँमा मात्र पाइन्छ । यसको छाला धेरै बाक्लो हुन्छ । यसको दृष्टि कमजोर भए पनि सुन्ने र सुँघ्ने शक्ति धेरै हुन्छ । यसलाई एकान्तमा बस्न मनपर्छ र यसको अगाडि पऱ्यो भने यसले हामीलाई हमला गर्न सक्छ । चितवनमा जाँदा हात्तीमा चढेर गैँडा चरिरहेको हेर्न रमाइलो हुन्छ ।

एक सिङे गैँडा

पाटे बाघ

घडियाल

हिउँ चितुवा

पाटे बाघः यसलाई जङ्गलको राजा भनेर चिनिन्छ । यसलाई दुर्गा भगवतीको वाहन भनिन्छ । यसको पहेँलो जिउमा काला लामा पाटाहरू हुन्छन् । यो सानो क्षेत्रमा रहन सक्तैन । नेपालमा यसको सङ्ख्या २५० जति छ ।

घडियालः नेपालमा पाइने गोही जातमा घडियाल मुख्य हो । यसको टाउको लामो हुन्छ । यसको माथि र तल दाँतहरूको पङ्क्ति हुन्छ । माछा यसको मुख्य आहार हो । यसले जमिनका र पानीका अरू जीवहरू पनि खान्छ । दक्षिण एसियाका ठूला नदी र शाखा नदीहरू यसका वासस्थान हुन् ।

हिउँ चितुवा: हिउँ चितुवा हिमालमा पाइन्छ । बाघले जस्तै यसले पनि ठूलो क्षेत्र ओगट्छ । लेकै लेकमा, भीरमा र ढुङ्गे पहाडमा रुख नभएको ठाउँमा पनि यो रहन्छ । छोटो थुतुनो अनि फराकिलो निधार र ठाडो चिउँडोले यसलाई चिन्न सकिन्छ । यसको जिउ हल्का खैरो तर अगाडिको भाग सेतो हुन्छ ।

GRAMMAR

➤ 12.1 भएर *BECAUSE OF* neg. नभएर

You have already learned भएर as *via*. Literally, this means *being*. In our text: मान्छेहरूको नराम्रो व्यवहार भएर वनविनाश हुँदै छ *Lit. the people's behavior being bad, the forest is being destroyed*. The implication of this sentence is, *because of the peoples' bad behavior*....So, भएर in this context means *because of*. To understand how *being* can imply *because of*, consider the following:

*It **being** important, I had to go*	implies	***because** it was important...*
*The rhinos vision **being** weak, it relies on ...*	implies	***because** the rhinos vision is weak...*
*The tiger **being** king of the jungle...*	implies	***because** the tiger is king...*

➤ 12.2 HISTORICAL PAST (PAST HABITUAL).

This tense is used to express an action that was done habitually or regularly or continued over a period of time. It is often translated in English as *used to do, would do (repeatedly)* and *did (for some time)*. For example:

म हिन्दी सिकाउँथें ।	*I used to teach Hindi.*
म भारतमा पढ्थें ।	*I used to go to study in India.*
दिनदिनै घाम लाग्थ्यो ।	*Every day it would shine.*
म लुगा खोलामा धुन्थें ।	*I washed my clothes in the river (regularly)*
पहिले जङ्गली सिसौको धेरै प्रयोग गरिन्थ्यो ।	*Before, the wild Dalbergia tree was used a lot (but now isn't).*

The conjugations for historical past are:

*म	-थें	-दिनथें
हामी	-थ्यौं	-दैनथ्यौं
तिमी	-थ्यौ	-दैनथ्यौ
तपाईं/वहाँ	-नुहुन्थ्यो	-नुहुन्नथ्यो
उनी	-थे	-दैनथे
ऊ	-थ्यो	-दैनथ्यो

* normally ले with subject is not used even for transitive verbs.

➤ 12.3 PARTICLE रे.

This discourse particle always comes at the end of a sentence and conveys the meaning *so they say, I heard*. It is used similarly to the English, "Don't quote me on this, but..."

➤ 12.4 भनेर.

Literally, भनेर means *saying that*. However, it has several uses.

- *as.* बाघलाई जङ्गलको राजा भनेर चिनिन्छ । *the tiger is known* ***as*** *the king of the jungle.*
  Used this way, भनेर only modifies a noun phrase, ie. *king of the jungle.*

- *because X is considered:*
  बाघ जङ्गलको राजा हो भनेर मान्छेलाई डर लाग्छ । ***because*** *the tiger is considered the king ...*

- *thinking that: (saying to oneself)*
  पानी पर्छ भनेर म गइनँ । ***thinking that*** *it might rain, I didn't go.*
  उसलाई थकाइ लाग्छ भनेर हामी बिस्तारै गयौँ । ***thinking that*** *he might get tired, we went slowly.*

- it is used literally in reported speech (to be covered in detail next chapter):
  उहाँले म जान्छु भनेर भन्नुभयो । *He* ***said that*** *he is leaving.*

➤ 12.5 त FOR द.

In our text we have सक्तैन. This is because occasionally द is written as त (mostly in Western Nepal). For example, बस्दा is written as बस्ता. For you phonologists, this is simply a reflection of voiceless assimilation.

➤ 12.6 NOUNS INTO ADJECTIVES WITH -ए.

पाटा *stripe* + -ए = पाटे *striped*
सिङ *horn* + -ए = सिङे *horned*
काँडा *thorn* + -ए = काँडे *thorned*
ढुङ्गा *stone* + -ए = ढुङ्गे *stony*

This is also a productive derivation for nicknames (often rude and pejorative):

कुहिरो *mist* + -ए = कुहिरे *misty (eyed)--pejorative term for whites*
कालो *black* + -ए = काले *blackie*

COMPLEX VERBS

- **-इरहेको** — ***the continual, repeated X-ing of...***

गैँडा चरिरहेको	*the grazing of rhinos*
गाडी चलिरहेको	*the driving/moving of vehicles*
नानी सुतिरहेको	*the sleeping of the baby*
ऊ आइरहेको	*his coming (over and over)*

- **-इरहनु** — ***to continue, keep on...***(see ch 8)

म नेपाली सिकिरहन्छु ।	*I continue to learn Nepali.* (present freq)
म खाइरहन्छु ।	*I will keep on eating*
म गइरहन्छु ।	*I will continue going*
मैले खाइरहेँ ।	*I kept on eating* (past habitual freq)
म गइरहेँ ।	*I kept on going*
मैले दिइरहेँ ।	*I kept on giving*

- **-इराख्नु** — ***to continue, keep on...***

म नेपाली सिकिराख्छु ।	*I continue to/keep on learning Nepali.*
मैले खाइराखेँ ।	*I kept on eating*
म गइराखेँ ।	*I kept on going*

- **-न दिनु** — ***to allow to...***

मलाई जान दिनुस् ।	*Allow me to go.*
उसलाई पढ्न देऊ न !	*Allow him to read.*
उहाँलाई त्यहाँ बस्न देऊ न !	*Allow him to sit there.*

PRACTICE

1. Using भएर, translate and complete the sentences:
   a) महत्त्वपूर्ण भएर...
   b) गैँडाको दृष्टि कमजोर भएर...
   c) जनसङ्ख्या त्यति थोरै भएर...
   d) बाघ जङ्गलको राजा भएर...

e) उनीहरूको नराम्रो व्यवहार भएर...
f) Because it was very cold...
g) Because the path was uphill...
h) Because it is so different...
i) Because it was so difficult...
j) Because the elephant was so heavy...

2. Conjugate the following verbs for the historical past (for each pronoun, positive and negative): छाउनु, उमार्नु, चढ्नु, रहनु, चिन्नु

3. Using ...भनेर चिनिनु, translate the following:
a) My father is known for being a happy man.
b) The shopkeeper is known for being an honest (straight) person.
c) The doctor is known for being a tall person.
d) Nepal is known for being mountainous country.
e) India is known for being a hot place.

4. Translate and complete the following sentences:
a) मेरो बा सुखी मान्छे हो भनेर...
b) साहुजी सोझो मान्छे हो भनेर...
c) डाक्टर अग्लो मान्छे हो भनेर...
d) दृश्य अत्यन्त सुन्दर छ भनेर...
e) because Nepal is considered mountainous country (translate only)
f) because India is considered a hot place (translate only)
g) because the path is considered narrow (translate only)

5. Using भनेर, translate and complete the following sentences:
a) पानी पर्ला भनेर...
b) तरकारी धेरै महँगो छ भनेर...
c) उहाँ छिटो आउनुहुन्छ भनेर...
d) उहाँले फोन गर्नुहुन्छ भनेर...
e) यो महत्त्वपूर्ण छैन भनेर...
f) Thinking that my mother was very sick...
g) Thinking that it had great benefit (profit)...
h) Thinking that the sun would shine again...
i) Thinking that the tiger would attack me...

6. Based on the conjugations for the simple indefinite and simple past, give the following conjugations using -इरहनु (the first one for each is given).

म	खाइरहन्छु	खाइरहँदिनँ	खाइरहें	?	खाइरहेको छु ।	खाइरहन्थें
हामी	?	?	?	खाइरहेनौं	?	?
तिमी	?	?	?	?	?	?
तपाईं/उहाँ	?	?	?	?	?	?
ऊ	?	?	?	?	?	?
उनी	?	?	?	?	?	?

7. Translate the following sentences using -इरहनु.
    a) I won't keep on telling you.
    b) We won't keep on eating daal bhaat.
    c) You (mid) will keep on asking for money.
    d) I will keep on talking.
    e) He (high) will keep on waiting.
    f) I won't keep on thatching my hut all day.
    g) He (mid) will keep on going.
    h) They will keep on settling in the Terrai.
    i) I kept on talking.
    j) I didn't keep on talking to him.
    k) We kept on looking.
    l) We didn't keep on looking all day.
    m) You (mid) kept on studying.
    n) You (mid) didn't keep on eating.
    o) He (high) kept on forgetting.

8. Repeat half of the sentences in #7 using -इराख्नु.

9. Translate the following using -न दिनु:
    a) Will she allow you to go?
    b) Allow me to sit here.
    c) Allow me to go to Pokhara.
    d) He let him go to Pokhara.
    e) Don't allow him to come inside.

10. Study the following sentences that show reasons:

i. ऊ बिरामी छ; त्यसकारण ऊ आउन सकेन ।	त्यसकारण
ii. ऊ बिरामी छ; त्यसैले ऊ आउन सकेन ।	त्यसैले
iii. ऊ आउन सकेन; किनभने ऊ बिरामी थियो ।	किनभने
iv. बिरामी भएर ऊ आउन सकेन ।	भएर
v. बिरामी भएका (कारण)ले ऊ आउन सकेन ।	-एको (कारण)ले
vi. बिरामी हुनुको कारणले ऊ आउन सकेन ।	नुको कारणले
vii. बिरामी भएकोले ऊ आउन सकेन ।	ना(को कारण)ले
viii. बिरामी हुनाले ऊ आउन सकेन ।	-एको (हुना)ले
ix. बिरामी हुनाको कारणले ।	हुनाको कारणले

Now for each of the following pairs of sentences, construct a sentence for each of the sentence patterns above.

a) धेरै पानी पऱ्यो । बाटो बिग्रियो ।

b) ऊ नयाँ केटो थियो । उसलाई धेरै डर लाग्यो ।

c) छुट्टी थियो । सबै पसल बन्द थिए ।

d) ऊ धेरै गरिब थियो । उसले छोराछोरीलाई स्कूलमा पढाउन सकेन ।

e) उसको काम थिएन (फुर्सद थियो) । ऊ सिनेमा हेर्न गयो ।

f) खुब पानी पऱ्यो । बाली *(crops)* राम्रो भयो ।

11. Study how the following sentences are connected:

i. गैँडा चरिरहेको थियो । मैले देखेँ ।	गैँडा चरिरहेको ~~थियो ।~~ मैले देखेँ ।
ii. गैँडाले घाँस खायो । उसले देख्यो ।	गैँडाले घाँस खा***एको*** उसले देख्यो ।
iii. गैँडा चरिरहेको थियो । त्यो देखेर हामीलाई....	गैँडा चरिरहको ~~थियो ।~~ त्यो देखेर हामीलाई....

Now for each of the following pairs of sentences, connect them as above:

(a)
i. शेरा खेलिरहेको थियो । उहाँले हेर्नुभयो ।
ii. शेरा खेल्यो । मैले देखेँ ।
iii. शेरा खेलिरहेको थियो । त्यो देखेर .... (complete)

(b)
i. नानी रोइरहेको थियो । मैले सुनिनँ ।
ii. नानी रोयो । मैले सुनिनँ ।
iii. नानी रोइरहेको थियो । त्यो सुनेर .... (complete)

(c) i. साथी आइरहेको थियो । उहाँले थाहा पाउनुभयो ।

ii. ______________________________

iii. ______________________________

(d) i. म राम्रोसँग सिकिरहेको थिएँ । त्यो देखेर उहाँलाई खुसी लाग्यो ।

ii. ______________________________

iii. ______________________________

(e) i. उनीहरू कुरा गरिरहेका थिए । उहाँले सुन्नुभयो होला ।

ii. ______________________________

iii. ______________________________

(f) i. नानी सुतिरहेको छ । तपाईंले देख्नुभएन ?

ii. ______________________________

iii. ______________________________

LET'S TALK

1. Without letting the other person see, fill in the phrase म...हुँ with the name of an animal, a vegetable or a geographical feature. Your tutor then has to ask questions until they can guess what you are. You can only answer *yes* or *no*. Play the game several times, reversing roles.

2. Discuss which is more important *and* the importance of each one:
   a) लेक or वन
   b) दृष्टि or सुन्ने शक्ति
   c) किरा or वन्यजन्तु

3. Take turns talking about what a(n) A can do with a(n) B:

A	**B**
गोही	माछा
डाक्टर	औषधि
किरा	फूल
मान्छे	रौँ
शिक्षक	किताब

4. Tell your tutor about the plants and animals of your home country. Does your home country and Nepal have any plants and animals in common?
5. Taking turns using the phrase -को प्रयोग हुन्छ/गरिन्छ give as many uses for *each* of the following as possible: पात, रुख, छाला, हात्ती, बाँस, वन, खोला, पोखरी
6. Discuss what things are really important/urgent for you to do in the near future.
7. Tell each other what you did just before class, using the phrase म(ले) भर्खर...:
8. Tell a story. Each of you are to build a story together by contributing one sentence at a time, in turns. For example, your tutor may begin by saying, *There was a big forest with lots of animals.* You then have to think of an appropriate second sentence. For example, *In that forest, there was a big tiger.* Then it's your tutor's turn to continue with the next sentence, followed by yourself, and so on.
9. The optimist versus the pessimist. Your tutor begins with a positive sentence like, *Boiling drinking water is good for your health.* You are then to produce a negative statement based on your tutor's. For example, *To boil water you have to cut down trees for wood.* Come up with at least twenty statements, then **reverse roles**.
10. Using the historical past, take turns making statements about things you used to do. You should come up with at least twenty statements each.
11 Describe to each other life in your home countries during your grandfathers' lifetime. Touch on the following areas: prices of things, method of travel, health practices, climate and weather (any differences?), environment (any differences?) and anything else you can think of saying.
12. Discuss what your parents didn't allow you to do when you were a child using -न दिनु.

IN THE COMMUNITY

Take a trip to the zoo (चिडियाखाना). Time required for completion: a total of 2.5 hrs. *conversation.*

The temptation will be to walk through the zoo only looking. However, you are to *talk* yourself through the zoo. Also, if you have kids, take them some other time so that you can focus on language learning this time around. You should minimally spend 2.5 hours in *conversation* with people. There will probably be considerable "down time" so you may have to go back twice to meet this requirement.

1. Spend time at the exhibits where you know the animal's name. Ask people where they are found? what do they eat? how many there are? if they attack people? have they ever seen one in the wild? etc.

2. Find someone who has...
   a) ...been to Chitawan. Find out as much as you can about their experience there.
   b) ...seen a leopard in the wild. Where? Were they afraid?
   c) ...ridden an elephant.
   d) ...the opinion that tigers should not be protected.

3. Find out as much as you can about the डाँफे (in the aviary section).

4. Ask a zoo worker if the following plants can be found in the zoo: सल्ला, बाँस, सिसौ, साल. If so, can they point them out to you?

5. Write down the names of the animals you don't know. Make special effort to learn: jackal, deer, bear, monkey and rabbit.

6. Observe the number of tribal looking people and make a mental note of how many other languages you think you hear being spoken. Also observe peoples' attitudes towards the animals. What seems to be the favorite animal?

Hint: the aviary section of the zoo is probably the best place to engage in conversation with people. That's where there are sitting benches (and the restrooms!) and where many people like to picnic.

DID YOU KNOW?

Deforestation is ranked as one of Nepal's biggest problems, causing erosion, water supplies to dry up and flooding in the lowlands.

Nepal contains 10% of the world's bird species!

Many plants and animals are considered sacred because they are the embodiment of one of the gods:

- the *pipal* tree, *dubo* grass and the *tulasi* plant -- Narayan (Vishnu)
- banyan-Lakshmi
- cow-Lakshmi
- the fish -- Matsya (Vishnu)
- the turtle -- Kurma (Vishnu)
- the boar -- Varaha (Vishnu)
- elephant -- Ganesh
- monkey -- Hanuman

It is believed by some that (taken from Nepalese Customs and Manners):

- Eating elephant ears will give you a headache.
- If you point at the fruit of a tree, the fruit will grow bad
- The man who plants bamboo can die if he steps into its shadow or it flowers.
- The bull is Mahadev's (Shiva) steed, so Newar farmers will not plow in KTM valley (because Mahadev's temple is in the valley).
- A minute piece of rhinoceros horn is required for a radio to receive and transmit.
- The high mountains are the home of the beast the yeti.
- The fox has a horn that appears when it howls.
- Elephants have pearls embedded in their heads.

UNIT FOUR

Nepali Attire and Society

CHAPTER 13

THE STORY OF THE OLD GOAT

बूढी बाखीको कथा

VOCABULARY					
बूढी	old woman	पूजा	worship	साँचो	key; also true
बाखी	she-goat	निधो	decision	बन्द	closed
कथा	story	-भनेर टार्नु	pretending X (for an excuse)	खोल्नु	to open
मर्नु	to die	टीका	tika (on forehead)	फोर्नु	to break open
दुष्ट	evil, corrupt, wicked	हाड	bone	भाग्नु	to flee, run away
ईर्ष्यालु	malicious, jealous	तैपनि	nevertheless, even then	हिस्स पर्नु	be baffled,
हरेक	each and every	फाल्नु	throw away, *syn* फ्याँक्नु	घच्घच्याउनु	rattle (door)
				धक्धक्याउनु	knock
गाली गर्नु	to rebuke, scold, abuse	गाड्नु	to bury	छक्क पर्नु	to be amazed
माया गर्नु	to love	भलो	welfare	बिर्सनु	to forget
(-न) छोड्नु	to stop doing X, quit ... ing	फल	fruit, reward result	लोभी	greedy
सहनु	endure, tolerate	फल्नु	to fruit	कराउनु	yell, cry out
तर्फ/तिर	side (of)	अन्जीर	fig	पिट्नु	to beat, hit
सोझो	honest, simple	लाखे	Newari demon	वरिपरि	surrounding, around X
ईर्ष्या गर्नु	to be jealous	-मुनि	below, under	काट्नु	to cut
खुवाउनु	to feed	खसाल्नु	drop	पर्खनु	to wait
दोबर	double, X2	फोहर	filth, *syn.* फोहोर	काग	crow
पाल्नु	to tend, raise, keep	खुरुक्क	at once	सूचना	information, notice
लच्छिन	lucky sign	नुहाउनु	to bathe	छाती	chest
चराउनु	to graze (tr)	दुलो	hole (mouse den)	रुनु	to cry
खानेकुरा	food, thing-to-eat	मुसो	mouse	लोककथा	folk tale/story
निकाल्नु	to take out, bring out, push out	सुनाउनु	to tell	सकेजति	as much as one can
मोटाउनु	to fatten, gain weight	पस्नु	to enter	बुद्धिमान्	intelligent, wise
जिद्दी	obstinance, insistance	फेरि	again	मूर्ख	stupid, foolish
माग्नु	to ask for, beg	छुरा	knife	कुरूप	ugly, unattractive

लुकाउनु	to hide (tr)	उध्याउनु	to sharpen	नरम	polite (also soft)
टुक्रा	piece	ढुकुटी	treasury, treasure room	ठाडो	rude, blunt, steep up, erect
नङ	finger / toe nail	सुन	gold	दया गर्नु	be kind, have mercy
अड्काउनु	to jam, fasten, stop moving	चाँदी	silver	निर्दयी	merciless, callous
बताउनु	to explain	जवाहरात	jewels, precious stones	अल्छी	lazy
रिस	anger	सिँढी	stair step	मिहिनेत गर्नु	to work hard
आगो हुनु	id. on fire mad	थुक्नु	to spit, थुक *n.* spit	तँ	you (low honorific)
-ने बित्तिकै	immed after	गोल	charcoal (circle)		
मार्नु	to kill	आग्लो	bar (across door)		
झिक्नु	take out, bring out	धनसम्पत्ति	riches, wealth		

USEFUL PHRASES

- नरिसाउनुस् है ! *Don't be angry, okay? (Please, don't be offended, OK?)*
- त्यत्तिकै छोड्नुस् न ! *Leave it just like that.*
- एकछिन पर्खनुस् । *Please wait a moment.*
- म छक्क परेँ । *I was amazed (surprised).*

TEXT

पुनखुँ सानै छँदा उसकी आमा मरेकीले उसका बाले उसकी सानीआमा ल्याए । तर सानीआमाचाहिँ धेरै दुष्ट र ईर्ष्यालु थिई । ऊ पुनखुँलाई खान थोरै दिन्थी तर काम भने देखेजति गराउँथी । ऊ हरेक कुरामा पुनखुँलाई गाली गर्थी । बिस्तारै-बिस्तारै बाबुचाहिँले पनि उसलाई माया गर्न छोडे । यस संसारमा उसको आफ्नो कोही नभएकोले उसले यी सबै कुरा सहनै पर्थ्यो ।

केही वर्षपछि सानीआमाको तर्फबाट एउटी बहिनी भई । सोझी पुनखुं बहिनी पाउँदा खुसी भए पनि सानीआमाले उसलाई पहिलेभन्दा धेरै ईर्ष्या गर्न थाली । पुनखुँलाई अब त धेरै गाह्रो भयो । बहिनी अलि ठूली भई । सानीआमा आफ्नी छोरीलाई मीठो र राम्रो खुवाएर पुनखुँलाई रोटी मात्र खुवाउँथी। पुनखुँको काम भने दोबर बढेको थियो । पुनखुँको दुःख उनीहरूले पालेको बूढी बाख्रीलाई थाहा थियो । त्यो बूढी बाख्री लच्छिनको रहेछ । त्यसले पुनखुँलाई मद्दत गर्ने विचार गऱ्यो । दिउँसो चराउन जाँदा त्यस बाख्रीले पुनखुँलाई मीठोमीठो खानेकुरा निकालेर दिन्थ्यो । त्यसैले घरमा रोटी मात्र खानु परे पनि ऊ मोटाउन थाली । यो कुरा कसैलाई थाहा थिएन ।

एक दिन बाख्री चराउन जाँदा पुनखुँले बहिनीलाई पनि सँगै लगी । पुनखुँले केही कुरो खाएको थाहा पाई जिद्दी गरेर बहिनीले आफूलाई पनि अलिकति खानेकुरा मागी । पुनखुँले जति लुकाए पनि खानेकुरा लुकाउन सकिन । पुनखुँले यो कुरो कसैलाई भन्न पाइँदैन अनि मात्र म तँलाई खान दिन्छु भनी । बहिनीले हुन्छ भनेपछि पुनखुँले उसलाई पनि आधा खानेकुरो दिई । छिटोछिटो खाइसकेपछि बहिनीले एक टुक्रा खाना नङमा अड्काएर घर लगी । घरमा गएर त्यसले आमालाई दिदीले खाने गरेको कुरा सबै बताई । सानीआमा बूढी बाख्री देखेर रिसले आगो भई । उसको बाबु घरमा आउनेबित्तिकै उसले बाख्रीलाई मार्ने कुरा झिकी । भोलिपल्ट पूजा गरेर बाख्री मारेर खाने निधो भयो ।

यो कुरा बाख्रीलाई थाहा भयो । त्यसले पुनखुँलाई भन्यो- "बहिनीलाई खानेकुरा नदेऊ भन्दाभन्दै दियौ । अब तिम्रा आमाबालाई सबै कुरा थाहा भयो । उनीहरूले भोलि मलाई मार्ने भए । तिमीचाहिँ उनीहरूले बोलाउँदा नजानू । पेट दुखेको छ भनेर टार्नू । उनीहरूले टीका लगाउन बोलाउलान् तर तिमी नजानू । उनीहरूले एक टुक्रा मासु खान आऊ भनेर बोलाउलान् । तैपनि तिमी नजानू । तर मेरा हाडहरू फाल्नको लागि बोलाएपछि तिमी जानू अनि ती हाड तिमीले एक ठाउँमा गाड्नू । तिम्रो भलो हुनेछ ।"

बाख्रीले भनेजस्तै पुनखुँले बाख्रीको हाड एक ठाउँमा गाडिदिई । त्यहाँ भोलिपल्ट धेरै फल फलेको अन्जीरको ठूलो रुख उम्रेछ । पुनखुँले रुख चढेर अन्जीर टिप्दै खाँदै गर्न थाली । त्यत्तिकैमा केही लाखेहरू रुखमुनि आएर भन्न थाले- "ए, हामीलाई पनि अन्जीर खसाल न !" पुनखुँचाले पनि अन्जीर खसाल्न थाली । चारपाँचपटक खसाल्दासम्म पनि उनीहरूले फोहरमा पऱ्यो, अर्को देऊ न भने । पछि तिनीहरूले तिमी आफै तल आएर देऊ न भने । सोझी पुनखुँले ल हुन्छ भनेर तल गएर दिन जाँदा तिनीहरूले उसलाई खुरुक्क बोकेर आफ्नो घरमा लगे ।

घरमा लगेपछि तिमी यहाँ बसेर रोटी पकाइराख; हामी चैँ (चाहिँ) नुहाएर आउँछौँ भनेर लाखेहरू बाहिर गए । उसले रोटी पकाइरहँदा दुलोबाट एउटा मुसो आयो । त्यसले एउटा रोटी दियौ भने एउटा कुरा सुनाउँछु भनी पुनुखुँलाई भन्यो । एउटा रोटी दिएपछि ऊ दुलोभित्र पस्यो । एकछिनपछि त्यो फेरि आयो र पहिलेजस्तै भन्यो । रोटी पाएपछि त्यो फेरि दुलोभित्र पस्यो । यसरी चारपाँचवटा रोटी खाएपछि मुसाले केही कुरा भन्न सुरु गऱ्यो- "अहिले लाखेहरू छुरा उद्याउन गएका छन् । एकछिनपछि तिनीहरू आउनेछन् र तिमीलाई मारेर खानेछन् । त्यसैले तिनीहरू आउनुभन्दा अघि तिमी यहाँबाट छिटो भाग्नुपर्छ । यहाँबाट जानुअघि तिनीहरूको ढुकुटीबाट सकेजति सुनचाँदी र जवाहरात लिएर जाऊ । जाने बेलामा भरेङको हरेक सिँढीमा थुकेर एकएक टुक्रा गोल राख अनि ढोकामा साँचोले बाहिरबाट आग्लो लगाएर जाऊ ।" पुनखुँ त्यसै गरेर धनसम्पत्ति लिएर घरमा गई । लाखेहरू फर्कँदा

उनीहरुले घरको ढोका बन्द भएको देखे । तिनीहरूले पुनखुँलाई बोलाए । तर भित्रबाट थुकले हजुर मात्र भनिरहच्यो । ढोका खोल्न कोही आएन । पछि ढोका फोरेर भित्र जाँदा तिनीहरूले पुनखुँ भागिसकेको थाहा पाए । तिनीहरू हिस्स परे ।

यता राति घरमा पुगेपछि पुनखुँले ढोका घचघच्याई । सानीआमा ढोका खोल्न आई । त्यत्तिको धन देखेपछि सानीआमाले छक्क परेर सबै कुरा सोधी । पुनखुँले पनि अन्जीर टिप्न गएदेखिको सबै कथा सुनाई तर मुसाको कुरा भन्न बिर्सी ।

लोभी सानीआमाले आफ्नी छोरीलाई पनि त्यसै गराउने मन गरी । त्यसैले उसले छोरीलाई अन्जीरको रुखं चढ्न पठाई । लाखेहरूले आएर पहिलेजस्तै अन्जीर मागे । उसलाई पनि लाखेहरूले बोकेर आफ्नो घरमा लगे । तिनीहरूले उसलाई रोटी पकाउन लगाए र नुहाएर आउँछौं भनेर बाहिर गए । पहिलेजस्तै मुसो आएर रोटी देऊ भनेर कराउन थाल्यो । तर उसले मुसालाई पिटेर पठाई । मुसो दुलोभित्र भाग्यो । त्यसले उसलाई भलो हुने कुरा बताउन पाएन । पछि लाखेहरू आए । उसलाई बीचमा राखेर लाखेहरू वरिपरि बसे । सबैले उसको मासु एकएक टुक्रा गरी काटेर खान थाले । उसको जिउको सबै मासु लाखेहरूले काटेर खाए ।

यता सानीआमाचाहिँ छोरी कहिले आउली र धनसम्पत्ति ल्याउली भनी पर्खी । तर छोरी फर्किन । भोलिपल्ट लाखेहरूले छोरीका हाडहरू बाटोमा फाल्न ल्याए । यो कुरा पनि सानीआमालाई थाहा भएन । पछि एउटा कागले यस कुराको सूचना दियो । छोरी मरिसकेको थाहा पाएपछि ऊ छाती पिटेर रोई । तर के गर्ने ? ढिलो भइसकेको थियो ।

Phrases:

छँदा: *When* or *while.* Combination of छ and दा(खेरि). Synon. with हुँदाखेरि, but more colloquial.

सानी आमाको तर्फबाट: *From the side of her step mother.*

मेरो तर्फबाट नमस्ते भनिदिनुस्: *Say hi from me (my side).*

टीका लगाउन बोलाउलान्: *They'll probably call you to put on a tika (9.3).*

बूढी बाख्री देखेर ऊ रिसले आगो भई: *Seeing the old goat, she was infuriated (lit. on fire with anger)*

त्यसले उसलाई...बताउन पाएन: *He didn't get a chance (wasn't available) to explain to her...*

उसले अन्जीर खसाल्दासम्म उनीहरूले "..." भने: *The whole time she dropped the figs they said...*

पुनखुँचा: -चा is a Newari suffix added to names. Compared to -जी, -चा is not honorific. Used of someone in their presence, it can be pejorative.

-ने मन गर्नु: *to want to do X.*

ढिलो भइसकेको थियो: *It was already too late.*

GRAMMAR

➤ 13.1 भने *AS FOR* **.** We have yet another use of भने which is synonymous with चाहिं. It emphasizes the word it follows, meaning something like *as for* or *speaking of.* In our text: तर काम भने... *speaking of work...*

➤ 13.2 रहेछ FOR NEW INFORMATION.

रहेछ at the end of a sentence means that the speaker has just become aware of the fact or that the information stated is new information. It also conveys surprise (past or present). Following nouns or adjectives (see *Complex Verbs* for its use with verbs):

सुन रहेछ ।	It's gold, I see. (I thought it was something else)
ठूलो रहेछ ।	*It's big, I see. (I expected it to be much smaller)*
म पोखरा गएँ । त्यहाँ ताल रहेछ ।	*I went to Pk. (I was surprised to find) there is a lake there.*

After हो or होइन to describe surprise at something being (or not being):

सुन हो ? हो रहेछ ।	*Is it gold? It turns out it is!*
ठूलो हो ? होइन रहेछ ।	*Is it big? No, I guess it isn't.*
सुन रहेनछ ।	*It's not gold, I see. (but I thought it would be)*

➤ 13.3 AFFECTIONATE IMPERATIVE –नू. Used often in colloquial speech this imperative (command) falls somewhere between the तपाईं imperative (बस्नुस्) and the तिमी imperative (बस) in terms of politeness. In our text: नजानू *don't go.*

➤ 13.4 REPORTED SPEECH.

There are two main ways of reporting speech:

1) The use of भन्नु and quotation marks (if in writing):

उसले भन्यो, "म जान्छु" ।	*He said "I am going".*
उसले "म जान्छु" भन्यो ।	*He said that he was going. or, He said, "I am going."*

2) The use of भन्नु together with भनेर/भनी (you learned in 12.4 as *saying that*):

उसले म जान्छु भनेर भन्यो ।	*He said "I am going".* (Lit. saying I'm going he said)
उसले म जान्छु भनी भन्यो ।	*He said "I am going".*

Note: if you say उसले ऊ जान्छ भनेर भन्यो, the ऊ always implies two different people. So, if you want to say *He said (that) I was lazy* you have to say उसले तिमी अल्छी छौ भनेर भन्यो. In other words, *He said "You are lazy."*

भनेर can introduce a relative clause and stand alone to literally mean *saying that*: **उहाँले म** जान्छु भनेर भन्नुभयो ***he** said that **he** is leaving*. Important: unlike English, in Nepali the pronouns are different.

➤ 13.5 DEFINITE FUTURE –ने–.

The definite future is used do describe a future event that is sure to happen or absolutely certain. To express this you simply insert a -ने- into the simple indefinite to get खानेछु, खानेछौं, खानुहुनेछ, etc. For example:

म	-नेछु	-नेछैन
हामी	-नेछौं	-नेछैनौं
तिमी	-नेछौ	-नेछैनौ..

COMPLEX VERBS

• **(ले) -एको रहेछ**	***surprise new info...***(past event)
ऊ आएको रहेछ ।	*It came, I see. (but I didn't expect it)*
यो नउमालेको रहेछ ।	*It's unboiled, I see. (but I thought it was)*
उहाँ**ले** नेपाली बोल्नुभएको रहेछ ।	*He spoke Nepali! (I'm surprised)*
उस**ले** खाएको रहेछ ।	*He's (already) eaten, I see. (but I didn't know it)*
उसले खाएको रहेनछ ।	*He hasn't eaten, I see. (negative)*
उसले नखाएको रहेछ ।	*He hasn't eaten, I see. (alt. negative for ऊ)*
• **-दो रहेछ / दा रहेछन्**	***surprise new info...***(present or general fact)
उहाँ नेपाली बोल्नुहुँदो रहेछ ।	*He speaks Nepali, I see. (but I didn't expect it)*
उहाँ नेपाली बोल्नुहुँदो रहेनछ ।	*He doesn't speak Nepali, I see. (negative)*
उनीहरू नेपाली बोल्दा रहेछन् ।	*They speak Nepali, I see. (but I didn't expect it)*
ऊ खाँदो रहेछ ।	*He eats, I see. (not what I expected)*
ऊ नखाँदो रहेछ ।/खाँदो रहेनछ ।	*He does not eat, I see. (not what I expected)*
• **-एछ**	***surprise new info...***(storytelling)
यो उम्रेछ ।	*I see that it has sprouted.*
मैले किरा खाएछु ।	*Oh my! I've eaten a bug.*
• **-ने बित्तिकै**	***as soon as, immediately after...***
यो खबर सुन्नेबित्तिकै म आएँ ।	*As soon as I heard the news, I came.*
खबर सुन्नेबित्तिकै म आउँछु ।	*Immediately after hearing the news, I'll come.*
घरमा आउनेबित्तिकै ऊ रोयो ।	*As soon as he came in the house, he cried.*
खानेबित्तिकै दिसा लाग्छ ।	*As soon as one eats it, one gets diarrhea.*
• **-दा...दै and दै...दै**	***while X-ing, Y...***
म जाँदाजाँदै पानी पऱ्यो ।	*While I was walking it began to rain.* (two actions don't start together)
मैले जाँदैजाँदै कुरा गरें ।	*While walking I talked.* (two actions simultaneous, same subject)
उसलाई नदेऊ भन्दाभन्दै दियौ ।	*While saying don't give it, you did.*
भन्दाभन्दै	*despite (my) saying X, Y*

• **-न लगाउनु**	***involve someone in X...***
उनीहरूले रोटी पकाउन लगाए ।	*They involved (her) in making bread.*
मैले साथीलाई काम गर्न लगाएँ ।	*I involved my friend in work.*
• **-ने भयो**	***will certainly, definitely will...***
मलाई मार्ने भए ।	*They will kill me--it's already decided.*
पानीको धारा आउने भयो ।	*Taps will definitely be coming (installed)..*
हामीले खाने भयौं ।	*We're eating, no question about it!*
• **-ए(को)जति**	***as much as...***
सकेजति सुन लिएर जाऊ ।	*Go, taking as much gold as you can.*
ऊ काम भने देखेजति गराउँथी ।	*As for work, as much as she saw she made do.*
म सकेजति मद्दत दिन्छु ।	*I will help as much as I can.*
• **-न छोड्नु**	***to stop, leave...***
तिनीहरूले उसलाई माया गर्न छोडे ।	*They stopped loving her/him.*
मैले काम गर्न छोडें ।	*I stopped working.*
मैले उहाँलाई यो काम गर्न छोडें ।	*I left him to do this work.*

PRACTICE

1. Using भने as an emphatic, translate and complete the following:
   a) खुसीको खबर भने...
   b) तपाईंको भलो भने...
   c) Speaking of the rude shopkeeper...
   d) Speaking of the lazy employee...

2. Take turns telling each other to go towards something using तर्फ.

3. Taking turns (for each word), use रहेछ in connection with the following list. However, for each sentence you make using रहेछ you first have to make a statement that explains your discovery. For example, for the word बूढी you might state (your first sentence) त्यो मान्छे बिस्तारी हिंड्छ. This explains the discovery (your second sentence) बूढी रहेछ.

बूढी	दुष्ट	मुसो	बन्द
लुकाउनु	रुनु	ठाडो	मार्नु

4. Repeat #3 using a) the negative रहेनछ and b) the short form -एछ.

5. Translate the following sentences uing एको रहेछ:
   a) You spoke Nepali! (surprise)
   b) She scolded her own mother!
   c) You stopped working!
   d) He has hidden my book!
   e) She threw away good food!

6. Repeat #5 using the negative -एको रहेनछ.

7. Translate the following sentences uing दो/दा रहेछ/रहेछन्
   a) They speak Nepali! (surprise)
   b) She scolds her own mother!
   c) You never work!
   d) In Nepal they tend goats!
   e) She throws away good food!

8. Repeat #7 using the negative -दो/दा रहेनछ(न्)

9. Taking turns for each sentence, translate and complete each sentence *twice*:
   a) औषधि खानेबित्तिकै...
   b) घरमा पस्नेबित्तिकै...
   c) हाड गाड्नेबित्तिकै...
   d) मान्छेको नाम जान्नेबित्तिकै...
   e) As soon as the tree sprouts...
   f) As soon as he ate a bug...
   g) As soon as electricity reached his village...

10. Translate the following using ...भन्दाभन्दै:
   a) Despite my saying don't drink the water, he drank it.
   b) Despite my saying don't go, he went.
   c) Despite my saying go to sleep, they kept talking.
   d) Despite my saying take a bath, they went to sleep.
   e) Despite my saying wash your hands, they didn't.

11. Using the structures दा...दै **and** दै...दै build sentences using the following verbs:

   बोल्नु चराउनु नुहाउनु खोज्नु

12. Use -न लगाउनु to build a sentence with each of the following verbs:

    बोल्नु सुनाउनु माग्नु पिट्नु काट्नु

13. Translate using -एजति:
    a) Say as much as you can.
    b) Eat as much as you can.
    c) Take as much as you can see.
    d) Give me as much as you have.

LET'S TALK

For this section, bring to class: A news magazine with lots of pictures of people.
For this section: Prepare a folk tale to tell your tutor.

1. Using the word छँदा or हुँदा with each sentence, talk about things that happened or things you did when you were small. Take turns.
2. Recount to each other the events of your day using a series of -ने बित्तिकै's.
3. Your tutor makes a simple statement. Quote what your tutor said in as many ways possible. **Reverse Roles.**
4. Talk about your definite plans for the future using the definite future tense. Then repeat your dialogue using -ने हुनु (as though anything is ever that sure!).
5. No doubt many things have changed for you since arriving in Nepal. Using -एदेखि tell your tutor what things have *and* haven't changed.
6. Using the news magazine you brought to class, flip through the pictures and describe the emotions people are displaying. What type of personalities do you think they have? Here are some of the words that you can use:

राम्रो	अग्लो	रिसले आगो हुनु	नरम
नराम्रो	बलियो	हिस्स पर्नु	ठाडो
सिधा	दुष्ट	छक्क पर्नु	दया गर्नु
रमाइलो	ईर्ष्यालु	लोभी	निर्दयी
मिलनसार	गाली गर्नु	बुद्धिमान्	अल्छी
होसियार	माया गर्नु	मूर्ख	मिहिनेत गर्नु
सुन्दर	सोझी/सोझो	कुरूप	

7. Take turns describing the following people:

Jesus Christ	Mother Teressa	Hitler
your landlord	a farmer	a teenager

8. Retell the story of the old goat to your tutor as best as you can.

9. Tell your tutor the folk tale that you thought of (in preparation for class).

10. Tell each other about the person in your life who has influenced you most.

11. You are to go fishing for words. From the list below, randomly pick a word and describe to your tutor a person who is characterized by that word. ***However, you must not use the word itself!*** When your tutor identifies the word you are after, check that word off. Then reverse roles. Do this until you have described and found each and every word. Start with the phrase:
म एक किसिमको मान्छेको बारेमा कुरा गर्छु । तपाईं भन्नुस्, यो कुन किसिमको मान्छे हो ?

राम्रो	सुन्दर	माया गर्नु	बुद्धिमान्	निर्दयी
नराम्रो	अग्लो	सोझी/सोझो	मूर्ख	अल्छी
सिधा	बलियो	रिसले आगो हुनु	कुरूप	मिहिनेत गर्नु
रमाइलो	दुष्ट	हिस्स पर्नु	नरम	
मिलनसार	ईर्ष्यालु	छक्क पर्नु	ठाडो	
होसियार	गाली गर्नु	लोभी	दया गर्नु	

12. Using the phrase --ए देखि, discuss what things you stopped doing (several phrases each):
    a) since when you finished school.
    b) since when you lived in your own house.
    c) since when you first came to Nepal.
    d) since when you got your first job.

13. Using the phrase -न छोड्नु, discuss what things you will stop doing (several phrases each):
    a) when you finish this textbook.
    b) when you move to a village.
    c) when you return to your home country.

IN THE COMMUNITY

Using the folk tale you prepared for class, exchange folk tales with at least 4 people (or until you have spent at least 3 hours *in conversation* trying).

As an alternative to this, spend at least 3 hours using any number of the "Let's Talk" exercises in the community (you can adapt them as needed).

DID YOU KNOW?

The use of spit and charcoal in the story is related to "tantric" practice. Tantrism is considered by some to be a sect of Hinduism but by others as a mixture of pre-Hindu religions that reject many Hindu ideas. The central idea is that rebirth can be avoided through the manipulation of objects (ritual) and engaging in magical rites. Most of the sexual imagery on many of the temples come out of tantrism.

In one sense, tantric worship refers merely to physical ritual. But in a more popular sense, it is synonymous with black magic and witchcraft. This is because tantrism invokes both good and bad "energy" through magical rites. There are even tantric practitioners that can be hired to bring harm to someone else, though this is largely shunned. His materials may include charcoal, spit, clothing or hair of the person you want to bring harm to, or even the enemy's horoscope. In our story, spit and charcoal are employed to ward off the demons.

In Nepal...

- As in Hansel and Gretel, there are many stories about the wicked step-mother.
- Plump is considered beautiful.
- Burping while eating, cutting in line, asking how much something cost and asking someone's age are not considered to be rude.
- It is very rude (downright unacceptable!) to step over any part of someone. If someone is sitting with their legs out for example and you need to get by, you would never step over their legs.

- If a job is below your caste or position it is not considered lazy to sit and watch others work around you.
- In the hills, it is almost expected that a husband will beat his wife.
- There is a strong losing face concept, so that rebuking someone in public or showing public anger will result in deep resentment.
- Husbands and wives never show physical affection in public.
- The Western value of independence is often interpreted as selfishness. For example, when Westerners expect their grown children to pay for their own education, land, house, etc. they are seen as being selfish. Likewise, not supporting your own parents out of your own income is considered selfish.
- Those with power and wealth are described as being "wise" because their words are heeded.
- Nepalis think it is brutal to kill even a suffering animal while a westerner would consider it an act of mercy.
- Though by law an inheritance is to be shared equally by all sons, a father's wealth is usually inherited by the oldest son. The mother's wealth is inherited by the youngest son. The oldest son is responsible to manage the father's estate after the father's death, and the youngest the mother's. A daughter is not entitled to any inheritance unless she is unmarried for 35 years. If she marries, she loses her right.

CHAPTER 14

NEPALI ATTIRE
नेपालको भेषभूषा

VOCABULARY					
भेषभूषा	attire/adornment	तिलहरी	gold pendant	जुनसुकै	whatsoever
भौगोलिक	geographic	नौगेडी	necklace (of nine gold beads)	धर्म	religion; duty, goodness, righteousness
वातावरण	surroundings, environ.	मङ्गलसूत्र	necklace	नेपालीत्व	Nepaliness
परम्परा	tradition	रुचाउनु	like, prefer	जुत्ता	shoe(s)
निर्भर गर्नु	to depend (on), rely on	नक्कली	fake	पन्जा	glove(s)
उदाहरण	example, illustration	सन्दर्भ	context	दोपट्टा	scarf, shawl
स्वाभाविक	natural, normal	दौरा	Nepali shirt	पेटी	belt
मझौला	medium (size, quality)	टोपी	Nepali hat	मोजा	sock(s)
खालको	type of, kind of, sort of	पुरुष	man, male	फुकाल्नु	take off (shoes, clothes)
विविधता	variations, diversities	राष्ट्रिय	national	खल्ती	pocket
खुब	very, extremely	महिला	woman, female	चुरा	bangle
पहिरन	clothes, attire	सारी	sari	टप	ear pin
चाडपर्व	festivals	चोलो	sari top	झुम्की/झुम्का	tasseled earring
उत्सव	celebration	-को सट्टामा	in substitution of	फूली	nose pin
परम्परागत	traditional	ज्यापू	Newar farmer	औंठी	ring
आधुनिक	modern	परिवार	family	पोते	string bead necklace
पोशाक	dress, uniform	बुन्नु	to weave, knit	माला	garland
भिन्दै	different	कपडा	cloth, material	फरिया	sari (low grade)
आजभोलि	nowadays	घरबुना	loom woven cloth	टाँक लगाउनु	to button
प्रभाव	influence, effect	तयार गर्नु	make ready, prepare	टाँक खोल्नु	to unbutton
गहनापात	jewelry, ornaments	धागो	thread, string	सिउनु	to sew, stitch

ढाँचा	fashion, style, design, pattern	महिनौं	many months	सिलाउनु	have sewn, stitched
कमिज	shirt	हराउनु	lose (tr), be lost (intr), defeat, disappear	कपास	cotton (raw)
कुर्ता	shirt	प्रदर्शनी	exhibition, show	धोती	loin cloth
सुरुवाल	Nepali pant	सांस्कृतिक	cultural	ऊन	wool
म्याक्सी	housecoat	हिसाब	accounting; calculation	सक्कली	real, genuine
कतिपय	many of/most of			सुहाउनु	to suit, look nice

USEFUL PHRASES

- यो तपाईंलाई सुहाउँछ । — *It suits you. It looks nice on you.*
- यो कहिले तयार हुन्छ ? — *When will it be ready?*
- यो लाइहेर्नुस् । — *Try it on.*
- यो जुनसुकैले/जोसुकैले गर्न सक्छ । — *Anyone can do it.*
- जे होस्, — *Anyway. Whatever the case may be.*
- त्यसको सट्टामा.. — *In place of that...*
- आउनुभएकोमा (तपाईंलाई) धन्यवाद छ । — *Thank you for coming.*

TEXT

कुनै ठाउँको भेषभूषा त्यहाँको भौगोलिक वातावरण र परम्परामा निर्भर हुन्छ । उदाहरणको लागि जाडो ठाउँमा न्यानो लुगा लगाउनु र गर्मी ठाउँमा पातलो लुगा लगाउनु स्वाभाविक हो । त्यसैले हिमाली भेगमा मान्छेहरू बाक्लो लुगा लगाउँछन् अनि तराईमा पातलो लुगा लगाउँछन् । मान्छेहरू पहाडमा अलि मझौला खालको लुगा लगाउँछन् । तर यहाँका भेषभूषामा विविधता भने खुब पाइन्छ । फेरि मौसमअनुसार पनि पहिरन फरक हुन सक्छ । जस्तै- गर्मी महिनामा र जाडो महिनामा लगाउने लुगाहरू फरक हुन्छन् । अर्को कुरा, यहाँ चाडपर्व र उत्सवमा लगाइने परम्परागत तथा आधुनिक पोसाक र साधारण पोसाकहरू पनि भिन्दै हुन्छन्। आजकल विदेशी र आधुनिक फेसनको प्रभावको कारणले परम्परागत पहिरन र गहनापातको ढाँचा फरक

हुँदै छ । उदाहरणको लागि कोट, पाइन्ट, सर्ट (कमिज), कुर्ता, सुरुवाल, म्याक्सी साधारणतया यहाँका मानिसहरूले लगाउने गरेको देखिन्छ । यीमध्ये कतिपय पहिरन उत्सव र पर्वहरूमा प्रयोग हुँदैनन् । त्यस्तै, कोही महिलाहरू तिलहरी र नौगेडीको ठाउँमा मङ्गलसूत्र लगाउन रुचाउँछन् । नक्कली गहना र प्लास्टिकका गहना लगाउनेहरू पनि यहाँ कम छैनन् । नेपालको सन्दर्भमा दौरासुरुवाल र टोपी पुरुषहरूको राष्ट्रिय पोसाकमा पर्दछन् । तर आजभोलि त्यस्तो राष्ट्रिय पोसाक कतिजनाले लगाउँछन् र! त्यस्तै महिलाहरूको पोसाक सारीचोलो हो । तर महिलाहरू पनि मौसमअनुसार चोलोको सट्टा ब्लाउज अथवा अरू नै मनपराउँछन् ।

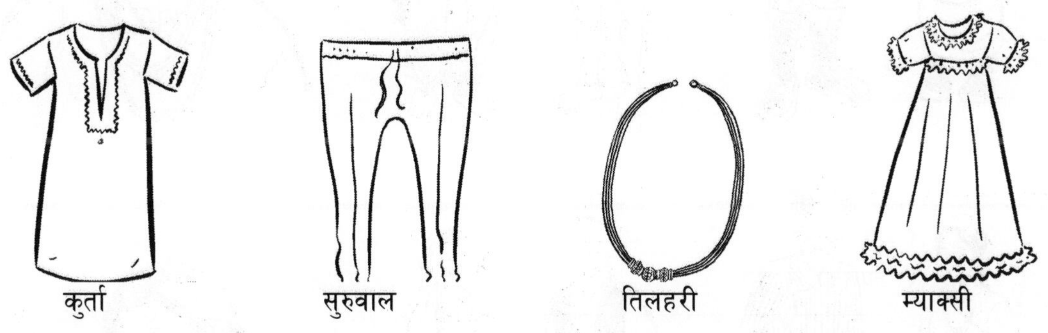

पहिले खास गरी ज्यापूहरू आफ्नै परिवारबाट तयार गरिएको हातले बुनेको कपडा प्रयोग गर्थे । ज्यापुनीहरू घरबुना तयार गर्न बाटोबाटोमा नै धागो तयार गरिरहन्थे । यस कामको लागि महिनौँ लाग्थ्यो ।

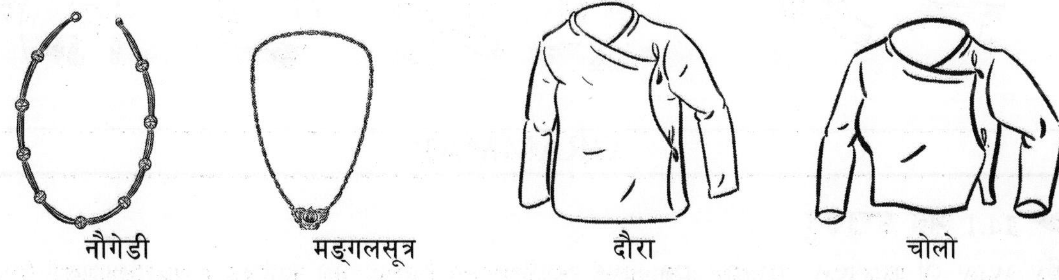

आजभोलि परम्परागत पहिरन र गहनाहरू हराउँदै छन् । तिनीहरू प्रदर्शनीको लागि मात्र प्रयोग गरिन्छन् । परम्परागत भेषभूषा हराउनु सांस्कृतिक हिसाबले

नराम्रो हो । जे होस्, जुनसुकै भेषभूषा भए पनि, जुनसुकै भाषा बोले पनि, जुनसुकै धर्म माने पनि, फरक-फरक संस्कृति भए पनि हामी नेपाली हौँ । नेपाल हाम्रो देश हो । नेपालीत्व हामीमा हुनुपर्छ ।

GRAMMAR

➤ 14.1 मन पराउनु

By way of review, many passive sentences have an active counterpart (6.3). You will remember the passives requires -लाई, while the active does not:

मलाई दालभात मन पर्छ ।	*Dal bhat is liked by me.*
म दालभात मन पराउँछु ।	*I like dal bhat.*

➤ 14.2 PAST HABITUAL FREQUENTIVE -इरहन्थे

This tense is used to express *used to keep on X-ing*. The subject of transitive verbs require -ले with this tense (but many speakers often don't):

उनीहरू धागो तयार गरिरहन्थे ।	*They used to keep on preparing threads.*
म दाल भात खाइरहन्थें ।	*I used to keep on eating dal bhat.*
उहाँ(ले) धेरै कुरा बताइरहनुहुन्थ्यो ।	*He used to keep on explaining lots of things.*

➤ 14.3 X हिसाबले *IN X MANNER, IN X WAY.*

The primary meaning of हिसाब is *account(s), accounting*. It is also used for *bill, calculation* and *mathematics*. But in the frame [X हिसाबले] it is used figuratively to mean *in X manner, in X way, in terms of X*. Study the following sentences to get a feel for its range of meaning.

तपाईं यो काम आफ्नो हिसाबले गर्नुस् ।	*Do it in your own way. (Cf. By your own account...)*
सांस्कृतिक हिसाबले त्यो नराम्रो हो ।	*In terms of culture, it's bad.*
एक हिसाबले तपाईंको कुरा ठीक हो/छ ।	*In a way, you are right. (Cf. By some accounts...)*
अर्को हिसाबले यो ठीक छैन ।	*In another way, it's not right. (Cf. By other accounts)*
मेरो हिसाबले...	*According to my guess...(Cf. By my calculation...)*
ऊ नराम्रो हिसाबले आयो ।	*He came with bad intentions. (idiomatic)*

➤ 14.4 जुनसुकै *WHATSOEVER.*

You have already learned the relative pronoun जुन (10.5). Its use in this text with सुकै is simply an emphatic form. In the same way that -नै is used, -सुकै is used emphatically with relative pronouns.

जुन ➡ जुनसुकै *whatsoever*	जहाँ ➡ जहाँसुकै *absolutely wherever*
जो ➡ जोसुकै *whosoever*	जहिले ➡ जहिलेसुकै *absolutely whenever*

Note the following possible confusion (in English and Nepali!):

जुनसुकै मान्छे *whatever person* = जोसुकै *whosoever*
जुनसुकै ठाउँ *whatever place* = जहाँसुकै *wherever*
जुनसुकै बेला *whatever time* = जहिलेसुकै *whenever*

➤ 14.5 कतिपय *MANY (OF).*

कतिपय मान्छे(हरू)	*many people*	कतिपय समयमा	*many times*
कतिपय ठाउँमा	*in many places*	कतिपय पहिरन	*many attire*

➤ 14.6 RHETORICAL QUESTIONS.

A very common discourse feature of Nepali is the rhetorical question. In our text we have the sentence त्यस्तो राष्ट्रिय पोशाक कति जनाले लगाउँछन् र ? This question is not meant to illicit a response but implies the strong statement *Not many people wear the national dress*. The statement is very emphatic. It should also be noted that rhetorical questions can sound rude and are very colloquial. The sense is often, "Come on, you should know...". Rhetorical questions are marked by the particle र.

कहाँ हो र ? = होइन।	*(has the sense, "Of course not!")*
कहाँ गएँ र ? = म गइनँ।	*(has the sense, "Of course I didn't go!")*
कहाँ जान्छु र ? = म जाँदिनँ।	*(has the sense, "Of course I won't go!")*
कहाँ हुन्छ र ? = हुँदैन	*(has the sense, "Of course you can't!")*

➤ 14.7 हराउनु

This verb is often confusing to those learning Nepali. Following is a list of common phrases associated with this verb:

म हराएँ ।	*I got lost.*
मैले कलम हराएँ ।	*I lost my pen.*
मेरो कलम हरायो ।	*My pen is lost.*
उहाँले मलाई हराउनुभयो ।	*He caused me to lose. He won. He defeated me.*
म हारें ।	*I lost. (a game)*
हराउँदै छ ।	*Is disappearing, being lost. (eg. custom)*

COMPLEX VERBS

• -इबस्नु — *to continue, keep on...*(some dialects)

ऊ किताप पढिबस्यो ।	*He kept on reading a book.*
हामी काम गरिबस्यौं ।	*We kept on working.*
तपाईं यो गरिबस्नुस् ।	*Keep on doing this.*

• -दै दैन — *absolutely not..., not ... at all.*

ऊ खाँदै खाँदैन ।	*He absolutely will not eat.*
ऊ जाँदै जाँदैन ।	*He absolutely will not go.*
हामी त्यो गर्दै गर्दैनौं।	*We absolutely will not do that.*

- **-न खोज्नु / -ने कोशिस गर्नु** — ***try, seek to..., attempt to***

धेरै मान्छेहरूले हिमाल चढ्न खोज्छन् ।	*Many people try to climb the Himalayas.*
(उनीहरू) आधुनिक फेसनको लुगा लगाउन खोज्छन् ।	*(They) seek to wear modern fashions.*
हामी(ले) त्यहाँ जान खोज्यौं ।	*We tried to go there.*

- **-इहेर्नु / -एर हेर्नु** — ***try (out), test...***

लाइहेर्नुस्	*Try it on.*
खाइहेर्नुस् । मीठो छ ।	*Try it out--taste and see. It's tasty.*
चलाइहेर्नुस् । राम्रो छ ।	*Try il out--drive and see. It's good.*

- **-एकोमा** — ***for x-ing...***

आउनुभएकोमा तपाईंलाई धन्यवाद छ ।	*Thank you for coming.*
तपाईंले यो दिनुभएकोमा मलाई खुसी लाग्यो ।	*I'm happy for your giving it. (I'm happy you gave it)*
तपाईंलाई भेट्न पाएकोमा (मलाई) खुशी लाग्यो।	*Nice to meet you.*
तपाईंलाई भेटेर (मलाई) खुशी लाग्यो।	

PRACTICE

Bring for this section: A book or magazine with lots of pictures of people in different clothes. Idea: National Geographic has pictures of clothes from around the world.

1. Complete the following sentences. Both you and your tutor should produce a unique sentence for each of the following:

   a) मेरो नेपाली भाषा सिक्ने .... मा निर्भर गर्छ ।
   b) राम्रो मीठो स्याउ .... मा निर्भर गर्छ ।
   c) म कहाँ जान्छु भन्ने .... मा निर्भर गर्छ ।
   d) शहरका बाटाहरू .... मा निर्भर गर्छ ।
   e) हाम्रो ज्याला .... मा निर्भर गर्छ ।
   f) कुनै ठाउँको हावापानी .... मा निर्भर गर्छ; किनभने ....
   g) हाम्रो यात्रा .... मा निर्भर गर्छ; किनभने ....
   h) नेपालको जनसङ्ख्या .... मा निर्भर गर्छ; त्यसकारण ....
   i) मान्छेहरूको भेषभूषा .... मा निर्भर गर्छ ।

2. Complete the following sentences. Both you and your tutor should produce a unique sentence for each of the following:
   a) आजभोलि खुब तरकारी पाइन्छ । उदाहरणको लागि ....
   b) ट्याक्सीहरू टाढा जान मोलतोल गर्छन् । उदाहरणको लागि ....
   c) दिदी हाम्रो घरको काममा मद्दत गर्छिन् । उदाहरणको लागि ....
   d) सबैजना एकएक थोक लिएर आउँछन् । उदाहरणको लागि ....
   e) नेपालमा अरू पनि रोग पाइन्छन् । उदाहरणको लागि ....
   f) .... । उदाहरणको लागि वैशाखजेठमा सबभन्दा गर्मी हुन्छ ।
   g) .... । उदाहरणको लागि सगरमाथा ।
   h) .... । उदाहरणको लागि ऊनको लुगा र धोती ।

3. Complete the following sentences. Both you and your tutor should produce a unique sentence for each of the following:
   a) विदेशी र आधुनिक फेसनको प्रभावको कारणले ....
   b) धर्मको प्रभावको कारणले ....
   c) रिसको प्रभावको कारणले ....
   d) फँडानीको प्रभावले ....
   e) .... को प्रभावले सुविधा बढ्दै जान्छ ।
   f) .... को प्रभावको कारणले धेरै पैरो जान्छ ।
   g) .... को प्रभावले बिरामीहरू कम हुँदै छन् ।
   h) संस्कृतिको प्रभावको कारणले ....

4. Complete the following sentences. Both you and your tutor should produce a unique sentence for each of the following:
   a) नेपालीहरू आफ्नो हिसाबले ....
   b) हिन्दू धर्मको हिसाबले ....
   c) स्वास्थ्यको हिसाबले ....
   d) नेपालको वन फँडानीको हिसाबले ....
   e) विकासको हिसाबले पहाडभन्दा ....

5. Translate the following general statements, remembering to use -ले when necessary:
   a) Everyone dies.
   b) Mothers feed their children.
   c) Women wear jewelry.
   d) People everywhere drink Coke.
   e) People like festivals.

6. Translate the following:
   a) In the context of Nepal, many villages don't have electricity.
   b) In this context, wearing a hat inside the house is alright.
   c) In what context did he say that?
   d) In the context of festivals, they still wear that.
   e) That is not the right context.

7. Conjugate the past habitual frequentive for each pronoun for each of the following verbs (positive and negative) : छोड्नु, माग्नु, हराउनु

8. Translate and complete each of the following sentences using the emphatic relative pronoun:
   a) जुनसुकै भाषा बोले पनि...
   b) Whatever dress I wear...
   c) जसलाई भेटे पनि...
   d) Whatever place you go...
   e) जहाँसुकै नेपाली बोले पनि...
   f) Wherever you are...

9. Re-express the following statements in the form of a rhetorical question.
   a) हिमाली भेगमा मान्छेहरू बाक्लो लुगा लगाउँछन् ।
   b) गर्मी महिनामा र जाडो महिनामा लगाउने लुगाहरू फरक हुन्छन् ।
   c) प्लास्टिकका गहना लगाउनेहरू पनि कम छैनन् ।
   d) परम्परागत भेषभूषा हराउनु सांस्कृतिक हिसाबले नराम्रो हो ।
   e) नेपाल हाम्रो देश हो ।

10. Translate the following sentences using -इबस्नु.
    a) I won't keep on telling you.
    b) We won't keep on eating daal bhaat.
    c) Don't keep on asking for money.
    d) I will keep on talking.
    e) He (high) will keep on waiting.

11. Translate the following sentences using -दै दैन:
    a) I absolutely will not tell you again.
    b) We absolutely will not eat cow meat.
    c) I absolutely will not wear that sari.
    d) They absolutely will not talk to me.
    e) I absolutely will not ask for money.

12. Translate the following sentences using -न खोज्नु:

    a) Try to do this as quicky as possible.
    b) Try to speak only Nepali for one week.
    c) They tried to go home.
    d) He tried to hide the money.
    e) Don't try to wear those pants.

13. Translate the following sentences using -इहेर्नु:

    a) Eat it and see (try it out). It tastes good.
    b) Read it and see (try it out). The book is good.
    c) Sit and see. The chair is strong.
    d) Drive it and see. It has power.

14. Translate the following sentences using -एकोमा:

    a) Thank you for coming.
    b) Thank you for telling me.
    c) I'm glad you came.
    d) We're glad you told us.
    e) He's very angry you didn't come.

LET'S TALK

1. Certain things are common in Nepal that are not common in your home country. For example, it is common for women in Nepal to wear *tikas* and it is common for women in the US to wear pants. Using the phrase स्वभाविक हो, take turns telling each other something that is common in your country that is not common in the other. Come up with *at least fifteen* phrases each. Think back over the topics of the previous chapters for ideas: weather, clothing, health, etc.
2. Turn your chairs so that you are facing away from each other. Without looking, take turns describing what the other person is wearing. Whoever can say the most correct sentences wins.
3. Using the words भिन्दै and उस्तै , take turns describing the things that you are wearing that are similar and different giving reasons why. Come up with *at least fifteen* phrases each.
4. Leaf through a magazine and talk about the different clothes *and jewelry* that people are wearing. Have you ever worn something like what is pictured? Do you like what is pictured? When would you wear something like what is pictured? etc., etc., etc.

5. No doubt you have lived through many clothing fashions. Using the past habitual (-इरहन्थें) talk about the things that you used to wear (regularly). Take turns. (Note: the regular past habitual could also be used).

6. Take turns describing the current clothing fads of your country. Then take turns describing what you think of the other person's country's fads.

7. Using the word हराउनु, what clothing fashions are being lost in your country?

8. Take turns describing what you wear for the following occasions:

   going to the market
   going to visit a friend
   attending a friend's wedding
   doing household chores
   celebrating a holiday (pick two each)
   going to a government office for official work

9. Describe the significance of any jewelry you may be wearing as best as you can.

10. Using the word प्रभाव take turns discussing the influence of the West on the East *and visa versa.* How do you feel about those influences?

11. Using the phrase -को सट्टामा, take turns answering:

    a) What do people in the hills use in place of electricity?
    b) What do you buy in place of expensive apples?
    c) What do you wear in place of national dress?
    d) As a substitute for an umbrella, what do you use?
    e) As a substitute for a bus, what transportation do you like?

12. Which list suits you best *and why*? Why don't the other lists suit you?

LIST A	LIST B	LIST C	LIST D	LIST E
रातो कमिज	निलो ब्लाउज	कुर्ता	आधुनिक सारी	धोती
निलो जुत्ता	पोते	सुरुवाल	सुनको फूली	टोपी
ऊनको मोजा	कालो जुत्ता	नेपाली टोपी	धेरै झुम्काहरू	मात्रै
ठूलो माला	रातो चुरा	कालो पेटी	टीका	
सुनको टप	फरिया	नक्कली औंठी	हरियो चुरा	
हरियो पाइन्ट	सुनको औंठी	आधुनिक दोपट्टा		

IN THE COMMUNITY

Adapt four or five questions from "Let's Talk" to serve as a basis for conversation. Use them loosely to generate conversation in the community. The assignment is complete when you have talked to 4 individuals, or until your conversation time totals 3 hours. Suggestion: if you go with #4 (leafing through a magazine), try using pictures of someplace you've been to or of people you know. That will open up all kinds of conversation opportunities.

DID YOU KNOW?

- Clothes should not be bought on a Monday, nor should new clothes be worn on a Monday.
- Wedding clothes are red (not white) and only married women are permitted to wear red clothing thereafter. A widow, however, is not permitted to wear red clothing. Only married women are permitted to wear a red *pote,* wear red bangles and dye the part in her hair red. All women except widows (including unmarried women) should wear at least some bangles.
- White clothing symbolizes mourning (not black). After the death of a parent, a son must wear pure white clothing for an entire year, including shoes.
- When eating, a Brahman man is technically permitted to wear only a dhoti.
- Even in hot weather, small children are often bundled up.
- A special ear piercing ceremony is performed when a child is one month old.
- Newari women are not permitted to pierce their noses.
- If you go out unknowingly wearing any clothing inside out, your plans for that day will be unsuccessful.
- If you see a married woman who isn't wearing any jewelry, bad luck will follow.
- The national dress must be worn in the presence of the king.
- Some ethnic groups, including Newar Jyapus, take off their caps when eating.

CHAPTER 15

NEPALI SOCIETY
नेपाली समाज

Vocabulary					
समाज	society	सदस्य	member	कार्यालय	office, workplace
जात	caste, species	प्रभावित	influenced, impressed, affected	हाकिम	boss, in-charge
वर्ग	social class	बुहारी	daughter-in-law	मुखिया	village leader, chieftain
स्तर	status, level, standard quality	प्रत्यक्ष	obvious, visible, direct	अध्यक्ष	director, chair(man) person
छूत	"touchable"	पार्नु	to make, cause	मालिक	master, owner, *syn.* -धनी
चलन	custom, practice	अधिकार	authority, right	शासक	ruler
धनी	rich, wealthy	प्रश्न	question	मजदुर	laborer, factory worker
गरिब	poor	चित्त बुझाउनु	persuade, convince	सेवक	servant
उच्च	high; noble class	निश्चय	certainly	सम्पन्न	successful, affluent
निम्न	low (standard)	जेठो	eldest (in family)	रीति	custom, manner
मध्यम	middle (standard)	बाबु	father	रिवाज	tradition, practice
बिताउनु	to spend (time)	बाजे	grandpa	रीतिरिवाज	etiquette
कानुन	law, regulation, act	डाडु	ladle (long handle)	हुन त...तर	although; of course... but ...
बराबर	equal; frequently	पन्यूँ	rice serving spoon	प्रत्येक	each and every
जिउनु	to live (a life), be alive	निर्णयकर्ता	decider	बेइज्जत गर्नु	slander, insult
संयुक्त	in common; united, joined	कमाइ	earnings, income	खर्च	expenditure
जाति	ethnic group	भर पर्नु	depend, rely on	खेत	irrigated field
निर्धारण	determination	-समेत	including	बेच्नु	to sell
देखावटी	showiness, pretence	स्थान	place (formal)	गच्छे	financial capability, for spending
इज्जत	status, prestige	केटो	boy		
जीवनपद्धति	lifestyle	केटी	girl	थर	subcaste, clan

संस्कार	rite, sacrament	जनता	people, population	नातेदार	relative
मूली	chief, headman	नेता	leader	नाता	relationship
अचेल	now-a-days	माग	demand, requisition	बूढाबूढी	elders
प्रभावशाली	all influential	पूर्ति	supply, fulfilment	राजनीति	politics
निर्णय	decision			स्वीकार गर्नु	to accept, approve

USEFUL PHRASES

- हाम्रो चलन कस्तो छ भने... — *Our custom/practice is (such that)...*
- मैले नेपालमा एक वर्ष बिताएँ। — *I spent a year in Nepal.*
- म निर्णय गरेर तपाईंलाई थाहा दिन्छु। — *I'll let you know after deciding.*
- तपाईंको केही प्रश्न छ ? — *Do you have any questions?*
- तपाईंको कुरामा मैले चित्त बुझाएँ। — *I am convinced of your point.* *Syn.* मेरो चित्त बुझ्यो।
- आज निश्चय पानी पर्छ। — *It will certainly rain today.*
- म तपाईंको भर पर्छु। — *(I) depend on you.*
- हुन त यो मेरो किताब हो; तर (पनि)... — *Yeah, this is my book. But...*
- म तपाईंको कुरा स्वीकार गर्छु। — *I accept (agree with) what you say.*
- यसको के काम ? — *This is worthless--what's this good for!*

TEXT

नेपाली समाजमा विभिन्न जात, वर्ग र स्तरका मान्छेहरू छन्। नेपालमा जातका दृष्टिले ठूलो जात, सानो जात, छूतअछूत भन्ने चलन छ। धनी, गरिब र शक्तिअनुसार यहाँको समाजमा उच्च वर्ग, मध्यम वर्ग र निम्न वर्ग पनि छन्। त्यस्तै मध्यम स्तर र निम्न स्तरको जीवन बिताउनेहरू पनि यहाँ छन्। तर यहाँ कानुनअनुसार सबैजना बराबर छन्। एउटै घर अथवा परिवारमा पनि विभिन्न स्तरको जीवन जिउनेहरू पनि हुन सक्छन्। संयुक्त परिवारलाई एउटै घर भन्न सकिन्छ। तर संयुक्त परिवार मन नपराउनेहरू धेरै छन्। जात, जाति र धनले जीवनस्तर निर्धारण गर्छ। कहिलेकाहीं मान्छेहरू देखावटी जीवनस्तरले पनि आफ्नो इज्जत देखाउन चाहन्छन्। जे होस्, जात, जाति, वर्ग र स्तरअनुसार जीवनपद्धति, चाडहरू, चलन, संस्कार फरकफरक हुन सक्छन्।

साधारणतया एउटा परिवारमा घरको मूली एकजना हुन्छ । घरको मूली सबभन्दा प्रभावशाली मानिन्छ । उसको निर्णय सबै सदस्यले मान्छन् । तर उसको निर्णय छोराहरूबाट प्रभावित हुन सक्छ । छोरीबुहारीहरूले उसको निर्णयमा प्रत्यक्ष प्रभाव पार्न सक्दैनन् भन्छन् । तर आजभोलि महिलाको अधिकारको प्रश्न बलियो हुँदै छ । त्यसैले छोरीबुहारीको पनि चित्त बुझाउनु जरुरी हुँदै छ । गाउँघरमा र अरू धेरै ठाउँमा यस्तो नहुन पनि सक्छ ।

अब प्रश्न उठ्छ, यो निर्णय गर्ने अधिकार कसको हुन्छ ? निश्चय नै घरको मूली अर्थात् सबभन्दा जेठो बाबु अथवा बाजेकै हुनुपर्छ । तर व्यवहारमा कहिलेकाहीँ यस्तो नहुन सक्छ । जसको हातमा डाडुपन्यूँ हुन्छ उही निर्णयकर्ता हुन्छ । अर्थात् जसको हातमा परिवारको सम्पत्ति छ र जसको कमाइमा अरू भर पर्छन् उही निर्णयकर्ता हुन्छ । यतिसम्म कि घरको मूलीले समेत उसैको कुरा सुन्नुपर्छ । यस्तो स्थान महिला र केटाकेटीले कमै पाउँछन् । महिलाहरू पुरुषहरूभन्दा कम प्रभावशाली मानिन्छन् ।

त्यस्तै नेपाल देश पनि एउटा घर हो । जनता यसका परिवार हुन् । अचेल यहाँका नेताहरूको हातमा डाडुपन्यूँ छ । आजभोलि महिला नेताहरूको पनि माग बढ्दो छ । तर यहाँ महिला नेताको पूर्ति हुन सकेको छैन ।

कार्यालय पनि एउटा घर हो । हाकिम कार्यालयको मूली हो । सबै कर्मचारी त्यसका सदस्य हुन् । गाउँको मुखिया, संस्थाको अध्यक्ष, पार्टीको अध्यक्ष, मालिक, शासक इत्यादि धेरै किसिमका मूलीहरू हुन्छन् । जनता, कर्मचारी, मजदुर, सेवक सबै आआफ्नो परिवारका सदस्य हुन् ।

कुनै परिवार ठूलो हुन्छ, कुनै परिवार सानो हुन्छ । कुनै परिवारमा धेरै सदस्य हुन्छन्, कुनै परिवारमा थोरै सदस्य हुन्छन् । कुनै परिवारको ठूलो इज्जत हुन्छ । कुनै परिवार धनी र सम्पन्न हुन्छ । धनी र सम्पन्न परिवारको सदस्य हाकिम, डाक्टर अथवा नेता भए त्यस परिवारको इज्जत नै अर्को हुन्छ । त्यस्तो परिवारको रीतिरिवाज ठूलो इज्जतको हुन्छ ।

हुन त प्रत्येक मान्छेको आफ्नै इज्जत हुन्छ अनि उसलाई कसैले बेइज्जत गरेको मनपर्दैन । उसले आफ्नो इज्जतको लागि देखावटी खर्च गर्न सक्छ । कोही त यसको लागि निकै खर्च गरेर घरखेत बेच्न पनि पछि पर्दैनन् । तर त्यस्तो घरखेत बेचेर पाइने इज्जतको के काम ? त्यसैले आफ्नो गच्छेअनुसारको मात्र खर्चव्यवहार गर्नुपर्छ ।

GRAMMAR

➤ 15.1 DERIVATIONS OF भन्नु.

Which one is it: भनी, भने, भनेर, भन्ने, etc.! All the ones you've learned are included below:

भने	पानी पर्‍यो भने बाटो हिलो हुन्छ ।	*If* it rains, the road will get muddy.
	तिनीहरूले अर्को देऊ न भने ।	***They said*** "Give us another!"
	म भने रक्सी खाँदिनँ ।	***whereas/As for*** me, I don't drink alcohol.
SEQUENCES	भनेपनि, भनेअनुसार, भनेजति, भनेजस्तै, भने हुन्छ, भनेपछि, भनेसम्म, नभनेसम्म	

भन्ने	टीम नेपाल भन्ने संस्था	An organization ***called*** TEAM.
	यहाँ छूतअछूत भन्ने चलन छ ।	There's the custom ***of*** touchable and...
	मासु पाइँदैन भन्ने (कुरा) मलाई थाहा छ।	I know ***that*** meat is not available.
	मैले कसलाई भन्ने ?	Who shall I tell? (***informal future***)
SEQUENCES	भन्ने बेलामा, भन्ने हुनाले, भन्ने चलन	

भनी / भनेर	हुन्छ भनेर / भनी म गएँ ।	***Having said*** okay, I left.
	उसले "नमस्ते" भन्यो ।	He said, "Namaste"
	उसले नमस्ते भनी ।	She said Namaste (***fem. conjugation***)
	उसलाई जङ्गलको राजा भनेर / भनी चिनिन्छ ।	He's known ***as*** the king of the jungle.
	भोक नलागोस् भनेर / भनी म खाना खान्छु ।	I'll eat ***so that*** I won't be hungry.
	म यहाँ नेपाली सिक्न भनेर / भनी आएँ ।	I came ***intending to*** learn Nepali.

भनेको	मैले त्यो भनेको	I said that *(informal past)*
	मैले भनेको कुरा	The thing *that* I said.
SEQUENCES	भनेको कारण, भनेको जस्तै, भनेको देखेर, भनेको मन पर्नु, भनेको रहेछ, भनेको हुनाले, भनेको बेलामा, "....." भनेको के हो। (Note: भनेको जस्तो = भने जस्तो, भनेको जति = भने जति....)	

भन्नेको **भन्नेले** **भन्नेलाई**	राम भन्नेको पसल	The store of the guy called Ram.
	राम भन्नेले फोन गर्‍यो ।	The guy called Ram phoned.
	राम भन्नेलाई यो दिनुस् ।	Give this to the guy called Ram.

➤ 15.2 पार्नु *TO MAKE, TO CAUSE.*

By now you should have recognized that गर्नु and हुनु are used with numerous nouns. For example, *to do a decision* (*decide*), *to do an expenditure* (*spend*), etc.

In the same way, पार्नु is used with numerous nouns to mean *to make or cause X*:

अचम्म पार्नु	*to make amazed (amaze)*
आगो पार्नु	*to make a fire (light)*
छक्क पार्नु	*to make surprised (surprise)*
टुक्रा पार्नु	*to make into pieces*
ठूलो पार्नु	*to make big (enlarge)*
तयार पार्नु	*to make ready (get X ready)*
खुशी पार्नु	*to make happy*
प्रभाव पार्नु	*to influence/impress*

➤ 15.3 पर्नु *TO FALL.*

Another verb that is used frequently in conjunction with various nouns is पर्नु. You've already had मनपर्नु and in this text भर पर्नु (*depend on*). Other usages:

अचम्म पर्नु	*to be amazed (lit. fall amazed)*
असिना पर्नु	*to hail (used literally)*
बिरामी पर्नु	*to get sick (lit. fall sick)*
...लाई गाह्रो पर्नु	*to be difficult*
...लाई समस्या पर्नु	*to have a problem*
...मा/लाई किरा पर्नु	*to be infested (with bugs)*

➤ 15.4 –समेत *TOGETHER WITH, INCLUDING.*

मसमेत त्यहाँ तीनजना थिए ।	*Including me, there were three there.*
मलाई दालभातसँग तरकारीसमेत चाहिन्छ ।	*I need vegetables together with my daal bhat.*
घरको मूलीले समेत उसको कुरा मान्नुपर्छ ।	*(Everyone) including the headman has to accept ...*

➤ 15.5 ...नै अर्को *DISTINCTIVE, UNIQUE.*

...को इज्जत नै अर्को छ।	*has distinctive prestige*
...को बुद्धि नै अर्को छ।	*has a distinctive wit*
...को स्वाद नै अर्को छ।	*has a distinctive taste*
...को महत्त्व नै अर्को छ।	*has distinctive importance*
...को काम नै अर्को छ।	*has distinctive work*

➤ 15.6 हुन सक्छ *MAYBE, POSSIBLE.*

यो हुन सक्छ ।	*it may be/might happen*	नहुन सक्छ	*it may not be/might not happen*
ऊ जान सक्छ ।	*he may go*	ऊ नजान सक्छ	*he might not go*

Note how the last example is negated. If it had been negated as ऊ जान सक्दैन the meaning would have been *he can't go*. If we say 'यो हुन सक्दैन', it means, *can not be done or if may not be.*

➤ 15.7 यतिसम्म कि... *TO SUCH AN EXTENT THAT.*

उसले जे पनि गऱ्यो । यतिसम्म कि उसले (एकदिन) भरियाको काम गऱ्यो ।

He did anything. Even to the extent that he did a porter's work!

ऊ जसलाई पनि गाली गर्छ । यतिसम्म कि ऊ आमालाई पनि गाली गर्न छोड्दैन ।

He chews everyone out. To such an extent that he doesn't even spare his mother!

➤ 15.8 सक्नु OVERVIEW.

सकिनु	चामल छैन, सकियो ।	*There's no rice; it is **finished**. (Passive)*
-न सक्नु	तपाईं यहाँ बस्न सक्नुहुन्छ ।	*You are **permitted** to sit here. (Permission)*
	म यो काम गर्नसक्छु ।	*I **can (am able to)** do this job. (Ability)*
-न सकिन्छ	रात पर्नुअघि पुग्न सकिन्छ ।	*It **can** be reached before dark. (Ability)*
-इसक्नु	मैले भात खाइसकेँ ।	*I have **already** eaten. (Completion)*

COMPLEX VERBS

- **-न पछि नपर्नु** — ***don't delay, lag behind...***

बेच्न पछि नपर्नुस् ।	*Don't delay selling (do sell it)! Wait no longer!*
खान पछि नपर्नुस् ।	*Don't delay eating! Don't put it off anymore!*
फाल्न पछि नपर्नुस् ।	*Don't delay throwing away (throw it away)!*

- **-इहाल्नु** — ***quickly, immediately...; with finality***

मैले खाना खाइहालेँ ।	*I ate the food very quickly. I wolfed it down.*
ऊ गइहाल्यो ।	*He's gone! Out the door!*
म गइहाल्छु ।	*I'm definately about to go.*
वर्षा आइहाल्छ ।	*Monsoon is coming definitely; it's almost here.*
खाना चिसो भइहाल्यो ।	*The food is already cold.*
भइहाल्छ ।	*Idiomatic: Good enough. It'll do.*

PRACTICE

For this chapter, bring to class: one dice, two game pieces -- a ripped piece of paper will do.

1. Circle the correct form of भन्नु in the following sentences:
   a) यो सजिलो छ । त्यो - [भने/भन्ने/भनेको] - सजिलो छैन ।
   b) छूतअछूत - [भने/भन्ने/भनेको] - चलन छ ।
   c) ऊ आयो - [भने/भन्ने/भनी] - म पनि जान्छु ।
   d) पानी पऱ्यो - भने/भन्ने/भनी - बाटो हिलो हुन्छ ।
   e) राम - [भने/भन्ने/भनेको] - मान्छे ।
   f) ऊ गयो । म - [भने/भन्ने/भनेको] - गइनँ ।
   g) टीम - [भने/भन्ने/भनेको] - संस्था ।
   h) फोहोर बाटोमा फाल्नुहुँदैन - [भने/भन्ने/भनेको] - छैन ।

i) उनले नमस्ते - [भने/भन्ने/भनी] ।

j) कुरा गरौं - [भने/भनेको/भनेर] - फोन गरेको ।

k) जङ्गलको राजा - [भने/भन्ने/भनी] - चिनिन्छ ।

l) मैले त्यो - [भनें/भन्नेको/भन्ने] ।

m) सबैजनाको अगाडि - [भने/भन्ने/भनेर] - क्यार ।

n) हुन्छ - [भने/भन्ने/भनेर] - गरें ।

o) तपाईंलाई केही भन्छु - [भने/भनेको/भनेर] - आएँ ।

p) तिनीहरूले नमस्ते - [भने/भन्ने/भनी] ।

q) त्यो नभन्नुस् - [भने/भन्ने/भनेर - भनें] ।

r) मलाई थाहा छैन, कसलाई - [भने/भन्ने/भनेर] ।

s) मैले त्यो - [भनें/भनेको/भन्नेको] ।

2. Translate and complete the following sentences (take turns for each one):

a) If I don't return in one hour...

b) They said, "_____".

c) She said, "_____".

d) As for my status...

e) The girl called "_____"...

f) The custom of caste is...

g) I know that...

h) Having said "I'm leaving", so,...

i) Having said that he was leaving...

j) He is known as the rich ruler.

k) So that I won't be tired, I am going to...

l) What I said was, "_____"

3. Draw lines to form a correct sequence and *form a sentence for each one*:

	पछि
	अनुसार
भने--------------------✍	पनि
	जस्तै
भन्ने	कारण
	बेलामा
भनेको	हुनाले
	जति
	देखेर
	सुनेर

4. Translate the following sentences using पार्नु or पर्नु:
   a) Having said that, I amazed my friends.
   b) I made a fire with dried leaves.
   c) I broke the bread into small pieces.
   d) After eating that food I fell sick.
   e) This question is really difficult for me.
   f) While traveling, we encountered a problem.

5. Translate the following sentences using समेत:
   a) Together with the apples we had lots of fruit.
   b) Including all the servants, twelve people lived in the house.
   c) Including my children, there are four in my family.

6. Translate the following sentences using -नै अर्को:
   a) The work that he has to do is distinctive -- he feeds tigers.
   b) The food is distinctive -- everything is hot.
   c) His status is distinctive -- higher than even the village leader.
   d) His boy is distinctive -- he never talks.
   e) Her attire is distinctive -- even her shoes are orange.

7. Translate the following sentences using -हुन सक्छ or नहुन सक्छ:
   a) He might not be ready.
   b) She might not eat spicy food.
   c) I might be able to finish by 5 o'clock.
   d) The patient might die.
   e) He might not be able to explain (it).

8. Translate and complete the following sentences (take turns for each one):
   a) ऊ जे पनि खान्छ । यतिसम्म कि...
   b) She agrees with everything. To such an extent that...
   c) I rely on him very much. To such an extent that...
   d) ...बेलामा मलाई फोन गर्न पछि नपर्नुस् ।
   e) Don't hesitate to sell...

9. Translate and complete the following sentences:
   a) गाउँलेहरू...मा भरपर्छन् ।
   b) Sick people rely on...
   c) The poor rely on...

10. Translate the following using -इहाल्नु:

a) I wolfed down my daal bhaat.

b) It looks like it's going to rain. I'm going.

c) He's not here. He already left.

d) Stand up quickly.

e) We finished this chapter quickly.

f) I don't have 6 rupees; can I give you 5? Good enough.

LET'S TALK

1. Discuss the things that indicate high status in your home culture. Nice clothes? Money? Work? Ethnicity? Language? Age? Land? etc. Take turns (make sure your tutor is giving you equal time).

2. Discuss your home culture's attitude and treatment of old people. How much do their children care for them? How are they supported? What age is considered old? Take turns.

3. For your home culture, discuss how often relatives normally visit and under what conditions. For what occasions?

4. Using just one dice, move through the following game board. For each topic you land on, give as full an answer as possible. If you land on "Ask A Question", you may ask the other player another question you like.

Start ➲	The importance of money	Something you lost recently	**Ask a question**	Your feelings about caste	What you did yesterday	Your ideal climate to live in	A good friend	You have to be careful about...
								Ask a question
What would you do about KTM's filth	The wisest person you have met	An important thing you forgot to do	**Ask a question**	Something you would never sell.	Something you no longer do	The biggest influence on your life		Your feelings about politics
Is it ever okay to hit a child?						Your favorite festival		Something you like doing
Something you cannot tolerate		Things you do to stay healthy	What's to the North, S, E and W of you?	The value of vaccines		Your feelings about wealth		Your taste in clothes
The most evil person you know of		A great ruler		Where you'd like to take a holiday		Something you depend on		Where you do your shopping
Your feelings about development		Something that makes you very angry		**Ask a question**		Your favorite national dress		Something you are good at doing
A time you scolded someone		Your feelings about your gov't		**PLAY AGAIN?**		A Western custom you can't accept		Your plans for next week
The benefits of electricity		Something you are experienced in				An Eastern custom you can't accept		What you do in the evenings
Ask a question		What do you like to do in your free time	A time you were very afraid	**Ask a question**	A law that has no value	Something you heard about on the news		Your most important possession
Describe a crocodile								Your feelings about this game
The importance of re-forestation	A time you were attacked by an animal	The most famous person you've met	Your most beautiful place	The highest altitude you've been to	Your most recent shopping trip	Your most difficult journey	**Ask a question**	Something different about your country

5. In your home culture, how much authority does the eldest son have? What if a younger sibling disagrees with an older brother? Who gets a parents' possessions when a parent dies? Take turns.

6. Below is a list of statements. Take turns stating whether or not you agree with each statement. *Give your reasons.* First read the statement, then alternate between the phrases: म यो कुरा मान्छु/मान्दिन, किनभने... and म यो कुरा स्वीकार गर्छु/गर्दिनँ किनभने....

   a) सबैजना बराबर छन् ।
   b) धनी र गरिबअनुसार हामी सबैजना बराबर छौँ ।
   c) नेपालमा संयुक्त परिवारलाई एउटै घर भन्न सकिन्छ ।
   d) अमेरिकामा संयुक्त परिवारलाई एउटै घर भन्न सकिन्छ ।
   e) धेरैजसो नेपालको नेताहरू आफ्नो इज्जत देखाउन चाहन्छन् ।
   f) व्यवहारमा जात भन्ने महत्त्वपूर्ण हो (नेपालमा) ।
   g) नेपालमा महिलाहरूको धेरै अधिकार छ ।
   h) नेपालमा महिलाहरूको अधिकार ठीकैको छ ।

IN THE COMMUNITY

Adapt "Let's Talk" (excluding #4) to serve as a basis for conversation with at least 4 individuals (or until your conversation time totals 3 hours).

DID YOU KNOW?

There are many different perceptions as to where one falls on the caste scale, with even local variations. Many of the Tibeto-Burman hill tribes are really outside the caste system. For example, Buddhists (including Newari Buddhists) don't fit into the caste scheme. Interestingly, it's common for a low caste to change their name when they move to a new area to lose stigma.

It is not considered polite to ask someone their caste. However, their last name (their थर) often reveals their caste. Here are the most common:

	Non-Newari	*Newari Hindu*
Brahmin	*Kumain (West Nepal):* Bhatta, Bista, Dotel, Joshi, Kadriya, Khatiwada, Lohini, Patiola, Pandey, Paneru, Pant, Pyakurel, Soti, Upreti... *Purbiya (East Nepal):* Acharya, Adhikari, Aryal, Baral, Baskota, Bastola, Basyal, Bhandari, Bhatta, Bhattarai, Chamlagain, Chapagain, Dahal, Devkota, Dhungel, Ghimire, Gotame, Khanal, Lamichane, Nepal, Paudel, Pokhrel, Regmi, Rijal, Rimal, Sharma, Sudebi, Upadhyaya...	Deobhaju (Rajojpadhyaya)
Chetri	Bam, Basnet, Chand, Kalyal, Karki, Khand, Malla, Pal, Pande, Rana, Shahi, Shah, Singh, Thapa...	Shrestha (also generic for Chetri), Karmacharya, Pradhan, Joshi, Amatya, Rajbhandari...
Baisya	*(mostly Tibeto-Burman hill tribes)* Magar (Pun, Budha, Kham, etc), Gurung, Sunuwar, Lhomi, Sherpa, Rai (Khulung, Thulung, Khaling, etc), Limbu, Tamang, Thakali...	Kumale (Prajapati) - Potters Mali - Gardeners Chippa (Ranjitkaar) -Dyers Manandhar - Oil pressers Jyapu (Dangol, Maharjan) - Farmers Napit - Barbers Nakarmi - Blacksmiths
Sudras	Kami - blacksmith Sarki - shoemaker Kadara, Damai - tailors, musicians Gaine - minstrel Badi - musicians	Kulu - Tanner Kasain - Butchers Kusle - Musicians Dhobi - Washermen Pode - Skinners, sweepers

UNIT FIVE

Nepali Life

CHAPTER 16

DAILY LIFE
दैनिक जीवन

VOCABULARY					
दैनिक	daily	ज्यामी	day laborer	व्यस्त	busy
चेलीबेटी	young women	जिम्मेबारी	responsibility	दिनचर्या	daily chores
उमेर	age	मुग्लान	India; foreign land	*आइमाई	woman
दाउराघाँस	firewood-grass	कुवा	water(ing) hole, artison well	पूजाआजा	worship & prayers
मेलापात	agricult. teamwork	मट्टीतेल	kerosene	पसले	shopkeeper, merchant
चुलो	oven, stove	चियासिया	tea and snack	भोज	feast, banquet
आँगन	courtyard	गृहकार्य	homework	भोजनालय	restaurant
सबैजसो	almost all	दुवै	both	महिनाबारी	monthly
छोरीबेटी	daughters/girls	जागिरे	employed; office worker	ठेक्का	lease, contract
मिल्नु	united; match	नोकर	servant	प्राय:	generally
एक्लै	single, alone	कुर्नु	watch, guard, wait	स्वतन्त्र	independent, free
ओसार्नु	move, carry (tr.)	होटेल	restaurant, hotel	पेसा	occupation, profession
फकाउनु	persuade, incite, comfort	वा	or	जानकारी	info; knowledge
पीठो	flour	कामकाजी	working (people)	घाम ताप्नु	warmup in the sun, bask
पिँध्नु	grind	चिन्ता	worry, anxiety	कपाल कोर्नु	comb hair
घट्ट	mill	सताउनु	torment, persecute	दाँत माझ्नु	brush teeth
धाउनु	to frequent	तयारी	ready, ready made, prepared, is tant (food)	गफ(सफ) गर्नु	to chat
जाँतो	grindstone	स्थिति	condition, situation	आगो बाल्नु	to light a fire
गोठ	goat shed, cow shed	वहन गर्नु	bear responsibility	लिप्नु	to mud walls/floors
भ्याउनु	manage to do (in time)	पूरा गर्नु	to complete, fulfill	परिश्रम/मिहिनेत	toil, hard labor, hard work
तेल	oil	अनेक	several, many	चौतारा	stone resting place
थाप्लो	head (bearing responsiblity)	कार्यक्रम	program, timetable, schedule	बेकार	unemployed; useless
कारखाना	factory, workshop	बन्नु	to be made	लाहुरे	Indian Gurkha
गलैंचा	carpet	सरसफाइ	cleaning work	व्यापारी	businessman, merchant, trader
बाट्नु	to plait, twine (rope)	सिनेमा	cinema, film	स्त्री	woman
		आफन्त	one's own relatives, kins	साँच्चै	really, truly

* Synonyms for woman: आइमाई, महिला, स्वास्नीमान्छे, स्त्री, नारी etc.

USEFUL PHRASES

- तपाईंको उमेर कति भयो ? — *What is your age (how old are you)?*
- तपाईंको बिहा भयो ? भएको छैन/भइसक्यो — *Are you married? No/yes.*
- एक्लै होइन, मिलेर गर्नुस् । — *Don't do it alone; do it together.*
- धेरै व्यस्त छु । म गर्न भ्याउँदिनँ । — *I'm very busy. I don't have time to do (it).*
- तपाईं यहाँ धाउनुहुन्छ ? — *Do you come here frequently?*
- यो कसको जिम्मेबारी हो ? — *Who's responsibility is this?*
- चिन्ता नगर्नुस्, केही हुँदैन । — *Don't worry. Nothing will happen.*
- यो कहाँ बनेको हो? — *Where was/is it made?*
- चियासिया खाऔं, गफसफ गरौं। — *Let's have tea/snack and chat.*

TEXT

एउटा नेपालीको दैनिक जीवन कस्तो हुन्छ ? यो कुरा भन्नुअघि ऊ को हो ? कहाँ बस्छ ? कहाँको हो ? उसको परिवार कस्तो छ ? यी सबै कुरा विचार गर्नुपर्छ ।

गाउँघरमा धेरैजसो चेलीबेटीले सानै उमेरदेखि धेरै काम गर्नुपर्छ । ठूलो भएपछि त ऊ सबभन्दा ढिलो सुत्छे अनि सबभन्दा छिटो उठ्छे । उसको जीवन दाउराघाँस, मेलापात र चुलोआँगनमा बित्छ । घरको सबैजसो काम उसैले गर्नु पर्छ । उसले यी कामहरू घरका अरू छोरीबेटीसँग मिलेर अथवा एक्लै गर्नु पर्छ । भात पकाउनु, दाउरा र पानी ओसार्नु, भाइबहिनी फकाउनु, आमासँग मेलापात जानु, पीठो पिँध्न घट्ट धाउनु अथवा जाँतो चलाउनु आदि उसका मुख्य काम हुन् । उसले गोठको काम पनि भ्याउनु पर्छ । नुन-तेलको लागि बजार जाने काम पनि उसैको थाप्लोमा पर्छ । यतिले नपुगे शहरबजारमा गएर कारखानामा काम गर्नु, गलैँचा बुन्नु, ऊन बाट्नु, ज्यामी काम गर्नु पनि उसका अरू जिम्मेबारी हुन सक्छन्।

छोराहरूचाहिँ मीठो खान्छन्, स्कूल जान्छन् र साथीहरूसँग खेल्छन् । छोराहरू ठूला भएपछि पुगे खेतमै काम गर्छन्, नपुगे भारी बोक्छन्, शहरमा गएर ज्यामी, भरियाको काम गर्छन्, कारखानामा काम गर्छन् अथवा मुग्लान पस्छन् ।

तर शहरबजारमा जीवन फरक हुन्छ । त्यहाँ छोरीहरू पनि स्कूल जान्छन् । शहरमा गाउँको जस्तो गाह्रो जीवन हुँदैन । शहरमा दाउरा खोज्न जानु पर्दैन, पानीको लागि कुवा धाउनुपर्दैन, लामो बाटो हिँड्नु पर्दैन, गोठको काम गर्नु पर्दैन, मेलापात जानु पर्दैन र सबैथोक किन्न पाइन्छ । शहरमा धेरैजसोले मट्टीतेलको स्टोभमा खाना पकाउँछन् । तर आजभोलि ग्यासले खाना पकाउने चलन शहरमा बढ्दो छ । शहरका केटाकेटीहरू खाना खाएर दिउँसोको खाजा लिएर स्कूल जान्छन् । उनीहरू स्कूलबाट फर्केपछि चियासिया खाएर गृहकार्य गर्छन्, रेडियो सुन्छन् र टेलिभिजन हेर्छन् । साँच्चै टेलिभिजनले त मान्छेलाई अल्छी नै बनाएको छ ।

आमाबाबु दुवै जागिरे छन् भने घरको धेरैजसो काम नोकर र घर कुर्ने बूढा-बूढीको थाप्लोमा पर्छ । बिहान खाना खाएर अफिस जानैपऱ्यो । दिउँसोको खाजा क्याफेटेरियामा अथवा होटेलमा खाइन्छ । अफिसबाट फर्केपछि थकाइ लाग्छ । चियासिया खाएर आराम गर्नैपऱ्यो । बेलुकाको खाना खानुअघि वा पछि टेलिभिजन हेर्ने समय निकाल्नैपऱ्यो । अनि घरको काम गर्ने फुर्सद कहिले पाउनु?

घरको कामसमेत भ्याउने कामकाजी महिलाहरू पनि कम छैनन् । त्यति मात्र होइन, केटा-केटीको स्कूलको चिन्ताले पनि तिनलाई सताउँछ । स्कूल पठाउन तयारी गर्नेदेखि लिएर गृहकार्य गर्नसमेत आमाले मद्दत गर्नुपर्नेहुन्छ । यस स्थितिमा उनीहरू घरको धेरै जिम्मेबारी वहन गर्छन् । श्रीमान्श्रीमती दुवै मिलेर काम पूरा गर्नेहरू पनि धेरै पाइन्छन् ।

हप्तामा एक दिन शनिवार अफिस र स्कूलमा छुट्टी हुन्छ । त्यस दिनको लागि अनेक कार्यक्रम बन्छन् । त्यस दिन लुगा धुने, सरसफाइ गर्ने, घुम्न जाने, सिनेमा हेर्ने, साथीकहाँ वा आफन्तकहाँ जाने योजना हुनसक्छ । सबै जना छुट्टीमा पनि व्यस्त नै हुन्छन् । हप्ताभरिको बाँकी काम सबैजना यही छुट्टीमा नै गर्ने विचार राख्छन्। यसोउसो गरी दिन बितेको थाहा हुँदैन । कसैलाई अचम्म लाग्ला हामीलाई शनिवार पनि फुर्सद नभएको देखेर ।

फेरि कति साहुजीहरू भने सधैं व्यस्त नै रहन्छन् । दिनभरि पसलमा बस्नु उनीहरूको दिनचर्या हुन्छ । घरमा आइमाईहरू र काम गर्ने मान्छेहरू बस्छन् । आइमाईहरू पूजाआजा गर्छन् अनि खाना तयार गर्छन् । धेरैजसो पसलेहरू घरमै दिउँसोको खाना खान जान्छन् । चाडपर्व र भोजहरूमा आइमाईहरू निकै व्यस्त देखिन्छन् । अरू बेला उनीहरूलाई अलिअलि फुर्सद हुन्छ । साहुनीहरूलाई पैसाको दु:ख नहुन सक्छ ।

बाहिर जिल्लाबाट भर्खर शहर आएका धेरै मानिसहरू डेरामा एक्लै अथवा साथीसँग बस्छन् र परिवारसँग बस्दैनन् । तिनीहरू कुनै एउटा भोजनालयमा महिनाबारी तिरेर ठेक्कामा बिहानबेलुका दालभात खान्छन् र दिउँसो जहाँ भए पनि

चियासिया खान्छन् । उनीहरूको घरको काम प्राय: हुँदैन र कुनै जिम्मेबारी हुँदैन । तिनीहरू स्वतन्त्र हुन्छन् ।

यसरी सबै मान्छेको एउटै दैनिक जीवन हुँदैन, फरकफरक हुन्छ । त्यसैले मलाई धेरै मान्छेहरूका पेसा र दैनिक जीवनको बारेमा जानकारी लिन मन लाग्छ ।

Phrases:

-को काम पनि भ्याउनुपर्छ: *She needs to manage/have time for...*

-को थाप्लोमा पर्नु: Lit. *To fall on one's head.* Idiom for *to be the responsibility of.*

-ले पुग्छ: X is sufficient. एक किलोले पुग्छ *One kilo is sufficient.* यतिले नपुगे... *If this (much) isn't sufficient...*

मुग्लान पस्नु: Lit. *to enter India* (der. Moghul). Idiom for *to go to India in search of employment.*

बढ्दो छ: The same as बढ्दै छ.

स्कूल पठाउन तयारी गर्नेदेखि लिएर गृहकार्य गर्न...: *From getting ready to send them to school to helping them with their homework...*

यसोउसो गरी: *In this way and that...*

दिन बितेको थाहा हुँदैन: *The day passes away unknowingly (Before you know it, the day is gone).*

-को दु:ख: *the problem of X.* पैसाको दु:ख *the problem of money.*

जहाँ भए पनि: *Wherever it is possible...*

मलाई जानकारी लिन मन लाग्छ: *I feel like/want to gather knowledge.*

GRAMMAR

➤ 16.1 मिल्नु AND मिलाउनु.

As you may have noticed by now, there are many uses of मिल्नु and मिलाउनु.

उसले छोरीबेटीसँग मिलेर यो गर्नुपर्छ ।	*She has to do it **together/united with** the girls.*
तपाईंको र मेरो विचार मिल्छ ।	*Your idea and my idea **jive/match**.*
उहाँका छोराछोरीको अनुहार मिल्छ ।	*The faces of his children **resemble/match**.*

उनीहरू मिल्छन्/मिलेर बस्छन् ।	*They live in* ***harmony****.*
दुईवटा बाटा मिल्छन् ।	*The two roads* ***meet/join****.*
खुट्टामा जुत्ता मिल्छ ।	*The shoe* ***fits*** *on the foot.*
त्यहाँ जान मिल्छ ।	*It's* ***okay*** *to go there. You're* ***allowed to*** *go there.*
बेकामेहरू दिनभरि मिलेर गफसफ गर्छन् ।	*The unemployed people* ***get together*** *and talk all day.*
हिसाब मिल्यो ।	*The accounts tallied.*

बाले हाम्रो झगडा मिलाउनुभयो ।	*Father* ***reconciled/resolved*** *our fight / dispute.*
यो भोलिको लागि मिलाइएको छ ।	*It is* ***arranged*** *for tomorrow.*
मलाई/उसलाई चिनी र केरा मिलाएर खुवाऊ ।	*Feed me/him bananas* ***mixed*** *with sugar.*
उसले मेरो घडीअनुसार आफ्नो घडी मिलायो ।	*He* ***adjusted/synchronized*** *his watch to mine.*
हात मिलाउनु	*To shake hands*
भिसा मिलाउनु	*To arrange visas*
हिसाब मिलाउनु	*To reconcile accounts*

➤ 16.2 –नु पर्छ VERSUS –नु पर्‍यो.

In many situations you will hear पर्‍यो used instead of पर्छ. They are actually used fairly synonymously and can be interchanged. However, there is a sense that the use of the past tense expresses more urgency and is more compelling. The action must be done in the immediate future.

म अफिस जानै पर्‍यो ।	*I must to go to the office!*
आराम गर्नै पर्‍यो ।	*(I) have to rest!*
समय निकाल्नै पर्‍यो ।	*I have to find the time.*
ढिलो भयो, अब जानु पर्‍यो ।	*It's late. (We) have to go (now)!*
तपाईंले मेरो एउटा काम गरिदिनु पर्‍यो ।	*You have to do a job for me (a request).*

➤ 16.3 PAST TENSE FOR PRESENT SITUATIONS.

As illustrated in 16.2, the simple past tense may not always be restricted to a past action or event. When something is expected to happen but hasn't yet, often the simple past tense is used (in a question). A negative response is in the present perfect. You also saw this in 10.8, where *it* ***is*** *raining* can be said पानी पर्‍यो. Some other examples include:

बस आयो ?	*Is the bus here?*	बस आएको छैन ।	*The bus hasn't come.*
घाम लाग्यो ?	*Is the sun shining?*	घाम लागेको छैन ।	*The sun isn't shining.*
खाने बेला भयो ?	*Is it time to eat?*	खाने बेला भएको छैन ।	*It isn't time to eat.*
भोक लाग्यो ?	*Are you hungry?*	भोक लागेको छैन ।	*I'm not hungry.*
बाढी आयो ?	*Is there a flood?*	बाढी आएको छैन ।	*It hasn't flooded.*
भात पाक्यो ?	*Is the rice cooked (ready)?* (Implies: Is the meal ready?)	भात पाकेको छैन ।	*The rice isn't cooked.*

When responding in the positive, -इसक्यो is often used.

बस आयो ?	*Is the bus here?*	बस आइसक्यो ।	*The bus has already come.*
घाम लाग्यो ?	*Is the sun shining?*	घाम लागिसक्यो ।	*The sun is shining.*
खाने बेला भयो ?	*Is it time to eat?*	खाने बेला भइसक्यो ।	*It is already time to eat.*
भोक लाग्यो ?	*Are you hungry?*	भोक लागिसक्यो ।	*I'm already hungry.*
बाढी आयो ?	*Is there a flood?*	बाढी आइसक्यो ।	*It has already flooded.*
भात पाक्यो ?	*Is the rice cooked (ready)?*	भात पाकिसक्यो ।	*The rice has finished cooking.*

➤ 16.4 जानकारी *INFORMATION, KNOWLEDGE.*

-को बारेमा जानकारी लिनु	*To gather knowledge about...*
-को बारेमा जानकारी दिनु	*To provide knowledge about...*
मेरो जानकारीमा...	*To my knowledge...*
नेपालको बारेमा जानकारी हुँदा फाइदा हुन्छ।	*It's beneficial when you have knowledge about Nepal.*
यसको बारेमा मलाई जानकारी छैन।	*I don't have any knowledge about this.*
मलाई यसको जानकारी छैन।	*I don't have any knowledge about this.*
*तपाईंले यसको जानकारी पाउनुभो ?	*Did you get the acknowledgment about this?*
*मलाई यसको जानकारी चाहियो ।	*I need acknowledgment of this.*
*उहाँलाई जानकारी पठाउनुस् ।	*Send him an acknowledgment.*

*The implication in the last three sentences is a legal receipt of acknowledgment. By signed receipt, जानकारी serves as proof of knowledge.

COMPLEX VERBS

- **-न भ्याउनु** — ***have time to...***

मैले काम गर्न भ्याएँ।	*I had time to work.*
मैले पानी लिन भ्याएँ ।	*I had time to get water (time permitted me to).*
सबैले नेपाली सिक्न भ्याउँदैनन् ।	*Not everyone has time to learn Nepali.*

- **–नु पर्नेहुन्छ** — ***...need to ; necessary to*** (generally)

पानी लिन टाढा जानु पर्नेहुन्छ ।	*(You) need to go far to get water.*
सबैले नेपाली सिक्नु पर्नेहुन्छ ।	*It's necessary for everyone to learn Nepali.*
औषधि खानु पर्नेहुन्छ ।	*It's necessary to take medicine.*
	..will need to (generally, future)
पानी लिन टाढा जानु पर्नेहुन्छ ।	*(You) will need to go far to get water (generally).*
सबैले नेपाली सिक्नु पर्नेहुन्छ ।	*Everyone will need to learn Nepali (generally).*
औषधि खानु पर्नेहुन्छ ।	*It will be necessary to take medicine (generally).*

- **–नु पर्नेछ** — ***...will need to*** (definite future)

पानी लिन टाढा जानु पर्नेछ ।	*(You) will need to go far to get water (eg. next week).*
सबैले नेपाली सिक्नु पर्नेछ ।	*Everyone will need to learn Nepali (eg. next year).*
तिमीले औषधि खानु पर्नेछ ।	*You will need to take medicine (eg. on the trip).*

- **–न पाइन्छ** — ***allowed, able*** (passive)

भोलि मलाई जान पाइन्छ ।	*I'll be able to go tomorrow.*
हामीलाई तपाईंकहाँ आउन पाइँदैन ।	*We're not allowed to come to your place.*

PRACTICE

For this chapter, bring to class: Photos relating to village and urban life.

1. Using the phrase -न पाइन्छ, translate the following:
   a) Tomorrow, I will be available to come.
   b) In Nepal you are allowed to drive on the left side of the road.
   c) You can hear the news later.
   d) Am I allowed to say that?
   e) Are you available to chat?
   f) Are we allowed to chat here?

2. Repeat #1 using the negative phrase -न पाइँदैन.

3. Noting that #1 used the passive पाइन्छ, repeat #1 using the active पाउँछ/पाउँदैन (and conjugate accordingly).

4. Translate the following, then respond in the negative and positive:
   a) Has the bus come?
   b) Is it raining?
   c) Is the food ready now?
   d) Is it time to go?
   e) Is class finished?
   f) Do you understand now?
   g) Do you have a headache now?
   h) Is the cooking gas finished?

5. Using the phrase -ले पुग्छ, give amounts that you think would be sufficient for the following items. If your tutor disagrees, your tutor is to say त्यतिले पुग्दैन. You then say त्यतिले नपुगे... and try another amount.
   a) ___ Rps to buy a kilo of apples
   b) ___ kilos of rice to feed a Nepali family of four for a week
   c) ___ people to lift a car
   d) ___ days to plant a paddy of rice
   e) ___ hours to do your homework
   f) ___ weeks to make a carpet

6. Express the following sentences using मिल्नु or मिलाउनु.
   a) Do your homework together.
   b) Your thinking agrees with mine.
   c) The ages of the girls are the same (match).
   d) Go left where the two roads meet.
   e) These pants don't fit me.
   f) It's not okay to wear shoes in the office.
   g) Can you arrange a job for me?
   h) Arrange a time to come to my house.
   i) Adjust your watch to the time on the radio.

7. Tense review. Translate the following and review the tense for any you have trouble with.
   a) We went to the market.
   b) He goes to the market on Tuesdays.
   c) I am going to the market later.
   d) Shall we go to the market?
   e) I am going to the market (spoken while walking).
   f) Hey boy! Go to the market!
   g) They have gone to the market.
   h) She will (definitely) be going to the market.
   i) We used to go to the market.

8. Translate the following:
   a) I didn't have time to do my homework.
   b) She didn't have time to do the dishes.
   c) Time permitted him to go.
   d) Time permitted me to cook before they came.
   e) I had time to go shopping.

9. Translate and complete each of the following using -नु पर्नेहुन्छ:
   a) वनविनाश भयो भने...
   b) जापानमा बसे...
   c) बिरामी भए...
   d) It's necessary to speak Japanese. Therefore...
   e) The village people are poor. Therefore, it's necessary for them to...

10. Restate the sentences in #9 in the negative.

11. Translate and complete the following using -नुपर्नेछ:
   a) तिनी घर आएकी छैनन् । तिनले...
   b) म भोलि जापान जाँदै छु । मैले...
   c) म बिरामी छु । ...
   d) He forgot his money. He will need to...
   e) They found lots of money in the woods. They will need to...

12. Restate the sentences in #11 in the negative.

13. Fill in the following table:

मलाई बैठकको जानकारी छ।	मलाई बैठकको बारेमा थाहा छ।	मैले बैठकको बारेमा जानकारी पाएँ।
	...लाई नेपालको बारेमा थाहा थियो	
		...ले नेपालको राजनीतिबारे जानकारी पायो।
...लाई अस्पतालको जानकारी...		
	तपाईंलाई कामको बारेमा थाहा छैन।	

LET'S TALK

1. Describe your schedules to each other when:
   a) You were in secondary school
   b) You worked at another job
   c) You were on a long distance trip

2. Describe to each other your current daily schedule.

3. Using pictures of village and urban life, describe to your tutor as best as you can what is going on in the pictures.

4. Use the phrase थाप्लोमा पर्नु to describe your respective responsibilities.

5. Take turns giving one answer for each sentence using the phrase गर्नुपर्ने हुन्छ. What is necessary to do...
   a) When you get a high fever.
   b) When your buffalo have run out of food.
   c) When your house catches on fire.
   d) When you are extremely busy.
   e) When you are worried about your responsibilities.
   f) When you are at the age of 75.
   g) When you have no more oil or salt.

6. Finish the following sentences in as many ways as you can.

जहाँ भए पनि म...	...बढ्दो छ ।
यस स्थितिमा...	यहाँको स्थितिमा...

7. Consider the following statements of opinion. Take turns stating whether or not they "मिल्छ" with your opinion. *If not, give your reasons why.*
   a) आइमाईहरूले घरको सबैजसो काम गर्नुपर्छ ।
   b) केटाहरूको जीवनभन्दा केटीहरूको जीवन गाह्रो छ ।
   c) शहर र गाउँको जीवन फरक छ ।
   d) सबै मान्छेको दैनिक जीवन एउटै हुँदैन ।
   e) जात मान्ने चलन ठीक हो ।
   f) प्रत्येक मान्छेको आफ्नो इज्जत हुन्छ ।
   g) टेलिभिजनको प्रभाव राम्रो हुन्छ ।

8. Take turns describing the typical life of the following person in your home country:
   a) a student
   b) a farmer
   c) a housewife (a home maker/गृहिणी)
   d) a businessman in a city
   e) a doctor

IN THE COMMUNITY

Converse in the community for a total of 3 hours (or to at least 4 different people) and compare their daily routines. Include such elements as:

a) waking and sleeping times
b) eating times
c) do they do puja daily? when?
d) various chores they do
e) amount of leisure time (फुर्सद)
f) seasons or occasions that make them busy

If any of the people you talk to used to live in a village, ask about the differences between village and city life. Which do they prefer? Why? If they lived in the village, did they have to get water? how far? Have they ever worked overseas (particularly India)? Doing what? As usual, provide them with the above information about yourself so that the conversation is less one-sided.

DID YOU KNOW?

Villages have usually been established where there was water. However, as a result of deforestation, the water in many areas has shifted far away. Because of this, in some areas one member of the family's time will almost be solely occupied with fetching water, sometimes having to walk up to two hours one way.

Unlike the West, Nepalis don't impose a nap time or bedtime on children. They sleep when they fall asleep.

Daily *puja*:
In most Hindu homes *puja* is a part of every morning's routine. It is usually performed by an older member of the household, usually the oldest woman. Younger members of the family will often simply bow to the idol rather than performing *puja* duties. Food offerings (*prasad*) from the *puja* are then distributed to the other members of the family to eat as a blessing. In wealthy families, a Brahmin priest may be employed to perform such duties. In this modern age, however, there is an increasing number who show no interest in doing any *puja* whatsoever. It is also common for a member of a household to

perform an evening light offering with the ringing of a bell. This one is less detailed than the morning puja, and in the evening one can hear the ringing of bells and see wick lights being waved in a circle from many rooftops.

Many pious Hindus will frequent a neighborhood temple regularly, and on auspicious days they will frequent prominent temples depending on the occasion or day of the week. For example, Saturday is a popular day for Dakshin Kali, Shova Bhagwati, and Mahankal. Pashupati is popular on Monday, Kathmandu Ganesh is popular on Tuesdays, Bagalamukhi on Thursdays.

Eating time:

In Nepal, eating time varies depending on a person's occupation. Valley farmers will eat *daal bhaat* at dawn so that he can work in the field or make it to a vegetable market. He'll then eat a heavy snack (*chiuraa* and *tarkaari*) around 1 o'clock, followed by a final meal of *daal bhaat* at 6 o'clock in the evening. An office worker will eat his first meal at 9:30 before going to work, have a snack at work or a "hotel", followed by the final meal at 7 or 8 p.m. A businessman or shopkeeper will eat breakfast around 8 o'clock, lunch at 2 o'clock, snack at 5 and the final meal around 10 o'clock.

Busy months for farmers:

In the Kathmandu valley, farmers are busy year round because so many different kinds of crops can be grown. In areas that depend on the monsoon for agriculture, life is busy 3-4 months of the year. In areas that grow maize, millet or buckwheat, life is busy only 2-3 months of the year. Many people from these areas migrate to urban areas in the down time in search of temporary employment, often going to India.

CHAPTER 17

ANIMAL HUSBANDARY
पशुपालन

VOCABULARY					
विकट	Interior	ढङ्ग	manner, style	माहुरी	bee
पशुपालन	animal husbandry	बाँध्नु	to tie, bind	उन्नत	improved quality
कृषि अर्थव्यवस्था	agro-economy	उपयुक्त	appropriate, fitting	विकासे	developed, improved
भूमिका	role	व्यवसाय	occupation, business, trade	प्राविधिक	technical; technician
गाई	cow	चिसो	damp, cold	आधुनिकीकरण	modernization
भैँसी	buffalo (fem)	कार्य	work, act, deed	आत्मनिर्भर	self dependent/suffic.
बाखो	goat	उपाय	method, solution	सम्भावना	probability, feasibility
एक अर्को	each other, one another	चौर	meadow, field	सञ्चालन गर्नु	conduct, operate
सहायक	assistant, subsidiary, tributary	खर्क	hillside grazing land	हाल	news, at present, recently
पैदावार	crop, produce	भैँडो	sheep	केन्द्र	center, hub
मलमूत्र	dung-urine, excreta	च्याङ्ग्रो	hill goat	स्थापना हुनु	be founded
बारी	dry field, garden	चौँरी	yak	पालन	tending, care
मल	manure, fertilizer	खच्चर	mule	अङ्गोरा	Angora (rabbit)
गोबर	cow dung	गधा	donkey	मूल्यवान्	valuable; precious
जोत्नु	plow	बोकाउनु	get/have carried	थुप्रै	a lot, many, heaps
दाइँ गर्नु	thresh by oxen	बेँसी	lowland, base of hill	फुल	egg
गाडा	cart	जीविका चलाउनु	earn livelihood	उत्पादन	produce, production
तान्नु	pull	गुरुङ	Gurung (ethnic)	गुणस्तरीय	standard, quality
दूध	milk	बढी	a lot, so much, more	चल्ला	chick, duckling
पशु	animal	सन्तुष्ट	satisfied, content	पौष्टिक	nutritious
प्राप्त हुनु	be obtained, received	गोरु	ox	दाना	animal feed
बोसो	fat, grease, lard	सुँगुर	pig, hog	खोर	pen, sty, cage, jail
खुर	hoof	कुखुरो	chicken	प्रबन्ध	arrangement
सिङ	horn	हाँस	duck	भारतीय	Indian
खेर जानु	go to waste, vain	खरायो	rabbit	विकट	difficult (place)
ज्यादै	too much				

USEFUL PHRASES

- तपाईंको भनाइको अर्थ के हो ? — *What do you mean?*
- अब जानुको कुनै अर्थ छैन । — *There's no point in going now.*
- उल्टो अर्थ नलगाउनुस् । — *Don't misunderstand/misconstrue (me).*
- तपाईंले यो प्राप्त गर्नुभएको छ ? — *Have you received it?*
- धेरै नदिनुस्, खेर जान्छ । — *Don't give (me) lots; it will go to waste.*

TEXT

नेपालको कृषिअर्थव्यवस्थामा पशुपालनको महत्त्वपूर्ण भूमिका छ । यसमा गाई, भैँसी र बाख्रा प्रमुख छन् । कृषि र पशुपालन नङ र मासुजस्तै हुन् । यी एक अर्काका सहायक हुन् । धेरै कृषि पैदावारहरूलाई पशुहरूको आहारका रूपमा लिइन्छ भने पशुबाट फालिएको मलमूत्र खेतबारीको लागि कम्पोष्ट मल बन्दछ । आजभोलि गोबर ग्यासको प्रयोग पनि बढ्दै छ । खेत जोत्न, दाइँ गर्न, गाडा तान्न, भारी बोक्न पनि पशुहरू धेरै प्रयोग गरिन्छन् । दूध, मासु, ऊन, छाला पनि पशुबाटै प्राप्त हुन्छ । पशुका बोसो, हाड, खुर र सिङसमेत खेर जाँदैनन् ।

नेपालमा पशुपालन ज्यादै पुरानो ढङ्गबाट चलेको छ । वनविनाश रोकिने किसिमले पशुहरू बाँधेर पाल्ने चलन राम्रो हो । जहाँ खेती उपयुक्त हुँदैन त्यहाँ पशुपालन नै मुख्य व्यवसाय हुन्छ । नेपालको उत्तरी क्षेत्रमा कृषिकार्य (खेतीको काम) कठिन हुन्छ; किनभने त्यहाँ विकट भौगोलिक स्थिति, चिसो हावापानी र धेरै उचाइ छ।

त्यहाँ पशुपालन नै राम्रो पेसा हो । त्यसकारण लेकमा बस्नेहरूको मुख्य पेसा नै पशुपालन हो । त्यहाँका मानिसहरू खाली चौर र खर्कहरूमा भेँडा, च्याङ्ग्रा, चौँरी, खच्चर, गधा आदि चराउने गर्छन् । त्यहाँ गधा र खच्चर भारी बोकाउने काममा प्रयोग गरिन्छन् भने भेँडा, च्याङ्ग्रा, चौँरी गाईचाहिँ मासु, दूध, ऊन तथा छालाको लागि पालिन्छन् । तैपनि यी सबै जनावरहरूको मुख्य काम बेँसीको सामान पहाड र पहाडको सामान बेँसी ओसार्नु हो । यसैबाट उत्तरी भेगका धेरै मान्छेहरू जीविका चलाउँछन् । खास गरी सेर्पा र गुरुङ जाति यस पेसाबाट बढी प्रभावित र सन्तुष्ट देखिन्छन् ।

मध्यपहाडी क्षेत्र, तराई र उपत्यकाका मानिसहरू कृषिपछि सहायक पेसाको रूपमा गाई, गोरु, भैँसी, बाखा, सुँगुर, कुखुरा, हाँस, खरायो, माहुरी आदि पाल्ने गर्छन् । यसमा कुनैकुनै पशुहरू खेत जोत्न, गाडा तान्न, भारी बोक्न, दाइँ गर्न प्रयोग गरिन्छन् भने कुनैकुनै पशुहरू मासु, दूध र छालाको लागि पाल्ने गरिन्छन् । यहाँ उन्नत जातको (विकासे) पशु, प्राविधिक ज्ञान र पशुस्वास्थ्य ज्ञानको आवश्यकता छ।

पशुपालन व्यवसायलाई आधुनिकीकरण गरी हामी मासु, दूध आदि कुरामा आत्मनिर्भर हुनुपरेको छ । यसको विकासको सम्भावना भएका क्षेत्रहरूमा पशु विकास कार्यक्रमको सञ्चालन गरिएको छ । हाल ललितपुर, चितवन, पोखरा, नुवाकोट, मकवानपुर, जुम्ला आदि ठाउँहरूमा पशु विकास फार्महरू सञ्चालन भएका छन् । ठाउँठाउँमा पशु स्वास्थ्य केन्द्रको पनि स्थापना भएका छन् ।

आजभोलि खरायो पालन पनि सुरु हुँदै छ । छाला, मासु र ऊनको लागि खरायो पालिन्छ । यसमा अङ्गोरा जातको खरायो प्रमुख छ । खरायोको छाला र ऊनबाट बनेका विभिन्न सामान मूल्यवान् हुन्छन् । त्यसको बजार व्यवस्था राम्रो बनाउनुपर्ने देखिन्छ । खरायोको मासु पनि राम्रो मानिन्छ ।

मासु र फुलको लागि कुखुरापालन महत्त्वपूर्ण छ । नेपालमा विभिन्न हचाचरी र पोल्ट्री फार्महरूले थुप्रै मासु र फुल उत्पादन गर्छन् । यसको अलावा सानो स्तरमा घरघरमा कुखुरापालन गर्नेहरू ठाउँठाउँमा भेटिन्छन् । प्राविधिक ज्ञान, गुणस्तरीय विकासे चल्ला, पौष्टिक दाना र खोरको प्रबन्ध यसका आवश्यकता हुन् । धेरैजसो पौष्टिक दाना र हचाचरीको मेसिन, औषधि इत्यादि भारतबाट आउँछन् । अरू विदेशी मेसिन महँगो पर्छ । कहिलेकाही" फुल र मासुको बजारसमेत भारतीय बजारमा भर पर्छ ।

Phrases:

बन्दछ: A literary convention that is the same as बन्छ.

पहाडको सामान बेँसी ओसार्नु: *transport goods from the hills to the lowlands.*

यताको सामान उता गर्नु: *transport goods from here to there.*

उन्नत जातको: *improved variety*

कार्यक्रमहरू सञ्चालन गरिएको छ: *programs have been conducted*

पशु स्वास्थ्य केन्द्र: *veterinary clinic* स्वास्थ्यकेन्द्र: *health post*

साना स्तर: *small scale*

GRAMMAR

➤ 17.1 –समेत *EVEN.* (*Syn.* पनि)

In addition to meaning *together with, including* (15.4), समेत also can mean *even.*

बोसो, हाड, र सिङसमेत खेर जाँदैन ।	*Even the fat, bones and horns do not go to waste.*
मेरा बा र आमासमेत धेरै हिँड्न सक्नुहुन्छ ।	*Even my mother and father can walk a long way.*
सानो गाउँमा समेत बिजुली छ ।	*Even small villages have electricity.*
कुनै कुनै बाहुनहरू फुलसमेत खाँदैनन् ।	*Some brahmins don't even eat eggs.*
पशुले समेत पौष्टिक खाना खानु पर्छ ।	*Even animals need to eat nutritious food.*

➤ 17.2 PASSIVES MARKED FOR NUMBER.

Consider the following three sentences found in our text:

गुरुङ जाति...सन्तुष्ट देखिन्छन् ।	*Gurungs appear content.*
पशुहरू प्रयोग गरिन्छन् ।	*Animals are used.*
कुखुरापालन गर्नेहरू भेटिन्छन् ।	*People who raise chickens are encountered.*

All of these end in -छन् rather than -छ. In these sentences the object is plural: गुरुङ जाति, पशुहरू, पालन गर्नेहरू. In passive sentences, if the object is plural the verb is marked with -छन्.

COMPLEX VERBS

• -ने किसिमले — *in a way that x's...*

वनविनाश रोकिने किसिमले	*In a way that stops forest destruction*
(उसले) यो खेर जाने किसिमले गऱ्यो ।	*(He) did it in a way that was wasteful.*
(उसले) अरूलाई सताउने किसिमले गफसफ गऱ्यो ।	*(He) chatted in a way that tormented others.*
प्राप्त हुने किसिमले	*In a way that could be obtained*
उल्टो अर्थ लगाउने किसिमले	*In a way that misconstrues/miscommunicates.*

• -ने गर्नु — *do as a practice, habit...*

उनीहरू खरायो पाल्ने गर्छन् ।	*They practice rabbit raising.*
उनीहरू खच्चर चराउने गर्छन् ।	*They have the practice of grazing mules.*
म रक्सी खाने गर्दिनँ ।	*I don't have the habit of drinking alcohol.*
उनीहरू खोरमा राख्ने गर्छन् ।	*They put (them) in a pen (as a practice).*
तिनीहरूलाई मासु र दूधको लागि पाल्ने गरिन्छ ।	*They are raised for milk and meat (as a practice).*

• -नु परेको छ — *necessary to be... has been necessary to ...*

(हामी) आत्मनिर्भर हुनु परेको छ ।	*(We) have to be self-sufficient.*
	Compare (not much difference!):
आत्मनिर्भर हुनु पऱ्यो ।	*It is (or was) necessary to be self-sufficient.*
आत्मनिर्भर हुनु पर्छ ।	*It's necessary to be self-sufficient* (generally).

आत्मनिर्भर हुनु पर्ने हुन्छ ।	*It's necessary to be self sufficient* (generally).
आत्मनिर्भर हुनु पर्नेछ ।	*(We'll) need to be self sufficient.*

- **-नु पर्ने देखिन्छ** — ***seems/appears necessary to...***

यसलाई राम्रो बनाउनु पर्ने देखिन्छ ।	*It seems necessary to build it well.*
यसो हेर्दा जानु पर्ने देखिन्छ ।	*It seems necessary to go. (when we look)*
यसो हेर्दा खानु पर्ने देखिन्छ ।	*It seems necessary to eat (it). (when we look)*

PRACTICE

For this chapter, bring to class: Photos relating to animal husbandry.

1. Using the phrase -ने किसिमले, take turns constructing sentences with the following verbs:

   बताउनु   सुनाउनु   निर्भर गर्नु   तयार गर्नु   खेर नजानु   बेइज्जत नगर्नु

2. Translate and complete each of the sentences twice:

   a) गाईभैँसीसमेत...

   b) गाईको गोबरसमेत...

   c) Even the restaurants of Kathmandu...

   d) She doesn't even like...

   e) Will a boy who torments even his mother and father...?

3. Complete each of the sentences with two reasons each:

   a) ...त्यसकारण जानुपर्ने देखिन्छ ।

   b) ...त्यसकारण धाउनुपर्ने देखिन्छ ।

   c) ...त्यसकारण आगो बाल्नुपर्ने देखिन्छ ।

   d) ...त्यसकारण पोसाक लगाउनुपर्ने देखिन्छ ।

   e) ...त्यसकारण आफ्नो लुगा बुन्नुपर्ने देखिन्छ ।

   f) ...त्यसकारण माया गर्नुपर्ने देखिन्छ ।

4. Following are several situations. Using the phrase -नु पर्ने देखिन्छ, produce a sentence in response to each sentence below (what does it seem necessary to do as a result).

    a) मेरो छोरो एकदम बिरामी छ ।
    b) पशुहरूलाई दाना सकियो ।
    c) कोठा धेरै चिसो छ ।
    d) आफन्तले मलाई बोलाउनुभएको छ ।
    e) पैसा सिद्धियो ।
    f) चिनी छैन ।
    g) पानी पऱ्यो ।
    h) भोक लाग्यो ।

5. Translate and complete the following using -नु परेको छ, -नु पऱ्यो, -नु पर्छ, -नु पर्ने हुन्छ, and -नु पर्नेछ:

    a) उहाँ घर आउनुभएको छैन; त्यसकारण ....
    b) म भोलि जापान जान्छु; त्यसकारण ....
    c) म बिरामी छु; त्यसकारण ....
    d) He forgot his money. Therefore ....
    e) They found lots of money in the woods. Therefore ....

6 Complete each of the following:

    a) त्यहाँ जानुको कुनै अर्थ छैन; किनभने ....
    b) .... मा काम गर्नुको कुनै फाइदा छैन; किनभने ....
    c) .... भन्नुको कुनै फाइदा छैन; किनभने ....
    d) .... सिक्नुको कुनै फाइदा छैन; किनभने ....
    e) .... किन्नुको कुनै फाइदा छैन; किनभने ....

LET'S TALK

1 Together with your tutor, discuss the role of

    a) cows in Nepal; in your home country.
    b) men in Nepal; in your home country.
    c) women in Nepal; in your home country.
    d) animal husbandry in Nepal; in your home country.
    e) carts in Nepal; in your home country.

2. Using the phrases below, produce sentences about something that is done as a practice or a habit. Each of you is to produce two sentences for each phrase; the first one positive, the second one negative.

...खाने गर्नु	...गाडा तान्ने गर्नु	...बन्ने गर्नु
...ओसार्ने गर्नु	...धाउने गर्नु	...गफसफ गर्ने गर्नु

3. Without letting your tutor see what is written, write down म...हुँ , filling in the blank with the name of an animal. For example, म गाई हुँ. Your tutor then asks questions that can only be answered "yes" or "no" and tries to figure out what you are. Reverse roles so that each of you have three turns being an animal and three turns guessing.

4. Discuss the pictures you have brought to class.

5. Compare between Nepal and your home country for the following animals:
गाई, भैंसी, बाखा, भेँडा, चौँरी, खच्चर, गधा, गोरु, सुँगुर, कुखुरा, हाँस, खरायो
   a) appearance of
   b) frequency of
   c) use of
   d) importance of
   e) diet of

6. Compare between Nepal and your home country methods of:
   a) fertilizing fields
   b) irrigating fields
   c) plowing fields
   d) threshing grain
   e) milking livestock
   f) grazing livestock
   g) tending livestock
   h) feeding livestock

7. Discuss together diet prohibitions of different religions and cultures.

8. Role play. You are a reporter for Nepal TV and your tutor is a villager. The reporter is doing a story on the use of domestic animals in the village and interviews the villager. Ask as many *who, what, where, when* and *why* questions as you can. Then reverse roles.

9. Role play through the community assignment (in the classroom).

IN THE COMMUNITY

This community assignment has no time constraints, but it does require that *all* of the questions be asked of at least *two* different people. Or alternatively, elicit two answers for each of the following questions. You will likely have to ask these question of someone who is (or was) a farmer or someone who lives in a rural area. If you can't think of how to ask a question in Nepali, try to think of other ways you could approach the same question.

1) Which animal is regarded as the most valuable:
   a) cow b) bull c) buffalo
   d) buffalo bull (राँगो) e) goat f) pig
2) How much does each of the following cost:
   a) cow b) bull c) buffalo
   d) buffalo bull (राँगो) e) goat f) pig
3) What is the most important role/use of a cow?
4) How much milk (liters) does a cow produce? a buffalo?
5) Is cow's milk or buffalo's milk more expensive?
6) Do you eat meat? Is there any kind of meat you can't eat? If so, what kinds and why?
7) Why do farmers dig by hand in Kathmandu (if they know)?
8) What sort of things is cow-dung used for? How is it used in puja?
9) When are fields fertilized?
10) Have they ever raised chickens or ducks?
11) What is the value of chickens?
12) How many eggs will a chicken produce in a week?
13) Are domestic animals ever rented or hired? For how much?
14) Whose job is it to graze livestock?

DID YOU KNOW?

It is illegal to slaughter cows in Nepal even after a cow has grown old and is no longer useful for farming. As a result, old cattle are often let go to wander astray. Rumor has it, though, that recently old cattle are smuggled into India (especially from the Western Terai) where Muslim butchers slaughter them. Some of this meat is then smuggled back into the country. In areas where the people are animistic, there is no religious prohibition against eating beef. They will eat cattle that died falling from a hillside (sometimes encouraging a fall).

Momos are often made from the meat of old male buffaloes that are no longer useful as farm animals.

Interesting proverbs:

भीरबाट खसेको गाईलाई रामराममात्र भन्न सकिन्छ, काँध थाप्न सकिँदैन ।

One can only say "Ram, Ram" to a cow falling from a cliff; a shoulder can't be given to stop it.

Meaning: Someone is not in a position to help another person, though they are headed for certain trouble. Even though they can sympathize, "their hands are tied".

मान्छे बूढो भएपछि निहुँ खोज्छ, गोरु बूढो भएपछि भीर खोज्छ ।

As an old ox looks for a cliff (to fall off of), so an old man looks to grumble.

Meaning: Nepalis will claim that when cattle get old, they attempt suicide by nature. In the same way, old people tend to complain by nature.

साउनमा आँखा फुटेको गोरुले सधैं हरियो देख्छ ।

A cow that burst its eye during the month of Saun (during monsoon) sees green forever.

Meaning: Used of a person who repeats a story over and over with great embellishment; someone who only remembers "the glory days".

कानो गोरुलाई औंसी न पुर्ने ।

To a one eyed ox, new moon or full moon (it doesn't matter).

Meaning: Used of someone who doesn't care whether something is good or bad.

CHAPTER 18

AGRICULTURE IN NEPAL
नेपालमा कृषि

VOCABULARY					
आधारित	based (on)	नगदे	cash (crop, etc.)	लहरै	in rows, lines
करिब	about, approx.	बाली	crop	लाप्पा खेल्नु	mud wrestle
प्रतिशत	percent (per 100)	नपुग हुनु	be insufficient, deficient	पर्म	work exchange
अधिकांश	most, more than 50%	आपूर्ति	supply	गाउनु	sing
भूमि	earth, ground, land	छेउ	side, edge	गीत	song
आकासे / 'शे	of sky, rain dependent	गरा	terrace	छुपुछुपु	way of planting rice
उब्जनी	produce, crop	खला	plots	आली	ridge dividing rice field
भिरालो	steep, precipitous	थुन्नु	trap, detain, imprison	दोहोरी	duet (song)
मकै	corn, maize	अड्नु	stop, halt (intr)	रहिरहनु	continue to remain
टारी	unirrigated field	जग्गा	land (plot of)	झार	weed, thicket
धान	paddy (rice)	हिले	muddy	उखेल्नु	uproot
गहुँ	wheat	रासायनिक मल	chemical fert.	मनमोहक हुनु	to be charming
लेकाली	mountainous (high hills)	अत्यधिक	excessive(ly)	पाक्नु	to ripen; be cooked
झन्	the more, still	कीटनाशक	insecticide	पारिलो घाम	warm (Sun)
तसर्थ	thus, therefore	भ्यागुता	frog	गुदी	kernel
समथर	plain (land)	सर्प	snake	कडा	hard, harsh (bun)
चाप	pressure	गँगटो	crab	बिछ्याउनु	lay out bedding
कोदो	millet	रोप्नु	plant, transplant	मनै लोभिनु	be attracted
जौ	barley	साथै	along with	भित्र्याउनु	take in, import
निर्यात	export	बीउ	seed	योग्य	fit, able, worthy, qualified
घट्नु	to decrease (intr)	छुट्टै	separate(ly)	किसान	farmer
कामदार	worker, employee	ब्याड	bed (nursery)	बाढी	flood
बिदेशिनु	emigrate	उमारिनु	be grown, sprout	सफल	successful, fruitful
बचत	profit, saving(s)	हिल्याउनु	to puddle (fields)	तातो	hot (to touch)
कमी	lack	बाउसे	"puddler"	फलाउनु	to fruit, grow (tr)
अन्य	others (*syn.* अरू)	रोपाइँ	rice planting	उत्तम	excellent, best

USEFUL PHRASES

- झन् राम्रो । — *Even/more better!*
- महँगो भयो, अलिकति घटाउनुस् । — *It's (too) expensive; please reduce (the price).*
- सफल भयो ? — *Was it successful? Did it work out?*
- समयको बचत — *saving of time*
- जहाँ इच्छा, त्यहाँ उपाय । — *Where there's a will, there's a way.*
- यो काम गर्न योग्य छ । — *This work's worth doing/He's fit for this work.*
- गहुँ कसरी उम्रँदै छ ? राम्रोसँग उम्रँदै छ । — *How's the wheat growing? Well.*
- अहिले केके उमार्नुहुन्छ ? — *What all are you growing now?*

TEXT

नेपालको अर्थव्यवस्था खास गरी कृषिमा आधारित छ । करिब ८० प्रतिशत जनसङ्ख्या यस पेसामा लागेको छ । तर कृषिपेसामा लागेका सबै मानिसहरू कृषिमा मात्र भर पर्छन् भन्न सकिन्न । किनभने उनीहरू वर्षमा करिब तीनचार महिना मात्र कृषिकार्यमा व्यस्त हुन्छन् । खास गरी वर्षा हुन्जेल उनीहरूको फुर्सद हुँदैन । त्यसैले उनीहरूको प्रमुख पेसा कृषि नै मानिन्छ ।

नेपालको कृषि परम्परागत ढङ्गले नै चलिरहेको छ । यहाँ सिँचाइको सुविधा थोरै भएकोले अधिकांश कृषिभूमि आकासे पानीमा भर पर्छ । नेपालको कृषि धेरैजसो आकासे पानीमा भर पर्ने हुनाले यहाँ मौसमको प्रभाव निकै पर्छ । अर्थात् जहाँ धेरै पानी पर्छ त्यहाँ धेरै उत्पादन हुन्छ । त्यसैले नेपालको पूर्वी तराई सबभन्दा बढी उब्जनी हुने ठाउँ हो भने सुदूर पश्चिमी पहाड सबैभन्दा थोरै उब्जनी हुने क्षेत्र हो । जहाँ धेरै उब्जनी हुन्छ त्यहाँ धेरै जनसङ्ख्या पनि हुन्छ । त्यसैले सुदूर पश्चिमी पहाडमा मानिसको थोरै बसोबास पाइन्छ ।

पहाडको भूभाग धेरैजसो भिरालो हुन्छ । यो क्षेत्र फलफूल खेतीको लागि बढी उपयुक्त हुन्छ । बारीमा मकै र टारीमा धान अनि गहुँको खेती प्रमुख रूपमा गरिन्छ । हुन त हिमाली भेगमा अर्थात् लेकाली क्षेत्रमा उब्जनी थोरै हुन्छ तर यो क्षेत्र भैँडा र चौँरीको पालनका लागि उपयुक्त छ । तसर्थ तराईको समथर भागमै जनसङ्ख्याको चाप बढ्दो छ ।

पहिले नेपालबाट धेरै अन्न (धान, गहुँ, मकै, कोदो, जौ आदि) विदेश अर्थात् भारतमा निर्यात गरिन्थ्यो तर आजभोलि देशमै जनसङ्ख्या बढेकोले र उत्पादन घटेकोले निर्यात कम हुँदै छ । फेरि खेतीको मौसममा धेरै भारतीय कामदारलाई काममा लगाइन्छ (हिजोआज नेपालमा भारतीय कामदारको सङ्ख्या सबै क्षेत्रमा बढ्दै छ) । तिनीहरूलाई ज्यालाको रूपमा अन्न नै दिने गरिन्छ । उत्पादनको ठूलो भाग यसरी पनि बिदेशिन्छ । त्यसैले बचतमा कमी आउँछ । भारतीय कामदारको प्रयोग गरिन्जेल बचत बढाउन सकिँदैन ?

तराईमा सबभन्दा बढी अन्न र तरकारी तथा अन्य नगदे बालीको उत्पादन हुन्छ । अर्थात् त्यहाँको लागि चाहिनेभन्दा धेरै बढी उत्पादन तराईमा हुन्छ । तर पहाडमा चाहिनेजति उत्पादन हुँदैन । त्यसैले पहाडमा नपुग भएको अन्न र अरू कुरा तराईबाट आपूर्ति गरिन्छ ।

हुन त धानको खेती खास गरी बर्खामा गरिन्छ; तर सिँचाइको सुविधा भएका ठाउँमा वर्षमा दुई बाली पनि गरिन्छ । बीचमा अरू एक बालीसमेत गरेर तीन बाली गर्नेहरू पनि छन् । तराईको समथर भागमा र पहाडका उपत्यकामा, खोलाछेउको

टारीमा, बेँसीमा वा जहाँ गरामा अथवा खलामा पानी थुन्न सकिन्छ त्यहाँ धानको खेती गरिन्छ । पानी नअड्ने भिरालो जग्गामा धानको खेती गरिन्न । कुनै समयमा धानको खेतमा हिले माछा पनि खुब हुन्थ्यो अथवा माछापालन पनि गरिन्थ्यो । तर रासायनिक मलको अत्यधिक प्रयोग र कीटनाशक औषधिले माछा, भ्यागुता, सर्प, गँगटा इत्यादि हराउँदै छन् ।

धान रोप्नुअघि खेत जोतेर तयार गरिन्छ । काठमाडौँ उपत्यकामा खेत जोतिँदैन । यहाँ किसानहरू हातैले खेत खन्छन् । हिजोआज ट्र्याक्टरले पनि खेत खनिन्छ । यसरी खेत खन्नुको साथै यहाँ धानको बीउ छुट्टै ब्याडमा उमारिन्छ । त्यसपछि पानी पर्दाखेरि खेतलाई हिल्याइन्छ ।

खेत खन्ने, जोत्ने, हिल्याउने काम पुरुषहरूले गर्छन् । तिनीहरूलाई (हिल्याउनेहरूलाई) बाउसे पनि भन्छन् । त्यसपछि खास गरी आइमाई, केटीहरूले लहरै धान रोप्छन् । त्यसबेला केटाहरू हिलोमा लाप्पा खेलेर रमाइलो पनि गर्छन् । धेरै ठाउँमा एकअर्काको खेतमा काम गर्न पर्मको व्यवस्था पनि हुन्छ । रोपाइँ गर्दै गाइने रोपाइँको असारे गीत पनि त्यत्तिकै रमाइलो हुन्छ । छुपुछुपु धान रोप्दै गरेका केटीहरू र आलीमा बसेका केटाहरूका बीचमा दोहोरी पनि चल्छ । यसरी दोहोरी चलुन्जेल धान रोप्नु रमाइलो पनि हुन्छ रे ! धेरैजसोले साउनसम्ममा रोपाइँ

सिध्याइसक्छन् । रोपाइँ गरेपछि केही महिनासम्म खेतमा पानी रहिरहने व्यवस्था पनि गर्नुपर्छ । बीचमा एकदुईपटक झार अथवा अन्य घाँस उखेल्नुपर्छ । यो काम स्त्रीपुरुष दुवैले गर्छन् । यसबेला हरिया धानखेतका फाँटहरू मनमोहक हुन्छन् । पाक्ने बेलामा पारिलो घाम लाग्यो भने धानको गुदी छिटो कडा भएर राम्रो हुन्छ । यसबेला फाँटहरू सुन बिछ्याएका जस्ता पहेँला देखिन्छन् । त्यो हेर्दा मनै लोभिन्छ ।

साढे तीन महिनाजतिमा धानबाली काटेर भित्र्याउन योग्य हुन्छ । त्यसबेला किसानहरू आफ्नो मिहिनेतको फल पाएर निकै खुसी देखिन्छन् । ठीक समयमा पानी पर्ने हो र बाढीपहिरोले दु:ख नदिने हो भने वर्षको मुख्य बाली निकै सफल हुन्छ । अर्को कुरा तराईको तातो पानीमा फलाएको चामलभन्दा पहाडको चिसो पानीमा फलाएको चामल उत्तम मानिन्छ ।

Phrases:

सबै कृषिमा मात्र भर पर्छन् भन्न सकिन्न: *It can't be said that everyone depends only on agriculture.*

तराई सबभन्दा बढी उब्जनी हुने ठाउँ हो **भने** पश्चिमी पहाड सबैभन्दा थोरै उब्जनी हुने ठाउँ हो:

__Whereas__ the Terai produces the most, the W. hills produce the least.

Literally, if the Terai has the most produce, then the W. hills have the least.

समेत गरेर: *including.* Syn. समेत गरी

कुनै समयमा: *once upon a time*

खेतमा पानी रहिरहने व्यवस्था गर्नुपर्छ: *there should be an arrangement for keeping water in the field.*

सुन बिछ्याएकाजस्ता पहेँला देखिन्छन्: *will look yellow like a bed of gold*

निकै सफल हुन्छ: *will be a big success*

GRAMMAR

➤ 18.1 –मा लाग्नु *BE ENGAGED/INVOLVED IN (PROFESSION).*

कृषिमा लाग्नु	*engaged in agriculture (as a profession)*
शिक्षाको पेसामा लाग्नु	*engaged in the teaching profession*

The causative of this is -मा लगाउनु, *to engage/involve someone in the work of...*

कृषिमा लगाउनु	*engage someone (in the work of) agriculture*
भारतीय कामदारलाई काममा लगाउनु	*engage Indian laborers in work...*

➤ 18.2 जहाँ...त्यहाँ *WHEREVER...THERE.*

This was already covered in 10.3, but by way of review:

जहाँ धेरै उब्जनी हुन्छ, त्यहाँ ... ।	*Wherever there's lots of produce, there's...*
जहाँ धेरै पानी पर्छ त्यहाँ धेरै उब्जनी हुन्छ ।	*Wherever there's lots of rain, there's...*
जहाँ तपाईं जानुहुन्छ, त्यहाँ म जान सक्दिनँ ।	*Wherever you go, there I can't (go)...*

➤ 18.3 FORMING VERBS FROM ADJECTIVES.

विदेशी *foreign(er)* ➡ विदेशिनु *emigrate*
तातो *hot* ➡ तातिनु *to be heated*
लामो *long* ➡ लम्मिनु *to lengthen (to be elongated)*

COMPLEX VERBS

● **-ने जति** — ***as much as...*** (general fact)

पहाडमा चाहिने जति उत्पादन हुँदैन।	*As much as is needed in the hills is not produced (fact).*

Compare **ए(को) जति:**

पहाडमा चाहिएको जति उत्पादन भएन।	*As much as was needed in the hills was not produced (particular point in time)*

● **-ने हो भने** — ***if...*** (for passives)

पानी पर्ने हो भने...	*If it is to rain...*
दु:ख दिने हो भने...	*It you are to give trouble...*
चीजबिज किन्ने हो भने..	*If stuff is to be bought...*
साँच्चै भन्ने हो भने...	*If it is to be truly said ...*

● **-ने गरी** — ***so that, in a way that...***

तिमी सबैले सुन्ने गरी ठूलो स्वरमा बोल ।	*Speak in a loud voice so that all can hear.*
सबैले बुझ्ने गरी स्पष्टसँग लेख ।	*Write clearly in a way that is understandable.*
स्पष्ट गरी लेख ।	*Write in a way that is clear (write clearly).*

- **-ने काममा लाग्नु** — ***be engaged in the work of...***

  (उहाँ) भाषा सिक्ने काममा लाग्नुभयो । — *(He) is engaged in the work of language learning.*

  भाषा सिकाउने काममा लाग्नु — *be engaged in the work of teaching a language.*

- **-ने काममा लगाउनु** — ***engage someone in the work of...***

  (उसले) उसलाई भाषा सिक्ने काममा लगायो। — *(He) engaged him in the work of language learning.*

  भाषा सिक्ने काममा लगाउनु — *engage (someone) in the work of learning language*

- **-उन्जेल** — ***as long as...*** (active sentences)

  वर्षा हुन्जेल उनीहरूको फुर्सद हुँदैन । — *They don't have leisure time as long as it is monsoon.*

  दोहोरी चलुन्जेल धान रोप्न रमाइलो हुन्छ। — *Planting paddy is a fun as long as a duet is going.*

  गरुन्जेल — *as long as (someone) does*

  खाउन्जेल — *as long as (someone) eats*

- **-इन्जेल** — ***as long as...*** (passive sentences)

  वर्षा भइन्जेल हिमाल देखिँदैन । — *The Himals can't be seen as long as it is monsoon.*

  यहाँ भइन्जेल हामीलाई नेपाली बोल्नुपर्छ । — *Nepali needs to be spoken as long as we're here.*

  दिन भइन्जेल हामीले काम गर्नुपर्छ । — *As long as it is to be day, we need to work.*

  गरिन्जेल — *as long as it's being done*

  खाइन्जेल — *as long as it's being eaten*

- **-न त** VERB, **तर**... — ***it's true that...but...; of course X...but...***

  पानी पर्न त पऱ्यो तर गर्मी थियो । — *It's true that it rained, but it was hot.*

  खान त खाएँ तर अझै भोक लागेको छ । — *Yes, I ate, but I'm still hungry.*

  सुत्न त सुतेँ तर अलिकति मात्र । — *Yes, I slept, but only a little.*

PRACTICE

1. Take turns making sentences using -ने जति with the following verbs:

   a) घट्नु
   b) रोप्नु
   c) उमारिनु
   e) गाउनु
   f) भन्नु
   g) सक्नु

2. Repeat #1 using -एको जति.

3. Translate and complete each of the following sentences:
   a) टिकट किन्ने हो भने...
   b) समय बचाउने हो भने...
   c) मकै रोप्ने हो भने...
   d) If there is to be a flood...
   e) If fruit is to be grown...

4. Repeat #3, but supply subjects for each of the sentences.

5. Using the phrase -ने गरी, take turns constructing sentences with the following words:

   बताउनु सुनाउनु रोप्नु गाउनु भन्नु खेल्नु

6. Translate the following using either -इन्जेल or -उन्जेल:
   a) As long as there was a storm he was afraid.
   b) As long as it's hot there are mosquitoes.
   c) As long as I read the book I didn't study.
   d) As long as he walked he talked.
   e) As long as there is money, people will steal.
   f) As long as there is rain, the wheat will grow.
   g) He slept while (as long as) he rode the bus.
   h) as long as we work
   i) as long as work is done

7. Give an answer to each of the following questions at least twice using न त VERB, तर:
   a) तपाईंले खाना खानुभयो ?
   b) यो पानी खान हुन्छ ?
   c) तपाईं साथीकहाँ जानुभयो ?
   d) Have you read this book?
   e) Did you do your homework?

8. Translate the following using -न सिध्याउनु or -न सिध्याइसक्नु:
    a) I have finished eating.
    b) I have already finished eating.
    c) We haven't finished this book.
    d) They have finished reading.
    e) We have already finished reading.

9. Translate and complete the following:
    a) हुन त मैले खान सिध्याएँ तर...
    b) हुन त यो पानी खान हुन्छ तर...
    c) Yeah, I went to my friends house. But...
    d) Although I have read this book, I still...
    e) Of course I have finished my homework. But...

LET'S TALK

1. Estimate the following using a) करिब and b) जति:
    a) rooms in the building
    b) cups of water in a bucket
    c) countries in Asia
    d) number of times you go shopping in a week
    e) number of months you've been studying Nepali

2. Using -को पेसामा लाग्नु talk about the various professions your family is involved in.

3. Using -ने काममा लगाउनु, talk about the chores you have your househelp do.

4. Using -ने काममा लगाउनु, talk about the work men in Nepal have women do. What about vice-versa?

5. Discuss what sort of agriculture is going on right now...
    a) In Kathmandu valley.
    b) In the terrai.
    c) In the hills.
    d) In your home country.
    e) In your immediate neighborhood (छिमेकमा).

6. Repeat after your tutor the entire agricultural cycle (from plowing to storing) for the following crops: मकै धान गहुँ आलु

7. Where in Nepal are the following crops *not* grown?
    मकै धान गहुँ आलु जौ

IN THE COMMUNITY

In this chapter you have learned about several crops in Nepal as well as where and when they are grown. But you have not learned much about the *tools* of agriculture. Take a full day trip to an outlying village (or two half days) and first observe any type of agriculture that might be going on. What method is being used, with what tools?

After initial observation, talk to some of the villagers and ask them to describe the following:

a) the method of plowing
b) the method of fertilizing
c) the method of planting/sowing
d) the method of irrigating
e) the method of harvesting
f) the method of threshing

Ask them if the above methods are unique to their ethnic group?

Looking at the surrounding fields, ask some villagers at what stage of the agricultural cycle the fields are? What were the fields used for before now? What will the fields be used for next?

DID YOU KNOW?

90% of the population are subsistence farmers operating outside the cash economy.

Large amounts of land were developed in the Terrai in the late '70s, along with the introduction of improved seeds and chemical fertilizers. Nepal was then able to export large amounts of rice. However, as people from the hills flood the Terrai, production is fast losing out to population growth and Nepal will soon be forced to import rice.

The average land-holding size is around .5 hectares in the hills and 1.5 hectares in the Terrai. In a good year in the hills, .5 hectares yields around 1000 kg of rice and 500 kg of vegetables. Tenant farmers are still common, and as much as 50% of what a farmer produces goes to the land owner as rent.

[Nepal—Lonely Planet]

Until 1950, land tenure was basically feudal. Following this, there were numerous land reforms, though legislation was largely left unimplemented. Ceilings were placed on how much land could be owned, and land above those ceilings was to be bought and redistributed to tenants or landless farmers. However, in the end only 1% was redistributed! The ceilings were arbitrarily high and most landlords transferred land to grown children and relatives to defeat the reforms. 1964 reforms certified 10-20% of tenants, giving them the potential to claim title to the land they tilled. Landowners now often use Indian labor to avoid this. [Nepal, A Himalayan Kingdom in Transition. Karan and Ishii].

The highest concentration of festivals falls between the time of rice planting to the time of harvest, illustrating the importance of agriculture (the world over).

CHAPTER 19

MEANS OF ENTERTAINMENT
मनोरञ्जनका साधन

VOCABULARY					
मनोरञ्जन	entertainment	रक्सी	alcohol	सभागृह	City Hall
साधन	means, resource	जुवा	gambling	नाचघर	theater
त्यतापट्टि	there, that side	जात्रा	festival (with procession)	नाटक	drama, stage play
ध्यान	attention; meditation	मेला	fair	दृश्यावलोकन	sightseeing
सोच्नु	ponder, think	जादू	magic	भ्रमण	travel, tour
युवा/युवती	young boy/girl	चिट्ठा	raffle, lottery	मजा	fun, enjoyment
मन्दिर	temple	अति	extremely	-को दाँजोमा	in comparison to
फलैंचा	elevated resting place	भीड	crowd	जताततै	everywhere
तास	playing cards	अवरुद्ध	blocked, stopped, interrupted	रोदी घर	social hall(Gurung)
पाङ्ग्रो	wheel, tire	बटुवा	pedestrian, traveler, hiker	चौराली	worship place at hilltop
गुडाउनु	to roll (tr)	फागु	Hindu festival (Holi)	स्थल	place, site
डन्डी बियो	see *Did You Know*	नववर्ष	New Year	सोरठी	Gurung dance
ध्वाइँ	Newari hopscotch	विशेष	special, particular	घाटु	Gurung dance
तेलकासा	Newari tag	तीर्थयात्रा	pilgrimage	मारुनी	male dancer dressed as fem.
खोपी	see *Did You Know*	चिडियाखाना	zoo	भजन	hymn, praise song
अधबैंसे	adult (post-youth)	मनाउनु	celebrate, observe	कीर्तन	incantation
पाका	elders (lit. ripe people)	सङ्ग्रहालय	museum	दोहोरो	double, two-in-one
मन बहलाउनु	amuse, entertain oneself	नाच्नु	dance	लेख	writing, article
मक्ख पर्नु	be happy, glad (inside)	खुला	open	लेख्नु	to write
नकल गर्नु	mimic, imitate	यसबाहेक	besides this	साध्य	practicable
नकल पार्नु	to decorate (speech)	शारीरिक व्यायाम	physical exercise	मजाको	interesting, pleasant
खेतबारी	field under tillage	खेल	game	गुच्चा	marble(s)
उत्पादक	productive, fruitful	पौडी खेल्नु	to swim	रक्सी लाग्नु	become intoxicated
मतलब	meaning	बेलाबेलामा	from time to time	बाजा	musical instrument
-बाहेक	except, excluding	प्रज्ञाभवन	Academy Hall	बजाउनु	play (instrument)
गजल	Gazal	सोचाइ	thinking , idea		

USEFUL PHRASES

- त्यहाँ जाने कुनै साधन छैन । — *There's no means of going there.*
- ध्यान राख्नुस्, नबिर्सनुस् । — *Mind it, don't forget!*
- तपाईंले यसको बारेमा के सोच्नुभयो ? — *What do [lit. did] you think about this?*
- म भन्न सक्दिनँ, सोचिरहेको छु । — *I can't say, I'm thinking it over.*
- उसलाई यसको (केही) मतलब छैन । — *It makes no difference to him.*
- यो कति बजे खुल्छ ? यो खुलेको छ । — *What time does it open? It's open.*
- मजासँग बित्यो । — *(It) passed pleasantly/enjoyably.*
- विशेष गरी... — *Especially...*

TEXT

एकजना साथीले नेपालमा मनोरञ्जनका साधन थोरै पाइन्छन् भनेको थियो । मनोरञ्जनको साधन नपाउँदा नरमाइलो हुन्छ रे! काममा व्यस्त हुँदा मेरो त्यतापट्टि ध्यान पनि गएन । फुर्सदको समयमा मान्छेहरू केके गर्छन् होला भन्ने सोचाइ मेरो मनमा आउँछ।

एकपल्ट म कीर्तिपुर घुम्न गएको थिएँ । त्यहाँ धेरै युवाहरू मन्दिरको फलैँचामा बसेर तास खेलिरहेको देखेर मलाई अचम्म लाग्यो । किनभने तिनीहरूले त्यहाँ सधैँ यसरी नै समय बिताउने गरेको मैले थाहा पाएँ । त्यही चोकमा मैले केही साना केटाकेटीहरू कोही पाङ्ग्रा गुडाउँदै, कोही डन्डीबियो, कोही घ्वाइँ, तेलकासा र कोही खोपी खेल्दै गरेको देखेँ । केही अधबैंसे र बूढापाकाहरू पनि गफ गर्दै थिए । कोही तास खेलेको हेरेर अनि कोही केटाकेटी खेलेको हेरेर मन बहलाउँदै थिए । कोही गफ गरेको सुनेर मक्ख परिरहेका थिए । केही केटाकेटीहरू एकअर्कालाई नकल पारीपारी लोककथाहरू सुनाउँदै थिए । यी सबै हेरेर मलाई रमाइलो पनि लाग्यो । तर कीर्तिपुरको त्यस मन्दिर वरिपरि सधैँ यस्तै हुन्छ भनेको मैले सुनेँ । त्यहाँ आइमाई र युवतीहरू यसरी मनोरञ्जन गरिरहेका देखिएनन् । उनीहरू घरको र खेतबारीको काममा व्यस्त हुन्छन् रे ! सधैँ यस्तै हो भने मलाई त्यहाँका मान्छेहरूले समय खेर फालिरहेकोजस्तो लाग्यो । त्यो समय केही उत्पादक क्षेत्रमा प्रयोग गर्न सकिन्थ्यो होला । यो मेरो मतलबको कुरा थिएन । त्यसैले मैले केही बोलिनँ ।

काठमाडौँमा यसबाहेक अरू पनि तरिकाले मनोरञ्जन गरिन्छ । गजल/दोहोरी रेस्टुरेन्टमा डिनरको मनोरञ्जनका साथै होटेलहरूमा रक्सी, क्यासिनो, जुवा इत्यादि खान-खेलन पाइन्छन् । परम्परागत चाडपर्वमा, जात्रामा, मेलामा मनोरञ्जन गर्नेहरू यहाँ कम हुँदै छन् । रमाइलो मेलामा सर्कस, जादू र चिट्ठाको मनोरञ्जन पनि लिइन्छ ।

आजभोलि शहरमा जहाँ गए पनि मान्छे धेरै छन् । शहरमा सधैँ जात्रा र मेला जस्तो हुन्छ । झन् जात्रामा त अति नै भीड हुन्छ । त्यो जात्रा हेर्न आउनेहरूको मात्र भीड होइन । धेरैजसो जात्राले अवरुद्ध भएका बटुवाहरू पनि त्यहाँ हुन्छन्। यहाँका जात्रामेलाहरूमा गाइजात्रा, इन्द्रजात्रा, घोडेजात्रा, फागु, दशैँ-तिहारका बजारहरू,

नववर्ष मेला र जात्रा (विशेष गरी भक्तपुर र ठिमीमा), विशेष तीर्थयात्रा मेला आदि प्रमुख छन् ।

अर्को बढ्दो मनोरञ्जनको साधन सिनेमा, भिडिओ फिल्म, टेलिभिजन, रेडियो इत्यादि हुन् । फेरि धेरै मानिसहरू चिडियाखाना (जहाँ पिकनिक मनाउनको लागि पनि गइन्छ) र सङ्ग्रहालयहरू घुम्न जान्छन् । यी सबैले नपुगेर केही मानिसहरू विभिन्न ठाउँमा पिकनिक मनाउन जान्छन् । खानु, पिउनु, जुवातास खेल्नु, नाच्नु-गाउनु पिकनिकका मनोरञ्जनहरू हुन् । दिउँसो आराम गर्न रत्नपार्कमा जानेहरू पनि छन् । तर रत्नपार्क सधैं खुला हुँदैन ।

यसबाहेक शारीरिक व्यायाम र मनोरञ्जनको लागि यहाँका मानिसहरू विभिन्न खेलहरू पनि खेल्छन् । यस्ता खेलहरू हेरेर समय बिताउनेहरू पनि कम छैनन् । यस्ता खेलहरूमा गल्फ, क्रिकेट, फुटबल, पौडी, टेनिस, भलिबल, जुडो, कराँते इत्यादि प्रमुख छन् । फेरि बेलाबेलामा प्रज्ञाभवन, सभागृह र नाचघरमा विभिन्न नाटक, सांस्कृतिक कार्यक्रम इत्यादि हेर्न धेरै मान्छेहरू जान्छन् । कुनैकुनै कार्यक्रम हेर्न धेरै महँगो पर्छ ।

नेपालीहरूकै लागि पनि यहाँ मनोरञ्जनका साधनको कमी छैन । विदेशीहरूको लागि त अझ धेरै नै पाइन्छ । होटेलमा नै हेरिने सांस्कृतिक कार्यक्रम, विभिन्न दृश्यावलोकन र अन्य भ्रमणको मजा नै अर्को ।

काठमाडौंको दाँजोमा गाउँघरमा मनोरञ्जनको साधन थोरै मात्र पाइन्छ । जुवा, तास, रक्सी जताततै पाइन्छ । गुरुङहरूको रोदी घर, गाउँघरको चौराली, चौतारी इत्यादि त्यहाँका मनोरञ्जनका स्थल हुन् । विभिन्न पर्वहरूमा नाचिने सोरठी, घाटु, मारुनी नाचहरू रमाइलै हुन्छन् । बिहानबेलुका मन्दिरमा जाने, भजनकीर्तन गाउने इत्यादिबाट पनि दोहोरो फाइदा पाइन्छ रे ! सबै कुरा यस सानो लेखमा लेखेर साध्य छैन ।

Phrases:

सधैं यसरी समय बिताउने गरेको थाहा पाएँ: *I found out they always spend their time like this.*

समय खेर फालिरहेको जस्तो लाग्यो: *I felt as though they were wasting time.*

यो मेरो मतलबको कुरा थिएन: *This was none of my concern.*

सांस्कृतिक कार्यक्रम: *cultural program*

-को कमी छैन: *there is no shortage of...*

GRAMMAR

➤19.1 PAST PERFECT.

In our text, we have the sentence: एकपल्ट म कीर्तिपुर घुम्न गएको थिएँ *One day I had gone strolling in Kirtipur.* This is the past perfect *had X-ed:* **-ले is required for transitive verbs.**

मैले खाएको थिएँ ।	*I had eaten/ate.*
म गएको थिएँ ।	*I had gone.*
हामी गएका थिएनौँ ।	*We had not gone.*
ढिलो भइसकेको थियो ।	*It was already too late.*

The past perfect tense is conjugated as follows:

SUBJECT	POSITIVE	NEGATIVE
म	-एको थिएँ	-एको थिइनँ
हामी(हरू)	-एका थियौँ	-एका थिएनौँ
तपाईं/उहाँ(हरू)	-नुभएको थियो	-नुभएको थिएन
ऊ	-एको थियो	-एको थिएन
उनी(हरू)	-एका थिए	-एका थिएनन्
तिमी(हरू)	-एका थियौ	-एका थिएनौ

➤19.2 PAST CONTINUOUS.

The past continuous tense is formed as follows:

① चलाउनु + ② रहनु + ③ एको + ④ थियो = चलाइरहेको थियो

to run to keep on had past = had been keeping on running

Essentially this means *was running*. In our text we have:

① मक्ख पर्नु + ② इरहनु + ③ एको + ④ थियो = परिरहेको थियो

be happy to keep on had past = had been keeping on being happy

Essentially this means *were happy*. The past continuous tense is conjugated as follows:

SUBJECT	POSITIVE	NEGATIVE
म	-इरहेको थिएँ	-इरहेको थिइन
हामी	-इरहेका थियौं	-इरहेका थिएनौं
तपाईं	-इरहनुभएको थियो	-इरहनुभएको थिएन
ऊ	-इरहेको थियो	-इरहेको थिएन
उनी	-इरहेका थिए	-इरहेका थिएनन्
तिमी	-इरहेका थियौ	-इरहेका थिएनौ

As with the present continuous tense, there is an almost synonymous alternative that is conjugated using -दै instead of -इरहनु. For example:

SUBJECT	POSITIVE
म	-दै थिएँ
हामी	-दै थियौं

उनीहरू लोककथाहरू सुनाउँदै थिए । *They were telling folk stories.*
उनीहरू मन बहलाउँदै थिए । *They were entertaining themselves.*
कोही मक्ख परिरहेका थिए । *Some were happy.*

➤19.3 बढ्दो / घट्दो *INCREASING/DECREASING.*

बढ्दो महँगी *increasing cost (of living)*
बढ्दो माग *increasing demand* घट्दो माग *decreasing demand*
बढ्दो जनसङ्ख्या *increasing population* घट्दो जनसङ्ख्या *decreasing population*

➤19.4 -बाहेक *EXCEPT, BESIDES, EXCLUDING.*

ऊसँग भैंसीबाहेक अरू केही छैन । *Except for a buffalo, he has nothing.*
रामबाहेक यो काम अरू कसैले गर्न सक्दैन । *Besides Ram, no one can do this job.*
स्याउबाहेक कति पऱ्यो ? *Excluding apples, how much did it cost?*

➤19.5 -को दाँजोमा *IN COMPARISON TO.*

उपचारको दाँजोमा रोग लाग्न नदिनु राम्रो	*Compared to treatment, it's better to ...*
पोखराको दाँजोमा काठमाडौँ ठूलो छ ।	*As compared to Pokhara, Kathmandu is big.*
काठमाडौँको दाँजोमा पोखरा सानो छ ।	*Compared to Kathmandu, Pokhara is small.*

➤19.6 -को कमी *LACK OF, SHORTAGE OF.*

काठमाडौँमा पानीको कमी छ ।	*In KTM there is a shortage of water.*
त्यहाँ मनोरञ्जनका साधनको कमी छैन ।	*There is no shortage of means of entertainment .*

➤19.7 कम *LESS, FEW; A LOT, MANY.*

कम can be confusing because in certain contexts it means *less, too few, too little*. In other contexts, **with sentence stress and high pitch**, it means the opposite: *really, a lot, many*:

जानेहरू कम छन् ।	*Only a few go.*
कममा दिन सक्दिनँ ।	*I can't give it to you for less.*
चिनी कम छ, पुग्दैन ।	*There's not enough sugar.*
गाउँ कम रमाइलो छैन ।	*The village is very enjoyable.*
यसको बारेमा तिमीले जति भने पनि कम हुन्छ।	*Whatever you say about it is insufficient.*
कम बोल्नुस्, धेरै सुन्नुस् ।	*Speak little, listen lots.*
त्यहाँ कम मान्छे थिए !	*There were lots of people!* **(high pitch and stress)**
त्यो काम कम गाह्रो छ !	*That job is really difficult.*

COMPLEX VERBS

• -एको थाहा पाउनु *to find out...*

उनीहरूले त्यहाँ समय बिताएको मैले थाहा पाएँ ।	*I found out they spent their time there.*
उसले कसरी गरेको भन्ने मैले थाहा पाएँ ।	*I found out how (he) did it.*

- **-दै गर्नु (*Syn.* -दै जानु, -इराख्नु, -इरहनु, -इबस्नु)** ***keep on, continue...***

तपाईं भन्दै गर्नुस्, म सुन्दै जान्छु ।	*You continue talking, I'll continue listening.*
तपाईं भन्दै जानुस्, म सुन्दै गर्छु ।	*You continue talking, I'll continue listening.*
कोही खोपी खेल्दै गरेको मैले देखें ।	*I saw them playing along (khopi).*

- **-न सकिन्थ्यो** ***could have (been)..., If used to be possible to...***

त्यो प्रयोग गर्न सकिन्थ्यो ।	*(It) could have been used.*
जुवा खेल्न सकिन्थ्यो, तर मसँग पैसा थिएन।	*(I) could have gambled, but I didn't have money.*
साँझ पर्नुअगाडि पुग्न सकिन्थ्यो ।	*(He) could have arrived before dark.*
भित्र जान सकिन्थ्यो तर ऊ बाहिर बस्यो ।	*(He) could have gone inside, but he stayed outside.*

- **-एर साध्य छैन** ***impossible, beyond possibility...***

भनेर साध्य छैन	*impossible to say*
गरेर साध्य छैन	*beyond the possibility of doing*
खाएर साध्य छैन	*impossible to eat*
किनेर साध्य छैन	*not possible to buy*

- **-न मजा आउनु/लाग्नु** ***get enjoyment from...***

उसलाई सिनेमा हेर्न मजा आउँछ ।	*He gets enjoyment from watching movies.*
मलाई तास खेल्न मजा आउँछ ।	*I get enjoyment from playing cards.*
तपाईंलाई के गर्न मजा आउँछ ?	*What do you gain enjoyment from?*

PRACTICE

1. Using the phrase -एको थाहा पाउनु, construct two sentences for each of the following verbs:

   नकल पार्नु   पौडी खेल्नु   लेख्नु   रक्सी लाग्नु   रोप्नु   गीत गाउनु

2. Using the phrase -दै गर्नु, translate and complete the following:

   a) तपाईं कुरा गर्दै गर्नुस्...
   b) तिमी किताप पढ्दै गर...
   c) Keep on having fun.
   d) Keep on singing--don't be embarrassed!
   e) Keep on writing until you're finished.

3. Repeat #2 using the phrase -दै जानु.

4. Conjugate the following verbs for both the past perfect and the past continuous. Use both positive and negative: खेल्नु लेख्नु रोप्नु गाउनु

5. Translate the following sentences using the past perfect:

a) We hadn't done anything.
b) I had given him the book.
c) They had asked me to dance.
d) You had not called me for a long time.
e) They had finished planting the rice.

6. Translate the following sentences using the past continuous:

a) We were talking.
b) I was studying my book.
c) They were dancing.
d) They were making lots of noise.
e) I was trying to sleep.

7. Repeat #5 and #6, but state the negative of each sentence.

8. Translate and complete each of the sentences twice:

a) म जुवा खेल्न सक्थें; तर...
b) उहाँले गीत गाउन सक्नुहुने थियो; तर...
c) उनीहरूले अरू खाना खान सक्ने थिए; तर...
d) हामीले उसलाई पैसा दिन सक्ने थियौं; तर...
e) He could have arrived before dark, but...
f) The man could have lied, but...
g) The money could have been used for food, but...
h) It could have rained, but...
i) He could have written me a letter...
j) The book could have been easier, but...

9. Here is a list of things bought and their prices:

apples	40 Rps
carrots	30 Rps
bananas	20 Rps
potatoes	10 Rps
spinach	5 Rps

Use the word बाहेक to translate and complete the following sentences:

a) Besides the apples, everything cost...
b) Besides the carrots, everything cost...
c) Besides the bananas, everything cost...
d) Besides the potatoes, everything cost...
e) Besides the spinach, everything cost...

10. Translate and complete each of the following sentences *twice* using भन्दा:

a) Compared to Kathmandu...
b) Compared to you...
c) Compared to me...
d) Compared to Nepal...
e) Compared to the Kathmandu zoo...

11. Repeat #10 using -को दाँजोमा.

12. Translate the following sentences using कम:

a) There's not enough sugar. Give me some more.
b) Please give it to me for less.
c) Your job is not easy; it's very difficult.
d) What a crowd! There are lots of people!
e) Don't talk so much! (Talk less).

LET'S TALK

1. Using the phrase -एको थाहा पाउनु, talk about the things you've found out about Nepal in the following areas:

shopping geography caste agriculture entertainment

2. Using the phrase बढ्दो [noun] –को कारणले, talk about the consequences of:

increased cost of living
increasing population
increasing deforestation
increased gambling
increased sightseeing
increased crops

3. Using -को कमीको कारणले or -को कमी भएकोले talk about the consequences of:

the shortage of water in KTM
the lack of electricity in the hills
the lack of health care in the hills
the shortage of work in KTM
the lack of food in different areas
the lack of money for some people

4. In class, learn and play at least one Nepali game.

5. In class, teach and play at least one traditional game from your home country.

6. Tell your tutor what things (at least five) you couldn't do when you arrived in Nepal, but that you can do now.

7. Tell your tutor what things (at least five) you could have done when you arrived in Nepal, but you didn't.

8. Using the phrase -को दाँजोमा, compare the following for your respective countries:

amount of gambling	amount of free time
amount of temples	amount of crowds
number of festivals	number of games
the type of weather	the type of entertainment

9. Using the phrase -एर साध्य छ/छैन, state whether you believe the following is possible or not for yourself. *State your reasons why.* If impossible, what could you do?

   a) To swim a distance of 1 km.
   b) To dance a Gurung dance.
   c) To think all day long.
   d) To play cards until 4 a.m.
   e) To travel from Paris to Kathmandu by car.

   Do you know anyone or know of anyone who has done any of the above? Give details for each one.

10. Using -न मजा आउनु talk about the things you get enjoyment from doing. Use -न मजा आउँछ in describing your hobbies. Do you enjoy anything now that you didn't used to enjoy? Do you not enjoy doing something now that you used to enjoy?

IN THE COMMUNITY

Choose one of the following:

1. With a Nepali friend(s), learn and play at least two Nepali games. Teach and play at least one game from your home country.

2. With a Nepali friend, go to a cinema and watch a Nepali film (not Hindi).

3. With a Nepali friend, go to a cultural program *that is for a Nepali audience.* There are several theaters in town that put on various dramas and cultural programs (the cultural center kitty-corner to Rani Pokhari, for example). Often they are more of a variety show with short plays, dances, magic acts, etc. and they last several hours. Both men and women attend (children too!). Most theaters feature weekly shows and tickets are easy to obtain. Your tutor can help you pursue this, and there are numerous theaters listed in the yellow pages under "Culture Training Centres".

DID YOU KNOW?

डन्डीबियो:

A game, in which a small stick (*biyo*) is placed over a hole. Holding a larger stick (*dandi*) underneath the *biyo*, the player knocks the *biyo* into the air. Once in the air, there are two objectives: hit the *biyo* as many times as possible, and hit the *biyo* as far as possible. If the *biyo* is knocked twice, the distance from the *biyo* to the hole is measured with the *dandi*. If the *biyo* is knocked three times, the distance is measured with the *biyo* (resulting in a higher score). If the *biyo* is knocked four times, the measurement is doubled, etc. There are many local variations, including catchers who, if they catch the *biyo*, get the striker out. Interestingly, there is a different counting system used for this game.

खोपी: (lit. small hole; hole in the wall for keeping things)

A hole is made in the ground at which coins are thrown. The players stand at a mark about 10 feet away and each throw a coin at the hole. The player whose coin comes closest to the hole is called the *nir* and he takes a coin from each player and throws them all towards the hole. One of the other players then chooses one of the coins (*cekhe*) that the *nir* must hit with a coin thrown from the mark. If he hits it, he wins all the coins. If he hits a coin other than the *cekhe* or his coin lands in the hole, he is penalized by having to add one coin to the hole. Then the player that was originally second closest takes a go at hitting the *cekhe*. If he isn't successful, the player that was originally third closest takes a go at hitting the *cekhe*, and so on. There are many local variations to this game.

रोदी घर:

The Gurung's have a sanctioned system whereby young men and women in their teens get together for an evening of eating, singing and dancing. The place they meet is called the *rodi ghar*. Though not always, the night often ends in great license. Though this is a Gurung term, there are many similar practices among many of Nepal's Tibeto-Burman peoples. The Kham Magars of Rukum call it "the sitting of the young men", in other places it's देउडा नाच, छोटी खेल्नु, etc.

Cf. भजन, कीर्तन and मन्त्र:

Bhajan is a religious song of worship made up of many verses. *Kirtan* is similar, only it is the singing of a short verse or refrain over and over aloud. For example, the Hare Krishna's repeated singing of *Hari Hari, Krishna Krishna, Ram Ram*...is considered a *kirtan*. A *mantra* is a *kirtan* that is sung in one's head or heart (*man*), over and over. If a *mantra* is sung aloud, it is said to produce no results or even adverse effects.

CHAPTER 20
A NEPALI WEDDING
एउटा नेपाली बिहे

VOCABULARY

*see Appendix 2: kinship chart

बिहे/बिहा	wedding	बाँड्नु	divide, distribute	स्वागत	welcome
छोटकरीमा	in short	जन्ती	bridegroom procession	नयाँ	new; novice; latest
वर्गीय	of social class	प्रस्थान गर्नु	departure (to do)	सम्बन्ध	connection, relation
काहिँलो	4th youngest son/bro	सामाजिक	social	जोड्नु	join, fix, connect
लमी	mediator; match-maker	ऐन	law, Act	पर्सिपल्ट	two days later
नाइँ	no	स्वयंवर	girl choosing husband	माइती	women's parent's home
पक्का गर्नु	make sure, certain, confirm	साइत	auspicious time	रमाउनु	be pleased, rejoice
निश्चित	sure, certain	कान्छो	youngest son/bro	ससुराली	wife's parent's home
औपचारिक	formal, official	कौसी	verandah, flat roof top	ज्वाइँ	son-in-law; husb of young sis
पोका	packet, bundle	पुरोहित	domestic priest	परिकार	variety (of food)
दुलहा	bridegroom	निर्देशन	instruction, direction	सानोतिनो	small, petty, minor
संयोग	coincidence, chance	रात	night (noun)	पर्सि	day-after-tomorrow
पक्ष	side, party; aspect	सिद्धिनु	end, be finished	माहिला	2nd oldest son/bro
आश्वस्त हुनु	be assured	चहलपहल	commotion, hustle bustle	नाति	grandson
थप	addition(al)	अन्तमा	in/at the end	नातिनी	granddaughter
पालो	time, turn (of a #)	रुवाबासी	wailing, lamenting	बज्यै	grandma (also हजुरआमा)
उभिनु	stand up; be standing	बिछोड	difficult goodbye	भतिजो/जी	nephew/niece
दुलही	bride	तोड्नु	break	भाउज्यू	wife of older bro.
छिनिनु	be arranged, settled	सम्धी	*kinship term	भिनाज्यू	husband of older sis.
मसला	spice, condiment	बिदा	leave, good-bye	ससुरा	father-in-law
उपहार	gift	-साथ	with	सासू	mother-in-law
सिँगारिनु	be decorated, adorned	दाज्यू/दाजु	older brother (also दाइ)	मामा	mother's brother.
सुपारी	betel nut	एकैसाथ	together, along with	काका	father's younger bro.
निम्तापत्र	invitation card	विधिपूर्वक	accord. to law/ritual	फुपू	father's sister

* Used by husband's parents when addressing wife's father, or by wife's parents when addressing husband's father. सम्धिनी is used for the respective mother.

USEFUL PHRASES

- तपाईं कहिले जाने, पक्का गर्नुस् । — *Please confirm when you'll be going.*
- निश्चित समय भन्नुस् अनि म आउँछु । — *Give me a definite time and I'll come.*
- संयोगले... — *By coincidence/chance...*
- हाम्रो केही पनि सम्बन्ध छैन । — *We have no connection/relation.*

TEXT

नेपालमा विभिन्न जातजातिको बसोबास छ । सबै जातिको आफआफ्नै रीतिरिवाज र परम्परा छन् । सबैको बिहा उस्तै हुँदैन । जे होस्, अब म मेरो एकजना साथीको बिहाको बारेमा छोटकरीमा भन्न चाहन्छु ।

मेरो साथी मध्यमवर्गीय नेवार परिवारका थिए । उनको बिहे २०४५ साल जेठमा हिन्दू रीतिअनुसार भएको थियो । उनको र उनका काहिँलो दाइको बिहा सँगै भएको थियो । बिहा हुनुभन्दा दुई हप्ताअघि एकजना लमीले केटीको कुरा ल्याएको थियो । त्यसअघि कहिल्यै बिहेको बारेमा नसोचेको अथवा बिहा गर्ने विचार नगरेको भए पनि त्यसपटक चाहिँ उनले नाइँ भन्न सकेनन् । बा, आमा र परिवारलाई चित्त बुझेपछि अझ पक्का गर्नुअघि केटी हेर्न जाने दिन निश्चित भयो । बा, ठूलो दाइ, ठूली दिदी, लमी र उनी गरी जम्मा पाँचजना ट्याक्सीमा चढेर बानेश्वरको एउटा घरमा पुगे । लमीले कुरा मिलाइसकेको थियो । साधारण औपचारिक कुराकानीपछि कसैले कुरा गर्दै, कसैले चियानास्ता ल्याउँदै र कसैले ढोकैबाट हुनेवाला दुलहालाई हेरे । संयोगले उनले चिनेको मान्छे एकजना पनि त्यहाँ रहेछ । त्यसैले उनलाई त्यहाँ अलि सजिलो भयो अनि केटी पक्ष पनि अलि आश्वस्त भयो । किनभने हुनेवाला दुलहाको बारेमा उनीहरूले थप जानकारी पाए । अब पालो आयो केटी हेर्ने । एउटा कोठामा

केटी उभिएकी थिई । सबैले पालैपालो हुनेवाला दुलही अर्थात् त्यस केटीलाई हेरे र मनपराएर फर्के । अब कुरा छिनियो अर्थात् बिहा पक्का भयो ।

बिहाको चार दिनअघि विभिन्न रोटी, फलफूल, मसला, लुगा, गहना आदिको उपहारको साथै १० वटा सिँगारिएका ठूला सुपारी केटीको घरमा पठाइए । निम्तापत्र बाँडियो । जन्तीको दिनमा दुलहाको घरमै जन्ती जम्मा भए । जम्मा भएको जन्ती दुई ठाउँमा जानुपर्थ्यो । बस र अरू गाडीको व्यवस्था पनि थियो । मसलाको पोका बाँडिसकेपछि बैन्ड बाजा र अरू सामानसँगै जन्ती प्रस्थान गऱ्यो । बाजाको पछाडि बिहाको सामान अनि त्यसको पछाडि दुलहा बसेका दुईवटा कार थिए । जन्तीमा दुलहा जाने चलन नेवारहरूको लागि धेरै पुरानो थिएन । जन्तीमा करिब एक सयजना जति थिए । सामाजिक व्यवहार ऐन २०३३ अनुसार एउटा जन्तीमा बाजावालासमेत गरी ५१ जनासम्म मात्र लान पाइन्थ्यो ।

त्यही राति करिब साढे एघार बजेतिर स्वयंवरको साइत थियो । म मेरो साथीको जन्तीमा थिएँ । उनी कान्छाचाहिँ दुलाहा थिए । कौसीमा भीडको बीचमा दुवैतिरका पुरोहितहरूको निर्देशनमा स्वयंवरको काम सम्पन्न भयो । त्यसपछि दुलहाको लागि एउटा कोठा दिइयो जहाँ उनले साथीहरूसँग रातभरि तास खेलेर बिताए । त्यही दिन दुलहीको घरमा भोज सिद्धिएको थियो । भोलिपल्ट बिहानैदेखि त्यहाँ चहलपहल थियो । दुलहीले सबै आफन्तहरूलाई बिदाइको सुपारी दिइन् र उनीहरूले पनि एउटाएउटा उपहार दिए । त्यसपछि दुलहीले दुलहालाई पहिले दुलहाले नै पठाएका दशवटा सुपारी दिइन् । अन्तमा दुलहीले आफ्ना आमा-बालाई सुपारी दिइन् । त्यहाँ दुलहीका आफन्तहरूको रुवाबासी चलेको थियो । किनभने त्यो बिछोडको बेला थियो । अब उनीहरूकी छोरी अर्काकी बुहारी हुन्छे । सम्धीहरूसँग बिदा मागेर जन्ती फर्के । अब पहिलेजस्तै बैन्ड बाजा अघि लगाएर दुलहादुलही भएको कारसँग जन्ती खुसीसाथ फर्के। त्यस्तै कामहरू काहिँलो दाज्यूकहाँ पनि भएको थियो होला । म त्यहाँ गएको भए दुईवटै बिहा हेर्ने थिएँ । दुवै दुलहाहरू एकैसाथ घरमा पुगे । दुलहादुलहीहरूको विधिपूर्वक स्वागत गरियो । घरमा पुगेपछि दुलहाहरूका आफन्तहरूले नयाँ दुलहीहरूबाट सुपारी लिए । त्यो सम्बन्ध जोड्ने सुपारी थियो । त्यही दिन बेलुका पार्टीभोज थियो ।

त्यसको पर्सिपल्ट दुलहीको माइतीतर्फबाट उपहारसहित मुख हेर्न आए । छोरीलाई खुसी देखेर सबै रमाए । छोरीलाई खुसी नदेखेको भए के हुन्थ्यो होला ? मुख हेर्न आउने सबैले पैसा दिए । त्यही रात दुलहालाई ससुरालीमा स्वागत गरियो । ज्वाइँबाट सम्बन्धको रूपमा सुपारी लिने काम भयो । ज्वाइँलाई राम्रा मीठा परिकारहरूको भोज ससुरालीले खुवाए । दुलहा र दुलही राती नै घर फर्के । त्यसपछि सानोतिनो पिकनिक पनि तिनीहरूले मनाए । बिहाभरि दुलहीले राता लुगा र गहनाहरू लगाइन् । केही दिनसम्म रमाइलो चली नै रह्यो ।

GRAMMAR

➤ **20.1 साथ** derives adverbs from adjectives in the same way that सँग does (5.6):

खुसीसाथ = खुसीसँग

➤ **20.2 –ने थिएँ** ***WOULD'VE X–ED.***

म बस्ने थिएँ	*I would have stayed.*
मैले खाने थिएँ	*I would have eaten.*
म जाने थिएँ	*I would have gone.*
राम्रो हुने थियो	*It would have been nice.*
मैले गर्ने थिएँ	*I would have done (it).*

SUBJECT*	POSITIVE	NEGATIVE
म	-ने थिएँ	-ने थिइनँ
हामी	-ने थियौं	-ने थिएनौं
तपाईं/उहाँ (हरू)	-नुहने थियो	-नुहने थिएन
ऊ	-ने थियो	-ने थिएन
उनी (हरू)	-ने थिए	-ने थिएनन्
तिमी (हरू)	-ने थियौ	-ने थिएनौ

* use -ले with subject for transitive verbs.

➤ 20.3 *IF X HAD HAPPENED, Y WOULD'VE*

We now build on 20.2 to learn how to say *If X had happened, Y would have happened*. For the first phrase *if X had happened*, simply add -एको भए (using -ले for transitive verbs):

पानी परेको भए...	*If it had rained...*
म बसेको भए...	*If I had stayed...*
हामीले खाएको भए...	*If we had eaten...*
तपाईं जानुभएको भए...	*If you had gone...*

Add the second phrase conjugated as you learned in 20.2:

पानी परेको भए म जाने थिइनँ ।	*If it had rained, I would not have gone.*
म बसेको भए काम चल्ने थियो ।	*If I had stayed, the work would have continued.*
हामीले खाएको भए बिरामी हुने थियौं ।	*If we had eaten, we would have gotten sick.*
तपाईं जानुभएको भए राम्रो हुने थियो ।	*If you had gone, it would have been nice.*

IMPORTANT:
In spoken forms, the final phrase is often abbreviated and conjugated exactly as you conjugate the historical past (12.2):

पानी परेको भए म जाँदिनथें ।	*If it had rained, I would not have gone.*
म बसेको भए काम चल्दैनथ्यो ।	*If I had stayed, the work would not have continued.*
हामीले खाएको भए बिरामी हुन्थ्यौं ।	*If we had eaten, we would have gotten sick.*
तपाईं जानुभएको भए राम्रो हुन्थ्यो ।	*If you had gone, it would have been nice.*

You will know this is not the historical past, however, because of its connection to the first phrase.

Note the synonyms:

जाने थिइनँ = जाँदिनथें = जान्नथें = नजाने थिएँ

➤ 20.4 भएको भए *IF X , THEN Y (BUT NO X).*

The same exact pattern as that taught in 20.3 can be used for *if x, then y,* where X is not a reality--for hypothetical situations. However, this is only true for the verb हुनु. For example:

तपाईं भएको भए म जान्थें ।	*If I was you, I would leave.*
म डाक्टर भएको भए धेरै पैसा कमाउँथें ।	*If I were a doctor, I would earn lots of money.*
म अग्लो भएको भए टाउको ठोक्ने थिएँ ।	*If I were tall, I would hit my head.*

In the above sentences, the first phrase does not have *had,* but all of the second phrases have *would.*

➤ 20.5 *EVEN IF X HAD HAPPENED, Y WOULDN'T HAVE.*

To say *Even if X had happened, Y wouldn't have happened,* for the first phrase simply add -एपनि (using -ले for transitive verbs):

पानी परे पनि...	*Even if it had rained...*
म बसे पनि...	*Even if I had stayed...*
हामीले खाए पनि...	*Even if we had eaten...*
तपाईं जानुभए पनि...	*Even if you had gone...*

Add the second phrase conjugated as you learned in 20.2:

पानी परे पनि म जाँदिनथें ।	*Even if it had rained, I wouldn't have gone.*
म बसे पनि काम चल्दैनथ्यो ।	*Even if I'd stayed, the work wouldn't have continued.*
हामीले खाए पनि बिरामी हुँदैनथ्यौं ।	*Even if we had eaten, we wouldn't have gotten sick.*
तपाईं जानुभए पनि राम्रो हुँदैनथ्यो ।	*Even if you had gone, it wouldn't have been nice.*

➤ 20.6 *REVIEW OF CONDITIONALS.*

If it rains...	(यदि) पानी पऱ्यो भने	म आउँदिनँ ।	*...I will not come.*
" " "	(यदि) पानी परे	म आउँदिनँ ।	*...I will not come.*
Even if it rains...	पानी परे(ता)पनि	म आउँछु ।	*...I will come.*
If it had rained...	पानी परेको भए	म आउँदिनथें ।	*...I wouldn't have come.*
Even if it had rained...	पानी परेको भए पनि	म आउँथें ।	*...I would have come.*

There are several other conditional sentences, but they are fairly rare. For example, पानी परे पनि म आउँथें *Even if it rains, I'd have come.* If you can use all of the ones in the above chart, you will be doing well.

➤ 20.7 -वाला.

The use of -वाला reflects Hindi influence and means something like *the X guy* and indicates possession or agency. हुनेवाला means *soon-to-be*.

हुनेवाला दुलहा	*groom-to-be*
रिक्सावाला	*ricksaw guy (driver)*
फलफूलवाला	*fruit guy (vendor)*
घरवाली	*wife (slang)*
जग्गावाला	*land guy (owner)*
साथी आउनेवाला छ ।	*My friend is soon to come.*

COMPLEX VERBS

- **-ने विचार** — ***plan of, intention of...***

बिहा गर्ने विचार	*intention of marriage*
मेरो बिहा गर्ने बिचार छ ।	*I'm planning to get married.*
घर बनाउने विचार	*plan to build a house*
बजार जाने बिचार	*plan to go to the market*

- **-ने विचार गर्नु** — ***plan to, intend to...***

म बिहा गर्ने विचार गर्छु ।	*I will plan to get married.*
म घर बनाउने विचार गर्छु ।	*I will think about building a house.*
हामीले बजार जाने विचार गऱ्यौं । तर पानी पऱ्यो ।	*We planned on going to the market, but...*

- **-नासाथ/नासाथै** — ***immediately after, as soon as...***

यो खबर सुन्नासाथै म आएँ ।	*As soon as I heard the news, I came.*
खबर सुन्नासाथै म आउँछु ।	*Immediately after hearing news, I'll come.*
घरमा आउनासाथै ऊ रोयो ।	*As soon as he came in the house, he cried.*

- **-नु पर्थ्यो/पर्ने थियो** — ***should have...***

म बस्नु पर्थ्यो/बस्नु पर्ने थियो ।	*I should have stayed.*
मैले खानु पर्थ्यो ।	*I should have eaten.*
तपाईं जानु पर्थ्यो ।	*You should have gone.*
मैले गर्नु पर्थ्यो ।	*I should have done (it).*

ALSO: used to be (was) necessary to...

मैले खानु पर्थ्यो ।	*I used to have to eat.*
तपाईं जानु पर्थ्यो ।	*You used to have to go.*
मैले गर्नु पर्थ्यो ।	*I used to have to do (it).*
(पहिलेका) मान्छेहरूले धेरै काम गर्नु पर्थ्यो ।	*It used to be necessary for people to work hard.*
धेरै टाढा जानु पर्दैनथ्यो ।	*It didn't used to be necessary to go far.*

- **-नु हुँदैनथ्यो** — ***should not have...***

म बस्नु हुँदैनथ्यो ।	*I should not have stayed.*
मैले खानु हुँदैनथ्यो ।	*I should not have eaten.*
तपाईं जानु हुँदैनथ्यो ।	*You should not have gone.*
मैले गर्नु हुँदैनथ्यो ।	*I should not have done (it).*

- **-न मन पर्थ्यो** — ***would like to...***

मलाई बस्न मन पर्थ्यो/मन पर्ने थियो ।	*I would like to stay.*
मलाई खान मन पर्थ्यो/मन पर्ने थियो ।	*I would like to eat.*
तपाईंलाई जान मन पर्थ्यो/मन पर्ने थियो ।	*You would like to go.*
मलाई गर्न मन पर्थ्यो/मन पर्ने थियो ।	*I would like to do (it).*

ALSO: used to like to...

मलाई बस्न मन पर्थ्यो ।	*I used to like to stay.*
मलाई खान मन पर्थ्यो ।	*I used to like to eat.*
तपाईंलाई जान मन पर्थ्यो ।	*You used to like to go.*
मलाई गर्न मन पर्थ्यो ।	*I used to like to do (it).*

- **-नेथिएँ** — ***would have...*** (see 20.2)
- **-एको भए...नेथिएँ** — ***if X had... then Y*** (see 20.3)
- **-एपनि...दिनथैं** — ***Even if X had... Y still wouldn't*** (see 20.5)

PRACTICE

1. Translate the following:
   a) Intention of marriage
   b) plan to build a house
   c) We planned on going to the market.
   d) I intend on finishing this book in a month.
   e) He planned on calling me.

2. Translate and complete each of the following *twice*:
   a) मैले त्यो केरा खाए...
   b) मैले फोन गरे...
   c) ट्याक्सी लिए...
   d) मकै रोपे...
   e) उहाँले मलाई अरू पैसा दिए...
   f) If we pay attention...
   g) If we play cards...
   h) If we gamble...
   i) If you go...
   j) If I stay...
   k) If I stay longer...
   l) If it's nice...
   m) If it's easy...
   n) If we swim in the river...
   o) If you get better...

3. Translate and complete each of the following *twice*:
   a) मैले त्यो केरा खाए पनि...
   b) मैले तपाईंलाई फोन गरे पनि...
   c) ट्याक्सी लिए पनि...
   d) उसले मकै रोपे पनि...
   e) उहाँले मलाई अरू पैसा दिए पनि...
   f) Even if we pay attention...
   g) Even if we play cards...
   h) Even if we gamble...
   i) Even if you go...
   j) Even if I stay...
   k) Even if I stay longer...
   l) Even if it's nice...
   m) Even if it's easy...
   n) Even if we swim in the river...
   o) Even if you get better...

4. Translate the following:
   a) I would have eaten that banana.
   b) I would have called you.
   c) I would have taken a taxi.
   d) He would have planted corn.
   e) He would have given me more money.
   f) We would have paid attention.
   g) We would have played cards.

h) We would have gambled.
i) You would have been able to go.
j) I would have stayed.
k) I would have stayed longer.
l) It would have been nice.
m) It would have been easy.
n) We would have swam in the river.
o) You would have gotten better.

5. Translate and complete each of the following *twice*:

a) म त्यो केरा खान्थेँ तर...
b) तपाईंलाई फोन गर्थें तर...
c) ट्याक्सी लिन्थेँ तर...
d) मकै रोप्नुहुन्थ्यो तर...
e) उहाँले मलाई अरू पैसा दिनुहुन्थ्यो तर...
f) We would have paid attention, but...
g) We would have played cards, but...
h) We would have gambled, but...
i) You would have been able to go, but...
j) I would have stayed, but...
k) I would have stayed longer, but...
l) It would have been nice, but...
m) It would have been easy, but...
n) We would have swam in the river, but...
o) You would have gotten better, but...

6. Translate and complete each of the following *twice*:

a) मैले त्यो केरा खाएको भए...
b) मैले तपाईंलाई फोन गरेको भए...
c) मैले ट्याक्सी लिएको भए...
d) उसले मकै रोपेको भए...
e) मलाई अरू पैसा दिनुभएको भए...
f) If we had paid attention...
g) If we had played cards...
h) If we had gambled...
i) If you had been able to go...
j) If I had stayed...
k) If I had stayed longer...
l) If it had been nice...
m) If it had been easy...
n) If we had swam in the river...
o) If you had gotten better...

7. Translate and complete the following *twice* once in positive and then in negative. For the first, use the long form, for the second use the short form (like historical past):
   a) If..., I would have eaten that banana.
   b) If..., I would have called you.
   c) If..., I would have taken a taxi.
   d) If..., he would have planted corn.
   e) If..., he would have given me more money.
   f) If..., we would have paid attention.
   g) If..., we would have played cards.
   h) If..., we would have gambled.
   i) If..., you would have been able to go.
   j) If..., I would have stayed.
   k) If..., I would have stayed longer.
   l) If..., it would have been nice.
   m) If..., it would have been easy.
   n) If..., we would have swam in the river.
   o) If..., you would have gotten better.

8. Translate and complete each of the following *twice*:
   a) मैले त्यो केरा खाएको भए पनि...
   b) मैले तपाईंलाई फोन गरेको भए पनि...
   c) ट्याक्सी लिएको भए पनि...
   d) उसले मकै रोपेको भए पनि...
   e) उहाँले मलाई अरू पैसा दिनुभएको भए पनि...
   f) Even if we had paid attention...
   g) Even if we had played cards...
   h) Even if we had gambled...
   i) Even if you had been able to go...
   j) Even if I had stayed...
   k) Even if I had stayed longer...
   l) Even if it had been nice...
   m) Even if it had been easy...
   n) Even if we had swam in the river...
   o) Even if you had gotten better...

9. Translate the following:
   a) I should have eaten that banana.
   b) I should have called you.
   c) I should have taken a taxi.
   d) He should have planted corn.
   e) He should have given me more money.
   f) We should have paid attention.
   g) We should have played cards.

h) We should have gambled.
i) You should have been able to go.
j) I should have stayed.
k) I should have stayed longer.
l) It should have been nice.
m) It should have been easy.
n) We should have swam in the river.
o) You should have gotten better.

10. Translate the following:

a) I shouldn't have eaten that banana.
b) I shouldn't have called you.
c) I shouldn't have taken a taxi.
d) He shouldn't have planted corn.
e) He shouldn't have given me more money.
f) We shouldn't have played.
g) We shouldn't have played cards.
h) We shouldn't have gambled.
i) You shouldn't have gone.
j) I shouldn't have stayed.
k) I shouldn't have stayed longer.
l) It shouldn't have been difficult.
m) It shouldn't have been hot.
n) We shouldn't have swam in the river.
o) You shouldn't have gotten sick.

11. Translate the following:

a) It used to be necessary for people to walk a long ways.
b) It used to be necessary to take a bus.
c) It didn't used to be necessary to take a bus.
d) It used to be necessary for me to walk.
e) It used to be necessary for us to rest.

12. Translate the following:

a) I used to like to eat bananas.
b) I used to like to call you.
c) I used to like to take a taxi.
d) He used to like to plant corn.
e) We used to like to play cards.
f) I would like to eat a banana.
g) I would like to call you.
h) I would like to take a taxi.
i) He would like to plant corn this year.
j) We would like to play cards.

LET'S TALK

1. Using the phrase -ने विचार छ, what are your plans for the following:
   a) shopping this week
   b) what you'll do in three months
   c) what you'll do in one year
   d) when you'll return to your home country
   e) what you'll do on your next birthday
   f) what you'll take to the village

2. State five things that *would*...
   a) ...be nice
   b) ...not be nice
   c) ...be easy
   d) ...be hard

3. Taking turns, give *three* full sentences for each of the following:
   a) If I had eight children...
   b) If I had no friends...
   c) If I was the king of Nepal...
   d) If I was you...
   e) If I had lots of money...
   f) If I had (not) gotten married...

4. Tell your tutor about what you would be doing right now if you had not left your home country.

5. Give each other several commands to do. Whoever receives the command can choose to do that or to do something else. If the receiver of the command does something other than commanded, then the giver states *You should not have X-ed, you should have Y-ed.*

6. Looking back at your time in Nepal so far, what would you do differently. Use the phrase *I should have*...and *I shouldn't have*....For example, *I should have eaten at home more. I shouldn't have eaten in restaurants so much.* Make at least ten statements.

7. Comparing when you first arrived in Nepal, what did you used to have to do that you don't have to now. For example, *I used to have to speak slowly.* Make at least ten statements.

8. Using the phrase मनपर्ने थियो, talk about what you would like to do for the following:
   a) your next vacation
   b) dinner tonight
   c) work tomorrow
   d) your next trip out of the valley
   e) your friend's birthday

9. If you are married, describe your wedding. If not, describe a wedding you witnessed in your home country. What things are similar / different as compared to a Nepali wedding? What colors were used? Who attended? How long was it? etc....

10. Discuss which you think is better: a love marriage or an arranged marriage? Give your reasons why.

11. Discuss what you think are the prerequisites to a good marriage. Money? Love? Parental approval? A certain age?

12. Describe the most unusual wedding you have ever attended.

13. If married, discuss how your life would be different if you were single. If single, discuss how your life would be different if you were married.

14. Recount to each other the events of your day using a series of -नासाथै's.

IN THE COMMUNITY

Of course the ideal assignment would be to attend a Nepali wedding! If you can, fantastic. If you already have, perhaps you'll have pictures that you can talk about with someone. Otherwise, choose from one of the following:

1) Find someone who:
   - ❑ had a love marriage
   - ❑ married the *bel* fruit as a girl (or has a sister that has)
   - ❑ married younger than the age of 15
   - ❑ has a close relative with more than one wife

2) Choose three of the questions from the above "Let's Talk" 9-13 and converse in the community for a total of 3 hours.

3) If you're married and have pictures to show, talk with several friends for a total of 3 hours and compare your wedding to a Nepali wedding.

DID YOU KNOW?

THE STEPS IN THIS CHAPTER'S MARRIAGE:

- A mediator or matchmaker proposes a bride or groom to their parents.
- The parents consider the proposal, gather more information, and gain the consent of the proposed bride and groom before proceeding.
- The parents and matchmaker personally meet with the proposed couple and after everyone is satisfied, there is verbal confirmation. The wedding date is fixed and half the matchmaker fee is paid.
- For the engagement ceremony, the groom sends the bride ten large betel nuts as well as gifts.
- On the wedding day, the groom's party gathers at the groom's house. After the groom's party receives gifts of dried fruit and *paan* (betel leaf with spices), they march to the bride's house accompanied by a brass band.
- The groom's party is welcomed at the bride's house with gifts of dried fruit and *paan* , and many stay to witness and help with the wedding.
- The bride and groom exchange garlands and jewelry.
- The following day, the bride bids farewell to her family by exchanging betel nuts then the bride and groom go in a procession to the groom's house. There, the bride establishes relations with the groom's family by exchanging betel nuts with them.
- A few days later, the bride's family comes to see the bride.

TYPES OF MARRIAGES IN NEPAL

- **Infant**: Children are sometimes even promised to each other before birth!
- **Monogamous**: One man, one wife
- **Polygamous**: One man, two or more wives. In some cases, a man marries all the sisters simultaneously, in other cases the wives may be unrelated.
- **Polyandrous**: One wife, several husbands. In Nepal, all cases of polyandry are to related brothers.
- **Arranged**: By far the most common, where parents arrange a marriage.
- **Capture**: Though this custom is declining, the Kham Magar for example, will capture their bride by force. Sometimes it's prearranged and simply acted out, sometimes the bride will be unsuspecting (but the parents will know).
- **Elopement**: Common and fairly accepted.

- **By service**: With the Rajbansis, for example, the groom lives with and works for the bride's parents until he earns enough to pay the bride price.
- **By purchase**: The groom's side pays the bride's side (bride-price) or the bride's side pays the groom's side (dowry). The Tamangs are required to pay dowry only when the couple has a child. Among the Gurung, if you marry outside the rightful kin, payment has to be made.
- **By exchange**: Both sides exchange goods or money.
- **To inanimate objects**: common among the Newar.

(Marriage Customs In Nepal, *Majupurias*)

In Nepal, bigamy is legal if the wife contracts leprosy or a venereal disease, or has no surviving children after 10 years of marriage. Bigamy is also legal if the wife becomes lame, blind, or insane. (Marriage Customs In Nepal, *Majupurias*)

In Nepal, 16% of women and 30% of men have been married more than once. (Marriage Customs In Nepal, *Majupurias*)

In Nepal, 40% of marriages are consummated with girls under the age of 14 years. (UNICEF report).

UNIT SIX

Religion & Government

CHAPTER 21

DASHAIN
दशैं

VOCABULARY

दसौं	tenth	जतिसुकै	however much	जमरा	young barley shoot
ढाकिनु	be covered	यात्रु	traveler, pilgrim, pax, passenger	सातौं	seventh
छाना	roof (sloping)	भर्नु / भरिनु	fill/ be filled	फूलपाती	7th day of Dashain
आनन्द	pleasure, joy	जाँड	rice-beer	उखु	sugar cane
बस्तुभाउ	domestic animal	खोलो	river (syn. खोला)	अदुवा	ginger
थप्नु	add, increase	बगाउनु	dispense lavishly	बोट	plant
पिङ खेल्नु	swing (to play)	सुनौलो	golden	भुप्पा	bunch (flower, grapes, bananas)
चङ्गा उडाउनु	fly a kite	मौका	opportunity	ज्यावल	tool(s)
इच्छा	wish, will, desire	सबका सब	each and everyone	दरबार	palace, mansion
आशा	hope, expectation	मोज गर्नु	enjoy	उपस्थित हुनु	to be present
विद्यार्थी	student	मज्जा गर्नु	enjoy, have fun	निजामती	civil (servant)
थाप्नु	hold; receive, take	सुर	preoccupation, consciousness	मान्यजन	respected people
कारोबार	transaction	नौरथा	Dashain pilgrimage	उपस्थिति	presence
नाफा	profit	तीर्थस्थल	shrine, pilgrimage site	अष्टमी	8th day of lunar fortnight
बिक्री गर्नु	to sell	नवदुर्गा	name of goddess	पीठ	shrine (of goddess)
सकेसम्म	as much as possible	भगवती	title (name) of goddess	श्री ५ महाराजाधिराज	King's title, HM the King
खसी	goat (castrated)	दर्शन गर्नु	visit (god or superior)	सवारी	royal tour/visit
बोका	he-goat	घुइँचो	crowd	होइबक्सिनु	be (royal honorific)
मोल	price, cost	रमिता	show, spectacle, sight	महानवमी	Great 9th Day
मरमसला	spices and such	जलपूर्ण	full-of-water	काटमार	slaughter (lit. cut-kill)
च्यूरा	pounded rice snack	कलश	worship water jug	बलि	sacrifice, offering
गेडागुडी	peas and beans	पवित्र	holy	चढाउनु	to offer, uplift
बिक्नु	be sold, it sells	माटो	mud, clay, soil	विजया दशमी	Victorious 10th Day

भत्ता	bonus pay, allowance	बालुवा	sand	अघिल्लो	former, previous
पेस्की	advance (money)	बिछ्याउनु	to spread out	आशीर्वाद	blessing
दङ्ग	delighted, thrilled	छर्नु	scatter, sow	कुमारी	Living Goddess; virgin
जुटाउनु	collect, provide, supply	टीका लगाइमाग्नु	get tika (from)	खचाखच हुनु	crowded, crammed
बडा दसैँ	big dashain	रिन	debt, loan	द्वारा	by means of, see. 23.3

USEFUL PHRASES

- म खाना दिन्छु, तपाईं आफ्नो थाल थाप्नुस् । *I'm serving food, hold out your plate.*
- मलाई खाना पुग्यो । नथप्नुस् । *That's enough food for me. Don't add (anymore).*
- म नेपाली सिक्ने इच्छाले आएँ । *I've come with the intention of learning Nepali.*
- तपाईंको आशा केके छन् ? *What are your hopes?*
- मौका आउँछ, त्यो पर्खँदैन । *Opportunity comes; it doesn't wait.*
- सकेसम्म कोसिस गर्नुस् । *Try as hard as possible.*
- तपाईं सकेसम्म आउनुस् । *Come as best as you are able.*
- सकेसम्म छिटो आउनुस् । *Come as early/quickly as possible.*
- मैले एक घण्टा पढे पुग्छ । *One hour is enough for me to study.*

TEXT

दसैँ हिन्दूहरूको ठूलो चाड हो । यो चाड असोज-कार्तिक महिनामा पर्छ । चाड सुरु भएको दसौँ दिन मुख्य दिन भएकाले त्यसै दिनलाई दसैँ भन्ने चलन छ । चैते दसैँ पनि सानो रूपमा मनाइन्छ । त्यसलाई सानो दसैँ भनिन्छ । चैतमा गर्मी हुने, सुख्खा हुने, अल्छी लाग्ने, धुलो उड्ने, रोग लाग्ने इत्यादि कारणले त्यसबेला भोज गर्नु खास उपयुक्त नभएकाले बडा दसैँ असोजमा सारिएको हो भन्छन् । यसबेला मौसम रमाइलो हुन्छ । यसबेला न जाडो हुन्छ न गर्मी नै हुन्छ । यति बेला वर्षा सिद्धिइसकेकाले पहाड, जङ्गल इत्यादि भर्खर धोएकाजस्तो सफा देखिन्छन् । यति बेला बादल नभएको

निलो आकाश देखिन्छ । यति बेला हिमाल पनि कुहिरो र बादलले ढाकिएको हुँदैन । यसबेला छानामा बसेर भिन्दै किसिमको सफा वातावरणको आनन्द लिन सकिन्छ ।

फेरि नेपालका धेरै किसान वा कृषिमा भर पर्नेहरू सबै यसबेला अति खुसी देखिन्छन् । किनभने यति बेला वर्षको मुख्य बाली धान पाकिरहेको हुन्छ अर्थात् यति बेला धान काट्ने बेला भइसकेको हुन्छ । पहाडमा धान नहुने ठाउँमा मकै बाली भित्र्याइसकिएको हुन्छ । यसरी भित्र्याएको र पाकेको बाली हेरेर उनीहरू रमाइरहेका हुन्छन् । साउनभदौको घाँस खाएर मोटाएका बस्तुभाउले पनि यति बेला केही आनन्द थपिदिन्छन् ।

केटाकेटीहरू यसबेला मीठो खाने, राम्रो नयाँ लुगा लगाउने, पिङ खेल्ने, चङ्गा उडाउने तथा अरू रमाइलो गर्ने दिनहरूको आशामा रमाइरहेका हुन्छन् । स्कूल र क्याम्पसमा पनि यति बेला चाहिएजति बिदा हुने भएकाले रमाइलो गर्ने समय धेरै हुन्छ। बाहिर पढिरहेका विद्यार्थीहरू पनि दसैंमा आफ्नो घर फर्कन्छन् र आफूभन्दा ठूलाबाट टीका थापेर भोज खान्छन् ।

विभिन्न व्यापारीहरू दसैंअघि र दसैंमा हुने ठूलो कारोबार र नाफाको आशामा खुसी र व्यस्त हुन्छन् । सामान जम्मा गर्ने, धेरै बिक्री गर्ने र सकेसम्म धेरै नाफा जम्मा गर्ने कामले व्यापारीहरूलाई फुर्सदै हुँदैन । कपडा पसलमा, लुगा पसलमा खुब

भीड हुन्छ । फलफूल र रोटीका पसलमा पनि दसैंमा भीड हुन्छ । खसीबोका, राँगो, कुखुरा, हाँस बेच्नेहरू त यति बेला आफ्नै मोल खोज्छन् । दसैंमा मरमसला, च्यूरा, गेडागुडी पनि त्यत्तिकै बिक्छ । जता हेर्‍यो उतै भीड मात्र देखिन्छ ।

कर्मचारीहरू पनि भत्ता, पेस्की र बिदाको कारणले दसैंमा दङ्ग नै हुन्छन् । उनीहरू पनि दसैं मनाउन चाहिने सामान जुटाउन व्यस्त हुन्छन् । जतिसुकै टाढा रहे पनि नेपालीहरू आफ्नै घरमा दसैं मनाउन आउँछन्/जान्छन् । त्यसकारण दसैंअघि र दसैंपछि बसहरू पनि यात्रुहरूले भरिएर खचाखच हुन्छन् । हप्तौं अघिदेखि बसको टिकट बुक भइसक्छ ।

वर्षको एकपल्ट आउने यति ठूलो र यति रमाइलो चाडमा रमाइलो गर्नेहरू कम हुँदैनन् । मासुको भोज खाने, रक्सीजाँडको खोलो बगाउने, जुवातास खेलेर पैसा उडाउने, चङ्गा उडाएर मनोरञ्जन गर्ने मानिसहरू यतिबेला जताततै भेटिन्छन् । जुवा खेल्नेहरूको लागि त यो एउटा सुनौलो मौका नै हो ।

जस्तोसुकै गरिब भए पनि, अरू बेला कहिल्यै राम्रोसँग खान नपाए पनि दसैंमा सबैले मासुभात त खानै पर्छ; नयाँ लुगा त लाउनै पर्छ । दसैंमा सबका सब मोजमज्जा गर्ने सुरमा हुन्छन् । यसै सुरमा कतिले त यो पनि बिर्सन्छन् र थाहा पाउँदैनन् कि यो दसैं किन मनाइन्छ ? यसको महत्त्व के हो ? यो कसरी मनाउन थालियो ?
किन चाहिए यी सब कुरा ? भोज खान पाइयो र रमाइलो गर्न पाइयो; त्यति भए पुग्दैन र ?

दसैंका पहिलो नौ दिनलाई नौरथा भनिन्छ । नौरथाभरि काठमाडौंका विभिन्न तीर्थस्थलमा बिहान सबेरै मेला भर्ने चलन छ र नवदुर्गाको पूजा गरिन्छ । यी दिनहरूमा भगवतीका मन्दिरहरूमा दर्शन गर्न आउनेहरूको घुइँचो हुन्छ । कोहीकोही युवायुवतीहरू रमिता हेर्नको लागि पनि मन्दिर जान्छन् । त्यस बेला बिहानको ताजा हावा खान पनि रमाइलै हुन्छ ।

नौरथाको पहिलो दिनमा जलपूर्ण कलशको स्थापना गरिन्छ । त्यसको नजिकै पवित्र माटो, बालुवा आदि बिछ्याएर जौ, मकै आदि छरेर जमरा राख्ने काम हुन्छ । दसैंको सातौं दिनलाई फूलपाती भनिन्छ । फूलपातीका दिन जमरा कोठामा उखु र अदुवाको बोट, फूलको झुप्पा ल्याएर पूजा गरिन्छ । त्यसै दिन काम गर्ने

ज्यावलहरूको पनि पूजा गरिन्छ । यसै दिन गोरखा दरबारबाट ल्याइएको फूलपातीलाई काठमाडौँमा ठूलो स्वागत गरिन्छ । त्यस बेला टुँडिखेलमा निजामती कर्मचारीहरू र अन्य मान्यजनहरूको उपस्थिति हेर्न रमाइलो हुन्छ । अष्टमीको दिनमा विशेष पूजा सुरु हुन्छ । यस दिन पीठहरूमा ठूलो भीड हुन्छ । त्यसैले ठाउँठाउँमा सवारीसाधनहरूको जाम हुन सक्छ । महानवमीमा ठूलो सङ्ख्यामा काटमार हुन्छ । यस दिन भगवतीका मन्दिरहरूमा बलि चढाउनेहरूको ठूलो भीड हुन्छ । यस दिन खास गरी बोका, भेँडा, राँगो, कुखुरा हाँसको बलि चढाइन्छ । मोटर, मोटरसाइकलमा समेत यस दिन बोका, हाँसआदिको बलि चढाइएको देखेर विदेशीहरूलाई अचम्म लाग्छ ।

दसौँ दिन विजया दशमीको मुख्य दिन हो । पहिले आफ्नै घरमा टीका लगाइसकेपछि अरू आफन्तको घरमा गएर आफूभन्दा ठूलाबाट टीका लगाइमाग्ने दिन पनि यहीँबाट सुरु हुन्छ । यो दिन र अघिल्लो दिन बजार पूरै बन्द हुन्छ । टीका लगाइदिने बेलामा ठूलाद्वारा सानालाई आशीर्वाद दिइन्छ । कुमारी घरमा गएर कुमारीको टीका थाप्न जानेहरूको घुइँचो पनि यस दिन कम हुँदैन ।

दसैं सबैको लागि उत्तिकै रमाइलो नहुन सक्छ । धेरैलाई यसले रिन बोकाएर जान्छ । दसैँमा जुवातास, रक्सी आदिको धेरै प्रयोग हुन्छ । धेरै खाना र रक्सीबाट कोहीकोही त बिरामीसमेत पर्छन् । जे होस्, नेपालमा यस चाडको ठूलो महत्त्व छ ।

Phrases:

इत्यादि कारणले... *because of such reasons...*

...त्यसबेला भोज गर्नु खास (गरी) उपयुक्त नभएकाले... *Because it's not really appropriate to feast at that time...*

...असोजमा सारिएको भन्छन्: *They say it's been moved to Asoj*

साउनभदौको घाँस खाएर मोटाएका बस्तुभाउ: *Animals fattened by the grass of Saun and Bhadau.*

मीठो खाने...तथा अरू रमाइलो गर्ने दिन: *days of eating good food...and having other such fun.*

सामान जम्मा गर्ने...कामले: *with the work of accumulating goods...*

वर्षको एकपल्ट आउने...यति रमाइलो चाड: *such an enjoyable festival that comes once a year.*

मासुको भोज खाने...मनोरञ्जन गर्नेहरू: *people who eat a meat feast...have fun.*

आफूभन्दा ठूलाबाट टीका लगाउने दिन: *the day of receiving tika from those older than oneself...*

जताततै भेटिन्छ: *It's seen (encountered) everywhere.*

GRAMMAR

➤ 21.1 न X...न Y *NEITHER X NOR Y.*

न कालो न सेतो	*Neither black nor white.*
न जाडो न गर्मी हुन्छ ।	*It's neither cold nor hot.*
ऊ न लेख्छ न पढ्छ ।	*He neither writes nor reads.*

Refer also 4.5 ...पनि (-) ... पनि (-) and 22.4 न त ...

➤ 21.2 REVIEW OF हुनु FOR GENERAL STATEMENTS (8.2).

In this chapter we have several more examples of हुन्छ used for statements of general fact--for things that are always true:

(यतिबेला) धान पाकिसकेको हुन्छ ।	*The rice finishes ripening [at this time of year].*
(यसबेला) काट्ने बेला भइसकेको हुन्छ ।	*It becomes harvest time [at this time of year].*
(यसबेला) जमरा राख्ने काम हुन्छ ।	*It's time to put in the barley shoots [at this time...]*

➤ 21.3 ORDINAL NUMBERS AND ADJ WITH –औँ.

In this chapter you have two examples of ordinal (order) numbers: *seventh* and *tenth.* These are formed by adding -औँ to a number. Note: the first four ordinal are irregular.

पहिलो	*first*	सातौँ	*seventh*
दोस्रो	*second*	दसौँ	*tenth*
तेस्रो	*third*	बीसौँ	*twentieth*
चौथो	*fourth*	सयौँ	*hundredth/hundreds of*
पाँचौँ	*fifth*	हजारौँ	*thousandth/thousands of*

-औँ is also added to form *many weeks* and *many months:* हप्तौँ and महिनौँ

हप्तौँ लाग्छ।	*It takes many weeks.*

➤ 21.4 ROYAL HONORIFIC.

Obviously the royal honorific is used for royalty. However, it is also used in a couple of other situations:

1) It is fairly common for wives to use the royal honorific for their husbands. For example, let's say you phone a man but the wife answers. If you ask if he's home, it would not be unusual to hear her say होइबक्सिन्छ *he's here.*
2) Flattery and sarcasm. The royal honorific is sometimes used just as in English when a sarcastic teenager says, "Yes, your highness!"

The royal honorific is formed by simply adding -इबक्सिनु to the verb root:

INDEF	PAST	PRES PER	PRES CONT	HIST PAST
गरिबक्सिन्छ	गरिबक्सियो	गरिबक्सेको छ	गरिबक्सिँदै छ	गरिबक्सिन्थ्यो
लेखिबक्सिन्छ	लेखिबक्सियो	लेखिबक्सेको छ	लेखिबक्सिँदै छ	लेखिबक्सिन्थ्यो

Note: it is गरिबक्सियो, **not** गरिबक्सिनुभयो.

There are also verbs that are specific to royal speech. For example:

जानु/आउनु	is	सवारी होइबक्सिनु
खानु	is	ज्यूनार गरिबक्सिनु
हेर्नु	is	नजर गरिबक्सिनु
बस्नु	is	राज होइबक्सिनु

➤ 21.5 -कि FOR REPORTED SPEECH AND *THAT* (Cf. 13.4).

In 13.4 you learned the "correct" way of reporting speech. However, there is another common way, though it is considered incorrect to use in writing (Hindi borrow). Because it follows the English word order, it is often easier for native English speakers.

उसले भन्यो कि ऊ जान्छ ।	*He said he's going* (both *he's* can refer to same person).
मैले भनें कि पानी पऱ्यो ।	*I said that it's raining.*
उहाँले भन्नुभयो कि म नेपाली बोल्दिनँ ।	*He said that I don't speak Nepali.*
मैले बुझिनँ कि ऊ किन अहिले आउँछ ?	*I didn't understand why is he coming now.?*
मलाई थाहा थिएन कि ऊ अहिले आउँछ ।	*I didn't know that he's coming now.*

COMPLEX VERBS

- **–ए पुग्छ** — ***is enough to, suffices...***

  मैले एक घण्टा पढे पुग्छ । — *One hour is enough for me to study.*

- **–न पुग्नु** — ***be finished, ended...***

  मलाई पढ्न पुग्यो । — *I have finished my studies (sufficiently studied).*

  हामीलाई खान पुग्यो । — *We've finished eating; we've had enough.*

  तिमीलाई चङ्गा उडाउन पुगेको छैन । — *You haven't finished flying the kite?*

PRACTICE

1. By way of review (14.4), translate and complete each using सुकै:

   a) जतिसुकै गरिब भए पनि...
   b) मैले जेसुकै गरे पनि...
   c) जोसुकैले चङ्गा उडाए पनि...
   d) Whatever he says...
   e) Whoever flies a kite...
   f) Whoever sacrifices a goat...
   g) Wherever you look...
   h) Wherever there's a will...
   i) Whenever he flies a kite...
   j) Whenever you seek pleasure...

2. Consider the following phrases and describe them by what they are **not** (using न X न Y *in full sentences*):

   a) a red taxi
   b) the room you're in
   c) this chapter
   d) the weather today
   e) your country
   f) the way you get around town
   g) Kathmandu
   h) a food you find delicious
   i) what you did yesterday
   j) what you do with your leisure time
   k) what you will do tomorrow
   l) walking downhill
   m) mosquitoes
   n) drinking and gambling
   o) your previous job

3. Count to twenty, using ordinal numbers: ie. *first, second, third, fourth...*

4. Translate each of the following sentences in three ways:
   i) using "..." भन्नु ii) using भनेर भन्नु iii) using कि
   a) He said he is going. (Both *he's* are the same person)
   b) He said he is going. (Both *he's* are not the same person)
   c) She said, "Try as hard as possible."
   d) Ram said, "I'll come as quickly as possible."
   e) I said that I'm not going.
   f) Did he say that he would like to sleep?*
   g) "I don't speak Nepali," he said.
   h) I said, "Don't bother me!"
   i) She said that she will never get married.
   j) Did you say that this isn't hard?*

   * with questions the use of 'कि' for indirect speech is not preferred.

5. Translate the following using -ए पुग्छ:
   a) One hour is enough for me to finish this job.
   b) One month is enough for me to finish this book.
   c) Three days is enough for him to reach the village.
   d) Three years is enough for us to build a hospital.
   e) Six hours is enough for me to sleep.

6. Translate the following using ...लाई -न पुग्नु:
   a) I've finished reading the book.
   b) We've finished paying the employees.
   c) Have you finished staying in that house?
   d) They finished their studies.
   e) I've finished thatching the roof.

LET'S TALK

1. Tell your tutor as much about Dassai as you can.

2. Describe to your tutor the most significant holiday/festival of your home country and then discuss the following:
   a) How is it similar to Dassai?
   b) How is it different from Dassai?
   c) What are the negative and positive aspects of Dassai?
   d) What are the negative and positive aspects of the significant holiday of your home country?
   e) What is the farthest you've traveled to celebrate a holiday? Explain.

3. Together with your tutor, take turns finishing the following sentences:
    a) If I had 1 million rupees, I would...
    b) Everybody should...
    c) I have never...
    d) Parents should always...
    e) This world would be a better place if...
    f) I like people who...
    g) I'd like to be more...and less...
    h) Some day I'm going to...
    i) If I could be somewhere else now, I'd...

4. Take turns discussing what would happen...
    a) if Kathmandu ran out of water?
    b) if everyone in Kathmandu got a car or motorcycle?
    c) if men were not allowed to be doctors or pilots?
    d) if drinking in Nepal was prohibited?

5. Take turns discussing what you would do...
    a) if you were invited to meet the King?
    b) if your little sister aged 13 told you she was going to get married?
    c) if a priest warned you not to go outside tomorrow?
    d) if you found a bag of money on the road?
    e) if you found a snake in your bed?
    f) if you got lost in the mountains?
    g) if your village neighbor beat their child every day?
    h) if a friend asked to give you a *tika* during Dassai?

6. Both of you state three ways in which you think you are similar. Both of you state three ways in which you think you are different.

7. Using -ए पुग्छ, estimate how much time suffices for you to...:
    a) finish one chapter of this book.
    b) eat daal bhat.
    c) get ready for class.
    d) drive to Pokhara.
    e) walk home.

IN THE COMMUNITY

Whatever time of year it is, there is almost certain to be a festival somewhere in Kathmandu this week or next, be it big or small. Some of them will not be described in the tour books or marked on a calendar, so you may have to do some digging. And being based on a lunar calendar, you may have to ask around to figure exactly when it is (as they often do!). Whatever the case, plan to observe the next upcoming festival even if it's relatively insignificant.

By talking to those present, find out as much as you can about the festival. How did it originate? What is its significance? Who does and does not participate? How important is it? Why are the people you talk to there? Is there food involved? etc. Spend at least 4 hours talking to and observing people there at the festival.

As an alternative for men, if it's kite flying season learn to fly a kite (Nepali women never fly kites). Have a Nepali explain the different types of reels, strings and kites. Learn each step: choosing a good kite, stringing it, getting it up, controlling it, etc. What are the different strategies in a kite fight? Above all else, have fun!

DID YOU KNOW?

Sacrifice is accepted as one of the most effective means of reaching salvation. Different types of sacrifice have their own values. Animal sacrifice is but one type of sacrifice. The five kinds of animal sacrifice are the male (never the female) of the water buffalo, the goat, the chicken, the duck and the sheep. These symbolize anger, lust, timidity, apathy and stupidity respectively. The main value of their sacrifice is to gain control over the respective vice.

The Festivals of Nepal, *Dhurba Krishna Deep*.

Three different New Years are celebrated in Nepal: Tibetan New Year (Losar) usually in February, Lunar New Year in mid-April and the Newar New Year in October.

It is customary (and so expected) that all employees will receive a bonus for the month of dassai, usually one month's pay.

MAJOR FESTIVALS OF NEPAL

Dec-Jan	Seto Machhendranath	public bath of White M.
	Maghe Sankranti	cold weather bathing
	Bhimsen Puja	merchant patron saint
	1001 Lights	procession at Bodhnath
Feb	Losar	Tibetan New Year
Feb-Mar	Shiva Raatri	Lord Shiva's Night
	Holi	red powder and water fights
Mar-Apr	Chakandeo Jatra	merchant becomes god
	Balaju Mela	bathing at Balaju at full moon
	Ghonde Jatra	festival of horses
	Sapana Tirtha Mela	dreams for the New Year
Apr-May	Bishket Jatra	death of two serpent demons
	Nawabarsa	Lunar New Year
	Mata Tirtha Puja	Mother's Day
	Raato Macchendranath	chariot pull for monsoon rain
	Buddha Jayanti	Buddha's Birth

May-June	Sithinakha	Kumar's Birth
June-July	Tribhuvan Jayanti	Tribhuvan's birth (Democracy Day)
July-Aug	Ghanta Karna	night of the Devil
	Gunla	month of Lord Buddha
	Naga Panchami	day of the Snakes
	Janai Purnima	The Sacred Thread
Aug-Sep	Gai Jatra	procession of sacred cows
	Krishna Jayanti / Janmashtami	Krishna's birth
	Gokarna Aunsi	Father's Day
	Tij	women's Festival
Sep-Oct	Indra Jatra	Goddess of rain-masks, dancing
	Kumari Jatra	procession of Living Goddess
	Sorah Sraddha	16 days of ancestor worship
	Dashain	Durga triumphs over evil
	Pachali Bhairab Jatra	God of Terror rides again
Oct-Nov	Newari New Year	a merchant frees people from debt
	Tihar / Dipawali	Laxmi's festival of lights
	Haribodhini Ekadasi	return of Vishnu
	Mahalaxmi Puja	Laxmi--wealth and harvest
Nov-Dec	Gujeswari Jatra	worship of secret Goddess
	Indraini Puja	festival of Goddess Indraini
	Bala Chaturdasi	Bala and the Dead
	Bibaaha / Bibaha Panchami	wedding of Sita and Rama
	Yomarhi Punhi	rice cakes for the harvest moon

CHAPTER 22

HINDUISM
हिन्दू धर्म

VOCABULARY					
स्वर्ग	heaven, paradise	सम्भिनु	be considered	झुटो / झुठो	false
नर्क	hell	इष्टदेव	family god	सूक्ष्म	tiny, minute
मर्त्यलोक	place-of-death	देव	god (cf. "deo")	अंश	part, particle
पाप गर्नु	to sin	धर्मशास्त्र	Scripture (religious)	छुनु	touch
फल	fruit; result	उल्लेख	mention, description	आकार	shape
यातना	torment (noun)	उल्लिखित	mentioned	जगत्	world, universe
भोग्नु	undergo, experience, bear	सीमा	limit(ation), borderline	मूर्ति	idol, image, statue
सुख	comfort, ease	शास्त्र	Scripture	तस्बिर	picture, portrait
निर्धारित	determined, fixed	धकेल्नु	push, shove	देवता	deity, god
स्थायी	permanent	सुअवसर	good opportunity	या (वा अथवा कि)	or
भवसागर	Ocean of Existence	ईश्वर	God	धर्मावलम्बी	follower of X religion
पुनर्जन्म	rebirth, reincarnation	उपासना	worship (mental)	देवी	goddess
* लाख	100,000	निरन्तर	incessant	सज्नु / सजिनु	be decorated, adorned
** जुनी	one life in the circle of lives	बरु	or else, or rather	प्रतिष्ठा	consecration (temple, idol)
घुमीफिरी	spinning, circling	याद राख्नु	to remember, keep in mind	झुन्ड्याउनु	hang (up)
जन्म	birth	गल्ती गर्नु	make a mistake	टालो	patch
कर्म	work; duty; lot	सजाय	punishment	जोगी	ascetic, hermit
छुटकारा	freedom, release	विश्वास	faith, trust, belief	तपस्या	asceticism, meditation
अवस्था	condition, circumstance	आदर्श	ideal	शुद्ध	clean, pure (ritually), unadulterated
मुक्ति	freedom, salvation (from rebirth)	नत्र	otherwise, lest	आस्तिक (opp. नास्तिक)	religious, devout; theist
साधना	exercise, practice	डुमै (डुम नै)	part. low caste	क्षमा गर्नु	forgive, excuse
भोग	undertaking	जथाभाबी	randomly, haphazardly	दण्डवत् गर्नु	bow down, worship
मोक्ष	salvation (from rebirth)	डराउनु	be afraid	परमेश्वर	God
चक्र	wheel, circle, disc	अन्त्य	end	पूजारी	priest
आत्मा	soul, spirit	प्राणी	creature, being	जलाउनु (लास)	cremate, burn
पूर्वजन्म	previous life	ईश्वरीय	divine	मृत्यु	death

USEFUL PHRASES

* In Nepal, the commas in one *lakh* are placed as follows: 1,00,000
** One life in the circle of 8.4 million lives.

- तपाईं जस्तो काम गर्नुहुन्छ, त्यस्तै फल पाउनुहुन्छ । *As you sow, so shall you reap.*
- हामी तपाईंको सुखको कामना गर्दछौं । *We wish your happiness.*
- तपाईं कुन धर्म मान्नुहुन्छ ? *Which religion do you follow?*
- अरूलाई मद्दत गर्नु धर्म हो । *It is virtuous to help others.*
- तपाईंको काम छ भने मलाई सम्झनुस् । *If you have work, remember me.*
- मलाई गल्ती/गलत नसम्झनुस् । *Don't get me wrong/misunderstand me.*
- त्यो नामलाई याद राख्नुस् । *Remember that name.*
- जथाभाबी नबोल्नुस् । *Don't run off at the mouth.*
- झर्को नमान्नुस् है ? *Don't be irritated/offended, okay?*

TEXT

हिन्दू धर्म

१. स्वर्ग, नर्क र मर्त्यलोक

पाप गर्ने नर्क जान्छन् र धर्म गर्ने अर्थात् राम्रो काम गर्ने स्वर्ग जान्छन्। पापको फलअनुसार नर्कमा यातना भोग्नुपर्छ। पापको किसिमअनुसार धेरै समयसम्म वा थोरै समयसम्म ठूलो यातना वा सानो यातनाको फल भोग्नुपर्छ। यसरी पापको फल भोगेपछि आफूले गरेको धर्मको फल भोग्न स्वर्ग जान पाइन्छ। स्वर्गमा दु:ख भनेको हुँदैन। स्वर्गमा सुख भोग्न पाइन्छ। ठूलो धर्म, सानो धर्मअनुसार स्वर्गको सुख भोग्ने समय निर्धारित हुन्छ। ठूलो धर्म गरे धेरै समय स्वर्गमा बस्न पाइन्छ। तर स्वर्गको त्यो सुख स्थायी हुँदैन। आफूले गरेको धर्मअनुसार स्वर्गको सुख भोगेपछि फेरि यस संसार अथवा भवसागरमा आउनुपर्छ अर्थात्

पुनर्जन्म लिनुपर्छ। यसरी भवसागरमा चौरासी लाख जुनी घुमीफिरी एकपल्ट मान्छेको जन्म पाइन्छ। पूर्वजन्ममा धर्मकर्म गरेको भए चौरासी लाख जुनी पूरा घुम्नुपर्दैन अनि छिट्टै मान्छेको जुनी पाइन्छ। यही मान्छेको जुनी एउटा यस्तो मौका हो जुन बेला मान्छेले धर्मकर्म गर्न सक्छ। अझ अवस्था मिल्यो भने मान्छेले मुक्तिको लागि साधना गर्न सक्छ। किनभने स्वर्ग र नर्कको भोग मुक्तिभन्दा फरक कुरा हो।

२. मोक्ष/मुक्ति

मोक्ष/मुक्तिको अर्थ साधारणतया भवसागरमा फेरिफेरि जन्म लिनुपर्ने चक्रबाट मुक्ति वा छुट्कारा पाउनु भन्ने बुझिन्छ । भवसागरबाट मुक्ति पाएपछि मान्छेले फेरिफेरि जन्म लिनुपर्दैन (भवसागरमा जन्म लिनु आफै पनि दुःख भोग्नुपर्ने अवस्था मानिन्छ) । यस अवस्थामा उसको आत्माले समेत मोक्ष पाएको सम्झिन्छ र त्यो आत्मा आफ्नै इष्टदेवमा लीन भएको अर्थात् आफ्नो इष्टदेवसँग एक भएको पनि मानिन्छ । मुक्ति पाउनेहरू वैकुण्ठ कि कैलाशमा पुगेर विष्णु कि शिवको परिवारजस्तो भएर पनि रहन्छन् भनिन्छ । मान्छेले धर्मकर्मको साथै मोक्षको लागि पनि साधना गर्नुपर्छ भन्ने धारणा पनि हिन्दू धर्ममा पाइन्छ।

मरेको मानिस जलाउन लागेको

३. पाप र धर्म

कुनकुन कर्म पाप हो र कुनकुन कर्म धर्म हो भन्ने कुरा हिन्दू धर्मशास्त्रमा उल्लिखित छ भनिन्छ । कुनै काम कुनकुन अवस्थामा पाप हो ? यसको सीमा के हो भन्ने कुरा धर्मशास्त्रमा उल्लिखित छ भनिन्छ । त्यस्तै कुराहरू धर्मको बारेमा पनि छन् रे ! तर धर्मशास्त्रहरू पुरै पढेका र बुझेका कतिजना छन् र ? कसलाई ती शास्त्रहरू अध्ययन गर्ने फुर्सद छ ? ती शास्त्रहरू जताततै पाइन्छन् र ?

पापले नर्कतिर धकेल्छ अनि धर्मले स्वर्ग तथा अन्य सुअवसरहरू दिन्छ । तर मोक्षको लागि चाहिँ पापबाट टाढा रहेर धर्ममा लागेर आफ्ना ईश्वरको उपासना गरेर निरन्तर साधनामा लाग्नुपर्छ भन्ने विचार पाइन्छ ।

धेरैको विचार के छ भने स्वर्ग र नर्कको कुरा झुटो हो । मरेपछि को कहाँ जान्छ कसलाई के थाहा ? को के हुन्छ, के थाहा ? बरु यो पनि याद राख्नुपर्छ कि आफ्नो जीवनमा गरेको पाप र धर्मको फल यही जन्ममा पाइन्छ । कसैले गल्ती गरेको छ भने त्यस गल्तीको सजाय भोग्न उसले अर्को जन्म पर्खनुपर्दैन । पुनर्जन्म हुन्छ नै भनेर सबैले विश्वास गर्दैनन् । यो पाप र धर्मको कुरा त आदर्श जीवन, आदर्श समाजको लागि नभई नहुने कुरा हो । नत्र मरेपछि डुमै राजा भनेर जथाभाबी गरी हिँड्नेहरू पनि यहाँ कम छैनन् । मरेपछि पाउने पापको फलको लागि को डराउँछ र ? त्यस्तै मरेपछि पाउने धर्मको फलको आशा कसले गर्छ ?

४. आत्मा

आत्मा प्रत्येक प्राणीमा बास गरेको सुरु र अन्त्य नभएको एउटा ईश्वरीय सूक्ष्म अंश हो । यसलाई न त देख्न सकिन्छ न त छुन नै सकिन्छ । यसको आकारप्रकार छैन । मन र आत्मा फरक हुन् । सबैमा उही आत्मा हुन्छ भनिन्छ । प्राणी मरे पनि आत्मा मर्दैन बरु अर्को जन्ममा सर्छ । मोक्ष प्राप्त भएपछि मात्र आत्मा ईश्वरमा लीन हुन्छ । सबै आत्माको स्रोत ईश्वर हो र जगत्को अन्तमा सबै आत्मा ईश्वरमै लीन हुन्छन् । यसको बारेमा जति भने पनि कम हुन्छ ।

५. मन्दिर, मूर्ति र तस्बिरहरू

हिन्दू मन्दिरहरू धेरै किसिमका छन् । सबै मन्दिरमा एउटै देवता या ईश्वरको मूर्ति हुँदैन । धेरैजसो मन्दिरमा मुख्य देवता र वरिपरि अन्य देवताका मूर्ति पनि साधारणतया देखिन्छन् । कर्क पेट्रिकका अनुसार *"काठमाडौँमा घरहरू जति मन्दिर र मान्छेका टाउकाहरू जति मूर्ति छन् ।"*

प्राय: हिन्दू धर्मावलम्बीहरूका पूजाकोठा विभिन्न देवीदेवताहरूका मूर्ति र तस्बिरहरूले सजिएका हुन्छन् । प्रतिष्ठा गरिएका मूर्तिहरूको पूजा गरिन्छ । यतिसम्म कि झुन्डयाइएका फ्रेममा सजिएका तस्बिरले पनि टीकाटालो पाउँछन् ।

देवीदेवताहरूका तस्बिरहरू र तान्त्रिक

हिन्दू धर्मका अरू पनि धेरै पक्षहरू छन् जुन यहाँ लेखेर साध्य छैन ।

Phrases:

स्वर्गमा दु:ख भनेको हुँदैन: *There is no such thing as suffering in heaven.*

मान्छेको जुनी: *man's life, incarnation*

अझ अवस्था मिल्यो भने... *still more, if the situation allows...*

भवसागरमा जन्म लिनु आफै पनि दु:ख भोग्नुपर्ने अवस्था मानिन्छ:

To be born in the ocean of existence itself is considered a situation where sufferings are a must.

मरेपछि डुमै राजा: *Nepali proverb: After death even an untouchable becomes a king.*

GRAMMAR

➤ 22.1 भनेको हुँदैन *THERE ISN'T X.*

स्वर्गमा दु:ख भनेको हुँदैन ।	*There is no suffering in heaven.*
संसारमा असम्भव भनेको केही हुँदैन।	*There's nothing in the world that's impossible.*

➤ 22.2 REPETITION OF -एर.

In our text we find the repetition of -एर in the formation of a long sentence. This is a common way of conjunction that means something like ***in/by*** *w-ing and x-ing and y-ing, z...*

पापबाट टाढा रहेर, धर्ममा लागेर ईश्वरको उपासना गरेर साधनामा लाग्नुपर्छ ।
In staying far from sin, going on in good deeds and worshipping your god, one must go on practicing.

In some senses it means something like ***after*** *w-ing and x-ing and y-ing, z...*

म बजार गएर तरकरी किनेर घर फर्कें । After going to the bazaar and buying veggies, I went home.

➤ 22.3 के हो भने AND के छ भने.

Both phrases essentially mean the same thing and can be used interchangeably. The difference is grammatical, rather than semantic.

मैले नबुझेको के हो भने...	*What I didn't understand is (that) ...*
मैले भनेको के हो भने...	*What I said is/was ...*
धेरैको विचार के छ/हो भने	*The idea that many have/Many's idea is that...*
मेरो विचार के हो भने...	*The idea I have is/My idea is that...*
उहाँको समस्या के हो भने...	*The problem he has is/His problem is ...*

➤ 22.4 न त X...न त Y *NEITHER X NOR Y* *(same as 21.1).*

यो न त देख्न सकिन्छ न त छुन सकिन्छ ।	*This can be neither seen nor touched.*
यो न देख्न सकिन्छ न छुन सकिन्छ ।	*This can be neither seen nor touched.*
न त कालो न त सेतो ।	*Neither black nor white.*
न कालो न सेतो ।	*Neither black nor white.*

COMPLEX VERBS

• न–VERB ROOT–ई नहुने THING — *Thing that must be x-ed. Essential thing.*

(Lit. thing that must not not be x-ed)

हाम्रो लागि पानी नभई नहुने कुरा हो ।	*Water is essential for us (can't do without!).*
सफा हावा हामीलाई नभई नहुने कुरा हो ।	*Clean air is a must for us (can't do without!).*
धर्ममा विश्वास नभई नहुने कुरा हो ।	*In religion, faith is essential (can't do without!).*
नसिकी नहुने भाषा	*the lang we must not not learn (essential to learn)*
नगई नहुने ठाउँ	*essential place to go*
नहेरी नहुने दृश्य	*a must-see sight*

• –न हुने NOUN (neg. –न –नहुने N) *something okay to... (something not okay to...)*

जान हुने ठाउँ	*place okay to go to*
खान हुने कुरा	*something okay to eat*
हेर्न हुने दृश्य	*sight that's okay to see*

• –न डराउनु (passive... लाई ... न डर लाग्नु) *be afraid to...*

म नेपालमा गाडी चलाउन डराउँछु ।	*I'm afraid to drive a car in Nepal.*
म तपाईंलाई भन्न डराउँछु ।	*I'm afraid to tell you.*
उहाँ त्यहाँ जान डराउनुहुन्छ ।	*He's afraid to go there.*

PRACTICE

1. By way of review, translate and complete the following:
   a) ऊ जे पनि खान्छ । यतिसम्म कि...
   b) She agrees with everything. To such an extent that...

2. Repeating Practice #2 from chapter 21, consider the following phrases and describe them by what they are **not**. However, this time use नत X नत Y *in full sentences*:
   a) a red taxi
   b) the room you're in
   c) the weather today
   d) the way you get around town
   e) Kathmandu
   f) what you did yesterday
   g) what you do with your leisure time
   h) what you will do tomorrow
   i) walking downhill
   j) mosquitoes
   k) drinking and gambling

3. Translate the following sentences using कि:
   a) He said that you run off at the mouth.
   b) He said that when he dies he wants to be cremated.
   c) I thought that we had already finished.
   d) I heard that tomorrow there's going to be a holiday.
   e) My hope is that I will speak Nepali like you.

4. Translate the following sentences using -एर साध्य छैन:
   a) It's not possible to speak Nepali like you.
   b) It's impossible to understand him.
   c) He runs off at the mouth. It's impossible to believe him.
   d) It's impossible to not sin.

5. Construct sentences with the following verbs by repeating -एर:

a)	जन्मनु	भोग्नु	मर्नु	
b)	बिक्री गर्नु	कमाउनु	आराम गर्नु	
c)	बिहे गर्नु	बच्चा पाउनु	काम गर्नु	बिताउनु
d)	जुवा खेल्नु	रक्सी खानु	गफसफ गर्नु	बस्नु
e)	पढ्नु	ध्यान दिनु	लेख्नु	सिक्नु

6. Using के हो भने, translate and complete the following:
   a) मेरो विचार के हो भने...
   b) उसको सजाय के हो भने...
   c) My mistake was that...
   d) That game is...
   e) What I didn't understand was...

7. Translate the following using न-VERB ROOT-ई नहुने THING:
   a) food essential to eat
   b) place essential to go
   c) Water is essential for us to live.
   d) name essential to remember
   e) work essential to do
   f) lesson essential to finish
   g) language essential to learn
   h) religion essential to follow
   i) God essential to worship
   j) good deed essential to do

8. Rephrase as many in #7 as possible using -न हुने THING. Eg. *food that's okay to eat.*

9. Translate the following using -न डराउनु:
   a) I'm afraid to cross the river. I'll probably die.
   b) He's afraid to sleep in dark rooms.
   c) Don't be afraid to speak Nepali.
   d) Why are you afraid to tell me?
   e) Don't be afraid to do right.

LET'S TALK

1. You are being sent to a cold, remote area to study the डाँफे and will be all alone for one month. There are no villages nearby and no shelter. Using नभई नहुने कुरा both of you make a list of the top ten things you think of as being absolutely essential to take. Then compare your lists and discuss the things that were different. After seeing each other's lists, how would you change yours?

2. Using the phrase भनेको हुँदैन, talk about what you believe to be absent in heaven. Then, *both of you* share your beliefs about heaven. If you don't

believe in a heaven, why? If so, who goes there? Who doesn't? Where is it? How long do you stay? Are there different kinds of heaven? Who is the ruler of heaven? Do people ever have to leave heaven? If so, why? Are there other animals in heaven? Other beings in heaven? Ask each other any additional questions.

3. Using the phrase भनेको हुँदैन, talk about what you believe to be absent in hell. Then, *both of you* share your beliefs about hell. Who goes there? Who doesn't? Where is it? How long do you stay? Are there different kinds of hell? Who is the ruler of hell? Do people ever get to leave hell? If so, why? Are there other animals in hell? Other beings in hell? Ask each other any additional questions.

4. *Both of you* share your beliefs about reincarnation.

5. *Both of you* share your beliefs about salvation. How is it achieved? What happens after receiving or attaining salvation? Is it permanent? Is it difficult or easy to obtain? What is a person saved from? Ask each other any additional questions.

6. *Both of you* share your beliefs about sin and good deeds. What is the consequence (नतिजा/फल) of each? What is the role of good deeds? Ask each other any additional questions.

7. *Both of you* share your beliefs about the soul. Does it exist? Is it divine? Is it permanent? Is it created? What happens to it after physical death? Do only humans have a soul? Ask each other any additional questions.

8. *Both of you* share your beliefs about idols. Are they holy? Are they divine? If so, since they are manmade how did they become divine? What is their main purpose? Ask each other any additional questions.

9. *Both of you* share your beliefs about God. Who is God? What is God like? How many gods are there? Are all the Hindu gods forms of One God? Can or does God ever do bad? Ask each other any additional questions.

IN THE COMMUNITY

Some Hindus can argue the case of monotheism and can expound a complex symbolism behind different rituals. For the average Hindu, however, Hinduism is a set of cultural traditions that one follows for success in this life. The afterlife is really of little concern. For fertility you are required to do such-and-such. For good crops you are required to do such-and-such. To honor your elders you are required to do such-and-such. They can't explain reincarnation, the soul, heaven, etc. in any great detail. In other words, it's *doing*, not believing. Doing it right is much more important than working out exactly what you believe.

In this community assignment, try to get a feel for what the average Hindu believes by talking to several acquaintances (for at least 3 hours of conversation). How much can they tell you about heaven? reincarnation? the soul? God? What is salvation and how is it achieved? Ask them what a Hindu believes? Does their answer detail belief or action? etc.

As an alternative assignment, approach a "holy man" (ascetic) at Pashupati and talk to him about his life as a holy man. Does he have family? Where all has he traveled? How long has he been a holy man? Why did he choose this life? etc. Caution: most holy men at Pashupati are in it as a profession. In talking to you they will probably expect money. If so, offer them a cup of tea at a nearby tea shop. Also, many of them are from India and speak little Nepali. Even those that speak Nepali will spice up their language with lots of Sanskrit. After all, they're holy men! For this assignment, only one hour of conversation is required.

DID YOU KNOW?

When learning Nepali religious words, the temptation is to "pack" them with our world view without understanding how they are used in the Hindu context. We can assume a definition that is our own, forgetting that the words come packed with the beliefs and values of the Hindu world view. Following is an exposition of the religious implications for some of the words found in the last few chapters.

आत्मा *spirit, soul*

The *soul* is considered to be a minute particle of the Supreme God that is a part of all living beings. Some forms of Hinduism understand that particle to impregnate all matter (because God is omnipresent), and thus the worship of trees, rocks, rivers, etc.

परमेश्वर *God*

Parameshwar is literally, *param* + *ishwar*, or Supreme God. It is used interchangeably with *iswor*. There are various views on who *parameshwar* is: 1) A formless being above all the other gods, 2) a formless being that manifests himself in all the gods and, 3) the deity that ranks the highest in the pantheon of gods. Those of the last persuasion primarily worship the deity they rank highest, ie. Vishnu, Shiva, etc.

Whatever the understanding, it is believed that the bodies of the righteous are the temples of *parameshwar* , and as such, *parameshwar* indwells them. (The unrighteous are indwelled by *asur*, *da:nab*, or *ra:ksas*--'demons' or 'satan').

पाप *sin*

"Sin: in orthodox Hindu thought is the performing of acts that are not morally acceptable in human culture; it is not transgression against the laws of a Divine Being whom some call "God," but is a violation of man's own identity as Brahman or the Divine Being itself; the punishment for wrong action is the accumulation of more *karma* which will delay his liberation by requiring him to be reborn into as many lives as it takes to work off the accumulated *karma*..."--Dictionary of Oriental Philosophy.

The law of *karma* (cause and effect) requires the sinner to 1) work off the deed in hell, 2) be reborn into the life-cycle at a level determined by how much sin/good deeds one has done. If reborn as a human, there is another chance at achieving salvation, but if reborn as a plant or an animal, the soul must move up the ladder of species one at a time until finally reaching the level of humans again.

जुनी र पुनर्जन्म *cycle of life* and *reincarnation*

Because of a cyclical concept of the universe, creation and birth is not a single event, but something that is repeated again and again. There is no absolute beginning or end, but an ever repeating cycle of creation (Brahma), maintenance (Vishnu), and destruction (Shiva).

The cycle of the universe is nothing more than the life cycle of Brahma. When Brahma wakes from a nights sleep, creation of life begins. This starts the *Satayuga* Age--the Golden age where there is no evil. Following this is the *Thretayuga* Age--here evil appears. Then comes the *Dwaparayuga* age, where good and evil struggle for supremacy. In our current universe, Krishna's death ends the *Dwaparayuga* age. Following this is the age of *Kaliyuga* (heralded in by the death of Krishna). In this age, evil gains the upper hand and Vishnu is forced to destroy the world in the form of *Kalki,* who rides in on a white horse and destroys the world with his bow. With the destruction of all life (*Pralaya*), the cycle of *Satayuga - Thretayuga - Dwaparayuga - Kaliyuga* begins again. We are now said to be in the 5,000th year of *Kaliyuga,* with 425,000 years before the cycle begins again.

After 1,000 of those cycles, Brahma is ready to go to sleep. 4,320,000,000 million human years have now passed, and Brahma will be asleep for an equal amount of time. During his sleep the universe is thrust into chaos and confusion until Brahma wakes up to begin another day. With this comes another cycle of 4,000 ages.

Brahma is said to have just completed his 50th year (Brahma years!), and he will die after his 100th year. Brahma is not immortal, but like everything else experiences the cycle of life. When he dies, everything ceases to exist--humans, deities, demons...everything. That it to say, everything is reabsorbed into the godhead and loses all identity. This is how Hindus describe the ultimate salvation, the ultimate *mukti. Mukti* is the ultimate end of everything, good and evil. If *mukti* can be obtained prematurely, the soul escapes that vicious cycle it would otherwise have to travel through (8.4 million life cycles).

After being dead for 100 years, Brahma is reborn to begin another life of 100 years. Thus, our current universe is simply one in an infinite chain of universes.

स्वर्ग *heaven*

There are three uses of *heaven*.

1. A temporary place where good deeds are rewarded before the *soul* is reincarnated. It is a place of enjoyment and bliss. Prior to going here,

the *soul* pays off the debt of *sin* in *hell*. Some understand this place to be the kingdom of Indra, the god of rain, where he also rules over 330 million other gods.

2. One of two permanent places where one goes if *salvation* (one type of) is achieved. One being *baikkuntha*(*dhàm*), the kingdom of Vishnu and his *incarnations* (ie. Krishna, Rama, etc.). The other being *kailas*, the kingdom of Shiva. Which one is achieved is determined by the deity one primarily worships.

3. *brahmalok*, (also satyalok) the realm or plane of formless being and spiritual bliss. This is not final *salvation* (oneness with Brahma), however.

CHAPTER 23

POLITICS OF NEPAL
नेपालको राजनीति

VOCABULARY					
दलगत	party system	चुन्नु	elect, pick, choose	फुल्नु	to flower, blossom
राजनीति	politics	संसद्	Parliament	जय	hail, victory
बहुदलीय	multi-partied	सांसद / सभासद्	member of Parl.	राजनीतिज्ञ	politician
साँचो	true, genuine; key	द्वारा	by, through	मन्त्रालय	Ministry (of gov't)
प्रजातन्त्र	(people's) democracy	दल	party	प्रधानमन्त्री	Prime Minister
अधिराज्य	kingdom	उम्मेदवार	candidate	राष्ट्रपति	President (country), parliamentary
संविधान	constitution, statute	सक्षम	capable, qualified	सभापति	Council Chairman
लिखित	written	न्याय	justice	सचिव	Secretary
राजतन्त्र	monarchy	पद्धति	system	अध्यक्ष	Chairman, chairperson
निरङ्कुश	autocratic	आधारभूत	basic, fundamental	हडताल	strike (political)
संवैधानिक	constitutional	संसदीय	parliamentary	चुनाव	election
राज्य	kingdom, state, nation	सर्वोच्चता	greatness, supremeness	आम चुनाव	general election
कारबाही	operation, action	अन्तर्गत	under (system, org)	जुलुस	mob, procession, march
		सम्मान	honor		
हस्तक्षेप	interference, intervention	अयोग्य	unworthy, unfit	गाउँ विकास	Village Development
जन	people (in compounds)	असक्षम	incapable, unable, unqualified	समिति	Committee
प्रतिनिधि	representative	बेइमान	dishonest	(गा.वि.स.)	(V.D.C.)
गठन गर्नु	to form (committee)	उपयोगिता	usefulness, utility	अङ्गीकार गर्नु	to adopt (as a part)
सभा	council, conference, assembly	बाँदर	monkey	द्वन्द्व	Insurgency
प्रति	over, towards; per	नरिवल	coconut	सम्बिधान सभा	constituent assembly
उत्तरदायी	responsible	असफल	unsuccessful, failure	समानुपातिक	proportional
शासन गर्नु	to rule, govern	सम्मान	honor, respect	समावेशी	Inclusive
हक	right, entitlement	बुद्धिजीवी	wise/learned people, elite	अन्तरिम	Interim
सिमित	limit, limited, fixed	वाक्क लाग्नु	be fed-up with	लोकतन्त्र	Democracy (Synonym प्रजातन्त्र)
पञ्चायती	village council	सङ्घर्ष	struggle	संघिय	Federal
शङ्का गर्नु	doubt, suspect	दुर्भाग्य	misfortune	सहमतिय	Consentious
सार्वभौमसत्ता	sovereignty	पद	rank, post (also verse)	सरकार	government
धारा	section, article (of law)	उद्देश्य	aim, intention, objective, purpose	गणतन्त्र	Republic

बमोजिम	according to (legal)	आश्वासन	assurance	गणतान्त्रिक	Republican, Republic
स्वविवेक	personal conscience	इमानदार	honest, faithful	जारी हुनु	to be issued
विशेषाधिकार	privilege	एकता	unity		

USEFUL PHRASES

- घुस नखानुस् । *Don't take bribes.*
- घुस नखुवाउनुस् । *Don't give bribes.*
- प्रजातन्त्र दिवस *Democracy Day (national holiday)*
- तपाईं अर्काको कुरामा किन हस्तक्षेप गर्नुहुन्छ? *Why do you interfere in another's affairs?*
- तपाईं मलाई किन शङ्का गर्नुहुन्छ ? *Why do you doubt me?*
- कानुनबमोजिम *according to the law*
- उसले चुनावमा कति भोट पायो ? *How many votes did he get in the election?*
- त्यो कुरा सुनेर मलाई वाक्क लाग्यो । *Hearing that, I'm disgusted!*
- जीवनमा तपाईंको के उद्देश्य छ ? *What is your aim in life?*
  or तपाईंको जीवनको उद्देश्य के हो ?

TEXT

सम्वैधानिक राजतन्त्र र बहुदलीय व्यवस्था

नेपाल अधिराज्यको संविधान २०४७ का निम्नलिखित पक्षहरू महत्त्वपूर्ण छन्:

नेपाल अधिराज्यको संविधान, २०४७

१. **संवैधानिक राजतन्त्र**: यस संविधानमा निरङ्कुश राजतन्त्रको सट्टामा संवैधानिक राजतन्त्रको व्यवस्था गरिएको छ । संवैधानिक राजतन्त्रमा राजाले राज्यव्यवस्थाको कामकारबाहीमा कुनै किसिमको हस्तक्षेप गर्दैनन् । यस व्यवस्थामा जनप्रतिनिधिले सरकार गठन गर्छ । सरकार जनप्रतिनिधिसभाप्रति उत्तरदायी हुन्छ । राजाले राज्य गर्दछन् तर शासन गर्दैनन् । नेपालको संविधान २०४७ ले राजाको (श्री ५ को) हक-अधिकार सीमित गरेको छ ।

२. **सार्वभौमसत्ता जनतामा**: नेपाल अधिराज्यको संविधान २०४७ को धारा ३ अनुसार नेपालको सार्वभौमसत्ता जनतामा रहनेछ । यसको प्रयोग यस संविधानमा व्यवस्था भएबमोजिम हुनेछ । तर यस सार्वभौमसत्ताको प्रयोगको पनि सीमा छ । फेरि राजाको स्वविवेकमा पनि केही शक्ति र विशेषाधिकार छोडिएको छ ।

जे होस्, जनताले चाहेको प्रतिनिधि चुनावद्धारा संसद्मा पठाइन्छ । यी प्रतिनिधिहरूलाई सांसद भनिन्छ । यी जनप्रतिनिधिहरूद्वारा सार्वभौमसत्ताको उचित सम्मान हुने विश्वास गरिन्छ । यी जनप्रतिनिधिहरू विभिन्न दल (पार्टी) बाट आएका र स्वतन्त्र पनि हुन्छन् ।

३. **न्यायपद्धति**: यस संविधानले स्वतन्त्र र सक्षम न्यायपद्धतिलाई अङ्गीकार गरेको छ। स्वतन्त्र र सक्षम न्यायपद्धति प्रजातन्त्रको लागि नभई नहुने कुरा हो ।

४. **संसदीय सर्वोच्चता**: यस संविधानले संसदीय शासनपद्धतिलाई स्वीकार गरेको छ। तर संसदीय संविधानअन्तर्गतको सरकार जनप्रतिनिधिहरूमा भर पर्छ । जनप्रतिनिधिहरू अयोग्य, असक्षम, बेइमान भएमा विश्वासयोग्य हुँदैनन् । त्यसो भएमा बहुदलीय राजनीतिको उपयोगिता हुँदैन । यसो भएमा प्रजातन्त्र बाँदरको हातमा नरिवलजस्तै हुनेछ । अनि यो प्रजातन्त्र असफल भएमा पुरानै निरङ्कुश व्यवस्था आउन सक्छ ।

धेरै बुद्धिजीवीहरूलाई अहिले नै यो व्यवस्थादेखि वाक्क लागिसक्यो । त्यत्रो सङ्घर्षबाट ल्याइएको प्रजातन्त्र पनि कमजोर भएमा ठूलो दुर्भाग्य हुनेछ । संसद्को प्रतिनिधि बन्नु र पदको लागि सङ्घर्ष गर्नु मात्र नेताहरूको उद्देश्य हुनुहुँदैन । नेताहरूले जनतालाई झुटो आश्वासन दिनुहुँदैन । उनीहरू इमानदार हुनुपर्छ । उनीहरूले राष्ट्रिय एकताको लागि काम गर्नुपर्छ ।

२०४७ को सम्विधानपछि अन्तरिम सम्विधान २०६३ जारी भइ यसको आठौं संशोधित अन्तरिम सम्विधान २०६७ जेष्ठ १४ गते पुनः जारी गरिएको छ। अन्ततः २०७२ साल अशोज ३ गते संघिय लोकतान्त्रिक गणतन्त्र नेपालको संविधान जारी भएको छ।

आशा गरौं लोकतन्त्र फुलोस्, फलोस् र बलियो होस् । **जय नेपाल !**

Phrases:

निम्नलिखित: *the following (lit. the below written...)*

प्रतिनिधिसभा: *House of Representatives (syn.* संसद)

जनप्रतिनिधि: *people's representative*

व्यवस्थाअन्तर्गत: *under a system*

केही शक्ति छोडिएको छ: *Some power is left (spared).*

यी जनप्रतिनिधिहरूद्वारा सार्वभौमसत्ताको उचित सम्मान हुने विश्वास गरिन्छ:
Sovereignty is believed to be properly honored through peoples' representatives.

प्रजातन्त्र बाँदरको हातमा नरिवलजस्तै हुनेछ: *Democracy will be like a coconut in the hands of a monkey. (misused--they will not know its importance)*

-को लागि सङ्घर्ष गर्नु मात्र नेताहरूको उद्देश्य हुनुहुँदैन:
It must not be the aim of political leaders only to struggle for...

झुटा आश्वासन: *false assurance*

लोकतन्त्र फलोस्, फुलोस् र बलियो होस्: *May democracy fruit, flower and be strong.*

GRAMMAR

➤ 23.1 ADDITIONAL DOUBLE NEGATIVES.

You will remember from chapter 22 the following double negative:

न-VERB ROOT-ई नहुने THING *(thing that must not not be x-ed. Thing that must be x-ed)*

This structure was used to describe an essential *thing*: a noun. But what about something that is essential *to do*: a verb? For that, consider the following double negatives:

g-VERB ROOT-ई हुँदैन	***Should not not X***
म(लाई) नगई हुँदैन ।	*It is essential for me to go. (I should not not go).*
तिमी(ले/लाई) नखाई हुँदैन ।	*You have to eat it!*
हामी(ले/लाई) नपढी हुँदैन ।	*We have to study!*

g-VERB ROOT-ई भएन	***had to X (PAST TENSE) (also used for urgency persent)***
म(लाई) नगई भएन ।	*It was essential for me to go. (I had to go).*
तिमी(ले/लाई) नखाई भएन ।	*You had to eat it! (wouldn't have done not to)*
हामी(ले/लाई) नपढी भएन ।	*We had to study!*

➤ 23.2 बमोजिम *ACCORDING TO.*

बमोजिम is a formal word that is used in legal contexts. It is also used in conjunction with the verb भन्नु. When modifying nouns--NOUN बमोजिम:

हाकिमको भनाइबमोजिम	*according to what the boss said (lit. his sayings)*
संविधानबमोजिम	*according to the constitution*
कानुनबमोजिम	*according to the law*

➤ 23.3 -द्वारा *BY MEANS OF.*

द्वारा is synonymous with -बाट. However, it is literary and is not heard in colloquial speech. When it is used, it is often with passive and causative verbs:

हामीद्वारा लेखिएको किताप	*the book written by us*
मद्वारा स्याउ खाइयो ।	*An apple was eaten by me.*
मैले उहाँद्वारा काम गराएँ ।	*I got work done through him.*

COMPLEX VERBS

- **-एमा** — ***if, in the case of...***

जनप्रतिनिधिहरू बेइमान भएमा...	*If the peoples' representatives are dishonest...*
त्यसो भएमा...	*If that happens/in that case...*
यो प्रजातन्त्र असफल भएमा...	*If this democracy turns out to be unsuccessful...*
यो प्रजातन्त्र कमजोर भएमा...	*If this democracy grows weak...*
पानी परेमा...	*If it rains...*

- **-एबमोजिम** — ***according to...*** (formal; used with भन्नु)

तपाईंले भनेबमोजिम	*according to what you said*
संविधानमा व्यवस्था भएबमोजिम	*according to what's arranged (mentioned) in the Constit.*
सिकेबमोजिम	*according to what's learned*
जानेबमोजिम	*according to what's known*

PRACTICE

1. Using -को सट्टामा translate the following:
   a) I'm working in place of him.
   b) In place of a bike, he now has a motorcycle.
   c) Instead of the king, the people have sovereignty.
   d) Instead of going to Pokhara, I'm going to Dharan.
   e) Give me this in place of that.

2. Using न-ई हुँदैन translate the following:
   a) You just have to eat it!
   b) You just have to go to Pokhara!
   c) He has to rule honestly!
   d) The election must be successful!
   e) What to do? I have to give a bribe!
   f) My income is not enough. I have to take a bribe!

g) He just has to make a sacrifice!
h) You have to study more!
i) I have to work in the office!
j) I have to finish this book!

3. Using न-ई भएन translate the following:
a) I just had to eat it!
b) I had to go to Pokhara!
c) He had to rule honestly!
d) The election had to be successful!
e) What to do? I had to give a bribe!
f) My income is not enough. I had to take a bribe!
g) He just had to make a sacrifice!
h) You had to play less!
i) I had to work in the office!
j) I had to finish this book!

4. Translate and complete each of the following *twice* using -एमा:
a) मैले त्यो केरा खाएमा...
b) मैले तपाईंलाई फोन गरेमा...
c) ट्याक्सी लिएमा...
d) उनले मकै रोपेमा...
e) उहाँले मलाई अरू पैसा दिएमा...
f) If we pay attention...
g) If we play cards...
h) If we gamble...
i) If you go...
j) If I stay...
k) If I stay longer...
l) If it's nice...
m) If it's easy...
n) If we swim in the river...
o) If you get better...

5. Translate and complete the following using (-ए) बमोजिम:
a) कानुनबमोजिम...
b) मेरो हिसाबबमोजिम...
c) उहाँले भनेबमोजिम...
d) According to this book...
e) According to what you've taught...

6. Translate the following using द्वारा:
   a) The apple was eaten by me.
   b) It was done through him.
   c) I got it done through him.
   d) It should be done only through me.
   e) The news was heard by radio.

LET'S TALK

1. Take turns finishing the following sentences:
   a) If I were the Prime Minister of Nepal, I would...
   b) Most politicians are...
   c) What I think about politics is...
   d) Elections are important because...
   e) True justice is impossible because...
   f) ...is like a coconut in the hands of a monkey.
   g) My life's aim is to...
   h) ...was unsuccessful.
   i) I am fed up with...
   j) In my opinion...(politician)...is honest because...
   k) Marches are good / bad because...

2. Discuss the pros and cons of democracy in Nepal.

3. Ask your tutor how Nepal has changed for the better since democracy. For the worse. Does your tutor favor a stronger monarchy?

4. Discuss the various political parties in your respective countries.

5. Do you agree with or disagree with the following statements. *Give your reasons why.*
   a) Most politicians are genuine and honest.
   b) Democracy has been beneficial to Nepal.
   c) The king should have more power than he has now.
   d) Nepal was better before democracy.
   e) Candidates are usually chosen fairly.
   f) Women are not qualified to vote.
   g) People who can't read are qualified to vote.
   h) Democracy in Nepal has been successful.
   i) It is sometimes okay to give a bribe.
   j) It's possible to have unity throughout the world.

6. Describe someone who is:
   a) genuine
   b) responsible
   c) very qualified
   d) unqualified
   e) honest

7. Campaign speech. Take turns role playing that you are a politician making a campaign speech and the other person is your audience. Make up information to cover the following points:
   a) What is your party name?
   b) How are you qualified for the job?
   c) What is the biggest need in Nepal?
   d) What would you do for Nepal?
   e) Would you do anything about pollution in KTM?
   f) etc.

8. Take turns telling each other how you feel about the current leader(s) of your respective countries.

IN THE COMMUNITY

Caution: Talking politics is a Nepali past-time. However, it can also be a very hot issue. Given that you are a guest in this country, it is probably wise that you remain politically neutral and avoid criticism.

Option One:
In the community, get a feel for different peoples' political views by talking for at least 3 hours of conversation. Cover the following points:

Are they satisfied with the current government?
How do they feel about the monarchy?
Do they think things have improved or gotten worse since democracy?
What political party do they favor or are they all the same?
Where they are from, what is the most popular political party?
What do they think about the Maoist movement?
Did they like the panchayat system?
If they were Prime Minister, what would be the first thing they would do?

Option Two:
Find someone who was part of the march to the palace on April 8, 1990 and was present when the crowd was fired on. Ask them as much as you can about the incident.

Option Three:

Find someone who:

- ❑ Voted in the last elections
- ❑ Favors the RPP party.
- ❑ Favors a return to the panchayat system
- ❑ Believes the king should have more power
- ❑ Believes the king has too much power
- ❑ Has personally met a Minister of any ministry
- ❑ Someone who can name five political parties and knows their symbol

DID YOU KNOW?

1990 was a year to remember in Nepali politics. The Nepali Congress joined forces with several other banned communist parties (United Left Front) and started what has come to be known as the People's Movement--*Jana Andolan*. The movement called for the restoration of democracy and the abolition of the Panchayat System, a system established by King Birendra's father. A large mob marched to the Royal Palace on April 8th and after being fired upon, at least 50 people were killed.

As a result, in November 1990 a new constitution was adopted that transferred sovereign power to the people and allowed for a multi-party parliamentary system. The first parliamentary elections were held in May 1991. Since then it has been a bit of a rocky road for democracy:

Event	Emerging Party	Emerging Prime Minister
1991 elections	Nepali Congress	Girija Prasad Koirala
1994 mid-term poll	communist CPN-UML	Man Mohan Adhikari
1995 no-confidence vote	Congress led coalition	Sher Bahadur Deuba
1996 no-confidence vote	RPP led coalition	Lokendra Bahadur Chand
1997 no-confidence vote	RPP faction	Suriya Bahadur Thapa
1998 Thapa resigns	Nepali Congress Parl.	Girija Prasad Koirala
1999 elections	Nepali Congress	Krishna Prasad Bhattarai

Political Situation of Nepal

On May 22, 2002, King Gyanendra dissolved the House of Representatives, and declared mid-term elections upon recommendation of Prime Minister Sher Bahadur Deuba. On January 29, 2003, dialogue was held with the Maoists and ceasefire announced. In Sept. 2005, the Maoist declared a unilateral ceasefire, which ended in Jan. 2006. In November 2005, the two sides signed a 12-point agreement. In April 2006, massive pro-democracy protests were organized by seven opposition parties, supported by the Maoists, which went on for weeks and on April 24, 2006, King relinquished power to the people.

The government and the Maoists signed the landmark Comprehensive Peace Accord in November 2006, ending 10 years of conflict. The Maoists and the political parties endorsed the interim constitution on 15 January, 2007 and the Maoists stepped into the parliament for the first time. In March 2007, the Maoists achieved another political milestone: they joined the interim government. An agreement hold the Constituent Assembly Election in June 2007 was decided, but was again rescheduled to November 22, 2007.

Finally, the cabinet meeting held on Dec 28, 2007, declared Nepal a Federal Republic, to be implemented by the first meeting of the Constituent Assembly. On January 11, 2008, the cabinet meeting set the new date for Constituent Assembly Election as April 10th 2008. Twice deferred, Nepal's historic Constituent Assembly (CA) election was finally held on April 10, 2008. The Communist Party of Nepal (Maoist) won 220 out of 575 elected seats, followed by the Nepali Congress with 110 seats. The final list of members elected under the proportional representation system was released on May 8, 2008 and the CA was convened on May 28, 2008.

Out of 26 newly nominated members, 15 come from indigenous nationalities and six from marginal tribes. The cabinet on July 4, 2008 selected two legal experts and six women to the CA. The first President of Nepal was elected on July 21, 2008. Dr. Ram Baran Yadav from Nepali Congress was elected to the post by the Consitituent Assembly members. On July 24th 2008, Nepal's Constituent Assembly elected Subash Chandra Nembang of CPN-UML as its chairman. Pushpa Kamal Dahal Prachanda, chairman of the Communist Party of Nepal (Maoist), was elected the first Prime Minister of the Federal Democratic Republic of Nepal on August 15, 2008.

Madhav Kumar Nepal became Prime Minister of Nepal on 25 May 2009 after Prachanda resigned over a conflict with the President over the dismissal of the army's chief of staff. Nepal resigned on June 30, 2010 purportedly to help the government move past its current deadlock and to pave the way for a national consensus government, as demanded by the opposition.

Following are the 25 nominated parties of Nepal in the Constituent Assembly including the independent:

S. No.	Name of Party	No. of Seats
1.	Communist Party (Maoists)	229
2.	Nepali Congress	115
3.	Communist Party of Nepal (UML)	108
4.	Madhesi People's Rights Forum, Nepal	54
5.	Tarai Madhes Loktantrik Party	21
6.	Sadhvaawana Party (Mahato)	9
7.	Communist Party of Nepal (ML)	9
8.	Janamorcha Nepal	8
9.	Rastriya Prajatantra Party	8
10.	Communist Party of Nepal (United)	5
11.	Nepal Workers and Peasants Party	5
12.	Rastriya Prajantra Pary of Nepal	4
13.	Rastriya Janamorcha	4
14.	Nepal Sadhvawana Party (Anandidevi)	3
15.	Rastriya Janashakti Party	3
16.	Communist Party of Nepal (Unified)	2
17.	Federal Democratic National Forum	2
18.	Nepali Janata Dal	2
19.	Rastriya Janamukti Party	2
20.	Chure Bhawar Rastriya Ekata Party Nepal	1
21.	Dalit Janajati Party	1
22.	Nepal Rastriya Party	1
23.	Nepal Loktantrik Samajbadi Dal	1
24.	Nepal Pariwar Dal	1
25.	Samajwadi Prajatantrik Janata Party Nepal	1
26.	Independent	2
	Total	**601**

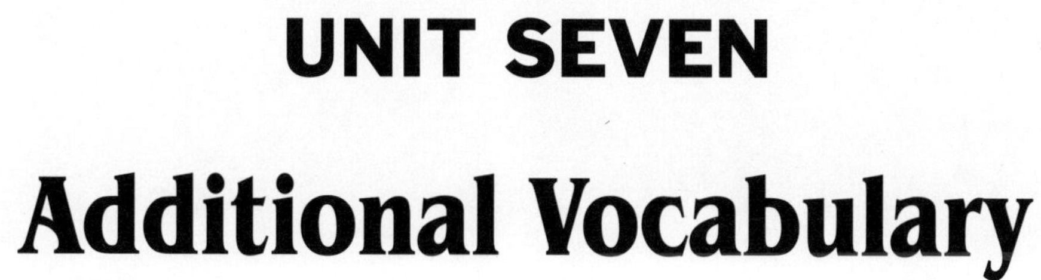

UNIT SEVEN

Additional Vocabulary

- **Domestic Vocabulary**
- **Medical Vocabulary**
- **Administrative Vocabulary**
- **Religious Vocabulary**
- **Construction Vocabulary**

DOMESTIC VOCABULARY

1. अङ्गूर grape
2. अँध्यारो dark
3. उखु sugar cane
4. अचानु cutting board for meat
5. अचार pickle, salsa, relish
6. अन्डा egg
7. अदुवा ginger
8. अनार pomegranate
9. अमिलो sour
10. अम्बा guava
11. आँखीझ्याल latticed widow (lit. eyed)
12. आँगन small courtyard
13. आगो fire
14. आरुबखडा plum
15. आलु potato
16. ओछ्यान bedding
17. ओछ्यान मिलाउनु tidy up the bed
18. ओर्लनु go downstairs, descend
19. ईंट brick
20. इनार water well
21. इस्त्री iron (clothes)
22. उज्यालो light, bright
23. उडुस bedbug
24. उपियाँ flea
25. उमाल्नु boil (water)
26. उसिन्नु boil (food, things)
27. ऊन wool
28. ऊनी woolen
29. ऐना mirror, window glass
30. कडा hard (to touch), feel
31. कप cup
32. कपडा cloth
33. कपास cotton (ball, swab)
34. कमिला ant
35. कम्बल blanket
36. कसौडी pot (small mouth, thick bronze, no handles)
37. कस्नु tighten, fasten
38. करेन्ट लाग्नु be shocked with electricity
39. काँक्रो cucumber
40. काँचो raw, unripe
41. काँटा fork
42. काँटी matches, matchstick
43. काउली cauliflower
44. कागती lemon (small)
45. काट्नु cut, chop
46. कित्ली kettle
47. किनमेल गर्नु go shopping
48. किला nail
49. कुकुर dog
50. कुचो broom
51. कुचो लगाउनु sweep
52. कुना corner
53. कुर्ची / मेच chair
54. कुहिनु rot, spoil
55. केरा banana
56. केराउ peas
57. केलाउनु cull, sort, take rocks out of rice
58. कैंची scissors
59. कोदालो spade, hoe (short handle)
60. खण्ड drawer, compartment, part
61. खल / खलौटो mortar (stone bowl, used with musli)
62. खस्रो rough (surface)

63. खाजा snack, light meal
64. खाट bed (with legs)
65. खुर्सानी chilli, red pepper
66. खेर जानु go to waste
67. खोर animal pen, cage, coop
68. गनाउनु / गन्हाउनु stink (to)
69. गन्ध stinky smell
70. गाजर carrot
71. गुन्द्री straw mat
72. गुलाब rose
73. गुलियो sweet
74. गोलो round, spherical
75. गोलभेँडा tomato
76. घण्टी bell
77. घरपति landlord
78. घरेलु domestic; domesticated, tame
79. घ्यू clarified butter, ghee
80. चक्कू knife, kitchen knife (small)
81. चपाउनु chew (food, betel)
82. चपाती unleavened, whole wheat bread
83. चम्चा spoon
84. चर्पी latrine
85. चलाउनु stir (to)
86. चानचुन change, loose coins, petty
87. चाना पार्नु slice (to)
88. चामल rice (uncooked)
89. चिनी sugar
90. चिप्ले किरा snail, slug
91. चिप्लो smooth (surface); slippery
92. चिम light bulb
93. चिया-पत्ती tea leaves, dust tea
94. चिसो cold (liquid, food); damp
95. चीजबीज goods, supplies
96. चुलो oven, stove (mud); hearth
97. चुल्याँसी / चुलेसी curved blade for cutting veggies
98. चौलानी rice water
99. च्यात्नु tear, tear up, rip
100. चियादानी teapot
101. च्यूरा beaten rice
102. छत roof (flat)
103. छहारी shade
104. छाँया shadow
105. छाना roof (sloping)
106. छिँडी ground floor of house
107. छिन्नु break (rope, string)
108. छिन्नु be cut, sliced
109. छिमेकी neighbor
110. छेस्किनी bolt (to secure window / door)
111. छोडाउनु peel, shell, scrape (to)
112. छोड्नु leave, stop doing
113. छोप्नु cover (to)
114. छुरी knife (larger)
115. जमिन ground, floor
116. जम्नु freeze, congeal (liquid)
117. जिरा cumin seed
118. जुगा leech
119. जुम्रा louse (lice)
120. जोगी तरकारी mixed vegetables
121. जोड्नु join, connect, link
122. झिँगा fly (insect)
123. झिक्नु remove (from something)
124. झुल mosquito net
125. झ्याल window
126. टकटक्याउनु shake out, brush off (remove dust)
127. टिप्नु pick (fruit, veggies)

128. टुक्र्याउनु dice, make into pieces
129. टयाङ्की water storage tank
130. ठोक्नु hit (eg. head on door)
131. डकर्मी mason
132. डालो / डाला basket (with small legs)
133. डेक्ची pot (large, flat bottom, no handles)
134. डेरा rented flat
135. डोको basket (bamboo, for carrying loads)
136. डोरी rope
137. ढकनी lid (of a pot)
138. ढक्की basket (for vegetables)
139. ढल drain, sewage drain
140. ढोका लगाउनु close a door
141. तताउनु heat up
142. तन्ना bedsheet/spread/cover
143. तन्ना floor covering
144. तर्बुजा watermelon
145. तल्ला floor, story
146. ताजा fresh
147. तान्नु pull, drag
148. ताप्के pot (with handle)
149. तार wire
150. तार्नु fry (to)
151. ताल्चा मार्नु lock (a padlock)
152. तावा frying pan (without handle)
153. तितो bitter
154. तोरी mustard
155. तोरीको तेल mustard oil
156. थाप्नु hold out/open/on
157. थाल plate (large), platter
158. दराज cupboard, shelves
159. दर्जन dozen
160. दही yogurt
161. दाबिलो wooden spoon for stirring corn meal
162. दालचिनी cinnamon
163. दुध milk
164. धनिया coriander
165. धमिलो muddy, cloudy, dirty (water)
166. धागो thread
167. धारा tap, faucet
168. धुनु wash (clothes, face, limbs)
169. धुवाँ smoke
170. धुलो dust, powder
171. धुलो उडाउनु stir up dust
172. धोबी washerman
173. ध्वाँसो soot (from smoke)
174. नाङ्लो winnowing tray
175. नाप्नु measure
176. नास्ता breakfast
177. नास्पाती apple–pear
178. निबुवा lime (big)
179. निभाउनु put out (flame), turn out (light), extinguish
180. निल्नु swallow
181. नुहाउनु bathe
182. नुन salt
183. नुनिलो salty
184. पकाउनु cook
185. पखाल्नु wash (rice, vegitable); rinse
186. पछार्नु beat clothes (by swinging)
187. पट्टी bandage
188. पत्ती razor blade
189. पर्खाल compound wall
190. पाउ roughly 1/2 pound or 200 gr
191. पानीको ढ्वाङ water cistern, metal drum
192. पानीमा भिजाउनु soak in water

193. पाहुना house guest
194. पिन्नु mince (to)
195. पिरो spicy hot
196. पिस्नु grind
197. पीठो flour
198. पुछ्नु clean off, wipe
199. पेचकस screw driver
200. पोको पार्नु pack (to)
201. पोल्नु roast (to); burn
202. प्याज onion
203. प्वाल hole
204. फटाउनु/च्यात्नु tear something
205. फर्सी pumpkin, squash
206. फाट्नु(दूध) go sour (milk)
207. फाल्नु throw out/away
208. फिंजाउनु spread (to)
209. फिका bland (food), black (tea), light (color)
210. फिट्नु stir (to)
211. फिल्टर filter
212. फुक्नु blow (eg. on a fire)
213. फुल्नु to flower, blossom
214. फोहोर dirt(y), garbage
215. फ्याँक्नु throw out/away
216. बगैंचा garden
217. बटुको cup (without handle), small bowl
218. बढार्नु sweep (floor), brush (carpet)
219. बत्ती light
220. बत्ती बाल्नु turn on light (lit. burn)
221. बत्ती मार्नु (निभाउनु) turn off light (lit. kill)
222. बदाम peanut, almond
223. बङ्ग्याउनु bend (a stick)
224. बन्चरो axe, hatchet
225. बन्दा कोबी cabbage
226. बस्तु farm animals
227. बाँकी राक्नु save, store, put away, spare
228. बाँध्नु bind, tie up
229. बाँस bamboo
230. बाकस box, trunk, suitcase
231. बाक्लो thick (blanket, mixture)
232. बाङ्गो crooked
233. बाटा basin, dishpan (washing hands/clothes)
234. बार fence, hedge
235. बार मसला curry powder
236. बाल्नु light (candle, stove, paper)
237. बाल्टिन bucket, pail
238. बासी खाना stale food
239. बास्ना smell (only good)
240. बाहाल rent (of house)
241. बिक्री हुनु be sold
242. बिग्रनु become broken, ruined
243. बिरालो cat
244. बिर्को lid, cover, cap (of container)
245. बिस्कुट cookie, biscuit
246. बेच्नु sell
247. बेसार turmeric
248. बैठक sitting/living room
249. भुटेको मकै roasted corn
250. भट्मास soybean
251. भर्नु fill, fill up
253. भऱ्याङ stair(case), ladder
253. भाँडा pot(s), dishes(s)
254. माड काढ्नु strain off water from cooking rice
255. भाडामा rented, leased (lit. on rent, hir

256. भान्छा kitchen; polite for meal
257. भन्टा eggplant, brinjal
258. भिझ्नु get wet, be soaked
259. भित्ता wall (of room)
260. भुइँ floor, ground
261. भुट्नु roast (to)
262. भोगटे grapefruit
263. मकै corn/maize
264. मख्खन butter
265. मटान hallway
266. मट्टीतेल kerosene
267. मनतातो lukewarm
268. मरिच black pepper
269. मसला spice
270. मसिनो soft, fine
271. माकुरा spider
272. माझ्नु wash, scour (pots, dishes), scrub
273. माहुरी bee
274. मिठाई sweets, candy
275. मिसाउनु mix (to)
276. मुस्ली pestle (for grinding in khal)
277. मुला radish
278. मेवा papaya
279. मैदा white wheat flour
280. मैनबत्ती candle
281. मैलो dirty (clothes)
282. मोल्नु marinate
283. मोही butter milk, whey
284. रस soup, gravy; juice
285. रिकापी small plate, saucer
286. रोटी bread
287. लसुन garlic
288. लाइन जानु electricity to go out
289. लामखुट्टे mosquito
290. लुगा धुनु wash clothes
291. वफाउनु steam (to)
292. शीतल cool
293. शीतल ताप्नु cool off in the shade
294. सफा गर्नु clean
295. सयपत्री (फूल) marigold
296. सरसफाइ sanitation, cleanness
297. सलाई match (to light fire)
298. ताला लगाउनु lock (turn a key)
299. साँध लगाउनु sharpen (blade)
300. साङ्लो cockroach
301. सारो/साह्रो hard (to touch)
302. सिँढी step (of flight of stairs)
303. सिउनु sew (to)
304. सिकर्मी carpenter
305. सिमी beans
306. सियो needle
307. सिरक quilt filled with cotton
308. सिरानी pillow
309. सिलाउनु have sewn
310. सिसी bottle
311. सुँघ्नु smell (to)
312. सुकसुक गर्नु sniff (to)
313. सुकाउनु dry (tr)
314. सुकुमेल cardamom (small)
315. सुकुल straw mat
316. सुक्नु get dry
317. सुती linen (cloth)
318. सुन्तला orange (tangerine)
319. सुरुवा पकाउनु stew (to)
320. सेकाउनु/सेक्नु grill (to)
321. सेपिलो shady and damp (place)
322. सेर roughly two pounds

323. स्टोभ — stove (kerosene, gas, electric)
324. स्याउ — apple
325. स्वादिलो — tasty, delicious
326. हँसिया — sickle
327. हराउनु — to lose; defeat
328. हल्लाउनु — shake
329. हाड — bone
330. हाता — grounds, compound, premises
331. हाल्नु — pour or throw in/on
332. हिलो — mud
333. हेरबिचार — supervision, looking after

MEDICAL VOCABULARY

1.	अङ्कुशे जुका	hook worm
2.	अंग	organ (part of body)
3.	अङ्ग-भङ्ग	broken limb
4.	अण्डकोष	testicle
5.	अण्डकोष सुन्निनु	hernia
6.	अनुहार	face; countenance
7.	अन्धो	blind, blind person
8.	अपाङ्ग	crippled, disabled
9.	अप्रेसन गर्नु	operate, surgery (to do)
10.	अर्बुद रोग	cancer
11.	अशक्त	very weak, seriously ill
12.	अस्ताउनु	to die (idiom)
13.	अस्थि विमोचन	bone fracture
14.	आँखा	eye
15.	आँखा चिम्लनु	to die (idiom)
16.	आँखा झिम्क्याउनु	blink eye, wink
17.	आँखा पाक्नु	eye infection
18.	आँखा बिझाउनु	eyes water
19.	आँखाको नानी	eye pupil
20.	आँसु	tear(s)
21.	आऊँ	dysentery
22.	आगो लाग्नु	catch fire, ignite, burn
23.	आन्द्रा	intestine
24.	आन्द्रा सुन्निने	appendicitis
25.	आराम गर्नु	rest (to)
26.	उत्तानो पर्नु	lie face up, prone
27.	उपचार गर्नु	treat
28.	उपाय	remedy, solution
29.	उल्टी गर्नु	vomit
30.	ओछ्यान पर्नु	bed ridden
31.	ओठ	lips
32.	औँलाको हाड	phalange
33.	औँला	finger
34.	औलो	malaria
35.	औषधि	medicine
36.	कट्कट् खानु	gnawing pain
37.	कण्ठ रोग	goiter
38.	कन्याउनु	scratch (itchy spot)
39.	कपाल	hair (of head)
40.	कपास	cotton
41.	कफ	phlegm
42.	कब्जियत	constipation
43.	कमजोर हुनु	weak (to be)
44.	कम्मर	lower back; waist
45.	करङ्ग	rib
46.	कलेजो	liver
47.	करेन्ट लाग्नु	get electric shock, domestic
48.	काँडाले बिझेको	pierced by thorn
49.	काँध	shoulder
50.	काख	lap
51.	काखी	armpit
52.	काट्नु	cut (to)
53.	कान	ear
54.	कान पाक्नु	ear infection
55.	कानको जाली	eardrum
56.	काने गुजी	ear wax
57.	कान्छी औँला	little finger

58. काम्नु shiver
59. कीटाणु bacteria
60. कुपोषण malnutrition
61. कुर्कुच्चा heel
62. कुल्ला गर्नु rinse (mouth)
63. कुष्ठ रोग leprosy
64. कुहिनु infect (sore); rot (food)
65. कुहिनो elbow
66. कैँची scissors
67. कोख womb
68. कोठी mole
69. कोढी / कुष्ठरोगी leper
70. क्षयरोग tuberculosis
71. खकार sputum
72. खकार्नु cough, hack
73. खटिरा abscess, wound; blister
74. खील corns
75. खुट्टा leg, foot
76. खुट्टाको औँला toe
77. खत बस्नु scar (to have)
78. खुम्च्याउनु bend over
79. गर्भ खेर जानु miscarry (go to waste)
80. खोँडे ओँठ harelip
81. खोकी लाग्नु cough (to have)
82. खोप vaccination, vaccine
83. गर्भ रहनु be pregnant, conceive
84. गर्भपात abortion
85. गलगाँड goiter
86. गलफुले mumps
87. गाडीले किचेको crushed by vehicle
88. गानो गोला colic
89. गाला cheek
90. गिजा gum (of mouth)
91. गुदद्वार anus
92. गोटा पर्नु constipated (to be)
93. गोली tablet, pill (lit. bullet)
94. गोलीगाँठो ankle
95. ग्यास्ट्रिक gastric, stomach problem,
96. घुँडा knee
97. घाँटी neck, throat
98. घाँटी बस्नु hoarse
99. घाँटीको हाड collar-bone
100. घाउ wound, sore
101. घाउ पाक्नु sore infect (lit. ripen)
102. घुम्ती शिविर mobile camp.
103. घोप्टो पर्नु lie face down (prostrate)
104. चक्की tablet (pill)
105. चक्कू knife (small)
106. चपाउनु chew
107. चर्पी latrine
108. चलाउनु move (to), operate, run, drive
109. चसचस घोच्नु have pricking pain
110. चाक buttock
111. चिउँडो chin
112. चिप्रा conjunctival pus
113. चिलाउनु itch
114. चिसो लाग्नु hypothermia
115. चुरोट खानु smoke cigarette
116. चुर्ना जुका thread / pin worm
117. चेप्टो खुट्टा flat feet
118. चोट लाग्नु injure, hurt (to be)
119. चोट(पटक) injury, hurt
120. चोर औँला index-finger
121. छाद्नु vomit
122. छाती breast; chest
123. छाती पोल्नु heart burn (to)
124. छान्नु strain, filter
125. छाला skin
126. छारे रोग epilepsy

127.	छिन्नु	cut off, sever, slice
128.	जँचाउनु	examine (to be), get examined
129.	जन्माउनु	give birth
130.	जाँगर नआउनु	lazy (to feel)
131.	जाँच	exam, test
132.	जाँच्नु	examine, check, test
133.	जाति हुनु	get well, healthy
134.	जिउ	body
135.	जिब्रो	tongue
136.	जिब्रो निकाल्नु	stick out tongue
137.	जीउ गल्नु	tired (to be)
138.	जीवन जल	oral rehydration solution
139.	जुगा/जुका	worm, parasite
140.	जुम्रा	lice
141.	जोर्नी	joint
142.	जोर्नी फुक्लेको	dislocated
143.	ज्वरो	fever
144.	झमझमाउनु	tingle; throb
145.	झिँगा लाग्नु	have flies (on)
146.	झुक्नु	bend over
147.	झोल	liquid
148.	टन्टनाउने	tight feeling
149.	टाउको	head
150.	टाउको दुख्नु	headache (to have)
151.	टाटो	burn scar
152.	ठेउला	chicken-pox
153.	डकार्नु	belch, burp
154.	डन्डीफोर	pimple
155.	डुब्नु	to drown (intr)
156.	डेढो	squint (eye)
157.	ढाड	backbone; trunk
158.	ढुङ्गा	stone (eg. gall)
159.	तिघ्रा	thigh
160.	तौल	weight
161.	थप्नु	add
162.	थाप्नु	hold (with both hands)
163.	थिच्नु	press
164.	थुक	spittle
165.	थुक निल्नु	swallow spittle
166.	थुक्नु	spit (to)
167.	थुपार्नु	dumping, heap up
168.	थोपा	drop
169.	दम	asthma
170.	दल्नु	apply and rub
171.	दाँत	tooth
172.	दाग	scar, mark
173.	दाद	ringworm
174.	दादुरा	measles
175.	दिसा	stool
176.	दिसा कब्जियत हुनु	constipated (to be)
177.	दुख्नु	hurt, pain
178.	दुब्लो	lean, thin, skinny
179.	दुर्घटना	accident (eg. car)
180.	दूधको मुन्टा	nipple
181.	दूभी	white patches on skin
182.	दैनिक	daily
183.	धनुष्टङ्कार	tetanus
184.	धमिलो देख्नु	weak vision, (to have)
185.	धुलो	dust
186.	धुवाँ	smoke
187.	नङ्ग	nail (eg. finger)
188.	नछुने हुनु	be untouchable (menstruate)
189.	नलीहाड	shin (bone)
190.	नसर्ने रोग	non-communicable disease
191.	नसा	vein; nerve
192.	नाइटो	navel
193.	नाक	nose
194.	नाक लाग्नु	bad smell
195.	नाकको प्वाल	nostril (nose hole)

196. नाडी wrist
197. नाडी हेर्नु pulse (to take)
198. नाथ्री फुट्नु have nose bleeding
199. नाप्नु measure
200. नाम्ले जुगा tapeworm
201. निको हुनु get better (to), be healed
202. निचोर्नु squeeze
203. निधार forehead
204. निन्द्रा लाग्नु feel sleepy
205. निमोनिया pneumonia
206. नीलडाम bruise
207. नुहाउनु bathe (to)
208. पक्षघात paralysis
209. पखाला diarrhea
210. पचाउनु digest
211. पट्टी लगाउनु bandage (to)
212. पित्त थैलीमा पत्थर gall stone
213. परिवार नियोजन family planning
214. परेला eye-lash
215. पलक eye-lid
215. पसार्नु extend (to)
217. पसिना sweat
218. खुट्टा foot
219. पाइतला sole (of foot)
220. पाखुरा arm
221. पागल हुनु crazy (to be)
222. पाठेघर ovary, uterus
223. पातलो thin, lean; watery
224. पाद आउनु flatulate
225. पानी शुद्ध गर्नु purify water
226. पानीमा राखिछोड्नु leave in water (soak)
227. पिँडुला calf
228. पिठ्यूँ back
229. पित्तको थैली gall bladder
230. पिनास sinus
231. पिलो आउनु abscess (to have)
232. पिलो कचल्टिने abscess suppurating
233. पिसाब urine
234. पिसाब थैली bladder
235. पिसाब फेर्ने ठाउँ perineum (place of urination)
236. पिसाब रोकिनु to have urine retention
237. पीप pus
238. पीलो boil
239. पुट्ठा hip
240. पुरिया paper packet for med.
241. पेट stomach
242. पेट गडबड upset stomach
243. पेट ढुस्स फुल्नु stomach bloat
244. पेट बोक्नु pregnant (to be)
245. पोतो rash
246. पोतो बस्नु discoloration (to have)
247. पोलिनु burnt (to be)
248. पोल्नु burn (sensation)
249. पोसिलो nutritious
250. प्राथमिक उपचार first aid
251. फित्ते जुका tapeworm
252. फियो spleen
253. फिला/तिघ्रा thigh
254. फुलो पर्नु cataract (to have)
255. फुल्नु bloat, swell, become swollen
256. फूर्ति energy, drive
257. फैलाउनु spread (to)
258. फोक्सो lung
259. फोक्सो सुनिने bronchitis
260. फोहोर गर्नु make dirty
261. बङ्गारा molar teeth jaw
262. बच्चा child

263. बहिरो deaf, deaf person
264. बहुमूत्र, मधुमेह diabetes
265. बहुला mad, insane
266. बहुलापन insanity
267. बाँच्नु live (to)
268. बाडुली hiccough
269. बाथ rheumatism; gout; arthritis
270. बान्ता गर्नु vomit
271. बित्नु die (to)
272. बिफर small pox
273. बिरामी sick; sick person
274. बिरामी हुनु sick (to be)
275. बिष (बिख) poison
276. बिषालु poisonous
277. बिसेक हुनु get better, well
278. बूढी औंला thumb
279. बेर्नु wrap up
280. बेहोस हुनु faint, become senseless
281. भिरिङ्गी syphilis
282. भूँडी belly
283. भोक लाग्नु feel hungry
284. भ्यागुते रोग diphtheria
285. मृगौलामा पत्थर kidney stone
286. मन mind
287. मन तातो luke warm
288. मर्कनु sprain
289. मर्नु die (to)
290. मल खाल्डो manure pit
291. मलम ointment
292. मलमूत्र excreta
293. मस्तिष्क ज्वरो meningitis
294. महामारी epidemic, plague
295. महिनाबारी menstruation, period
296. मांसपेशी muscle (formal)
297. माझीऔंला middle finger
298. मात्रा dose, amount
299. मानसिक रोग mental disease
300. मासु muscle, flesh
301. मिर्गौला / मृगौला kidney
302. मिसाउनु mix
303. मुख mouth
304. मुख बार्नु diet (to)
305. मुख सुक्नु dry mouth (to)
306. मुटु heart
307. मुटु हल्लनु palpitate
308. मुटुको चाल palpitation
309. मुट्ठी पार्नु make fist
310. मुसा wart
311. मूर्च्छा पर्नु faint
312. मूल नसा artery
313. मैला dirt
314. मोटो fat
315. मोतीबिन्दु cataract
316. म्यादे ज्वरो typhoid
317. योनि vagina
318. यौन अङ्ग sex organs
319. यौन रोग STD
320. रक्तचाप blood pressure
321. रक्सी खानु drink alcohol
322. रगत blood
323. रगत-मासी blood + mucus (in dycentry)
324. रगत बगाउनु shed blood
325. रगतको कमी anemia (lack of blood)
326. रछ्यान sewage
327. रातोपिरो robust, vigorous, healthy
328. रिँगटा लाग्नु feel dizzy
329. रुघा cold flu
330. रुचि appetite
331. रोग disease
332. रोग लाग्नु disease (to catch)

333. रोगी patient (chronic), sick persor
334. रौं hair, fur
335. लङ्गडो lame
336. लक्षण symptom
337. लड्नु fall (to)
338. लहरेखोकी whooping cough
339. लाउनु apply (eg. ointment)
340. लाटो/लाटी dumb (male/fem)
341. लामो सास deep breath
342. लिङ्ग penis; gender
343. लुतो scabies
344. लुलो पार्नु relax, make limp
345. लू sun-stroke, heat stroke
346. वाकवाक लाग्नु to be nauseated
347. वातावरण environment
348. वीर्य semen
349. विष poison
350. विषालु poisonous
351. व्यायाम physical exercise
352. शरीर body
353. सन्धि-बन्धन ligaments
354. सफा clean
355. समुदाय community
356. सरसफाइ sanitation
357. सरुवा communicable (disease)
358. सर्नु move, transfer
359. सर्ने तरीका mode of transmission
360. सर्ने रोग communicable disease
361. सर्पको डसाइ snake bite
362. साबुन soap
363. साल placenta
364. सास फेर्नु breath
365. सास रोक्नु hold breath
366. सास लिएर छोड्नु breath and then release
367. साहिँली औंला ring-finger
368. सिंगान nasal mucus
369. सिंगान फाल्नु blow nose
370. सिकिस्त worse, grave (illness), serious
371. सियो needle
372. सुई लगाउनु give injection; shots
373. सुत्केरी resting woman after delivery
374. सुन्निनु swell, to be swollen
375. सुरक्षा safety
376. सुर्ती tobacco
377. सूत्र formula
378. स्तनपान breast feeding
379. स्वच्छता hygiene
380. स्वच्छ hygenic
381. स्वस्थ healthy
382. स्वास्थ्य health
383. स्वास्थ्य कार्यकत health worker
384. स्वास्थ्य केन्द्र health post
385. स्वास्थ परीक्षण health exam
386. हत्केला palm
387. हाँडे mumps
388. हाँडी gland
389. हाड bone
390. हाड भाँचिनु bone fracture
391. हाडछाला skin and bones
392. हात hand
393. हात्तीपाइले रोग elephantiasis, phylaria
394. हिंड्नु walk (to)
395. हिउँले खानु frost bite
396. हेरचाह care, maintenance
397. हेरविचार गर्नु look after (to)
398. हैजा cholera
398. हैरान worn out, tired, exhausted

ADMINISTRATIVE VOCABULARY

1. अञ्चल — zone
2. अड्डा — office (govt.)
3. अदालत — court (of law)
4. अधिकार — rights, authority, power
5. अधिराज्य — kingdom
6. अध्यक्ष — chairman (of org. or party)
7. अध्यागमन — immigration
8. अनिवार्य — compulsory, obligatory, mandatory
9. अनुमति — permission, approval
10. अनुमति पत्र — permit, license
11. अनुमति माग्नु — ask for permission
12. अनुसन्धान — research, investigation
13. अन्तर्राष्ट्रिय — international
14. अन्तिम मिति — deadline, expiry date
15. अभिलेख — archives, records
16. अर्थ — finance, economy
17. असम्भव — unlikely; impossible
18. अस्वीकार गर्नु — refuse, deny; disagree
19. अफिसर — officer; official
20. आन्तरिक — internal
21. आन्दोलन — campaign, movement
22. आपसमा मिल्नु — unite, join forces
23. आम्दानी — income
24. आयकर — income tax
25. आयात-कर — import duty
26. आयात गर्नु — import (to)
27. आवाज उठाउनु — raise a voice
28. उत्सव — ceremony, event,
29. उत्सव मनाउनु — to celebrate
30. उपदेशक/ सल्लाहकार — advisor, counselor
31. उपलक्ष्य — occasion (auspicious)
32. उपाय — way out, solution
33. उमेदवार — election candidate; candidate
34. ऐन — law, legal code
35. कर — tax, toll, duty
36. कर्मचारी — civil servant; employee
37. कागज-पत्र — papers, documents
38. कानुन — law
39. कानुनी — legal (opp. illegal)
40. काममा फसेको — busy, tied up with work
41. कार्यक्रम — plan, agenda, program
42. कार्यालय — office, workplace
43. कालो धन — black money, illicit funds
44. किनारा लगाउनु — decide, finalize
45. किरिया खानु — to take (eat) an oath, swear
46. केन्द्र — center, hub
47. खबर गर्नु — notify, give a message
48. खरदार — civil servant (under subba)
49. खर्च — expenditure, expenses
50. खाता — ledger, account book
51. खाता खोल्नु — open a bank account
52. गते — Nepali calendar date
53. गुट — political group, faction
54. गुन तिर्नु — repay a favor
55. गुन लगाउनु — do favor, oblige someone
56. गैरकानुनी — illegal
57. गोप्य — confidential, secret
58. गृह नीति — domestic policy
59. गृह मन्त्रालय — Home Ministry
60. गाउँ विकास समिति — Village Development Committee

61. गा.वि.स. (VDC)
62. घुस खानु take a bribe
63. घुस दिनु give a bribe
64. चुनाव election
65. चुनावमा उठ्नु run for office, stand for election
66. छलफल गर्नु discuss
67. छाप rubber stamp, impression
68. छाप लाउनु stamp (to)
69. जन सहभागिता people's participation
70. जनता populace, people
71. जरिमाना गर्नु fine, penalize
72. जागिर employment (official), job
73. जागिर खानु be get employed
74. जागिर खोस्नु dismiss, fire from a job
75. जानकारी information, acknowledgement
76. जिम्मेवारी responsibility, obligation
77. जिल्ला district
78. जिल्ला प्रमुख कार्यालय District Office HQ
79. जुलुस procession, march; mob
80. टिकट postage stamp
81. टिकट काट्नु buy/book a ticket
82. थाना police station
83. ठेकेदार contractor
84. ठेक्का contract
85. ठेगाना address, place of residence
86. डाक्नु summon, send for
87. तलब salary (monthly wage)
88. तारिख Western calendar date
89. तोक्नु decide, fix, determine
90. त्रैमासिक tri-monthly (quarterly)
91. दरखास्त application (written)
92. दरखास्त दिनु apply for
93. दर-रेट exchange rate; rate, price
94. दर्ता entry (in register)
95. दर्ता गर्नु register a document
96. दर्शन गर्नु audience with VIP, gods, etc.
97. दल political party; group, association
98. दान दिने, दाता donor
99. दुर्गम क्षेत्र remote area
100. दोष लगाउनु accuse, blame, charge
101. नगर town, city (in admin. context)
102. नतिजा result
103. नाइके head, chief, leader
104. नागरिकता citizenship
105. नाघ्नु disobey, step over
106. नामावली list of names (name list)
107. निकाल्नु expel, fire (from job), take out, push out
108. निगम company, corporation
109. निजामती civil (of service)
110. निम्ता गर्नु invite
111. निम्तो invitation
112. नियम principle, law, rule
113. नियमविरुद्ध illegally, against law
114. निर्णय गर्नु decide, resolve
115. निर्देशक director of institute
116. निर्वाचन election
117. निवेदन application, request, appeal
118. नीति policy, rule
119. पत्र letter, document
120. पत्रकार journalist
121. पत्रिका magazine, journal, newspaper
122. पद post, position
123. पदोन्नति गर्नु promote (post)
124. परराष्ट्र मन्त्रालय Foreign Ministry

125. परिचय गराउनु introduce
126. परिचय-पत्र identity card
127. परियोजना project (eg. literacy)
128. पि.ए./व्यक्तिगत सहायक Personal Assistant (PA)
129. पिउन peon (errand runner)
130. पुलिस police(man)
131. पेस्की लिनु take an advance (money)
132. पेसा occupation, profession
133. प्रगति progress, development
134. प्रजातन्त्र (people's) democracy
135. प्रतिनिधि representative, delegate
136. प्रतिवेदन report
137. प्रतिशत percentage; percent
138. प्रधान chief, main
139. प्रधानमन्त्री Prime Minister
140. प्रवक्ता spokesman
141. प्रमाणपत्र certificate
142. प्रमुख जिल्ला अधिकारी Chief District Officer
143. प्र.जि.अ. CDO
144. प्रशासन administration, rule
145. प्रहरी police(man)
146. फाँट department; detailed list
147. फैसला judgement, verdict (legal)
148. वक्ता speaker
149. बक्सनु present, give (royal honorific)
150. बचत गर्नु save, economize (time, money
151. बचत खाता खोल्नु open a bank account (saving A/c)
152. बजेट budget
153. बढुवा promotion (in one's work)
154. बधाई congratulations
155. बधाई दिनु congratulate
156. बन्दोबस्त मिलाउनु work out a plan, organize
157. बसाल्नु set up, establish
158. बहाल rent
159. बहिदार civil servant cleark; book-keeper
160. बहुदलीय multi-party
161. बासिन्दा citizen, national, resident
162. बिदा holiday, leave (time off)
163. बिन्ती application, request (humble)
164. बिल bill, fee; invoice
165. बुझ्नु sign for (letter, parcel)
166. बैठक session, meeting
167. ब्याज interest (financial) on principal
168. भत्ता allowance, bonus pay
169. भन्सार customs (office)
170. भन्सार लगाउनु levy customs duty
171. भाग लिनु participate, to take part
172. भाडा rent, (hire); fare
173. भाषण lecture, speech, talk
174. भेटघाट meeting
175. भेट्नु meet
176. भेला हुनु to meet in a group
177. भेला हुनु gather, assemble
178. भोट vote, ballot; Tibet
179. मन्जुर गर्नु approve, agree
180. मन्जुरी approval, consent
181. मन्जुरीनामा a letter of consent
182. मतदान casting of votes
183. मतभेद difference of opinion
184. मध्यस्थ arbitrator, mediator
185. मनाही/निषेध prohibited, forbidden
186. मन्त्रालय Ministry (of gov't)
187. महत्त्वपूर्ण व्यक्ति important person, VIP

188. महसुल bill, fee, duty
189. महाशाखा administrative department
190. महोदय Sir, honorable (senior officials)
191. मासिक monthly
192. मासिक शुल्क monthly fees
193. मुखिया civil servant (under khardar)
194. मुद्दा legal case
195. मेल agreement, understanding
196. मौका opportunity, chance
197. मौसुफ royal pronoun
198. यातायात transportation, traffic
199. योग्य qualified, able, (fit for)
200. योग्यता qualification(s), ability
201. योजना plan
202. रकम money, funds
203. रसिद receipt
204. राजकुमार prince
205. राजतन्त्र monarchy
206. राजदूत ambassador
207. राजदूतावास embassy
208. राजधानी capital city
209. राजनीति politics
210. राजनीतिज्ञ politician
211. राजनैतिक political
212. राष्ट्र (nation)
213. राष्ट्र बैङ्क National bank
214. राष्ट्रपति president (of country)
215. राष्ट्रवादी nationalist(ic)
216. राष्ट्रिय national
217. राष्ट्रिय ऋण national debt
218. राहदानी passport
219. रिट दिनु take legal action, file a writ
220. रेखदेख गर्नु supervise, take care of
221. लाइन लाग्नु form a line, line up
222. लाइसेन्स license
223. लोक सेवा आयोग Public Service Commission
224. लोकतन्त्र democracy, people's republic
225. वकिल attorney, lawyer, advocate
226. वादविवाद Debate
227. वार्षिक annual, yearly
228. वार्षिक वृध्दि annual increment
229. वासलात balance sheet
230. विकास progress; development
231. विज्ञापन notice, advertisement
232. विधान सभा legislative assembly
233. विभाग department
234. विमानसेवा air service
235. विरोध गर्नु oppose; resist
236. विरोधी opponent antagonist
237. विश्व world
238. विषय subject, topic
239. शासन गर्नु govern, rule; administer
240. शाही royal
241. शुभनाम good/auspicious name
242. शुल्क dues, fees
243. श्री ५ address to royal family
244. -संग लाग्नु associate (intr)
245. संविधान The Law, Constitution
246. संयुक्त united, joint
247. संयुक्त राष्ट्र United Nations
248. संस्कृति culture
249. संस्थान institute
250. सङ्गठन union, organization
251. सच्याउनु revise, amend, correct
252. सञ्चय कोष provident fund
253. सदस्य member
254. सन्देश news, information
255. सभा meeting, assembly, council

256. सभापति district president, chairman
257. समाजसेवी social worker
258. समाधान solution
259. समाधान गर्नु solve
260. समारोह celebration, social event
261. समिति committee
262. समुदाय community, social group
263. सम्झौता agreement, treaty
264. सम्भव possible
265. सम्मेलन चल्नु hold conference / convention
266. सरकार government
267. सरदार chief, headman
268. सरुवा हुनु transferred (to be)
269. सल्लाह advice, counsel
270. सहभागी participant, partaker
271. सहायता help, aid, assistance
272. सही signature
273. साझा cooperative, joint venture; common
274. सूचना पाटी notice board
275. सूचना information, communication
276. सूची list
277. सेवा service, help (of the needy)
278. सैनिक military, army
279. स्थानीय local, indigenous
280. स्थापित गर्नु establish, set up
281. स्वतन्त्र independent, free
282. स्वदेश native land, own country
283. स्वागत welcome
284. स्वास्थ्य मन्त्रालय Ministry of Health
285. हक right(s)
286. हडताल गर्नु strike (political)
287. हमला attack, charge
288. हल्ला rumor
289. हस्ताक्षर signature
290. हाकिम boss, director, manager
291. हाजिर हुनु attend (a meeting), be present
292. हिसाब account(s), accounting
293. हुलाक post office
294. हुलमुल crowd, mob
295. मन्त्री Minister
296. सचिव Secretary
297. विशेष सचिव Joint Secretary
298. उपसचिव Under Secretary
299. शाखा अधिकृत Section Officer
300. सुब्बा civil servant (under Section Officer)

RELIGIOUS VOCABULARY

1. अगुवाइ गर्नु lead, guide
2. अङ्गरक्षक body guard
3. अजम्मरी immortal, eternal (youth)
4. अर्थ खोल्नु interpret (lit. open meaning)
5. अधिकार authority, right
6. अधीनमा under (one's) control
7. अनन्त जीवन eternal life (unending)
8. अनमोल priceless
9. अनुग्रह grace
10. अन्धकार darkness
11. अन्तिममा at the last (end)
12. अपराध guilt(y); crime
13. अपार unlimited
14. अयोग्य unfit, unqualified unable
15. अलग गर्नु separate, set apart
16. अस्तित्व existence
17. अशुद्ध unclean (ritually) impure
18. अहङ्कार pride arrogance
19. आत्मा soul, spirit
20. आत्मालोक world of spirits (dead)
21. आत्मिक spiritual
22. आदर गर्नु honor, revere
23. आनन्द joy, peace
24. आराधना worship
25. अराउनु/अह्राउनु order, command (to)
26. आशा hope, expectation
27. आशा राख्नु hope (to)
28. आशिष दिनु bless (give blessing)
29. आशीर्वाद दिनु bless (give blessing)
30. आश्चर्य कर्म miracle
31. आज्ञा command(ment)
32. आज्ञाकारी obedient
33. इच्छा will, wish
34. इनाम reward, prize
35. इन्कार गर्नु deny
36. इमानदार faithful, sincere, honest
37. इष्टदेव family god
38. ईश्वर God
39. ईश्वरवक्ता prophet
40. उखान parable/proverb
41. उज्यालो clear, bright; light
42. उठाउनु lift up
43. उदाहरण example
44. उद्धार salvation, redemption/ rescue
45. उद्धार गर्नु redeem (free); to rescue
46. उपवास बस्नु fast (from food)
47. उपहार gift, present
48. उपासना worship (mental)
49. एकता unity, harmony
50. कर्तव्य duty
51. करार covenant/agreement
52. कसम/किरिया खानु swear an oath
53. कृपा kindness, grace
54. क्रोध anger, wrath
55. खडा गर्नु erect, set upright; establish
56. खराब guilty (spoiled)
57. खिसी गर्नु scorn, mock
58. खेदो persecution
59. गाउनु sing
60. गीत song
61. ग्रहण गर्नु accept and receive
62. घुँडा टेक्नु kneel down (surrender)

63. घोप्टो पर्नु prostrate, lie prone
64. घोषणा गर्नु announce
65. चढाउनु to offer (eg. sacrifice)
66. चरण feet, step
67. चिन्ता worry
68. चुन्नु pick, choose, elect
69. चेला disciple
70. छान्नु choose, select
71. छुटकारा freedom, release
72. छोड्नु leave, forsake
73. जग foundation
74. जनहरू people
75. जन्म birth
76. जम्मा गर्नु gather, bring together; to total
77. जम्मा हुनु get together
78. जय victory
79. जयजयकार गर्नु praise
80. जाती पार्नु make fine, healthy, heal
81. जिउँदो alive
82. जीवन life
83. जीवित alive
84. जुनी one life in a circle of lives
85. जोगी ascetic, hermit
86. ज्योति light, brilliance
87. झुठो बोल्नु lie (fib)
88. टिक्नु last, endure
89. ठहरिनु be proven (legal term)
90. ठान्नु think, assume
91. डाक्नु call, summon, invite
92. डोऱ्याउनु lead (along)
93. तीर्थस्थल shrine, pilgrimage site
94. तोड्नु break (law/rules)
95. त्यागनु forsake, give up, abandon
96. थुन्नु imprison, trap
97. दण्ड penalty, fine
98. दण्ड दिनु to punish
99. दण्डवत् गर्नु bow down (to), worship
100. दया mercy, kindness
101. दयालु kind, merciful
102. दर्शन vision
103. दर्शन गर्नु visit (superior)
104. दर्शन दिनु (pay) give audience
105. दुःख भोग्नु undergo pain, sorrow
106. दुःख भोग्नु suffer, bear pain
107. देखा पर्नु appear
108. देवता god (cf. "deo")
109. देवता deity
110. देवी goddess
111. दोष लगाउनु blame, lay guilt, accuse
112. दोषी guilty
113. धर्म religion
114. धर्मकर्म religious deed
115. धर्मग्रन्थ religious book
116. धर्मशास्त्र Scripture
117. धर्मात्मा religious person, pious
118. धर्मावलम्बी follower of X religion
119. धार्मिक religious
120. धार्मिकता righteousness
121. धर्मी righteous
122. धर्मी ठहरिनु justify (lit. prove righteous)
123. ध्यान गर्नु meditate
124. ध्यान meditation
125. ध्यान दिनु pay attention
126. नजरमा in the sight/gaze of
127. नमुना example, pattern, sample
128. नम्र humble
129. नरक hell
130. नाउँ लिनु use the name of, invoke
131. नाश हुनु be ruined, destroyed
132. निको पार्नु heal (make well)

133. निर्धारित determined, fixed
134. नियम rule, law, principle
135. निरन्तर (always) continuous
136. निराश disappointed
137. निसाफ गर्नु judge
138. न्याय गर्नु judge (v)
139. पछुताउनु repent
140. -लाई पछ्याउनु follow
141. -को पछि लाग्नु follow
142. पत्ता लगाउनु discover, find out
143. पत्याउनु believe
144. परमेश्वर God (lit. Supreme God)
145. परम्परा अनुसार according to tradition
146. परीक्षा गर्नु test (tempt)
147. पवित्र holy
148. पवित्रता purity, holiness
149. पश्चात्ताप गर्नु repent
150. पाप sin
151. पापमोचन forgiveness of sin
152. पाप स्वीकार गर्नु confess (sin)
153. पापी sinful; sinner
154. पालन गर्नु observe, follow (rules)
155. पीठ shrine (of goddess)
156. पीर मान्नु worry, be anguished
157. पुकार्नु call (a name), invocate
158. पुर्खा ancestor
159. पुनर्जन्म rebirth, reincarnation
160. पूज्नु to worship
161. पूजाहारी priest
162. पूरा हुनु become complete, be fulfilled
163. पृथ्वी The Earth
164. प्यारो dear, beloved
165. प्रकट हुनु be manifest, clear, revealed
166. प्रतिज्ञा गर्नु promise
167. प्रतिष्ठा consecration (temple, idol)
168. प्रभु Lord
169. प्रवेश गर्नु enter, make entry (formal)
170. प्रशंसा गर्नु praise
171. प्रस्ट, स्पष्ट clear, plain, evident
172. प्राण life (opp. death)
173. प्रायश्चित्त atonement
174. प्रायश्चित गर्नु atone
175. प्रार्थना गर्नु pray
176. प्रेत ghost
177. प्रेम गर्नु to love
178. फल result (lit. fruit)
179. फल्नु bear fruit
180. फसाउनु mislead, entangle, entrap
181. फेर्नु change, alter
182. फैलिनु be spread out, scattered
183. बचन statement; Word, promise
184. बचाउनु defend, protect, save
185. बन्धन bondage, restriction
186. बलिदान sacrifice
187. बहाना बनाउनु make pretence, pretend
188. बाँच्नु escape, survive
189. बाटो way (lit. road)
190. बिधवा widow
191. बिन्ती request, petition
192. बुद्धि wisdom
193. बौरी उठ्नु rise from the dead
194. ब्रत लिनु fast (from food)
195. भक्ति devotion, piety
196. भजन hymn, song of praise
197. भर्नु fill
198. भरपुर हुनु be filled (with)
199. भलाइ गर्नु do welfare
200. भवसागर Ocean of Existence
201. भूत demon

202. भूत लागेको possessed (by demon)
203. भूतआत्मा spirit, demon
204. भूल मान्नु admit error/mistake
205. भेटी offering (to gods/priest)
206. भेद बुझ्नु know mysteries, secrets
207. मर्त्यलोक place-of-death
208. मन heart
209. मनदेखि from the heart
210. मन्दिर temple
211. महान् great
212. महिमा glory
213. महिमित glorified
214. माने meaning
215. माफ माग्नु ask for forgiveness
216. माया गर्नु to love
217. मारिनु/मार्नु be killed/kill
218. मिलाप harmony, reconciliation
219. मित्र friend
220. मुक्ति salvation, freedom
221. मुख्य पूजाहारी chief priest
222. मूर्ति idol
223. मूर्तिपूजा idol worship
224. मृत्यु death
225. मेट्नु delete, cancel; wipe off, erase
226. यातना torment (noun)
227. योग्य worthy, able, qualified, fit
228. रगत blood
229. रमाउनु rejoice
230. रहस्य mystery
231. रक्षक protector
232. रक्षा गर्नु protect
233. राज गर्नु rule, govern; dwell (formal)
234. राजी हुनु be willing
235. राज्य kingdom
236. रूप form, shape
237. लास corpse
238. लिन आउनु come to take
239. वंश dynasty, lineage
240. विश्व The World
241. विश्वास faith
242. विश्वास गर्नु believe, trust, have faith
243. विश्वासयोग्य faithful (worthy of faith)
244. विश्वासीहरू believers
245. विश्वस्तता faithfulness
246. व्यर्थमा in vain
247. शान, गौरव glory
248. शक्ति power, might, energy
249. शक्तिसाथ with power, might
250. शक्तिशाली काम miracle (powerful deed)
251. शपथ covenant, oath
252. शरण shelter, protection, asylum
253. शरणार्थी asylum seeker, refugee
254. शरीर body
255. शत्रु enemy
256. शान्ति peace
257. शासन गर्नु rule (to)
258. शिक्षक teacher
259. शुद्ध clean, undefiled, pure
260. श्राप curse
261. सङ्कट trouble
262. सङ्गति fellowship, meeting
263. सञ्चालन गर्नु conduct, run (business)
264. सजाय दिनु give punishment
265. सताउनु persecute, torment
266. सत्य truth
267. सत्यता truth(fulness)
268. सदासर्वदा ever always
269. सधैँको लागि forever, always
270. सन्तान children, offspring, family
271. सन्तुष्ट हुनु to be satisfied, content

272. सन्तुष्टि satisfaction
273. सपना dream
274. सबैतिर everywhere (towards everywhere)
275. समझ mind (understanding)
276. सम्झाउनु remind; admonish
277. संयम self-control
278. सर्वज्ञानी omniscient, all knowing
279. सर्वव्यापी omnipresent, all pervasive
280. सर्वशक्तिमान् omnipotent, almighty
281. सर्वोच्च highest
282. सहनु bear, suffer, endure
283. साँच्चै truly
284. सामु in front of, before
285. सावधान caution
286. सावधानी precaution
287. सांसारिक worldly
288. सिंहासन throne (lit. lion seat)
289. सुख happiness
290. सुनाउनु tell (to)
291. सेवा गर्नु serve
292. सोच्नु think, ponder
293. स्थायी permanent
294. स्तुति गर्नु praise
295. सृष्टि गर्नु to create
296. सृष्टिकर्ता creator
297. स्वर्ग heaven, paradise
298. स्वर्गीय divine, heavenly; late
299. स्वतन्त्रता freedom
300. स्वीकार्नु accept, approve
301. स्वर voice
302. हराउनु be lost, lose; defeat
303. हृदय heart
304. क्षमा गर्नु/दिनु forgive

CONSTRUCTION VOCABULARY

1.	अङ्कुसी	hook
2.	अन्तराप	slide bolt (hasp)
3.	अर्धचन्द्र	crescent (lit. half moon)
4.	अधिकतम	maximum
5.	आलमुनियम	aluminium
6.	आइबिम	I-beam
7.	आगो निभाउने यन्त्र	fire extinguisher
8.	आवश्यकता अनुसार	according to the need
9.	आधा गोलो रेती	half round file
10.	इस्पात	steel
11.	ईंट्टा/ईंटा/ईंट	brick
12.	उचाइ	height
13.	उब्जाउनु	to grow
14.	उत्पादन गर्नु	to produce
15.	उपकरण	equipment
16.	उपयोग गर्नु	to use, to make use of, utilise
17.	एङ्गल	angle
18.	ओसार्नु	to carry from one place to another
19.	औजार सूची	equipment list
20.	औजार	tools
21.	कस्नु	to tie (up), fasten
22.	कर्मी	workers
23.	कब्जा	hinge
24.	कराही	pan (iron, big)
25.	कार्यशाला	workshop (formal)
26.	करौंती	saw
27.	आरी	saw
28.	कम खर्चिलो	less expensive, economical
29.	कस्नु	to fasten, tighten (drive a screw, bolt, nut, rope, etc.)
30.	क्लाम्प	vice, g-clamp, c-clamp
31.	काट्नु	to cut
32.	काठ	wood, timber
33.	काठको किला	wooden, peg
34.	कामी	blacksmith
35.	काममा लाउनु	to put to work, appoint
36.	काममा लाउनु (भर्ना गर्नु)	to hire
37.	कारखाना	workshop (factory)
38.	कालो चस्मा	goggles (lit. black glasses)
39.	काँस	bronze
40.	किफाएती	cheap, economical
41.	किलिप	wire clip
42.	किला, काँटी	nails
43.	कुल्ली	labourer, porter
44.	कुल्ली, ज्यामी	labourer, porter
45.	कुटो	small spade
46.	कुलो, नाली	water channel, ditch
47.	कैंची	truss
48.	कोइला	coal
59.	कोदालो	spade, hoe
50.	खरको छाना	grass (thatched) roof
51.	खन्नु	to dig
52.	खम्बा	a pole, pillar
53.	खर्च गर्नु	to spend
54.	खराज	lathe

55. खस्नु fall (from above)
56. खानी mine
57. खुर्पा, बेल्चा trowels
58. खागसी sand paper, abrasive paper
59. गल crowbar, jumping bar
60. गन स्टोभ blow torch
61. गाडा wheel barrow, pushing cart
62. गारो wall (of a building)
63. गिँड्नु to cross cut
64. गोरुगाडा ox cart
65. ग्यास gas
66. ग्यास पाइप gas pipe
67. ग्यास वेल्डिङ गर्नु to weld with gas welding
68. ग्रिल grill
69. ग्राइन्डर लाउनु to grind, to use a grinder
70. गहिरो deep
71. गुना काट्नु to thread (eg. pipe)
72. गेज नाप्नु to measure guage
73. गैंची (गैंती), पिक pickaxe
74. गोलाइ diameter
75. गोलो रेती round file
76. गोलो पिँध round bottom
77. घन hammer (big, heavy)
78. घन (हथौडा) hammer
79. घिर्नी pulley, puller
80. घोट्नु to polish, rub
81. चक्का wheel
82. चालचलन behaviour
83. चारकुने पाइप square pipe
84. चारकुने रेती square file
85. चाँदी silver
86. चिर्नु, गिँड्नु to cut in half, split, or rip a board
87. चिर्नु to split, saw, cleave
88. चिनो लाउनु to mark (out)
89. चुकुल, तिखो किलो stake, wedge, spike
90. चून lime
91. चुहिनु to leak (out)
92. चेप्ट्याउने flattener
93. चौडाइ bredth, width
94. च्याप्नु to hold fast
95. च्याप्टो flat
96. च्याप्टो रेती flat file
97. च्याप्न हुने पेन्चिस vice grip pliers
98. छड / डन्डी steel rod
99. छपनी छाप्ने ढुङ्गा flagstone
100. छड्के काट्नु to cut slanted, at an angle
101. छाउने ढुङ्गा roof slate, stone shingle
102. छाना roof
103. छाला leather (also, skin)
104. छालाको पन्जा leather gloves
105. छाप्रो hut
106. छेस्किनी tower bolt
107. छिनाले काट्नु to cut with a chisel
108. छिनो / छिना chisel
109. छोप्नु to cover
110. जग-हाल्नु to lay foundation
111. जलविद्युत hydro-electricity
112. जनशक्ति manpower
113. जडान connection
114. जडान गर्नु to fix
115. जाली screen, net, filter
116. जाँच / परीक्षा examination, test
117. जोड्नु to join, connect, fix, attach
118. जोगाउनु / बचाउनु to protect/save, preserv
119. ज्याला wages (daily)
120. ज्यावलहरू tools, instruments
121. ज्याबल र औजार tools and equipment

122. ज्यावल घोट्ने ढुङ्गा — sharpening stone, whetstone
123. झिक्नु — to remove, take out (opp. घुसार्नु to insert)
124. झोलुङ्गेपुल — suspension bridge
125. झ्यालको खापा — window casement, window pane
126. टायल — tile
127. ट्याङ्की — tank
128. ठेक्काको काम — piece work, contract work
129. ठेक्कामा काम गर्नु — to work on contract
130. ठेक्कादार, ठेकेदार — supplier, contractor
131. ठेक्का — contract
132. ठोक्नु — to hit, hammer, drive (nail)
133. डकर्मी — mason
134. डाइले काट्नु — to cut with a die
135. ड्रिल गर्नु — to drill
136. ड्रिलमा धार लाउने गेज — drill sharpening guage
137. डोरी — rope string, thread
138. ढल — watershed
139. ढलान गर्नु — to lay concerete, cast with concrete
140. ढिङ्ग्री (नट) कस्नु — to tighten, fasten a nut
141. ढुवानी — shipment, transportation
142. ढोका — door
143. ढोकाको चौकोस — door frame
144. ढोकाको खापा — door casement
145. तलतिर बङ्ग्याउनु — to bend down
146. तताएर टेम्पर राख्नु — temper by heat
147. तयार — ready, prepared
148. तमोट ताम्राकार — coppersmith
149. तालिम — training
150. तार — wire
151. तामा — copper
152. तारबुरुस — wire brush
153. ताँवा — copper
154. तीनकुने पाइप — tringular pipe
155. तीनकुने रेती — triangular file
156. तिखो पार्नु — to sharpen (tip)
157. थोप्ले चिनो लाउनु — to punch, center punch
158. थोप्ले छिना — hole-punch
159. दराज — cupboard
160. दायाँतिर बङ्ग्याउनु — to bend right
161. दुरुपयोग गर्नु — to misuse
162. दुईधारे रेती — double edged file
163. दोब्र्याउनु — to fold, double over
164. दैनिक ज्याला — daily wages
165. धलौटे फलाम, किट — cast iron
166. धार लाउनु — to sharpen (blade)
167. धाराको सामानहरू — plumbing fixtures, supplies
168. धारा, धारो — tap
169. धातु — metal
170. धुवाँ नआउने चुलो — smokeless oven
171. नट — nut
172. नट खोल्नु — to unscrew (open) nut
173. नक्सा, चित्र — pattern, map, picture, blueprint
174. न्यूनतम — minimum
175. नाइके — headman, foreman

176. नाप measurement
177. नाला a drain-pipe
178. नाप्नु to measure
179. बाङ्गो crooked
180. निकास outlet, wall socket
181. निकाल्नु to take out (opp. घुसार्नु to insert)
182. निचोर्नु squeeze, wring out (eg. sponge)
183. निर्माण construction
184. निर्माण सामग्रीहरू hardware supplies
185. पर्खाल boundary wall
186. परीक्षाफल result
187. पग्लनु to melt
188. परियोजना project
189. पातलो ढुङ्गा slab stone
190. पानी थाप्नु to fill water container (hold a pot for filling water)
191. प्लग plug
192. प्लाइवुड plywood
193. प्वाल पार्नु to make a hole
194. पाइप pipe
195. पाता sheet (eg. tin)
196. पाइपको मिस्त्री plumber
197. पाले watchman
198. पित्तल brass
199. पिटेर/ठोकेर बनाउनु to forge
200. पिट्नु to beat, flatten
201. पुर्जा parts, accessories
202. पुर्नु to fill up, cover with soil
203. पूर्णाङ्क full mark, score (eg. exam)
204. पेच किला screw
205. पेन्चीसले समात्नु to hold with pliers
206. फल्याक (तखता) a board, plank, shelf
207. फलाम iron
208. (फलामे) डन्डी (steel) rod
209. फलाम काट्ने करौँती/हेक्सा hacksaw
210. फलाँसी wood chisel, mortise chisel
211. फर्लासी, रामो chisel (wood)
212. फाइल गर्नु to file
213. फुट्नु to be broken (glass, tube, ball, mirror, pipe)
214. फुटाउनु to break
215. फेर्नु, बदल्नु replace, change
216. बल्ब होल्डर bulb holder, socket
217. बङ्ग्याउनु to bend
218. बनाउनु to make
219. बटाम गर्नु to make right angled (90°)
220. बटाम square (90°), t-square
221. बटाम protractor
222. बर्मा drill saw, hand drill (manual)
223. बाउसी bousee
224. बाग vice, clamp vice, clamp
225. बचाउनु to protect, save
226. बन्चरो axe, hatchet
227. व्यवस्था मिलाउनु to arrange, manage
228. बालुवा sand, fine aggregate
229. बाल्टिन bucket
230. बार लाउनु to make a fence
231. बाँडा/सुनार goldsmith
232. बाँस bamboo
233. बिजुली electricity
234. बिंड handle
235. बिजुलीको मिस्त्रे electrician

236. बेल्चा, सावेल shovel
237. बोक्नु to carry
238. बोल्ट bolt
239. बोल्ट कस्नु to tighten a bolt
240. बोरा sack, big bag
241. भर्ना गर्नु to hire, enrol, admit
242. भरपर्दो reliable
243. भरिया porter
244. भत्कनु to be destroyed, broken, to be demolished
245. भारी load: heavy
246. भित्ता, गारो wall (of a room)
247. भुइँ floor
248. भूकम्प, भुइँचालो earthquake
249. मर्मत गर्नु to repair
250. मार्तोल/पेचकस screwdriver
251. मिलाउनु to make fit
252. मिसिनु to join; to be mixed (in)
253. मुङ्ग्रो wooden mallet
254. मुहान, स्रोत source
255. मूढा log
256. मेसिन, यन्त्र machine
257. मोटाइ thickness
258. योजना planning, plan
259. रसाउनु to leak, seep
260. रन्दा wooden plane
261. राख्नु to put, place, (set on)
262. रिपिट गर्नु to rivet
263. रेत मार्नु to file
264. रेत/रेती file
265. रेन्चु/रेन्च spanner, crescent wrench
266. रोडा (गिट्टी) gravel, coarse aggregate
267. लट्ठी thin stick, staff, cane
268. लम्बाइ length
269. लब्धाङ्क पत्र mark sheet, exam booklet
270. वितरण गर्नु to distribute
271. विकास development
272. वेल्डिङ तार welding electrode
273. वेल्डिङ गर्नु to weld
274. सम्भार maintenance
275. सहयोग help, assistance, aid, cooperation
276. सफा गर्नु to clean
277. सकेट socket
278. सम्याउनु to plain, to level
279. संरक्षण गर्नु to protect, preserve
280. स्थापना establishment
281. स्याहार maintenance, mending
282. साङ्लो/सिक्री chain
283. सामग्री materials
284. सामान things, stuff, equipment, supplies
285. सामूहिक रुपमा in co-ordination (collectively)
286. स्विच switch
287. सिकर्मी carpenter
288. सिँचाइको साधन means of irrigation
289. सिमेन्ट cement
290. सिलिङ्ग (पटाइ) ceiling
291. सिलाबर aluminium
292. सिधा काट्नु to cut straight
293. सिलिन्डर काट्नु to cut a cylinder, bore
294. सिलिन्डर खन्नु to dig a cylinder, hole
295. स्टील steel
296. सुरको ढुङ्गा corner stone

297. सुन — gold
298. सुलिस पाता — flat steel rod, strip steel
299. सुरुङ — tunnel
300. सुविधा — facility, convenience
301. सुविधायुक्त — with full facility, comfortable
302. सेन्टर पन्च — center punch
303. सोली — oil funnel, funnel
304. सोझ्याउनु — to straighten, make straight
305. सोझो — straight
306. श्रमदान — voluntary work
307. हथौडा — hammer (small, light)
308. हाते औजार — hand equipment, hand tools
309. हिलो, गिलो माटो — mud
310. हिफाजत गर्नु — to protect, take care of
311. हेक्सा — hacksaw
312. हेमर — hammer (medium)

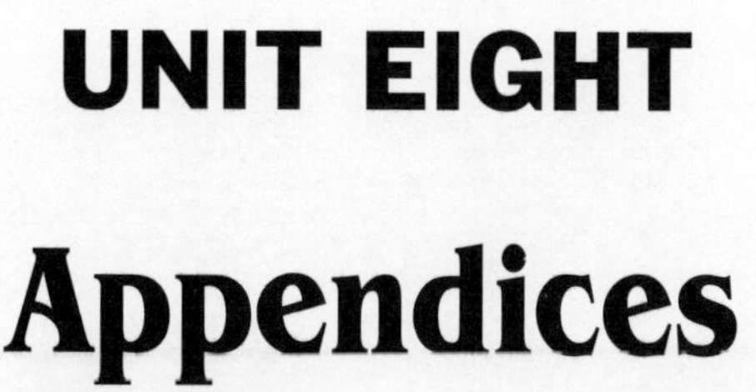

UNIT EIGHT

Appendices

1. Chapter Checklist
2. Nepali Numbers
3. Verb Building Blocks
4. Primary Conjugations of खानु
5. Primary Conjugations of हुनु
6. Primary Blood Relations
7. Complex Verbs by Semantic Category
8. Complex Verbs Alphabetically
9. Key to Practice Exercises
10. English Translation of Texts
11. Nepali – English Glossary
12. English – Nepali Glossary

APPENDIX 1

CHAPTER CHECKLIST

Each step must be fully completed before moving on to the next chapter.

Name:______________________ **Chapter:**_____

☑ Step One: Preparation
hours required:___ days required:___

- ❒ Tape: listened to and mimicked the vocabulary and useful phrases
- ❒ Memorized all vocabulary and useful phrases
- ❒ Read grammar section carefully and thoroughly
- ❒ Tape: listened to the text at least twice

☑ Step Two: With Your Teacher
hours required:___ days required:___

- ❒ Mimicked and drilled vocabulary, with attention to pronunciation
- ❒ Covered grammar for clarification
- ❒ Read and worked through the text
- ❒ Answered and asked comprehension questions on the text
- ❒ Completed the *Practice* section **orally** (before writing out answers).
- ❒ Wrote out answers to the *Practice* section (outside of class).
- ❒ Fully completed *Let's Talk* section
- ❒ Optional: went over *In the Community* with the tutor for hints.
- ❒ Mimicked the vocabulary of the upcoming chapter

☑ Step Three: In the Community
hours required:___ days required:___

- ❒ Fully completed *In the Community*, spending at least 3 hrs. in conversation.

1. New or reinforced cultural observations:

2. Noteworthy experiences:

3. Something that worked really well:

4. Something that didn't work at all:

5. Overall progress:

APPENDIX 2

NEPALI NUMERALS

०	शून्य	३१	एकतीस
१	एक	३२	बत्तीस
२	दुई	३३	तेत्तीस
३	तीन	३४	चौंतीस
४	चार	३५	पैंतीस
५	पाँच	३६	छत्तीस
६	छ	३७	सैंतीस
७	सात	३८	अठ्तीस
८	आठ	३९	उनन्चालीस
९	नौ	४०	चालीस
१०	दश		
११	एघार	४१	एकचालीस
१२	बाह्र	४२	बयालीस
१३	तेह्र	४३	त्रियालीस
१४	चौध	४४	चवालीस
१५	पन्ध्र	४५	पैंतालीस
१६	सोह्र	४६	छयालीस
१७	सत्र	४७	सतचालीस
१८	अठार	४८	अठ्चालीस
१९	उन्नाईस	४९	उनन्चास
२०	बीस	५०	पचास
२१	एक्काईस	५१	एकाउन्न
२२	बाईस	५२	बाउन्न
२३	तेईस	५३	त्रिपन्न
२४	चौबीस	५४	चवन्न
२५	पच्चीस	५५	पच्पन्न
२६	छब्बीस	५६	छपन्न
२७	सत्ताईस	५७	सन्ताउन्न
२८	अठ्ठाईस	५८	अन्ठाउन्न
२९	उनन्तीस	५९	उनन्साठी
३०	तीस	६०	साठी

६१	एकसठी	९१	एकानब्बे
६२	बयसठी	९२	बयानब्बे
६३	त्रिसठी	९३	त्रियानब्बे
६४	चौंसठी	९४	चौरानब्बे
६५	पैंसठी	९५	पन्चानब्बे
६६	छयसठी	९६	छयानब्बे
६७	सतसठी	९७	सन्तानब्बे
६८	अठसठी	९८	अन्ठानब्बे
६९	उनान्सत्तरी	९९	उनान्सय
७०	सत्तरी	१००	(एक) सय
७१	एकहत्तर	१०१	एक सय एक
७२	बहत्तर	२००	दुई सय
७३	त्रिहत्तर	१०००	(एक) हजार
७४	चौहत्तर	२०००	दुई हजार
७५	पचहत्तर	१०,०००	दस हजार
७६	छयहत्तर	१,००,०००	(एक) लाख
७७	सतहत्तर	१०,००,०००	दस लाख
७८	अठहत्तर	१,००,००,०००	एक करोड
७९	उनासी		
८०	असी		
८१	एकासी		
८२	बयासी		
८३	त्रियासी		
८४	चौरासी		
८५	पचासी		
८६	छयासी		
८७	सतासी		
८८	अठासी		
८९	उनानब्बे		
९०	नब्बे		

Ordinal Numbers (see 21.3)

पहिलो	First	आठौं	Eighth	सत्तरीयौं	Seventieth
दोस्रो	Second	नवौं	Ninth	असीयौं	Eightieth
तेस्रो	Third	दसौं	Tenth	नब्बेऔं	Ninetieth
चौथो	Fourth	बीसौं	Twentieth	सयौं	Hundredth
पाँचौं	Fifth	चालीसौं	Fortieth		
छैटौं	Sixth	पचासौं	Fiftieth		
सातौं	Seventh	साठीयौं	Sixtieth		

For Cards and Dice

एक्का	one / Ace
दुवा	two
तीर्की	three
चौका	four
पन्जा	five
छक्का	six
सत्ता	seven
अठ्ठा	eight
नहर	nine
दहर	ten
गुलाम	Jack
बजीर	Queen
बास्सा	King

X times

दोब्बर	x 2
तेब्बर	x 3
चौबर	x 4
पाँच गुना	x 5
छ गुना	x 6

Playing Cards

पान	heart
इंट	Diamond
चीर	Club
सुरथ	Spade

APPENDIX 3

VERB BUILDING BLOCKS
(conjugations for first person)

I ate.	**खा	एँ			sim past (5.3)
I used to eat.	खान्	थेँ			past hab (12.2)
I eat/will eat	खान्	छु			sim indef (2.3)
		-ing			
I was eating.	खाँ	दै	थिएँ		past cont (19.2)
I am eating.	खाँ	दै	छु		pres cont (6.4)
		keep on			
I kept on eating.	**खा	इरह	एँ		past freq (8.4)
I used to keep on eating.	खा	इरहन्	थेँ		past hab freq (14.2)
I (will) keep on eating.	खा	इरहन्	छु		pres freq (8.4)
			had/ have		
I was eating (had been keeping on).	खा	इरह	एको	थिएँ	past cont (19.2)
I am eating (have been keeping on).	खा	इरह	एको	छु	pres cont (8.4)
I had eaten.	**खा		एको	थिएँ	past per (19.1)
I have eaten.	**खा		एको	छु	pres per (9.5)
		definite			
I will definitely eat.	खा	ने	छु		def fut (13.5)
I will probably eat.	*खा	उँला			indef fut (9.3)
Shall I eat? Let me eat.	खा				injuct (4.6)
Let's eat.	खा	औँ			injuct (4.6)

* -ले optional for subject of transitive verbs

** -ले required for subject of transitive verbs

APPENDIX 4

PRIMARY CONJUGATIONS OF खानु

	म	तपाईं, ऊहाँ(हरू)	हामी	तिमी(हरू)	उनी(हरू)	
Sim Past (5.3) ****I ate.***	खाएँ खाइनँ	खानुभयो खानुभएन	खायौं खाएनौं	खायौ खाएनौ	खाए खाएनन्	खायो खाएन
Past Perf (19. 3) ****I had eaten.***	खाएको थिएँ खाएको थिइनँ	खानुभएको थियो खानुभएको थिएन	खाएका थियौं खाएका थिएनौं	खाएका थियौ खाएका थिएनौ	खाएका थिए खाएका थिएनन्	खाएको थियो खाएको थिएन
Past Hab (12.2) ***I used to eat.***	खान्थें खाँदिनथें	खानुहुन्थ्यो खानुहुन्नथ्यो	खान्थ्यौं खाँदैनथ्यौं	खान्थ्यौ खाँदैनथ्यौ	खान्थे खाँदैनथे	खान्थ्यो खाँदैनथ्यो
Past Cont (19. 4) ***I was eating.***	खाँदै थिएँ -	खाँदै हुनुहुन्थ्यो -	खाँदै थियौं -	खाँदै थियौ -	खाँदै थिए -	खाँदै थियो -
Past Cont (19. 4) ***I was eating.***	खाइरहेको थिएँ खाइरहेको थिइनँ	खाइरहनुभएको थियो खाइरहनुभएको थिएन	खाइरहेका थियौं खाइरहेका थिएनौं	खाइरहेका थियौ खाइरहेका थिएनौ	खाइरहेका थिए खाइरहेका थिएनन्	खाइरहेको थियो खाइरहेको थिएन
Past Freq (13.10) ****I kept on e-ing.***	खाइरहें खाइरहिनँ	खाइरहनुभयो खाइरहनुभएन	खाइरहचौं खाइरहेनौं	खाइरहचौ खाइरहेनौ	खाइरहे खाइरहेनन्	खाइरहचो खाइरहेन
Past Hab Freq (14.3) ***I used to keep on eating.***	खाइरहन्थें खाइरहँदिनथें	खाइरहनुहुन्थ्यो खाइरहनुहुन्नथ्यो	खाइरहन्थ्यौं खाइरहँदैनथ्यौं	खाइरहन्थ्यौ खाइरहँदैनथ्यौ	खाइरहन्थे खाइरहँदैनथे	खाइरहन्थ्यो खाइरहँदैनथ्यो
Sim Indef (2.3, 3.8) ***I eat/will eat.***	खान्छु खाँदिनँ / खान्नँ	खानुहुन्छ खानुहुन्न /	खान्छौं खाँदैनौं / खान्नौं	खान्छौ खाँदैनौ / खान्नौ	खान्छन् खाँदैनन् / खान्नन्	खान्छ खाँदैन

Pres Per (9.5) ****I have eaten.***	खाएको छु खाएको छैन	खानुभएको छ खानुभएको छैन	खाएका छौं खाएका छैनौं	खाएका छौ खाएका छैनौ	खाएका छन् खाएका छैनन्	खाएको छ खाएको छैन
Pres Cont (6.5) ***I am eating.***	खाँदै छु -	खानुहुँदै छ / खाँदै हुनुहुन्छ -	खाँदै छौं -	खाँदै छौ -	खाँदै छन् -	खाँदै छ -
Pres Cont (8.4) ***I am eating.***	खाइरहेको छु खाइरहेको छैन	खाइरहनुभएको छ खाइरहनुभएको छैन	खाइरहेका छौं खाइरहेका छैनौं	खाइरहेका छौ खाइरहेका छैनौ	खाइरहेका छन् खाइरहेका छैनन्	खाइरहेको छ खाइरहेको छैन
Pres Freq (13.10, 12) ***I will k***	खाइरहन्छु खाइरहन्नँ	खाइरहनुहुन्छ खाइरहनुहुन्न	खाइरहन्छौं खाइरहँदैनौं	खाइरहन्छौ खाइरहँदैनौ	खाइरहन्छन् खाइरहँदैनन्	खाइरहन्छ खाइरहँदैन
Def Fut (13.7) ***I'll definitely eat.***	खानेछु खानेछैन	खानुहुनेछ खानुहुनेछैन	खानेछौं खानेछैनौं	खानेछौ खानेछैनौ	खानेछन् खानेछैनन्	खानेछ खानेछैन
ndef Fut (9.4) ****I'll probably eat.***	खाउँला नखाउँला	खानुहोला नखानुहोला	खाऔंला नखाऔंला	खाऔला नखाऔला	खालान् नखालान्	खाला नखाला
Imper (3.10, 9.1) ***(Do) eat.***	- -	खानुस् नखानुस्	- -	खाऊ नखाऊ	- -	- -
Injunct (4.6) ***Shall I eat?*** ***Let's eat.***	खाऊँ नखाऊँ	- -	खाऔं नखाऔं	खाए नखाए	खाऊन् नखाऊन्	खाओस् नखाओस्

*** -ले** optional for subjects of transitive verbs
**** -ले** required for subjects of transitive verbs

APPENDIX 5

PRIMARY CONJUGATIONS OF हुनु

	म	तपाई», उहाँ(हरू)	हामी	तिमी(हरू)	उनी(हरू)	
Sim Past (5.3) ***I was.***	थिएँ थिइनँ	हुनुहुन्थ्यो हुनुहुन्नथ्यो	थियौं थिएनौं	थियौ थिएनौ	थिए थिएनन्	थियो थिएन
Sim Past (5.3) ***I became.***	भएँ भइनँ	हुनुभयो हुनुभएन	भयौं भएनौं	भयौ भएनौ	भए भएनन्	भयो भएन
Past Perf (19. 3) ***I had been.***	भएको थिएँ भएको थिइनँ	हुनुभएको थियो हुनुभएको थिएन	भएका थियौं भएका थिएनौं	भएका थियौ भएका थिएनौ	भएका थिए भएका थिएनन्	भएको थियो भएको थिएन
Past Hab (12.2) ***I used to be.***	हुन्थें हुँदिनथें	हुनुहुन्थ्यो हुनुहुन्नथ्यो	हुन्थ्यौं हुन्नथ्यौं	हुन्थ्यौ हुँदैनथ्यौ	हुन्थे हुँदैनथे	हुन्थ्यो हुँदैनथ्यो
Past Cont (19. 4) ***I was being.***	हुँदै थिएँ हुँदै थिइनँ	हुनुहुँदै थियो हुनुहुँदै थिएन	हुँदै थियौं हुँदै थिएनौं	हुँदै थियौ हुँदै थिएनौ	हुँदै थिए हुँदै थिएनन्	हुँदै थियो हुँदै थिएन
Past Cont (19. 4) ***I was being.***	भइरहेको थिएँ भइरहेको थिइनँ	भइरहनुभएको थियो भइरहनुभएको थिएन	भइरहेका थियौं भइरहेका थिएनौं	भइरहेका थियौ भइरहेका थिएनौ	भइरहेका थिए भइरहेका थिएनन्	भइरहेको थियो भइरहेको थिएन
Past Freq (13.10) ***I kept on being.***	भइरहें भइरहिनँ	भइरहनुभयो भइरहनुभएन	भइरहचौं भइरहेनौं	भइरहचौ भइरहेनौ	भइरहे भइरहेनन्	भइरहचो भइरहेन
Past Hab Freq (14.3) ***I used to keep on being.***	भइरहन्थें भइरहँदिनथें	भइरहनुहुन्थ्यो भइरहनुहुन्नथ्यो	भइरहन्थ्यौं भइरहँदैनथ्यौं	भइरहन्थ्यौ भइरहँदैनथ्यौ	भइरहन्थे भइरहँदैनथे	भइरहन्थ्यो भइरहँदैनथ्यो

Sim Indef (2.3, 3.8) ***I am***	हुँ / छु होइन / छैन	हनुहुन्छ / हुनुहुन्छ हुनुहुन्न / हुनुहुन्न	हौं / छौं होइनौं / छैनौं	हौ / छौ होइनौ / छैनौ	हुन् / छन् होइनन् / छैनन्	हो / छ होइन / छैन
Sim Indef (2.3, 3.8) ***I 'll be/become***	हुन्छु हुँदिनँ	हुनुहुन्छ हुनुहुन्न	हुन्छौं हुँदैनौं	हुन्छौ हुँदैनौ	हुन्छन् हुँदैनन्	हुन्छ हुँदैन
Pres Per (9.5) ***I have been.***	भएको छु भएको छैन	हुनुभएको छ हुनुभएको छैन	भएका छौं भएका छैनौं	भएका छौ भएका छैनौ	भएका छन् भएका छैनन्	भएको छ भएको छैन
Pres Cont (6.5) ***I am being.***	हुँदै छु -	हुनुहुँदै छ, हुदै हुनुहुन्छ -	हुँदै छौं -	हुँदै छौ -	हुँदै छन् -	हुँदैछ -
Pres Cont (8.4) ***I am being.***	भइरहेको छु भइरहेको छैन	भइरहनुभएको छ भइरहनुभएको छैन	भइरहेका छौं भइरहेका छैनौं	भइरहेका छौ भइरहेका छैनौ	भइरहेका छन् भइरहेका छैनन्	भइरहेको छ भइरहेको छैन
Pres Freq (13.10) ***I'll keep on being.***	भइरहन्छु भइरहँदिनँ	भइरहनुहुन्छ भइरहनुहुन्न	भइरहन्छौं भइरहँदैनौं	भइरहन्छौ भइरहँदैनौ	भइरहन्छन् भइरहँदैनन्	भइरहन्छ भइरहँदैन
Def Fut (13.7) ***I'll definitely be.***	हुनेछु हुनेछैन	हुनुहुनेछ हुनुहुनेछैन	हुनेछौं हुनेछैनौं	हुनेछौ हुनेछैनौ	हुनेछन् हुनेछैनन्	हुनेछ हुनेछैन
Indef Fut (9.4) ***I'll probably be.***	हुँला नहुँला	हुनुहोला नहुनुहोला	होऔंला नहोऔंला	होऔला नहोऔला	होलान् नहोलान्	होला नहोला
Imper (3.10, 9.1) ***(Do) be.***	- -	हुनुहोला, हुनुस् नहुनुस्	- -	होऊ नहोऊ	- -	- -
Injunct (4.6) ***Shall I be?*** ***Let's be.***	होऊँ नहोऊँ		होऔं नहोऔं	भए नभए	होऊन् नहोऊन्	होस् नहोस्

APPENDIX 6

PRIMARY BLOOD RELATIONS

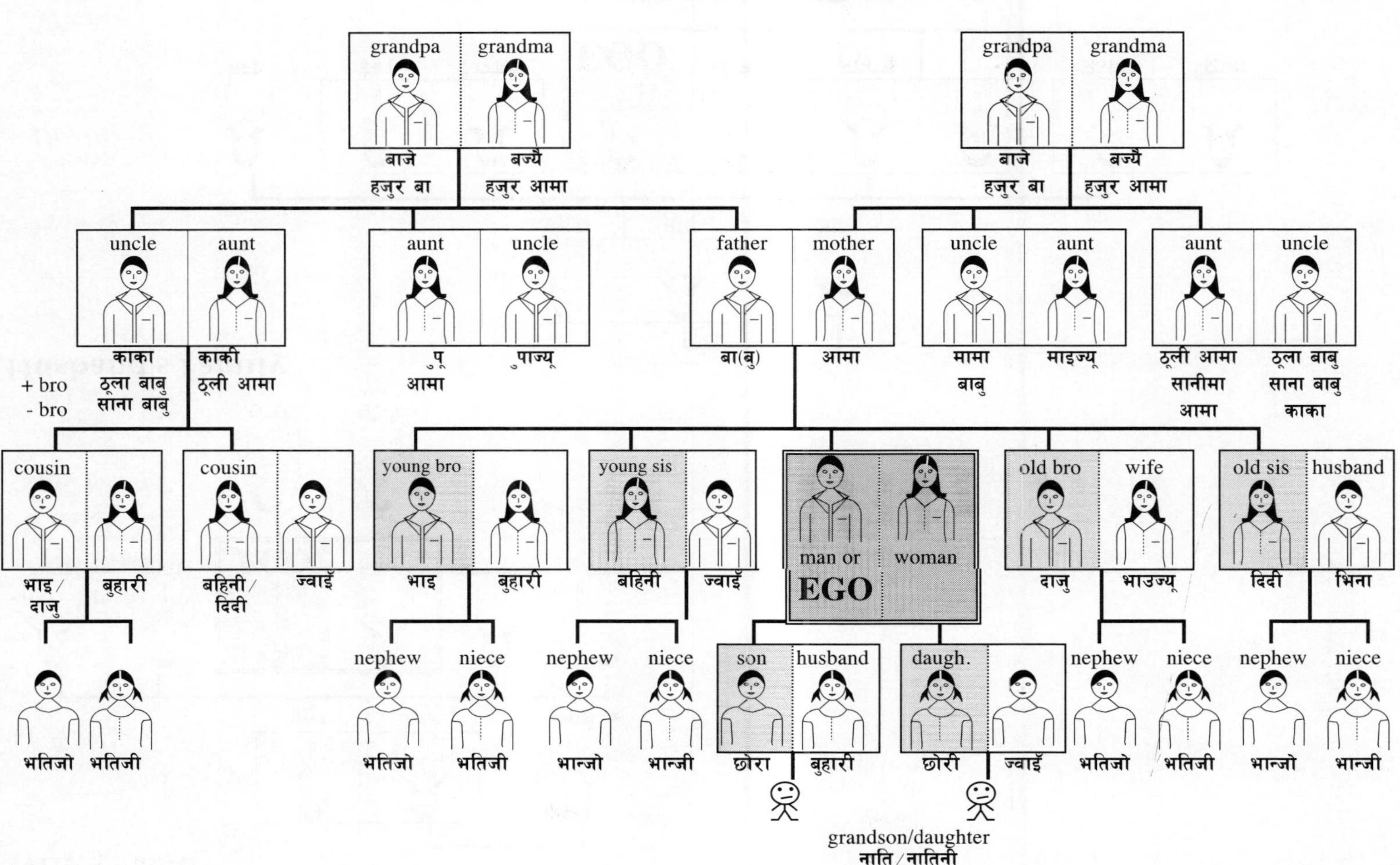

Wife's Family

Husband's Family

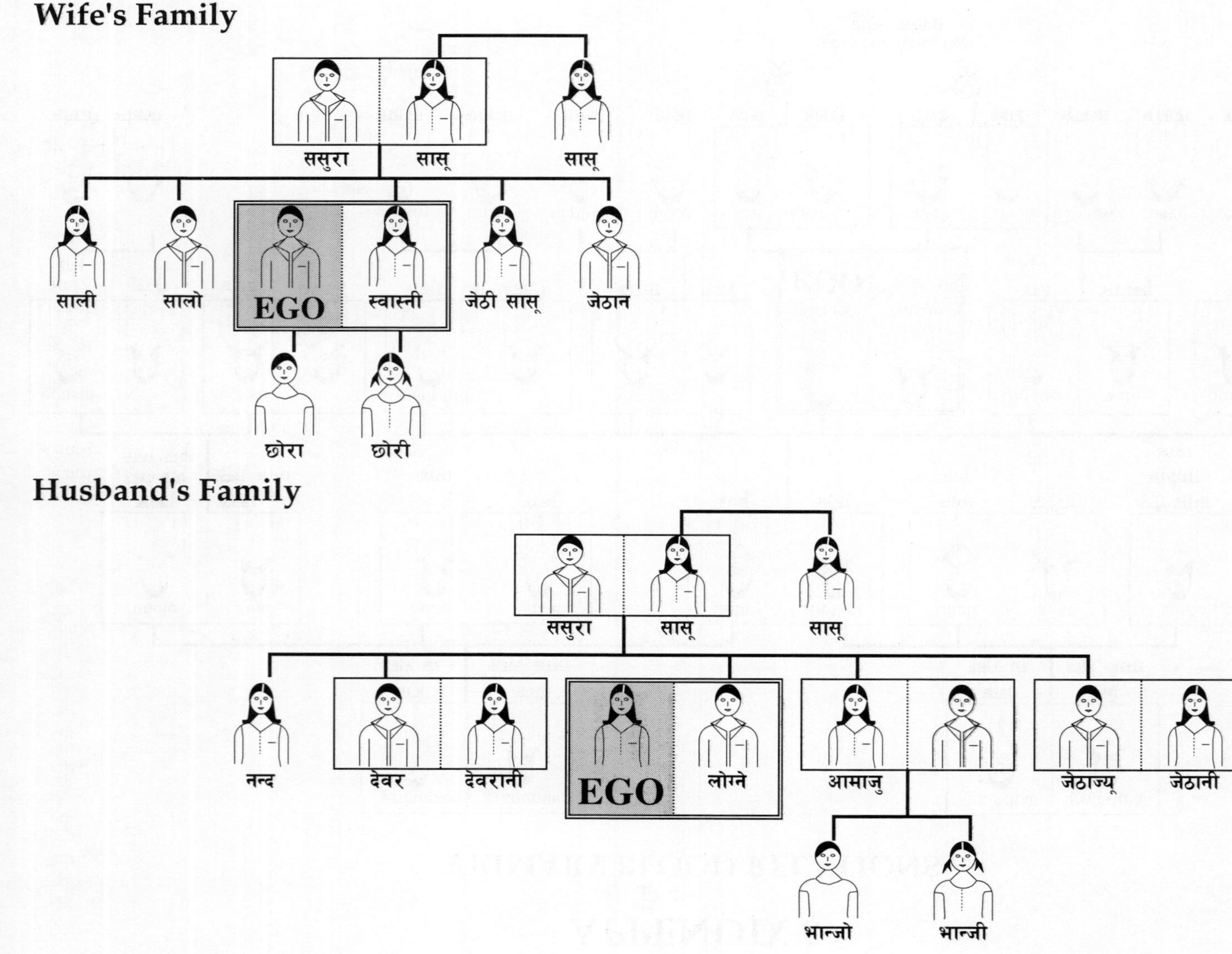

APPENDIX 7

COMPLEX VERBS BY SEMANTIC CATEGORY

AMOUNT		CHAPTER
-न (को/का लागि/लाई) MEASURE लाग्नु	**MEASURE *required to...***	8
नेपाली सिक्न(का लागि) एक वर्ष लाग्छ ।	*It takes one year to learn Nepali.*	
-ए(को)जति	***as much as...***	13
तिमी सकेजति सुन लिएर जाऊ ।	*Go, taking as much gold as you can.*	
-ने जति	***as much as...*** (general fact)	18
पहाडमा चाहिनेजति उत्पादन हुँदैन ।	*As much as is needed in the hills isn't produced (fact).*	
-ए पुग्छ	***is enough to, suffices...***	21
मैले एक घण्टा पढे पुग्छ ।	*One hour is enough for me to study.*	
-ए पनि	***_ever...***	10
जहिले आए पनि	*whenever you come*	
जहाँ बसे पनि	*wherever you sit*	
जे भए पनि	*whatever it is (however)*	
जे गरे पनि	*whatever you do*	
-न बाँकी छ	***...remaining to do***	11
विकासको काम धेरै गर्न बाँकी छ ।	*There's a lot of development work left to do.*	

CAPABILITY		
-न आउनु	***to know how to...***	5
मलाई नेपाली बोल्न आउँछ ।	*I know how to speak Nepali.*	
-न जान्नु	***to know how to...***	5
म नेपाली बोल्न जान्दछु ।	*I know how to speak Nepali.*	
-न सक्नु	***to be able to..***	7
पहिलो दिन हामी धेरै हिंड्न सकेनौं ।	*The first day we weren't able to walk much.*	

CONDITION AND POSSIBILITY

-एमा	***if, in the case of...***	23
यो प्रजातन्त्र असफल भएमा...	*If this democracy turns out to be unsuccessful...*	
-ने हो भने	***if...*** (for passives)	18
पानी पर्ने हो भने...	*If it is to rain...*	
-ए(ता)पनि	***even though, even if...***	11
पानी परे(ता)पनि म जान्छु ।	*Even if it rains, I will go / Even though it rains...*	
-न सकिन्थ्यो	***could have (been)...***	19
जुवा खेल्न सकिन्थ्यो; तर पैसा थिएन ।	*(I) could have gambled, but I didn't have money.*	
-एको भए...ने थिएँ.	***if X had... then Y*** (see 20.3)	20
जुवा खेलेको भए पैसा सिद्धिने थियो ।	*If I had gambled, the money would be finished.*	
-ए पनि...दिन्नथें.	***Even if X had... Y still wouldn't*** (see 20.5)	20
जुवा नखेलेपनि पैसा सिद्धिने थियो ।	*Even if I hadn't gambled, the money would've finished...*	
-ने थिएँ	***would have...*** (see 20.2)	20
(म) जुवा खेल्ने थिएँ ।	*(I) would have gambled.*	

COOPERATION

-न मदत गर्नु	***to help...***	5
उहाँले खाना पकाउन मदत गर्नुभयो ।	*He helped cook the food.*	
-इदिनु	***to do for..***	6
हुनुहुन्छ, म बोलाइदिन्छु ।	*He's here. I'll get him (for you).*	
-न लगाउनु	***involve someone in X...***	13
मैले साथीलाई काम गर्न लगाएँ ।	*I involved my friend in work.*	

DESIRE AND EMOTION

-न चाहनु	***to want to...***	4
अहिले डेरामा जान चाहन्छ ।	*He wants to go to his apartment now.*	

-न मन पर्नु	***to like to...***	**5**
मलाई दालभात खान मन पर्छ ।	*I like to eat daal bhat.*	
-न मन पर्थ्यो	***would like to...***	**20**
मलाई बस्न मन पर्थ्यो/मन पर्ने थियो ।	*I would like to stay.*	
-न मन लाग्नु	***feel like, want to...***(takes -लाई)	**9**
मलाई गाउँमा घुम्न मन लाग्यो ।	*I feel like strolling in the village.*	
-न खोज्नु	***try, seek to...***	**14**
धेरै मान्छेहरूले हिमाल चढ्न खोज्छन् ।	*Many people try to climb the Himalayas.*	
-न मजा आउनु/लाग्नु	***get enjoyment from...***	**19**
उसलाई सिनेमा हेर्न मजा आउँछ ।	*He gets enjoyment from watching movies.*	
-न डराउनु	***be afraid to...***	**22**
म नेपालमा गाडी चलाउन डराउँछु ।	*I'm afraid to drive a car in Nepal.*	

FINALITY / OBLIGATION

-नु पर्ने हुन्छ	***..will need to*** (generally, future)	**16**
पानी लिन टाढा जानु पर्ने हुन्छ ।	*(You) will need to go far to get water (generally).*	
-नु पर्नेछ	***...will need to*** (definite future)	**16**
पानी लिन टाढा जानु पर्नेछ ।	*You'll need to go far to get water (eg. next week)*	
-ने भयो	***will certainly, definitely will...***	**13**
उनीहरूले मलाई मार्ने भए ।	*They will kill me--it's a done deal.*	
-दै दैन	***absolutely not...***	**14**
ऊ जाँदै जाँदैन ।	*He absolutely will not go.*	

INFORMATION RECEIVED

(ले) -एको रहेछ	***surprise new info...***(past event)	**13**
उहाँले नेपाली बोल्नुभएको रहेछ ।	*He spoke Nepali! (I just found out)*	
-दो रहेछ / दा रहेछन्	***surprise new info...***(present / general)	**13**
उहाँ नेपाली बोल्नुहुँदो रहेछ ।	*He speaks Nepali, I see. (but I didn't expect it)*	
-एछ	***surprise new info...***(storytelling)	**13**
मैले किरा खाएछु ।	*Oh my! I've eaten a bug.*	

-ए(को) अनुसार	***according to...***	**10**
मैले भने(को) अनुसार गर्नुस् ।	*Do according to what I said.*	
-एबमोजिम	***according to...*** (formal; with भन्नु)	**23**
तपाईंले भनेबमोजिम	*according to what you said*	
-एको थाहा पाउनु	***to find out...***	**19**
मैले उनीहरूले त्यहाँ समय बिताएको थाहा पाएँ ।	*I found out they spent their time there.*	
-न त VERB, तर...	***it's true that, of course...but...***	**18**
म सुत्न त सुतेँ तर अलिकति मात्र ।	*Yes, I slept. But only a little.*	

INTENTION

-ने विचार	***plan of, intention of...***	**20**
बिहा गर्ने विचार	*intention of marriage*	
-ने विचार गर्नु	***plan to, intend to...***	**20**
म बिहा गर्ने विचार गर्छु ।	*I will plan to get married.*	
-न जानु	***to go (in order) to...***	**5**
मेरो श्रीमान् नेपाली सिक्न जानुभयो ।	*My husband went in order to learn Nepali.*	
-न (को लागि/लाई)	***in order to...*** (purpose / intention)	**8**
म तरकारी किन्न(को लागि)लाई जान्छु ।	*I'm going in order to buy vegetables.*	

MANNER

-ने किसिमले	***in a way that x's...***	**17**
खेर जाने किसिमले गर्‍यो ।	*(He) did it in a way that was wasteful.*	
-ने गरी	***so that, in a way that...***	**18**
सबैले सुन्ने गरी ठूलो स्वरमा बोल ।	*Speak in a loud voice so that all can hear.*	
-ए(को) जस्तो गर्नु	***do as if, pretend...***	**9**
उसले सुतेजस्तो गर्‍यो ।	*He pretended to sleep.*	
-ए(को) जस्तो/ए(को) जस्तै	***as... / as, exactly as...***	**9**
मैले नेपाली बोलेजस्तो बोल्नुस् ।	*Speak Nepali as I speak (it).*	
-न पछि नपर्नु	***don't delay, lag behind...***	**15**
बेच्न पछि नपर्नुस् ।	*Don't delay selling (do sell it)! Wait no longer!*	

-न गाह्रो हुनु — ***is difficult to...*** 7

सुत्न एकदम गाह्रो थियो । — *It was very difficult to sleep.*

-इहाल्नु — ***quickly, immediately...; with finality*** 15

मैले खाना खाइहालें । — *I ate the food very quickly. I wolfed it down.*

वर्षा आइहाल्छ । — *Monsoon is coming quickly; it's almost here.*

-न हतार गर्नु — ***hurry to...*** 11

बस समाउन हतार गर्नुस् । — *Hurry to catch the bus.*

-इहेर्नु — ***try (out), test...*** 14

खाइहेर्नुस् । मीठो छ । — *Try it out--taste and see. It's tasty.*

-न बिर्सनु — ***to forget to..*** 6

मैले तपाईंलाई फोन गर्न बिर्सें । — *I forgot to call you.*

NECESSITY, OBLIGATION

-नु पर्छ — ***should, must, have to...*** 8

हामीले त्यहाँ अस्पताल बनाउनु पर्छ । — *We are required to build a hospital there.*

-नु पर्ने हुन्छ — ***...need to ; necessary to*** (generally) 16

सबैले नेपाली सिक्नु पर्ने हुन्छ । — *It's necessary for everyone to learn Nepali.*

-नु परेको छ — ***necessary to be...*** 17

(हामीले) आत्मनिर्भर हुनु परेको छ । — *(We) have to be self-sufficient.*

-नु पर्ने देखिन्छ — ***seems/appears necessary to...*** 17

यसलाई राम्रो बनाउनु पर्ने देखिन्छ । — *It seems necessary to build it well.*

-नु पर्थ्यो / पर्नेथियो — ***should have...*** 20

म बस्नुपर्थ्यो / बस्नु पर्नेथियो । — *I should have stayed.*

न-VERB ROOT-ई नहुने THING — ***Thing that must be x-ed. Essential thing.*** 22

हाम्रो लागि पानी नभई नहुने कुरा हो । — *Water is essential for us (can't do without!).*

-नु पर्दैन — ***don't have to, not necessary to...*** 8

त्यहाँ अस्पताल बनाउनु पर्दैन । — *It's not necessary to build a hospital there.*

-नु हुँदैनथ्यो — ***should not have...; didn't used to have to...*** 20

म बस्नु हुँदैनथ्यो । — *I should not have stayed; I didn't used to have to stay.*

POSSIBILITY

-न पाउनु	***get a chance to...*** (active)	**6**
उसले कुरा गर्न पाएन ।	*He didn't get chance to talk.*	
-न पाइन्छ	***able (also allowed)*** (passive)	**16**
भोलि मलाई जान पाइन्छ ।	*I'll be able to go tomorrow.*	
-न सकिनु	***to be possible to...***	**7**
साँझ पर्नुअगाडि पुग्न सकिन्छ ।	*It's possible to arrive before dusk.*	
-न भ्याउनु	***have time to...***	**16**
सबैले नेपाली सिक्न भ्याउँदैनन् ।	*Not everyone has time to learn Nepali.*	
-एर साध्य छैन	***impossible, beyond possibility...***	**19**
गरेर साध्य छैन	*(It) is beyond the possibility of doing*	

REASON (BECAUSE)

-एको कारणले (गर्दा)/एकोले	***because, by reason of...***(past)	**7/9**
पानी परेका (कारण)ले (गर्दा) म गइनँ ।	*Because of it raining, I didn't go.*	
-ना(का कारण)ले (गर्दा)	***because, by reason of...***(past / present)	**9**
पानी पर्ना(को कारण)ले (गर्दा) म जाँदिनँ ।	*Because it rains, I don't go.*	
-एका (हुना)ले (गर्दा)	***because, by reason of...***(past)	**10**
पानी परेका (हुना)ले (गर्दा) म गइनँ ।	*Because of it raining, I didn't go.*	
-ने हुनाले	***because...***(general reasons)	**10**
सुख्खा हुने हुनाले...	*Because it is dry (generally)...*	
-एको देखेर	***seeing, having seen...***	**9**
पानी परेको देखेर म गइनँ ।	*Seeing it was raining, I didn't go.*	
-एकामा	***for x-ing...***	**14**
आउनुभएकामा धन्यवाद छ ।	*Thank you for coming.*	

PERMISSIBILITY AND ALLOWANCE

-नु ठीक छ/हो	***okay to..***	**6**
यहाँ बस्नु ठीक छ ?	*Is it okay to sit here?*	
-नु/न हुन्छ	***permissible, can, okay to...***	**8**
त्यहाँ अस्पताल बनाउनु/बनाउन हुन्छ ।	*It's okay to build a hospital there.*	

-ए(पनि) हुन्छ	***okay if, doesn't matter if...***	**11**
त्यहाँ अस्पताल बनाए(पनि) हुन्छ ।	*It's okay if you build a hospital there.*	
-न हुने NOUN	***something okay to...***	**22**
जान हुने ठाउँ	*place okay to go to*	
-न दिनु	***to allow to...***	**12**
उहाँलाई त्यहाँ बस्न देऊ न !	*Allow him to sit there.*	
-न पाइँदैन	***allowed (also able)*** (passive)	**16**
क्लासमा चुरोट खान पाइँदैन ।	*Smoking is not allowed in the classroom.*	
-नु हुँदैन	***must not, should not ...***	**8**
त्यहाँ अस्पताल बनाउनु हुँदैन ।	*It's not okay to build a hospital there.*	

START AND FINISH

-न थाल्नु	***to begin to...***	**7**
साँझ पर्नुअघि बास खोज्न थाल्यौं ।	*We began to look for shelter before dusk.*	
-न सुरु गर्नु	***to begin to...***	**7**
हामीले साँझ पर्नुअघि बास खोज्न सुरु गर्‍यौं ।	*We began to look for shelter before dusk.*	
-न लाग्नु	***about to...; started...***	**10**
पानी पर्न लाग्यो ।	*It's about to rain.*	
मैले काम गर्न लागें ।	*I started working.*	
-इसक्नु	***finish...; have already...; have had...***	**8**
मैले भात खाइसकें ।	*I have already eaten/I've finished eating.*	
-न पुग्नु	***be finished, ended...***	**21**
मलाई पढ्न पुग्यो ।	*I have finished my studies (sufficiently studied).*	
-न छोड्नु	***to stop, leave...***	**13**
उसले उसलाई माया गर्न छोड्यो ।	*(He) stopped loving her.*	
मैले उहाँलाई यो काम गर्न छोडें ।	*I left him to do this work.*	
-ने काममा लाग्नु	***engage in the work of...***	**18**
(उहाँ) भाषा सिक्ने काममा लाग्नुभयो ।	*(He) engaged in the work of language learning.*	
-ने काममा लगाउनु	***engage someone in the work of...***	**18**
(उसले) उसलाई भाषा सिक्ने काममा लगायो ।	*(He) engaged him in the work of language learning.*	

TIME: CONTINUOUS

–दै जानु *continue on, keep on...* 10

तपाईं भन्दै जानुस्, म सुन्दै जान्छु । *You keep on talking, I'll keep on listening.*

–दै गर्नु *continue, keep on...* 19

तपाईं भन्दै गर्नुस्, म सुन्दै जान्छु । *You continue talking, I'll continue listening.*

–इराख्नु *continue, keep on...* 12

म नेपाली सिकिराख्छु । *I continue to/keep on learning Nepali.*

–इरहनु *continue, keep on...*(see ch 8) 12

म नेपाली सिकिरहन्छु । *I continue to learn Nepali* (present freq).

–इरहेको *the continual, repeated X-ing of...* 12

नानी सुतिरहेको *the sleeping of the baby*

–ने गर्नु *do as a practice, habit...* 17

म रक्सी खाने गर्दिनँ । *I don't have the habit of drinking alcohol.*

TIME: POINT IN TIME

–एको TIME भयो *...ago , since* 8

म नेपाल आएको १ वर्ष भयो । *I came to Nepal a year ago (been here a year).*

मैले खाना पकाएको १ घण्टा भयो । *It's been 1hr. since I cooked food (finished an hr ago).*

–दा(खेरि) *while ...* 9

नेपालमा बस्दा(खेरि) खाने पानी उमाल्नु पर्छ । *While living in Nepal, drinking water ...*

–दा...दै and दै...दै *while X-ing, Y...* 13

म जाँदाजाँदै पानी पऱ्यो । *While I was walking it began to rain.*

मैले जाँदैजाँदै कुरा गरें । *While walking I talked.*

–ने बेलामा *when, at the time of...* 10

पानी पर्ने बेलामा मान्छे भित्र जान्छन् । *When it rains, people go inside.*

–ने बेला भयो *time to...* 10

खाने बेला भयो । *It's time to eat.*

–उन्जेल *as long as...* (active sentences) 18

वर्षा हुन्जेल उनीहरूको फुर्सद हुँदैन । *They don't have leisure as long as it is monsoon.*

-इन्जेल — ***as long as...*** (passive sentences) — **18**

वर्षा भइन्जेल हिमाल देखिँदैन । — *The Himals can't be seen as long as it is monsoon.*

-न मनपर्थ्यो — ***used to like to...*** — **20**

मलाई बस्न मन पर्थ्यो/मन पर्ने थियो । — *I would like to stay.*

TIME: SEQUENCE (First X, Then Y)

-एपछि — ***after...*** — **4**

साँझ परेपछि ट्याक्सीहरू मोलतोल गर्छन् । — *After turning dusk, taxi (drivers) bargain.*

-ने बित्तिकै — ***immediately after, as soon as...*** — **13**

यो खबर सुन्नेबित्तिकै म आएँ । — *As soon as I heard the news, I came.*

-नासाथ/नासाथै — ***immediately after, as soon as...*** — **20**

यो खबर सुन्नासाथै म आएँ । — *As soon as I heard the news, I came.*

-नु(भन्दा) अघि/अगाडि — ***before...*** — **7**

बास खोज्नु(भन्दा) अघि/अगाडि साँझ पर्‍यो । — *It turned dusk before we looked for shelter.*

-नुभन्दा पहिल्यै — ***before...*** — **9**

साँझ पर्नुभन्दा पहिल्यै पुग्न सकिन्छ । — *It's possible to arrive before dusk.*

न-एसम्म — ***until...*** — **7**

ऊ नआएसम्म बस्नोस् । — *Wait until he comes (as long as he hasn't come...)*

-एदेखि — ***since, from when...*** — **11**

म पोखराबाट फर्केदेखि पानी परेको छ । — *Since I returned from Pokhara it has been raining.*

APPENDIX 8

COMPLEX VERBS ALPHABETICALLY

(Alphabetical by head word. For example, -एपछि is sorted as पछि)

Devanagari Alphabetical Order (top to bottom, left to right)

ं *(nasal)*	ँ *(nasal)*	अ	आ – ा	
इ – ि	ई – ी	उ – ु	– ृ	
ए – े	ऐ – ै	ओ – ो	औ – ौ	
क क्ष	ख	ग	घ	ङ
च	छ	ज ज्ञ	झ	ञ
ट	ठ	ड	ढ	ण
त त्र	थ	द	ध	न
प		ब	भ	म
य	र	ल	व	
श श्र श्रृ	ष	स	ह	

		Chapter
-नु(भन्दा) **अगाडि**/अघि	***before...***	7
हिँड्नु(भन्दा) अघि/अगाडि हामीले खायौं ।	*Before we walked, we ate.*	
बास खोज्नु(भन्दा) अघि/अगाडि साँझ पऱ्यो ।	*It turned dusk before we looked for shelter.*	
-नु(भन्दा) **अघि**/अगाडि	see -नु(भन्दा) **अगाडि**/अघि	7
-ए(को) **अनुसार**	***according to...***	10
मैले भने(को) अनुसार गर्नुस् ।	*Do according to what I said.*	
मैले मेरो बाले भने(को) अनुसार गर्नु पर्छ ।	*I have to do according to what my father says.*	

-न आउनु *to know how to...* **5**

मलाई हिन्दी बोल्न आउँदैन । *I don't know how to speak Hindi.*

मलाई नेपाली बोल्न आउँछ । *I know how to speak Nepali.*

-इन्जेल ***as long as...*** (passive sentences) **18**

वर्षा भइन्जेल हिमाल देखिँदैन । *The Himals can't be seen as long as it is monsoon.*

यहाँ भइन्जेल हामीलाई नेपाली बोल्नु पर्छ । *Nepali needs to be spoken as long as we're here.*

-उन्जेल ***as long as...*** (active sentences) **18**

वर्षा हुन्जेल उनीहरूको फुर्सद हुँदैन । *They don't have leisure time as long as it is monsoon.*

दोहोरी चलुन्जेल धान रोप्न रमाइलो हुन्छ । *(People) have fun planting as long as a duet is going.*

-एको **कारण**ले (गर्दा) / एकोले ***because, by reason of...***(past events) **9**

ढिलो आएको (कारण)ले (गर्दा)... *By reason of being late...*

पानी परेको (कारण)ले (गर्दा), म गइनँ । *Because of it raining, I didn't go.*

-ना(को **कारण**)ले (गर्दा) ***because, by reason of...***(past / present) **9**

ढिलो आउना(को कारण)ले (गर्दा) *By reason of being late...*

पानी पर्ना(को कारण)ले (गर्दा) म गइनँ । *Because of it raining, I didn't go.*

-ने **काम**मा लगाउनु ***engage someone in the work of...*** **18**

(उसले) उसलाई भाषा सिक्ने काममा लगायो । *(He) engaged him in the work of language learning.*

भाषा सिक्ने काममा लगाउनु । *engage (someone) in the work of learning language*

-ने **काम**मा लाग्नु ***engage in the work of...*** **18**

(उहाँ) भाषा सिक्ने काममा लाग्नुभयो । *(He) engaged in the work of language learning.*

भाषा सिकाउने काममा लाग्नु *engage in the work of teaching language*

-ने **किसिमले** ***in a way that x's...*** **17**

वनविनाश रोकिने किसिमले । *In a way that stops forest destruction.*

(उसले) अरूलाई सताउने किसिमले गफसफ गऱ्यो । *(He) chatted in a way that tormented others.*

-दा(**खेरि**) ***while ...*** **9**

नेपालमा बस्दा(खेरि) खाने पानी उमाल्नु पर्छ । *While living in Nepal, drinking water ...*

नेपाली सिक्दा(खेरि) सुत्नु हुँदैन । *While studying Nepali, sleeping is not allowed.*

-न खोज्नु ***try, seek to...*** **14**

धेरै मान्छेहरूले हिमाल चढ्न खोज्छन् । *Many people try to climb the Himalayas.*

(उनीहरूले) आधुनिक फेसनको लुगा लगाउन खोज्छन् । *(They) seek to wear modern fashions.*

-ने गरी ***so that, in a way that...*** **18**

(तिमी) सबैले सुन्ने गरी ठूलो स्वरमा बोल । *Speak in a loud voice so that all can hear.*

(तिमी) बुझ्ने गरी स्पष्टसँग लेख । *Write clearly in a way that is understandable.*

-दै गर्नु ***keep on, continue...*** **19**

तपाईं भन्दै जानुस्, म सुन्दै गर्छु । *You continue talking, I'll continue listening.*

मैले कोही खोपी खेल्दै गरेको देखें । *I saw some (of them) playing along (khopi).*

-ने गर्नु ***do as a practice, habit...*** **17**

उनीहरू खच्चर चराउने गर्छन् । *They have the practice of grazing mules.*

म रक्सी खाने गर्दिनँ । *I don't have the habit of drinking alcohol.*

-न गाह्रो हुनु ***is difficult to...*** **7**

सुत्न एकदम गाह्रो थियो । *It was very difficult to sleep.*

उकालो बाटो हिँड्न गाह्रो छ । *It is difficult to walk on uphill trails.*

-न चाहनु ***to want to...*** **4**

ऊ अहिले डेरामा जान चाहन्छ । *He wants to go to his apartment now.*

ट्याक्सीहरू मोलतोल गर्न चाहन्छन् । *Taxi (drivers) want to bargain.*

-एछ ***surprise new info...***(storytelling) **13**

त्यो उम्रेछ । *I see that it has sprouted.*

मैले किरा खाएछु । *Oh my! I've eaten a bug.*

-न छोड्नु ***to stop, leave...*** **13**

(उसले) उसलाई माया गर्न छोड्यो । *(He) stopped loving her.*

मैले उहाँलाई यो काम गर्न छोडें । *I left him to do this work.*

-ए(को)जति ***as much as...*** **13**

(तिमी) सकेजति सुन लिएर जाऊ । *Go, taking as much gold as you can.*

म सकेजति मदत दिन्छु । *I will help as much as I can.*

-ने जति ***as much as...*** (general fact) **18**

पहाडमा चाहिनेजति उत्पादन हुँदैन । *As much as is needed in the hills isn't produced.*

-ए(को) जस्तो ***as...*** **9**

मैले पकाएजस्तो खाना पकाउनुस् । *Cook as I cook.*

-ए(को) **जस्तो** गर्नु — ***do as if, pretend...*** — **9**

उसले सुतेजस्तो गऱ्यो । — *He pretended to sleep.*

उसले रोग लागेकोजस्तो गऱ्यो । — *He pretended he was sick.*

ए(को) **जस्तै** — ***exactly as...*** — **9**

म तपाईंले भनेजस्तै गर्छु । — *I'll do exactly as you say.*

-दै जानु — ***continue on, keep on...*** — **10**

गर्मी बढ्दै जान्छ । — *It continues to get hotter.*

जाडो पनि बढ्दै जान्छ । — *It also continues to get colder.*

-न **जानु** — ***to go (in order) to...*** — **5**

मेरो श्रीमान् नेपाली सिक्न जानुभयो । — *My husband went to learn Nepali.*

उहाँ खाना पकाउन जानुभयो । — *He went to cook the food.*

-न **जान्नु** — ***to know how to...*** — **5**

म हिन्दी बोल्न जान्दछु । — *I know how to speak Hindi.*

म नेपाली बोल्न जान्दछु । — *I know how to speak Nepali.*

-नु **ठीक** छ/हो — ***okay to..*** — **6**

के ल्याउनु ठीक हो, भन्नुस् न ! — *Tell me what's okay to bring.*

यहाँ बस्नु ठीक छ ? — *Is it okay to sit here?*

-न **डराउनु** — ***be afraid to...*** — **22**

म नेपालमा गाडी चलाउन डराउँछु । — *I'm afraid to drive a car in Nepal.*

तपाईंलाई भन्न डराउँछु । — *I'm afraid to tell you.*

-न **त** VERB, **तर**... — ***it's true that...but...; of course X...but...*** — **18**

पानी पर्न त पऱ्यो तर गर्मी थियो । — *It's true that it rained, but it was hot.*

मैले खान त खाएँ तर अझै भोक लागेको छ । — *Yes, I ate. But I'm still hungry.*

-न **थाल्नु** — ***to begin to...*** — **7**

उसले बोल्न थाल्यो । — *He began to speak.*

हामीले खोलो तर्न थाल्यौं । — *We began to cross the river.*

-एको **थाहा** पाउनु — ***to find out...*** — **19**

मैले तिनीहरूले त्यहाँ समय बिताएको थाहा पाएँ । — *I found out they spent their time there.*

कसरी गरेको मैले थाहा पाएँ । — *I found out how (he) did it.*

-नेथिएँ — ***would have...*** (see 20.2) — **20**

म बस्नेथिएँ । — *I would have stayed.*

-इदिनु — ***to do for..*** — **6**

उहाँ हुनुहुन्छ, म बोलाइदिन्छु । — *He's here. I'll get him (for you).*

ऊ मेरो काम गरिदिन्छ । — *He does my work (for me).*

-न दिनु	***to allow to...***	**12**
उसलाई पढ्न देऊ न !	*Allow him to read.*	
उहाँलाई त्यहाँ बस्न देऊ न !	*Allow him to sit there.*	
-एदेखि	***since, from when...***	**11**
म पोखराबाट फर्केदेखि पानी परेको छ ।	*Since I returned from Pokhara it has been raining.*	
अन्जीर टिप्न गएदेखिको कथा ।	*The story from when (she) went to pick figs.*	
-नुपर्ने देखिन्छ	***seems/appears necessary to...***	**17**
यसलाई राम्रो बनाउनुपर्ने देखिन्छ ।	*It seems necessary to build it well.*	
त्यहाँ जानुपर्ने देखिन्छ ।	*It seems necessary to go.*	
-एको देखेर	***seeing, having seen...***	**9**
मैले खाली ट्याक्सी आएको देखेर त्यसलाई रोकेँ ।	*Seeing an empty taxi come, I stopped it.*	
अरूले धाराको पानी सिधै खाएको देखेर...	*Seeing others directly drinking tap water...*	
-दै...दै and दा...दै	***while X-ing, Y...***	**13**
म जाँदाजाँदै पानी पऱ्यो ।	*While I was walking it began to rain.*	
मैले जाँदैजाँदै कुरा गरेँ ।	*While walking I talked.*	
-दै दैन	***absolutely not...***	**14**
ऊ खाँदै खाँदैन ।	*He absolutely will not eat.*	
ऊ जाँदै जाँदैन ।	*He absolutely will not go.*	
-ए पुग्छ	***is enough to, suffices...***	**21**
मैले एक घण्टा पढे पुग्छ ।	*One hour is enough for me to study.*	
-न पुग्नु	***be finished, ended...***	**21**
मलाई पढ्न पुग्यो ।	*I have finished my studies (sufficiently studied).*	
हामीलाई खान पुग्यो ।	*We've finished eating; we've had enough.*	
-एपछि	***after...***	**4**
पीपलबोटमा पुगेपछि...	*After reaching the peepul tree...*	
साँझ परेपछि ट्याक्सीहरू मोलतोल गर्छन् ।	*After turning dusk, taxi (drivers) bargain.*	
-न पछि नपर्नु	***don't delay, lag behind...***	**15**
बेच्न पछि नपर्नुस् ।	*Don't delay selling (do sell it)! Wait no longer!*	
फाल्न पछि नपर्नुस् ।	*Don't delay throwing away (throw it away)!*	

-ए **पनि**	***_ever...***	**10**
जति खाए पनि	*however much you eat*	
जहिले आए पनि	*whenever you come*	
जहाँ बसे पनि	*wherever you sit*	
जे गरे पनि	*whatever you do*	
-ए(ता)**पनि**	***even though, even if...***	**11**
देश सानो भए(ता)पनि...	*Even though the country is small...*	
पानी परे(ता)पनि म जान्छु ।	*Even if it rains, I will go* or	
पानी नपरे(ता)पनि वन राम्रो छ ।	*Even though it doesn't rain, the forest is nice.*	
-ए**पनि**...-थें	***Even if X had... Y still wouldn't.***	**20**
पानी परे पनि म जाँदिनथें ।	*Even if it had rained, I wouldn't have gone.*	
-ए(**पनि**) हुन्छ	see -ए(पनि) **हुन्छ**	**11**
-नु **परेको छ**	***necessary to be...***	**17**
(हामी) आत्मनिर्भर हुनु परेको छ ।	*(We) have to be self-sufficient.*	
-नु **पर्छ**	***should, must, have to...***	**8**
तपाईंले नेपाली सिक्नु पर्छ ।	*You must learn Nepali.*	
हामीले त्यहाँ अस्पताल बनाउनु पर्छ ।	*We are required to build a hospital there.*	
-नु **पर्थ्यो/पर्नेथियो**	***should have...***	**20**
म बस्नु पर्थ्यो / बस्नु पर्नेथियो ।	*I should have stayed.*	
मैले खानु पर्थ्यो ।	*I should have eaten.*	
-नु **पर्दैन**	***don't have to, not necessary to...***	**8**
तपाईंले नेपाली सिक्नु पर्दैन ।	*It's not necessary for you to learn Nepali.*	
त्यहाँ अस्पताल बनाउनु पर्दैन ।	*It's not necessary to build a hospital there.*	
-नु **पर्ने**छ	***...will need to*** (definite future)	**16**
पानी लिन टाढा जानु पर्नेछ ।	*You'll need to go far to get water (eg. next week)*	
सबैले नेपाली सिक्नु पर्नेछ ।	*Everyone will need to learn Nepali (eg. next year)*	
-नु **पर्ने** देखिन्छ	see -नुपर्ने **देखिन्छ**	**17**
-नु **पर्ने**हुन्छ	***...need to ; necessary to*** (generally)	**16**
(तिमी) पानी लिन टाढा जानु पर्नेहुन्छ ।	*(You) need to go far to get water.*	
औषधि खानु पर्नेहुन्छ ।	*It's necessary to take medicine.*	
	..will need to (generally, future)	**16**
पानी लिन टाढा जानु पर्नेहुन्छ ।	*(You) will need to go far to get water (generally)*	
औषधि खानु पर्नेहुन्छ ।	*It's will be necessary to take medicine (generally)*	

-नुभन्दा **पहिल्यै** — ***before...*** 9

हिँड्नुभन्दा पहिल्यै हामीले खायौँ । — *Before we walked, we ate.*

साँझ पर्नुभन्दा पहिल्यै त्यहाँ पुग्न सकिन्छ । — *It's possible to arrive before dusk.*

-न **पाइन्छ** — ***allowed, able*** (passive) 16

हामीलाई तपाईंकहाँ आउन पाइँदैन । — *We're not allowed to come to your place.*

-न **पाउनु** — ***get a chance to, allow to...*** 6

मैले किताप पढ्न पाएँ । — *I got a chance to read the book.*

भोलि म तपाईंलाई भेट्न पाउँदिनँ । — *I won't be available to see you tomorrow.*

-**एबमोजिम** — ***according to...*** (formal; used with भन्नु) 23

तपाईंले भनेबमोजिम — *according to what you said*

सिकेबमोजिम — *according to what's learned*

-न **बाँकी** छ — ***...left to do*** 11

विकासको काम धेरै गर्न बाँकी छ । — *There's a lot of development work left to do.*

मेरो काम गर्न बाँकी छ । — *I have work left to do.*

-ने **विचार** — ***plan of, intention of...*** 20

बिहा गर्ने विचार — *intention of marriage*

मेरो बिहा गर्ने विचार छ । — *I'm planning to get married.*

-ने **विचार** गर्नु — ***plan to, intend to...*** 20

म बिहा गर्ने विचार गर्छु । — *I will plan to get married.*

म घर बनाउने विचार गर्छु । — *I will think about building a house.*

-**नेबित्तिकै** — ***as soon as, immediately after...*** 13

यो खबर सुन्नेबित्तिकै म आएँ । — *As soon as I heard the news, I came.*

खानेबित्तिकै दिसा लाग्छ । — *As soon as one eats it, one gets diarrhea.*

-न **बिर्सनु** — ***to forget to..*** 6

मैले पैसा ल्याउन बिर्सें । — *I forgot to bring money.*

तपाईंले टिप्न बिर्सनुभयो । — *You forgot to write it down.*

-ने **बेलामा** — ***when, at the time of...*** 10

पानी पर्ने बेलामा मान्छे भित्र जान्छन् । — *When it rains, people go inside.*

बतास चल्ने बेलामा धुलो उड्छ । — *When it blows, dust rises.*

-ने **बेला** भयो — ***time to...*** 10

खाने बेला भयो । — *It's time to eat.*

जाने बेला भयो । — *It's time to go.*

-एको **भए**...नेथिएँ — ***if X had... then Y*** (see 20.3) 20

-ने हो **भने**	***if...*** (for passives)	18
पानी पर्ने हो भने...	*If it is to rain...*	
साँच्चै भन्ने हो भने...	*If it is to be truly said ...*	
-नु(**भन्दा**) अघि/अगाडि	see -नु(भन्दा) **अगाडि/अघि**	7
-**नुभन्दा** पहिल्यै	see -नुभन्दा **पहिल्यै**	9
-ने **भयो**	***will certainly, definitely will...***	13
तिनीहरूले मलाई मार्ने भए ।	*They will kill me--it's a done deal.*	
हामी खाने भयौं ।	*We're eating, no question about it!*	
-एको TIME **भयो**	***...long ago , since***	8
नेपालमा आएको कति भयो ?	*How long ago did you come to Nepal (here now)?*	
म नेपालमा आएको १ वर्ष भयो ।	*I came to Nepal a year ago (been here a year).*	
मैले खाना पकाएको १ घण्टा भयो (tr) ।	*It's been 1hr. since I cooked food (finished).*	
मलाई डर लागेको १ घण्टा भयो ।	*I have been afraid for an hour.*	
	An hour ago, I was afraid (but not now).	
-न **भ्याउनु**	***have time to...***	16
मैले पानी लिन भ्याएँ ।	*I had time to get water (time permitted me to).*	
सबैले नेपाली सिक्न भ्याउँदैनन् ।	*Not everyone has time to learn Nepali.*	
-न **मजा** आउनु/लाग्नु	***get enjoyment from...***	19
उसलाई सिनेमा हेर्न मजा आउँछ ।	*He gets enjoyment from watching movies.*	
तपाईंलाई के गर्न मजा आउँछ ?	*What do you gain enjoyment from?*	
-न **मदत** गर्नु	***to help...***	5
उनी हामीलाई घरको काम गर्न मदत गर्छिन् ।	*She helps us do the housework.*	
उहाँले खाना पकाउन मदत गर्नुभयो ।	*He helped cook the food.*	
-न **मन** पर्नु	***to like to...***	5
मलाई दालभात खान मन पर्छ ।	*I like to eat daal bhat.*	
मलाई तरकारी किन्न मन पर्छ ।	*I like to buy vegetables.*	
-न **मन** पर्‍यो	***wanted to...***	20
मलाई बस्न मन पर्‍यो/मन पर्नेथियो ।	*I wanted to stay.*	
मलाई खान मन पर्‍यो/मन पर्नेथियो ।	*I wanted to eat.*	
	ALSO: used to like to...	
मलाई बस्न मन पर्‍यो ।	*I used to like to stay.*	
मलाई खान मन पर्‍यो ।	*I used to like to eat.*	

-न **मन** लाग्नु	***feel like, want to...***(takes -लाई)	**9**
मलाई गाउँमा घुम्न मन लाग्यो ।	*I feel like strolling in the village.*	
खान मन लाग्छ होला ।	*(You) will probably feel like eating.*	
-**एमा** ***if, in the case of...***	**23**	
जनप्रतिनिधिहरू बेइमान भएमा...	*If the peoples' representatives are dishonest...*	
यो प्रजातन्त्र असफल भएमा...	*If this democracy turns out to be unsuccessful...*	
-एका**मा**	***for x-ing...***	**14**
आउनुभएकामा धन्यवाद छ ।	*Thank you for coming.*	
दिनुभएकामा खुसी लाग्यो ।	*I'm happy for your giving it (happy you gave).*	
-**इरहनु**	***to continue, keep on...***	**12**
म नेपाली सिकिरहन्छु ।	*I continue to learn Nepali.* (present freq)	
म खाइरहन्छु ।	*I will keep on eating*	
-**इरहेको**	***the continual, repeated X-ing of...***	**12**
गैंडा चरिरहेको	*the grazing of rhinos*	
गाडी चलिरहेको	*the driving/moving of vehicles*	
(ले) -एको **रहेछ**	***surprise new info...***(past event)	**13**
नउमालेको रहेछ ।	*It's unboiled, I see (but I thought it was) .*	
उहाँ**ले** नेपाली बोल्नुभएको रहेछ ।	*He spoke Nepali (I just found out)!*	
-दो **रहेछ**/दा **रहेछन्**	***surprise new info...***(present / general fact)	**13**
उहाँ नेपाली बोल्नुहुँदो रहेछ ।	*He speaks Nepali, I see (but I didn't expect it) .*	
ऊ खाँदो रहेछ ।	*He eats, I see (not what I expected) .*	
-**इराख्नु**	***to continue, keep on...***	**12**
म नेपाली सिकिराख्छु ।	*I continue to/keep on learning Nepali.*	
म गइराख्छु ।	*I will continue going .*	
-न **लगाउनु**	***involve someone in X...***	**13**
उनीहरूले रोटी पकाउन लगाए ।	*They involved (her) in making bread.*	
मैले साथीलाई काम गर्न लगाएँ ।	*I involved my friend in work.*	
-ने काममा **लगाउनु**	see -ने **काम**मा लगाउनु	**18**
-न (कालागि/**लाई**)	see -न (को **लागि**/लाई)	**8**
-न (को **लागि**/लाई)	***in order to...***	**8**
औषधि किन्नको लागि बाहिर जानु पर्दैन ।	*One doesn't have to go outside in order to buy medicines.*	
भिसा मिलाउन ऊ मदत गर्छ ।	*In order to arrange visas, he helps.*	
म तरकारी किन्नलाई बजार जान्छु ।	*I'm going to the market to buy vegetables.*	

-न **लाग्नु**	***about to...; started...***	**10**
पानी पर्न लाग्यो ।	*It's about to rain.*	
गर्मी हुन लाग्यो ।	*It's about to become hot.*	
-ने काममा **लाग्नु**	see -ने **काम**मा लाग्नु	**18**
-न (का लागि/लाई) MEASURE **लाग्नु**	**MEASURE *required to...***	**8**
नेपाली सिक्न(का लागि) एक वर्ष लाग्छ ।	*It takes one year to learn Nepali.*	
त्यो किन्न(लाई) दुई रुपियाँ लाग्छ ।	*That requires two rupees to buy.*	
-एका**ले**	***because..***	**7**
थकाइ लागेकाले हामीले आराम गर्‍यौं ।	*Because we were tired we rested.*	
साँझ परेकाले पुग्न सकेनौं ।	*Because it fell dusk, we couldn't reach (it).*	
-एका कारणले (गर्दा)/एका**ले**	see -एको **कारण**ले (गर्दा)/एकोले	**9**
-न **सुरु** गर्नु	***to begin to...***	**7**
साँझ पर्नुअघि बास खोज्न सुरु गर्‍यौं ।	*We began to look for shelter before dusk.*	
हामीले खोला तर्न सुरु गर्‍यौं ।	*We began to cross the river.*	
-इसक्नु	***finish...; have already...; have had...***	**8**
मैले भात खाइसकें ।	*I have already eaten/I've finished eating.*	
दुई महिना भइसक्यो ।	*It's already been two months.*	
-न सिध्याइ**सक्नु**...	see -न **सिध्याइ**सक्नु	**18**
-न **सक्नु**	***to be able to..***	**7**
पहिलो दिन हामी धेरै हिँड्न सकेनौं ।	*The first day we weren't able to walk much.*	
हामीले धेरै खोलाहरू तर्न सक्यौं ।	*We were able to cross many rivers.*	
-न **सकिनु**	***to be possible to...***	**7**
साँझ पर्नुअगाडि पुग्न सकिन्छ ।	*It's possible to arrive before dusk.*	
पहिलो दिन धेरै हिँड्न सकिँदैन ।	*It's not possible to walk much on the first day.*	
-न **सकिन्थ्यो**	***could have (been)...***	**19**
जुवा खेल्न सकिन्थ्यो; तर पैसा थिएन ।	*(I) could have gambled, but I didn't have money.*	
भित्र जान सकिन्थ्यो; तर ऊ बाहिर बस्यो ।	*(He) could've gone inside, but he stayed outside.*	
न-एस**म्म**	***until...***	**7**
नखाएसम्म नहिँड्नुस् ।	*Don't walk until you've eaten.*	
नसुतेसम्म कुरा गरें ।	*I talked until I slept.*	
-नासाथ/नासाथै	***immediately after, as soon as...***	**20**
घरमा आउनासाथै ऊ रोयो ।	*As soon as he came in the house, he cried.*	

-एर **साध्य** छैन	***impossible, beyond possibility...***	**19**
भनेर साध्य छैन	*impossible to say*	
गरेर साध्य छैन	*beyond the possibility of doing*	
-न **सिध्याउनु**...	***to finish...***	**18**
खान सिध्याएँ ।	*I finished eating.*	
किताप पढ्न सिध्याएँ ।	*I finished reading the book.*	
-न **हतार** गर्नु	***hurry to...***	**11**
बस समाउन हतार गर्नुस् ।	*Hurry to catch the bus.*	
बस समाउनका लागि हिँड्न हतार गर्नुस् ।	*In order to catch the bus, walk hurredly.*	
-**इहाल्नु**	***quickly, immediately...; with finality***	**15**
मैले खाना खाइहालें ।	*I ate the food very quickly. I wolfed it down.*	
ऊ गइहाल्यो ।	*He's gone! Out the door!*	
खाना चिसो भइहाल्यो ।	*The food is already cold.*	
भइहाल्छ ।	*Idiomatic: Good enough. It'll do.*	
-नु हुँदैन	***must not, should not ...***	**8**
नेपाली सिक्नु हुँदैन ।	*You are not allowed to learn Nepali.*	
त्यहाँ अस्पताल बनाउनु हुँदैन ।	*It's not okay to build a hospital there.*	
-नु **हुँदैन**थ्यो	***should not have...***	**20**
म बस्नु हुँदैनथ्यो ।	*I should not have stayed.*	
मैले खानु हुँदैनथ्यो ।	*I should not have eaten.*	
	ALSO: used to be (was) necessary to...	
म बस्नु पर्थ्यो ।	*I used to have to stay.*	
मैले खानु पर्थ्यो ।	*I used to have to eat.*	
-एको (**हुना**)ले (गर्दा)	***because, by reason of...***(past events)	**10**
ढिलो आएको (हुना)ले (गर्दा)...	*Because of being late...*	
पानी परेको (हुना)ले (गर्दा) म गइनँ ।	*Because of it raining, I didn't go.*	
-ने **हुनाले**	***because...***(general reasons)	**10**
सुख्खा हुने हुनाले...	*Because it is dry (generally)...*	
पानी आउने हुनाले...	*Because water comes (generally)...*	
-न **हुने** NOUN	***something okay to...***	**22**
जान हुने ठाउँ	*place okay to go to*	
खान हुने कुरा	*something okay to eat*	
न-VERB ROOT-ई **नहुने** THING	***Thing that must be x-ed. Essential thing.***	**22**
हाम्रो लागि पानी नभई नहुने कुरा हो ।	*Water is essential for us (can't do without!).*	
सफा हावा हामीलाई नभई नहुने कुरा हो ।	*Clean air is a must for us (can't do without!).*	

-ए(पनि) हुन्छ	***okay if, doesn't matter if...***	**11**
नेपाली सिके(पनि) हुन्छ ।	*It's okay if you learn Nepali.*	
त्यहाँ अस्पताल बनाए(पनि) हुन्छ ।	*It's okay if you build a hospital there.*	
-नु/न हुन्छ	***permissible, can, okay to...***	**8**
नेपाली सिक्नु/सिक्न हुन्छ ।	*You can learn Nepali; it's okay.*	
त्यहाँ अस्पताल बनाउनु/बनाउन हुन्छ ।	*It's okay to build a hospital there.*	
-इहेर्नु	***try (out), test...***	**14**
लाइहेर्नुस् ।	*Try it on.*	
खाइहेर्नुस् । मीठो छ ।	*Try it out--taste and see. It's tasty.*	

APPENDIX 9

KEY TO PRACTICE EXERCISES

Chapter 1

1. *hun - equative* (These books are mine.)
2. *chhan - descriptive* (These fences are strong.)
   hun - equative (These fences are strong fences.)
3. *ho - equative* (That pen is a blue pen.)
4. *chha - existential* (Is there a nice pen?)
   ho - equative (Is that a nice pen?)
5. *ho - equative* (The room is a small room.)
6. *chha - descriptive* (The room is big.)
   ho - equative (The room is a big room.)
7. *hun - equative* (Those books are yours.)
8. *chha - descriptive* (That big bag is red.)
   ho - equative (That big bag is a red bag.)
9. *ho - equative* (your pen = a nice pen)
10. *chha - locative* (The bag is on the table.)
11. *ho - equative* (the door = a brown door)
12. *ho - equative* (Is that your red pen?)
    chha - existential (Do you have a red pen?)
13. *ho - equative* (this = a big house)
14. *chha - locative* (There is a book on the table.)
15. *ho - equative* (Is that a yellow bag?)
    chha - existential (Is there a yellow bag?)
16. *chha - locative* (There is a chair in the room.)
17. *ho - equative* (Is that your house?)
    chha - existential (Do you have a house?)
18. *chha - locative* (The curtain's on the window.)
19. *ho - equative* (this = a pen.)
20. *ho - equative* (Is that your notebook?)
    chha - existential (Do you have a notebook?)
21. *chha - loc.* (There's a blue book on the chair.)
22. *chhan - descriptive* (These pens are bad.)
    hun - equative (These pens are bad pens.)
23. *chha - locative* (There's a pencil in the bag.)
24. *chha - descriptive* (That book is small.)
    ho - equative (That book is a small book.)
25. *chha - locative* (There is a pen on the paper.)
26. *chha - descriptive* (This pen is blue.)
    ho - equative (This pen is a blue pen.)
27. *chha - locative* (There is a bag on the floor.)
28. *chhan - descriptive* (These houses are big.)
    hun - equative (These houses are big houses.)

29. *chha - locative* (The paper is on the table.)
30. *chha - descriptive* (My house is blue.)
    ho - equative (My house is a blue house.)
31. *chha - descriptive* (The wall is white.)
    ho - equative (The wall is a white wall.)
32. *chha - locative* (There's a curtain on the window.)

Chapter 3

3. a) पाउनुहुन्छ b) पाइन्छ c) चाहनुहुन्छ d) पाइन्छ e) गर्छु f) गरिन्छ
4. a) तपाईंलाई b) मलाई c) मलाई d) हामीलाई e) तपाईंलाई
   f) तपाईंलाई g) मलाई
5. a) त्यो त... b) ...छैन होला c) म त... d) सस्तोचाहिँ e) हस् लिनुस् f) ल...
   g) आलु त/चाहिँ h) ...होला i) ...दिनुस् न j) ल/हस्... k) बस्नुस् न
   l) मचाहिँ... m) ल...दिनुस् न
7. a) लुगा धुने साबुन b) चाहिने तरकारी c) गर्ने आमा d) बस्ने बा e) ...बोल्ने साहुजी
9. a) बजार जाने ? b) कति किन्ने ? c) कति दिने ? d) (तपाईं) ...धुनुहुन्छ? e) हामी फलफुल खान्छौं
10. a) अरू तरकारी दिनुस् । b) अरू दुईटा स्याउ लिनुस् । c) अर्को एक किलो स्याउ किन्नुस् ।
    d) अर्को स्याउ खानुस्। e) अरू दालभात खानुस्।

Chapter 4

1. a) टेबुलमा नै/टेबुलमै b) आमा नै/(आमै c) घरमा नै/घरै d) मेरो नै/मेरै
4. a) किनमेल गरेपछि तरकारी खान्छु । b) तपाईं बोलेपछि मेचमा बस्नुस् ।
   c) कितापमा सिकाएपछि हामी बोल्छौं । d) म टेबुलमा बसेपछि सिकाउनुस् ।
5. a) तरकारी किन्न b) पैसा दिन c) काम गर्न d) हिंन्दी सिकाउन ।
6. a) त्यो कलम निलो पनि छैन रातो पनि छैन । b) त्यो ट्याक्सी राम्रो पनि छैन नराम्रो पनि छैन ।
   c) पाँच रुपियाँ पनि होइन सात रुपियाँ पनि होइन । d) सुन्तला महँगो छैन सस्तो पनि छैन ।
7. a) (हामी) तरकारी किन्न जाऔं ? b) जाऔं । c) नेपाली बोलौं । d) स्याउ खाऔं ?

Chapter 5:

6. a) म मेचमा बसेर सिकाउँछु । b) तपाईं हात धोएर खानुस् ।
   c) ऊ त्यहाँ गएर साबुन किन्छ । d) उहाँ पैसा दिएर सामान लिनुहुन्छ ।
7. a) म नबसी(कन) सिकाउँछु । b) म नखाईकन लुगा धुन जान्छु ।
   c) हामी तरकारी नकिनिकन गयौं ।
8. a) काम गर्ने साहुजी b) घरमा बसेकी मेरी बहिनी c) नेपाली बोल्ने ड्राइभर
   d) घरमा बस्ने मेरी बहिनी e) काम गरेको साहुजी f) सुकेको रोटी
   g) कुचो लगाउने बहिनी h) पाटन जाने बाटो i) उमाल्ने पानी
   j) नेपाली बोल्ने ड्राइभर k) रोक्ने ट्याक्सी l) रोकेको ट्याक्सी
   m) उमालेको पानी n) कुचो लगाएको दिदी
11. a) म तरकारी किन्न जान्छु । b) उहाँ नेपाली सिक्न जानुहुन्छ । c) उनीहरू ट्याक्सी लिन जान्छन् ।

Chapter 6

1. a) म घर जाँदै छु । b) म घरमा जाँदै छु । c) म बजारमा जाँदै छु ।
4. a) तपाईंलाई g) म h) तपाईंलाई i) मलाई j) तपाईं k) तपाईं
   n) मलाई o) मलाई

5. a) म गाजर खाइदिन्छु । b) मेरो भाइले सुन्तला खाइदियो । c) म बिस्तारै नेपाली बोलिदिन्छु ।
d) बसिदिनुस् ।e) अलिअलि नेपाली बोलिदिनुस् ।
f) तपाईं हामीलाई नेपाली सिकाइदिनुस्, हामी तपाईंलाई अङ्ग्रेजी सिकाइदिन्छौं ।
6. a) नि b) क्यारे c) र d) ओहो e) हजुर f) है
7. a) यहाँ बस्नु ठिक छ ? b) भोलि तपाईंलाई फोन गर्नु ठिक छ ?
c) क्लासमा गफ गर्नु ठिक छ ? d) क्लासमा खानु ठिक छ ?
8. a) हिजो तपाईंले फोन गर्न बिर्सनुभयो । b) मैले तपाईंलाई मेरो नाम भन्न बिर्सें ।
c) हामीले तरकारी किन्न बिर्स्यौं । d) मैले, "हजार" भन्न बिर्सें ।
9. a) मैले उहाँलाई भेट्न पाएँ । b) माफ गर्नुस्, मैले तपाईंलाई फोन गर्न पाइनँ । c) ऊ घर जान पायो ।

Chapter 7

13. a) यो पानी खान सकिन्छ । b) दश मिनेटमा बजारमा पुग्न सकिन्छ । c) त्यो नदी तर्न सकिन्छ ।
14. a) उसले पानी खान थाल्यो/सुरु गऱ्यो । b) म बजार जान थालें/मैले बजार जान सुरु गरें ।
c) हामीले खोला तर्न थाल्यौं/सुरु गऱ्यौं । d) तपाईं पहिले बोल्न थाल्नस्/सुरु गर्नुस् ।
e) उनीहरू त्यहाँ जान थाले/उहाँहरू त्यहाँ जान थाल्नुभयो ।

Chapter 8

8. a) मैले खाइसकें । b) त्यहाँ अस्पताल बनिसक्यो ।
c) म आएको दुई घण्टा भइसक्यो । d) मैले त्यो सिकिसकें ।
10. a) म नेपाल आएको एक वर्ष भयो । b) उहाँ नेपाल आउनुभएको दुई वर्ष भयो ।
c) तपाईं क्लासमा आउनुभएको कति भयो ? d) म क्लासमा आएको एक घण्टा भयो ।
11. a) म नेपाली सिक्नका लागि आएको छु । b) म तरकारी किन्नका लागि जान्छु ।
c) तिनी सोमबार हाम्रो घर सफा गर्नको लागि आउँछिन् ।
d) ऊ हामीलाई एउटा खबर दिनको लागि आएको छ ।
e) ऊ हामीलाई खबर दिनका लागि आएको छ । f) नेपालीमा कुरा गर्नका लागि मलाई फोन गर्नुस् ।
13. a) हिजो एकजना रबिन भन्ने साथी आउनुभयो । b) भोलि हामी धुलिखेल भन्ने ठाउँमा घुम्न जान्छौं ।
c) राम्चा भन्ने(साहुजी)को पसलमा नेपाली टोपी पाइन्छ ।
d) म शमा भन्ने शिक्षकसँग नेपाली सिक्छु ।
e) भेटीकन सिटी भन्ने संसारको सानो देशमा पोप जोन पाल बस्नुहुन्छ ।

Chapter 9

6. a) वाकवाक लागी ऊ सुत्यो । b) मेरो भाइ धेरै कुरा सोधी बस्छ ।
7. a) वाकवाक नलागी ऊ सुत्यो । b) मेरो भाइ धेरै कुरा नसोधी बस्छ ।
8. a) काठमाडौंभन्दा पोखरा राम्रो छ । b) पोखराभन्दा काठमाडौं ठूलो छ ।
c) पोखराभन्दा रुकुम टाढा छ ।d) रोटीभन्दा म:म: मिठो छ ।
10. a) मलाई ज्वर आयो। b) मलाई ज्वर आएन।
c) मलाई ज्वर आयो। d) मलाई ज्वर आएको छैन।
11. a) त्यो साहुजी मेरो बाजस्तै देखिन्छ । b) मेरी दिदी मेरी आमाजस्तै हुनुहुन्छ ।
c) यो आँपजस्तो मिठो छ । d) त्यो संस्था टीमजस्तै छ ।
12. a) मैले गरे(को) जस्तो उहाँ गर्न सक्नुहुन्न ।
b) नेपालमा किनमेल गर्नु मेरो देशमा किनमेल गर्नुजस्तो होइन ।
c) नेपालीले पकाएजस्तै पकाउनुस् ।

13. a) ज्वर आएजस्तो गर्नुस् । b) जिउ दुखेजस्तो गर्नुस् ।
14. a) यसबाहेक b) औलोबाहेक नेपालमा अरू रोग पनि छन् ।
c) मबाहेक कोही गएन । d) नूनबाहेक हामीलाई अरू केही चाहिँदैन ।

Chapter 10

10. a) छ बज्यो ...ने बेला भयो । b) सवा दश बज्यो ...ने बेला भयो । c) साढे बाह्र बज्यो ...ने बेला भयो ।
d) सवा दुई बज्यो ...ने बेला भयो । e) पौने सात बज्यो ...ने बेला भयो । f) दश बज्यो ...ने बेला भयो ।
11. a) पानी पर्न लाग्यो । b) जाडो मौसम आउन लाग्यो । c) हामी जान लाग्यौं ।
13a. i) देख्न नसक्ने मान्छे ii) जुन मान्छेले देख्न सक्दैन iii) जसले देख्न सक्दैन
b. i) दृष्टि नभएकालाई अन्धो भनिन्छ ।
ii) जुन मान्छेको दृष्टि छैन त्यसलाई अन्धो भनिन्छ ।
iii) जसको दृष्टि छैन त्यसलाई अन्धो भनिन्छ ।
c. i) सन्तान नभएको मान्छे ii) जुन मान्छेको सन्तान छैन iii) जसको सन्तान छैन
d. i) मेरो घरमा काम गर्ने मान्छे
ii) जुन मान्छे मेरो घरमा काम गर्छ iii) जो मेरो घरमा काम गर्छ

Chapter 11

2. f) नउमालेको पानी खाए हुन्छ । g) उसले हिन्दी बोले हुन्छ । h) उनी भोलि आए हुन्छ ।
i) पसल घरनिर भए हुन्छ । j) म होसियार भए हुन्छ । k) मैले महँगो तरकारी मात्र किने हुन्छ ।
3. a) पानी परे तापनि म पिकनिक जान्छु । b) गाडी ढिलो भए पनि म रिसाएको छैन ।
c) त्यो क्षेत्र सुदूर भए पनि मान्छेहरू त्यहाँ बस्छन् ।
d) पानी नपरेको एक हप्ता भए तापनि बिरुवाहरू अझै हरिया छन् । e) धेरै हिउँ पग्ले पनि नदी सानो छ ।
f) मेरो विचारमा आकाशमा बादल नभए(ता) पनि पानी पर्छ ।
g) झरना सुन्दर भए(ता) पनि त्यो पानी नपिउनुस् ।
h) नेपालमा विकास भए(ता) पनि धेरै विकास गर्न बाँकी छ ।
i) नेपाल सानो देश भए(ता) पनि संसारभरि प्रसिद्ध छ ।

4.

near the mountain	पहाडनिर	between the village and lake	गाउँ र तालमध्ये
towards the border	सिमानानिर	on the other side of the ridge	डाँडापारि
beyond the sea	समुद्रभन्दा माथि	from my house to...	घरदेखि/बाट अफिससम्म
towards the stream	खोलातिर	in the room	कोठामा
in front of the hotel	होटेलको अगाडि	to/as far as the river	नदीसम्म
below the house	घरतल	facing him	उहाँका अघि
on top of the summit	शिखरको टुप्पामा	among the diseases	रोगहरूमध्ये
near the car	गाडीनिर	behind the school	स्कूलपछाडि
between PK and KTM	पोखरा र काठमाडौंमध्ये	all over the village	गाउँभरि
outside the school	स्कूलबाहिर	in the bag	झोलामा
among the problems	समस्याहरूमध्ये	in front of the gate	ढोकाका अगाडि
outside the clinic	क्लिनिकबाहिर	in three hours	तीन घण्टामा
beyond the forest	वनभन्दा माथि	inside the house	घरभित्र
on the other side of the forest	वनपारि	all evening long	बेलुकाभरि
below the hospital	अस्पतालतल	facing the road	बाटोअघि
behind the house	घरको पछाडि	inside the book	किताबभित्र

6. a) मेरो धेरै काम गर्न बाँकी छ । b) धेरै विकास गर्न बाँकी छ ।
7. a) सिध्याउन हतार गर्नुस् । b) खाइसक्न हतार गर्नुस् ।
c) म ट्याक्सी लिन हतार गर्दै छु । d) उनीहरूले घर जान हतार गरे ।

Chapter 12

3. a) मेरो बा सुखी मान्छे भनेर चिनिनुहुन्छ । b) साहुजी सोझो मान्छे भनेर चिनिनुहुन्छ ।
c) डाक्टर अग्लो मान्छे भनेर चिनिनुहुन्छ । d) नेपाललाई पहाडी देश भनेर चिनिन्छ ।
4. e) नेपाल पहाडी देश हो भनेर... f) भारत गर्मी ठाउँ हो भनेर...
g) बाटो साँघुरो छ भनेर...
7. a) म तिमीलाई भनिरहँदिनँ । b) हामी दाल भात खाइरहँदैनौं । c) तिमी पैसा मागिरहन्छौ ।
d) म कुरा गरिरहन्छु । e) उहाँ पर्खिरहनुहुन्छ । f) म दिनभरि मेरो छाप्रो छाइरहँदिनँ ।
9. a) उनी तपाई»लाई जान दिन्छिन् । b) मलाई यहाँ बस्न दिनुस् । c) मलाई पोखरा जान दिनुस् ।
10a. i) धेरै पानी पर्‍यो । त्यसकारण बाटो बिग्रियो । ii) धेरै पानी पर्‍यो । त्यसैले बाटो बिग्रियो ।
iii) बाटो बिग्रियो किनभने धेरै पानी पर्‍यो । iv) धेरै पानी परेर बाटो बिग्रियो ।
v) धेरै पानी परेका (कारण)ले बाटो बिग्रियो । vi) धेरै पानी परेको हुनाले बाटो बिग्रियो ।
11a. i) शेरा खेलिरहेको उहाँले हेर्नुभयो । ii) शेरा खेलेको मैले देखेँ ।
iii) शेरा खेलिरहेको देखेर उहाँहरूलाई खुसी लाग्यो ।

Chapter 13

3. a) त्यो मान्छे श्रीमतीलाई पिट्छ । ऊ दुष्ट रहेछ । b) दुलाभित्र के छ ? ए...सानो मुसा रहेछ ।
c) म दूध किन्न गएँ । तर पसल बन्द रहेछ ।
4a. a) त्यो आइमाई फुर्तिसँग हिँड्छे । त्यो बूढी रहिनछ । b) उसले मसँग राम्रो कुरा गर्‍यो । ऊ दुष्ट रहेनछ ।
c) मैले दुलाभित्र खोजेँ । तर त्यहाँ मुसो रहेनछ । d) उसले दूध किनेर ल्यायो । पसल बन्द रहेनछ ।
4b. a) उहाँ हिँड्न सक्नुहुन्न । बूढी हुनुभएछ । b) ऊ श्रीमतीलाई पिट्दो रहेछ । ऊ दुष्ट भएछ ।
c) दुलोभत्र मुसो छैन । मुसो भागेछ । d) म ढिलो पुगेँ । पसल बन्द भएछ ।
5. a) तपाईंले नेपाली बोल्नुभएको रहेनछ । b) उसले आफ्नी आमालाई गाली गरेकी रहिछ ।
c) तिमीले काम गर्न छोडेका रहेछौ । d) उसले मेरो किताब लुकाएको रहेछ ।
6. a) तपाईंले नेपाली बोल्नुभएको रहेछ । b) उसले आफ्नी आमालाई गाली गरेकी रहिनछ ।
c) तिमीले काम गर्न छोडेका रहेनछौ । d) उसले मेरो किताब लुकाएको रहेनछ ।
7. a) उनीहरू नेपाली बोल्दा रहेछन् । b) ऊ आफ्नै आमालाई गाली गर्दी रहिछे ।
c) तिमी कहिल्यै काम गर्दा रहेनछौ । d) नेपालमा उनीहरू बाख्रा पाल्दा रहेछन् ।
10. a) मैले नखाऊ भन्दाभन्दै उसले त्यो पानी खायो । b) मैले नजानुस् भन्दाभन्दै उहाँ जानुभयो ।
11. a) उहाँ बोल्दाबोल्दै रुनुभयो । उसले बोल्दैबोल्दै खायो ।
b) गाउँमा केटाकेटीहरू दिउँसो गाई चराउँदाचराउँदै सुत्छन् । उनीहरू गाई चराउँदैचराउँदै खेल्थे ।
12. a) उहाँले मलाई बैठकमा बोल्न लगाउनुभयो । b) हामीले बाहुनलाई कथा सुनाउन लगायौं ।
13. a) सकेजति भन्नुस् । b) सकेजति खानुस् ।
c) सकेजति लिनुस् । d) तपाईंसँग भएजति मलाई दिनुस् ।

Chapter 14

5. a) सबैजना मर्छन् / हरेक मान्छे मर्छ b) आमाले छोराछोरीलाई खुवाउँछिन् ।
c) स्वास्नीमानिसहरूले गहना लगाउँछन् । d) मान्छेहरू सबै ठाउँमा 'कोक' खान्छन् ।

6. a) नेपालको सन्दर्भमा धेरै गाउँहरूमा बिजुली छैन । b) यस सन्दर्भमा घरभित्र टोपी लगाउनु ठीक छ ।
c) उहाँले कुन सन्दर्भमा त्यसो भन्नुभयो ? d) चाडपर्वको सन्दर्भमा उनीहरू अझै त्यो लगाउँछन् ।
9. a) किन लगाउँदैनन् र ? b) किन हुँदैनन् र ?
10. a) म तपाईंलाई भनिबस्दिनँ । b) हामी दालभात खाइबस्दैनौं ।
c) पैसा मागी नबस । d) म कुरा गरिबस्छु ।
11. a) म तपाईंलाई फेरि भन्दै भन्दिनँ । b) हामी गाईको मासु खाँदै खाँदैनौं ।
c) म त्यो सारी लगाउँदै लगाउँदिनँ । d) उनीहरू मसँग कुरा गर्दै गर्दैनन् ।
12. a) यो काम सकेसम्म चाँडै/छिटो गर्न खोज्नुस् । b) एक हप्तासम्म नेपाली बोल्न खोज्नुस् ।
c) उनीहरू(ले) घर जान खोजे । d) उसले पैसा लुकाउन खोज्यो ।
13. a) खाइहेर्नुस् । मीठो छ । b) यो किताप राम्रो छ । पढिहेर्नुस् ।
14. a) आउनुभएकोमा धन्यवाद । b) मलाई भन्नुभएकोमा धन्यवाद ।
c) तपाईं आउनुभएकोमा मलाई खुसी लाग्यो । d) तपाईंले हामीलाई भन्नुभएकोमा खुशी लाग्यो ।

Chapter 15

1. a) भने b) भन्ने c) भने d) भने e) भन्ने f) भने g) भन्ने
h) भन्ने i) भने j) भनेर k) भनी l) भनें m) भनेर n) भनेर
o) भनेर p) भने q) भनेर r) भन्ने s) भनेको
2. a) म एक घण्टामा फर्किनँ भने... c) तिनले भनिन्, "_____"
d) मेरो स्तर भने... e) सीता भन्ने केटी... f) जातको चलन भने...
g) ...भन्ने मलाई थाहा छ । h) "म जान्छु" भनेर... i) उसले म गएँ भनेर...
j) तिनी धनी शासक भनेर चिनिन्छन् । k) थकाइ नलागोस् भनेर...
l) मैले भनेको के हो भने...
3. भनेपछि, भनेअनुसार, भने पनि, भनेजस्तै, भन्ने बेलामा, भनेजति, भनेको जति, भनेको सुनेर, भन्ने हुनाले, भनेका कारण
4. a) त्यो भनेर मैले साथीलाई छक्क पारें । b) मैले सुकेको पातले आगो पारें ।
c) मैले रोटी सानो-सानो टुक्रा पारें । d) त्यो खाना खाएपछि म बिरामी परें ।
e) मलाई यो प्रश्न साँच्चै गाह्रो पर्‍यो । f) यात्रा गर्दाखेरि हामीलाई एउटा समस्या पर्‍यो ।
5. a) स्याउसमेत (गरेर) हामीसँग धेरै फलफूल थियो । b) सबै काम गर्नेहरू समेत घरमा बाह्र जना बस्थे ।
6. a) उसले गर्नुपर्ने काम नै अर्को छ -- उसले बाघलाई खुवाउँछ । b) खाना नै अर्को --सबैकुरा पिरो छ ।
c) उहाँको स्तर नै अर्को छ-गाउँको मुखियाभन्दा पनि उच्च । d) उहाँको छोरा नै अर्को ... कहिल्यै कुरा गर्दैन ।
7. a) ऊ तयार नहुन सक्छ । b) तिनले पिरो खाना नखान सक्छन् ।
c) म पाँच बजेसम्ममा सिध्याउन सक्छु। d) बिरामी मर्न सक्छ ।
10. a) मैले भात खाइहालें । b) पानी पर्लाजस्तो छ । म त गइहालें ।
c) ऊ यहाँ छैन । गइहाल्यो । d) उठिहाल्नुस् ।

Chapter 16

1/2. a) भोलि आउन पाइन्छ/पाईंदैन । b) नेपालमा बाटोको बायाँतिर गाडी चलाउन पाइन्छ/पाईंदैन ।
c) समाचार पछि सुन्न पाइन्छ/पाईंदैन ।
3. a) भोलि म आउन पाउँछु/पाउँदिनँ । b) तपाईं नेपालमा बाटाको बायाँतिर गाडी चलाउन पाउनुहुन्छ/पाउनुहुन्न ।
c) तपाईं समाचार पछि सुन्न पाउनुहुन्छ/पाउनुहुन्न ।
4. a) बस आयो ? आएको छैन । आइसक्यो । b) पानी पर्‍यो ? परेको छैन । परिसक्यो ।
c) खाना तयार भयो ? भएको छैन । भइसक्यो । d) जाने बेला भयो ? भएको छैन । भइसक्यो ।

6. a) मिलेर गृहकार्य गर्नुस् । b) तपाईंको र मेरो विचार मिल्छ ।
c) केटीहरूको उमेर मिल्छ । d) दुईटा बाटो मिल्ने ठाउँमा बायाँतिर जानुस् ।
e) यो पाइन्ट मलाई मिल्दैन । f) अफिसमा जुत्ता लगाउन मिल्दैन ।

8. a) मैले गृहकार्य गर्न भ्याइनँ । b) तिनले भाडा माझ्न भ्याइनन् । c) उहाँले जान भ्याउनुभयो ।

Chapter 18

1. a) सहन सक्नेजति जाडो घटेको छैन । b) चाहिनेजति रुख रोप्न सकिएको छैन ।
c) खानलाई पुग्नेजति अन्न उमारिन्छ ?

2. a) मैले विचार गरेकोजति मोल घट्यो । b) किसानहरूले चाहिएकोजति धान रोपे ।
c) तपाईंले भनेकोजति तरकारी उमारिएको छैन ।

4. a) तपाईंले टिकट किन्नुहुने हो भने.. b) मैले समय बचाउने हो भने...
c) हामीले मकै रोप्ने हो भने...

5. a) सबैले बुझ्ने गरी बताउनुस् । b) उहाँलाई मनपर्ने गरी सुनाउनुस् ।

6. a) आँधी चलुन्जेल उहाँलाई डर लाग्यो । b) गर्मी हुन्जेल/भइन्जेल लाम्खुट्टे आउँछ ।
c) किताब पढुन्जेल मैले अध्ययन गरिनँ । d) हिँडुन्जेल उहाँले कुरा गर्नुभयो ।
e) पैसा हुन्जेल मान्छेहरू चोर्छन् । f) वर्षा हुन्जेल/भइन्जेल गहुँ हुर्कन्छ ।

8. a) मैले खान सिध्याएँ । b) मैले खान सिध्याइसकें ।
c) हामीले यो किताब सिध्याएका छैनौं । d) उनीहरूले पढ्न सिध्याइसके ।

Chapter 19

1. a) उसले नकल पारेको थाहा पाउनुभयो ? b) आज मैले पौडी खेलेको उहाँले थाहा पाउनुभयो ।

5. a) हामीले केही गरेका थिएनौं । b) मैले उहाँलाई किताप दिएको थिएँ ।
c) उनीहरूले मलाई नाच्न भनेका थिए । d) उनीहरूले धान रोप्न सिध्याएका छन् ।

6. a) हामी जाँदै थियौं/गइरहेका थियौं । b) म मेरो किताप पढ्दै थिएँ/पढिरहेको थिएँ ।
c) उनीहरू नाच्दै थिए/नाचिरहेका थिए । d) उनीहरू धेरै हल्ला गर्दै थिए/गरिहेका थिए ।

11. a) काठमाडौंको दाँजोमा नेपालका अरू सहरमा कम जनसङ्ख्या छ । b) तपाईंको दाँजोमा ....
c) मेरो दाँजोमा .... d) नेपालको दाँजोमा भारत ठूलो छ ।

12. a) चिनी कम छ । अरू अलिकति दिनुस् । b) कममा दिनुस् / कम गर्नुस्
c) तपाईंको काम कम गाह्रो छैन । d) कम भीड छ! धेरै मान्छे थिए ।

Chapter 20

1. a) बिहा गर्ने विचार b) घर बनाउने विचार
c) हामीले बजार जाने विचार गर्‍यौं । d) एक महिनामा मेरो यो किताब सिध्याउने बिचार छ।

4. a) म त्यो केरा खान्थें/खाने थिएँ । b) तपाईंलाई फोन गर्थें/गर्ने थिएँ ।
c) ट्याक्सी लिन्थें/लिने थिएँ । d) मकै रोप्नु हुन्थ्यो/रोप्नु हुने थियो ।
e) अरू पैसा दिनु हुन्थ्यो/दिनु हुने थियो । f) हामीले ध्यान दिने थियौं ।

9. a) मैले त्यो केरा खानु पर्थ्यो । b) तपाईंलाई फोन गर्नु पर्थ्यो ।
c) ट्याक्सी लिनु पर्थ्यो । d) मकै रोप्नु पर्थ्यो ।
e) उहाँले मलाई अरू पैसा दिनु पर्थ्यो । f) हामीले ध्यान दिनु पर्थ्यो ।

10. a) मैले त्यो केरा खान हुँदैनथ्यो । b) तपाईंलाई फोन गर्न हुँदैनथ्यो ।
c) ट्याक्सी लिन हुँदैनथ्यो । d) मकै रोप्न हुँदैनथ्यो ।
e) उहाँले मलाई अरू पैसा दिन हुँदैनथ्यो । f) हामीले खेल्नु हुँदैनथ्यो ।
11. a) मान्छेहरू लामो बाटो हिँड्नु पर्थ्यो । b) बस लिनुपर्थ्यो / बसमा जानु पर्थ्यो ।
c) बस लिनु पर्दैनथ्यो । d) म हिँड्नु पर्थ्यो ।
12. a) मलाई केरा खान मन पर्थ्यो । b) तपाईंलाई फोन गर्न मन पर्थ्यो ।
c) मलाई ट्याक्सी लिन मन पर्थ्यो । d) उहाँलाई मकै रोप्न मन पर्थ्यो ।
e) हामीलाई तास खेल्न मन पर्थ्यो । f) मलाई केरा खान मन पर्थ्यो ।

Chapter 21

3. See Appendix 2: Numerals.
4a. i) उसले "म जान्छु" भन्यो । ii) उसले म जान्छु भनेर भन्यो । iii) उसले भन्यो कि ऊ जान्छ ।
a. i) उसले "ऊ जान्छ" भन्यो । ii) म जान्छु भनेर उसले भन्यो । iii) उसले भन्यो कि उहाँ जानुहुन्छ ।
c. i) तिनले भनिन्... ii) तिनले सकेसम्म कोसिस गर्नुस् भनेर भनिन् ।
iii) तिनले भनिन् कि सकेसम्म...
d. i) रामले भन्यो, "म..." ii) रामले म...भनेर भन्यो । iii) रामले भन्यो कि ऊ सकेसम्म...
e. i) मैले भनें, "म..." ii) मैले म जाँदिनँ भनेर भनें । iii) मैले भनें कि म जाँदिनँ ।
5. a) यो काम सिध्याउन मलाई एक घण्टा भए पुग्छ
b) यो किताप सिध्याउन मलाई एक महिना भए पुग्छ । c) उसलाई गाउँमा पुग्न तीन दिन भए पुग्छ ।
d) अस्पताल बनाउन तीन वर्ष भए पुग्छ । e) मलाई सुत्न छ घण्टा भए पुग्छ ।
6. a) मलाई यो किताप पढ्न पुग्यो । b) कर्मचारीहरूलाई तलब दिन पुग्यो ।
c) तपाईंलाई त्यो घरमा बस्न पुग्यो ? d) उनीहरूलाई पढ्न पुग्यो ।

Chapter 22

3. a) उसले भन्यो कि तिमी जथाभाबी बोल्छौ ।
b) उहाँले भन्नुभयो कि मरेपछि उहाँलाई जलाएको चाहनुहुन्छ ।
c) मैले विचार गरें कि हामीले सिध्याइसक्यौं । d) मैले सुनें कि भोलि छुट्टी छ ।
e) मेरो आशा छ कि म तपाईंजस्तै नेपाली बोलूँ ।
4. a) तपाईंले जस्तो नेपाली बोलेर साध्य छैन । b) उहाँलाई बुझेर साध्य छैन ।
5. a) जन्मेपछि धेरै दुःख भोगेर मर्नु पर्छ ।
b) धेरै सामान बिक्री गरेर पैसा कमाएर आराम गर्नेहरू छन् ।
c) गाउँमा मान्छेहरू छिटो बिहे गरेर धेरै बच्चा पाएर दिनदिनै धेरै काम गरेर बिताउँछन् ।
7. a) नखाई नहुने खाना b) नगई नहुने ठाउँ
c) हामीलाई बाँच्नको लागि पानी नभई नहुने कुरा हो ।
d) नसम्झी नहुने नाम e) नगरी नहुने काम
8. a) खान हुने कुरा b) जान हुने ठाउँ
9. a) म नदी तर्न डराउँछु । म मर्छु होला । b) ऊ अँध्यारो कोठामा सुत्न डराउँछ ।
c) तपाईं नेपाली बोल्न नडराउनुस् । d) किन तपाईं मलाई भन्न डराउनुहुन्छ ?

Chapter 23

1. a) म उहाँको सट्टामा काम गर्छु ।
   b) साइकलको सट्टामा अहिले उसको मोटरसाइकल छ ।
   c) राजाको सट्टामा जनतामा सार्वभौमसत्ता छ ।
   d) पोखरा जानुको सट्टामा म धरान जान्छु ।
   e) मलाई यसको सट्टामा त्यो दिनुस् ।
2. a) तिमीले यो नखाई हुँदैन ।
   b) तिमी पोखरा नगई हुँदैन ।
   c) उनले इमानदारीसँग राज्य नगरी हुँदैन ।
   d) चुनाव सफल नभई हुँदैन ।
   e) के गर्ने ? घुस नखुवाई हुँदैन ।
   f) मेरो कमाइ पुग्दैन । मैले घुस नखाई हुँदैन ।
3. a) मैले यो नखाई भएन ।
   b) म(लाई) पोखरा नगई भएन ।
   c) उनलाई इमानदारीसँग राज्य नगरी भएन ।
   d) चुनाव सफल नभई भएन ।
   e) के गर्ने ? घुस नखुवाई भएन ।
   f) मेरो कमाइ पुग्दैन । मैले घुस नखाइ भएन ।
6. a) मद्वारा स्याउ खाइयो ।
   b) उहाँद्वारा यो गरियो ।
   c) मैले यो काम उहाँद्वारा गराएँ ।
   d) चुनाव सफल नभई भएन ।
   e) रेडियोद्वारा खबर सुनियो ।

APPENDIX 10

ENGLISH TRANSLATION OF TEXTS
(Chapter 9-23)

*(**Note:** Translation is literal in order to illustrate certain structures.)*

CHAPTER 9: CONCERNING HEALTH

Mike, who slept having eaten delicious food yesterday evening, suddenly got up at two o'clock at night. He had a bit of a fever and felt a little cold. His body also ached a little. After some time, his stomach hurt a little. He also had diarrhea and was nauseated. He didn't know of (couldn't remember having) this kind of stomach upset ever before. He thought (wondered), "Will I be bedridden now? Will I not be able to see anything else in Nepal? Will I have to return to my own country?"

The next day, he got up very late. (His) stools were still thin like water. He went to the doctor. The doctor was an old friend of his. Having studied his symptoms he said, "You have diarrhea. In (during) this season, most foreigners get diarrhea. It may be because of bacteria. You may get better on your own. In order to get better quickly, it's best to take a kind of antibiotic. You should (need to) eat food that has lots of liquid. You should drink water that has *Jiwan Jal* (oral rehydration solution) mixed in because you have already wasted (lost) lots of water and salt from your body." He was surprised to hear what the doctor said. After two days, he got better and began to stroll around.

While staying in Nepal, foreigners need to be careful (in regards to their health). They need to be alert particularly in all matters of eating and drinking. Seeing Nepalis eat food they consider tasty, you yourself may also feel like eating (the same). Seeing others drink tap water directly, you yourself may also feel like doing the same, right? For you to be able to do that will probably take a long time. As for now, don't even do so by forgotting. Not only foreigners, but Nepalis as well get stomach problems from food and drink (things). Diarrhea and gastro-intestis are commonly found illnesses in Nepal. Knowingly or unknowingly the wrong food eaten becomes just like poison (causes the same effect).

Besides this, other diseases are also found in Nepal. For example: malaria in the Terai (from the bite of a mosquito), hepatitis, meningitis, encephalitis, TB, venereal diseases, etc. Sometimes the cold flu also gives a little trouble. Some diseases contaminate (move) and spread like an epidemic. Some diseases don't move that easily. For some diseases vaccinations are available, and for some diseases they are not. Some vaccinations are expensive , others are cheap. Before coming to Nepal, one needs to know a little bit about these things. It's better to prevent disease than to treat it.

For illnesses, one shouldn't buy and take medicine on your own. A doctor's advice is important. Which medicine, how to take it, how many tablets to take in a day, at what time, etc.--all this should be done having asked a doctor. In the city there are lots of doctors and doctors clinics. But in the village they are not available. For common illnesses a health worker can give help. But for major illnesses one must go (come) to a city. Treatment for some diseases may not be possible in Nepal. In other words, for those diseases it may be necessary to go to a foreign country.

CHAPTER 10: NEPAL'S WEATHER AND CLIMATE

Look at a map of Nepal. Nepal is spread from Mechi in the East to Mahakali in the West. But the weather of all these places of Nepal are not the same. The weather here is different according to (depending on) the place. The most rain falls in Nepal's Eastern Terai. However far we go towards Nepal's west (that's how much) less rain falls. In West Nepal it rains the least. Furthermore, it rains less in the hills than here in the Terai. It rains the very little in the hilly region of West Nepal.

In the same way, most of the rain falls in Asar and Saun. And here, in the winter it is dry. Between the winter and rainy seasons, sometimes storm winds blow and it rains with thunder. Sometimes it even hails here. At that time, it's mostly dry and dusty. But the weather between monsoon and winter seasons is very pleasant. It doesn't rain as much at this time and the natural view looks green and clean.

Because of low elevation from (above) sea level, the Terai is hot. As we go towards the West, (so) the heat increases. It is the hottest in Nepal's West Terai. Here, it is less hot in the hills than in the Terai. It is coldest in the Himals. As we go towards the North, (so) the ground elevation increases. Therefore the cold also increases.

In this way, it is hottest in Chait and Baishakh and coldest in Push and Magh. Because it is hot and dry in Baishakh and Jeth water becomes a problem. We sweat, get sick and life is difficult. In Push and Magh (in other words, the winter) it is not only cold; it's also dry. At that time it's foggy and misty. Sometimes in the morning, there is also dew and frost. Thick clothes, quilts, jackets, sweaters and a lot of food are the requirements of this time.

CHAPTER 11: THE COUNTRY NEPAL (GEOGRAPHY)

Nepal is between China and India. Even though this country is small it is extremely beautiful. There are different kinds of natural beauty. The natural beauties are: many big and small rivers, streams, waterfalls, lakes, green forests, white mountains, etc.

In the Northern part there is the high Himalayan Mountain Range. There is even Nepalese territory on the other side of some of the Himals. The Himalayas divide the border of Nepal and Tibet. Nepal's Northern region is called the Himalayan region. The big rivers have been flowing with the melted snow of the Himals. If lots of snow melts, the rivers get very big. The highest mountain in the world, Sagarmatha, is in Nepal. Because of this summit, Nepal is famous throughout the world.

Because there is snow (snow upon snow) twelve months (all year), there are no kinds of vegetation. Towards the base of the Himals a little thorny vegetation is seen (found). A little below that vicinity, a thin inhabitancy of people begins to be seen. There, there are mainly Tibetan and Sherpa settlements. There, in the winter months (particularly) the snow falls thick. Because Himalayas are the source of (some) main big rivers the water is clean.

(Now), after the Himal Region let's talk about the hilly region. From the Eastern hills to the mid-Western hills, settlements of people are seen well (plentiful). In the far Western hills it is a little desolate and hot. In the hilly region, there is all type of people's habitation. There is also various kinds of vegetation in the hilly regions here. Many villages and cities are in this region. There are also commercial areas here. Here is the pleasant terrain of valleys, rivers, streams ridges, etc. (However), the problem of transportation hasn't yet decreased here. In many places motor-able roads and electricity has not yet arrived.

The Terai is a large plain. Because of low elevation from (above) sea level, the Terai is hot. The Terai itself is the best plain for agriculture. Furthermore, because even if you dig a little bit water comes in the Terai, there is convenience of irrigation. The Terai can be called the granary of Nepal. In this very region there are also industrial cities. The most populated region is here. One of the problems here is people's tendency to settle a village (settlement) by denuding the jungle. There is more development work yet to be done in the Western Terai than the Eastern Terai. If the Western Terai was more developed, the population would also probably increase there also.

CHAPTER 12: NEPAL'S WILDERNESS (BIOLOGY)

Many know the importance of forests. Some people probably don't know the importance of this. However, much of the forests have already been destroyed. Many disadvantages have resulted from this. Illegal felling of trees has not been stopped. The forests are being destroyed because of the population increasing and people's bad behavior.

Now lets talk about some of the trees, plants and wild animals of Nepal's forests.

- **Saal:** The wood of this tree is used for building houses. Many saal trees are found in the jungles of the Terai. This is also the tree that has most been destroyed. But if it is protected in the places where it is cut down, it comes (sprouts) and grows on its own. This tree is also used for its branches and leaves. Saal tree leaves are used commercially. This (trees) proper management is important.

- **Pine:** Another tree often found in Nepal is the pine. There are many kinds of pine. Various kinds of pine are found from the hills to the highlands. Its wood is a little soft. In the hilly region it is often used for reforestation.

- **Bamboo (thick and thin):** Thick and thin bamboo is used for many, many things. It is used is for lots of things: thatching houses making houses, making huts, etc. Newly sprouted bamboo shoots are also often used for food. Bamboo (a thick and thin) are wild and they are also cultivated.

- **Sisau:** Sisau is a standard wood for making nice furniture. Formerly, wild sisau was used a lot. But nowadays it is cultivated. They say its cultivation brings lots of profit.

Some wild animals:

- **One horned rhino:** This is only found in Nepal, India, Burma and some places in Africa. It's skin is very thick. Though its vision is weak it has powerful hearing and smelling. It likes solitary places and it may attack us if we're in front of it. When going to (at) Chitwan, it's fun to mount an elephant and watch the grazing of rhinos.
- **Striped tiger:** This is known as the king of the jungle. It's said to be the vehicle of goddess Durga. On its yellow body are long, black stripes. It cannot live in a small area. In Nepal its population is around 250.
- **Alligator (slender nosed):** The main crocodile species in Nepal is the slender nosed alligator. Its head is long. It has rows of upper and lower teeth. Fish is its main diet. It also eats other lives (living things) of the land and water. Its habitat is the large rivers and tributaries of South Asia.
- **Snow leopard:** The snow leopard is found in the Himals. Just like the tiger is covers a large area. It lives in the highlands, cliffs and rocky hills as well as the places without trees. It can be recognized by its short snout, wide forehead and steep chin. Its body is light brown but its front part is white.

CHAPTER 13: THE STORY OF THE OLD GOAT

Because Punkhuñ's mother died when she was small, her father brought a stepmother (took another wife). As for the stepmother, she was very wicked and malicious. She gave Punkhuñ only a little bit of food; as for work, she made her do however much she saw. She scolded punkhuñ for everything. Gradually, the father also stopped loving her. Because she (Punkhuñ) didn't have anyone else in the world (that was her own), she had to tolerate all these things.

After a few years, (Punkhuñ) got a little sister from the side of the stepmother. Even though simple Punkhuñ was happy to get a sister, the stepmother began to hate her (Punkhuñ) even more than before. Now it become very difficult for Punkhuñ. Little Sister got a little bigger. The stepmother fed her own daughter tasty and good food but fed Punkhuñ only bread. As for P's work, it had increased double. An old goat that they tended knew about Punkhuñ's trouble. It turns out, the old goat had a lucky sign. It thought about helping Punkhuñ. When grazing in the afternoon, the old goat used to take out good food and give it to Punkhuñ. Because of that, even though at home she had to eat only bread, she began to get fatter. No one knew about this.

One day when going to graze the goat, P. also took her Little Sister with (her). Having found out that Punkhuñ had eaten something, (Little Sister) insisted and asked for a little food for herself. Punkhuñ could not hide it the food however much she tried to (hide it). P. said

"You must not tell anyone this thing; only then will I give you some food." After Little Sister said okay, P. gave her half the food. After Little Sister ate up quickly, she jammed a piece of food under her finger nail and took it home. After going home, she fully explained to her mom (Punkhuñ)'s eating. Seeing the old goat the stepmother was infuriated (on-fire-mad). As soon as her father came home, she raised the issue of killing the goat. It was decided that the next day, having done *puja,* the goat would be killed and eaten.

The goat found this out. It said to Punkhuñ, "Despite (my) saying don't give food to Little Sister, you gave it." Now your parents know everything. Tomorrow they will surely kill me. As for you, don't go when they call you. Pretend that your stomach hurts. They may call you to put on *tika,* but don't go. Don't even go when they call you to eat a piece of (my) meat. Go after they call you to throw away my bones. Bury the bones in one place. For sure, it will be to your benefit.

Just as the goat said, Punkhuñ buried the goat's bones in one place. The next day, it turns out there was a big fig tree sprouted there ripe with fruit. Punkhuñ climbed the tree and started picking and eating the figs. At that very moment, some demons came under the tree and began saying, "Hey, drop us (some) figs too." Punkhuñ started to drop (some) figs. The whole of four or five times she dropped (them) they said, "It went into filth. Give us another." Later they said, "Come down yourself and give (them to us)." Simple Punkhuñ said "All right" and when she went down to give (the figs) they all of a sudden carried her off to their own house.

After taking her home they said, "You stay here and keep cooking bread. We will come (back) after bathing," and the demons went out. While cooking bread a mouse come out of a hole. It said to P., "If you give me a (piece) of bread I will tell you something." After she gave a piece of bread it entered (went back into) the hole. After a while, it came again and said as before. After getting some bread it again went into the hole. Like that, after eating four or five pieces of bread he started to say something. "The demons have gone to gone to sharpen knives. After a while they will come and, having killed you, they will eat you. So, before they come you must flee from here quickly. Before leaving from here, take as much gold, silver and jewelry from their treasury as you can and go. At the time of going, spit and put on every step of the stairs (or every rung of the ladder) a piece of charcoal. Then bolt the door bar from the outside with a key and go." Having done that, Punkhuñ took the riches and went home. When the demons returned they saw the door of the house had been shut. They called for Punkhuñ. But the spit kept saying repeatedly from the inside "hajur." No one came to open the door. Later, (they) broke open the door and when the went in they found out that Punkhuñ had already fled. They were baffled.

At this side (meanwhile), after reaching home at night, Punkhuñ rattled the door. The stepmother came to open the door. After seeing so much wealth the step mother was amazed and asked about everything. Punkhuñ told the whole story from when she went to pick the figs. But she forget to tell about the mouse.

The greedy stepmother wanted her own daughter to do the same. So, she sent her own daughter to climb the fig tree. The demons came and asked for the figs just as before. The demons carried her to their house too. They engaged her in cooking bread and, saying that they would come having bathed, went out. Just as before, the mouse came and cried out to be given bread. But she sent the mouse off with a beating. The mouse fled into the hole. Therefore it wasn't able to explain what would be to her benefit. Later the demons came. Placing her in the middle the demons sat around. Piece by piece, they all began to cut and eat her flesh. The demons cut and ate all the flesh of her body.

At this side (meanwhile), the stepmother waited wondering when she would come and bring the wealth. But the daughter didn't return. The next day the demons brought the daughters bones to throw on the path. The stepmother didn't even come to know this. Later, a crow gave news of this. Finding out her daughter was already dead, she beat her chest and cried. But what to do; it was already too late.

CHAPTER 14: NEPALI ATTIRE

The attire of a certain place depends on its geographical environment and traditions. For example, it's natural to wear warm clothes in a cold place and to wear thin clothes in a hot place. Therefore, in the Himalayan region, people wear thick clothes and in the Terai (people) wear thin clothes. In the hills people wear medium type of clothes. However, there are many variations in their attire here. Furthermore, clothes may differ according to the weather here. For example, in hot and cold months, the clothes that are worn are different. Another thing is, here, the dress of traditional and modern festivals and celebrations is different from ordinary dress. These days, due to the influence of foreign and modern fashion, the style of traditional clothing and jewelry is changing. For example, coats, pants, shirts, *kurtas*, trousers and housecoats are commonly seen worn by the people here. Among these, most (of the) clothing is not used in festivals and celebrations. In the same way, some women like to wear *mangal sutras* in place of *tilaharis* and *naugedis*. Those that wear fake and plastic jewelry are not few here. In the context of Nepal, *daura suruwals* and *topis* fall in the national dresses of men. But nowadays, not many people wear such national dress. In the same way, women's national dress is the *sari* and *cholo*. But according to the weather, the women like to wear a blouse or something else instead of a *cholo*.

Previously, the *Jyapus* in particular used to use hand woven material prepared by their own family. The *Jyapunis* used to ready (their) hand looms by preparing thread on the roads. For this job, it used to take months.

Nowadays, traditional dress and jewelry are disappearing. They are used only for exhibitions. In terms of culture, the disappearing of traditional attire is not good. Whatever the case (anyway), whatever dress we wear, whatever language we speak, whatever religion we follow, even if have different cultures, we are (after all) Nepalis. Nepal is our country. We must have "Nepali-ness" in us.

CHAPTER 15: OUR SOCIETY (CASTE AND STATUS)

In our society there are people of various caste, class and status. In view of caste, in our society there is a custom of (having) high caste and low caste, touchable and untouchable. There are also high classes, middle classes and low classes according to rich/poor (wealth) and power in the society here. Likewise there are also those that spend a life of middle status and low status. According to law, they are all equal. Even in the same house or family it's possible there are those living at various standards of life. It's possible to call a joint family one house. However, there are many that don't like joint families. The standard of living is determined by caste, tribe and wealth. Sometimes for their own prestige, people want to display a pretentious standard of living. Whatever the case may be, it's possible that ones lifestyle, festivals, customs and culture may be different according to caste, tribe and class.

Ordinarily, one family has one head (man) of the house. The head (man) of the house is considered to be the most influential. Every member respects/obeys his decisions. But his decisions may be influenced by his sons. Daughters and daughters-in-law are said to have no apparent influence on his decisions. However, nowadays the question of women's rights is growing strong. Therefore, it's becoming important to convince daughters and daughters-in-law as well. It's also possible that this isn't so in villages and many other places.

Now, the question arises, whose authority is it to make such decisions. Surely it must be the headman; in other words the oldest father or grandfather. But in practice it sometimes may not be so. "He in whose hand is the ladle and serving spoon is the decision maker." That means, whoever's hand holds the family wealth and on whose earnings others depend. So much so that even the headman of the house has to listen to him. Such a position is hardly available to women and children. Women are considered less influential than men.

In that way, the country of Nepal is also a single home. The people are its family. Now-a-days in the hands of the leaders (politicians) are the ladle and serving spoon. Nowadays, there is even an increasing demand for female leaders. But the fulfillment of women leaders hasn't been possible here.

An office is also a house. The boss is the headman of the office. The employees are all the members. There are many kinds of headmen: the chief of a village, the chairman of an organization, the party president, masters, rulers, etc. The people, staff, laborers and servants are all members of the family.

Some families are large, some families small. In some families there are many members and in some families there are very few. Some families have great prestige. Some families are rich and well-to-do. If a member of a rich and well-to-do family is a boss, doctor or leader, that family's prestige is different indeed! Such families have customs and traditions of great prestige.

It's true--every person has his own prestige. And he doesn't like to be insulted by anyone else. For his own prestige it may be that he spends pretentiously. For this (prestige) some spend tremendously and don't hesitate to sell their estate. But of what use is the prestige gained by selling one's estate? Therefore, one should practice spending only according to one's capability.

CHAPTER 16: DAILY LIFE

What is the daily life of a Nepali like? Before answering this, who is he? Where does he live? Where is he from? What is his family like? All of these things should be considered.

In the rural areas most of the young women have to work very hard from an early age. After getting big (growing up) she goes to sleep the latest and gets up the earliest. Her life passes away in (the work of) getting firewood and grass, agricultural teamwork and in the kitchen and courtyard. She has to do almost all the housework. She has to do these jobs together with the other women of the house or by herself. She has to cook the rice, carry the firewood and water, comfort her younger brother and sister, go do agricultural teamwork with her mother, frequent the mill to grind flour or operate the grindstone. She also has to manage time for the cow shed jobs. The job of going to the market for salt and oil also falls on her head. (As) if this is not enough, her other responsibilities may even be to go to the cities/bazaar to work in the factories, weave carpets, twine wool or work as a day laborer.

As for boys, they eat good food, go to school and play with their friends. After growing up, if it suffices the boys work in the fields. If not, they carry loads, go to the cities and work as day laborers or porters, work in the factories or emigrate to India.

But life in the cities and bazaars is different. There, girls also go to school. Life in the cities is not as difficult as in the village. In the city one doesn't have to search for firewood. The water hole doesn't have to be frequented for water. One doesn't have to walk a long ways, do cow shed chores and do agricultural teamwork and everything is available for buying in the cities. In the cities usually they cook on kerosene stoves. These days, the practice of cooking food with gas is increasing in the cities. In the cities, having eaten (morning meal), children take their afternoon snacks and go to school. After returning from school and having tea-time, they do their homework. They listen to the radio and watch TV. Truly, TV has made people lazy.

If both of the parents are employed, most of the housework falls on the head of the servant and the elders who watch the home. After eating the morning meal, they must go to the office. An afternoon snack is eaten in the cafeteria or "hotel". After returning from the office they feel tired. Having had tea, they need to rest. Before or after eating the evening meal they have to find to time to watch TV. When do they find the time to do the household chores?

Working women who also manage time for household chores are not few. Not only that, they are also troubled by the worries of their children's school. It becomes necessary for the mother to give help in everything from sending (the children) to school to getting them and doing (their) homework. In this situation, they bear many responsibilities of the home. There are also many husbands and wives that complete work together.

There is a holiday every week on Saturday. Many schedules are made for that day. That day, there may be plans to wash clothes, do the cleaning, stroll about, watch a film, or go to a friend or relative's place. Even on a holiday every one is busy. The plan is to do the weeks remaining work on that holiday. The day passes unknowingly by doing this or that. Someone may be surprised to see us with no free-time on Saturdays either.

Furthermore, many shopkeepers remain busy all the time. Their daily chore is to stay in the store the whole day. The women and the workers (servants) stay at home. The women do the prayers and worship and get the food ready. Most of the shopkeepers go home for an afternoon meal. On festivals and feasts the women are seen to be extremely busy. At other times, they have a little free time. Shopkeepers may not have money problems.

Many people that have just come from the outside districts live alone in a rented room or with a friend. They don't live with (their) family. Paying a monthly payment they eat daal bhaat mornings and evenings by contract in some restaurant. They have tea in the afternoon wherever they are. Generally they don't have any household chores or responsibilities. They are free.

In this way, every person's daily life is not the same (one). They are different. Because of that, I like to gain information about many people's profession and daily life.

CHAPTER 17: ANIMAL HUSBANDRY

Animal husbandry has an important role in Nepal's agro-economy. In this, there is mainly the cow, buffalo and goat. Agriculture and animal raising are like fingernail and flesh (inseparable). They are supplementary to each other. Many agricultural crops take the form of animal feed, whereas the scattered dung of animals is made into compost fertilizer for the fields. These days, the use of dung gas (methane) is also increasing. The animals are used a lot for plowing the fields, threshing, pulling carts and even carrying loads. Milk, meat, wool and hides are also obtained from animals. Not even the fat, bones, hooves or horns of animals go to waste.

In Nepal, animal husbandry is going on in a very old style. The custom of tying animals and raising them in a way that stops forest destruction is good. Wherever it is not appropriate for fields, there the main occupation is animal husbandry. In Nepal's Northern region agricultural work (field work) is difficult because there are difficult geographical conditions, cool climate and very high altitude. There, animal husbandry is a good solution (way out). For that reason, in the highlands the main occupation of the inhabitants is animal husbandry. There, the people graze sheep, mountain goats, yaks, mules, donkeys, etc. in the empty fields and hillside grazing lands. There, donkeys and mules are used for the work of carrying loads whereas sheep, goats and yaks are raised for meat, milk, wool and hides. Nevertheless, the main job of these animals is to transport supplies from the lowlands to the hills and vice versa. From this very thing, the people of the Northern region earn a living. The Gurung and Sherpa tribes particularly are (seen to be) greatly influenced and content with this occupation.

In the middle hilly region, Terai and valleys, people raise cows, bulls, buffaloes, goats, pigs, chickens, ducks rabbits, bees, etc. as a subsidiary to agriculture. Among these (animals) some are used for plowing fields, pulling carts, carrying loads and threshing whereas some are raised for meat, milk and hides. In this (case) improved or developed species of animals, technical knowledge and knowledge about animal health are all necessary here.

In the animal husbandry business, we need to be self-sufficient in the matters of (producing) meat, milk, etc. through modernization. In areas where there is possibility for development, animal development programs have been conducted. Presently, animal development farms have been conducted in the places of Lalitpur, Chitawan, Pokhara, Nuwakot, Makwanpur, Jumla, etc. Animal health centers have also been set up in various places.

Nowadays, rabbit farming is also beginning. Rabbits are raised for hide, meat and wool. In this, the Angora species is primary. The various rabbit hide and woolen goods are valuable.

It appears necessary to make good (improve) its market management. Rabbit meat is also considered good.

Poultry farming is important for meat and eggs. In Nepal, various hatcheries and poultry farms produce lots of meat and eggs. Besides this, those who raise chickens in their homes on a small scale are found from place to place. Technical knowledge, high quality developed chicks, nutritious food and arrangement for cages are all necessary for this. Usually, the nutritious food, hatchery machines, medicine, etc. come from India. Other foreign machines are expensive. Sometimes, the market for eggs and meat depend on the Indian market.

CHAPTER 18: AGRICULTURE IN NEPAL

Nepal's economy is based particularly on agriculture. Around 90% of the population is engaged in this occupation. But it cannot be said that all the people engaged in agricultural occupation are dependent only on agriculture, because they are busy in agriculture only three or four months out of the year. In particular, they have no free time as long as it is monsoon. Therefore agriculture is considered to be their main profession.

Agriculture in Nepal is going on in traditional style. Because there is little facility for irrigation here, most of the cultivated land depends on water from the sky. Because Nepal's agriculture depends on water from the sky, the weather has tremendous influence here. In other words, wherever it rains a lot there is a lot of produce. Because of that, whereas the Eastern Terai of Nepal is the place there is the most produce, the middle hills is the region where there is the least production. Wherever there is lots of produce there is a large population. Because of that, there are few settlements in the far Western hills.

Most of the hill region is steep. This area is more suitable for fruit farming. Corn is mainly cultivated in the dry fields and wheat in the unirrigated fields. It's true that in the Himal region (in other words, the high hilly region) there is little production, but that area is suitable for raising sheep and goats. Therefore, the plains of the Terai have the increased pressure of population.

Previously, a lot of grain (rice, wheat, corn, millet, barley, etc.) used to be exported to foreign countries: that is, India. But these days exports are declining because of increased population and a decrease in production. Furthermore, in the seasons of cultivation, many Indian laborers are used for work. (These days Indian laborers are increasing in every area/sector.) Grain itself is the form of their wages. In this way as well, a large portion of grain is exported. So, there is a decrease in savings (net productions). Is not it possible to increase savings as long as Indian laborers are used?

The most production of grain, vegetables and other cash crops is in the Terai. In fact, there is more produce than is needed there in in Terai. However, in the hills the amount that is needed is not produced. Because of that, the lacking grain and other things are supplied from the Terai.

Of course, rice is cultivated primarily in the monsoon. However, where there is irrigation facility, two crops a year are done (cultivated). There are also those that cultivate three crops, (if) one crop between (the other two) is included. Rice is cultivated in the plain region of the

Terai, the hill valleys, the unirrigated fields beside the rivers and in the lowlands where water can be trapped in the terraces or plots. Rice is not cultivated in land that is not able to stop (store) water or is steep. At one time, there used to be a lot of mud fish in the rice fields and fish also used to be farmed. But due to the excessive use of chemical fertilizers and insecticides fish, frogs, snakes, crabs, etc. are disappearing.

Before planting rice the field is plowed and readied. In Kathmandu valley, plowing is not done. Here, the farmers dig the fields by hand. These days, fields are also dug by tractor. Along with digging in this way here they grow the rice seedlings separately in a nursery bed. After that, when it rains, the fields are puddled.

Men do the work of digging, plowing and puddling. They (the puddlers) are also called *bause*. After that, the women and girls (in particular) plant the rice in rows. At that time the boys also have fun wrestling in the mud. In many places, there is a managed (organized) work exchange of working each others' fields. The singing of *asare* planting songs while planting is also equally fun. There are also duets that go on between the boys sitting on the (paddy) walls and the girls that are planting rice tschk, tschk (sound). As long as there is a duet going, it's said that rice planting is fun. Most (people) will have finished the planting within the month of *Saun*. For some months after planting rice, water needs to be managed to be kept in the fields. In between, weeds and other grasses need to be uprooted once or twice. Both men and women do this job. At this time, the green rice fields are charming. At the time of ripening, the rice becomes nice if there is warm sun to quickly harden the kernel. At this time the fields look yellow like a bed of gold. It is charming (captivates heart and mind).

In about three and a half months, the rice crop become suitable to cut and bring in. At this time, having received the fruit of their labor, farmers are (seen to be) very happy. If it rains at the perfect time and there is no trouble from flood or landslide, the main crop of the year turns out to be very successful.

Another thing, the rice grown in the cold water of the hills is considered to be better quality than the rice grown in the warm waters of the Terai.

CHAPTER 19: MEANS OF ENTERTAINMENT

A friend had commented that there are few means of entertainment in Nepal. It is said that if a means of entertainment is not found, it isn't fun (boring). Being busy with work, it (what he said) didn't get my attention. (But) I wonder what all people do in (their) free time.

One time I had gone strolling in Kirtipur. There, I was amazed to see many youths playing cards on the temple steps because I found out they always spent their time in this way. In the same courtyard I saw some small children rolling wheels, some playing *dandi biyo*, some hopscotch, some tag and some *khopi*. Some adults and elders were also chatting. Some were amusing themselves by watching others play cards and watching the children play. Some were content (just) to listen to others chat. Some boys and girls were telling each other stories with great embellishment. Seeing all this things, I too was pleased. But I heard (learned) that it is always this way around that temple in Kirtipur. I didn't see any women or young women entertaining (themselves) in this way. I hear they are busy working in their homes and fields.

If it was always like this, I felt like people were wasting their time. The time could probably be used in some productive area (way). But, it meant nothing to me (was none of my business), so I didn't say anything.

In Kathmandu, there are other methods of entertainment besides these. There is dinner entertainment with Gazel singing, hotel casinos, drinking and gambling, etc available. The number of people here who entertain themselves at traditional festivals, fairs and *melas* (village gatherings) is decreasing. In fun fairs there is also circus entertainment, magicians and lotteries. These days, wherever you go in the city there are lots of people. It seems like there's always a festival or fair in the cities. There are even more crowds during festivals. It's not just the crowd of those who come to see the festival, but mostly they are also the passers-by blocked by the festival here. Among the main festivals here are Gaijatra, Indrajatra, Ghorajatra, Phagu (holi), the Dassaiñ and Tihar markets, New Years and festivals mainly in Bhaktapur and Thimi.

Other increasingly popular means of entertainment are the cinema, videos, TV, radio, etc. Furthermore, a lot of people go to visit the zoo (where they also go to have picnics) and the museums. Because there aren't enough of these for everyone, some people go to have picnics in various other places. The entertainment of a picnic is food, drinking, gambling with cards and dancing and singing. There are also those that go to Ratna Park to relax in the evening. But Ratna Park is not always open.

Besides this, people here also play various games for entertainment and physical exercise. The people who also spend their time watching these kinds of games are not few. Among these games the main ones are golf, cricket, football, swimming, tennis, volleyball, judo, karate, etc. Furthermore, many people go to see the Academy Hall, the city hall and other theaters to watch various plays, cultural programs, etc. Some shows are very expensive.

For Nepalis also, there are lots of ways for entertainment. There are even more for foreigners; distinctively, cultural programs in hotels, sightseeing tours and other travel enjoyment.

Compared to Kathmandu there are much fewer ways of entertainment in the villages. Gambling, cards and alcohol are found everywhere. The places of entertainment there are the *rodi* houses of the Gurung, the village hilltops and the resting places. In various festivals the *sorathi, ghatu* and *maruni* dances are pleasant. It is said there is double benefit to going to the temples in the morning and evening and singing hymns.

It is not possible to write everything in this small article.

CHAPTER 20: A NEPALI WEDDING

The people of various castes and tribes dwell in Nepal. Every tribe has its own customs, practices and traditions. All of the weddings are not the same. Whatever the case may be, I now want to tell in short about one of my friend's wedding.

My friend was a Hindu a middle-class Newar. He got married in the year 2045 in Jeth according to Hindu custom. He and his fourth eldest brother got married together. Two weeks before the wedding, a matchmaker (had) brought information about a girl. Even though before that he (my friend) had never thought about marriage of intended on getting married, at that time he could not say no. After the parents and family were satisfied, a day to go and see the girl was decided on before making it (the wedding) more certain. Five in total, the father, an older brother, an older sister, the matchmaker and himself got in a taxi and arrived at a house in Baneswor. The matchmaker had already arranged the matter. After the ordinary formal conversation, some watched the groom-to-be while talking, some while having tea and snacks and some right from the door.

By coincidence, there happened to be an acquaintance of his there. So, it was a little easier for him (to be) there. Also, the brides side was a little more assured because they got additional information about the groom-to-be.

Now the time to see the bride has arrived. The girl was standing in a room. Turn by turn with great interest, everyone (went and) returned after seeing the bride-to-be; that is, the girl. Now the matter was settled; that is, the wedding was certain.

Four days before the wedding, various breads, fruit, dried fruits, clothes and gifts of jewelry were sent to the girls house along with 10 big, decorated betel nuts. Invitation cards were distributed. On the day of the wedding procession, the procession gathered right at the groom's house. The gathered procession would have to go to two places. The was also an arrangement for buses and other cars. After distributing the packets of dried fruits, the band departed with instruments and other things. Behind the band were the wedding supplies and behind these were the two cars with the grooms. For Newars, it was a new custom (not old) for the groom to go (as well). In the procession there were around a hundred people. (According to the Social Practice Act of 2033, only 51 people including the band used to be able to be taken (go) in the wedding procession.)

That same night around 11:30 was the auspicious time for *swayambar* (when the girl chooses the husband). I was in my friends wedding procession. He himself was the younger groom. On the rooftop in the middle of a crowd, the *swayambar* was a success under the direction of (two) priests on both sides. After that a room was given (provided) for the groom where he spent the whole night playing cards with friends. On that very day, the feast at the bride's house had finished. The next day from morning on there was busy commotion. The bride gave farewell betel nuts to all her relatives, and each of them gave (her) a gift. Then the bridge gave the groom the ten betel nuts previously sent to her by the groom himself. Lastly the bridge gave betel nuts to her own parents. There, the bride's relatives went on wailing. The reason being, that was the time of difficult separation. Now their daughter was going to be someone else's daughter. Taking leave from the brides parents, the procession returned. Now, the procession returned happily with the bride and groom's car with the band in front as before. These things probably happened at the place of the fourth elder brother as well. If I had gone there, I would have seen two weddings. Both grooms arrived home together. The groom and bride were ritually welcomed. After arriving home, the grooms' relatives took (some) betel nuts from the brides. These were the betel nuts that connected relations. The evening of that day there was a party feast.

Two days after that, the people from the brides' parents' homes come with gifts to see her face. Seeing that the daughters looked happy, they were all glad. What would have happened if the daughters hadn't looked happy? All those that came to see their faces gave (them) money.

That evening, the groom was welcomed at the wife's parent's home. The job of joining relations (in the form of betel nuts) was completed. The son-in-law was fed a feast of delicious dishes by the father-in-law (wife's parent's home). The groom and bride returned home the same night. After that they had a few, insignificant picnics. The whole wedding, the bride wore red clothes and jewelry. The fun continued on for several days.

CHAPTER 21: DASHAIÑ

Dashaiñ is a great Hindu festival. This festival falls in the month of Asoj. Once the festival begins, because the tenth day (*dasauñ*) is the main day, there is the custom of calling this day Dashaiñ as well. Chaite Dashaiñ is also celebrated on a small scale. This is called "small Dashaiñ." Because Chait is hot, dry, lazy, dusty, disease ridden, etc. it is not really an appropriate time for feasting; therefore they say the big dashai festival was moved to Asoj. At this time, the weather is pleasant. At this time it's neither hot nor cold. At this time, because the monsoon is just finished, the hills, jungles and such look clean as though they were just washed. The sky appears cloudless and blue. The mountains aren't covered with mist or clouds. At this time, one can sit on the rooftop and take pleasure from the various surroundings.

The many farmers of Nepal and those who depend on agriculture seem very happy at this time. The reason being, the main crop of the year, rice, will be ripening. It other words, it will have become harvest time at this time. In the hills, the place where rice is not grown, the corn crop will already have been brought in (harvested). So, they will be happy to see (both) the harvested and the ripened crops. The animals fattened by the grass of Saun and Bhadau also add some joy at this time.

During this time children are happy with the hope of good food, the wearing of nice, new clothes, playing on a swing, flying kites and other fun things. Because there is as much school and campus vacation as is needed at this time there is lots of free time for fun. Students that are studying outside (away from home) also return to their own homes at dashaiñ and, having received *tika* from those older than them, eat feasts.

Various businessmen become happy and busy in the hopes of big business and profit before and during Dashaiñ. There is no free time for the businessmen because of the work of gathering goods, lots of sales and as much gathering of profits as possible. There are crowds at the material and clothing stores. There are also crowds at the fruit and bread (sweets) shops at Dassaiñ. Those that sell goats (castrated and uncastrated), water buffalo, chickens and ducks try to get their own price at that time. (Such) a lot of spices, beaten rice, and peas-beans are also sold in dashain. Wherever you look only crowds are seen.

Employees are also thrilled because of bonus pay, advances and vacation at Dassaiñ. They also become busy collecting the supplies needed for celebrating Dashaiñ. However far away Nepalis live from their homes, they come home to celebrate Dashaiñ. For that reason, before and after Dashaiñ the buses are filled with travelers and space is insufficient. But Tickets are fully booked weeks ahead of time.

For such an important and such a fun festival that comes but once a year, those that enjoy it are not few. Everywhere one encounters (people) eating feasts of meat, (people) lavishly dispensing of alcohol and rice beer, those raising money by gambling with cards and those entertained with the flying of kites. For gamblers, this is a golden opportunity.

However poor one is and even though one never eats well any other time, one has to eat rice with meat at Dashaiñ. It's absolutely necessary to wear new clothes. At Dassaiñ each and everyone is in the mood for fun and enjoyment. In the midst of such preoccupation, sometimes the reason for celebrating Dashaiñ is forgotten or not found out. What is its importance? How did this begin to be celebrated? Why are all these things needed? They get to feast and enjoy. Is that not enough?

The first nine days of Dashaiñ are called *nauratha*. During the whole of *nauratha* there is the custom of doing *mela* (local gatherings) at various pilgrimage sites in Kathmandu very early in the morning and Goddess Navadurga is worshipped. During these days there are crowds of those coming to pay audience (to Bhagawati) at the temples of Bhagawati. Some youths also go to temples to see the spectacle. It's also enjoyable at that time to breathe the morning air.

On the day Dashaiñ begins, a ritual water jug full of water is set up. Near to that, holy mud, sand, etc. are spread out, barley, corn, etc. is scattered and the job of placing young barley shoots is done. The seventh day of Dassaiñ is called "phulpati". On the day of Phulpati, in the room where the young barley shoots are, worship is performed by bringing sugar cane, ginger plants and flower bunches. Even work tools are worshipped on this day. On this very day, the *phulpati* brought from the Gorkha Palace is welcomed. At that time it's fun to observe the presence of civil servants and other honorable people at 'Tudikhel'. Special worship starts on the eighth day of the lunar month. The shrines of goddesses become crowded on this day. His Majesty the King also visits various shrines of goddesses. Because of that, it's possible that the royal tour will cause traffic jams. On Mahanavami (9th day) large numbers (of animals) are slaughtered. At the temples of Bhagawati there are large crowds of those come to offer sacrifices on this day. In particular, goats, sheep, water buffalo, chickens and ducks are sacrificed on this day. Foreigners are surprised to see that goats and ducks are sacrificed for even cars and motorcycles on this day.

The tenth day of Dasaiñ, Vijaya Dashami, is the main day. After putting on a *tika* at one's own home, the day begins for going to one's relatives and getting *tikas* from those older than one's self. On this and the previous day, the bazaar is completely closed. At the time of putting on a *tika*, blessings are given by the older to the youngers. The crowds that go to Kumari House to receive *tika* from Kumari (Living Goddess) are not few on this day.

Dasaiñ may not be equally enjoyable for everyone. Many people are left carrying debts from it (Dasaiñ). Gambling, cards and alcohol etc. are used a lot in Dashai. Some people even fall sick from consuming a lot of food and alcohol. Whatever the case, this festival is of great importance in Nepal.

CHAPTER 22: HINDUISM

1. **Heaven, Hell and the Place of Death:** Sinners go to hell and the righteous or those who do good deeds go to heaven. One has to suffer torment in hell according to the fruit of sin. According to the type of sin, one has to undergo the fruit (of sin) (either) a long or short

time, and (either) great or small torment. In this way, after undergoing the fruit of sin, one can go to heaven to undergo the fruit of righteousness done by one's self. In heaven there is no such thing as suffering. One undergoes a time of happiness in heaven. The (length of) time one undergoes happiness is determined according to (either) big good deeds or small good deeds (the magnitude of good deeds). If big (significant) good deeds are done then one can stay in heaven a long time. However, the happiness of heaven is not permanent. After experiencing the happiness of heaven (according to one's own righteousness), one has to again come to this world or Ocean of Existence; in other words, one has to be reborn. In this way, birth as a man is available after having spun and circled 8.4 million lives in the Ocean of Existence. If good deeds and karma had been done in the previous life, one does not have to fully circle all of the 8.4 million lives; then, life as a man is again quickly available. When a man can do good deeds and karma, the person's life is a great (such an) opportunity. (Because) if the situation allows a man can practice for salvation. Because the experience of heaven and hell is different from salvation.

2. **Salvation/Freedom:** The meaning of salvation is generally understood to be freedom or release (known as *mukti*) from having to be born again and again in the Ocean of Existence. After receiving freedom from the Ocean of Existence, people aren't required to be born again and again. (To be born in the Ocean of Existence itself considered to be a situation where suffering must be undergone). In this situation, even his soul is considered to have found salvation and the soul taken into it's own family god. In other words, it is considered to have become one with the family god. It is said that having arrived at *Baikuntha* or *Kailash* those who receive salvation will live as one of Vishnu or Shiva's family. There is also the opinion in Hinduism that people must practice for salvation along with doing good deeds and karma.

3. **Sin and Good Deeds:** It is said that the Hindu scriptures mention which deeds are sin and which deeds are good deeds. What deed is sin under what situation? It is said that the borderlines are described in scripture. Similar things are said about good deeds, I hear. But how many people have studied and understand all of the scriptures? Who has time to study those scriptures? Are those scriptures available everywhere?

   Sin pushes a person towards hell and good deeds give (provide) heaven and other good opportunities. But there is also the opinion that for salvation one must continue staying far from sin, going on in good deeds and worshipping one's own god.

   What many think is heaven and hell are false (don't exist). After death, who knows who goes where? Who knows what happens to someone? Rather, it must be remembered that the fruit of sins done and (the fruit of) good deeds is received in this very birth. If someone has made a mistake, he doesn't have to wait for another life to experience that mistake's punishment. Not everyone believes that there is rebirth. The matter of sin and good deeds (morals) is absolutely necessary for ideal life and ideal society. Or else there will be no lack of people that continue on recklessly (doing anything they like) thinking that after dying even an untouchable becomes a king. Who is afraid of the fruit of sin that is received (only) after dying? In the same way, who hopes in the fruit of good deeds that is received (only) after dying?

4. **The Soul/Spirit:** The soul is a tiny, divine particle that inhabits every living thing and has no beginning or end. It is neither possible to be seen nor possible to be touched. It has no shape or kind. Mind and soul are different. They say the same soul is in everyone. Even if living things die, the soul doesn't; rather it moves to another birth. Only after receiving salvation the soul is taken (absorbed) into God . The source of every soul is God and at the end of the universe every soul will be taken into God. Whatever is said about this is little (not enough).

5. **Temples, Idols and Pictures:** There are many kinds of temples. Not every temple has the same idol of a deity or god. Usually the main deities and other surrounding idols of deities are generally seen. According to Kirk Patrick, there are as many temples in Kathmandu as houses and as many idols as there are people's heads.

   Usually the worship room of a follower of Hinduism is decorated with the idols of various goddesses and gods. Consecrated idols are worshipped. To such an extent that even pictures decorated in frames even get *tika* and such.

   In Hindusim, there are many other aspects that are beyond the possibility of writing about here.

CHAPTER 23: POLITICS OF NEPAL

Constitutional Politics and Multiparty System:

The following aspects of the Constitution of the Kingdom of Nepal 2047 (hereafter CKN) are important.

1. Constitutional Monarchy

Constitutional monarchy has been conducted in place of autocratic monarchy in this constitution. In the constitutional monarchy the king does not interfere in any affairs of state administration. The people's representatives form a government in this system. The government is responsible to the House of Representatives. The king reigns but does not rule. The CKN has limited the power of the king (H.M).

2. Sovereignty in the People

According to Article 3 of CKN, the sovereignty of Nepal remains with the people. Its use will be according to what is arranged in the constitution. But there is a limitation on the use of sovereignty. Furthermore, some power and privileges have been left to the king's personal conscience. Whatever the case, the representative needed by the people is sent through election to the parliament. These representatives are called parliamentarians. These representative are believed to make proper honor of sovereignty. These representatives are either from various political parties or are independent (candidates).

3. This constitution has adopted a free (independent), capable justice system. An independent, capable justice system is essential for democracy.

4. Supreme Parliament (Parliamentary Supremacy)

This constitution has accepted parliamentary governing system (gov't). But the government under parliament depends on peoples representatives. The people's representative does not become trustworthy if they are unworthy, incapable and dishonest. If that happens, party politics becomes useless. In that case democracy will be just like a coconut in the hands of a monkey. And if this democracy turns out to be unsuccessful, the same old autocratic system may prevail again.

Many learned people (intellectuals) have become fed-up with this system. It would be a great misfortune if this democracy which was achieved though such a big struggle, grows weak. It should not be the aim of the political leaders only to become a member of parliament and struggle for position. The leaders should not give false assurances to the people. They should be faithful (honest). They should work for national unity.

After the Constitution of 2047, an interim constitution 2063 was promulgated which was ammended for the eighth time to re-promulgate an interim constitution on the 14th of Jestha 2067, according to which a constitution of Federal Democratic Republic Nepal will be promulgated by 3rd Ashoj 2072 B.S.

Let us hope. May democracy flower, fruit and be strong. Hail Nepal!

APPENDIX 11

NEPALI-ENGLISH GLOSSARY
(with chapter indexed)

Devanagari Alphabetical Order (left to right)

ं *(nasal)*	ँ *(nasal)*	अ	आ – ा	
इ – ि	ई – ी	उ – ु	– ृ	
ए – े	ऐ – ै	ओ – ो	औ – ौ	
क क्ष	ख	ग	घ	ङ
च	छ	ज ज्ञ	झ	ञ
ट	ठ	ड	ढ	ण
त त्र	थ	द	ध	न
प		ब	भ	म
य	र	ल	व	
श श्र	ष	स	ह	

Note: Nasalized vowels precede unasalized vowels.

Spellings throughout the textbook have been standardized to the Nepali Brihat Shabdakosh.

अ

अंश	part, particle 22
अगाडि	in front, before 4
अग्लो	tall 11
अङ्गीकार	adopt (as a part of) 23
अघि	before; in front, ago 7
अघिल्लो	former, previous 21
अङ्ग्रेजी	English 2
अचम्म लाग्नु	amazed, surprised 9
अचानक	suddenly 9
अछूत	untouchable 7
अझै	still, yet 9
अञ्चल	Zone/Region 8
अड्काउनु	to jam, fasten 13
अड्नु	stop, halt 18
अति	extremely 19
अत्यधिक	excessive(ly) 18
अत्यन्त	extremely 7
अथवा	or 9
अदुवा	ginger 21
अधबैंसे	adult (post-youth) 19
अधिकांश	most, more than 50% 18
अधिकार	authority, right 15
अधिराज्य	kingdom 23

अध्यक्ष director, chairman, chairperson 15
अध्ययन study 9
अनि and (then) 5
अनुभवी experienced 8
अनुसन्धान research, investigation 8
अनुसार according to 10
अनेक several, many 16
अन्जीर fig 13
अन्तमा in/at the end 20
अन्तर्गत under (system, org) 23
अन्त्य end 22
अन्न grain 11
अन्य others 18, 8
अफिस office 4
अब now 4
अमेरिका America 2
अयोग्य unworthy, unfit 23
अरू other, else, more 3
अर्थात् that-is-to-say 9
अलावा (को) besides X 17
अलि little (a) 2
अल्छी lazy 13
अवस्था condition, circumstance 22
अवरुद्ध blocked, stopped, interrupted 19
अष्टमी 8th day of lunar month 21
असक्षम incapable, unqualified 23
असफल unsuccessful, failure 23
असार June-July 10
असिना पर्नु to hail 10
असोज Sept-Oct 10
अहिले now 4

आ

आँगन courtyard 16
आँधीबेहरी storm 10
आँप mango 3
आइतबार Sunday 5
आइमाई woman 16
आउनु come 4
आकार shape 22
आकाश sky 10
आकाशे of sky, rain dependent 18
आगो बाल्नु to light a fire 16
आगो हुनु id. on fire mad 13
आग्लो bar (across door) 13
आज today 3
आजकल nowadays 14
आजभोलि nowadays 4
आत्मनिर्भर self dependent, sufficient 17
आत्मा soul, spirit 22
आदर्श ideal 22
आदि etc. 12
आधा half 3
आधारभूत basic, fundamental 23
आधारित based (on) 18
आधुनिक modern 14
आधुनिकीकरण modernization 17
आनन्द pleasure, joy 21
आपूर्ति supply 18
आफन्त one's own relatives 16
आफू (one's) self 9
आमा mother 2
आराम rest, ease 7
आली ridge dividing rice field 18
आलु potato 3
आवश्यकता necessity 10
आशा hope 21
आशीर्वाद blessing 21
आश्वस्त हुनु be assured 20
आश्वासन assurance 23
आस्तिक religious, devout; theist 22
आहार diet, food 12

इ

इच्छा	wish, will, desire 21
इज्जत	status, prestige 15
इत्यादि	etc. 9
इन्जिनियर	engineer 8
इमानदार	honest, faithful 23
इमिग्रेशन	immigration 4
इस्त्री	iron (clothes) 5
ईश्वर	God 22
ईश्वरीय	divine 22
इष्टदेव	family god 22
ईर्ष्या गर्नु	to be jealous 13
ईर्ष्यालु	malicious, jealous 13

उ/

उकालो	uphill, rise 7
उखु	sugar cane 21
उखेल्नु	uproot 18
उचाइ	height, altitude 10
उचित	proper, reasonable, appropriate 12
उच्च	high; noble class 15
उजाड	desolate; wilderness 11
उठ्नु	get up, rise 7
उड्नु	fly (intr) 10
उत्तम	excellent, best 18
उत्तर	North 10
उत्तरदायी	responsible 23
उत्पादक	productive, fruitful 19
उत्पादन	produce, production 17
उत्सव	celebration 14
उदाहरण	example 14
उद्देश्य	aim, intention, objective, purpose 23
उद्याउनु	to sharpen 13
उनी	he, she 7
उन्नत	improved quality 17
उपकरण	equipment 8
उपचार	treatment 8
उपत्यका	valley 11
उपयुक्त	appropriate, fitting 17
उपयोगिता	usefulness, utility 23
उपस्थित हुनु	to be present 21
उपस्थिति	presence 21
उपहार	gift 20
उपाय	method, way; solution 17
उपासना	worship (mental) 22
उब्जनी	produce, crop 18
उभिनु	stand up; be standing 20
उमारिनु	be grown, sprout 18
उमाल्नु	boil (liquids, tr.) 5
उमेर	age 16
उम्मेदवार	candidate 23
उम्रनु	sprout, germinate 12
उल्लेख	mention, description 22
उसिन्नु	boil (solids) 5
उस्तै	same as, similar 10
उहाँ	he/she (polite) 2
ऊ	he, she, it 4
ऊन	wool 14

ए

एकअर्को	each other, one another 17
एकता	unity 23
एकदम	very, quite 5
एकान्त	loneliness 12
एकैसाथ	together, along with 20
एक्लै	single, alone, by oneself 16

ऐ

ऐन	law, Act 20
ऐना	glass; mirror 5

ओ

ओगट्नु to cover, occupy (area) 12
ओछ्यान bed(ing) 9
ओछ्यान पर्नु be bed-ridden 9
ओरालो downhill 7
ओसार्नु move, shift, carry (tr.) 16
ओहो wow!, hey! 6

औ

औंठी ring 14
औद्योगिक industrial 11
औपचारिक formal, official 20
औलो ज्वरो malarial fever 9
औषधि medicine 8

क

कच्चा weak; crude 1
कटानी cutting, deforestation 12
कठिन difficult 10
कडा hard 18
कता whither? 4
कति how much 3
कतिपय many of /most of 14
कतिवटा how many 1
कथा story 13
कपडा cloth, material 14
कपाल कोर्नु comb hair 16
कपास cotton (raw) 14
कम below, less 3
कमजोर weak, tender 12
कमलपित्त Hepatitis A 9
कमाइ earnings 15
कमी lack 18
कमिज shirt 14
कराउनु yell, cry out 13
करिब about, approx. 18
कर्म work; duty; lot 22
कर्मचारी employee 8
कलम pen 1
कलश worship water jug 21
कसरी how, in what way 9
कसको whose 1
कस्तो of what sort 1
कहाँ where 1
कहिले when; sometimes 7
कहिलेकाहीँ occasionally 5
कहीँकहीँ in some places 11
काँक्रो cucumber 3
काँटा fork 5
काँडे thorny 11
काका father's younger bro 20
काग crow 13
कागज paper 1
काटमार slaughter (lit. cut-kill) 21
काट्नु to cut 13
काठ wood, timber 12
काठ्माडौं Kathmandu 2
कानुन law, regulation 15
कान्छो youngest son/bro 20
कापी notebook 1
काम work 2
कामकाजी working (people) 16
कामदार worker, employee 18
कारखाना factory 16
कारण reason 9
कारबाही operation, action 23
कारोबार transaction 21
कात्तिक Oct-Nov 10
कार्य work, act, deed 17

कार्यकर्ता	worker (of org) 9
कार्यक्रम	program, timetable 16
कार्यालय	office, workplace 15
कालो	black 1
काहिँलो	4th youngest son/bro 20
कि	or 4; yes or no? 6
किताब	book 1
किनभने	because 7
किनमेल	shopping 3
किनार	edge, side 8
किन्नु	buy 3
किरा	insect, bug 12
किलो	kilo 3
किसान	farmer 18
किसिमको	kind of, sort of 9
कीटनाशक	insecticide 18
कीर्तन	incantation 19
कुखुरा	chicken 17
कुचो	broom 5
कुन	which 3
कुनैकुनै	some (emph) 9
कुमारी	Living Goddess; virgin 21
कुरा	thing 3
कुराकानी	talk, chat 6
कुरूप	ugly, unattractive 13
कुर्ता	shirt 14
कुर्नु	watch, guard, wait 16
कुवा	water(ing) hole 16
कुहिरो लाग्नु	to mist 10
कृषि	agriculture 11
कृषि अर्थव्यवस्था	agro-economy 17
के	what 1
केटा	boy 15
केटी	girl 15
केन्द्र	center, hub 17
केरा	banana 3
केलाउनु	cull, clean (rice) 5
केही	some (emph. of s]) 6
कोठा	room 1
कोदो	millet 18
कौसी	verandah, flat roof top 20
क्यारे	uncertainty 6
क्लिनिक	clinic 8
क्षमा गर्नु	forgive, excuse 22
क्षेत्र	area, region, field 11

ख

खचाखच हुनु	crowded, crammed 20
खच्चर	mule 17
खन्नु	to dig 11
खबर	news, message 6
खरायो	rabbit 17
खर्क	hillside grazing land 17
खर्च	expenditure, spending 15
खला	plots 18
खल्ती	pocket 14
खसाल्नु	drop, cause to fall 13
खसी	goat (castrated) 21
खाजा	snack 6
खाना	food, meal 5
खानु	eat 2
खानेकुरा	food, thing to-eat 13
खालको	type of, kind of 14
खाली	empty, vacant 4
खास गरी	actually, in fact 9
खुरुक्क	at once 13
खुला	open 19
खुवाउनु	to feed 13
खुसी	happiness, pleasure 7
खुब	very, extremely 14

खुर hoof 17
खेत irrigated field 15
खेतबारी field under tillage 19
खेती cultivation 12
खेर जानु go to waste, vain 17, 9
खेल game 19
खैरो brown 1
खोज्नु search for 7
खोप vaccination 9
खोपी game (see "Did You Know" 19)
खोर pen, sty, cage 17
खोला/खोलो river 7, 21
खोल्नु to open 13

ग

गँगटो crab 18
गच्छे capability 15
गजल Gazal 19
गठन गर्नु to form (committee) 23
गडबडी upset, disorder 9
गधा donkey 17
गफ(सफ) गर्नु to chat 16
गरा terrace 18
गरिब poor 15
गर्नु to do 2
गर्मी hot (weather) 7
गलत wrong; error 9
गलैंचा carpet 16
गल्ती गर्नु make a mistake 22
गहनापात jewelry, ornaments 14
गहुँ wheat 18
गाजर carrot 3
गाई cow 17
गाउँ village 7
गाउँ विकास समिति (गा.वि.स.) Village Development Committee-(V.D.C.) 23
गाउनु sing 18
गाडा cart 17
गाडी car, truck 4
गाड्नु to bury 13
गाली गर्नु to rebuke, scold 13
गाह्रो difficult, hard 7
गीत song 18
गुच्चा marble(s) 19
गुडाउनु to roll (tr) 19
गुणस्तरीय standard, quality 17
गुदी kernel 18
गुफा cave 11
गुरुङ Gurung (ethnic) 17
गृहकार्य homework 16
गेडागुडी peas and beans 21
गैँडा rhinoceros 12
गोठ goat shed, cow shed 16
गोबर cow dung 17
गोरु ox 17
गोल charcoal (also circle) 13
गोलभैँडा tomato 3
गोही crocodile 12

घ

घचघच्याउनु knock, rattle (door) 13
घट्ट mill 16
घट्नु to decrease (intr) 18
घडियाल slender nose alligator 12
घण्टा hour 8
घर house 1
घरबुना loom woven cloth 14
घरभेटी landlord 7
घाटी mountain pass 11

घाटु	Gurung dance 19
घाम ताप्नु	warm up in the sun 16
घाम लाग्नु	shine, be sunny 10
घुइँचो	crowd 21
घुमीफिरी	spinning, circling 22
घुम्ती	bend (in a road) 4
घुम्नु	wander, stroll 9
घ्वाइँ	Newari hopscotch 19

च

चक्की	tablet 9
चक्कु	knife (small) 5
चक्र	wheel 22
चङ्गा उडाउनु	fly a kite 21
चढाउनु	to offer 21
चढ्नु	to mount; ascend, climb, ride 12
चम्चा	spoon 5
चरा	bird 12
चराउनु	to graze (tr) 13
चर्नु	to graze (intr) 12
चलन	custom, practice 15
चलाउनु	drive, operate 4
चल्नु	move (intr) 10
चल्ला	chick, duckling 17
चहलपहल	commotion 20
चाँदी	silver 13
चाडपर्व	festivals 14
चाप	pressure 18
चामल	rice (uncooked) 5
चाहनु	to want 4
चाहिनु	to be needed 3
चाहिँ	emphatic particle 3
चिउँडो	chin 12
चिट्ठा	raffle, lottery 19
चिडियाखाना	zoo 19
चितुवा	leopard 12
चित्त बुझाउनु	persuade, convince 15
चिन्ता	worry, anxiety 16
चिन्नु	know, recognize 12
चिया	tea 6
चियासिया	tea and snack 16
चिसो	damp, cold 17
चीजबीज	goods, supplies 5
चीन	China 11
चुनाव	election 23
चुन्नु	elect, pick, choose 23
चुरा	bangle 14
चुलो	oven, stove 16
चेलीबेटी	young women 16
चैत	Mar-Apr 10
चोक	intersection 4
चोरी	theft 12
चोलो	sari top 14
चौँरी	yak 17
चौतारा/री	stone resting place 16
चौर	meadow, field 17
च्याङ्ग्रा	hill goat (long hair) 17
च्यूरा	pounded rice snack 21

छ

छक्क पर्नु	to be amazed 13
छर्नु	scatter, sow 21
छाउनु	to thatch 12
छाता	umbrella 10
छाती	chest 13
छाना	roof (sloping) 21
छाप्रो	hut 12
छाला	skin, hide, leather 12
छिँडी	ground floor 7
छिटो	quickly 6

छिन moment 4
छिनिनु be arranged, settled 20
छुटकारा freedom, release 22
छुट्टी holiday, leave 8
छुट्टै separate 18
छुट्ट्याउनु divide, separate 11
छुनु touch 22
छुपुछुपु way of planting rice 18
छुरा knife 13
छेउ side, edge 18
छेउछाउ vicinity 11
छोटकरीमा in short 20
छोटो short 12
छोड्नु (-न) to stop doing X 13
छोरा son 5
छोरी daughter 5
छोरीबेटी daughters/girls 16

ज

जगत् world, universe 22
जग्गा land (plot of) 18
जङ्गल jungle 11
जङ्गली wild 12
जतातातै everywhere 19
जति about, approx 8
जतिसुकै however much 21
जथाभाबी randomly, haphazardly 22
जन people (in compounds) 23
जनता people, population 15
जनसङ्ख्या population (human) 11
जन्ती bridegroom procession 20
जन्म birth 22
जमरा young barley shoot 21
जमिन land 10
जम्नु to freeze 10
जम्मा in total 3
जय hail; victory 23
जरुरी important, urgent 12
जलपूर्ण full-of-water 21
जलाउनु cremate 22
जवाहिरात jewels 13
जस्तो like, as if, as 9
जाँड rice-beer 21
जाँतो grindstone 16
जागिरे employed; office worker 16
जाडो लाग्नु feel cold 9
जात caste, species 12, 15
जाति ethnic group 15
जात्रा festival (with procession) 19
जादू magic 19
जानकारी info; knowledge 16
जानु go 3
जिउ body 9
जिउनु to live, be alive 15
जिद्दी obstinance, insistence 13
जिम्मेबारी responsibility 16
जिल्ला District 8
जीविका चलाउनु earn livelihood 17
जी/ज्यू Mr. (polite) 6
जीव life, living being 12
जीवन life; lifetime 10
जीवनपद्धति lifestyle 15
जीवनजल oral rehydration fluid 9
जुटाउनु collect, provide, supply 21
जुत्ता shoe(s) 14
जुनसुकै whatsoever 14
जुनी circle of life 22
जुलुस mob, procession, march 23
जुवा gambling 19
जेठ May-June 10

जेठो	eldest (in family) 15
जोगी	ascetic, hermit 22
जोड्नु	join, fix, connect 20
जोत्नु	plow 17
जौ	barley 18
ज्ञान	wisdom, knowledge
ज्यादै	too much 17
ज्यान	life 7
ज्यापू	Newar farmer 14
ज्यामी	day laborer 16
ज्याला	daily wages 7
ज्यावल	tool(s) 21
ज्वर आउनु	get fever 9
ज्वाइँ	son-in-law; husb of young sis 20

झ

झन्	the more, still 18
झरना	waterfall 11
झाडा पखाला	loose stool, diarrhea 9
झार	weed, thicket 18
झिक्नु	take out, bring out 13
झुन्ड्याउनु	hang (up) 22
झुप्पा	bunch (flower, banana...) 21
झुटो	false 22
झुम्की	tasseled earring 14
झोल	liquid; soup 9
झोला	bag 1
झ्याल	window 1

ट

टप	ear pin 14
टाँक खोल्नु	to unbutton 14
टाँक लगाउनु	to button 14
टाढा	far (distance) 4
टारी	unirrigated field 18
-भनेर टार्नु	pretending X 13
टालो	patch 22
टिप्नु	write down 6
टीका	tika 13
टुक्रा	piece 13
टुसा	bamboo shoot (thin) 12
टोक्नु	bite 9
टोपी	Nepali hat 14

ठ

ठाउँ	place 4
ठाडो	steep, erect; rude 12, 13
ठिक	right, correct 6
ठूलो	big 1
ठेक्का	lease, contract 16

ड

डन्डीबियो	see Did You Know 19
डर	fear 7
डराउनु	be afraid 22
डाँडा	ridge, hill 7
डाँडाकाँडा	mountains + hills 11
डाँफे	pheasant 12
डाडु	ladle (long handle) 15
डुम	part. low caste 22
डेढ	one and a half 8
डेरा	rented flat 4

ढ

ढङ्ग	manner, way, style 17
ढाँचा	fashion, style, design, pattern 14
ढाकिनु	be covered 21
ढीलो	late; slow 9

ढुकुटी treasury, treasure room 13
ढुङ्गे stoned, rocky 12
ढोका door 1

त

तँ you (low) 13
तथा and (literary) 10
तपस्या asceticism, meditation 22
तपाईं you (polite) 1
तयार गर्नु get ready, prepare 14
तयारी ready, ready made, prepared 16
तर but, however 4
तरकारी vegetable 3
तराई Terai 9
तरिका way, method 7
तर्नु to cross 7
तर्फ side (of) 13
तल below, down 6
तलब pay, salary 8
तसर्थ thus, therefore 18
तस्बिर picture, portrait 22
तातो hot (to touch) 18
तान्नु pull 17
तापक्रम temperature 10
तामा bamboo shoot 12
ताल lake 11
तास playing cards 19
तिनी he, she 5
तिमी you (med.) 9
-तिर towards 4
तिर्नु pay, repay 8
तिलहरी gold pendant 14
ती those 1
तीर्थयात्रा pilgrimage 19
तीर्थस्थल shrine, pilgrimage site 21
तुवाँलो लाग्नु to be hazy 10
तुसारो पर्नु to frost 10
तेर्सो level, flat 7
तेल oil 16
तेलकासा Newari tag game 19
तैपनि nevertheless, even then 13
तोड्नु break 20
त्यतापट्टि there, that side 19
त्यति that much 9
त्यसकारण therefore 5
त्यसैले because of that 8
त्यस्तै / त्यसो like that 9
त्यहाँ there 4
त्यो that 1

थ

थकाइ fatigue 7
थप addition(al) 20
थप्नु add, increase 21
थर subcaste, clan 15
थाप्नु hold; receive, take 21
थाप्लो head 16
थाल plate, platter 5
थाल्नु to begin 7
थाहा knowledge 6
थुक्नु to spit 13
थुतुनो snout 12
थुन्नु trap, detain 18
थुप्रै a lot, many 17
थोक thing 6
थोरै a little 10

द

दक्षिण South 10
दङ्ग delighted, thrilled 21

दण्डवत् गर्नु	bow down, worship	22
दया गर्नु	be kind, have mercy	13
दरबार	palace, mansion	21
दर्शन गर्नु	visit (god or superior)	21
दल	party	23
दलगत	party system	23
दसौँ	tenth	21
दाँजामा (को)	in comparison to	19
दाँत	tooth	12
दाँत माझ्नु	brush teeth	16
दाइँ गर्नु	thresh by oxen	17
दाइ	older brother	6
दाउराघाँस	firewood-grass	16
दाज्यू/दाजु	older brother	20
दाना	animal food; seed grain	17
दायाँ	right	4
दालभात	lentil and rice	2
दालमोठ	crunchy snacks	6
दिउँसो	afternoon	4
दिदी	older sister	2
दिनचर्या	daily chores	16
दिनु	give	3
दिनहुँ	daily	8
दिसा लाग्नु	get diarrhea	9
दुःख दिनु	bother, trouble	9
दुख्नु	hurt	9
दुवै	both	16
दुर्भाग्य	misfortune	23
दुलहा	bridegroom	20
दुलही	bride	20
दुलो	hole (mouse den)	13
दुष्ट	evil, corrupt, wicked	13
दूध	milk	17
दृश्य	view, sight	7
दृश्यावलोकन	sightseeing	19
दृष्टि	sight (sense); eye	12
देखाउनु	to show	4
देखावटी	showiness, pretence	15
देख्नु	to see	4
देखि	from	10
देव	god (cf. "deo")	22
देवता	deity, god	22
देवी	goddess	22
देश	country	2
दैनिक	daily	16
दोपट्टा	scarf, shawl	14
दोबर	double	13
दोहोरो	doubled, two-in-one	19
दोहोरी	duet (song)	18
दौरा	Nepali shirt	14
द्यौराली	worship place at hilltop	19
द्वारा	by, through	23

ध

धकेल्नु	push, shove	22
धनसम्पत्ति	riches, wealth	13
धनी	rich, wealthy	15
धन्यवाद	thanks	3
धरातल	terrain	11
धर्म	religion; duty; goodness	14
धर्मशास्त्र	Scripture	22
धर्मावलम्बी	follower of X religion	22
धाउनु	to frequent	16
धागो	thread, string	14
धान	paddy (rice)	18
धारा	section, article (of law)	23
धारा	water tap	9
धुनु	wash	3
धुलो	dust	10
धेरै	very	1

धेरैजसो most, mostly 8
धोती loin cloth 14
ध्यान attention; meditation 19

न

नकल पार्नु copy, imitate 19
नक्कली fake 14
नक्सा map 10
नगदे cash (crop, etc.) 18
नजिक near 5
नङ finger / toe nail 13
नत्र otherwise 22
नदी river 8
नपुग हुनु be insufficient 18
नयाँ new; novice; latest 20
नरम polite; soft 12, 13
नराम्रो bad 1
नरिवल coconut 23
नर्क hell 22
नवदुर्गा name of goddess 21
नववर्ष New Year 19
नाइँ no 20
नाचघर theater 19
नाच्नु dance 19
नाटक drama, stage play 19
नाता relationship 15
नातेदार relative 15
नातिनी granddaughter 20
नाती grandson 20
नाफा profit 21
नाम name 2
नारायणी Narayani 4
नाला stream 11
नास्ता morning snack 7
निकाल्नु to take out 13
निको well, healthy 9
निकै very 11
निगाला bamboo (thin) 12
निजामती civil (servant) 21
निधार forehead 12
निधो decision 13
निम्तापत्र invitation card 20
निम्न low (standard) 15
नियुक्ति appointment to a job 8
-निर near 4
निरङ्कुश autocratic 23
निरन्तर incessant 22
निर्णय decision 15
निर्णयकर्ता decider 15
निर्दयी merciless, callous 13
निर्देशन instruction, direction 20
निर्धारण determination 15
निर्धारित determined, fixed 22
निर्भर गर्नु to depend (on) 14
निर्यात export 18
निलो blue 1
निश्चय certainly 15
निश्चित sure, certain 20
नुन salt 16
नुहाउनु to bathe 13
नेता leader 15
नेपाल Nepal 2
नेपाली Nepali 2
नोकर servant 16
नौगेडी necklace 14
नौरथा Dasai pilgrimage 21
न्यानो warm 10
न्याय justice 23

प

पङ्क्ति line, row 12
पन्चान्नब्बे ninety-five 6
प्रभाव influence, effect 14

पकाउनु cook 5
पक्का गर्नु make sure, certain, confirm 20
पक्ष side, party; aspect 20
पग्लनु melt (intr) 11
पचपन्न fifty-five 6
पचहत्तर seventy-five 6
पचासी eighty-five 6
पच्चीस twenty-five 3
पछाडि behind 4
पछि after, behind 4
पञ्चायती village council 23
पटक time (1 of a #) 9
पठाउनु send 8
पढ्नु to study, read 6
पद rank, post, (also verse) 23
पद्धति system 23
पनि also, even 4
पन्जा glove(s) 14
पन्ध्र fifteen 3
पन्यूँ rice serving spoon 15
परमेश्वर God 22
परम्परा tradition 14
परम्परागत traditional 14
परिकार variety (of food) 20
परिचय introduction 2
परिवार family 14
परिश्रम toil, labor, hard work 16
पर्खनु to wait 13
पर्खाल wall (compound) 1
पर्दा curtain 1
पर्म work exchange 18
पर्सि day-after-tomorrow 20
पर्सिपल्ट two days later 20
पवित्र holy 21
पशु animal 17
पशुपालन animal husbandry 17
पश्चिम West 10
पसल shop, store, stall 3
पसले shopkeeper, merchant 16
पसिना sweat 10
पस्नु to enter 13
पहाड hill, mountain 10
पहाडी mountainous, hilly 10
पहिरन clothes, attire 14
पहिले firstly, before 8
पहिलो first 7
पहिल्यै already before 9
पहेँलो yellow 1
पाइनु to be available 3
पाउरोटी loaf bread 3
पाका elders (lit. ripe people) 19
पाक्नु to ripen; be cooked 18
पाङ्ग्रा wheel, tire 19
पाटा stripe 12
पाटे striped (black) 12
पात leaf 12
पातलो thin 9
पानी water 5
पाप गर्नु to sin 22
-पारि across, other side 11
पारिलो घाम warm (sun) 18
पार्नु to make, cause 15
पालन tending, care, protection 17
पालो time, turn (of a #) 20
पाल्नु to tend, raise, keep 13
पिँढी porch 7
पिँध्नु grind 16
पिङ खेल्नु swing (to play) 21
पिउनु drink 9
पिट्नु to beat, hit 13
पिरो spicy hot 7

पीठ	shrine (of goddess) 21
पीठो	flour 16
पीपलबोट	Peepal tree 4
पुग्नु	reach, arrive 4
पुच्छर	tail 12
पुछ्नु	wipe, clean off 5
पुनर्जन्म	rebirth, reincarnation 22
पुरानो	old 9
पुरुष	man, male 14
पुरोहित	domestic priest 20
पुल	bridge 4
पुलाउ	fried rice 6
पुस	Dec-Jan 10
पूजा	worship 13
पूजाआजा	worship & prayers 16
पूजारी	priest 22
पूरा गर्नु	to complete 16
पूर्ति	supply, fulfillment 15
पूर्व	East 10
पूर्वजन्म	previous life 22
पूर्वी	eastern 10
पृथ्वी	earth 11
पेट	stomach 9
पेटी	belt 14
पेसा	occupation, profession 16
पेस्की	advance (money) 21
पैंतालीस	forty-five 6
पैंतीस	thirty-five 6
पैंसट्ठी	sixty-five 6
पैदल	on foot, by foot 7
पैदावार	crop, produce 17
पैरो/पहिरो	landslide 11
पैसा	money 3
पोका	parcel,packet, bundle 20
पोखरी	pond 11
पोते	string bead necklace 14
पोसाक	dress, uniform 14
पौडी खेल्नु	to swim 19
पौष्टिक	nutritious 17
प्याज	onion 3
प्रकार	kind, sort 11
प्रज्ञाभवन	Academy Hall 19
प्रजातन्त्र	(people's) democracy 23
प्रति	over, towards; per 23
प्रतिनिधि	representative 23
प्रतिशत	percent (per 100) 18
प्रतिष्ठा	consecration (temple, idol) 22
प्रत्यक्ष	obvious, visible 15
प्रत्येक	each and every 15
प्रदर्शनी	exhibition, show 14
प्रधानमन्त्री	Prime Minister 23
प्रवृत्ति	tendency (people's) 11
प्रभाव	influence 14
प्रभावशाली	all influential 15
प्रभावित	influenced 15
प्रमुख	main 11
प्रयोग	use 12
प्रबन्ध	arrangement 17
प्रश्न	question 15
प्रसिद्ध	renown, famous 11
प्रस्थान गर्नु	departure (to do) 20
प्राकृतिक	natural 10
प्राणी	creature, being 22
प्राप्त हुनु	be obtained, received 17
प्राय:	generally 16
प्राविधिक	technical; technician 17

फ

फडानी	deforestation 11
फकाउनु	persuade 16

फरक different 10
फराकिलो wide 4
फरिया sari (low grade) 14
फर्कनु return; turn 9
फल fruit; result 13, 22
फलफूल fruit 3
फलाउनु to fruit, grow (tr) 18
फलैंचा elevated resting place 19
फल्नु to fruit 13
फाँट cultivated plain (plot of) 11
फाइदा profit, benefit, merit, advantage 12
फागु Hindu festival (Holi) 19
फागुन Feb-Mar 10
फाल्नु throw away 13
फुकाल्नु take off (shoes, clothes) 14
फुपू father's sister 20
फुर्सद leisure time 6
फुल egg 17
फुली nose pin 14
फुल्नु to flower, blossom 23
फूल flower 12
फूलपाती 7th day of Dasai 21
फेदी foot, bottom 11
फेरि again 13
फेरि also, furthermore 7
फैलिनु to be spread 9
फोर्नु to break open 13
फोहर filth 13

ब

बगाउनु dispense lavishly 21
बग्नु flow 11
बचत profit, saving(s) 18
बजाउनु play (instrument) 19
बजार market 3
बजे (at)...o'clock 5
बज्यै grandma 20
बटुवा traveler, hiker, pedestrian 19
बढ्दै जानु continue increasing 10
बढी a lot, so much, more 10, 17
बताउनु to explain 13
बतास wind 10
बनाउनु make, build 8
बन्द closed 13
बन्दाकोबी cabbage 3
बन्नु to be made 16
बमोजिम according to (legal) 23
बराबर equal; frequently 15
बरु or else, or rather 22
बलि sacrifice, offering 21
बलियो strong 1
बल्ल finally, at last 7
बसाउनु to settle 11
बस "bus" 7
बस्ती village, settlement 11
बस्तुभाउ domestic animal 21
बस्नु sit, stay, live at 2
बहिनी younger sister 6
बहुदलीय multi-partied 23
बाँकी remaining 11
बाँड्नु divide, distribute 20
बाँदर monkey 23
बाँध्नु to tie, bind 17
बाँस bamboo 12
बा father 2
बाक्लो thick 10
बाख्रा goat 17
बाख्री she-goat 13
बाघ tiger 12
बाजा musical instrument 19

बाजे	grandpa 15
बाट	from 7
बाटो	road 4
बाट्नु	to plait, twine (rope) 16
बाढी	flood 18
बादल लाग्नु	to become cloudy 10
बाबु	father 15
बायाँ	left 4
बार	fence, hedge 1
बारी	dry field, garden 17
बारेमा (-को)	about X 9
बाली	crop 18
बालुवा	sand 21
बास	lodging, stay 7
बाहिर	out(side) 6
-बाहेक	except 9, 19
बिक्नु	be sold, it sells 21
बिक्री गर्नु	to sell 21
बिछोड	difficult good-bye 20
बिछ्याउनु	lay out bedding 18
बिजुली	electricity 11
बिताउनु	to spend (time) 15
बित्तिकै (-ने)	as soon as, immed after 13
बिदा	leave, good-bye 20
बिदा लिनु	take leave 7
बिरामी	sick (person) 8
बिरुवा	seedling, sapling 12
बिर्सनु	to forget 9
बिस्तारै	slowly 6
बिहान	(in the) morning 5
बिहीबार	Thursday 5
बिहे/बिहा	wedding 20
बीउ	seed 18
बीचमा (-को)	in between/middle 10
बुद्धिजीवी	wise/learned people, elite 23
बुद्धिमान्	intelligent, wise 13
बुधबार	Wednesday 5
बुन्नु	to weave, knit 14
बुहारी	daughter-in-law; wife of young bro 15
बूढाबूढी	elders 15
बूढी	old woman 13
बेँसी	lowland, base of hill 17
बेइज्जत गर्नु	slander, insult 15
बेइमान	dishonest 23
बेकार	unemployed; useless 16
बेच्नु	to sell 15
बेर	time (short period) 9
बेला	time (point of) 9
बेलाबेलामा	from time to time 19
बेलुका	late afternoon, evening 7
बैठक	meeting-room 6
बैसाख	April-May 10
बोका	he-goat 21
बोकाउनु	get/have carried 17
बोट	plant 21
बोल्नु	speak 2
बोसो	fat, grease 17
ब्याड	bed (nursery) 18

भ

भएर	via (having been at) 7
भगवती	name of goddess 21
भजन	hymn, praise song 19
भण्डार	warehouse, storeroom 11
भतिजो/जी	nephew/niece 20
भत्ता	bonus pay, allowance 21
भदौ	Aug-Sept 10
-भन्दा	than, as compared to 9
भन्नु	say, tell 4

भर पर्नु	depend, rely on 15
भरि	throughout; full 11
भरिया	porter 7
भर्खर	just, just now 12
भर्नु / भरिनु	fill / be filled 21
भऱ्याङ	stairs, ladder 5
भलो	welfare 13
भवन	building (large) 8
भवसागर	Ocean of Existence 22
भाँडा	utensil 5
भाइ	younger brother 6
भाउज्यू	wife of older bro 20
भाग	part 11
भाग्नु	to flee, run away 13
भाडा	rent, hire 8
भारत	India 11
भारतीय	Indian 17
भारी	load, burden 7
भाषा	language 2
भिज्नु	get wet, soaked 10
भित्ता	wall (of house) 1
भित्र	inside, within 6
भित्र्याउनु	take in, import 18
भिना	husband of older sis 20
भिन्दै	different 14
भिरालो	steep, precipitous 18
भीड	crowd 19
भीर	precipice, cliff 8
भीरपाखा	terraced land 11
भुईं	floor 1
भूभाग	region, territory 11
भूमि	earth, ground, land 18
भूमिका	role 17
भेडा	sheep 17
भेग	locality 10
भेषभूषा	attire / adornment 14
भैंसी	buffalo 17
भोग	undertaking 22
भोग्नु	undergo 22
भोज	feast, banquet 16
भोजनालय	restaurant 16
भोटे	Tibetan (can be pejorative) 11
भोलि	tomorrow 6
भोलिपल्ट	the next day 7
भौगोलिक	geographical 14
भ्याउनु	manage to do (in time) 16
भ्यागुता	frog 18
भ्रमण	traveler, tour 19

म

म	I 1
मकै	corn, maize 18
मक्ख पर्नु	be happy, glad (inside) 19
मङ्गलबार	Tuesday 5
मङ्गलसूत्र	necklace 14
मङ्सिर	Nov-Dec 10
मजदुर	laborer 15
मजा	fun, enjoyment 19
मजाको	interesting, pleasant 19
मजा गर्नु	enjoy, have fun 21
मझौला	medium (size, quality) 14
मट्टीतेल	kerosene 16
मतलब	meaning 19
मदत	help 5
मधेस	the Terai 11
मध्य	middle 11
मध्यम	middle (standard) 15
मध्ये	among 11
मन	mind / heart 5
मन बहलाउनु	amuse, entertain oneself 19

मनमोहक हुनु to be charming 18
मनाउनु celebrate, observe 19
मनै लोभिनु be attracted 18
मनोरञ्जन entertainment 19
मनोहर attractive, beautiful 7
मन्त्रालय Ministry (of gov't) 23
मन्दिर temple 19
मरमसला spices and such 21
मरुभूमि desert 11
मर्त्यलोक place-of-death 22
मर्नु to die 13
मल manure, fertilizer 17
मलमूत्र dung-urine, excreta 17
मसला spice, condiment 20
मस्तिष्क ज्वर meningitis 9
महँगो expensive 3
महत्त्व importance 12
महत्त्वपूर्ण important 9
महानवमी Great 9th Day 21
महामारी plague, epidemic 9
महिना month 8
महिनाबारी monthly payment 16
महिनौँ many months 14
महिला woman, female 14
मा in, at, on 1
माइती women's parent's home 20
माग demand, requisition 15
माग्नु to ask for 13
माघ Jan-Feb 10
माछा fish 12
माझ्नु brush, scrub 5
माटो mud, clay, soil 21
मात्र only, merely 5
माथि up, over, above 6
मानिस person, man 11
मान्छे person, man 7
मान्नु agree 7
मान्यजन respected people 21
मामा mother's brother 20
माया गर्नु to love 13
मारुनी male dancer dressed as fem. 19
मार्नु to kill 13
माला garland 14
मालिक master, owner 15
मासु meat 6
माहिला 2nd oldest son/bro 20
माहुरी bee 17
मीठो tasty, delicious 5
मिलनसार sociable, friendly 7
मिलाउनु arrange, fix 8
मिल्नु united; match, jive 16
मिहिनेत गर्नु to work hard 13
मुक्ति salvation (from rebirth) 22
मुख mouth; face 5
मुखिया village leader 15
मुख्य main, chief 8
मुग्लान India; foreign land 16
मुनि below, under 13
मुसलधारे torrential (rain) 10
मुसा mouse 13
मूर्ख stupid, foolish 13
मूर्ति idol, image, statue 22
मूली chief, headman 15
मूल्यवान् valuable; expensive 17
मृत्यु death 22
मेघ गर्जनु thunder (cloud roar) 10
मेच chair 1
मेला fair 19
मेलापात agricult. teamwork 16

मैदान the plains. plain 11
मोक्ष salvation (from rebirth) 22
मोज गर्नु enjoy 21
मोजा sock(s) 14
मोटाउनु to fatten 13
मोड्नु to turn 4
मोल price, cost 21
मोलतोल bargaining 4
मौका opportunity 21
मौसम weather 9

य

यसबाहेक besides this 19
यसरी thus, in this way 7
यस्तो/यसो like this 9
यहाँ here 3
या or 22
यातना torment (noun) 22
यातायात transportation 11
यात्रा journey 7
यात्रु traveller, pilgrim 21
याद राख्नु to remember 22
यी these 1
युवा/युवती young boy/girl 19
योग्य fit, able, worthy 18
योजना plan, arrangement 8
यौन रोग venereal disease 9

र

र and 3
रक्सी alcohol 19
रक्सी लाग्नु become intoxicated 19
रङ्ग color 1
रमणीय pleasant 11
रमाइलो pleasant 7
रमाउनु be pleased, rejoice 20
रमिता show, spectacle, sight 21
रहनु to remain 12
रहिरहनु continue to remain 18
राख्नु put down, place 6
राजतन्त्र monarchy 23
राजनीति politics 15
राजनीतिज्ञ politician 23
राजा king 12
राज्य kingdom, state; reign, nation 23
रात night (noun) 20
रातो red 1
राती night (at) 9
राम्रो good 1
राष्ट्रपति President (country) 23
राष्ट्रिय national 14
रासायनिक मल chemical fert. 18
रिन debt, loan 21
रिबाज tradition, practice 15
रिस anger 13
रीति custom, manner 15
रितिरिवाज etiquette 15
रुख tree 12
रुघाज्वरो cold flu 9
रुचाउनु like, prefer 14
रुनु to cry 13
रुपियाँ/रुपैयाँ rupee 3
रुवाबासी wailing, lamenting 20
रूप form 11
रोक्नु stop; obstruct 4
रोग sickness, disease 9
रोटी bread 5
रोदी घर social hall(Gurung) 19
रोपाइँ planting 18

रोप्नु	plant, transplant 18
रौँ	fur, hair 12

ल

ल	alright, okay 3
लक्षण	symptom 9
लगाउनु/लाउनु	apply 5
लग्नु	take away 8
लच्छिन	lucky sign 13
लमी	mediator; match-maker 20
लहरै	in rows, lines 18
लाख	100,000 22
लाखे	Newari demon 13
लागि (को)	for the sake (of) 8
लाग्नु	feel (emotion) 7
लाग्नु	to begin, set off, go 10
लाप्पा खेल्नु	mud wrestle 18
लाम्खुट्टे	mosquito 7
लामो	long 12
लालीगुराँस	red rhododendron 12
लाहुरे	Indian Gurkha 16
लिखित	written 23
लिनु	take 3
लिप्नु	to mud walls/floors 16
लुकाउनु	to hide (tr) 13
लेक	highlands 12
लेकाली	mountainous (high hills) 18
लेख	writing, article 19
लेख्नु	to write 19
लोककथा	folk tale/story 13
लोभी	greedy 13
ल्याउनु	bring 6

व

वनस्पति	vegetation 11
वन	forest, woods 11
वन्यजन्तु	wild animal 12
वरिपरि	surrounding, around X 13
वर्ग	social class 15
वर्गीय	of social class 20
वर्ष	year 7
वर्षा	rain; rainy season 10
वहन गर्नु	bear responsibility 16
वा	or 16
वाकवाक	nausea 9
वाक्क लाग्नु	be fed-up with 23
वातावरण	surroundings, environ. 14
वासस्थान	habitat, dwelling 12
वाहन	vehicle 12
विकत	interior 1
विकास	development 11
विकासे	developed, improved 17
विचार गर्नु	think, consider 9
विजयादशमी	Victorious 10th Day 21
विदेश	foreign country 8
विदेशिनु	emigrate 18
विदेशी	foreign(er) 7
विद्यार्थी	student 21
विधिपूर्वक	according to law or ritual 20
विनाश	destruction 12
विभिन्न	various 11
विविधता	variations 14
विशेष	special, particular 19
विशेषाधिकार	privilege 23
विश्वास	faith, trust, belief 22
विष	poison 9
वैसाख	April-May 10
वृक्षारोपण	tree planting 12
व्यवसाय	occupation, business 17
व्यवस्था	management, arrangement 12
व्यवहार	behavior, practice, treatment 12

व्यस्त	busy 16
व्यापारी	businessman, merchant 16
व्यापारिक	business, commercial 11
व्यावसायिक	vocational 12

श

शक्ति	power, strength 12
शङ्का गर्नु	doubt, suspect 23
शनिवार	Saturday 5
शरीर	body 9
शहर	city 5
शाखा	branch, division, section 12
शारीरिक व्यायाम	physical exercise 19
शासक	ruler 15
शासन गर्नु	to rule, govern 23
शास्त्र	Scripture 22
शिक्षक	teacher 8
शिखर	summit 11
शीत पर्नु	to dew 10
शुक्रबार	Friday 5
शुद्ध	clean, pure (ritually) 22
श्री ५ महाराजाधिराज	King's title, HM the King 21
श्रीमती	wife 5
श्रीमान्	husband 5

स

-सँग	with, together 5
संयुक्त	in common; united, joined 15
संयोग	coincidence, chance 20
संरक्षण	protection, conservation 12
संविधान	constitution, statute 23
संवैधानिक	constitutional 23
संसद्	Parliament 23
संसदीय	parliamentary 23
संसार	world 11
संस्कार	rite 15
संस्कृति	culture 8
संस्था	an organization 8
सङ्ग्रहालय	museum 19
सङ्घर्ष	struggle 23
सकिनु	to be possible, can be 7
सकेजति	as much as one can 13
सकेसम्म	as much as possible 21
सक्कली	real, genuine 14
सक्नु	be able to 7
सक्षम	capable, qualified 23
सगरमाथा	Mt. Everest 11
सचिव	Secretary 23
सजाय	punishment 22
सजिलो	easy 7
सज्नु	be decorated, adorned 22
सञ्चालन गर्नु	conduct, operate 17
सट्टा	substitution 14
सतर्क	alert 9
सतह	surface; level 10
सताउनु	torment, persecute 16
सदस्य	member 15
सधैँ	always 5
सन्चै	health; well 6
सन्तुष्ट	satisfied, content 17
सन्दर्भ	context 14
सफा गर्नु	clean (up), tidy 5
सफल	successful, fruitful 18
सबकासब	each and everyone 21
सबभन्दा	(the) most of all 10
सबेरै	early morning 7
सबै	all 6
सबैजना	everyone 6
सबैजसो	almost all 16

सभा	council, conference, assembly 23	साँझ	evening, dusk 4
सभागृह	City Hall 19	सांसद	member of Parl. 23
सभापति	chairman (of a council) 23	सांस्कृतिक	cultural 14
समथर	plain (land) 18	साइत	auspicious time 20
समय लाग्नु	to require time 9	साउन	July-Aug 10
समस्या	problem 9	साग	spinach 3
समाज	society 15	साडी	sari 14
समुद्र	sea 10	सातौं	seventh 21
-समेत	together with, including 15	साथ	with 20
सम्झिनु	be considered 22	साथी	friend 9
सम्धी	kinship term 20	साथै	along with 18
सम्पन्न	successful, affluent 15	साधन	means, resource 19
सम्बन्ध	connection, relation 20	साधना	exercise, practice 22
सम्बन्धी	concerning, relating 9	साधारण	ordinary, general 9
सम्भावना	probability 17	साधारणतया	generally 9
-सम्म	up to, until 7	साध्य	practicable 19
सरकार	government 8	सानो	small 1
सरसफाइ	cleaning work 16	सानोतिनो	small, petty, minor 20
सर्नु	shift, move 9	साबुन	soap 3
सर्प	snake 18	सामाजिक	social 20
सर्वोच्चता	greatness, supremeness 23	सामान	supplies 7
सल्यान	Salyan 7	सार्वभौमसत्ता	sovereignty 23
सल्ला	pine tree 12	साल	tree - Shorea Robustas 12
सल्लाह	advice 9	सासू	mother-in-law 20
सवारी	royal tour / visit 21	साहुजी	shopkeeper (male) 3
ससुरा	father-in-law 20	साहुनी	shopkeeper (female) 3
ससुराली	wife's parent's home 20	सिँगारिनु	be decorated, adorned 20
सस्तो	inexpensive 3	सिँचाइ	irrigation 11
सहनु	endure, tolerate 13	सिँढी	stair step 13
सहायक	assistant, subsidiary 17	सिउनु	to sew, stitch 14
-सहित	with, including 10	सिकाउनु	teach 2
साँघुरो	narrow, tight 4	सिक्नु	learn 8
साँचो	key 13	सिङ	horn 17
साँचो	true, genuine,	सिङे	horned 12
साँच्चै	really, truly 16, 23	सिद्धिनु	end, be finished 20

सिधा	straight 4
सिनेमा	cinema, film 16
सिमाना	border, frontier 11
सिमी	bean 3
सिरक	quilt 10
सिलाउनु	have sewn, stitched 14
सिसाकलम	pencil 1
सिसौ	tree - Dalbergia Sissu 12
सीमा	limit(ation), borderline 22
सीमित	limit, limited, fixed 23
सुँगुर	pig 17
सुँघ्ने	smell (sense) 12
सुअवसर	good opportunity 22
सुक्नु	get dry (intran.) 5
सुख	comfort, ease 22
सुत्नु	sleep, lie down 7
सुदूर	far, remote, distant 11
सुन	gold 13
सुनाउनु	to tell 13
सुनौलो	golden 21
सुन्तला	orange 3
सुन्दर	beautiful 11
सुन्दरता	beauty 11
सुन्नु	listen, hear 6
सुन्ने	hearing (sense) 12
सुपारी	betel nut 20
सुर	preoccupation, consciousness 21
सुरु	beginning 7
सुरुवाल	Nepali pant 14
सुविधा	convenience, facility 11
सुहाउनु	to suit, look nice 14
सूक्ष्म	tiny, minute 22
सूचना	news, information 13
सेतो	white 1
सेवक	servant 15
सेर्पा	Sherpa 11
सोच्नु	ponder, think 19
सोझो	honest, simple 13
सोध्नु	ask 9
सोमबार	Monday 5
सोरठी	Gurung dance 19
स्रोत	source 11
स्कूल	school 2
स्तर	status, level 15
स्तरीय	quality, standard 12
स्त्री	woman 16
स्थल	place, site 19
स्थान	place (formal) 15
स्थापना हुनु	be founded, established 17
स्थायी	permanent 22
स्थिति	condition, situation 16
स्याउ	apple 3
स्याउला	branch (leafy) 12
स्वतन्त्र	independent, free 16
स्वयंसेवक	volunteer 2
स्वयंवर	girl choosing husband 20
स्वर्ग	heaven, paradise 22
स्वविवेक	personal conscience 23
स्वागत	welcome 20
स्वाभाविक	natural 14
स्वास्थ्य	health 9
स्वीकार गर्नु	to accept, approve 15

ह

हुँदैन	not allowed 3
हक	right, entitlement 23
हगि	right? 4
हजार	thousand 6
हजूर	Sir, lord (hon) 6
हडताल	strike (political) 23

हप्ता	week 5
हमला	attack, invasion 12
हराउनु	lose, defeat (tr), be lost (intr), disappear 14
हरियो	green 1
हरेक	each and every 13
हल्का	light (color, weight...) 12
हवाईजहाज	airplane 7
हस्/हवस्	okay 3
हस्तक्षेप	interference, intervention 23
हाँस	duck 17
हाकिम	boss, in-charge 15
हाड	bone 13
हात	hand; arm 5
हात्ती	elephant 12
हामी	we 3
हाल	news, at present 17
हावा	air, wind 11
हावापानी	climate 10
हिँड्नु	walk 7
हिउँ पर्नु	to snow 10
हिउँद	winter 10
हिजो	yesterday 7
हिजोआज	nowadays 8
हिन्दी	Hindi 2
हिमाल	snow-peak 7
हिमालय पर्वतमाला	Himal. Range 11
हिले	muddy 18
हिलो	mud 11
हिल्याउनु	to puddle (fields) 18
हिसाब	accounting; calculation 14
हिस्स पर्नु	be baffled, disappointed 13
हुन त...तर	although; of course...but 15
हुन सक्नु	to be possible 9
हुनु	to be 2
हुने हुनाले	because (it) is 10
हुरी	gale, storm 10
हुस्सु लाग्नु	to fog 10
हेरविचार	supervision 5
हेर्नु	to look, watch 4
है	okay? 6
होइन	isn't; no 4
होइबक्सिनु	be (royal honorific) 21
होटेल	restaurant, hotel 16
होला	probably 3
होसियार	careful 9

APPENDIX 12

ENGLISH-NEPALI GLOSSARY
(with chapter indexed)

Spellings throughout the textbook have been standardized to the *Nepali Brihat Shabdakosh*.

a little	थोरै 10
a lot	बढी 17; थुप्रै 17
able (adj)	योग्य 18;
about	जति 8; करिब 18
about X	बारेमा (-को) 9
above	माथि 6
Academy Hall	प्रज्ञाभवन 19
accept	स्वीकार गर्नु 15
according to	अनुसार 10
according to (legal)	बमोजिम 23
according to law/ritual	विधिपूर्वक 20
accounting	हिसाब 14
across	–पारि 11
act	कार्य 17
Act (law)	ऐन 20
action	कारबाही 23
actually	खास गरी 9
add	थप्नु 21
addition(al)	थप 20
adopt (as a part)	अङ्गीकार 23
adorned (to be)	सिँगारिनु 20; सज्नु 22
adornment	भेषभूषा 14
adult	अधबैंसे 19
advance (money)	पेस्की 21
advice	सल्लाह 9
afraid (to be)	डराउनु 22
after	पछि 4
after (immed.)	बित्तिकै (-ने) 13
afternoon	दिउँसो 4
afternoon (late)	बेलुका 7
again	फेरि 13
age	उमेर 16
ago	अघि 7
agree	मान्नु 7
agriculture	कृषि 11
agro-economy	कृषि अर्थव्यवस्था 17
aim (objective, purpose)	उद्देश्य 23
air, wind	हावा 11
airplane	हवाईजहाज 7
alcohol	रक्सी 19
alert	सतर्क 9
alive (to be)	जिउनु 15
all	सबै 6
alligator (long nose)	घडियाल 12
allowance (money)	भत्ता 21
almost all	सबैजसो 16
alone	एक्लै 16
along with	साथै 18; एकैसाथ 20
alright	ल 3
also	पनि 4; फेरि 7
although	हुन त...तर 15
altitude	उचाइ 10
always	सधैँ 5
amazed	अचम्म लाग्नु 9; छक्क पर्नु 13
America	अमेरिका 2
among	मध्ये 11

amuse oneself मन बहलाउनु 19
and र 3; तथा 10
and (then) अनि 5
anger रिस 13
animal पशु 17
animal (domestic) बस्तुभाउ 21
animal (wild) वन्यजन्तु 12
animal husbandry पशुपालन 17
anxiety चिन्ता 16
apple स्याउ 3
apply लगाउनु/लाउनु 5
appointment नियुक्ति 8
appropriate उपयुक्त 17
approximately जति 8; करिब 18
Apr-May बैसाख 10
approve स्वीकार गर्नु 15
area, field क्षेत्र 11
arm हात 5
around X वरिपरि 13
arrange मिलाउनु 8
arranged (to be) छिनिनु 20
arrangement योजना 8; प्रबन्ध 17
arrive पुग्नु 4
article लेख 19
article (of law) धारा 23
as जस्तो 9
as compared to भन्दा 9
as if जस्तो 9
as much as one can सकेजति 13
as much as possible सकेसम्म 21
as soon as बित्तिकै (-ने) 13
ascend चढ्नु 12
ascetic जोगी 22
asceticism तपस्या 22
ask सोध्नु 9
ask for माग्नु 13
assistant सहायक 17
assurance आश्वासन 23
assured (to be) आश्वस्त हुनु 20
at मा 1
at last बल्ल 7
at once खुरुक्क 13
attack, invasion हमला 12
attention ध्यान 19
attire पहिरन 14; भेषभूषा 14
attracted (to be) मनै लोभिनु 18
attractive मनोहर 7
Aug-Sept भदौ 10
auspicious time साइत 20
authority अधिकार 15
autocratic निरङ्कुश 23
available (to be) पाइनु 3
bad नराम्रो 1
baffled (to be) हिस्स पर्नु 13
bag झोला 1
bamboo बाँस 12
bamboo (thin) निगालो 12
bamboo shoot तामा 12
bamboo shoot (thin) टुसा 12
banana केरा 3
bangle चुरा 14
banquet भोज 16
bar (across door) आग्लो 13
bargaining मोलतोल 4
barley जौ 18
barley (young shoot) जमरा 21
based (on) आधारित 18
basic आधारभूत 23
bathe नुहाउनु 13
be हुनु 2
be (royal honorific) होइबक्सिनु 21
bean सिमी 3

bear responsibility	वहन गर्नु 16
beat (to be)	पिट्नु 13
beautiful	मनोहर 7; सुन्दर 11
beauty	सुन्दरता 11
because	किनभने 7
because (it) is	हुने हुनाले 10
because of that	त्यसैले 8
bed(ing)	ओछ्यान 9
bed-ridden (to be)	ओछ्यान पर्नु 9
bee	माहुरी 17
beer (rice)	जाँड 21
before	अगाडि 4; अघि 7; पहिले 8; पहिल्यै 9
begin	थाल्नु 7; लाग्नु 10
beginning	सुरु 7
behavior	व्यवहार 12
behind	पछाडि 4; पछि 4
below	कम 3; तल 6; मुनि 13
belt	पेटी 14
bend (in a road)	घुम्ती 4
benefit	फाइदा 12
besides this	यसबाहेक 19
besides X	अलावा (को) 17
best	उत्तम 18
betel nut	सुपारी 20
big	ठूलो 1
bird	चरा 12
birth	जन्म 22
bite	टोक्नु 9
black	कालो 1
blessing	आशीर्वाद 21
blocked (interrupted, stopped)	अवरुद्ध 19
blue	निलो 1
body	जिउ 9; शरीर 9
boil (liquids, tr.)	उमाल्नु 5
boil (solids)	उसिन्नु 5
bone	हाड 13
bonus pay	भत्ता 21
book	किताब 1
border	सिमाना 11
borderline	सीमा 22
boss	हाकिम 15
both	दुवै 16
bother	दु:ख दिनु 9
bottom	फेदी 11
bow down	दण्डवत् गर्नु 22
boy	केटा 15
boy (young)	युवा 19
branch (division)	शाखा 12
branch (leafy)	स्याउला 12
bread	पाउरोटी 3; रोटी 5
break	फोर्नु 13; तोड्नु 20
bride	दुलही 20
bridegroom	दुलहा 20
bridge	पुल 4
bring	ल्याउनु 6
bring out	झिक्नु 13
broom	कुचो 5
brother (older)	दाइ 6; दाज्यू/दाजु 20
brother (younger)	भाइ 6
brown	खैरो 1
brush	माझ्नु 5
buffalo	भैँसी 17
bug	किरा 12
build	बनाउनु 8
building (large)	भवन 8
bunch (flower, banana...)	झुप्पा 21
bundle	पोका 20
burden	भारी 7
bury	गाड्नु 13

bus	बस 7
business	व्यापारिक 11; व्यवसाय 17
businessman	व्यापारी 16
busy	व्यस्त 16
but	तर 4
button	टाँक लगाउनु 14
buy	किन्नु 3
by	द्वारा 23
cabbage	बन्दाकोबी 3
cage	खोर 17
calculation	हिसाब 14
callous	निर्दयी 13
can (be)	सकिनु 7; सक्नु 7
candidate	उम्मेदवार 23
capability	गच्छे 15
capable	सक्षम 23
car	गाडी 4
cards (playing)	तास 19
care	पालन 17
careful	होसियार 9
carpet	गलैँचा 16
carried (to get/have)	बोकाउनु 17
carrot	गाजर 3
carry (tr.)	ओसार्नु 16
cart	गाडा 17
cash (crop, etc.)	नगदे 18
caste	जात 12, 15
cause	पार्नु 15
cave	गुफा 11
celebrate	मनाउनु 19
celebration	उत्सव 14
center	केन्द्र 17
certain (adv)	निश्चित 20
certain (v)	पक्का गर्नु 20
certainly	निश्चय 15
chair	मेच 1

chairman, chairperson	अध्यक्ष 15
chairman (of council)	सभापति 23
chance	संयोग 20
charcoal	गोल 13
charming (to be)	मनमोहक हुनु 18
chat	कुराकानी गर्नु 6;
	गफ(सफ) गर्नु 16
chemical	रासायनिक 18
chest	छाती 13
chick	चल्ला 17
chicken	कुखुरा 17
chief	मुख्य 8; मूली 15
chin	चिउँडो 12
China	चीन 11
choose	चुन्नु 23
chores (daily)	दिनचर्या 16
cinema	सिनेमा 16
circle of life	जुनी 22
circling	घुमीफिरी 22
circumstance	अवस्था 22
city	शहर 5
City Hall	सभागृह 19
civil (servant)	निजामती 21
clan	थर 15
clay	माटो 21
clean (rice)	केलाउनु 5
clean (ritually)	शुद्ध 22
clean (up)	सफा गर्नु 5
clean off	पुछ्नु 5
cleaning work	सरसफाइ 16
cliff	भीर 8
climate	हावापानी 10
clinic	क्लिनिक 8
closed	बन्द 13
clothe	कपडा 14

clothes	पहिरन 14
cloudy (to become)	बादल लाग्नु 10
coconut	नरिवल 23
coincidence	संयोग 20
cold	चिसो 17
cold (to feel)	जाडो लाग्नु 9
cold flu	रुघाज्वरो 9
collect	जुटाउनु 21
color	रङ्ग 1
comb hair	कपाल कोर्नु 16
come	आउनु 4
commercial	व्यापारिक 11
comfort	सुख 22
commotion	चहलपहल 20
complete	पूरा गर्नु 16
concerning	सम्बन्धी 9
condition	स्थिति 16; अवस्था 22
conduct	सञ्चालन गर्नु 17
conference	सभा 23
connect	जोड्नु 20
connection	सम्बन्ध 20
consecration (temple, idol)	प्रतिष्ठा 22
consider	विचार गर्नु 9
considered (to be)	सम्भिनु 22
constitution	संविधान 23
content	सन्तुष्ट 17
context	सन्दर्भ 14
continue (to remain)	रहिरहनु 18
contract	ठेक्का 16
convenience	सुविधा 11
convince	चित्त बुझाउनु 15
cook	पकाउनु 5
cooked (to be)	पाक्नु 18
copy	नकल पार्नु 19
corn	मकै 18
correct	ठिक 6
corrupt	दुष्ट 13
cotton (raw)	कपास 14
council	सभा 23
council (of village)	पञ्चायती 23
country	देश 2
country (foreign)	विदेश 8
courtyard	आँगन 16
cover, occupy (area)	ओगट्नु 12
covered (to be)	ढाकिनु 21
cow	गाई 17
cow dung	गोबर 17
cow shed	गोठ 16
crammed	खचाखच हुनु 20
crab	गँगटो 18
creature	प्राणी 22
cremate	जलाउनु 22
crocodile	गोही 12
crop	पैदावार 17; उब्जनी 18; बाली 18
cross (to other side)	तर्नु 7
crow	काग 13
crowd	भीड 19; घुइँचो 21
crowded	खचाखच हुनु 20
crude	कच्चा 1
cry	रुनु 13
cry out	कराउनु 13
cucumber	काँक्रो 3
cull (rice)	केलाउनु 5
cultivation	खेती 12
cultural	सांस्कृतिक 14
culture	संस्कृति 8
curtain	पर्दा 1
custom	रीति 15; चलन 15

cut	काट्नु 13
cutting	कटानी 12
daily	दिनहुँ 8; दैनिक 16
damp	चिसो 17
dance	नाच्नु 19
daughter	छोरी 5
daughter-in-law	बुहारी 15
daughters	छोरीबेटी 16
day-after-tomorrow	पर्सि 20
death	मृत्यु 22
debt	रिन 21
Dec-Jan	पुस 10
decider	निर्णयकर्ता 15
decision	निधो 13; निर्णय 15
decorated (to be)	सिँगारिनु 20; सज्नु 22
decrease (intr)	घट्नु 18
deed	कार्य 17
deforestation	फँडानी 11; कटानी 12
deity	देवता 22
delicious	मीठो 5
delighted	दङ्ग 21
demand, requisition	माग 15
democracy (of people)	प्रजातन्त्र 23
demon (Newari)	लाखे 13
departure (to do)	प्रस्थान गर्नु 20
depend	निर्भर गर्नु 14; भर पर्नु 15
description	उल्लेख 22
desert	मरुभूमि 11
desolate	उजाड 11
destruction	विनाश 12
detain	थुन्नु 18
determination	निर्धारण 15
determined	निर्धारित 22
developed	विकासे 17
development	विकास 11

devout	आस्तिक 22
dew	शीत पर्नु 10
Dhangarhi	धनगढी 8
diarrhea	झाडापखाला 9
diarrhea (to get)	दिसा लाग्नु 9
die	मर्नु 13
diet	आहार 12
different	फरक 10; भिन्दै 14
difficult	गाह्रो 7; कठिन 10
dig	खन्नु 11
direction	निर्देशन 20
director	अध्यक्ष 15
disappointed (to be)	हिस्स पर्नु 13
disease	रोग 9
dishonest	बेइमान 23
disorder	गडबडी 9
dispense (lavishly)	बगाउनु 21
distribute	बाँड्नु 20
District	जिल्ला 8
divide	छुट्ट्याउनु 11; बाँड्नु 20
divine	ईश्वरीय 22
division	शाखा 12
do	गर्नु 2
donkey	गधा 17
door	ढोका 1
double	दोबर 13; दोहोरो 19
doubt	शङ्का गर्नु 23
down	तल 6
downhill	ओरालो 7
drama	नाटक 19
dress	पोसाक 14
drink	पिउनु 9
drive	चलाउनु 4
drop	खसाल्नु 13
dry (intr)	सुक्नु 5

duck हाँस 17
duckling चल्ला 17
duet (song) दोहोरी 18
dung-urine मलमूत्र 17
dusk साँझ 4
dust धुलो 10
duty धर्म 14; कर्म 22
dwelling वासस्थान 12
each & every हरेक 13; प्रत्येक 15; सबका सब 21
each other एकअर्को 17
ear pin टप 14
earring (tasseled) झुम्की 14
earnings कमाइ 15
Earth पृथ्वी 11
earth (ground) भूमि 18
ease सुख 22
East पूर्व 10
eastern पूर्वी 10
easy सजिलो 7
eat खानु 2
edge किनार 8; छेउ 18
egg फुल 17
elders बूढाबूढी 15; पाका 19
eldest (in family) जेठो 15
elect चुन्नु 23
election चुनाव 23
electricity बिजुली 11
elephant हात्ती 12
emigrate विदेसिनु 18
employed जागिरे 16
employee कर्मचारी 8; कामदार 18
empty खाली 4
end (n) अन्त्य 22
end (v) सिद्धिनु 20
end (in/at the) अन्तमा 20
endure सहनु 13
engineer इन्जिनियर 8
English अङ्ग्रेजी 2
enjoy मोज गर्नु 21; मजा गर्नु 21
enjoyment मजा 19
enter पस्नु 13
entertain oneself मन बहलाउनु 19
entertainment मनोरञ्जन 19
entitlement हक 23
environment वातावरण 14
epidemic महामारी 9
equal बराबर 15
error गलत 9
established (to be) स्थापना हुनु 17
etc. इत्यादि 9; आदि 12
ethnic group जाति 15
even पनि 4
even then तैपनि 13
evening साँझ 4; बेलुका 7
everyone सबैजना 6
everywhere जतातातै 19
evil दुष्ट 13
example उदाहरण 14
excellent उत्तम 18
except बाहेक 9, 19
exercise (physical) शारीरिक व्यायाम 19
excessive(ly) अत्यधिक 18
excreta मलमूत्र 17
excuse क्षमा गर्नु 22
exercise साधना 22
exhibition प्रदर्शनी 14; रमिता 21
expenditure खर्च 15
expensive महँगो 3; मूल्यवान् 17
experienced अनुभवी 8

explain	बताउनु 13
export	निर्यात 18
extremely	अत्यन्त 7; खुब 14; अति 19
face	मुख 5
facility	सुविधा 11
factory	कारखाना 16
fair	मेला 19
faith	विश्वास 22
faithful	इमानदार 23
fake	नक्कली 14
false	झुटो 22
family	परिवार 14
famous	प्रसिद्ध 11
far	टाढा 4; सुदूर 11
farmer	ज्यापू 14; किसान 18
fashion, design, pattern	ढाँचा 14
fasten	अड्काउनु 13
fat	बोसो 17
father	बा 2; बाबु 15
father-in-law	ससुरा 20
fatigue	थकाइ 7
fatten	मोटाउनु 13
fear	डर 7
feast	भोज 16
Feb-Mar	फागुन 10
fed-up with (to be)	वाक्क लाग्नु 23
feed	खुवाउनु 13
feel (emotion)	लाग्नु 7
female	महिला 14
fence	बार 1
fertilizer	मल 17
festival (with procession)	जात्रा 19
festivals	चाडपर्व 14
fever (to get)	ज्वर आउनु 9

field	चौर 17
field (dry)	बारी 17
field (irrigated)	खेत 15
field (under tillage)	खेतबारी 19
field (unirrigated)	टारी 18
fig	अन्जीर 13
fill/filled (to be)	भर्नु/भरिनु 21
film	सिनेमा 16
filth	फोहर 13
finger	नङ 13
finished (to be)	सिद्धिनु 20
fire	आगो 16
first	पहिलो 7
firstly	पहिले 8
fish	माछा 12
fit	योग्य 18
fitting	उपयुक्त 17
fix	मिलाउनु 8; जोड्नु 20
fixed	निर्धारित 22; सीमित 23
flat	तेर्सो 7
flee	भाग्नु 13
flood	बाढी 18
floor	भुइँ 1
flour	पीठो 16
flow	बग्नु 11
flower (n)	फूल 12
flower (v), blossom	फुल्नु 23
fly (a kite)	चङ्गा उडाउनु 21
fly (intr)	उड्नु 10
fog	हुस्सू लाग्नु 10
folk tale	लोककथा 13
follower (of X religion)	धर्मावलम्बी 22
food, meal	खाना 5; खानेकुरा 13
food (diet)	आहार 12
food (of animal)	दाना 17

foolish मूर्ख 13
foot फेदी 11
foot (on/by) पैदल 7
forehead निधार 12
foreign(er) विदेशी 7
forest वन 11
forget बिर्सनु 9
forgive क्षमा गर्नु 22
fork काँटा 5
form रूप 11
formal औपचारिक 20
former अघिल्लो 21
founded (to be) स्थापना हुनु 17
free स्वतन्त्र 16
freedom छुटकारा 22
free-time फुर्सद 6
freeze जम्नु 10
frequent धाउनु 16
Friday शुक्रबार 5
friend साथी 9
friendly मिलनसार 7
frog भ्यागुता 18
from बाट 7; देखि 10
from time to time बेलाबेलामा 19
frontier सिमाना 11
frost तुसारो पर्नु 10
fruit (intr) फल्नु 13
fruit (n) फल 13, 22; फलफूल 3
fruit (tr) फलाउनु 18
fruitful सफल 18; उत्पादक 19
full भरि 11
fun मजा 19
fun (to have) मजा गर्नु 21
fundamental आधारभूत 23
fur रौँ 12
furthermore फेरि 7
gale हुरी 10
gambling जुवा 19
game खेल 19
garden बारी 17
garland माला 14
guard कुर्नु 16
Gazal गजल 19
general साधारण 9
generally साधारणतया 9; प्राय: 16
genuine सक्कली 14; साँचो 16, 23
geographical भौगोलिक 14
germinate उम्रनु 12
get up उठ्नु 7
gift उपहार 20
ginger अदुवा 21
girl केटी 15; युवती 19
girls छोरीबेटी 16
give दिनु 3
glad (to be) मक्ख पर्नु 19
glass ऐना 5
glove(s) पन्जा 14
go जानु 3; लाग्नु 10
goat बाख्रा 17
goat (castrated) खसी 21
goat (he-goat) बोका 21
goat (long hair) च्याङ्ग्रा 17
goat shed गोठ 16
god देव 22; देवता 22
God परमेश्वर 22; ईश्वर 22
god (of family) इष्टदेव 22
goddess देवी 22
gold सुन 13
golden सुनौलो 21
good राम्रो 1

good-bye बिदा 20
good-bye (difficult) बिछोड 20
goodness धर्म 14
goods चीजबीज 5
govern शासन गर्नु 23
government सरकार 8
grain अन्न 11
grain seed दाना 17
granddaughter नातिनी 20
grandma बज्यै 20
grandpa बाजे 15
grandson नाति 20
graze (intr) चर्नु 12
graze (tr) चराउनु 13
grazing land (hillside) खर्क 17
grease बोसो 17
greatness सर्वोच्चता 23
greedy लोभी 13
green हरियो 1
grind पिँध्नु 16
grindstone जाँतो 16
ground भूमि 18
ground floor छिँडी 7
grow (tr) फलाउनु 18
grown (to be) उमारिनु 18
Gurkha (Indian) लाहुरे 16
Gurung (ethnic) गुरुङ 17
habitat वासस्थान 12
hail जय 23
hail (ice) असिना पर्नु 10
hair रौँ 12; कपाल 16
half आधा 3
halt अड्नु 18
hand हात 5
hang (up) झुन्डचाउनु 22
haphazardly जथाभाबी 22
happiness खुसी 7
happy (to be) मक्ख पर्नु 19
hard (substance) कडा 18
hard (to do) गाह्रो 7
hard work परिश्रम 16
hat टोपी 14
hazy (to be) तुवाँलो लाग्नु 10
he उहाँ 2; ऊ 4; तिनी 5; उनी 7
head थाप्लो 16
headman मूली 15
health सन्चै 6; स्वास्थ्य 9
healthy निको 9
hear सुन्नु 6
hearing (sense) सुन्ने 12
heart मन 5
heaven स्वर्ग 22
hedge बार 1
height उचाइ 10
hell नर्क 22
help मदत 5
Hepatitis A कमलपित्त 9
here यहाँ 3
hermit जोगी 22
hide छाला 12
hide (tr) pedestrian लुकाउनु 13
highlands लेक 12
hiker बटुवा 19
hill डाँडा 7; पहाड 10
hill (bottom of) बेँसी 17
hilly पहाडी 10
Hindi हिन्दी 2
hire भाडा 8
hit (to be) पिट्नु 13

hold	थाप्नु 21	in common	संयुक्त 15
hole (mouse den)	दुलो 13	in comparison (to)	दाँजोमा (को) 19
holiday	छुट्टी 8	in fact	खास गरी 9
holy	पवित्र 21	in front	अगाडि 4; अघि 7
homework	गृहकार्य 16	in short	छोटकरीमा 20
honest	सोझो 13; इमानदार 23	in some places	कहीं कहीं 11
hoof	खुर 17	in this way	यसरी 7
hope	आशा 21	in time (to manage to do)	भ्याउनु 16
horn	सिङ 17	in total	जम्मा 3
horned	सिङे 12	in what way	कसरी 9
hot (spicy)	पिरो 7	incantation	कीर्तन 19
hot (to touch)	तातो 18	incapable	असक्षम 23
hot (weather)	गर्मी 7	incessant	निरन्तर 22
hotel	होटेल 16	including	सहित 10; समेत 15
hour	घण्टा 8	increase	थप्नु 21
house	घर 1	increase (to continue)	बढ्दै जानु 10
how	कसरी 9	independent	स्वतन्त्र 16
how many	कतिवटा 1	India	भारत 11
how much	कति 3	Indian	भारतीय 17
however	तर 4	industrial	औद्योगिक 11
however much	जतिसुकै 21	inexpensive	सस्तो 3
hurt	दुख्नु 9	influence	प्रभाव 14
husband	श्रीमान् 5	influenced	प्रभावित 15
hut	छाप्रो 12	influential	प्रभावशाली 15
hymn	भजन 19	information	सूचना 13; जानकारी 16
I	म 1	inhabitation	बस्ती 11
ideal	आदर्श 22	insect	किरा 12
idol	मूर्ति 22	insecticide	कीटनाशक 18
imitate	नकल पार्नु 19	inside	भित्र 6
immigration	इमिग्रेसन 4	insistence	जिद्दी 13
import	भित्र्याउनु 18	instruction	निर्देशन 20
importance	महत्त्व 12	instrument (musical)	बाजा 19
important	महत्त्वपूर्ण 9; जरुरी 12	insufficient (to be)	नपुग हुनु 18
improved	बिकासे 17; उन्नत 17	insult	बेइज्जत गर्नु 15
in	मा 1	intelligent	बुद्धिमान् 13
in between	बीचमा (को) 10		

intention	उद्देश्य 23
interesting	मजाको 19
interference	हस्तक्षेप 23
intersection	चोक 4
intervention	हस्तक्षेप 23
intoxicated (to become)	रक्सी लाग्नु 19
introduction	परिचय 2
invitation card	निम्तापत्र 20
iron (clothes)	इस्त्री 5
irrigation	सिँचाइ 11
it	4
jam	अड्काउनु 13
Jan-Feb	माघ 10
jealous (adj)	ईर्ष्यालु 13
jealous (to be)	ईर्ष्या गर्नु 13
jewelry	गहनापात 14
jewels	जवाहिरात 13
join	जोड्नु 20
journey	यात्रा 7
July-Aug	साउन 10
June-July	असार 10
jungle	जङ्गल 11
just (now)	भर्खर 12
justice	न्याय 23
Kathmandu	काठमाडौं 2
kernel	गुदी 18
kerosene	मट्टीतेल 16
key	साँचो 13
kill	मार्नु 13
kilo	किलो 3
kind (to be)	दया गर्नु 13
kind of	किसिमको 9; प्रकारको 11; खालको 14
king	राजा 12
kingdom	अधिराज्य 23, राज्य 23
kite	चङ्गा 21
knife	चक्कू 5; छुरा 13
knit	बुन्नु 14
knock (door)	घचघच्याउनु 13
know	चिन्नु 12
knowledge	थाहा 6; ज्ञान 9; जानकारी 16
labor	परिश्रम 16
laborer	मजदुर 15; ज्यामी 16
lack	कमी 18
ladder	भऱ्याङ 5
ladle (long handle)	डाडु 15
lake	ताल 11
lamenting	रुवाबासी 20
land	जमिन 10; जग्गा 18; भूमि 18
land (terraced)	भीरपाखा 11
landlord	घरबेटी 7
landslide	पैरो/पहिरो 11
language	भाषा 2
late	ढीलो 9
law	कानुन 15
law, (Act)	ऐन 20
lay out (bedding)	बिछ्याउनु 18
lazy	अल्छी 13
leader	नेता 15
leader (of village)	मुखिया 15
leaf	पात 12
learn	सिक्नु 8
lease	ठेक्का 16
leather	छाला 12
leave (n)	बिदा 20
leave, to take	बिदा लिनु 7
left	बायाँ 4
lentil	दाल 2

leopard चितुवा 12
less कम 3
level तेर्सो 7; सतह 10; स्तर 15
lie down सुत्नु 7
life ज्यान 7; जीवन 10; जीव 12
-previous life पूर्वजन्म 22
lifestyle जीवनपद्धति 15
lifetime जीवन 10
light (color, weight...) हल्का 12
light (fire) आगो बाल्नु 16
like जस्तो 9
like (prefer) रुचाउनु 14
like that त्यस्तै/त्यसो 9
like this यस्तो/यसो 9
limit(ation) सीमा 22
limit(ed) सीमित 23
line पङ्क्ति 12
lined लहरै 18
liquid झोल 9
listen सुन्नु 6
little (a) अलि 2; थोरै 10
live जिउनु 15
live (at) बस्नु 2
livelihood (to earn) जीविका चलाउनु 17
living being जीव 12
Living Goddess कुमारी 21
load भारी 7
loan रिन 21
locality भेग 10
lodging बास 7
loin cloth धोती 14
loneliness एकान्त 12
long लामो 12
look हेर्नु 4
look nice सुहाउनु 14
lose (tr), defeat हराउनु 14
lost (to be), disappear हराउनु 14
lot (a) बढी 10, 17; थुप्रै 17
lottery चिट्ठा 19
love माया गर्नु 13
low (standard) निम्न 15
lowland बेँसी 17
mad (on fire) आगो हुनु 13
made (to be) बन्नु 16
magic जादू 19
main मुख्य 8; प्रमुख 11
maize मकै 18
make बनाउनु 8; पार्नु 15
make sure, confirm पक्का गर्नु 20
malarial fever औलो ज्वरो 9
male पुरुष 14; मान्छे 7; मानिस 11
malicious ईर्ष्यालु 13
man पुरुष 14
management व्यवस्था 12
mango आँप 3
manner रीति 15; ढङ्ग 17
mansion दरबार 21
manure मल 17
many अनेक 16; थुप्रै 17
many of कतिपय 14
map नक्सा 10
Mar-Apr चैत 10
marble(s) गुच्चा 19
march जुलुस 23
market बजार 3
master मालिक 15
match मिल्नु 16
material (clothe) कपडा 14
May-June जेठ 10

meadow चौर 17
meaning मतलब 19
means साधन 19
meat मासु 6
mediator लमी 20
medicine औषधि 8
meditation ध्यान 19; तपस्या 22
medium (size, quality) मझौला 14
meeting-room बैठक 6
melt (intr) पगलनु 11
member सदस्य 15
member (of Parl) सांसद 23
meningitis मस्तिष्क ज्वर 9
mention उल्लेख 22
merchant व्यापारी 16; पसले 16
merciless निर्दयी 13
mercy (to have) दया गर्नु 13
merely मात्र 5
message खबर 6
method तरिका 7; उपाय 17
middle बीचमा (को) 10
middle (standard) मध्य 11; मध्यम 15
milk दूध 17
mill घट्ट 16
millet कोदो 18
mind मन 5
Ministry (of gov't) मन्त्रालय 23
mirror ऐना 5
misfortune दुर्भाग्य 23
mist कुहिरो लाग्नु 10
mistake (to make) गल्ती गर्नु 22
mob जुलुस 23
modern आधुनिक 14
modernization आधुनिकीकरण 17
moment छिन 4
monarchy राजतन्त्र 23
Monday सोमबार 5
money पैसा 3
monkey बाँदर 23
monsoon वर्षा 10
month महिना 8
more बढी 10, 17
morning (early) सबेरै 7
morning (in the) बिहान 5
mosquito लाम्खुट्टे 7
most धेरैजसो 8; अधिकांश 18
most of all (the) सबभन्दा 10
mostly धेरैजसो 8
mother आमा 2
mother-in-law सासू 20
mount, climb, ride चढ्नु 12
mountain पहाड 10
mountainous पहाडी 10; लेकाली 18
mouse मुसा 13
mouth मुख 5
move (intr) सर्नु 9; चल्नु 10
move (tr) ओसार्नु 16
movie सिनेमा 16
Mr. (polite) जी/ज्यू 6
mud हिलो 11; माटो 21
muddy हिले 18
mule खच्चर 17
museum सङ्ग्रहालय 19
name नाम 2
narrow साँघुरो 4
national राष्ट्रिय 14
natural प्राकृतिक 10; स्वाभाविक 14
nausea वाकवाक 9
near निर 4; नजिक 5

necessity	आवश्यकता 10
necklace	मङ्गलसूत्र 14; नौगेडी 14; पोते 14
needed (to be)	चाहिनु 3
needs	आवश्यकता 17
Nepal	नेपाल 2
Nepali	नेपाली 2
nephew	भतिजो 20
nevertheless	तैपनि 13
new	नयाँ 20
news	खबर 6; सूचना 13; हाल 17
New Year	नववर्ष 19
next day	भोलिपल्ट 7
niece	भतिजी 20
night (at)	राती 9
night (noun)	रात 20
no	होइन 4; नाइँ 20
noble class	उच्च 15
North	उत्तर 10
nose pin	फुली 14
not (is)	होइन 4
notebook	कापी 1
Nov-Dec	मङ्सिर 10
novice	नयाँ 20
now	अब 4; अहिले 4
nowadays	आजभोलि 4; हिजोआज 8; आजकल 14; अचेल 15
nursery-bed	ब्याड 18
nutritious	पौष्टिक 17
o'clock (at)	बजे 5
observe	मनाउनु 19
obstinance	जिद्दी 13
obstruct	रोक्नु 4
obtained (to be)	प्राप्त हुनु 17
obvious	प्रत्यक्ष 15
occasionally	कहिलेकाहीँ 5
occupation	पेसा 16; व्यवसाय 17
Ocean of Existence	भवसागर 22
Oct-Nov	कात्तिक 10
of course...but	हुन त...तर 15
offer	चढाउनु 21
offering	बलि 21
office	अफिस 4; कार्यालय 15
official	औपचारिक 20
oil	तेल 16
okay	ल 3; हस्, हवस् 3
okay?	है 6
old	पुरानो 9
old woman	बूढी 13
omit	भुल्नु 9
on	मा 1
one and a half	डेढ 8
one another	एकअर्को 17
onion	प्याज 3
only	मात्र 5
open (adj)	खुला 19
open (v)	खोल्नु 13
operate	चलाउनु 4; सञ्चालन गर्नु 17
operation	कारबाही 23
opportunity	मौका 21; सुअवसर 22
or	कि 4; अथवा 9; वा 16; या 22
or else	बरु 22
or rather	बरु 22
orange	सुन्तला 3
ordinary	साधारण 9
organization	संस्था 8
ornaments	गहनापात 14

other (else, more) अरू 3
other side पारि 11
others अन्य 18
otherwise नत्र 22
out(side) बाहिर 6
oven चुलो 16
over माथि 6
over (towards) प्रति 23
owner मालिक 15
ox गोरु 17
packet पोका 20
paddy (rice) धान 18
palace दरबार 21
pant सुरुवाल 14
paper कागज 1
parcel पोका 20
Parliament संसद् 23
Parliamentary संसदिय 23
part भाग 11; अंश 22
particle अंश 22
party दल 23
party system दलगत 23
pass (mountain) घाटी 11
patch टालो 22
pay (v) तिर्नु 8
pay (n) तलब 8
payment (monthly) महिनाबारी 16
peak (of snow) हिमाल 7
pen कलम 1
pen (cage) खोर 17
pencil सिसाकलम 1
pendant (of gold) तिलहरी 14
people जनता 15
people (in compounds) जन 23
per प्रति 23

percent (per 100) प्रतिशत 18
permanent स्थायी 22
persecute सताउनु 16
person मान्छे 7; मानिस 11
persuade चित्त बुझाउनु 15; फकाउनु 16
petty सानोतिनो 20
pheasant डाँफे 12
pick चुन्नु 23
picture तस्बिर 22
piece टुक्रा 13
pig सुँगुर 17
pilgrim यात्रु 21
pilgrimage तीर्थयात्रा 19
place ठाउँ 4; स्थान 15; स्थल 19
place (to) राख्नु 6
plague महामारी 9
plain (cultivated) फाँट 11
plain (land) समथर 18
plain(s) मैदान 11
plan योजना 8
plant (n) बोट 21
plant (v) रोप्नु 18
planting (n) रोपाइँ 18
planting (of rice) छुपुछुपु 18
planting (of tree) वृक्षारोपण 12
plate, platter थाल 5
play (instrument) बजाउनु 19
play (of stage) नाटक 19
pleasant रमाइलो 7; रमणीय 11; मजाको 19
pleased (to be) रमाउनु 20
pleasure (joy) खुसी 7; आनन्द 21
plots खला 18

plow	जोत्नु 17	priest	पुरोहित 20; पूजारी 22
pocket	खल्ती 14	Prime Minister	प्रधानमन्त्री 23
poison	विष 9	privilege	विशेषाधिकार 23
polite	नरम 12	probability	सम्भावना 17
politician	राजनीतिज्ञ 23	probably	होला 3
politics	राजनीति 15	problem	समस्या 9
pond	पोखरी 11	procession	जुलुस 23
ponder	सोच्नु 19	procession (wedding)	जन्ती 20
poor	गरिब 15	produce	उत्पादन 17; पैदावार 17; उब्जनी 18
population (the)	जनता 15	production	उत्पादन 17
population (human)	जनसङ्ख्या 11	productive	उत्पादक 19
porch	पिँढी 7	profession	पेसा 16
porter	भरिया 7	profit	फाइदा 12; बचत 18; नाफा 21
portrait	तस्बिर 22	program	कार्यक्रम 16
possible (to be)	सकिनु 7; सक्नु 7; हुन सक्नु 9	proper (appropriate)	उचित 12
post (rank)	पद 23	protection, conservation	संरक्षण 12; पालन 17
potato	आलु 3	provide	जुटाउनु 21
power	शक्ति 12	pull	तान्नु 17
practicable	साध्य 19	punishment	सजाय 22
practice (rite)	चलन 15	pure (ritually)	शुद्ध 22
practice (exercise)	साधना 22	push	धकेल्नु 22
practice (rite)	रिबाज 15	qualified, capable	सक्षम 23
precipice	भीर 8	quality	स्तरीय 12; गुणस्तरीय 17
prefer	रुचाउनु 14	question	प्रश्न 15
prepare	तयार गर्नु 14	quickly	छिटो 6
presence	उपस्थिति 21	quilt	सिरक 10
present (to be)	उपस्थित हुनु 21	rabbit	खरायो 17
President (country)	राष्ट्रपति 23	raffle	चिट्ठा 19
pressure	चाप 18	rain	वर्षा 10
prestige	इज्जत 15	randomly	जथाभाबी 22
pretence	देखावटी 15	rank (post)	पद 23
pretending X	टार्नु 13	rattle (door)	घचघच्याउनु 13
previous	अघिल्लो 21	reach	पुग्नु 4
price	मोल 21		

read पढ्नु 6
ready, prepared, ready made तयारी 16
ready (to) तयार गर्नु 14
ready made, prepared तयारी 16
real साँचो, सक्कली 14
really, truely साँच्चै 16, 23
reason कारण 9
reasonable (appropriate) उचित 12
rebuke गाली गर्नु 13
receive थाप्नु 21
received (to be) प्राप्त हुनु 17
recognize चिन्नु 12
red रातो 1
Region अञ्चल 8
region भूभाग 11; क्षेत्र 11
regulation कानुन 15
reign राज्य 23
reincarnation पुनर्जन्म 22
rejoice रमाउनु 20
relating सम्बन्धी 9
relation सम्बन्ध 20
relationship नाता 15
relative नातेदार 15
relatives (one's own) आफन्त 16
release (n) छुटकारा 22
religion धर्म 14
religious आस्तिक 22
rely on भर पर्नु 15
remain रहनु 12
remaining बाँकी 11
remember याद राख्नु 22
remote, distant सुदूर 11
renown प्रसिद्ध 11
rent भाडा 8
rented flat डेरा 4
repay तिर्नु 8
representative प्रतिनिधि 23
research अनुसन्धान 8
resource साधन 19
responsibility जिम्मेबारी 16
responsible उत्तरदायी 23
rest आराम 7
restaurant भोजनालय 16; होटेल 16
resting place फलैंचा 19
result फल 13, 22
return फर्कनु 9
rhinoceros गैँडा 12
rhododendron (red) लालीगुराँस 12
rice (cooked) भात 2
rice (fried) पुलाउ 6
rice (uncooked) चामल 5
rich धनी 15
riches धनसम्पत्ति 13
ridge डाँडा 7
ridge (divides rice field) आली 18
right (author.) अधिकार 15; हक 23
right (correct) ठिक 6
right (side) दायाँ 4
right? हगि 4
ring औँठी 14
ripen पाक्नु 18
rise उठ्नु 7
rite संस्कार 15
river नदी 8; खोला/खोलो 7, 21
road बाटो 4
rocky ढुङ्गे 12
role भूमिका 17
roll (tr) गुडाउनु 19
roof (flat top) कौसी 20
roof (sloping) छाना 21

room	कोठा 1	self dependent	आत्मनिर्भर 17
row	पङ्क्ति 12	self sufficient	आत्मनिर्भर 17
rowed	लहरै 18	sell	बेच्नु 15; बिक्री गर्नु 21
rude	ठाडो 12, 13	send	पठाउनु 8
rule	शासन गर्नु 23	separate (adj)	छुट्टै 18
ruler	शासक 15	separate (v)	छुट्ट्याउनु 11
run away	भाग्नु 13	Sept-Oct	असोज 10
rupee	रुपैयाँ, रुपियाँ 3	servant	सेवक 15; नोकर 16
sacrifice	बलि 21	settle	बसाउनु 11
salary	तलब 8	settlement	बस्ती 11
salt	नुन 16	settled (to be)	छिनिनु 20
salvation	मुक्ति 22; मोक्ष 22	seventh	सातौँ 21
same as	उस्तै 10	several	अनेक 16
sand	बालुवा 21	sew	सिउनु 14
sapling	बिरुवा 12	sewn (to have)	सिलाउनु 14
sari	साडी ; फरिया 14	shape	आकार 22
sari top	चोलो 14	sharpen	उध्याउनु 13
satisfied	सन्तुष्ट 17	shawl	दोपट्टा 14
Saturday	शनिवार 5	she	उहाँ 2; ऊ 4; तिनी 5; उनी 7
savings (profit)	बचत 18		
say	भन्नु 4	she-goat (she-goat)	बाख्री 13
scarf	दोपट्टा 14	sheep	भेडा 17
scatter	छर्नु 21	Sherpa	सेर्पा 11
school	स्कूल 2	shift (intr)	सर्नु 9
scold	गाली गर्नु 13	shift (tr)	ओसार्नु 16
Scripture	धर्मशास्त्र 22; शास्त्र 22	shine	घाम लाग्नु 10
scrub	माझ्नु 5	shirt	दौरा 14; कुर्ता 14; कमिज 14
sea	समुद्र 10		
search for	खोज्नु 7	shoe(s)	जुत्ता 14
Secretary	सचिव 23	shop	पसल 3
section (of law)	धारा 23	shopkeeper	साहुजी, साहुनी 3; पसले 16
see	देख्नु 4	shopping	किनमेल 3
seed	बीउ 18	short	छोटो 12
seedling	बिरुवा 12	shove	धकेल्नु 22
self	आफू 9		

show	देखाउनु 4; प्रदर्शनी 14; रमिता 21	snack	खाजा 6
		snack (in morning)	नास्ता 7
showiness	देखावटी 15	snack (pounded rice)	च्यूरा 21
shrine	तीर्थस्थल 21; पीठ 21	snack (type of)	दालमोठ 6
sick (person)	बिरामी 8	snake	सर्प 18
sickness	रोग 9	snout	थुतुनो 12
side	किनार 8; छेउ 18	snow	हिउँ पर्नु 10
side (of)	तर्फ 13	so much	बढी 10, 17
sight (view)	दृश्य 7	soak (intr)	भिज्नु 10
sight (spectacle)	रमिता 21	soap	साबुन 3
sight (sense)	दृष्टि 12	sociable	मिलनसार 7
sightseeing	दृश्यावलोकन 19	social	सामाजिक 20
silver	चाँदी 13	social class	वर्ग 15
similar	उस्तै 10	society	समाज 15
simple	सोझो 13	sock(s)	मोजा 14
sin	पाप गर्नु 22	soft	नरम 13
sing	गाउनु 18	soil	माटो 21
single	एक्लै 16	sold (to be)	बिक्नु 21
sister (older)	दिदी 2	solution	उपाय 17
sister (younger)	बहिनी 6	some (emph)	केही 6; कुनैकुनै 9
sit	बस्नु 2	sometimes	कहिले 7
site	स्थल 19	son	छोरा 5
site (of pilgrimage)	तीर्थस्थल 21	son-in-law	ज्वाइँ 20
situation	स्थिति 16	song	गीत 18
skin	छाला 12	song (of praise)	भजन 19
sky	आकाश 10	sort	प्रकार 11
sky (of)	आकाशे 18	sort of	किसिमको 9
slander	बेइज्जत गर्नु 15	soul	आत्मा 22
slaughter	काटमार 21	soup	झोल 9
sleep	सुत्नु 7	source	स्रोत 11
slow	ढीलो 9	South	दक्षिण 10
slowly	बिस्तारै 6	sovereignty	सार्वभौमसत्ता 23
small	सानो 1; सानोतिनो 20; सूक्ष्म 22	sow	छर्नु 21
		speak	बोल्नु 2
smell (sense)	सुँघ्ने 12	special	विशेष 19

species	जात 12, 15	story	कथा 13
spectacle	रमिता 21	stove	चुलो 16
spend (time)	बिताउनु 15	straight	सिधा 4
spending	खर्च 15	stream	नाला 11
spice	मसला 20	strength	शक्ति 12
spices (and such)	मरमसला 21	strike (political)	हडताल 23
spinach	साग 3	string	धागो 14
spinning	घुमीफिरी 22	stripe	पाटा 12
spirit	आत्मा 22	striped (black)	पाटे 12
spit	थुक्नु 13	stroll	घुम्नु 9
spoon	चम्चा 5	strong	बलियो 1
spoon (for serving rice)	पन्यूँ 15	struggle	सङ्घर्ष 23
spread (to be)	फैलिनु 9	student	विद्यार्थी 21
spread out	बिछ्याउनु 21	study (n)	अध्ययन 9
sprout	उम्रनु 12	study (v)	पढ्नु 6
sprout (to be)	उमारिनु 18	stupid	मूर्ख 13
stairs	भऱ्याङ 5	sty (cage)	खोर 17
stand up	उभिनु 20	style, design, pattern	ढाँचा 14
standing (to be)	उभिनु 20	subcaste	थर 15
state, nation	राज्य 23	subsidiary	सहायक 17
statue	मूर्ति 22	substitution	सट्टा 14
status	स्तर 15; इज्जत 15	successful	सम्पन्न 15; सफल 18
stay	बस्नु 2	suddenly	अचानक 9
steep	ठाडो 12, 13; भिरालो 18	sugar cane	उखु 21
step (of stair)	सिँढी 13	suit	सुहाउनु 14
still	अझै 9; झन् 18	summit	शिखर 11
stitch	सिउनु 14	Sunday	आइतबार 5
stitched (to have)	सिलाउनु 14	sunny (to be)	घाम लाग्नु 10
stomach	पेट 9	supervision	हेरविचार 5
stop	रोक्नु 4; अड्नु 18	supplies	चीजबीज 5; सामान 7
stop doing X	छोड्नु (-न) 13	supply	आपूर्ति 18
stopped	अवरुद्ध 19	supply (v)	जुटाउनु 21
store	पसल 3	supremeness	सर्वोच्चता 23
storeroom	भण्डार 11	sure	निश्चित 20
storm	आँधीबेहरी 10; हुरी 10	sure (to make)	पक्का गर्नु 20

surface	सतह 10	tenth	दसौँ 21
surprised	अचम्म लाग्नु 9	Terai	तराई 9
surrounding X	वरिपरि 13	terrace	गरा 18
surroundings	वातावरण 14	terrain	धरातल 11
suspect	शङ्का गर्नु 23	territory	भूभाग 11
sweat	पसिना 10	than	भन्दा 9
swim	पौडी खेल्नु 19	thanks	धन्यवाद 3
swing (to play)	पिङ खेल्नु 21	that	त्यो 1
symptom	लक्षण 9	that much	त्यति 9
system	पद्धति 23	that side	त्यतापट्टि 19
tablet	चक्की 9	that-is-to-say	अर्थात् 9
tail	पुच्छर 12	thatch	छाउनु 12
take	लिनु 3; थाप्नु 21	the more	झन् 18
take away	लग्नु 8	theater	नाचघर 19
take in	भित्र्याउनु 18	theft	चोरी 12
take off (shoes, clothes)	फुकाल्नु 14	theist	आस्तिक 22
take out	निकाल्नु 13	there	त्यहाँ 4; त्यतापट्टि 19
talk	कुराकानी 6	therefore	त्यसकारण 5; तसर्थ 18
tall	अग्लो 11	these	यी 1
tap (water)	धारा 9	thick	बाक्लो 10
tasty	मीठो 5	thicket	झार 18
tea	चिया 6	thin	पातलो 9
tea and snack	चियासिया 16	thing	कुरा 3; थोक 6
teach	सिकाउनु 2	think	विचार गर्नु 9; सोच्नु 19
teacher	शिक्षक 8	thorny	काँडे 11
teamwork (agri)	मेलापात 16	those	ती 1
technical	प्राविधिक 17	thousand	हजार 6
technician	प्राविधिक 17	thread	धागो 14
teeth	दाँत 16	thresh (by oxen)	दाइँ गर्नु 17
tell	भन्नु 4; सुनाउनु 13	thrilled	दङ्ग 21
temperature	तापक्रम 10	through	द्वारा 23
temple	मन्दिर 19	throughout	भरि 11
tend, raise, keep	पाल्नु 13	throw away	फाल्नु 13
tendency (of people)	प्रवृत्ति 11	thunder (cloud roar)	मेघ गर्जनु 10
tender	कमजोर 12	Thursday	बिहीबार 5

thus यसरी 7; तसर्थ 18
Tibetan (can be pejorative) भोटे 11
tidy सफा गर्नु 5
tie, bind बाँध्नु 17
tiger बाघ 12
tight साँघुरो 4
tika टीका 13
timber काठ 12
time (of a #) पालो 20
time (one of a #) पटक 9
time (point of) बेला 9
time (short period) बेर 9
time (to require) समय लाग्नु 9
tiny सूक्ष्म 22
tire पाङ्ग्रा 19
today आज 3
toe nail नङ 13
together सँग 5; समेत 15; एकैसाथ 20
toil परिश्रम 16
tolerate सहनु 13
tomato गोलभेँडा 3
tomorrow भोलि 6
too much ज्यादै 17
tool(s) ज्यावल 21
tooth दाँत 12
torment सताउनु 16
torment (noun) यातना 22
torrential (rain) मुसलधारे 10
touch छुनु 22
tour भ्रमण 19
towards तिर 4; प्रति 23
tradition परम्परा 14; रिबाज 15
traditional परम्परागत 14
transaction कारोबार 21
transplant रोप्नु 18
transportation यातायात 11
trap थुन्नु 18
travel भ्रमण 19
traveler, padestrian बटुवा 19; यात्रु 21
treasury ढुकुटी 13
treatment उपचार 8
tree रुख 12
tree - pine सल्ला 12
tree - Dalbergia Sissu सिसौ 12
tree - Shorea Robustas साल 12
trouble दु:ख दिनु 9
truck गाडी 4
true साँचो 16, 23
truly साँच्चै 16, 23
trust विश्वास 22
Tuesday मङ्गलबार 5
turn मोड्नु 4; फर्कनु 9
turn (of a #) पालो 20
two-in-one दोहोरो 19
type of खालको 14
ugly कुरूप 13
umbrella छाता 10
unattractive कुरूप 13
unbutton टाँक खोल्नु 14
uncertainty क्यारे 6
under मुनि 13
under (system, org) अन्तर्गत 23
undergo भोग्नु 22
undertaking भोग 22
unemployed बेकार 16
unfit अयोग्य 23
uniform पोसाक 14
united, joint संयुक्त 15

united (to be) मिल्नु 16
unity एकता 23
universe जगत् 22
unqualified (incapable) असक्षम 23
unsuccessful (failure) असफल 23
until सम्म 7
untouchable अछूत 7
unworthy अयोग्य 23
up माथि 6
up to सम्म 7
uphill उकालो 7
uproot उखेल्नु 18
upset गडबडी 9
urgent जरुरी 12
use प्रयोग 12
usefulness उपयोगिता 23
useless बेकार 16
utensil भाँडा 5
utility उपयोगिता 23
vacant खाली 4
vaccination खोप 9
vain (to be in) खेर जानु 17
valley उपत्यका 11
valuable मूल्यवान् 17
variations विविधता 14
variety (of food) परिकार 20
various विभिन्न 11
vegetable तरकारी 3
vegetation वनस्पति 11
vehicle वाहन 12
venereal disease यौन रोग 9
verandah कौसी 20
very धेरै 1; एकदम 5; निकै 11; खुब 14
via (having been at) भएर 7
vicinity छेउछाउ 11
victory जय 23
view दृश्य 7
village गाउँ 7; बस्ती 11
Village Development Committee-(V.D.C.) गाउँ विकास समिति (गा.वि.स.) 23
virgin कुमारी 21
visible प्रत्यक्ष 15
visit (god or superior) दर्शन गर्नु 21
vocational व्यावसायिक 12
volunteer स्वयंसेवक 2
wages (daily) ज्याला 7
wailing रुवाबासी 20
wait पर्खनु 13; कुर्नु 16
walk हिँड्नु 7
wall (compound) पर्खाल 1
wall (of house) भित्ता 1
wander घुम्नु 9
want चाहनु 4
warehouse भण्डार 11
warm न्यानो 10
warm (sun) पारिलो घाम 18
warm up (in the sun) घाम ताप्नु 16
wash धुनु 3
wasted (to get) खेर जानु 17
watch हेर्नु 4; कुर्नु 16
water पानी 5
waterfall झरना 11
watering hole कुवा 16
way तरिका 7; ढङ्ग 17; उपाय 17
we हामी 3
weak कच्चा 1; कमजोर 12
wealth धनसम्पति 13
wealthy धनी 15

weather	मौसम	9
weave	बुन्नु	14
wedding	बिहे/बिहा	20
wedding procession	जन्ती	20
Wednesday	बुधबार	5
weed	झार	18
week	हप्ता	5
welcome	स्वागत	20
welfare	भलो	13
well	निको	9
West	पश्चिम	10
wet (to get)	भिज्नु	10
what	के	1
whatsoever	जुनसुकै	14
wheat	गहुँ	18
wheel	पाङ्ग्रा 19; चक्र 22	
when	कहिले	7
where	कहाँ	1
which	कुन	3
white	सेतो	1
whither?	कता	4
whose	कसको	1
wicked	दुष्ट	13
wide	फराकिलो	4
wife	श्रीमती	5
wild	जङ्गली	12
wilderness	उजाड	11
will (desire)	इच्छा	21
wind	हावा, बतास	10
window	झ्याल	1
winter	हिउँद	10
wipe	पुछ्नु	5
wisdom	ज्ञान	9
wise	बुद्धिमान्	13
wish (desire)	इच्छा	21
with	सँग 5; सहित 10; साथ 20	
within	भित्र	6
woman	महिला 14; स्त्री 16; आइमाई 16	
women (young)	चेलीबेटी	16
wood	काठ	12
woods	वन	11
wool	ऊन	14
work	काम 2; कार्य 17; कर्म 22	
work hard	मिहिनेत गर्नु	13
worker	कामदार	18
worker (of office)	जागिरे	16
worker (of org)	कार्यकर्ता	9
working (people)	कामकाजी	16
world	संसार 11; जगत् 22	
worry	चिन्ता	16
worship	पूजा गर्नु 13; दण्डवत् गर्नु 22	
worship & prayers	पूजाआजा	16
worship (mental)	उपासना	22
worthy	योग्य	18
woven cloth (loom woven)	घरबुना	14
wow! hey!	ओहो	6
wrestle (in mud)	लाप्पा खेल्नु	18
write	लेख्नु	19
write (take down)	टिप्नु	6
writing	लेख	19
written	लिखित	23
wrong	गलत	9
yak	चौंरी	17
year	वर्ष	7
yell	कराउनु	13
yellow	पहेँलो	1
yesterday	हिजो	7
yet	अझै	9
you	तपाईं 1; तिमी 9; तँ 13	
Zone	अञ्चल	8
zoo	चिडियाखाना	19

BIBLIOGRAPHY

Anderson, Mary M. (1988) *The Festivals of Nepal*. Bombay: Rupa and Co.

Burbank, Jon. (1995) *Culture Shock Nepal*. Singapore: Times Books International.

Deep, Dhurba K. (1992) *The Nepal Festivals*. Kathmandu: Ratna Pustak Bhandar.

Deep, Dhurba K. (1993) *Popular Deities, Emblems and Images of Nepal*. New Delhi: Nirala Publications.

Finlay, H., Everist R., and Wheeler T. (1996) *Nepal*. Lonely Planet Publications.

Karan, Pradyumna P. and Ishii, Hiroshi. (1997) *Nepal: A Himalayan Kingdom in Transition*. United Nations University Press.

Lall, Kesar. (1990) *Nepalese Customs and Manners*. Kathmandu: Ratna Pustak Bhandar.

Majupuria, I. and Majupuria T. C. (1989) *Marriage Customs in Nepal*. Bangkok: Craftsman Press.

Matthews, David. (1992) *A Course In Nepali*. London: School of Oriental and African Studies.

Reyna, Ruth. (1984) *Dictionary of Oriental Philosophy*. New Delhi: Munshiram Manoharlal Publishers.

Schmidt, Ruth and Dahal, Ballabh Mani (eds) (1996) *A Practical Dictionary of Modern Nepali*. Ratna Sagar.

Whelpton, John. (1994) "The General Elections of May 1991." *Nepal in the Nineties*. Hutt, Michael (ed). Delhi: Oxford University Press.